Preparing for the

REGENTS EXAMINATION

GEOMETRY

Richard J. Andres, Ph.D.
Retired Mathematics Teacher and SAT Instructor
Jericho High School
Jericho, New York

Joyce Bernstein, Ed.D.
Curriculum Associate for Mathematics
East Williston Union Free School District
Old Westbury, New York

AMSCO SCHOOL PUBLICATIONS, INC.
315 Hudson Street, New York, N.Y. 10013

Dedication

In remembrance of Edward P. Keenan, our Amsco mentor.

Special thanks to Peg and Marc for their encouragement, patience, and understanding.

And to Kate for her technical assistance.

Cover design by Meghan J. Shupe
Cover photo by Corbis (RF) Image

Please visit our Web site at: *www.amscopub.com*

Regents Examinations included: 1/10, 6/10, 8/10

Additional Practice Examinations can be found at Amsco's eLearning site: *amscoelearning.com*

When ordering this book, please specify either **R 81 W** or
PREPARING FOR THE REGENTS EXAMINATION: GEOMETRY

ISBN 978-1-56765-599-5

Copyright © 2008 by Amsco School Publications, Inc.

No part of this book may be reproduced in any form without written permission
from the publisher.

Printed in the United States of America

9 10   11

Contents

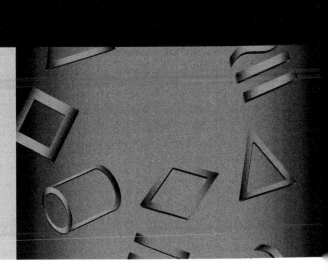

Chapter 3: Introduction to Geometric Proof

Chapter 4: Congruence of Lines, Angles, and Triangles

Chapter 5: Congruence Based on Triangles

Chapter 6: Transformations and the Coordinate Plane

Chapter 7 Polygon Sides and Angles

Chapter 8: Slopes and Equations of Lines

Chapter 9: Parallel Lines

Chapter 10: Quadrilaterals

Chapter 11: Geometry of Three Dimensions

Chapter 12: Ratios, Proportion, and Similarity

Chapter 13: Geometry of the Circle

Chapter 14: Locus and Constructions

Assessment: Cumulative Reviews

Geometry Regents Examinations

Index

Getting Started

About This Book

New York State has instituted a three-year, three Regents Examination series for high school mathematics. The second examination is the Geometry Regents. This book is intended to help students review the necessary mathematics in order to meet the performance standards described for the Geometry Regents in the 2005 New York State Core Curriculum for Mathematics. *Preparing for the Regents Examination: Geometry* is written to provide appropriate and substantive materials to help both students and teachers achieve the following objectives, applicable to the New York Geometry Regents or any modern geometry course.

1   To develop an understanding of geometric relationships in a plane and in space.
2   To develop an understanding of the meaning and nature of proof.
3   To teach the method of deductive proof.
4   To develop the ability to think creatively and critically.
5   To integrate geometry with arithmetic and algebra.

In addition to precisely stated definitions, postulates, theorems, and corollaries, this text provides clearly written explanations of all the necessary concepts along with essential Model Problems. Through lengthy and complete Practice exercises, the student comes to a clear understanding of the structure of geometry as well as the meaning and nature of mathematical proof.

Test-Taking Strategies

General Strategies

- Become familiar with the directions and format of the test ahead of time. There will be both multiple-choice and extended response questions where you must show the steps you used to solve a problem, including formulas, diagrams, graphs, charts, and so on, where appropriate.
- Pace yourself. You have three hours to complete the examination. Do not race to answer every question immediately. On the other hand, do not linger over any question too long. Keep in mind that you will need more time to complete the extended response questions than to complete the multiple-choice questions.
- Speed comes from practice. The more you practice, the faster you will become and the more comfortable you will be with the material. Practice as often as you can.
- Keep track of your place on the answer sheet. This way you can mark each successive answer easily. If you find yourself bogged down, skip the problem and move on to the next. Return to the problem later. Do not leave any answer spaces blank. There is no penalty for guessing. Make a note in the margin of the test booklet so that you can locate the skipped problem easily. Be careful when you skip a problem. Be sure to leave the answer line blank that corresponds to the question you skipped. When you return later to the skipped problem, find some reasonable response even if you must guess.
- Be cautious about wild guessing on any question. Remember that guess-and-check solutions require at least three guesses, selected in a logical way.

Specific Strategies

- Always scan the answer choices before beginning to work on a multiple-choice question. This will help you to focus on the kind of answer that is required. Are you looking for fractions, decimals, percents, integers, squares, cubes, and so on? Eliminate choices that clearly do not answer the question asked.
- Do not assume that your answer is correct just because it appears among the choices. The wrong choices are usually there because they represent common student errors. After you find an answer, always reread the problem to make sure you have chosen the answer to the question that is asked, not the question you have in your mind.
- Draw pictures when they are not provided. It is helpful to look at a visual representation of many geometry problems before attempting a solution.
- Look for the caution *Not drawn to scale.* Diagrams given in problems may appear to provide more information than they actually do provide.
- Sub-in. To sub-in means to substitute. You can sub-in friendly numbers for the variables to find a pattern and determine the solution to the problem.
- Backfill. If a problem is simple enough and you want avoid doing the more complex algebra, or if a problem presents a phrase such as $x = ?$, then just fill in the answer choices that are given in the problem until you find the one that works.
- Do the math. This is the ultimate strategy. Don't go wild searching in your mind for tricks, gimmicks, or math magic to solve every problem. Most of the time the best way to get the right answer is to do the math and solve the problem.

Essentials of Geometry

1-1 Undefined Terms

As we study topics in geometry, we will learn many new terms. We will define them terms by referring to other terms we have already defined. Of course, there must be a starting point—a small set of terms we accept without referencing to previously defined terms. We refer to these as *undefined terms*. The following are some terms and their definitions that we will be referring back to from time to time.

Set: A collection of distinct elements that are written inside braces { }.

- A set with no elements is known as the **empty set** or the **null set** and can be written as $\varnothing$ or { }.
- A set with a specific number of elements, such as {1, 2, 3, 4, 5}, is a **finite set**. If the set is very large, three dots … can be used to show "and so on in the same pattern." So {1, 2, 3, …, 98, 99, 100} is the set of counting numbers from 1 to 100.
- A set that has no last element and continues indefinitely, like {1, 2, 3, 4, …}, is an **infinite set**.

The following three undefined terms are the backbone of all other definitions in geometry.

Point: A location in space. A point has *no* dimensions—no length, no width, no height. It has only position. We represent a point as a dot and usually name it with a capital letter, such as point P.

$\bullet P$

Line: An infinite set of points, with no endpoints. A **straight line**, which could be represented by a string stretched tight, extends endlessly in two opposite directions. (Unless otherwise described, lines are assumed to be straight.) A line has only one dimension, length. We can name a line by any two points on it. For example, if the two points are A and B, we have line AB or $\overleftrightarrow{AB}$. We can also name a line by a single lowercase letter: line ℓ.

Plane: A set of points forming a flat surface that extends infinitely in all directions. A plane has two dimensions: length and width. It has no thickness. We can name a plane by using letters that identify three points on the plane that do not all lie on the same line. Points lying on the same plane are *coplanar*. We can also name a plane using one letter.

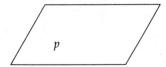
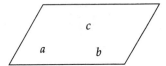

 Practice

---

1 The set of two-digit integers is:

   (1) finite
   (2) infinite
   (3) empty
   (4) unclear

2 The set of real numbers greater than 10 and less than 20 is:

   (1) finite
   (2) infinite
   (3) empty
   (4) unclear

3 The set of perfect square numbers less than zero is:

   (1) finite
   (2) infinite
   (3) empty
   (4) unclear

4 Represent the line through points A and B symbolically.

5 If we name a plane by using three points on the plane, why must they *not* all lie on the same line?

6

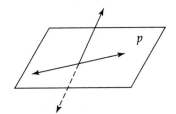

  a Label the line coplanar with plane P as line l.
  b Label the line that intersects plane P in exactly one spot as line m.

1-2 Real Numbers and Their Properties

We have already learned that the set of real numbers can be graphically represented by the real number line. Every real number corresponds to a point on the number line.

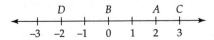

The numbers are referred to as *coordinates* of the points. The point to which each number corresponds is the *graph* of the point. The graph of 2 is *A*.

Properties of Addition and Multiplication on Real Numbers

The following table summarizes important properties of addition and multiplication on real numbers.

Property	Meaning	Examples
Commutative property of addition or multiplication	The order of the numbers does NOT affect the sum or the product.	$5 + 8 = 8 + 5 = 13$ $\frac{2}{3} + \frac{1}{4} = \frac{1}{4} + \frac{2}{3} = \frac{11}{12}$ $7 \bullet 4 = 4 \bullet 7 = 28$ $3(11) = 11(3) = 33$
Associative property of addition or multiplication	The way the numbers are paired does NOT affect the sum or the product.	$(1 + 2) + 3 = 1 + (2 + 3) = 6$ $\left(\frac{1}{2} \times \frac{1}{3}\right)\frac{1}{5} = \frac{1}{2}\left(\frac{1}{3} \times \frac{1}{5}\right) = \frac{1}{30}$ $(1 \times 3)(4) = 1(3 \times 4) = 12$
Distributive property	Multiplication can be distributed over addition or subtraction.	$2 \times (3 + 5) = (2 \times 3) + (2 \times 5) = 16$ $7 \times (4 - 1) = (7 \times 4) - (7 \times 1) = 21$
Additive identity	When zero is added to or subtracted from any number, the number remains unchanged.	$18 + 0 = 18$ $18 - 0 = 18$ $0 + 25 = 25$ $25 - 0 = 25$
Additive inverse	The sum of a number and its additive inverse (also called its **opposite**) is zero.	4 and –4 are additive inverses: $4 + (-4) = 0$ $\frac{3}{4}$ and $-\frac{3}{4}$ are additive inverses: $\frac{3}{4} + \left(-\frac{3}{4}\right) = 0$
Multiplicative identity	Any number multiplied by 1 remains unchanged.	$1 \times 15 = 15$ $-7 \times 1 = -7$
Multiplicative inverse or **reciprocal**	The product of any number and its multiplicative inverse (its reciprocal) is 1.	5 and $\frac{1}{5}$ are multiplicative inverses: $5 \times \frac{1}{5} = 1$
Zero product property	The product of zero and any number is zero.	$-8 \times 0 = 0$ $\pi \times 0 = 0$

Note: Zero has no reciprocal, because $\frac{n}{0}$ is undefined.

Closure

If we perform an operation on any number in a set with itself or with another member of the set, and the result is always still a number in the set, then the set is closed under that operation. The real numbers are **closed** under addition, subtraction, and multiplication. Whenever we add, subtract, or multiply two real numbers, the result is always a real number. The real numbers are *not* closed under division. The reason why this is true is left as an exercise.

MODEL PROBLEMS

For $-\frac{2}{3}$, name the following: **SOLUTIONS**

1 Additive inverse $\frac{2}{3}$, because $-\frac{2}{3} + \frac{2}{3} = 0$

2 Multiplicative identity   1, because 1 is the multiplicative identity for any number

3 Reciprocal $-\frac{3}{2}$ or $-1\frac{1}{2}$, because $\left(-\frac{2}{3}\right)\left(-\frac{3}{2}\right) = 1$

4 Additive identity   0, because 0 is the additive identity for any number

5 Multiplicative inverse $-\frac{3}{2}$, because the multiplicative inverse is the reciprocal, found above

 Practice

1 The additive inverse of –8 is:

    (1) $-\frac{1}{8}$

    (2) 0

    (3) $\frac{1}{8}$

    (4) 8

2 The reciprocal of $\frac{1}{5}$ is:

    (1) –5

    (2) $-\frac{1}{5}$

    (3) $\frac{1}{25}$

    (4) 5

3 Which statement illustrates the zero product property?

    (1) $\frac{0}{n} \bullet \frac{n}{0} = 1$

    (2) $n^0 = 0$

    (3) $0n = 0$

    (4) $0 - n = -n$

4 Which statement illustrates the distributive property?

    (1) $a(b + c) = ab + ac$

    (2) $a + b + c = c + b + a$

    (3) If $ab = c$, then $a = \frac{c}{b}$.

    (4) $1 \bullet abc = abc$

5 *Opposite* means the same as:

    (1) additive inverse
    (2) additive identity
    (3) reciprocal
    (4) zero product

Exercises 6–16: Identify the property illustrated by each statement.

commutative	**associative**
distributive	**additive identity**
additive inverse	**multiplicative identity**
multiplicative inverse	

6 $-6(10) = 10(-6)$

7 $1(64) = 64$

8 $6 + 10 = 10 + 6$

9 $6 + 0 = 6$

10 $6 + (10 + 8) = (6 + 10) + 8$

11 $3(4 \times 5) = (3 \times 4) \times 5$

12 $6 \times 8 = 8 \times 6$

13 $6(3 + 4) = (6 \times 3) + (6 \times 4)$

14 $-84 + 84 = 0$

15 $7(31 - 13) = (7 \times 31) - (7 \times 13)$

16 $\frac{p}{q} \bullet \frac{q}{p} = 1$

17 The number 1 is its own multiplicative inverse. Name another number with this property.

18 Which integer has *no* multiplicative inverse?

19 Which number is its own additive inverse?

20 Why are the real numbers not closed under division?

1-3 Lines and Line Segments

In Section 1-1, we discussed sets, points, lines, and planes as undefined terms. All other terms in geometry are *defined*. The following are some key definitions we will need to use as we discuss geometry that is associated with lines. All definitions are stated using terms that are undefined or terms that have already been defined.

Collinear points: A set of points all lying on the same line. Any two points are collinear.

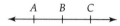

Noncollinear points: A set of three or more points that do not all lie on the same line.

Distance between two points on the real number line: The absolute value of the difference of the coordinates of the points. The symbol for the difference between points A and B is AB.

$$AB = |-1 - 0| = |-1| = 1$$

For any points A and B, $AB = BA$.

Betweenness: B is between A and C if and only if A, B, and C are distinct collinear points and $AB + BC = AC$. $\overleftrightarrow{ABC}$ represents a line on which B is between A and C.

Line segment: Part of a line, consisting of two endpoints and all the points on the line between them. A line segment is named by its endpoints. If the endpoints are A and B, we have line segment AB with notation $\overline{AB}$. Note that either endpoint can be mentioned first. $\overline{BA}$ is the same line segment as $\overline{AB}$. If point C is on the line between points A and B, the notation, which includes C is written as $\overline{ACB}$.

Length or measure of a line segment: The distance between the endpoints. The length of $\overline{AB}$ is denoted as AB.

A quick review of notation is useful:

Symbol	Meaning
$\overleftrightarrow{AB}$	a line through points A and B
$\overleftrightarrow{ACB}$	a line through points A and B with C between A and B
$\overline{AB}$	a line segment with endpoints A and B
$\overline{ACB}$	a line segment with endpoints A and B and C between A and B
AB	The length of $\overline{AB}$ or the distance from A to B

Congruent line segments: Line segments that have the same measure. The symbol for congruence is ≅. $\overline{AB} \cong \overline{CD}$ compares segments and indicates that they have the same length.

Note: AB and CD are lengths. We write $AB = CD$ to compare lengths. $\overline{AB}$ and $\overline{CD}$ are geometry figures. We write $\overline{AB} \cong \overline{CD}$ to compare figures.

Midpoint of a line segment: The point on the line segment that divides it into two congruent segments. In the figure below, M is the midpoint of $\overline{AB}$. $\overline{AM} \cong \overline{MB}$ and $AM = MB = \frac{1}{2}AB$.

A   M   B

Bisector of a line segment: Any line or subset of a line that intersects the segment at its midpoint.

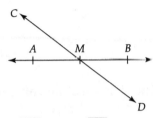

$\overleftrightarrow{CD}$ bisects $\overline{AB}$ at M.

Sum of two line segments: A line segment, $\overline{AC}$, is the *sum* of two line segments $\overline{AB}$ and $\overline{BC}$, if B is between A and C. $\overline{AC} = \overline{AB} + \overline{BC}$.

Practice

1. On a number line, the coordinate of A is 5 and the coordinate of B is −3. Find AB.

2. On a number line, the coordinate of C is −6 and the coordinate of D is −2. Find CD.

3. Points A, B, C, D, and E are collinear points. The following table shows the coordinate associated with each point.

Point	Coordinate
A	−2
B	0
C	1
D	3
E	4

   Name all line segments congruent to $\overline{AC}$.

4. Three line segments have the following measures: $AB = 4$, $BC = 6$, and $AC = 10$. What conclusions can you draw about points A, B, and C?

5. Three line segments have the following measures: $AB = 6$, $BC = 3$, and $AC = 8$. If A, B, and C are distinct points, what conclusions can you draw about points A, B, and C? Draw a diagram to help explain your answer.

6. Points P, Q, R, S, and T are collinear points. The following table shows the coordinate associated with each point.

Point	Coordinate
P	−5
Q	−3.5
R	−0.5
S	−1
T	3

   What point is the midpoint of $\overline{PT}$? Explain your answer.

Exercises 7–10: Determine if each relationship shown is written in correct notation. If the notation is correct, write a literal translation.

7   $AB = CD$

8   $AB \cong CD$

9   $\overline{AB} = \overline{CD}$

10 $\overline{AB} \cong \overline{CD}$

11 $\overleftrightarrow{APB}$ and $\overleftrightarrow{CPD}$ intersect at point P. If $AP = 7$, $AB = 14$, $CP = 7$, and $PD = 14$, which segment is the line segment bisector? Explain your answer.

12 $\overleftrightarrow{FG}$ bisects $\overline{RS}$ at M. If $FG = 8$ and $RS = 12$, find MS.

1-4 Angles

The definitions below will help us establish a formal understanding of angles.

Ray: Part of a line, consisting of one endpoint and all the points on one side of that endpoint. A ray is named by the endpoint and any other point of the ray. If the endpoint is A and the ray passes through B, we refer to the figure as ray AB or $\overrightarrow{AB}$. The first letter is always the endpoint.

Opposite rays: Two rays of the same line with a common endpoint and no other point in common.

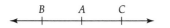 $\overrightarrow{AB}$ and $\overrightarrow{AC}$ are opposite rays.

An **angle** ($\angle$) is formed by two rays that share an endpoint. The rays are called its **sides**, and the endpoint is called the **vertex**. We can also say that angles are formed by **intersecting lines**—lines that meet or cross. In this case the vertex is the point of intersection.

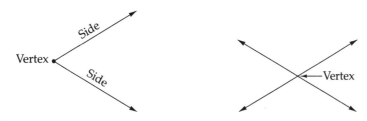

There are several ways to *name* an angle:

• By a capital letter that names its vertex, such as $\angle B$.
• By a lowercase letter or number placed inside the angle, such as $\angle x$ or $\angle 1$.
• By three capital letters, such as $\angle ABC$. The middle letter is the vertex, and the other two letters name points on different rays (or lines), in either order: $\angle ABC$ can also be named $\angle CBA$.

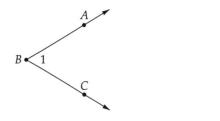

An angle divides the points of the plane that are not points of the rays forming the angles into two regions. If A is any point on one side of the angle and C is any point on the other side of the angle, neither point is the vertex, then any point P on $\overline{AC}$ between A and C belongs to the **interior region** of the angle. All other points of the plane, except the points on the angle itself, belong to the **exterior region** of the angle.

Angles are measured by **degrees** (°) and are classified by their measure. *The measure of angle ABC is 50 degrees* can be written m∠ABC = 50. **Congruent angles** are equal in measure. In the example on the previous page, ∠1 ≅ ∠x.

Classification of Angles

Angle	Definition
Right angle	An angle of exactly 90°. The symbol for a right angle is a square at the vertex.
Acute angle	An angle less than 90°.
Obtuse angle	An angle greater than 90° but less than 180°.
Straight angle	An angle of exactly 180°. A straight angle is a line.
Reflex angle	An angle greater than 180° but less than 360°.

→ MODEL PROBLEMS

1 Refer to the following angle:

a Name this angle in four different ways.

b Name its vertex and its sides.

SOLUTIONS

a Four names for the angle:
∠1, ∠S, ∠RST, ∠TSR

b Vertex: S. Sides: $\overrightarrow{SR}$ and $\overrightarrow{ST}$.

2 Refer to the illustration below:

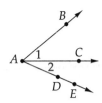

a Why is ∠A an incorrect name for any of the angles shown?

b Why is ∠EAD an incorrect name for ∠2?

c Give four correct names for ∠2.

SOLUTION

a All three angles have the same vertex, A. Therefore, the name ∠A does not identify any one of them.

b ∠EAD is an incorrect name for ∠2 because D and E are on the same side of the angle.

c Four names for ∠2 are: ∠CAD, ∠CAE, ∠DAC, ∠EAC.

Practice

1 Which statement is true of ray MN?

(1) It extends indefinitely in both directions.

(2) Its endpoint is N.

(3) It contains exactly two points, M and N.

(4) It is a portion of a line, beginning with point M.

2 Choose the correct name or names for ∠1.

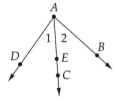

(1) ∠DAE

(2) ∠A and ∠DAE

(3) ∠CEA and ∠DAE

(4) ∠A, ∠CEA, and ∠DAE

3 In which case are points X, Y, and Z collinear?

(1) ∠XYZ is acute.

(2) ∠XYZ is a 90° angle.

(3) ∠XYZ is obtuse.

(4) ∠XYZ is a 180° angle.

4 The measure of a right angle is:

(1) less than 90°

(2) at least 90°

(3) equal to 90°

(4) approximately 90°

5 An obtuse angle could be made up of:

(1) a straight angle plus an acute angle

(2) three acute angles

(3) two smaller obtuse angles

(4) a smaller obtuse angle plus a right angle

Exercises 6 and 7: Refer to illustration below.

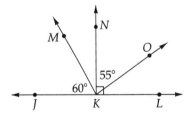

6 Name: 5 acute angles, 2 obtuse angles, 2 right angles, 1 straight angle.

7 What is the measure of: ∠LKO, ∠MKN, ∠MKO?

Exercises 8–11: Draw and label an angle to fit each description.

8   Acute angle *DEF*

9   Obtuse angle with sides $\overrightarrow{BR}$ and $\overrightarrow{BT}$

10 Right angle *V*

11 Reflex angle *GHI*

12 Draw an acute angle, ∠*ABC*, and the points on the angle as described below.

a   Draw point *I*, a point on the interior region of ∠*ABC*.

b   Draw point *E*, a point on the exterior region of ∠*ABC*.

1-5 Preliminary Angle and Line Relationships

The following table reviews basic relationships of angles and lines.

Property	Description	Examples
Congruent angles	Angles having the same measure.	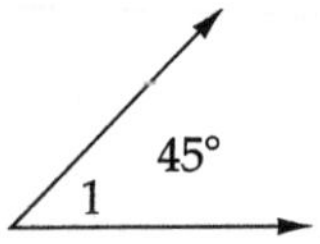 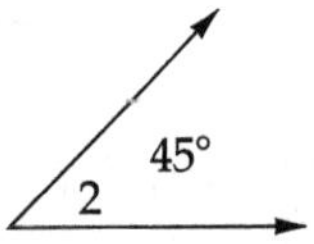 ∠1 and ∠2 are congruent; ∠1 ≅ ∠2.
Angle bisector	A line or ray that divides an angle into two congruent parts.	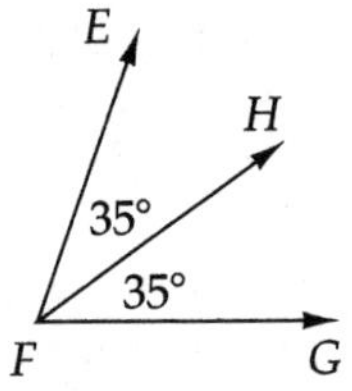 If line *FH* bisects ∠*EFG*, then ∠*EFH* ≅ ∠*HFG*.
Perpendicular (⊥) lines	Lines (or segments or rays) that form right angles.	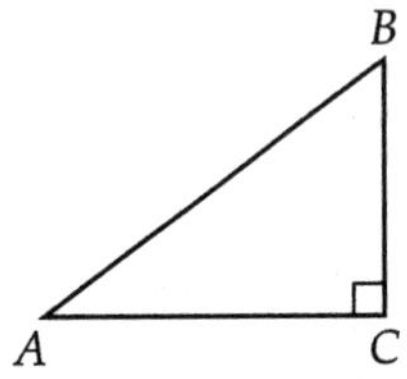 If line *BC* ⊥ line *AC*, then ∠*C* measures 90°.
Distance from a point not on a line to the line	The length of the perpendicular segment from the point to the line.	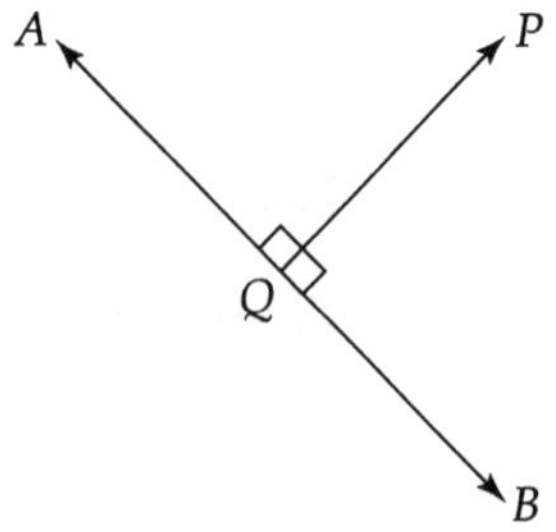 *Q* is called the foot of the perpendicular. $\overrightarrow{QP}$ ⊥ $\overleftrightarrow{AB}$. The distance from *P* to $\overleftrightarrow{AB}$ is *PQ*.

(continued)

Property	Description	Examples
Parallel (∥) lines	Lines that are the same perpendicular distance apart and do not intersect.	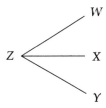 $AB = CD$ If $AB = CD$, then $\ell_1 \parallel \ell_2$.

Adding and Subtracting Angles

If two angles share a common vertex and a common side, and there is no point common to the interiors of both angles, we may add the angles:

$\angle WZY = \angle WZX + \angle XZY$ and m$\angle WZY$ = m$\angle WZX$ + m$\angle XZY$

Likewise, we can subtract:

$\angle XZY = \angle WZY - \angle WZX$ and m$\angle XZY$ = m$\angle WZY$ − m$\angle WZX$
$\angle WZX = \angle WZY - \angle XZY$ and m$\angle WZX$ = m$\angle WZY$ − m$\angle XZY$

 Practice

---

1 Straight angle ABC is bisected by $\overrightarrow{BD}$.

   a What is the measure of $\angle DBC$?
   b What congruent angles are formed?

2 $\angle MNP$ is a right angle. $\overrightarrow{NO}$ bisects $\angle MNP$.

   a Find m$\angle ONP$.

   b What congruent angles are formed?

Exercises 3 and 4: Refer to the figure below.

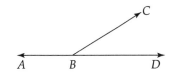

3 m$\angle ABD$ = m$\angle ABC$ + m$\angle$_____

4 m$\angle ABC$ = m$\angle ABD$ − m$\angle$_____

5 In the figure below, $\overline{BD}$ bisects $\angle CBE$. What is the measure of $\angle ABD$?

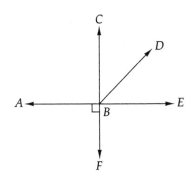

6 In the figure below, $l \perp m$ and $m \parallel n$. Find a relationship between l and n.

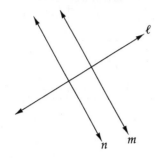

7 $\overrightarrow{BD}$ bisects $\angle ABC$ and m$\angle ABD$ is represented by $6x - 3$. What is the value of x?

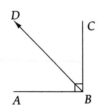

8 $\overrightarrow{EF}$ and $\overrightarrow{ED}$ are opposite rays. $\overrightarrow{EK}$ bisects $\angle DEF$. If m$\angle KED$ is represented by $10y - 5$, what is the value of y?

9 $\overrightarrow{AB}$ bisects $\angle CAT$. m$\angle CAB = 2x - 2$ and m$\angle BAT = x + 6$. Find m$\angle CAT$.

10 $\overrightarrow{FG}$ bisects $\angle AFC$ and $\overrightarrow{MN}$ bisects $\angle LMK$. $\angle AFC \cong \angle LMK$. m$\angle AFG = 4x + 7$ and m$\angle KMN = 6x - 1$. Find m$\angle AFC$.

1-6 Triangles

A **polygon** is a *closed* figure in the plane formed by three or more segments joined at their endpoints. The line segments are the *sides* of the polygon and the endpoints are the *vertices*. A figure is closed if, starting at any endpoint and tracing along the sides, we arrive back at that endpoint. A polygon is named by the letters of its vertices, starting with any vertex and going in order in either direction (clockwise or counterclockwise).

The following are key definitions and facts about triangles.

Triangle (△): A closed figure formed by three line segments.

Side: One of the line segments making up the triangle.

Vertex: A point where two sides of the triangle meet.

Interior angle: An angle within the triangle. A triangle has three interior angles.

Exterior angle: An angle formed outside the triangle by one side and the extension of the adjacent side.

Altitude or **height:** A line segment with one endpoint at any vertex of the triangle, extending to the opposite side and perpendicular to that side.

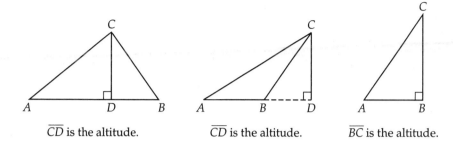

$\overline{CD}$ is the altitude. $\overline{CD}$ is the altitude. $\overline{BC}$ is the altitude.

Median: A line segment with one endpoint at any vertex of the triangle, extending to the **midpoint** (middle) of the opposite side.

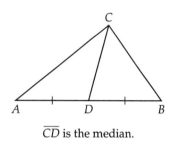

$\overline{CD}$ is the median.

Angle bisector: A line segment with one endpoint at any vertex of the triangle, extending to the opposite side so that it bisects (evenly divides) the vertex angle.

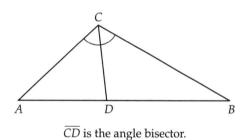

$\overline{CD}$ is the angle bisector.

Included Sides and Included Angles of a Triangle

In $\triangle ABC$, the endpoints of $\overline{AB}$ are points A and B, which are also the vertices of $\angle A$ and $\angle B$, respectively. $\overline{AB}$ is *included* between $\angle A$ and $\angle B$. Likewise, $\overline{BC}$ is *included* between $\angle B$ and $\angle C$ and $\overline{CA}$ is *included* between $\angle C$ and $\angle A$.

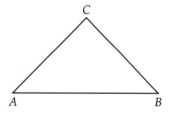

Similarly, we refer to angles *included* between two sides. $\angle A$ is *included* between $\overline{AB}$ and $\overline{AC}$, $\angle B$ is *included* between $\overline{BC}$ and $\overline{BA}$, and $\angle C$ is *included* between $\overline{CA}$ and $\overline{CB}$.

Opposite Sides and Opposite Angles of a Triangle

$\overline{BC}$ is the side *opposite* $\angle A$. $\angle A$ is the angle *opposite* $\overline{BC}$.
$\overline{AC}$ is the side *opposite* $\angle B$. $\angle B$ is the angle *opposite* $\overline{AC}$.
$\overline{AB}$ is the side *opposite* $\angle C$. $\angle C$ is the angle *opposite* $\overline{AB}$.

   The lowercase form of the angle letter opposite a side is often used as a shortcut name for the side. Thus, in $\triangle ABC$, a is another name for $\overline{BC}$, b is another name for $\overline{AC}$, and c is another name for $\overline{AB}$.

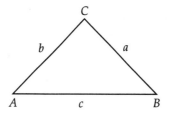

Classifying Triangles According to Sides

A triangle may be classified by the number of congruent sides.

Name	Description	Examples
Scalene triangle	No two sides are equal. No two angles are equal.	
Isosceles triangle	Two sides, called the **legs**, are equal. The third side is the **base**. Two angles, called the **base angles**, are equal. The third angle, called the **vertex angle**, is opposite the base. An altitude drawn from the vertex angle bisects the angle and the base.	$AB = BC$ $\angle A \cong \angle C$
Equilateral triangle	All three sides are equal. Equilateral triangles are **equiangular**: all angles are equal and each angle = 60°.	$AB = BC = AC$

Classifying Triangles According to Angles

A triangle may be classified by its angles.

Name	Description	Examples
Acute triangle	All angles are acute. That is, each angle is less than 90°.	*B* 70°, *A* 50°, *C* 60°
Obtuse triangle	One angle is obtuse. That is, one angle is between 90° and 180°	*B* 100°, *A* 50°, *C* 30°
Right Triangle	One angle is a right (90°) angle. The side opposite the right angle is the **hypotenuse**. The other two sides are the **legs**. The **Pythagorean theorem** is true for all right triangles: $a^2 + b^2 = c^2$.	*A*, *c*, *b*, *C*, *a*, *B* $a^2 + b^2 = c^2$

 MODEL PROBLEM

Classify each triangle by its sides or by its angles as appropriate. Sides or angles with the same number of hash marks have the same measure.

a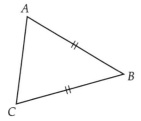

b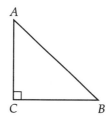

c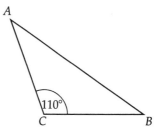

SOLUTION

    a   Isosceles triangle
    b   Right triangle
    c   Obtuse triangle

Practice

Exercises 1–5: Indicate whether the statement is true or false.

1   A triangle can have more than one right angle.

2   An equilateral triangle is equiangular.

3   In a right triangle, the side opposite the right angle is the shortest leg of the triangle.

4   The measure of a leg of an isosceles triangle is the shortest distance from the vertex to the base.

5   An obtuse triangle has exactly one angle between 90° and 180°.

6   The lengths of the legs of an isosceles triangle are $2x - 10$ and $x + 4$. What are the lengths of the legs of the triangle?

7   The lengths of the sides of an equilateral triangle are $3x + 1$, $5x - 9$, and $2y + 2$.

   a   What are the lengths of the sides of the triangle?
   b   What is the value of y?

8   $\triangle ABC$ is an isosceles triangle and $\angle A$ is the vertex angle. If $m\angle A = 4x - 4$, $m\angle B = 6x + 4$, and $m\angle C = 8x - 18$, find the measure of each angle.

Exercises 9–11: Sketch the figure named. Mark congruent sides and angles with identifying hash marks. Mark right angles appropriately.

9   Isosceles triangle ABC with vertex angle C.

10   Right triangle PQR with hypotenuse $\overline{PQ}$.

11   Acute triangle FGH that is scalene.

12   In $\triangle CDE$, $\angle C$ is included between which two sides?

CHAPTER REVIEW

1   Name the undefined geometry term that has no dimension.

2   Name the undefined geometry term that has one dimension and describe the dimension.

3   Name the undefined geometry term that has two dimensions and describe the dimensions.

4   P and Q are two points on a number line. The coordinate of P is 4 and the coordinate of Q is -5. Find the distance from P to Q.

5   Square root is not closed in the rational numbers. Why is this true?

6   In isosceles triangle XYZ, the base is side $\overline{XY}$.

   a   Which sides are congruent?
   b   Which angles are the base angles?

7   Points A and B lie on a line. The coordinate of A is -6. The midpoint of segment AB has coordinate -2. What is the coordinate of B?

8   $\overrightarrow{JK}$ is the angle bisector of $\angle LJM$. If $m\angle MJK = 36$, find $m\angle KJL$.

9   Points F, G, and H lie on a line. The bisector of $\overline{FH}$ passes through G. What term is used to describe G?

10   Explain why distinct bisectors of a line segment *cannot* be parallel to each other.

Exercises 11–14: Refer to the diagram below.

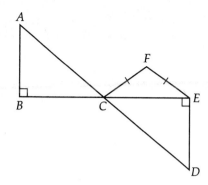

Exercises 15 and 16: Refer to the diagram below.

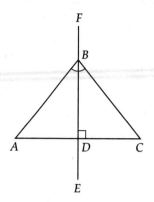

11 Name two straight angles.

12 What angle is the sum of ∠CED and ∠CEF?

13 Name two right triangles.

14 Name an isosceles triangle.

15 Name the bisector of ∠ABC two ways.

16 Which segment describes the distance from B to $\overline{AC}$?

Logic

2-1 Statements, Truth Values, and Negations

Open and Closed Sentences

Logic is the study of deductive reasoning, the process of using mathematical sentences to make decisions. A **mathematical sentence** is always in the form of a simple declarative sentence that states a complete idea.

A **statement** or **closed sentence** does not contain any variables or replacement pronouns. Each such statement has a truth value. It is either true or false, denoted by the symbols **T** and **F**. An example of a closed sentence is "Every week has seven days." The statement is true and its truth value is denoted as **T**. The statement "Wednesday follows Thursday" is false, with truth value denoted as **F**. Questions, commands, and exclamations are not statements because they do not have a truth value. They cannot be designated as true or false.

Open sentences contain unknown pronouns (*he, she, they, it*) or variables. The truth value of an open sentence cannot be established until that unknown or variable is replaced. Otherwise, open sentences have no truth value. The set of all replacements that will make an open sentence true is called the **solution set** for the open sentence. For example:

Sentence	Unknown	Solution Set
$x + 5 = 9$	The variable is x.	The solution set is {4}.
He was the sixteenth president of the United States.	The unknown pronoun is *he*.	The solution set is {Abraham Lincoln}.
$|x| = 10$	The variable is x.	The solution set is {−10, 10}.

→ MODEL PROBLEMS

Label each sentence as a true closed sentence, a false closed sentence, an open sentence, or not a statement.

		SOLUTIONS
1	Sit down and eat your dinner.	Not a statement
2	Why are you wearing a raincoat?	Not a statement
3	All squares are circles.	False closed statement
4	$6 + 2 = 5$	False closed statement
5	$4x + 1 = 13$	Open sentence
6	$8 < 4$	False closed statement
7	A triangle has three sides.	True closed statement
8	George Washington was the first president of the United States.	True closed statement
9	$2x - 5 = 3$	Open sentence

Negations

A statement and its negation have opposite truth values. In other words, if the statement "A week has seven days" is true, then its **negation**, "A week does not have seven days," is false.

Most explanations of logical relationships assign letters to statements, providing a helpful shorthand for writing them. The most common letters used are p, q, and r. For instance, if p represents "The White House is in Washington, D.C.," then we can say that p is a true statement. The shorthand symbol for negation is ~. If p is a true statement, then ~p is false. If p is false, then ~p is true.

Negations can be written in several ways. For example, look at the negation of the statement p: The Geometry Exam is given to all fourth-grade students. (false statement)

- ~p: It is not true that the Geometry Exam is given to all fourth-grade students. (true statement)
- ~p: It is not the case that the Geometry Exam is given to all fourth-grade students. (true statement)
- ~p: The Geometry Exam is not given to all fourth-grade students. (true statement)

A double negation has the same meaning as the original statement. For example, the two phrases

p: *I am hungry*
~(~p): *It is not true that I am not hungry*

have the same truth value.

Write the negation of the statement q: "Taking the Geometry Exam is a requirement for graduation."

SOLUTION

The negation can be stated in several different ways:

$\sim q$: It is not true that the Geometry Exam is a requirement for graduation.
$\sim q$: It is not the case that the Geometry Exam is a requirement for graduation.
$\sim q$: The Geometry Exam is not a requirement for graduation.

 Practice

1 "$4 + 1 > 8$" is:

  (1) a true closed sentence
  (2) a false closed sentence
  (3) an open sentence
  (4) not a statement

2 "A hexagon has four sides" is:

  (1) a true closed sentence
  (2) a false closed sentence
  (3) an open sentence
  (4) not a statement

3 "Get out!" is:

  (1) a true closed sentence
  (2) a false closed sentence
  (3) an open sentence
  (4) not a statement

4 "$x + 3 = 5$ for $x = 2$" is:

  (1) a true closed sentence
  (2) a false closed sentence
  (3) an open sentence
  (4) not a statement

5 What is the negation of the statement "$4 + 3 > 2$"?

  (1) $4 + 3 < 2$
  (2) $4 + 3 > 1$
  (3) $4 + 3 = 7$
  (4) $4 + 3$ is not greater than 2.

6 What is the negation of the statement "The coat is blue"?

  (1) The coat is green.
  (2) The coat is not blue.
  (3) The coat is sometimes blue.
  (4) It is not true that the coat is not blue.

7 If the negation of the statement is true, what is the truth value of the original statement?

  (1) true
  (2) false
  (3) no truth value
  (4) cannot be determined

8 What is the negation of the statement "$3 + 6 = 7$"?

  (1) $3 + 6 \neq 7$
  (2) $3 + 6 = 9$
  (3) $-3 + 6 = -7$
  (4) $3 + 6$ equals 7

9 Write a sentence that has no truth value.

10 Write a statement about triangles that is true.

Exercises 11–14: Use the replacement set {algebra, geometry, trigonometry, statistics} to rewrite each sentence as a true closed statement.

11 It is the study of analyzing data.

12 It is the study of operations on sets of numbers.

13 It is the study of triangles.

14 It is the study of shapes and sizes.

Exercises 15–20: Write the negation of each statement. State the truth value of the original statement and the truth value of its negation.

15 Chicago is a city in Indiana.

16 The sun rises in the west.

17 January is a winter month.

18 The area of a rectangle is length times width.

19 Each state has two senators.

20 All real numbers are rational.

2-2 Compound Statements

Compound statements can be made by joining simple statements with connectives such as *and*, *or*, and *if/then*.

Consider the following simple statements.

It is raining outside.
I stay at home.

From these two simple statements three basic compound statements can be formed.

- It is raining outside *and* I stay at home.
- It is raining outside *or* I stay home.
- *If* it is raining outside, *then* I stay at home.

Conjunctions

A **conjunction** is a compound sentence that is formed by connecting two simple sentences using the word *and*. The sentence "*p* and *q*" can be represented in symbols as $p \wedge q$.

p: Today I go to math class.

q: I am wearing a blue sweater.

Conjunction ($p \wedge q$): Today I go to math class *and* I am wearing a blue sweater.

For a conjunction to be true, both parts must be true. If either or both parts are false, the conjunction is false.

Examples

1 *p*: Buffalo is larger than Syracuse. (true statement)

    q: Rochester is larger than Yonkers. (true statement)

    $p \wedge q$: Buffalo is larger than Syracuse *and* Rochester is larger than Yonkers. (true statement)

2 *p*: Veterans Day is in August. (false statement)

    q: Mother's Day is in May. (true statement)

    $p \wedge q$: Veterans Day is in August *and* Mother's Day is in May. (false statement)

3 *p*: Harry Truman is the president of the
United States.   (false statement)

q: Napoleon Bonaparte is the president
of France.   (false statement)

p ∧ *q*: Harry Truman is the president of the
United States *and* Napoleon Bonaparte is
the president of France.   (false statement)

It is often helpful to summarize the truth values for a conjunction in a truth table, though this is not required on the Geometry Exam.

p	*q*	*p* ∧ *q*
T	T	T
F	T	F
T	F	F
F	F	F

Disjunctions

A **disjunction** is a compound sentence that is formed by connecting two simple sentences using the word *or*. The sentence "*p* or *q*" can be represented in symbols as *p* ∨ *q*. For the disjunction to be false, both parts must be false. When both parts or either part is true, the disjunction is true.

Using the same three sets of simple sentences discussed for conjunctions, we can see how the truth values differ when *and* is replaced with *or*.

Examples

1 *p*: Buffalo is larger than Syracuse.   (true statement)

q: Rochester is larger than Yonkers.   (true statement)

p ∨ *q*: Buffalo is larger than Syracuse *or*
Rochester is larger than Yonkers.   (true statement)

2 *p*: Veterans Day is in August.   (false statement)

q: Mother's Day is in May.   (true statement)

p ∨ *q*: Veterans Day is in August *or*
Mother's Day is in May.   (true statement)

3 *p*: Harry Truman is the president of the
United States.   (false statement)

q: Napoleon Bonaparte is the president
of France.   (false statement)

p ∨ *q*: Harry Truman is the president of the
United States *or* Napoleon Bonaparte is
the president of France.   (false statement)

The commutative property holds for conjunctions and disjunctions so that *p* ∧ *q* has the same truth value as *q* ∧ *p*, and *p* ∨ *q* has the same truth value as *q* ∨ *p*.

The truth values for conjunctions and disjunctions can be summarized in a truth table.

p	q	$p \wedge q$	$p \vee q$
T	T	T	T
F	T	F	T
T	F	F	T
F	F	F	F

 MODEL PROBLEM

Two is an even number.

Six is an odd number.

Which of the following is a conjunction formed by the two statements?

(1) Two is an even number and six is an odd number.
(2) Two is an even number or six is an odd number.
(3) If two is an even number, then six is an odd number.
(4) If two is not an even number, then six is not an odd number.

ANSWER: (1)

 Practice

Exercises 1–4: Choose the statement that has the same truth value as the given statement.

1 $4 + 7 = 3$ or $3 + 7 = 10$

  (1) $4 + 7 = 3$ and $3 + 7 = 10$
  (2) $3 + 7 = 10$ and $4 + 7 = 3$
  (3) $3 + 7 = 10$ or $4 + 7 = 3$
  (4) $4 + 7 \neq 3$ and $3 + 7 \neq 10$

2 Albany is the capital of New York and is located on Long Island.

  (1) Albany is not the capital of New York and is located on Long Island.
  (2) Albany is the capital of New York and is not located on Long Island.
  (3) Albany is the capital of New York or it is located on Long Island.
  (4) Albany is the capital of New York or it is not located on Long Island.

3 5 is an odd number or $6 + 4 = 12$.

  (1) 5 is an odd number and $6 + 4 = 12$.
  (2) 5 is not an odd number or $6 + 4 \neq 12$.
  (3) 5 is not an odd number and $6 + 4 = 12$.
  (4) 5 is not an odd number or $6 + 4 = 12$.

4 Daylight saving time ends in November and the clock is turned back one hour.

  (1) Daylight saving time does not end in November and the clock is turned back one hour.
  (2) Daylight saving time does not end in November and the clock is not turned back one hour.
  (3) Daylight saving time does not end in November or the clock is not turned back one hour.
  (4) Daylight saving time ends in November or the clock is not turned back one hour.

Exercises 5–9: Find the truth value of the compound sentence. Explain how you arrived at your answer.

5 Twelfth graders are seniors and a hamburger is a soft drink.

6 Twelve is a prime number or 36 is a perfect square number.

7 Nine is an odd number and π is an irrational number.

8 Fifteen is not evenly divisible by 4 or 16 is evenly divisible by 4.

9 July 4th is not a holiday or apples are fruits.

10 Suppose p = Every square has four sides.

q = Every triangle has three sides.

Write a disjunction using these two statements and describe its truth value. Explain your reasoning.

11 Let p = The sum of the measures of the angles of every triangle is 180°.

q = Every triangle has four angles.

Write a conjunction using these two statements and describe its truth value. Explain your reasoning.

2-3 Conditionals

A **conditional** is a compound sentence that is formed by connecting two simple sentences using the words *If . . .* , *then . . . .* In a standard conditional, the sentence between the words *if* and *then* is called the **premise**, the **hypothesis**, or the **antecedent**. The sentence after the word *then* is called the **conclusion** or the **consequent**. A conditional statement can be represented in symbols as $p \rightarrow q$ and is read "If p then q" or "p implies q."

Examples

1 Hypothesis (p):   A triangle is equilateral.
  Conclusion (q):   All of the angles have the same measure.
  Conditional ($p \rightarrow q$):   *If* a triangle is equilateral, *then* all of the angles have the same measure.

2 Hypothesis (p): $3x = 12$
  Conclusion (q): $x = 4$
  Conditional ($p \rightarrow q$):   *If* $3x = 12$, *then* $x = 4$.

3 Hypothesis (p):   I bring a jacket.
  Conclusion (q):   I will be warm.
  Conditional ($p \rightarrow q$)   *If* I bring a jacket, *then* I will be warm.

Conditional statements are not always written in "*If . . . then . . .*" form. However, they can be rephrased to "*If . . . then . . .*" form.

Examples of Hidden Conditionals

1 A quadratic equation is easy to solve if it is factored.

  Conditional form: *If* a quadratic equation is factored, *then* it is easy to solve.
  Hypothesis: A quadratic equation is factored.
  Conclusion: It is easy to solve.

2 The sides of rhombus are congruent.

Conditional form: *If* the figure is a rhombus, *then* the sides are congruent.
Hypothesis: The figure is a rhombus.
Conclusion: The sides are congruent.

3 The measure of an exterior angle of a triangle is found by adding the measures of the two nonadjacent interior angles.

Conditional form: *If* you add the measures of the two nonadjacent interior angles of a triangle, *then* you find the measure of the exterior angle.
Hypothesis: You add the measures of the two nonadjacent interior angles of a triangle.
Conclusion: You find the measure of the exterior angle.

The truth value of a conditional statement is false if and only if the hypothesis is true and the conclusion is false. The following examples show the correct truth values if today is Friday.

Examples

1 p: Today is Friday.   (true statement)
    q: Tomorrow is Saturday.   (true statement)
    $p \rightarrow q$: If today is Friday, then tomorrow
    is Saturday.   (true statement)

2 p: Today is Friday.   (true statement)
    q: Tomorrow is Monday.   (false statement)
    $p \rightarrow q$: If today is Friday, then tomorrow
    is Monday.   (false statement)

3 p: Today is Tuesday.   (false statement)
    q: Tomorrow is Saturday.   (true statement)
    $p \rightarrow q$: If today is Tuesday, then tomorrow
    is Saturday.   (true statement)

4 p: Today is Thursday.   (false statement)
    q: Tomorrow is Monday.   (false statement)
    $p \rightarrow q$: If today is Thursday, then tomorrow
    is Monday.   (true statement)

The following table summarizes the truth values for conditionals:

p	q	$p \rightarrow q$
T	T	T
T	F	F
F	T	T
F	F	T

The last two lines of this truth table usually invite some discussion. Since the hypothesis is false, the statement cannot be disproved.

Both parts of the statement "If Jane lives in California, then she lives in Los Angeles" are true. Choose the statement that is *false*.

(1) If Jane doesn't live in California, then she doesn't live in Los Angeles.
(2) If Jane lives in Los Angeles, then Jane lives in California.
(3) If Jane doesn't live in Los Angeles, then she doesn't live in California.
(4) If Jane lives in Los Angeles, then she does not live in California.

ANSWER: (4) In this case the hypothesis is true and the conclusion is false. Therefore, the conditional is false, as shown in the truth table above.

 Practice

1 Identify the hypothesis in the conditional statement.

You will feel better if you take this medicine.

(1) You will feel better.
(2) You take this medicine.
(3) You will not feel better.
(4) You will not take this medicine.

2 Identify the conclusion in the conditional statement.

I will stay in this afternoon if the teacher assigns homework.

(1) I will stay in this afternoon.
(2) The teacher assigns homework.
(3) I will not stay in this afternoon.
(4) The teacher doesn't assign homework.

Exercises 3–5: Identify the truth value to be assigned to the sentence.

3 If $3^2 = 9$, then $3^3 = 27$.

(1) true
(2) false
(3) no truth value
(4) cannot be determined

4 If $13 + 1 > 14$, then $17 + 1 > 18$.

(1) true
(2) false
(3) no truth value
(4) cannot be determined

5 "If x is divisible by 6, then it is divisible by 3" is true for every integer x.

(1) true
(2) false
(3) no truth value
(4) cannot be determined

Exercises 6–10: Identify each statement as a negation, conjunction, disjunction, or conditional.

6 If 6 is an even number, then 9 is greater than 6.

7 Chicago is a city and it is in the state of Indiana.

8 If it is January, then it must be cold.

9 The figure is a rectangle or its area is length times width.

10 All real numbers are not rational.

Exercises 11–15: Find a value of x that will make the statement *false*. Explain your reasoning.

11 If x is divisible by 6, then it is divisible by 4.

12 If x is a prime number, then it is odd.

13 If the slope of a line is x, then the line goes from upper left to lower right.

14 If x is a perfect square, then it is even.

15 If the square of x is rational, then x is rational.

Exercises 16 and 17: Identify the truth value to be assigned to the conditional. Explain your reasoning.

16 If every rectangle has only three sides, then $2 + 3 = 6$.

17 $4 > 10$ if $10 < 15$.

18 Given the statements

Hypothesis: The sun is shining.

Conclusion: It is not raining.

Describe the possible truth values of the hypothesis, the conclusion, and the conditional formed from these simple statements.

2-4 Converses, Inverses, and Contrapositives

Given the conditional statement

If I am 18 years old, then I can vote.

Hypothesis: I am 18 years old.

Conclusion: I can vote.

Three new conditionals can be formed from the given statement.

The **converse** of the given conditional is formed by interchanging its hypothesis and its conclusion. The converse of the original statement is

If I can vote, then I am 18 years old.

The **inverse** of the given conditional is formed by negating it hypothesis and conclusion. The inverse of the original statement is

If I am not 18 years old, then I cannot vote.

The **contrapositive** of the given conditional is formed by interchanging and negating its hypothesis and conclusion. The contrapositive of the original statement is

If I cannot vote, then I am not 18 years old.

The truth values of these statements can be summarized in a truth table where p is the hypothesis and q is the conclusion. The symbol ~ indicates negation and $\rightarrow$ indicates a conditional statement. The truth value of each conditional is determined by the truth value of its components.

p	q	$\sim p$	$\sim q$	Conditional $p \rightarrow q$	Converse $q \rightarrow p$	Inverse $\sim p \rightarrow \sim q$	Contrapositive $\sim q \rightarrow \sim p$
T	T	F	F	T	T	T	T
T	F	F	T	F	T	T	F
F	T	T	F	T	F	F	T
F	F	T	T	T	T	T	T

Two statements are **logically equivalent** when they always have the same truth value. Note that the truth value in the conditional and contrapositive columns are always the same. This means that the statements are logically equivalent. The truth values in the converse and inverse columns are also always the same, so these statements are also logically equivalent.

Knowing the truth value of a conditional statement does not imply anything about the truth value of the converse or the inverse.

Examples

Conditional	If two angles are consecutive angles of a parallelogram, the sum of their measures is 180°.	True
Converse	If the sum of the measures of two angles is 180°, the angles are consecutive angles of a parallelogram.	Not always true
Inverse	If two angles are not consecutive angles of a parallelogram, the sum of their measures is not 180°.	Not always true

 MODEL PROBLEM

Form the converse, inverse, and contrapositive of the conditional statement.

If the polygon has only three sides, then the polygon is a triangle.

SOLUTION

Hypothesis: The polygon has only three sides.
Conclusion: The polygon is a triangle.
Converse: If the polygon is a triangle, then the polygon has only three sides.
Inverse: If the polygon does not have only three sides, then the polygon is not a triangle.
Contrapositive: If the polygon is not a triangle, then the polygon does not have only three sides.

In this special case, all the above statements are true.

 Practice

1 Choose the converse of the statement "If the traffic light is red, then you stop your car."

(1) If you stop your car, then the traffic light is red.
(2) If you do not stop your car, then the light is not red.
(3) If the traffic light is not red, then you stop your car.
(4) If the traffic light is red, then you do not stop your car.

2 Choose the contrapositive of the statement "If two numbers are both even, then their sum is even."

(1) If two numbers are not both even, then their sum is not even.
(2) If two numbers are not both even, then their sum is even.
(3) If the sum of two numbers is not even, then the numbers are not both even.
(4) It the sum of two numbers is not even, then the numbers are both even.

3 Choose the inverse of the statement, "If the merry-go-round was oiled, then it will not squeak."

(1) If the merry-go-round was not oiled, then it will squeak.
(2) If the merry-go-round was not oiled, then it will not squeak.
(3) If the merry-go-round was oiled, then it will squeak.
(4) If the merry-go-round squeaks, then it was not oiled.

4 Choose the converse of the statement "If it is summer, then we are on vacation."

(1) If it is not summer, then we are not on vacation.
(2) If we are on vacation, then it is summer.
(3) It is summer and we are on vacation.
(4) If we are not on vacation, then it is not summer.

5 Choose the contrapositive of the statement "If a triangle has three congruent angles, then it is equilateral."

(1) If a triangle is equilateral, then it has three congruent angles.
(2) If a triangle does not have three congruent angles, then it is equilateral.
(3) If a triangle does not have three congruent angles, then it is not equilateral.
(4) If a triangle is not equilateral, then it does not have three congruent angles.

6 Choose the inverse of the statement "If I turned on the air conditioner, then the house is cool."

(1) If the house isn't cool, then I didn't turn on the air conditioner.
(2) If I didn't turn on the air conditioner, then the house isn't cool.
(3) If the house isn't cool, then I turned on the air conditioner.
(4) If the house is cool, then I turned on the air conditioner.

7 p: x is divisible by 5 q: x is divisible by 10

Which of the following is true for $x = 25$?

(1) conjunction, $p \wedge q$
(2) disjunction, $p \vee q$
(3) conditional, $p \rightarrow q$
(4) contrapositive, $\sim q \rightarrow \sim p$

Exercises 8–17: Write the converse, the inverse, and the contrapositive for each conditional statement.

8 If it is September, then school is open.

9 If the figure is a square, then it has four sides.

10 If I have cookies with my lunch, then someone will trade desserts.

11 If I typed my paper, then my teacher will be able to read it.

12 If I did not set my alarm, then I'll be late to school.

13 If I don't go to practice, then I will not be in the starting lineup.

14 If I don't make honor roll, then I will be unhappy.

15 If I go shopping, then I will not have money for the movies.

16 If I live close to school, then I won't take a school bus.

17 If I study French, then I don't study Latin.

18 Given the statement "The measures of congruent segments are equal."

  a Rewrite the statement as a conditional and state its truth value.

  b Write the converse of the conditional statement and state its truth value.

2-5 Biconditionals

A **biconditional** is a compound statement formed by the conjunction of a conditional statement and its converse. A biconditional is written using *if and only if*.

Example

Conditional ($p \rightarrow q$):   If two intersecting segments form a right angle, then they are perpendicular.

Converse ($q \rightarrow p$):   If two intersecting segments are perpendicular, then they form a right angle.

Biconditional ($p \leftrightarrow q$):   Two intersecting segments form a right angle *if and only if* they are perpendicular.

When both original statements have the same truth value—that is, when they are both true or both false—the biconditional is true. If the statements have different truth values, the biconditional is false. The truth values for the biconditional can be summarized in this truth table.

p	q	$p \rightarrow q$	$q \rightarrow p$	$p \leftrightarrow q$
T	T	T	T	T
T	F	F	T	F
F	T	T	F	F
F	F	T	T	T

 MODEL PROBLEMS

1 Given the following, write the conditional, converse of the conditional, and the biconditional.

   p: Two lines are parallel.

   q: Two lines never meet no matter how far they are extended.

SOLUTION

Conditional ($p \rightarrow q$): If two lines are parallel, then the two lines never meet no matter how far they are extended.

Converse ($q \rightarrow p$): If two lines never meet no matter how far they are extended, then the two lines are parallel.

Biconditional ($p \leftrightarrow q$): Two lines are parallel *if and only if* the two lines never meet no matter how far they are extended.

2 For what integer values of x is the statement "$x > 7$ if and only if $x > 5$" false?

SOLUTION

The biconditional statement means

If $x > 7$, then $x > 5$ *and* if $x > 5$ then $x > 7$.

"If $x > 7$, then $x > 5$" is true for any x since 7 is greater than 5, but

"If $x > 5$, then $x > 7$" is not true for $x = 6$ or 7.

In this case, since "If $x > 7$, then $x > 5$" is true and "If $x > 5$, then $x > 7$" is false, the whole statement is false.

ANSWER: $x = 6$ or 7

3 What is the truth value of the statement "A triangle has a 90° angle if and only if the triangle is a right triangle"?

SOLUTION

This means "if a triangle has a 90° angle, then the triangle is a right triangle" *and* "if the triangle is a right triangle, then the triangle has a 90° angle." Both statements are true, so the biconditional is true.

4 Biconditionals can be used to show that statements are logically equivalent.

Show that the two statements are equivalent.

Conditional $(p \rightarrow q)$: If a number is even, then the number is divisible by 2.

Disjunction $(\sim p \vee q)$: A number is not even or the number is divisible by 2.

SOLUTION

p: A number is even.

q: The number is divisible by 2.

The two statements being tested are $p \rightarrow q$ and $\sim p \vee q$.

The biconditional to test is $(p \rightarrow q) \leftrightarrow (\sim p \vee q)$. To be equivalent, two statements must always have the same truth values and the biconditional must always be true.
The truth table below can be used to show the truth values of the two statements and the biconditional.
In each case, the truth values are the same so the biconditional is true. Therefore, the statements are logically equivalent.

p	q	$\sim q$	$p \rightarrow q$	$\sim p \vee q$	$(p \rightarrow q) \leftrightarrow (\sim p \vee q)$
T	T	F	T	T	T
T	F	F	F	F	T
F	T	T	T	T	T
F	F	T	T	T	T

 Practice

1 Identify the truth value of the statement.

$x + 4 = 28$ if and only if $x = 24$.

(1) true for any value of x
(2) false for any value of x
(3) true for some values of x, false for others
(4) not a statement

2 Identify the truth value of the statement.

$x + 3 = 9$ if and only if $x + 5 = 12$.

(1) true for any value of x
(2) false for any value of x
(3) true for some values of x, false for others
(4) not a statement

3 Identify the truth value of the statement "In Euclidean geometry any two lines are skew if and only if the lines never meet."

(1) true
(2) false
(3) truth cannot be determined
(4) not a statement

4 The statement "I am sleepy if and only if I did not get eight hours of sleep" is logically equivalent to:

(1) If I am sleepy, then I did not get eight hours of sleep *and* if I did not get eight hours of sleep, then I am sleepy.
(2) I am sleepy or I did not get eight hours of sleep.
(3) I am sleepy if I did not get eight hours of sleep.
(4) I am sleepy and I did not get eight hours of sleep.

5 The statement "If Paul buys chicken, then he roasted it" is logically equivalent to:

(1) Paul buys chicken or he roasts it.
(2) Paul buys chicken and he does not roast it.
(3) Paul does not buy chicken or he roasts it.
(4) Paul does not buy chicken and he does not roast it.

6 A biconditional statement is formed by:
(1) the disjunction of two conditionals
(2) the conjunction of a conditional and its contrapositive
(3) the conjunction of a conditional and its inverse
(4) the conjunction of a conditional and its converse

7 Write this statement as a conditional statement that is logically equivalent to it:

Either I don't have money or I will earn it.

8 Write the converse of the statement "If today is Thursday, tomorrow is Friday" and give the truth value of the converse.

9 Write the converse of the statement "If a number is repeating decimal, then it is rational." Use the conditional and the converse to write a biconditional statement. For what numbers is the biconditional false?

10 Write the contrapositive of the statement "If two angles are complementary, then the sum of their measures is 45°." Describe a pair of angles that would make the statement and its contrapositive false. Describe another pair that would make both statements true.

2-6 Laws of Logic

In later chapters, we will study geometric proof. We will be given a set of hypotheses and use geometric theorems, postulates, and definitions to reach a desired conclusion. We will prepare for geometric proofs by studying some of the laws of logic and applying these laws to reach conclusions. Laws of logic involve **premises**, statements accepted as being true, and a **conclusion**, a related statement arrived at from the premises.

The Law of Detachment

The **Law of Detachment** states that when two given premises are true, where one is the conditional and the other is the hypothesis of the same conditional, the conclusion of the conditional is also true. For example, Danielle says the following:

"If today is Friday, then I get my allowance today."
"Today is Friday."

We conclude that Danielle gets her allowance today. The Law of Detachment allows us to prove this conclusion.

Let p represent "Today is Friday."
Let q represent "I get my allowance today."

Referring to our truth table for conditionals (page 25), the only row that shows a true value for p and a true value for $p \rightarrow q$ also shows a true value for q. If $p \rightarrow q$ is true and p is also true, then q must be true.

Using the symbol $\therefore$ to stand for *therefore*, the Law of Detachment is often written as:

$p \rightarrow q$	If p implies q is true
p	and p is true
$\therefore q$	therefore, q is true

Laws of logic are patterns and are not tied to particular symbols or the statements these symbols represent. The following are also examples of the Law of Detachment using different symbols.

$$r \rightarrow s \qquad \sim r \rightarrow t$$
$$\underline{r} \qquad\qquad \underline{\sim r}$$
$$\therefore s \qquad\qquad \therefore t$$

Sometimes conditional phrases are not written in *if-then* form. For example, "A polygon with three sides is a triangle" can be rewritten as "If a polygon has three sides, then it is a triangle." To use laws of logic that include conditionals, it is necessary to change phrases that contain *hidden conditionals* to phrases in *if-then* form. The argument proved above could just as well have been presented with the following premises:

"I get my allowance on Friday" and "Today is Friday."
The first premise is the same as "If today is Friday, then I get my allowance today."

The Law of the Contrapositive

The **Law of Contrapositive** states that a conditional statement and its contrapositive have the same truth value. They either are both true or both false. Written symbolically, we have:

$$p \rightarrow q \qquad \text{If } p \text{ implies } q \text{ is true}$$
$$\therefore \sim q \rightarrow \sim p \qquad \text{therefore, not } q \text{ implies not } p \text{ is also true}$$

The following table shows examples of conditionals and their contrapositive.

Conditional	Contrapositive
If I'm angry I stay away.	If I don't stay away I'm not angry.
If I'm tired I don't watch TV.	If I watch TV I'm not tired.
If I don't pay attention, I will fall.	If I don't fall, I paid attention.
If I don't practice, I won't win.	If I win, I practiced.

The Law of Disjunctive Inference

The **Law of Disjunctive Inference** states that when two given premises are true, where one is a disjunction and the other the negation of one of the disjuncts, the other disjunct is true. For example, Lillian says the following:

"Either I am shopping or I am resting."
"I am not shopping."

We conclude that Lillian is resting. The Law of Disjunctive Inference allows us to prove this conclusion.

Let p represent "I am shopping."
Let q represent "I am resting."

Referring to our truth table for disjunctions (page 23), a disjunction is false only when both statements are false. Therefore, if a disjunction is true, we know that at least one of the statements p and q must be true. If one statement is false, the other statement must be true.

The Law of Disjunctive Inference is often written as:

$p \lor q$ If p or q is true
$\underline{\sim p}$ and $\sim p$ is true (meaning p is not true or p is false)
$\therefore q$ therefore, q is true

also

$p \lor q$ If p or q is true
$\underline{\sim q}$ and $\sim q$ is true (meaning q is not true or q is false)
$\therefore p$ therefore, p is true

Remember, the pattern is important, not the symbols used.

The Law of Modus Tollens

The **Law of Modus Tollens** states that when two given premises are true, where one is a conditional and the other is the negation of the conclusion of that conditional, the negation of the hypothesis of the conditional is true. For example, Ilene says the following:

"If it's July, I am at camp."
"I am not at camp."

We conclude that "It is *not* July." The Law of Modus Tollens allows us to prove this conclusion.

Let p represent "It's July."
Let q represent "I am at camp."

Referring back to the truth table for conditionals, if $p \rightarrow q$ is true and q is false (and $\sim q$ is true), then p *must* also be false and thus $\sim p$ must be true.

The Law of Modus Tollens is often written as:

$p \rightarrow q$ If p implies q
$\underline{\sim q}$ and $\sim q$ is true
$\therefore \sim p$ therefore, $\sim p$ is true

The Chain Rule

The **Chain Rule** states that when given two premises that are true conditionals, of which the consequent of first is the antecedent of the second, the conditional formed using the antecedent of the first and the consequent of the second premise is true. Consider the following example:

Rick says:

"If I don't have a math test, I will work in the garden."
"If I work in the garden, my mother will be happy."

We conclude that if Rick doesn't have a math test, his mother will be happy.

The Chain Rule is written symbolically as follows:

$p \rightarrow q$ If p implies q is true
$\underline{q \rightarrow r}$ and q implies r is true
$\therefore p \rightarrow r$ therefore, p implies r is true

Note: Notice the pattern. The Chain Rule says that if two conditionals of the form $p \rightarrow q$ and $q \rightarrow r$ are true, then a third conditional of the form $p \rightarrow r$ is true.

MODEL PROBLEMS

1 Which law of logic validates the following argument?

Either my best friend is sleeping over or I am not happy. I am happy. Therefore, my best friend is sleeping over.

SOLUTION   Rewrite the argument symbolically.

Let p represent "My best friend is sleeping over."
Let q represent "I am happy."

Use the Law of Disjunctive Inference:

$p \vee \sim q$	Either my best friend is sleeping over or I am not happy.
q	I am happy. (Happy is the same as not(not happy) or $\sim(\sim q)$.)
$\therefore p$	Therefore, my best friend is sleeping over. (Disjunctive Inference)

ANSWER: Law of Disjunctive Inference

2 What conclusion can be drawn when the following premises are true? Name the law of logic used to reach the conclusion.

If I studied last night, I will pass the test.
I studied last night.

SOLUTION   Make the following assignments:

Let p represent "I studied last night."
Let q represent "I will pass the test."

Using the Law of Detachment:

$p \rightarrow q$	If I studied last night I will pass the test.
p	I studied last night.
$\therefore q$	Therefore, I will pass the test. (Detachment)

ANSWER: By the Law of Detachment, "I will pass the test."

3 What conclusion can be drawn when the following premises are true?

If the baby is not crying, then the baby is not hungry.
The baby is hungry.

SOLUTION   Make the following assignments:

Let p represent "The baby is crying."
Let q represent "The baby is hungry."

$\sim p \rightarrow \sim q$	If the baby is not crying, then the baby is not hungry.
q	The baby is hungry.
$\therefore p$	Therefore, the baby is crying. (Modus Tollens)

ANSWER: By Modus Tollens, "The baby is crying."

This example made use of the fact that $\sim(\sim p)$ is equivalent to p.

4 What conclusion can be drawn when the following premises are true?

Everyone is happy when it stops raining.
It stops raining.

SOLUTION   Rewrite the first phrase in *if-then* form and make the following assignments.

If it stops raining, then everyone is happy.
Let *p* represent "It stops raining."
Let *q* represent "Everyone is happy."

Using the Law of Detachment

$p \rightarrow q$	If it stops raining, then everyone is happy.
p	It stops raining
$\therefore q$	Therefore, everyone is happy. (Detachment)

ANSWER: By the Law of Detachment, "Everyone is happy."

 Practice

Make a conclusion and state the law of logic used.

1 Margaret is a doctor or a lawyer.
Margaret is not a lawyer.

2 If I wear braces, I will have straight teeth.
I wear braces.

3 If I save my money, I can rent a movie.
I can't rent a movie.

4 If I don't help my friend, she will be angry.
My friend is not angry.

5 If I take my umbrella, it will not rain.
I take my umbrella.

6 Joe is not a student or he is not a teacher.
Joe is a student.

7 If I eat dinner with Michael, I will not eat pizza.
I will eat pizza.

8 If I don't work out with the team, I will not play on Saturday.
I don't work out with the team.

9 If I practice the violin, I will perform with the orchestra.
If I perform with the orchestra, my friend will be jealous.

10 If I don't help my brother, he will fail his test.
If my brother fails his test, he cannot play football.

2-7 Proof in Logic

When we are given a list of true premises and we apply the laws of logic to these premises, we reach a true conclusion by means of a formal proof. The most commonly used format for proof involves two columns. The first column is labeled *statements*. It contains the given premises and statements derived from these premises and subsequent statements in a numbered list. The second column is labeled *reasons*. It contains numbered entries: either the word "Given" (if the corresponding statement entry is an original premise) or the law of logic and statement numbers used to arrive at the corresponding statement entry.

MODEL PROBLEM

Given: $p \rightarrow r$
         $\sim p \rightarrow q$
         $\sim r$

Prove: q

SOLUTION   List the *givens* first.

Statements	Reasons
1. $p \rightarrow r$	1. Given.
2. $\sim p \rightarrow q$	2. Given.
3. $\sim r$	3. Given.
4. $\sim r \rightarrow \sim p$	4. Law of the Contrapositive (1).
5. $\sim r \rightarrow q$	5. Chain Rule (4, 2).
6. q	6. Law of Detachment (5, 3).

ALTERNATIVE SOLUTION   List the *givens* as needed.

Statements	Reasons
1. $p \rightarrow r$	1. Given.
2. $\sim r \rightarrow \sim p$	2. Law of the Contrapositive (1).
3. $\sim p \rightarrow q$	3. Given.
4. $\sim r \rightarrow q$	4. Chain Rule (2, 3).
5. $\sim r$	5. Given.
6. q	6. Law of Detachment (4, 5).

Often, a conclusion can also be reached by listing the statements in several ways. For example, look at the following two alternate proofs for the model problem above.

Statements	Reasons
1. $p \rightarrow r$	1. Given.
2. $\sim p \rightarrow q$	2. Given.
3. $\sim r$	3. Given.
4. $\sim p$	4. Law of Modus Tollens (1, 3).
5. q	5. Law of Detachment (2, 4).

Statements	Reasons
1. $p \rightarrow r$	1. Given.
2. $\sim r$	2. Given.
3. $\sim p$	3. Law of Modus Tollens (1, 3).
4. $\sim p \rightarrow q$	4. Given.
5. q	5. Law of Detachment (3, 4).

1 Given: $p \lor q$
$r \to \sim q$
r
Prove: p

2 Given: $a \to b$
$c \lor a$
$\sim c$
Prove: b

3 Given: $e \lor \sim f$
$\sim f \to g$
$\sim e$
Prove: g

4 Given: $a \lor b$
$b \to c$
$c \to d$
$\sim d$
Prove: a

5 Given: $s \lor t$
$s \to r$
$r \to q$
$t \to v$
$\sim q$
Prove: v

6 Given: $d \to e$
$d \lor f$
$h \to \sim e$
h
Prove: f

7 Given: $\sim f \to g$
$\sim f \lor j$
$g \to \sim h$
$j \to k$
h
Prove: k

8 Given: $y \to z$
$x \to y$
$\sim z$
$x \lor t$
Prove: t

CHAPTER REVIEW

1 What is the truth value of the statement?

$9 + 4 > 10$ or $7 - 3 = 2$

(1) true
(2) false
(3) no truth value
(4) cannot be determined

2 What is the truth value of the statement?

If $6 + 7 = 11$, then $9 - 6 > 4$.

(1) true
(2) false
(3) no truth value
(4) cannot be determined

3 If a statement is false, what is the truth value of the negation of its negation?

(1) true
(2) false
(3) no truth value
(4) cannot be determined

4 Both of the given statements below are true.

Harry is a horse.
Harry is an animal.

Find the truth value of the statement "Harry is not a horse and Harry is not an animal."

(1) true
(2) false
(3) no truth value
(4) cannot be determined

5 Given the true statement "If I do not set my alarm, I will be late for school," which statement must also be true?

(1) If I am late for school, I did not set my alarm.
(2) If I set my alarm, I will not be late for school.
(3) If I am not late for school, then I did set my alarm.
(4) If I am late for school, then I set my alarm.

6 Given that the statement "Marie bowls on Monday" is true, which other statement must be true?

(1) If Marie is bowling it is Monday.
(2) If Marie is not bowling today, then today is not Monday.
(3) If it is not Monday, Marie is not bowling.
(4) Marie bowls only on Monday.

7 What can be said about the statement "If the figure is a square, it is a rhombus" and its converse "If the figure is a rhombus, it is a square"?

(1) The statement is always true but its converse cannot be determined.
(2) The statement is always false but its converse is always true.
(3) Both the statement and its converse are always false.
(4) Both the statement and its converse are always true.

Exercises 8 and 9: Identify the hypothesis and the conclusion.

8 The square of the longest side of a triangle is equal to the sum of the squares of the other sides if the triangle has a 90° angle.

9 If $\angle A$ and $\angle B$ are alternate interior angles, they are congruent.

Exercises 10–14: Use the statements below.

Daffodils are animals.   (false)
Daisies are flowers.   (true)

Find the truth value of each statement:

10 Daffodils are animals and daisies are flowers.

11 Daffodils are not animals and daisies are flowers.

12 Daffodils are animals or daisies are flowers.

13 Daffodils are animals or daisies are not flowers.

14 If daffodils are not animals, then daisies are not flowers.

15 For the conditional statement "If the altitude bisects the base, then the triangle is isosceles," write the inverse, the converse and the contrapositive. Then use the conditional and it converse to write a biconditional statement.

Exercises 16–19: Write *true* or *false* on the blank lines to make each statement true.

16 A conjunction $(p \wedge q)$ is true when both p and q are _____.

17 A disjunction $(p \vee q)$ is false when both p and q are _____.

18 A conditional $(p \rightarrow q)$ is false when p is _____ and q is _____.

19 A biconditonal $(p \leftrightarrow q)$ is _____ when both p and q have the same truth value.

Exercises 20–25: For each statement, write its converse. State the truth value of the conditional and its converse. If the conditional and the converse are both always true, write the biconditional. If either statement can be false, provide an example that makes it false.

20 If a number is an integer, then it is rational.

21 If a number is a perfect square, then it is not prime.

22 If the roots of a quadratic equation are equal, its parabola is tangent to the x-axis.

23 If a number is rational, then it is real.

24 If $x = \sqrt{32}$, then $x = 4\sqrt{2}$.

25 If a relation passes the vertical line test, then it is a function.

Exercises 26–28: Statement s is "If I don't study, I will get poor grades."

26 Write the inverse of statement s.

27 Write the converse of statement s.

28 Write the contrapositive of statement s.

Exercises 29–31: Rewrite each conditional statement using the words *"if"* and *"then"*.

29 My baby cousin gets a bottle whenever she cries.

30 Two adjacent sides of a rectangle form a right angle.

31 An equilateral triangle is equiangular.

32 Simplify the statement "It is not true that I don't like math."

Exercises 33–43: For each set of premises, make a logical conclusion and state the law of logic used.

33 The class president is a girl or a boy.
The class president is not a boy.

34 My teacher will be happy if I don't cut class.
I don't cut class.

35 If I go to the park, I will play baseball.
I will not play baseball.

36 If I learn to knit, I will make a sweater.
If I make a sweater, I will save money.

37 If I don't eat lunch, I won't have enough energy to work out.
I have enough energy to work out.

38 If I eat a healthy diet, I will feel good.
I eat a healthy diet.

39 Rick likes baseball or he likes lacrosse.
Rick doesn't like lacrosse.

40 If Marlene babysits, Kelsey is not in school.
Kelsey is in school.

41 If Jack is not using his computer, he is not happy.
Jack is happy.

42 I read novels when my teacher assigns them.
If I read novels, I watch less television.

43 I will join a club if I like school.
If I join a club, I won't get a job after school.

44 Given: a
$p \lor t$
$a \rightarrow {\sim}t$
Prove: p

45 Given: $x \rightarrow y$
${\sim}z \lor x$
z
Prove: y

46 Given: $a \rightarrow b$
$c \lor a$
${\sim}c$
Prove: b

47 Given: d
$a \lor {\sim}b$
${\sim}b \rightarrow c$
$c \rightarrow {\sim}d$
Prove: a

48 Given: ${\sim}m \lor n$
${\sim}m \rightarrow r$
$r \rightarrow {\sim}q$
$n \rightarrow z$
q
Prove: z

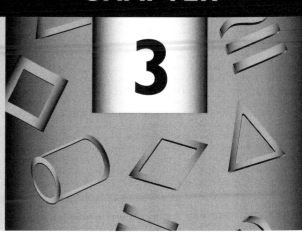

Introduction to Geometric Proof

3-1 Inductive Reasoning

Geometry has been developed as a mathematical discipline in response to observations of patterns. Key definitions related to these observations are as follows:

Conjecture: An educated guess; an unproven hypothesis based on observation, experimentation, data collection, etc.

Inductive reasoning: The process of observing data, recognizing patterns, and making generalizations about those patterns. Inductive reasoning results when a specific observation or set of observations is applied to a general case.

Earlier in your mathematical education, you learned to recognize and extend patterns involving numbers and shapes. For example, you might have been asked how many ways four people can shake hands. To solve this problem, you may have drawn a chart and crossed out duplicates:

A shakes hands with	B	C	D
B shakes hands with	~~A~~	C	D
C shakes hands with	~~A~~	~~B~~	D
D shakes hands with	~~A~~	~~B~~	~~C~~

Notice the pattern of handshakes and repeats. You can make a *conjecture*: four people can shake hands $3 + 2 + 1 = 6$ ways. Using *inductive reasoning*, you can make a more general conjecture: n people can shake hands in $(n - 1) + (n - 2) + (n - 3) + \ldots + 2 + 1$ ways. You can test the conjecture by using other numbers. Try the problem with six people:

A shakes hands with	B	C	D	E	F
B shakes hands with	~~A~~	C	D	E	F
C shakes hands with	~~A~~	~~B~~	D	E	F
D shakes hands with	~~A~~	~~B~~	~~C~~	E	F
E shakes hands with	~~A~~	~~B~~	~~C~~	~~D~~	F
F shakes hands with	~~A~~	~~B~~	~~C~~	~~D~~	~~E~~

Your conjecture states that six people can shake hands in $5 + 4 + 3 + 2 + 1 = 15$ ways. The chart verifies the conjecture with $n = 6$ people.

A conjecture is proved to be true only if it can be shown to be true for *all* cases. This is often an involved process. However, proving that a conjecture is false is much simpler. You can show that a conjecture is false by showing a **counterexample**, which is an example that disproves a general statement.

Example

Juanita made a conjecture that the product of two numbers is greater than their sum. Anisha found a counterexample:

Using the numbers 1 and 2, she showed that $1 \times 2 < 1 + 2$.

 **Practice**

Exercises 1 and 2: Make conjectures for each of the following problems. Test each conjecture once.

1 The number of diagonals in a polygon.

2 The sum of the integers from 1 to n.

3 Stephen told his sister that all odd numbers are prime numbers. Provide a counterexample to Stephen's conjecture.

4 Samantha said that all multiples of 3 are multiples of 6. Provide a counterexample to Samantha's conjecture.

3-2 Definitions and Logic

All definitions can be phrased as conditional statements. For example:

If a set of points all lie on the same line, then they are collinear. ($p \rightarrow q$)

The converse of all definitions is also a true conditional statement:

If points are collinear, then they lie on the same line. ($q \rightarrow p$)

If both a conditional statement and its converse conditional statement are true, the biconditional formed by the conjunction of these statements is also true:

A set of points all lie on the same line *if and only if* they are collinear. ($p \leftrightarrow q$)

Precise definitions in mathematics are written as biconditional statements.

Practice

Review the definitions given in Chapter 1 for the terms listed below. Rewrite each definition as a biconditional statement.

1   congruent line segments

2   midpoint of a line segment

3   bisector of an angle

4   perpendicular lines

5   polygon

3-3 Deductive Reasoning

Recall that inductive reasoning uses specific patterns and cases to form a conjecture. In Chapter 2, we used given facts and the laws of logic linked together to arrive at a conclusion. The proofs we studied in Chapter 2 are examples of deductive reasoning. **Deductive reasoning** is a process of showing that certain statements follow logically from agreed upon assumptions and proven facts, reasoning from the general to the specific.

The agreed upon assumptions are postulates and theorems. A *postulate* is a statement assumed to be true without proof. A *theorem* is a statement that can be proved by deductive reasoning.

Proofs may be written in one of two forms. They may be written in the two-column *Statements-Reasons* style used for our proofs in logic. They may also be written in a narrative style, where arguments are carefully developed and logically organized.

→ MODEL PROBLEM

Given: In $\triangle ABC$, $m\angle BAC = m\angle BCA$.
Prove: $\triangle ABC$ is an isosceles triangle.

SOLUTION

Statements	Reasons
1. $m\angle BAC = m\angle BCA$	1. Given.
2. $\angle BAC \cong \angle BCA$	2. Congruent angles are angles that have the same measure.
3. $\triangle ABC$ is isosceles.	3. An isosceles triangle is a triangle that has two congruent angles.

ALTERNATIVE SOLUTION   Using a narrative style.

Using the definition of congruence, if the measures of two angles are equal, the angles are congruent. Thus, two angles in $\triangle ABC$ are congruent. One of the defining characteristics of an isosceles triangle is that the base angles are congruent. Conversely, if the base angles of a triangle are congruent, the triangle is isosceles.

1

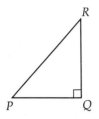

Given: In △PQR, $\overline{PQ} \perp \overline{QR}$.
Prove: △PQR is a right triangle.

Statements	Reasons
1. $\overline{PQ} \perp \overline{QR}$	1. _____
2. ∠PQR is a right angle.	2. _____
3. △PQR is a right triangle.	3. _____

2

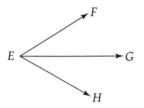

Given: m∠HEG = m∠FEG.
Prove: $\overrightarrow{EG}$ is the bisector of FEH.
Design a narrative style proof.

3

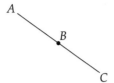

Given: AB = BC
Prove: B is the midpoint of $\overline{ABC}$.

Statements	Reasons
1. AB = BC	1. _____
2. $\overline{AB} \cong \overline{BC}$	2. _____
3. B is the midpoint of $\overline{ABC}$.	3. _____

4

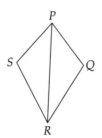

Given: In quadrilateral PQRS, $\overline{PR}$ bisects ∠SRQ.
Prove: m∠SRP = m∠QRP
Design a narrative proof.

3-4 Indirect Proof

When we studied logical proof, we learned that a statement and its negation have opposite truth values. Thus, if the truth value of a statement is false, its negation must be true. In an indirect geometric proof, we begin by assuming that the hypothesis is true and that the conclusion is false, making the negation of the conclusion true. We then proceed to show that this assumption leads to a contradiction.

To write an indirect proof:

- Assume that the *negation* of the desired conclusion is true.
- Use this negation along with the *givens*. Write *assumption* as the reason.
- You should arrive at a statement that contradicts either the given statement or a true statement derived from the given statement.
- Since the negation of the desired conclusion leads to a contradiction, the original assumption must be false.
- Thus the desired conclusion must be true.

Given: ∠JKL and ∠PQR such that m∠JKL ≠ m∠PQR.
Prove: ∠JKL and ∠PQR are *not* congruent angles.

Statements	Reasons
1. ∠JKL and ∠PQR are congruent angles.	1. **Assumption.**
2. m∠JKL = m∠PQR	2. Congruent angles have the same measure.
3. m∠JKL ≠ m∠PQR	3. Given.
4. ∠JKL and ∠PQR are not congruent angles.	4. Contradiction in lines 2 and 3, making the assumption false.

 Practice

Use an indirect proof for each.

1 Given: $\overline{CD}$ and $\overline{HK}$ such that $CD = HK$.
Prove: $\overline{CD}$ and $\overline{HK}$ are congruent segments.

2 Given: $\overline{AB} \perp \overline{CD}$
Prove: ∠ABC is a right angle.

3 Given: In ∠ABC, ∠A ≅ ∠B.
Prove: △ABC is an isosceles triangle.

4

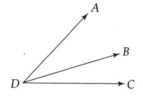

Given: m∠ADB ≠ m∠BDC
Prove: $\overrightarrow{DB}$ is *not* the bisector of ∠ADC.

3-5 Postulates, Theorems, and Proof

In geometry, some obvious statements are accepted without formal proof. Every-one simply agrees they are true. These statements are called *postulates*. When we apply deductive reasoning to undefined terms, definitions, and postulates, we are able to prove other statements called *theorems* that, in turn, become the building blocks for proof of still other theorems.

Postulate: A statement whose truth is accepted without proof.

Theorem: A statement that is proved using deductive reasoning.

The First Postulates

Extensions of the properties stated in Chapter 1 are restated in words as postu-lates. We use the relation "*a* is equal to *b*" or "*a* = *b*" to compare two elements of the same set, usually numbers, that are the same.

The Reflexive Property of Equality: $a = a$

Remember that equality refers to numeric measures, not lines, angles, or shapes. This postulate allows us to write $AB = AB$ as a statement in a proof to state that the length of AB is equal to itself. We can also write $m\angle A = m\angle A$ as a statement in a proof to state that the measure of an angle is equal to itself.

- Postulate. A quantity is equal to itself.

The Symmetric Property of Equality: If $a = b$, then $b = a$

If we are comparing two lengths, AB and CD, that are the same, we can write $AB = CD$ or $CD = AB$.

- Postulate. An equality may be expressed in either order.

The Transitive Property of Equality: If $a = b$ and $b = c$, then $a = c$

We know that equality is a property that can be "passed down."

- Postulate. Quantities equal to the same quantity are equal to each other.

The Substitution Postulate

Accepted without proof is the idea that we can replace a quantity—a number or a measure—with its equal.

- Postulate. A quantity may be substituted for its equal in any statement of equality.

Equivalence Relations

Any relation that is reflexive, symmetric, and transitive is said to be an **equivalence relation**. Certainly, "is equal to" is an equivalence relation. Congruence is also an equivalence relation.

$\overline{AB} \cong \overline{AB}$ A line segment (or angle or figure) is congruent to itself.

If $\overline{AB} \cong \overline{CD}$, then $\overline{CD} \cong \overline{AB}$ Congruence can be stated in either order.

If $\overline{AB} \cong \overline{CD}$ and $\overline{CD} \cong \overline{EF}$, then $\overline{AB} \cong \overline{EF}$ Segments (or angles or figures) congruent to the same segment (or angle or figure) are congruent to each other.

Constructing a Valid Deductive Proof

In order to produce a valid deductive proof, we must include the following:

- A diagram showing what is known is usually necessary.
- The *givens*. These are the premises or hypotheses supplied as facts. They are assumed to be true.
- The *prove* statement. This is the conclusion that is to be proved.
- The *proof* is a series of statements arrived at through deductive reasoning. Each statement should be justified by one of the *givens*, a definition, a postulate, or a previously proved theorem.

1 If $m\angle A = m\angle B$ and $m\angle B = m\angle C$, then $\angle A \cong \angle C$.

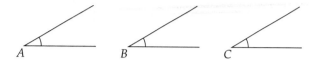

Given: $m\angle A = m\angle B$ and $m\angle B = m\angle C$
Prove: $\angle A \cong \angle C$

SOLUTION

Statements	Reasons
1. $m\angle A = m\angle B$	1. Given.
2. $\angle A \cong \angle B$	2. Angles that have the same measure are congruent.
3. $m\angle B = m\angle C$	3. Given.
4. $\angle B \cong \angle C$	4. Angles that have the same measure are congruent.
5. $\angle A \cong \angle C$	5. Transitive property of congruence (2, 4).

2 Given: $m\angle QPR + m\angle RQS = 90$, and $m\angle SPT = m\angle QPR$
Prove: $m\angle SPT + m\angle RQS = 90$

SOLUTION

Statements	Reasons
1. $m\angle QPR + m\angle RQS = 90$	1. Given.
2. $m\angle SPT = m\angle QPR$	2. Given.
3. $m\angle SPT + m\angle RQS = 90$	3. Substitution postulate (1, 2).

 Practice

1 Is "is parallel to" an equivalence relation for a set of coplanar lines?

2 Is "is perpendicular to" an equivalence relation for the set of line segments?

3 Is "is the bisector of" an equivalence relation for the set of line segments?

Exercises 4–6: State the postulate(s) that can be used to show that each conclusion is valid.

4 $DF = GH$, therefore $GH = DF$.

5 $\overline{AB} \cong \overline{AB}$

6 $\angle P \cong \angle Q$ and $\angle P \cong \angle R$, therefore $\angle Q \cong \angle R$.

Exercises 7–10: Write the missing parts of the proof.

7 Given: $\overline{PQ} \perp \overline{QR}$ and $\overline{XY} \perp \overline{YZ}$
Prove: $m\angle PQR = m\angle XYZ$

Statements	Reasons
1. $\overline{PQ} \perp \overline{QR}$	1. _____
2. $\angle PQR$ is a right angle.	2. _____
3. _____	3. A right angle is an angle whose degree measure is 90.
4. _____	4. Given.
5. _____	5. Perpendicular lines are two lines that intersect to form right angles.
6. $m\angle XYZ = 90$	6. _____
7. $90 = m\angle XYZ$	7. _____
8. _____	8. Transitive property of equality $(3, 7)$.

8 Given: $\overrightarrow{AC}$ is the angle bisector of $\angle BAD$.
$\overrightarrow{AD}$ is the angle bisector of $\angle CAE$.
Prove: $m\angle BAC = m\angle DAE$

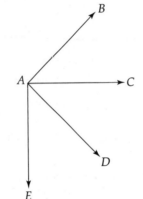

Statements	Reasons
1. _____	1. Given.
2. $\angle BAC \cong \angle CAD$	2. _____
3. _____	3. If two angles are congruent, they have the same measure.
4. _____	4. Given.
5. $\angle CAD \cong \angle DAE$	5. _____
6. $\angle BAC \cong \angle DAE$	6. _____
7. _____	7. If two angles are congruent, their measures are equal.

9 Given: $8 = x + y$ and $y = 3$
Prove: $x + 3 = 8$

Statements	Reasons
1. _____	1. Given.
2. _____	2. Given.
3. $8 = x + 3$	3. _____
4. $x + 3 = 8$	4. _____

10 Given: M is the midpoint of $\overline{AB}$
and $\overline{MB} \cong \overline{BC}$
Prove: $\overline{AM} \cong \overline{BC}$

A   M   B   C

Statements	Reasons
1. _____	1. Given.
2. _____	2. A midpoint divides a line segment into two congruent line segments.
3. $\overline{MB} \cong \overline{BC}$	3. Given.
4. $\overline{AM} \cong \overline{BC}$	4. _____

3-6 Remaining Postulates of Equality

In Chapter 1 we defined *betweenness*: B is between A and C if and only if A, B, and C are distinct collinear points and, adding the lengths of the segments, $AB + BC = AC$. We can also add the segments and find that $\overline{AB} + \overline{BC} \cong \overline{AC}$. $\overleftrightarrow{ABC}$ represents a line on which B is between A and C.

Stated more formally as the Partition Postulate:

• **Partition Postulate.** A whole is equal to the sum of its parts.

This postulate applies to any number of segments of the same line and to their lengths.

If B is between A and C, and C is between B and D,

A   B   C   D

$AB + BC + CD = AD$ and $\overline{AB} + \overline{BC} + \overline{CD} \cong \overline{AD}$.

This postulate also applies to angles and their measures.

If $\overrightarrow{AC}$ is in the interior of $\angle BAD$ and $\overrightarrow{AD}$ is in the interior of $\angle CAE$,

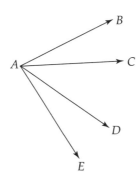

$m\angle BAC + m\angle CAD + m\angle DAE = m\angle BAE$ and
$\angle BAC + \angle CAD + \angle DAE = \angle BAE$.

The Addition Postulate of Equality applies to segments and angles, as well as the measures of segments and angles.

• **Addition Postulate of Equality**
If equals are added to equals, the sums are equal.
Example: If $m\angle a = m\angle b$ and $m\angle c = m\angle d$, then $m\angle a + m\angle c = m\angle b + m\angle d$.

If congruent segments or angles are added to congruent segments or angles, then the sums are congruent.
Example: If $\overleftrightarrow{ABC}$ and $\overleftrightarrow{DEF}$ are lines with $\overline{AB} \cong \overline{DE}$ and $\overline{BC} \cong \overline{EF}$, then $\overline{AC} \cong \overline{DF}$.

The Subtraction Postulate of Equality also applies to segments and angles, as well as the measures of segments and angles.

- **Subtraction Postulate of Equality**
  If equals are subtracted from equals, the differences are equal.

  Example: If $m\angle a = m\angle b$ and $m\angle c = m\angle d$, then $m\angle a - m\angle c = m\angle b - m\angle d$.

  If congruent segments or angles are subtracted from congruent segments or angles, then the differences are congruent.

  Example: If $\overleftrightarrow{ABC}$ is a line and B is between A and C, then $\overline{AB} = \overline{AC} - \overline{BC}$.

The multiplication postulate and the division postulate are aligned with the addition and the subtraction postulates. Proofs involving midpoints, segment bisectors, and angle bisectors often rely on these postulates. Therefore, pay special attention to the special cases involving doubles and halves.

- **Multiplication Postulate of Equality**
  If equals are multiplied by equals, the products are equal.
  Doubles of equal quantities are equal.

- **Division Postulate of Equality**
  If equals are divided by equals, the quotients are equal.
  Halves of equal quantities are equal.

 MODEL PROBLEMS

1   Given: $\angle BAC$ and D is a point in the interior region of $\angle BAC$.
    $\angle FEG$ and H is a point in the interior region of $\angle FEG$.
    $\angle BAC \cong \angle FEG$ and $\angle BAD \cong \angle FEH$
    Prove: $\angle DAC \cong \angle HEG$

SOLUTION   Construct a narrative proof.

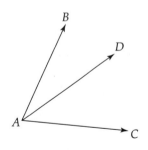 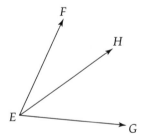

    Using the subtraction postulate of equality, when congruent angles are subtracted from congruent angles, the differences are congruent. $\angle BAC - \angle BAD = \angle FEG - \angle FEH$ or $\angle DAC \cong \angle HEG$.

2 Given: $\overline{AB} \cong \overline{CD}$, P is the midpoint of $\overline{AB}$, and Q is the midpoint of $\overline{CD}$.
Prove: $\overline{AP} \cong \overline{CQ}$

SOLUTION   Construct a narrative proof.

If two segments are congruent, they have the same measure. Therefore, $AB = CD$. Since P is the midpoint of $\overline{AB}$, $AP = \frac{1}{2}AB$. Since Q is the midpoint of $\overline{CD}$, $CQ = \frac{1}{2}CD$. Using the division postulate of equality, halves of equal quantities are equal. Therefore, $AP = CQ$. $\overline{AP} \cong \overline{CQ}$ because their measures are equal.

 Practice

Exercises 1–5: Draw a picture of the problem and name the postulate required to justify the conclusion.

1 Given: $\overline{ABC}$
Prove: $\overline{AB} + \overline{BC} = \overline{AC}$

2 Given: $\overline{AB}$ bisects $\angle BAC$, $\overline{EH}$ bisects $\angle FEG$;
$m\angle BAD = m\angle FEH$
Prove: $m\angle BAC = m\angle FEG$

3 Given: $\overline{AFB}$ and $\overline{CGD}$. $\overline{AF} \cong \overline{CG}$ and $\overline{FB} \cong \overline{GD}$
Prove: $\overline{AB} \cong \overline{CD}$

4 Given: $\overline{AFB}$ and $\overline{CGD}$. $\overline{AB} \cong \overline{CD}$ and $\overline{AF} \cong \overline{CG}$
Prove: $\overline{FB} \cong \overline{GD}$

5 Given: $\overline{AMB} \cong \overline{CND}$. M is the midpoint of $\overline{AB}$, N is the midpoint of $\overline{CD}$
Prove: $\overline{AM} \cong \overline{CN}$

Exercises 6–10: Write a formal or a narrative proof.

6

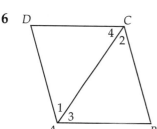

Given: $m\angle 1 = m\angle 2$
$m\angle 3 = m\angle 4$
Prove: $m\angle DAB = m\angle BCD$

7

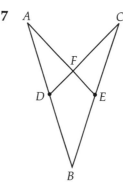

Given: $\overline{AB} \cong \overline{CB}$
$\overline{AD} \cong \overline{CE}$
Prove: $\overline{DB} \cong \overline{EB}$

8

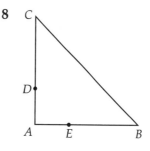

Given: $AB = AC$
$AD = \frac{1}{3}AC$
$AE = \frac{1}{3}AB$
Prove: $AD = AE$

9

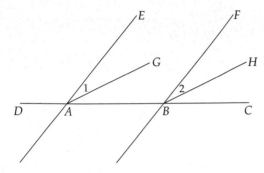

Given: m∠EAB = m∠FBC

$\overrightarrow{AG}$ is the angle bisector of ∠EAB

$\overrightarrow{BH}$ is the angle bisector of ∠FBC

Prove: m∠1 = m∠2

10

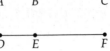

Given: AB = DE

AC = 3AB

DF = 3DE

Prove: AC = DF

CHAPTER REVIEW

Exercises 1–3: Name the property illustrated by the statement.

1 BC = BC

2 m∠1 = m∠2 and m∠2 = m∠3, therefore m∠1 = m∠3.

3 If $\overline{CD} \cong \overline{PQ}$, then $\overline{PQ} \cong \overline{CD}$.

4 Mr. Meyers asked his class to use indirect proof on the following problem:

Given: $\overrightarrow{AD}$ is the angle bisector of ∠BAC.

Prove: m∠BAD = $\frac{1}{2}$m∠BAC

What assumption should the class use?

Exercises 5–9: Draw a diagram showing what is known and write a proof to demonstrate that the conclusion is valid.

5 Given: $\overline{CMD}$; $\overline{CM} \cong \overline{MD}$
Prove: M is the midpoint of $\overline{CD}$

6 Given: $\overline{ABCD}$; $\overline{AB} \cong \overline{CD}$
Prove: $\overline{AC} \cong \overline{BD}$

7 Given: $\overline{AB} \cong \overline{CD}$; $\overline{AB}$ and $\overline{CD}$ bisect each other at E.
Prove: $\overline{AE} \cong \overline{CE}$

8 Given: $\overline{PQ} \perp \overline{QR}$; m∠PQR = m∠ABC
Prove: $\overline{AB} \perp \overline{BC}$

9 Given: $\overline{PQR}$ and $\overline{XYZ}$
PQ = XY and QR = YZ
Prove: $\overline{PR} \cong \overline{XZ}$

10

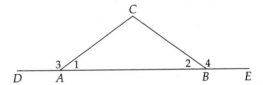

Given: ∠DAB and ∠EBA are straight angles.
m∠1 = m∠2
Prove: m∠3 = m∠4

11

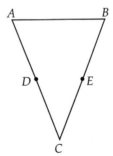

Given: $\overline{AC} \cong \overline{BC}$, $\overline{DC} \cong \overline{EC}$
Prove: $\overline{AD} \cong \overline{BE}$

12

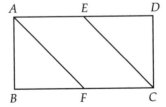

Given: $\overline{AD} \cong \overline{BC}$
E is the midpoint of $\overline{AD}$.
F is the midpoint of $\overline{BC}$.
Prove: $\overline{BF} \cong \overline{DE}$

CHAPTER 4

Congruence of Lines, Angles, and Triangles

In this chapter, we will continue to add to our toolbox of reasons that we can use to support the statements we make in more complicated geometric proofs. So far, we have specified a small set of undefined terms. We used these terms to build definitions. We next described properties of equality and created an initial list of postulates, assumptions we accept as true. In this chapter, we will expand our list of definitions and postulates necessary to continue our understanding of lines, line segments, and angles. We will use this set of undefined terms, definitions, properties, and postulates to create our first theorems, generalized conclusions that can be proven.

4-1 Setting Up a Valid Proof

Before we continue to augment our supply of reasons, be aware of the following two situations you will encounter in geometric proof problems.

1   A proof problem may appear as a conditional statement.
    So far, all deductive proof problems have had the following format:

Given:
Prove:

Sometimes the information needed for a proof is given as a conditional statement. The hypothesis must be restated as the *givens* and the conclusion must be restated as the *prove* statement.

Example
Rewrite the following conditional in the *given* and *prove* format.

If $\overline{AB} \cong \overline{CD}$ and M is the midpoint of $\overline{AB}$ and N is the midpoint of $\overline{CD}$, then $\overline{AM} \cong \overline{CN}$.

SOLUTION

Given: $\overline{AB} \cong \overline{CD}$
    M is the midpoint of $\overline{AB}$.
    N is the midpoint of $\overline{CD}$.
Prove: $\overline{AM} \cong \overline{CN}$

2 We may not assume special relationships are true because they appear that way in diagrams. Certainly, carefully drawn pictures will help us work through a proof. However, we cannot assume a conclusion is valid just because it *looks* like it is true. The only assumptions we can make from pictures are that lines that appear to be straight actually are straight and that points that appear to be on a given line are on the line.

Postulates of Lines, Line Segments, and Angles

A line, $\overleftrightarrow{AB}$, extends, without endpoints, in either direction. A line segment, $\overline{AB}$, is a part of $\overleftrightarrow{AB}$, has endpoints A and B, and is of finite length. We can *extend* $\overline{AB}$ to any length in either direction by selecting a point on $\overleftrightarrow{AB}$ but not on $\overline{AB}$ as a new endpoint.

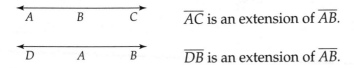

$\overline{AC}$ is an extension of $\overline{AB}$.

$\overline{DB}$ is an extension of $\overline{AB}$.

- Postulate. A line segment can be extended to any length in either direction.

  Because our line $\overleftrightarrow{AB}$ extends without bound in either direction, our two points, A and B, determine a unique line.

- Postulate. Through two given points, one and only one line can be drawn, *or two points determine a line.*

- Postulate. Two distinct lines cannot intersect in more than one point. $\overleftrightarrow{APB}$ and $\overleftrightarrow{CPD}$ intersect at P only.

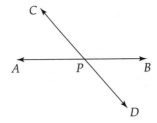

- Postulate. One and only one circle can be drawn with any given point as its center and the length of any given line segment as its radius.

  Only one circle can be drawn that has O as its center and r as its radius.

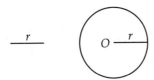

- Postulate. At a given point on a given line, one and only one perpendicular can be drawn to the line.

    At point P on $\overleftrightarrow{AB}$, only one line can be drawn perpendicular to $\overleftrightarrow{AB}$.

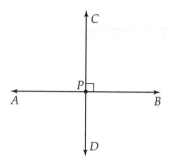

- Postulate. For any two distinct points, there is only one real number that is the length of the line segment joining the two points.

    For any segment $\overline{AB}$, there is only one real number, AB, representing the length of $\overline{AB}$.

The following postulate is called the **distance postulate**.

- Postulate. The shortest distance between two points is the length of the line segment joining these two points.

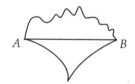

    This figure shows several *paths* from A to B. AB is the shortest length.
- Postulate. A line segment has one and only one midpoint.

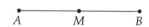

- Postulate. An angle has one and only one bisector.

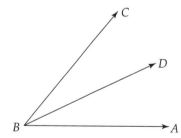

Restate the following conditional statement and complete the proof.

If $\overrightarrow{PB}$ is the angle bisector of $\angle APC$, then $m\angle APB = \frac{1}{2}m\angle APC$.

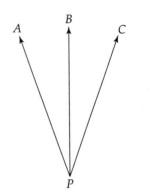

SOLUTION

Given: $\overrightarrow{PB}$ is the angle bisector of $\angle APC$.

Prove: $m\angle APB = \frac{1}{2}m\angle APC$

Statements	Reasons
1. $\overrightarrow{PB}$ is the angle bisector of $\angle APC$.	1. Given.
2. $\angle APB \cong \angle BPC$	2. Definition of angle bisector.
3. $m\angle APB = m\angle BPC$	3. Definition of congruent angles.
4. $m\angle APB + m\angle BPC = m\angle APC$	4. Partition postulate.
5. $m\angle APB + m\angle APB = m\angle APC$ or $2(m\angle APB) = m\angle APC$	5. Substitution postulate.
6. $m\angle APB = \frac{1}{2}m\angle APC$	6. Halves of equal quantities are equal.

Practice

Exercises 1–6: Rewrite the conditional statement if necessary and complete each proof. If a diagram is not supplied, draw a diagram to help visualize the proof.

1 If $\overleftrightarrow{ABC}$ is a straight line and $\overrightarrow{BD} \perp \overleftrightarrow{AC}$, then $\angle ABD \cong \angle CBD$.

Given: _____   Diagram:

_____

Prove: _____

Statements	Reasons
1. $\overleftrightarrow{ABC}$	1. Given.
2. _____	2. _____
3. $\angle ABD$ is a right angle.	3. Definition of perpendicular lines.
4. $\angle CBD$ is a right angle.	4. _____
5. $\angle ABD \cong \angle CBD$	5. _____

2 If $\overleftrightarrow{PQRS}$ is a straight line and $\overline{PR} \cong \overline{QS}$, then $\overline{PQ} \cong \overline{RS}$.

Given: _____   Diagram:
          _____

Prove: _____

Statements	Reasons
1. _____	1. _____
2. _____	2. _____
3. _____	3. Reflexive property of congruence.
4. $\overline{PR} - \overline{QR} \cong \overline{QS} - \overline{QR}$	4. _____
5. _____	5. _____

3

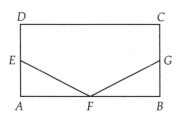

If $\overline{AD} \cong \overline{BC}$, $\overline{EF}$ bisects $\overline{AD}$, and $\overline{GF}$ bisects $\overline{BC}$, then $\overline{AE} \cong \overline{BG}$.

4

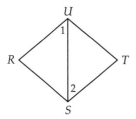

If $\angle URS \cong \angle UTS$ and $\overline{US}$ bisects both $\angle RUT$ and $\angle RST$, then $\angle 1 \cong \angle 2$.

5

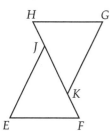

If $\overline{HJ} \cong \overline{FK}$, then $\overline{HK} \cong \overline{FJ}$.

6

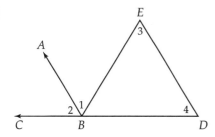

If $\overrightarrow{BA}$ bisects $\angle CBE$, $\angle 1 \cong \angle 3$, and $\angle 2 \cong \angle 4$, then $\angle 3 \cong \angle 2$.

7

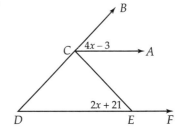

If $\overrightarrow{CA}$ bisects $\angle BCE$ and m$\angle ACE$ = m$\angle CED$, find m$\angle BCE$.

8

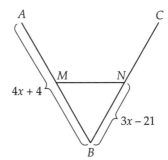

If $\overline{AB} \cong \overline{CB}$, M is the midpoint of $\overline{AB}$, and N is the midpoint of $\overline{CB}$, find AB.

9

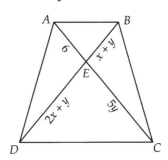

If AC = BD and DE = CE, find the value of BD.

10

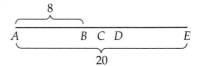

If AB = DE and BC = CD, find CE.

4-2 Proving Theorems About Angles

We begin to discuss theorems in this section. The theorem numbers refer to their placement in this book only. They are part of our proof toolbox used in later chapters. Proofs of theses theorems are left as exercises.

- Theorem 4.1. If two angles are right angles, then they are congruent.
- Theorem 4.2. If two angles are straight angles, then they are congruent.

Definitions Involving Pairs of Angles

Relationship	Description	Examples
Adjacent angles	Two angles having the same vertex, sharing one side and having no interior points in common.	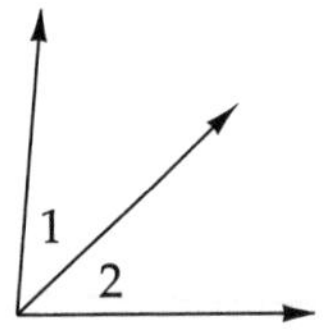 ∠1 and ∠2 are adjacent.
Complementary angles	Two angles, adjacent or nonadjacent, whose sum is 90°.	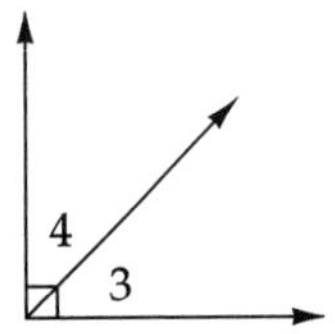 ∠3 and ∠4 are complementary.
Supplementary angles	Two angles, adjacent or nonadjacent, whose sum is 180°.	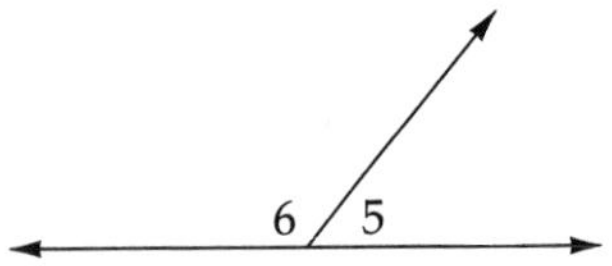 ∠5 and ∠6 are supplementary.
Vertical angles	Opposite angles formed by intersecting lines. Vertical angles are congruent: their measures are equal.	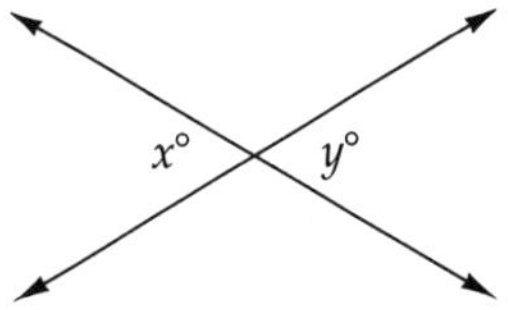 $x = y$ ∠x and ∠y are vertical angles.
Linear pairs of angles	Two adjacent angles whose sum is a straight angle.	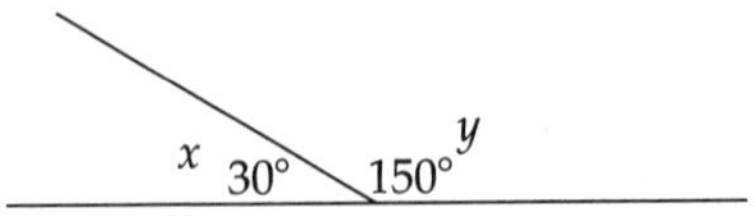 ∠x and ∠y are a linear pair.

- Theorem 4.3. If two angles are complements of the same angle, then they are congruent.

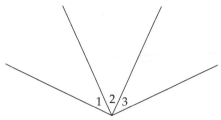

Given: ∠1 is the complement of ∠2 and ∠3 is the complement of ∠2.
Prove: ∠1 ≅ ∠3

- Theorem 4.4. If two angles are congruent, their complements are congruent.
- Theorem 4.5. If two angles are supplements of the same angle, then they are congruent.
- Theorem 4.6. If two angles are congruent, their supplements are congruent.
- Theorem 4.7. If two angles form a linear pair, then they are supplementary.
- Theorem 4.8. If two lines intersect to form congruent adjacent angles, then they are perpendicular.
- Theorem 4.9. If two lines intersect, the vertical angles are congruent.

 Practice

Exercises 1–9: Prove the indicated theorem using a narrative proof.

1 Theorem 4.1

2 Theorem 4.2

3 Theorem 4.3

4 Theorem 4.4

5 Theorem 4.5

6 Theorem 4.6

7 Theorem 4.7

8 Theorem 4.8

9 Theorem 4.9

Exercises 10–14: Write the following proofs in a narrative style.

10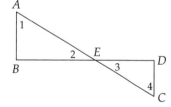

If $\overline{AC}$ and $\overline{BD}$ intersect at E, ∠1 is complementary to ∠2, and ∠3 is complementary to ∠4, then ∠1 ≅ ∠4.

11

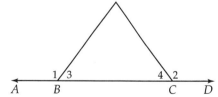

Given: $\overleftrightarrow{ABCD}$, ∠1 ≅ ∠2
Prove: ∠3 ≅ ∠4

12

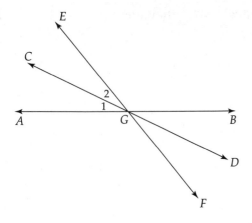

Given: $\overleftrightarrow{AGB}$, $\overleftrightarrow{CGD}$, $\overrightarrow{EGF}$, and $\angle 1 \cong \angle 2$
Prove: $\angle 1$ is supplementary to $\angle EGD$.

13

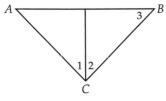

If $\angle ACB$ is a right angle and $\angle 1$ is complementary to $\angle 3$, then $\angle 2 \cong \angle 3$.

14

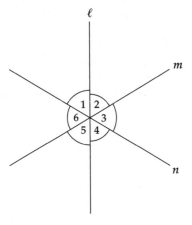

If ℓ, m, and n are straight lines, $\angle 1 \cong \angle 2$, and $\angle 2 \cong \angle 3$, then $\angle 4 \cong \angle 6$.

Exercises 15–19: Find the value of x.

15

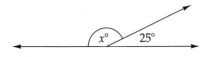

16

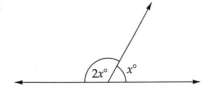

17

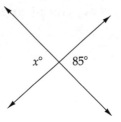

18

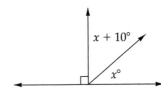

19

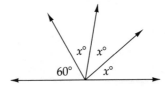

20 In the figure below, $\overleftrightarrow{AB}$ and $\overleftrightarrow{CD}$ intersect at E, $m\angle AEC = 6x - 20$, and $m\angle BED = 4x + 10$. Find the value of x.

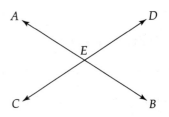

21 If $\angle x$ and $\angle y$ are complementary, $\angle y$ and $\angle z$ are supplementary, and $m\angle x = 50$, what is $m\angle z$?

22 Find the indicated measures.

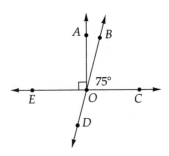

  a $m\angle DOE$
  b $m\angle AOB$
  c $m\angle DOC$

23 $\overleftrightarrow{PQ}$ and $\overleftrightarrow{RS}$ intersect at T. m$\angle PTR = 2x + 15$ and m$\angle QTS = 4x + 1$. Find m$\angle RTQ$.

24 $\overleftrightarrow{WX}$ and $\overleftrightarrow{YZ}$ intersect at V. m$\angle WVY = 3x + 25$ and m$\angle XVZ = 10x + 4$. Find m$\angle WVZ$.

25 $\overleftrightarrow{AB}$ and $\overleftrightarrow{CD}$ intersect at E. m$\angle AEC = 11y$, m$\angle CEB = 5x - 2y$, and m$\angle BED = 5x + 2y$. Find m$\angle AED$.

4-3 Congruent Polygons

We have already reviewed *congruence* (≅) with regard to lines and angles: congruent lines are equal in length, and congruent angles are equal in measure.

Congruent figures have the same size and same shape. When plane figures are congruent, one would fit exactly on top of the other. The parts that fit together, or match, are called *corresponding vertices*, *corresponding sides*, and *corresponding angles*.

Here are two important properties of **congruent figures**:

- Corresponding sides are congruent (equal in length).
- Corresponding angles are congruent (equal in measure).

We can also define congruency using a biconditional sentence. For example:

- Two polygons are congruent if and only if their corresponding sides are congruent and their corresponding angles are congruent.
- Two circles are congruent if and only if their radii are congruent.

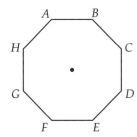 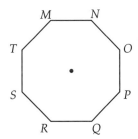

polygon *ABCDEFGH* ≅ polygon *MNOPQRST*

In a correct *congruence statement*, there is a one-to-one correspondence of points. The congruence statement above indicates that:

$\angle A \cong \angle M$	$\overline{AB} \cong \overline{MN}$
$\angle B \cong \angle N$	$\overline{BC} \cong \overline{NO}$
$\angle C \cong \angle O$	$\overline{CD} \cong \overline{OP}$
$\angle D \cong \angle P$	$\overline{DE} \cong \overline{PQ}$
$\angle E \cong \angle Q$	$\overline{EF} \cong \overline{QR}$
$\angle F \cong \angle R$	$\overline{FG} \cong \overline{RS}$
$\angle G \cong \angle S$	$\overline{GH} \cong \overline{ST}$
$\angle H \cong \angle T$	$\overline{HA} \cong \overline{TM}$

These relationships lead to the following definition:

- Two polygons are *congruent* if and only if there is a one-to-one correspondence between their vertices such that the corresponding angles are congruent and corresponding sides are congruent.

More useful as a reason in a proof, this definition can be restated as *corresponding parts of congruent polygons are congruent.*

The equivalence relations of congruence that have been applied to line segments and angles also hold for polygons.

The Reflexive Property of Congruence

- Any geometric figure is congruent to itself.

The Symmetric Property of Congruence

- A congruence may be expressed in either order.

The Transitive Property of Congruence

- Two geometric figures congruent to the same figure are congruent to each other.

Triangle Congruence

Proving congruence of triangles is especially interesting because it is possible to prove that two triangles are congruent *without* finding three pairs of congruent angles and three pairs of congruent sides.

- **Side-Angle-Side Postulate: SAS $\cong$ SAS.** Two triangles are congruent if two sides and the included angle of one triangle are congruent to two sides and the included angle of the other.

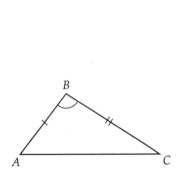 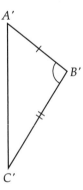

- **Angle-Side-Angle Postulate: ASA ≅ ASA.** Two triangles are congruent if two angles and the included side of one triangle are congruent to two angles and the included side of the other.

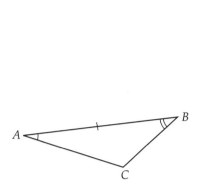
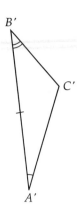

- **Side-Side-Side Postulate: SSS ≅ SSS.** Two triangles are congruent of three sides of one triangle are congruent to three sides of the other.

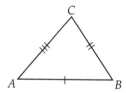
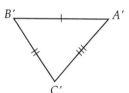

Note: If any two pairs of corresponding angles of a triangle are congruent, their measures have the same sum. The third angles must then also be congruent, so that the sum of all the interior angles is 180°. Thus, if two pairs of corresponding angles and a *nonincluded* side are given, the given side is actually included between a pair of corresponding congruent angles.

 MODEL PROBLEMS

1 △RST ≅ △XYZ. Complete each statement.

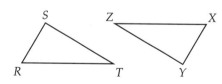

SOLUTIONS

$\overline{ST} \cong$?
$\overline{TR} \cong$?
$\angle T \cong$?
△SRT ≅ ?
△TSR ≅ ?

$\overline{ST} \cong \overline{YZ}$
$\overline{TR} \cong \overline{ZX}$
$\angle T \cong \angle Z$
△SRT ≅ △YXZ
△TSR ≅ △ZYX

2 For each pair of triangles, determine whether △I and △II are congruent.

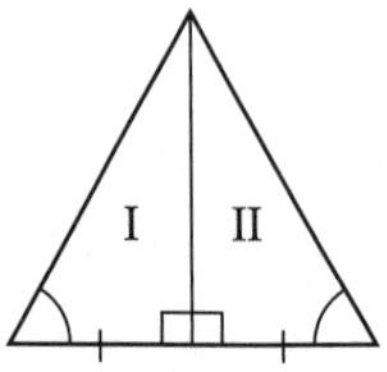

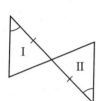

△I ≅ △II by SAS, since they share a side. They are also congruent by ASA and AAS.

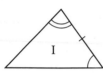

△I ≅ △II by ASA, since vertical angles are congruent.

△I ≅ △II by ASA.

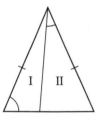

△I and △II are not congruent, because the congruent angles are not corresponding angles.

 Practice

---

1 △GHI ≅ △LMN. Which is *not* a congruence statement for these triangles?

   (1) △HGI ≅ △MLN
   (2) △HIG ≅ △MNL
   (3) △IHG ≅ △MNL
   (4) △GIH ≅ △LNM

2 Two squares are congruent if and only if:

   (1) any two corresponding angles are congruent
   (2) two pairs of corresponding angles are congruent
   (3) all four pairs of corresponding angles are congruent
   (4) a side of one is congruent to a side of the other

Exercises 3–5: Refer to pairs I to IV of triangles.

I   II

III   IV

3 Which pair of triangles are congruent by SAS?

(1) I
(2) II
(3) III
(4) IV

4 Which pair of triangles are congruent by ASA?

(1) I
(2) II
(3) III
(4) IV

5 Which pair of triangles can *not* be shown to be congruent?

(1) I
(2) II
(3) III
(4) IV

6 $\triangle ADB \cong \triangle BCA$. Complete each statement.

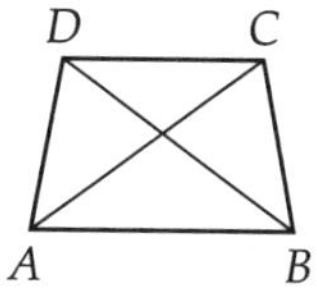

a $\overline{BD} \cong$?
b $\triangle ABD \cong$?
c $\overline{AD} \cong$?
d $\triangle DAB \cong$?

7 Write a congruence statement for each pair of triangles.

a

b

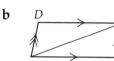

8 $\triangle ABC \cong \triangle EFG$

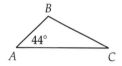 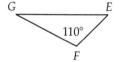

Find the measure of:

a $\angle E$
b $\angle B$
c $\angle C$

9 Provide an example that shows that this statement is *false*: "If the angles of one triangle are congruent to the angles of another triangle, then the two triangles are congruent."

Exercises 10 and 11: Draw and label polygons to fit the description.

10 $ABCD \cong MNOP$

11 $ABCDE \cong FGHIJ$

12 In the diagram below, $\overline{AE} \cong \overline{BE}$ and $\overline{CE} \cong \overline{DE}$.

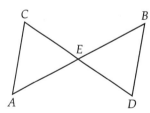

a Explain why $\triangle AEC \cong \triangle BED$.
b Given the following, find the lengths of the three sides of each triangle:
$AC = 2x$
$BD = x + 5$
$AE = x + 6$
$EC = x + 7$

13 In the diagram below, $\overline{AE} \cong \overline{BE}$, $\overline{CE} \cong \overline{DE}$, and $\angle ACE \cong \angle AEC$, m$\angle ACE = 5x$, and m$\angle BDE = 7x - 18$. Show that $\triangle DBE$ is a right triangle.

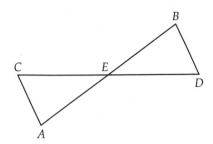

14 Find the value of AB, given the following:

$\triangle ABC \cong \triangle A'B'C'$

$\overline{AB} \cong \overline{A'B'}$

$AB = x^2 - 4x$

$A'B' = x + 14$

15 Alyssa says that two triangles are congruent if two pairs of sides are congruent and one pair of angles are congruent. Is she right? Explain.

Triangle Congruence Proofs

Whenever we are asked to prove that two triangles are congruent, we have to look at the *givens* and decide which postulate to use.

 MODEL PROBLEM

Given: $\overline{AEB}$ bisects $\overline{DEC}$ at E. $\angle 1 \cong \angle 2$.
Prove: $\triangle ADE \cong \triangle BCE$

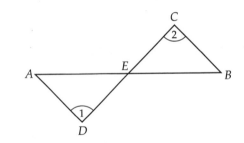

Statements	Reasons
1. $\overline{AEB}$ bisects $\overline{DEC}$ at E.	1. Given.
2. $\overline{DE} \cong \overline{EC}$	2. Definition of bisector.
3. $\angle 1 \cong \angle 2$	3. Given.
4. $\angle AED$ and $\angle BEC$ are vertical angles.	4. Definition of vertical angles.
5. $\angle AED \cong \angle BEC$	5. If two lines intersect, the vertical angles are congruent.
6. $\triangle ADE \cong \triangle BCE$	6. ASA $\cong$ ASA

1

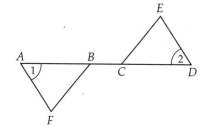

Given: $\overline{ABCD}$, $\angle 1 \cong \angle 2$, $\overline{AC} \cong \overline{BD}$, $\overline{AF} \cong \overline{DE}$
Prove: $\triangle ABF \cong \triangle DCE$

2

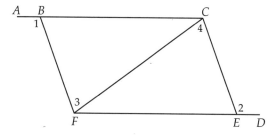

Given: $\overline{ABC}$, $\overline{DEF}$, $\angle 1 \cong \angle 2$, $\angle 3 \cong \angle 4$,
$\quad\overline{BF} \cong \overline{EC}$
Prove: $\triangle BCF \cong \triangle EFC$

3

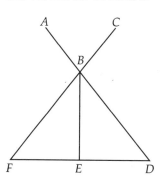

Given: $\triangle FBD$, $\overline{BE}$ is a median to $\overline{FD}$. $\overline{AD} \cong \overline{CF}$,
$\quad\overline{AB} \cong \overline{CB}$.
Prove: $\triangle FBE \cong \triangle DBE$

4

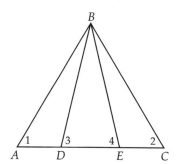

Given: $\overline{AE} \cong \overline{DC}$, $\angle 1 \cong \angle 2$, $\angle 3 \cong \angle 4$
Prove: $\triangle ADB \cong \triangle CEB$

5

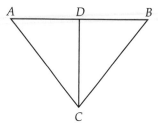

Given: D is the midpoint of $\overline{AB}$, $\overline{AC} \cong \overline{BC}$.
Prove: $\triangle ADC \cong \triangle BDC$

6

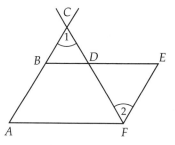

Given: $\overline{AB} \cong \overline{BC}$, $\overline{EF} \cong \overline{AB}$, $\angle 1 \cong \angle 2$, $\overline{BE}$
$\quad$ bisects $\overline{CF}$ at D.
Prove: $\triangle BCD \cong \triangle EFD$

7

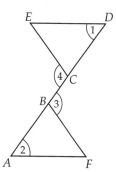

Given: $\overline{AC} \cong \overline{DB}$, $\angle 1 \cong \angle 2$, $\angle 3 \cong \angle 4$
Prove: $\triangle EDC \cong \triangle FAB$

8

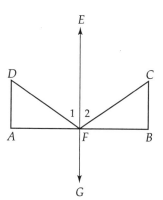

Given: $\overleftrightarrow{EG}$ is the perpendicular bisector of
$\quad\overline{AB}$, $\angle 1 \cong \angle 2$, $\overline{DF} \cong \overline{CF}$.
Prove: $\triangle ADF \cong \triangle BCF$

CHAPTER REVIEW

Exercises 1–4: Rewrite each conditional in *given* and *prove* format.

1 If ∠ABC and ∠DBE are vertical angles and ∠PQR ≅ ∠ABC, then ∠PQR ≅ ∠DBE.

2 If $\overleftrightarrow{AB}$ and $\overleftrightarrow{CD}$ intersect at E and ∠AEC ≅ ∠FGH, then ∠CEB is supplementary to ∠FGH.

3 If $\overleftrightarrow{AEB}$ and $\overleftrightarrow{CED}$ are perpendicular lines, then ∠AEC ≅ ∠AED.

4 If $\overleftrightarrow{AEB}$ and $\overleftrightarrow{CED}$ are perpendicular lines and F is not on $\overleftrightarrow{CD}$, then $\overrightarrow{FE}$ is not perpendicular to $\overleftrightarrow{AB}$.

Exercises 5–8: Write a narrative proof of each conditional statement.

5

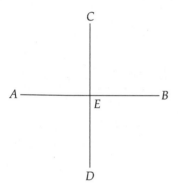

If E is the midpoint of $\overline{AB}$ and ∠AEC ≅ ∠BEC, then $\overleftrightarrow{CD}$ is the perpendicular bisector of $\overline{AB}$.

6

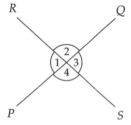

If ∠1 ≅ ∠2, then ∠3 ≅ ∠4.

7

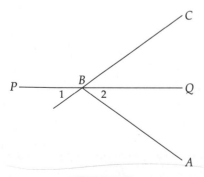

If $\overrightarrow{PQ}$ bisects ∠ABC, then ∠1 ≅ ∠2.

8

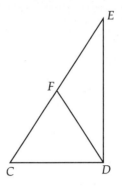

If ∠CDE is a right angle and ∠FCD ≅ ∠FDC, then ∠EDF is complementary to ∠FCD.

Exercises 9–12: $\overleftrightarrow{AB}$ and $\overleftrightarrow{CD}$ intersect at E.

9 If m∠AED = 4x + 20 and m∠BED = 9x – 48, find m∠CEB.

10 If m∠AED = 5x and m∠CEB = 7x – 26, find m∠DEB.

11 If m∠AED = 12x, m∠CEB = 6x + 10y, and m∠DEB = 10y, find m∠AEC.

12 If m∠AED = 6x, m∠CEB = 9y, and m∠DEB = 12y + 12, find m∠AEC.

13

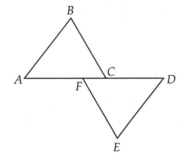

Given: $\overline{AC} ≅ \overline{DF}$, ∠A ≅ ∠D, ∠C ≅ ∠F
Prove: △ABC ≅ △DEF

14

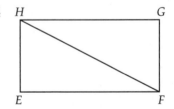

Given: $\overline{HE} ≅ \overline{FG}$, $\overline{HG} ≅ \overline{FE}$
Prove: △EFH ≅ △GHF

68 Chapter 4: Congruence of Lines, Angles, and Triangles

15

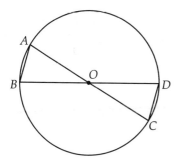

Given: A circle with center O, points A, B, C, and D on the circle, and $\overline{AOC}$ and $\overline{BOD}$ are straight lines.
Prove: $\triangle ABO \cong \triangle CDO$

16

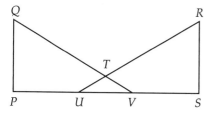

Given: $\overline{PQ} \cong \overline{RS}$, $\overline{QT} \cong \overline{RT}$, $\overline{TV} \cong \overline{TU}$, $\overline{PU} \cong \overline{VS}$, $\overline{QVT}$, $\overline{RTU}$
Prove: $\triangle PQV \cong \triangle SRU$

17

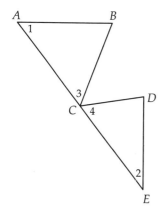

Given: C is the midpoint of $\overline{AE}$, $\angle 1 \cong \angle 2$, $\angle 3 \cong \angle BCD$, $\angle 4 \cong \angle BCD$
Prove: $\triangle ABC \cong \triangle EDC$

18

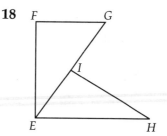

Given: $\angle FGE \cong \angle IEH$, $\angle FEG \cong \angle IHE$; I is the midpoint of $\overline{EG}$, and $EH = 2 \times EI$.
Prove: $\triangle FGE \cong \triangle IEH$

19

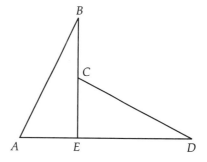

Given: $\angle AEB$ and $\angle CED$ are right angles. $\overline{AE} \cong \overline{CE}$ and $\angle A \cong \angle C$
Prove: $\triangle ABC \cong \triangle CDE$

20

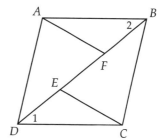

Given: $\overline{DF} \cong \overline{BE}$, $\overline{DC} \cong \overline{AD}$, $\overline{AB} \cong \overline{AD}$, $\angle 1 \cong \angle 2$
Prove: $\triangle ABF \cong \triangle DCE$

CHAPTER 5

Congruence Based on Triangles

5-1 Line Segments Associated With Triangles

As introduced in Chapter 1, the altitudes, medians, and angle bisectors of triangles are all lines drawn from a vertex of a triangle to the line opposite to the angle.

Altitude of a Triangle

An altitude of a triangle is a line segment with one endpoint at any vertex of the triangle, extending to the line containing the opposite side and perpendicular to that side.

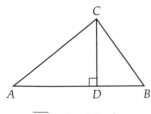
$\overline{CD}$ is the altitude.

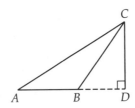
$\overline{CD}$ is the altitude.

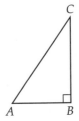
$\overline{BC}$ is the altitude.

Median of a Triangle

A median of a triangle is a line segment with one endpoint at any vertex of the triangle, extending to the midpoint (middle) of the opposite side.

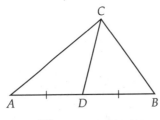
$\overline{CD}$ is the median.

Angle Bisector

An angle bisector of a triangle is a line segment with one endpoint at any vertex of the triangle, extending to the opposite side so that it bisects the vertex angle.

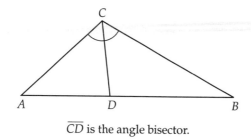

$\overline{CD}$ is the angle bisector.

In a scalene triangle, the altitude, the median, and the angle bisector drawn from any common vertex are three distinct line segments.

 **Practice**

1 Triangle *ABC* is an isosceles triangle and ∠*A* is the vertex angle. The altitude, the median, and the angle bisector are drawn from ∠*A*. How many distinct lines are drawn?

Exercises 2–6: In scalene triangle *ABC*, $\overline{CD}$ is an altitude, $\overline{CE}$ is a median, and $\overline{CF}$ is an angle bisector.

2 Draw triangle *ABC* and draw and label the altitude, the median, and the angle bisector drawn from ∠*C*.

3 State two line segments that are congruent.

4 State two line segments that are perpendicular to each other.

5 State two congruent angles, each of which has a vertex at *C*.

6 State two angles that are right angles.

5-2 Using Congruent Triangles to Prove Line Segments Congruent and Angles Congruent

We have learned that when two triangles are congruent, their corresponding sides are congruent and their corresponding angles are congruent. We can use this information about congruent triangles to prove that two line segments are congruent or two angles are congruent.

These are the steps to follow:

1 Select two triangles that contain the line segments or the angles that are to be proved congruent.
2 Prove that the two triangles are congruent.
3 Show that the line segments or angles to be proved congruent are corresponding sides or angles of the congruent triangles.
4 Corresponding parts of congruent triangles are congruent.

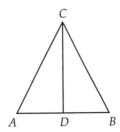

→ MODEL PROBLEM

Given: $\triangle ABC$; $\overline{CA} \cong \overline{CB}$ and $\overline{AD} \cong \overline{BD}$

Prove: $\angle ACD \cong \angle BCD$

Statements	Reasons
1. $\overline{CA} \cong \overline{CB}$	1. Given.
2. $\overline{AD} \cong \overline{BD}$	2. Given.
3. $\overline{CD} \cong \overline{CD}$	3. Reflexive property of congruence.
4. $\triangle ACD \cong \triangle BCD$	4. SSS $\cong$ SSS.
5. $\angle ACD \cong \angle BCD$	5. Corresponding parts of congruent triangles are congruent.

Note: When the triangles are compared in step 4, the three vertices of each triangle are listed so that corresponding vertices are in the same location. In this example, BCD, where the vertices are read counterclockwise, can be thought of as a reflection of $\triangle ACD$, where the corresponding vertices are read clockwise.

 Practice

Exercises 1–4: Refer to the corresponding figures below.

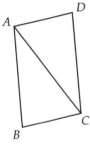

Ex. 1

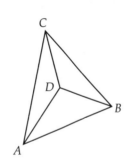

Ex. 2

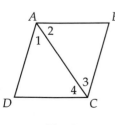

Ex. 3

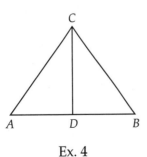

Ex. 4

1 If $\overline{AB} \cong \overline{CD}$ and $\overline{BC} \cong \overline{DA}$, prove that $\angle BAC \cong \angle DCA$.

2 If $\overline{BA} \cong \overline{BC}$ and $\overline{DA} \cong \overline{DC}$, prove that $\angle ABD \cong \angle CBD$.

3 If $\angle 1 \cong \angle 3$ and $\angle 2 \cong \angle 4$, prove that $\overline{AD} \cong \overline{CB}$.

4 If $\overline{CD}$ is the median drawn from $\angle C$ and $\overline{CD} \perp \overline{AB}$, prove that $\overline{CA} \cong \overline{CB}$.

5 $\triangle RST \cong \triangle R'S'T'$. If RS is represented by $4x - 1$, $R'S'$ is represented by $3x + 3$, and RT is represented by $x + 6$, find the $R'T'$.

6

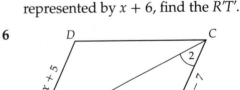

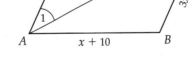

In quadrilateral $ABCD$, $\overline{AD} \cong \overline{CB}$ and $\angle 1 \cong \angle 2$. Find the lengths of all the sides of the figure.

7 In triangle RST, the median to side $\overline{ST}$ is also the altitude. If $\overline{RS}$ is represented by $3x + 11$ and $\overline{RT}$ is represented by $6x - 4$, find the value of x.

8

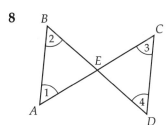

If $\angle 1 \cong \angle 3$, $\angle 2 \cong \angle 4$, and $\overline{AB} \cong \overline{CD}$, prove that $\overline{AC}$ and $\overline{BD}$ bisect each other.

9

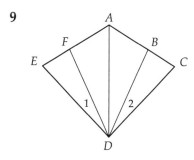

If $\overline{CD} \cong \overline{DE}$, $\angle 1 \cong \angle 2$, and $\overline{DA}$ bisects $\angle BDF$, prove that $\overline{AE} \cong \overline{AC}$.

10

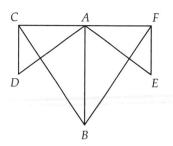

If $\overline{BA}$ is a median of $\triangle CBF$, $\overline{CD} \cong \overline{FE}$, and $\overline{FC}$ is perpendicular to both $\overline{CD}$ and $\overline{EF}$, prove that $\overline{DA} \cong \overline{AC}$.

5-3 Isosceles and Equilateral Triangles

For any isosceles triangle, the altitude, the median, and the angle bisector drawn from the vertex angle to the opposite side are the same line segment. This line segment separates the triangle into two congruent triangles. By comparing corresponding parts of these congruent triangles, we can prove the *Isosceles Triangle Theorem*.

- Theorem 5.1 (the Isosceles Triangle Theorem). If two sides of a triangle are congruent, the angles opposite these sides are congruent.

Note: The proof is left as an exercise.

A *corollary* is a theorem that can easily be deduced from another theorem. The Isosceles Triangle Theorem has two corollaries:

- Corollary 5.1.1. The median from the vertex angle of an isosceles triangle bisects the vertex angle.
- Corollary 5.1.2. The median from the vertex angle of an isosceles triangle is perpendicular to the base.

We may extend these patterns to the equilateral triangle, where all sides are congruent.

- Corollary 5.1.3. Every equilateral triangle is equiangular.

1 Prove the Isosceles Triangle Theorem.

2 Prove Corollary 5.1.1.

3 Prove Corollary 5.1.2.

4 Prove Corollary 5.1.3.

5 In $\triangle ABC$, if $\overline{AB} \cong \overline{BC}$, $m\angle A = 3x + 5$, and $m\angle B = 4x - 10$, find $m\angle C$.

6 In equilateral $\triangle ABC$, $m\angle B = 3x - 6$, $m\angle C = 3y + 6$. Find x and y.

7 Given equilateral $\triangle RST$, X is the midpoint of $\overline{RS}$, Y is the midpoint of $\overline{ST}$, and Z is the midpoint of $\overline{TR}$. Prove that $\triangle XYZ$ is an equilateral triangle.

8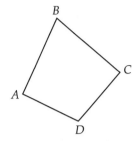

Given quadrilateral $ABCD$, $\overline{AB} \cong \overline{CB}$, $m\angle ABD = m\angle CBD$. Prove $\angle CAD \cong \angle ACD$.

9 In $\triangle ABC$, $m\angle A = 6x + 12$, $m\angle B = 8x - 8$, $m\angle C = 3x + 6$. What kind of triangle is $\triangle ABC$? Explain your answer.

10 If the measure of one base angle of an isosceles triangle is x, write an algebraic expression for the measure of the vertex angle.

5-4 Working With Two Pairs of Congruent Triangles

Sometimes we must establish the congruence of one pair of congruent triangles in a diagram in order to gain enough information to prove that a second pair of triangles in the same diagram are congruent.

 MODEL PROBLEM

Given: $\overline{AEC}$, $\overline{BED}$, and $\overline{GEF}$; $\overline{DE} \cong \overline{BE}$, $\overline{FE} \cong \overline{GE}$

Prove: $\triangle DEC \cong \triangle BEA$

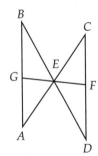

Statements	Reasons
1. $\overline{DE} \cong \overline{BE}$	1. Given.
2. $\overline{FE} \cong \overline{GE}$	2. Given.
3. $\angle GEB$ and $\angle FED$ are vertical angles.	3. Definition of vertical angles.
4. $\angle GEB \cong \angle FED$	4. If two angles are vertical angles, then they are congruent.
5. $\triangle GEB \cong \triangle FED$	5. SAS $\cong$ SAS.
6. $\angle EBG \cong \angle EDF$	6. Corresponding parts of congruent triangles are congruent.
7. $\angle AEB$ and $\angle CED$ are vertical angles.	7. Definition of vertical angles.
8. $\angle AEB \cong \angle CED$	8. If two angles are vertical angles, then they are congruent.
9. $\triangle DEC \cong \triangle BEA$	9. ASA $\cong$ ASA.

 Practice

1

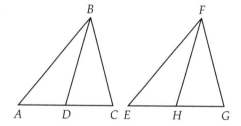

Given: $\triangle ABC \cong \triangle EFG$; $\overline{BD}$ and $\overline{FH}$ are medians.

Prove: $\overline{BD} \cong \overline{FH}$

2

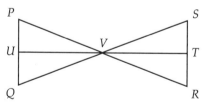

Given: $\overline{PR}$ and $\overline{QS}$ bisect each other at V; $\overline{UVT}$.

a   Prove: $\triangle PQV \cong \triangle RSV$
b   Prove: $\triangle PUV \cong \triangle RTV$

3

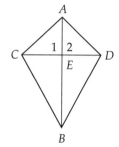

Given: $\overline{AC} \cong \overline{AD}$, $\overline{BC} \cong \overline{BD}$; $\overline{AB}$ intersects $\overline{CD}$ at E.

a   Prove: $\triangle ADE \cong \triangle ACE$
b   Prove: $\angle 1 \cong \angle 2$

4

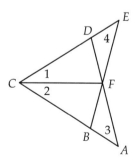

Given: $\overline{CF}$, $\overline{CBA}$, $\overline{DFA}$, $\overline{BFE}$; $\angle 1 \cong \angle 2$, $\overline{CD} \cong \overline{CB}$.

Prove: $\angle 3 \cong \angle 4$

5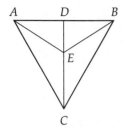

Given: $\overline{AC} \cong \overline{BC}, \overline{AE} \cong \overline{BE}$
Prove: $\overline{AD} \cong \overline{BD}$

6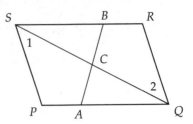

Given: $\overline{SP} \cong \overline{RQ}$, $\angle 1 \cong \angle 2$; $\overline{AB}$ bisects $\overline{QS}$ at C.

a Prove: $\triangle AQC \cong \triangle BSC$
b Prove: $\overline{AC} \cong \overline{BC}$

5-5 Proving Overlapping Triangles Congruent

When proofs involve overlapping triangles that share either sides or parts of sides, it is often helpful to separate the triangles.

 MODEL PROBLEM

Given: $\overline{DA} \cong \overline{CB}$ and $\overline{DB} \cong \overline{CA}$

Prove: $\angle ADB \cong \angle BCA$

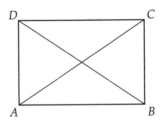

SOLUTION

Notice that the triangles overlap. Redraw the diagram, separating the triangles. Be careful to label the vertices accurately.

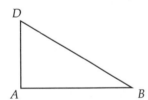   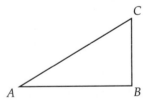

Statements	Reasons
1. $\overline{DA} \cong \overline{CB}$ (S $\cong$ S)	1. Given.
2. $\overline{BD} \cong \overline{CA}$ (S $\cong$ S)	2. Given.
3. $\overline{AB} \cong \overline{AB}$ (S $\cong$ S)	3. Reflexive property of congruence.
4. $\triangle ADB \cong \triangle BCA$	4. SSS $\cong$ SSS.
5. $\angle ADB \cong \angle BCA$	5. Corresponding parts of congruent triangles are congruent.

1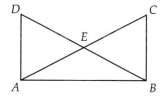

Given: $\overline{AD} \cong \overline{BC}$, $\overline{AC} \cong \overline{BD}$
Prove: $\triangle ABC \cong \triangle BAD$

2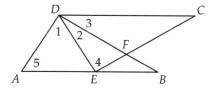

Given: $\overline{AD} \cong \overline{ED}$, $\angle 1 \cong \angle 3$, $\angle 4 \cong \angle 5$
Prove: $\triangle ADB \cong \triangle EDC$

3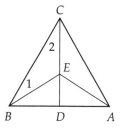

Given: $\angle 1 \cong \angle 2$, $\overline{AE} \cong \overline{BE}$; D is the midpoint of $\overline{AB}$.
Prove: $\triangle ADE \cong \triangle BDE$

4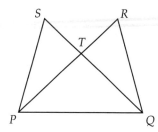

Given: $\overline{TP} \cong \overline{TQ}$; $\angle SPQ \cong \angle RQP$
Prove: $\triangle SPQ \cong \triangle RPQ$

5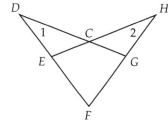

Given: $\overline{EF} \cong \overline{GF}$, $\overline{DF} \cong \overline{HF}$
Prove: $\angle 1 \cong \angle 2$

6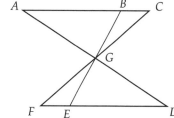

Given: $\overline{AD}$ and $\overline{FC}$ bisect each other at G
Prove: $\triangle AGB \cong \triangle DGE$

5-6 Perpendicular Bisectors of a Line Segment

The **perpendicular bisector** of a line segment is the line or segment of a line that is perpendicular to the line at its midpoint.

Recall from our discussion of isosceles triangles that the altitude and the median from the vertex angle to the opposite side are the same line segment.

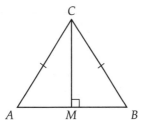

In the diagram, $\overline{CM}$ bisects $\overline{AB}$ and is perpendicular to $\overline{AB}$. Both C and M are equidistant from A and B. This circumstance suggests the following theorems. The proofs of these theorems are left as exercises.

- Theorem 5.2. If two points are each equidistant from the endpoints of a line segment, then the points determine the perpendicular bisector of the line segment.
- Theorem 5.3. If a point is equidistant from the endpoints of a line segment, then it is on the perpendicular bisector of the line segment.
  The converse of theorem 5.3 is also true:

- Theorem 5.4. If a point is on the perpendicular bisector of a line segment, then it is equidistant from the endpoints of the line segment.

Whenever a conditional statement and its converse are true, the biconditional statement combining the two statements is also true. Theorems 5.3 and 5.4 result in the following theorem:

- Theorem 5.5. A point is on the perpendicular bisector of a line segment if and only if it is equidistant from the endpoints of the line segment.

Any of the following statements is sufficient to prove that two intersecting lines or line segments are perpendicular:

- The lines intersect forming right angles.
- The lines intersect forming congruent adjacent angles.
- One line contains two points that are equidistant from the endpoints of a segment of the other line.

Concurrency of the Perpendicular Bisectors of a Triangle

- Theorem 5.6. The perpendicular bisectors of a triangle intersect at a point that is equidistant from the vertices of the triangle.

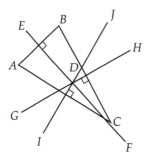

When three or more lines intersect in one point, we say they are *concurrent*. The point of *concurrency* of the perpendicular bisectors of a triangle is called the **circumcenter** of the triangle.

Given: $\overleftrightarrow{EF}$ is the perpendicular bisector of $\overline{AB}$, $\overleftrightarrow{GH}$ is the perpendicular bisector of $\overline{BC}$, $\overleftrightarrow{IJ}$ is the perpendicular bisector of $\overline{CA}$.

Prove: $\overleftrightarrow{EF}$, $\overleftrightarrow{GH}$, and $\overleftrightarrow{IJ}$ intersect at D.

Proof: It is sufficient to show that D is equidistant from A, B, and C. Let D be the intersection of $\overleftrightarrow{EF}$ and $\overleftrightarrow{GH}$, the perpendicular bisectors of $\overline{AB}$ and $\overline{BC}$, respectively. Then using theorem 5.4, D is equidistant from A and B and also from B and C. Thus, D is equidistant from C and A. Using theorem 5.3, since it is equidistant from C and A, D is on the perpendicular bisector of $\overline{CA}$. Therefore, D is equidistant from the three vertices and is on each of the three perpendicular bisectors. Since D is equidistant from A, B, and C, a circle with center at D and radius $DA = DB = DC$ can be drawn. The circle is said to circumscribe the triangle. The triangle is said to be inscribed in the circle.

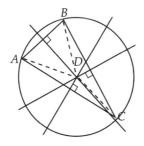

The altitudes of a triangle are concurrent. The point of concurrency is called the *orthocenter*.

The medians of a triangle are concurrent. The point of concurrency is called the *centroid*.

The angle bisectors of a triangle are concurrent. The point of concurrency is called the *incenter*.

 Practice

1 Prove theorem 5.2.

2 Prove theorem 5.5.

3 Given $\overline{PQ}$, describe the set of all points that are equidistant from P and Q.

4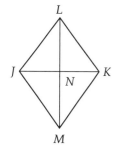

Given: $\overline{JL} \cong \overline{KL}$ and $\overline{JM} \cong \overline{KM}$
Prove: $\overline{JN} \cong \overline{KN}$

5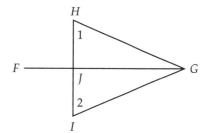

Given: $\overline{FG}$ is the perpendicular bisector of $\overline{HI}$.
Prove: $\angle 1 \cong \angle 2$

6 Given: $\overline{AB} \perp \overline{CD}$; $\overline{AB}$ and $\overline{CD}$ bisect each other.
Prove: If the segments $\overline{AC}$, $\overline{CB}$, $\overline{BD}$, and $\overline{DA}$ are drawn, the quadrilateral formed is equilateral.

7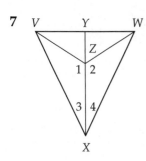

Given: $\overline{VYW}$, $\overline{YZX}$; $\angle 1 \cong \angle 2$, and $\angle 3 \cong \angle 4$
Prove: $\overline{XY}$ is the perpendicular bisector of $\overline{VYW}$.

8 The perpendicular bisectors of $\triangle ABC$ intersect at P. $AP = x - y$, $BP = 4y$, and $CP = 4$. Find x and y.

9 The perpendicular bisectors of $\triangle ABC$ intersect at P. $AP = 3x - y$, $BP = x + y$, and $CP = 4$. Find x and y.

10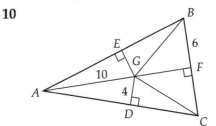

In $\triangle ABC$, the perpendicular bisectors meet at point G. Find CG.

5-7 Constructions

The constructions that follow are drawn with a straightedge and compass. If you use a ruler as a straightedge, you can use it to draw a straight line segment but not to measure distances or show that two distances are equal.

Constructing Congruent Line Segments

To Construct $\overline{CD}$ Congruent to $\overline{AB}$

- Using the straightedge, draw any segment longer than $\overline{AB}$ and mark point C near one end of the segment.
- On $\overline{AB}$, place the point of the compass on A and the pencil point on B.
- Without changing the compass setting, place the point of the compass at C and draw an arc intersecting your line segment.
- Label the point of intersection D.
- $\overline{CD} \cong \overline{AB}$.

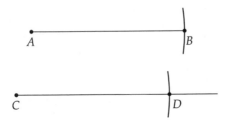

Constructing Congruent Angles

To Construct ∠FED Congruent to ∠ABC

- Draw point E and draw a line segment through it with a straightedge.
- Place the point of the compass on B and draw an arc intersecting $\overline{BA}$ and $\overline{BC}$. Label the points of intersection G and H.
- Without changing the compass setting, place the point of the compass at E and draw an arc longer than $\overset{\frown}{GH}$ through your line segment. Label the point of intersection D.
- Place the point of the compass on H and the pencil point on G.
- Without changing the compass setting, place the point of the compass at D and make a second arc that intersects the first. Label the intersection F.
- Draw $\overrightarrow{EF}$ with the straightedge.
- $∠FED \cong ∠ABC$.

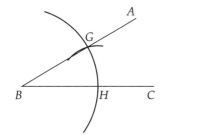 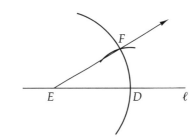

Constructing the Perpendicular Bisector of a Line Segment and the Midpoint of the Line Segment

To Construct the Perpendicular Bisector of $\overline{AB}$

- Open the compass to a radius that is greater than half of $\overline{AB}$.
- Place the point of the compass on A and draw an arc above $\overline{AB}$.
- Using the same radius, place the point of the compass on B and draw an arc that intersects the arc just drawn. Label this intersection point C.
- Using the same or a different radius, draw arcs from A and B that intersect below $\overline{AB}$.
- Label this intersection point D.
- Using a straightedge, draw $\overleftrightarrow{CD}$.
- Mark the point of intersection of $\overline{AB}$ and $\overleftrightarrow{CD}$ as M.

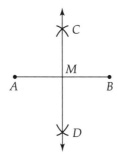

$\overleftrightarrow{CD}$ is the perpendicular bisector of $\overline{AB}$, and M is the midpoint of $\overline{AB}$.

To Construct the Bisector of ∠ABC

- With *B* as the center, draw an arc that intersects $\overline{BA}$ at *D* and $\overline{BC}$ at *E*.
- With *D* and *E* as centers, draw intersecting arcs. The radii of these two arcs must be the same. Be certain that the radius is large enough to allow an intersection.
- Label the intersection *F*.
- Draw $\overrightarrow{BF}$, the angle bisector.

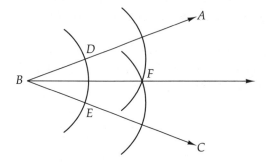

To Construct a Line Perpendicular to $\overleftrightarrow{AB}$ Through a Given Point *P* on $\overleftrightarrow{AB}$

- With the point of the compass at *P*, draw two arcs with the same radius; one intersecting $\overrightarrow{PA}$ and one intersecting $\overrightarrow{PB}$. Label the intersections *C* and *D* respectively.
- Increase the radius of the compass.
- With the point of the compass on *C*, draw an arc above $\overleftrightarrow{AB}$. With the point of the compass on *D*, draw an intersecting arc. Label the intersection *E*.
- Using a straightedge, draw $\overleftrightarrow{EP}$.

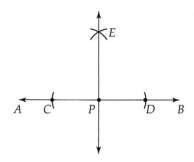

To Construct a Line Perpendicular to $\overleftrightarrow{AB}$ Through a Given Point *P* Not on $\overleftrightarrow{AB}$

- With the point of the compass at *P*, draw an arc that intersects $\overleftrightarrow{AB}$ twice. Label the points of intersection *C* and *D*.
- Using points *C* and *D* as centers, and using a slightly longer radius on the compass, draw arcs that intersect at point *E*.
- Using the straightedge to draw a line through *E* and *P*.
- $\overleftrightarrow{EP} \perp \overleftrightarrow{AB}$.

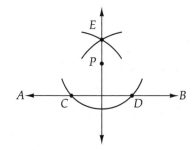

Since the line joining a point and its image over a line reflection is perpendicular to the line of reflection, a very similar construction to the one above can be used to find the image of line reflection.

 Practice

1   Use your compass to determine which two triangles are congruent.

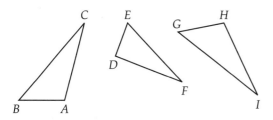

   (1) △ABC and △DEF
   (2) △ABC and △GHI
   (3) △DEF and △GHI
   (4) △BAC and △GHI

2   Draw a line segment and label it AB. Construct $\overline{AC}$ that is three times the length of $\overline{AB}$.

3   Draw an angle and label it RST. Construct SV so that ∠RSV has twice the measure of ∠RST.

4   Draw two line segments. Construct a third line segment that has a length equal to the sum of the two initial segments.

5   Draw two angles. Construct a third angle that has a measure equal to the difference of the two initial angles.

6   Give a geometric reason why the procedure of copying a line works. (Hint: Think of the compass as two sides of a triangle.)

7   Give a geometric reason why the procedure of a copying an angle works.

8   How would you use a compass and straightedge to construct an isosceles triangle?

9   Construct a right triangle.

10 Draw a triangle and construct an altitude.

11 Draw a scalene triangle and construct a median.

12 Draw a line segment AB. Let $\overline{AB}$ be one side of a square. Complete the square.

13 Draw a scalene triangle and construct the orthocenter.

14 Draw a scalene triangle and construct the centroid.

15 Draw a scalene triangle and construct the incenter.

16 Draw a scalene triangle and construct the circumcenter.

1

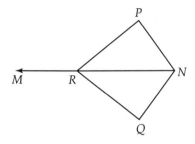

Given: $\overrightarrow{NM}$ is a ray that bisects $\angle PNQ$ and
$\angle RPN \cong \angle RQN$.
Prove: $\triangle RPN \cong \triangle RQN$

2

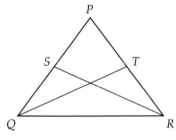

Given: In $\triangle PQR$, $\overline{PQ} \cong \overline{PR}$, $\overline{QT}$ and $\overline{RS}$ are
medians.
Prove: $\triangle PQT \cong \triangle PRS$

3

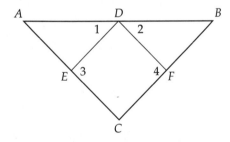

Given: $\angle 1 \cong \angle 2$, $\overline{DE} \cong \overline{DF}$, and $\angle 3 \cong \angle 4$
Prove: $\triangle ABC$ is an isosceles triangle.

4

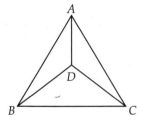

Given: $\triangle ABC$ is an equilateral triangle;
$\angle DCB \cong \angle DBC$.
Prove: $\overline{AD}$ bisects $\angle BAC$.

5

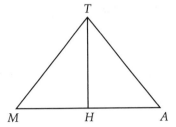

Given: $\overline{MHA}$; $\overline{TM} \cong \overline{TA}$; $\overline{TH}$ bisects $\angle MTA$.
Prove: $\overline{TH}$ is an altitude of $\triangle MTA$.

6

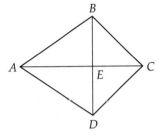

Given: $\overline{AB} \cong \overline{AD}$, $\overline{CB} \cong \overline{CD}$; $\overline{AEC}$
Prove: $\overline{AE}$ is an altitude of $\triangle DAB$.

7

Given: $\overline{AB} \cong \overline{BD}$, $\angle A \cong \angle D$, $\angle DBA \cong \angle CBD$
Prove: $\triangle ABE \cong \triangle DBC$

8

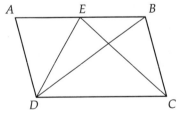

Given: $\overleftrightarrow{AB}$, $\overline{DA} \cong \overline{DE}$, $\angle ADE \cong \angle BDC$,
$\angle DAE \cong \angle DEC$.
Prove: $\triangle DAB \cong \angle DEC$

9

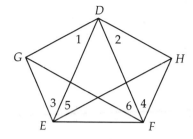

Given: $\overline{DE} \cong \overline{DF}$, $\angle 1 \cong \angle 2$, and $\angle 3 \cong \angle 4$
Prove: $\angle 5 \cong \angle 6$

10

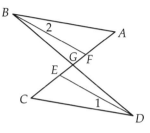

Given: $\overline{AC}$ and $\overline{BD}$ bisect each other at G; $\angle 1 \cong \angle 2$.
Prove: $\overline{EC} \cong \overline{FA}$.

11 Prove that in two congruent triangles, two corresponding angle bisectors are congruent.

12

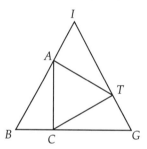

If $\triangle BIG$ is equilateral and $\overline{IA} \cong \overline{BC} \cong \overline{GT}$, prove that $\triangle CAT$ is equilateral.

13

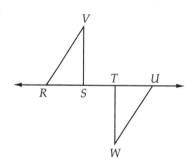

If $\overleftrightarrow{RU}$ is a straight line, $\overline{RT} \cong \overline{US}$, $\angle R \cong \angle U$, and $\angle VST \cong \angle WTS$, prove that $\triangle RVS \cong \triangle UWT$.

14

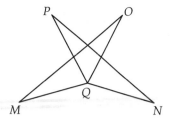

If $\overline{MQ} \cong \overline{NQ}$, $\overline{QP} \cong \overline{QO}$; $\overline{PQ} \perp \overline{MQ}$, $\overline{OQ} \perp \overline{NQ}$, prove that $\triangle MQO \cong \triangle NQP$.

15

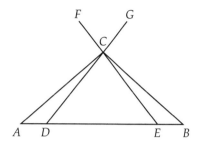

$\overleftrightarrow{AB}$, $\overleftrightarrow{EF}$, and $\overleftrightarrow{DG}$ are straight lines; $\overline{AC} \cong \overline{BC}$, and $\angle ACF \cong \angle BCG$.
Prove that $\triangle DCE$ is an isosceles triangle.

16 Draw two line segments, $\overline{AB}$ and $\overline{CD}$. Construct a line segment equal in length to the sum of the lengths of $\overline{AB}$ and $\overline{CD}$.

17 Draw line segment $\overline{AB}$ and divide it into four congruent parts.

18 Draw an obtuse angle and construct its bisector.

19 Draw scalene triangle ABC and the median to side AB.

20 Draw $\angle ABC$ and construct congruent $\angle A'B'C'$.

21 Draw $\triangle RST$ and construct the bisectors of each angle. Mark the intersection of the bisectors as point P.

22 Draw a line segment $\overline{AB}$ and one point, P, on the segment. Construct a segment perpendicular to $\overline{AB}$ through P.

23 Construct an equilateral triangle.

24 Draw a line segment $\overline{AB}$ and construct its midpoint.

6

Transformations and the Coordinate Plane

6-1 Cartesian Coordinate System

In this chapter we will investigate *transformations* of polygons with given vertices. A transformation occurs when the location, size, or orientation of a figure is changed. Many of the examples we will investigate involve figures drawn on the coordinate plane. Before we formally define each transformation, it is important to review some of the basic facts about the Cartesian coordinate system learned in pre-algebra and algebra.

The Cartesian coordinate system consists of a coordinate grid separated by the *x*-axis (a horizontal number line) and the *y*-axis (a vertical number line). The intersection of the *x*-axis and the *y*-axis is called the **origin**. The two axes divide the grid into four **quadrants**, numbered I to IV counterclockwise, as shown below.

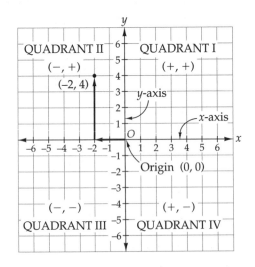

Every point on the grid can be identified with two numbers called **coordinates**:

- The first number is the *x*-**coordinate** (or **abscissa**). The absolute value of this number is the distance from the origin horizontally to the point on the *x*-axis.
- The second number is the *y*-**coordinate** (or **ordinate**). The absolute value of this number is the distance from the origin vertically to the point on the *y*-axis.

- For any point, the coordinates are written (x, y). When in this form, they are called an **ordered pair**. The coordinates of the origin are $(0, 0)$.
- Point $(-2, 4)$ on the graph has an x-coordinate of -2 and a y-coordinate of 4.
- The correct signs for coordinates in each quadrant are shown in parentheses.

Note: All graphs you draw must be labeled. The x-axis and y-axis must be labeled and the scale $(1, 2, 3, \ldots; 2, 4, 6, \ldots)$ must be indicated.

The following postulates are relationships regarding points and lines on the coordinate plane.

- Postulate. Two points are on the same horizontal line if and only if they have the same y-coordinates or ordinate values.
- Postulate. The length of a horizontal line segment is the absolute value of the difference of their x-coordinates or abscissas.
- Postulate. Two points are on the same vertical line if and only if they have the same x-coordinates or abscissa values.
- Postulate. The length of a vertical line segment is the absolute value of the difference of their y-coordinates or ordinates.
- Postulate. Each vertical line is perpendicular to each horizontal line.

Polygons on the Coordinate Plane

A polygon can be represented in the coordinate plane by locating its vertices and then drawing the sides connecting the vertices in either clockwise or counterclockwise order.

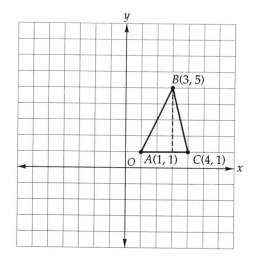

The graph above shows $\triangle ABC$. The vertices are $A(1, 1)$, $B(3, 5)$, and $C(4, 1)$.

Remembering the area formula for a triangle, $A = \frac{1}{2}bh$, we can use the postulates above to find the area of this triangle. The base, $\overline{AC}$, is a horizontal line. AC is the absolute value of the difference in the x-coordinates $= |1 - 4| = |-3| = 3$. The height is the vertical line segment drawn from vertex B to base $\overline{AC}$. The measure of the height is the absolute value of the difference in the y-coordinates. The y-coordinate (ordinate) of each point on $\overline{AC}$ is 1 and, therefore, the y-coordinate of the foot of the perpendicular segment drawn from B to $\overline{AC}$ is 1. Therefore, the measure of the height is $|5 - 1| = 4$. $A = \frac{1}{2}(3 \bullet 4) = 6$.

The Distance Formula

We will examine the distance between any two points in the coordinate plane that do not lie on the same horizontal or vertical line with an example:

Let the coordinates of A be $(1, 4)$ and the coordinates of B be $(4, 8)$. We will use the Pythagorean theorem to find AB.

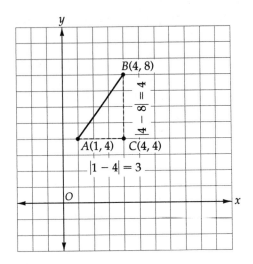

1. Draw a horizontal line segment through A and a vertical line segment through B to form a right triangle. Label the third vertex of the triangle C. The coordinates of C are $(4, 4)$.

2. Use the postulates above to find that the length of the horizontal segment is 3 and the length of the vertical segment is 4.

3. Use the Pythagorean theorem to find the length of the hypotenuse, which is the distance between the two points.
$AB^2 = AC^2 + BC^2$
$AB^2 = 3^2 + 4^2$
$AB^2 = 9 + 16$
$AB^2 = 25$
$AB = 5$

We will now derive a formula for the distance, d, from any two points $A(x_1, y_1)$ and $B(x_2, y_2)$. Draw a right triangle as we did in the example above. The horizontal and vertical segments meet at point C with coordinates (x_2, y_1).

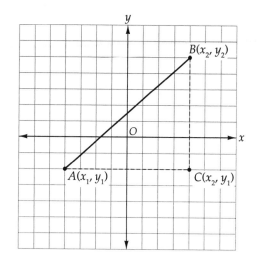

Then, $AC = |x_2 - x_1|$ and $BC = |y_2 - y_1|$

$(AB)^2 = (AC)^2 + (BC)^2$

Let d = the distance AB

$d^2 = (AC)^2 + (BC)^2$

$d^2 = |x_2 - x_1|^2 + |y_2 - y_1|^2$ Since squared values are positive, we can remove the absolute value signs.

$d^2 = (x_2 - x_1)^2 + (y_2 - y_1)^2$

$d = \sqrt{(x_2 - x_1)^2 + (y_2 - y_1)^2}$

The distance, d, between any two points (x_1, y_1) and (x_2, y_2) is found by the formula

$d = \sqrt{(x_2 - x_1)^2 + (y_2 - y_1)^2}$.

 MODEL PROBLEMS

1 Find the length of the line segment that joins $R(-3, 6)$ and $J(0, 2)$.

SOLUTION

Use the distance formula.

$d = \sqrt{(x_2 - x_1)^2 + (y_2 - y_1)^2}$

$d = \sqrt{[0 - (-3)]^2 + (2 - 6)^2} = \sqrt{3^2 + (-4)^2}$

$\quad = \sqrt{9 + 16} = \sqrt{25}$

$\quad = 5$

ANSWER: $RJ = 5$

2 Find (a) the area and (b) the circumference of a circle whose center is at $C(3, -3)$ and that passes through point $A(7, 1)$.

SOLUTION

The radius of the circle is AC. Use the distance formula to find its length.

$$d = \sqrt{(x_2 - x_1)^2 + (y_2 - y_1)^2}$$

Thus, $d_{AC} = \sqrt{(7 - 3)^2 + [1 - (-3)]^2} = \sqrt{4^2 + 4^2} = \sqrt{16 + 16} = \sqrt{16 \bullet 2} = 4\sqrt{2}$

a Now substitute $4\sqrt{2}$ for the *radius* in the formula for the area of a circle.

$$A = \pi r^2$$
$$= \pi(4\sqrt{2})^2$$
$$= \pi(16 \bullet 2) = 32\pi$$

b Substitute $4\sqrt{2}$ for the *radius* in the formula for the circumference of a circle.

$$C = 2\pi r$$
$$= 2\pi(4\sqrt{2})$$
$$= 8\sqrt{2}\pi$$

3 Use the distance formula to show that $\triangle ABC$, with vertices $A(-4, 3)$, $B(6, 1)$, and $C(2, -3)$, is a right triangle.

SOLUTION

In order for any triangle to be a right triangle, the Pythagorean theorem must hold. Use the distance formula to find the length of each side of the triangle and substitute the values in the Pythagorean theorem.

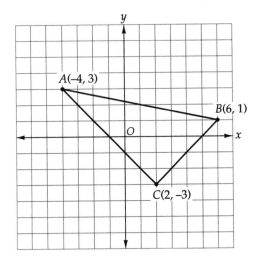

$$d = \sqrt{(x_2 - x_1)^2 + (y_2 - y_1)^2}$$
$$d_{AB} = \sqrt{[6 - (-4)]^2 + (1 - 3)^2}$$
$$d_{AB} = \sqrt{10^2 + (-2)^2}$$
$$d_{AB} = \sqrt{100 + 4} = \sqrt{104}$$
$$d_{BC} = \sqrt{(2 - 6)^2 + [(-3) - 1]^2}$$
$$d_{BC} = \sqrt{(-4)^2 + (-4)^2}$$
$$d_{BC} = \sqrt{16 + 16} = \sqrt{32}$$
$$d_{AC} = \sqrt{[2 - (-4)]^2 + [(-3) - 3]^2}$$
$$d_{AC} = \sqrt{6^2 + (-6)^2}$$
$$d_{AC} = \sqrt{36 + 36} = \sqrt{72}$$

The longest side, the hypotenuse, has to be $\sqrt{104}$. Substitute the values for the legs and the hypotenuse in the Pythagorean theorem.

$$a^2 + b^2 = c^2$$
$$(\sqrt{32})^2 + (\sqrt{72})^2 = (\sqrt{104})^2$$
$$32 + 72 = 104$$
$$104 = 104$$

ANSWER: Since the equation for the Pythagorean theorem is true, triangle ABC is a right triangle.

Practice

Exercises 1–6: Find the distance between each pair of points. (Answers may be left in simplest radical form.)

1 $(2, 5)$ and $(6, 8)$

(1) $\sqrt{7}$
(2) 5
(3) $\sqrt{105}$
(4) $\sqrt{233}$

2 $(-6, 4)$ and $(0, 4)$

(1) $2\sqrt{7}$
(2) 6
(3) 10
(4) $4\sqrt{10}$

3 $(-6, 4)$ and $(4, 4)$

(1) $\sqrt{6}$
(2) $\sqrt{8}$
(3) $\sqrt{68}$
(4) 10

4 $(-6, -2)$ and $(-6, 4)$

(1) $2\sqrt{5}$
(2) 6
(3) $2\sqrt{29}$
(4) $2\sqrt{35}$

5 $(-3, -5)$ and $(-2, -6)$

(1) $\sqrt{2}$
(2) $\sqrt{5}$
(3) $\sqrt{18}$
(4) $\sqrt{130}$

6 $(2, 20)$ and $(3, 5)$

(1) 4
(2) $\sqrt{226}$
(3) $\sqrt{298}$
(4) $5\sqrt{26}$

7 Find the coordinates of the points A and B in each figure.

a

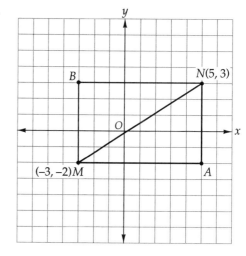

b

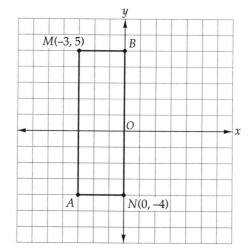

c

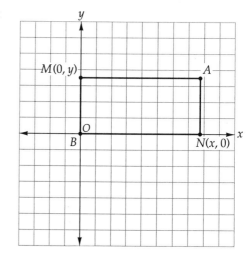

8 Find the area of the triangle whose vertices are $A(2, 1)$, $B(6, 1)$, and $C(5, 4)$.

9 Find the area of the triangle whose vertices are $A(-3, 8)$, $B(1, 8)$, and $C(0, 4)$.

10 Find the area of the triangle whose vertices are $A(2, 6)$, $B(2, 2)$, and $C(3, 3)$.

11 Find the area of the triangle whose vertices are $A(4, 8)$, $B(4, 2)$, and $C(-2, 5)$.

12 Square $ABCD$ has coordinates $A(1, 6)$, $B(5, 6)$, $C(5, 2)$, and $D(x, y)$. What are the coordinates of D? (Remember that all sides of a square have the same length.)

Exercises 13 and 14: Refer to the figure below.

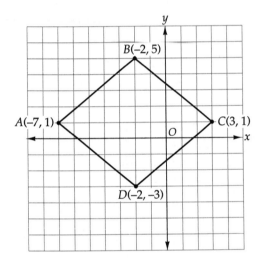

13 Find the area of quadrilateral $ABCD$ by adding the areas of halves of the figure.

14 Using the distance formula, find the perimeter of $ABCD$.

Exercises 15 and 16: Refer to the figure below.

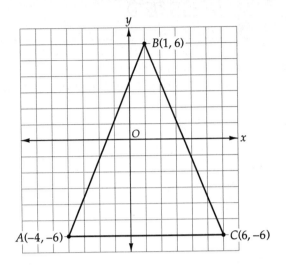

15 What is the area of $\triangle ABC$?

16 What is the perimeter of $\triangle ABC$?

Exercises 17–20: Identify the triangle with the given vertices as isosceles or scalene. Explain your reasoning.

17 $P(2, 3)$, $A(5, 7)$, $T(1, 4)$

18 $A(3, 4)$, $B(5, -3)$, $C(-2, 2)$

19 $M(-6, 2)$, $A(5, -1)$, $D(4, 4)$

20 $W(7, -1)$, $I(2, -2)$, $T(4, 9)$

21 Show that the triangle with vertices $(0, 0)$, $(2, 0)$, and $(1, \sqrt{3})$ is equilateral. Explain your reasoning.

22 What is the length of the diameter of a circle whose center is at point $(1, 2)$ and that passes through point $(4, -2)$?

23 The vertices of quadrilateral $ABCD$ are $A(3, 2)$, $B(3, -1)$, $C(7, -1)$, and $D(7, 2)$. Show that the diagonals are congruent. Explain your reasoning.

24 Use the distance formula to show that the triangle ABC, with vertices $A(-1, -2)$, $B(3, 2)$, and $C(1, 4)$, is a right triangle. Explain your reasoning.

6-2 Translations

A **transformation** occurs when the location, size, or orientation of an original figure is changed. Traditionally, the vertices of the original figure are labeled with letters, such as A, B, and C. We refer to the original figure as the **preimage**. The corresponding **transformation image** has points that are labeled with the prime sign, such as A', B', and C'. On the coordinate plane, an algebraic rule or **mapping** defines the transformation by assigning ordered pairs of the coordinate plane to new locations. Each of the transformations defined in this chapter is a one-to-one function. It is a set of ordered pairs in which the first element of each pair is a point of the plane and the second element is the image of that point under the transformation. Each preimage maps onto one and only one image.

A **translation** is a transformation in which each point in a figure *slides* a certain distance and in the same direction.

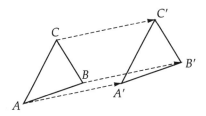

In the diagram above, $\triangle A'B'C'$ is the image of $\triangle ABC$. $AA' = BB' = CC'$ and $\triangle ABC \cong \triangle A'B'C'$. On the coordinate plane, the translation is defined by a **mapping rule**. $T_{a, b}(x, y) = (x + a, y + b)$. Under a translation, distance, angle measure, collinearity, betweenness, parallelism, and orientation are preserved.

 MODEL PROBLEMS

1 What is the image of point $P(-3, 2)$ under the transformation $T_{-2, 6}$?

SOLUTION

$T_{-2, 6}$ means add -2 to the x-value (-3) and add 6 to the y-value (2). Thus, the image of point P is ($-5, 8$).

ANSWER: $(-5, 8)$

2 A transformation maps $P(x, y)$ onto $P'(x - 4, y + 2)$. Under the same transformation, what are the coordinates of Q', the image of $Q(2, -3)$?

SOLUTION

Since the given transformation is a translation $T_{-4, 2}$, the point $Q(2, -3)$ is mapped onto Q' by adding -4 to the x-value (2) and 2 to the y-value (-3). Hence, the coordinates of Q' are ($-2, -1$).

ANSWER: $(-2, -1)$

3 If the coordinates of the vertices of $\triangle ABC$ are $A(-4, -1)$, $B(-1, 5)$, and $C(2, 1)$, what is the image of $\triangle ABC$ under the translation $T_{4,3}$?

SOLUTION

Translation $T_{4,3}$ means we must add 4 to each x-value and 3 to each y-value. Thus, $A(-4, -1)$ is mapped onto $A'(0, 2)$, $B(-1, 5)$ onto $B'(3, 8)$, and $C(2, 1)$ onto $C'(6, 4)$.

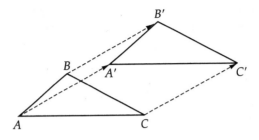

 Practice

---

1 The image of $H(-1, 3)$ under the translation $T_{2,-1}$ is:

(1) $(1, 2)$
(2) $(-3, 4)$
(3) $(-2, -3)$
(4) $(-2, 5)$

2 The transformation $T_{-2, 3}$ maps the point $(5, -5)$ onto the point whose coordinates are:

(1) $(-10, -15)$
(2) $(3, -2)$
(3) $(8, -7)$
(4) $(-2, 5)$

3 If translation T maps point $P(-3, 1)$ onto point $P'(5, 5)$, which is the translation T?

(1) $T_{2, 4}$
(2) $T_{2, 6}$
(3) $T_{8, 6}$
(4) $T_{8, 4}$

4 If the transformation $T_{x, y}$ maps point $M(1, -3)$ onto point $M'(-5, 8)$, what is the value of x?

(1) 4
(2) 1
(3) -5
(4) -6

Exercises 5 and 6: Express the translation in the form $T_{a, b}$.

5 $(x, y) \rightarrow (x, y + 2)$

6 $(x, y) \rightarrow (x - 3, y)$

Exercises 7 and 8: Find the image of the point $(5, -2)$ under the translation.

7 $T_{-1, 1}$

8 $T_{-2, -5}$

Exercises 9–12: Find the image or preimage, as specified, of the given point under translation T. Translation T is defined by $(x, y) \rightarrow (x + 3, y - 1)$.

9 Find the image of $(-1, 5)$.

10 Find the image of $(1, -2)$.

11 Find the preimage of $(-1, -3)$.

12 Find the preimage of $(1, 1)$.

Exercises 13 and 14: Find the values of a and b if the translation $T_{a, b}$ maps the first point onto the second.

13 $(2, 3) \rightarrow (5, 5)$

14 $(5, 0) \rightarrow (3, 2)$

15 If a translation maps (3, 1) onto (−4, 2), what is the image of (4, −1) under the same translation?

16 If a translation maps point (7, −2) to point (0, −3), what is the image of point (0, −2) under the same translation?

17 A transformation maps $P(x, y)$ onto $P'(x + 3, y − 5)$. What are the coordinates of Q whose image under the same transformation is $Q'(7, 2)$?

18 If the coordinates of the vertices of $\triangle KEN$ are $K(8, 5)$, $E(10, −3)$, and $N(−2, 2)$, then what are the coordinates of the vertices of the image of $\triangle KEN$ under the translation defined by $(x, y) \rightarrow (x − 6, y + 4)$?

19 The coordinates of the vertices of $\triangle DEW$ are $D(−3, 5)$, $E(4, 6)$, and $W(0, 2)$. Graph $\triangle DEW$ and complete the following:

   a Graph $\triangle D'E'W'$, the image of $\triangle DEW$ under the translation $T_{2, −3}$.

   b Graph $\triangle D''E''W''$, the image of $\triangle D'E'W'$ under the translation $T_{1, 4}$.

   c Name a single transformation that would map $\triangle DEW$ onto $\triangle D''E''W''$.

20 The coordinates of the vertices of quadrilateral *WASH* are $W(1, −2)$, $A(0, 1)$, $S(3, 4)$, and $H(5, 1)$. Graph quadrilateral *WASH* and complete the following:

   a Graph quadrilateral $W'A'S'H'$, the image of quadrilateral *WASH* under the translation $T_{−3, 2}$.

   b Graph, $W''A''S'H''$, the image of quadrilateral $W'A'S'H'$ under the translation $T_{7, −1}$.

   c Name a single transformation that would map quadrilateral *WASH* onto quadrilateral $W''A''S'H''$.

6-3 Line Reflections and Symmetry

A **line reflection** is a transformation in which a figure is reflected over a given line as if in a mirror. Each point of the reflection image is the same distance from a line of reflection as the corresponding point in the original figure. The line of reflection is also perpendicular to each line joining a point to its image. In Figure (a), line l is the bisector of $\overline{AA'}$, $\overline{BB'}$, and $\overline{CC'}$. In Figure (b), line m is the bisector of $\overline{AA'}$, $\overline{CC'}$, and $\overline{TT'}$.

(a)

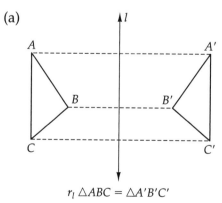

$r_l \triangle ABC = \triangle A'B'C'$

(b)

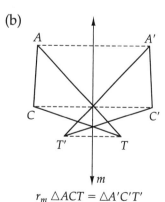

$r_m \triangle ACT = \triangle A'C'T'$

Note: The line of reflection is a *perpendicular bisector* of each line segment joining a point to its image.

Under a line reflection, distance, angle measure, collinearity, and betweenness are preserved. However, since the image "flips over" the line of reflection, the orientations of the preimage and image are opposite. If preimage $\triangle ABC$ is read clockwise, its image $\triangle A'B'C'$ would be read counterclockwise.

Line Reflection Mapping Rules

Reflections in the x-axis	$r_{x\text{-axis}}(x, y) = (x, -y)$
Reflections in the y-axis	$r_{y\text{-axis}}(x, y) = (-x, y)$
Reflections in the $y = x$ line	$r_{y = x}(x, y) = (y, x)$
Reflections in the $y = -x$ line	$r_{y = -x}(x, y) = (-y, -x)$

These rules are applied in the following model problems.

 MODEL PROBLEMS

1 Find a reflection in the x-axis of figure $ABCD$ with coordinates $A(-4, 3)$, $B(-3, 5)$, $C(4, 6)$, and $D(0, 2)$.

SOLUTION

Using our mapping rule, the image points are $A'(-4, -3)$, $B'(-3, -5)$, $C'(4, -6)$, and $D'(0, -2)$. Observe that the image of each point is the same perpendicular distance from the x-axis as the original points A, B, C, and D, and the x-axis or $y = 0$ line is the perpendicular bisector of $\overline{AA'}$, $\overline{BB'}$, $\overline{CC'}$, and $\overline{DD'}$.

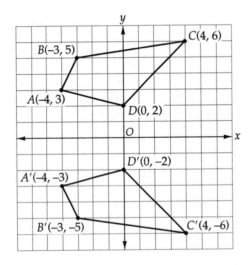

2 Find the reflection in the *y*-axis of $\triangle PQR$ with the coordinates $P(-8, -2)$, $Q(-4, 4)$, and $R(-3, -1)$.

SOLUTION

Using our mapping rule, the image points are $P'(8, -2)$, $Q'(4, 4)$, and $R'(3, -1)$. Again, observe that the image of each point is the same perpendicular distance from the *y*-axis as the original P, Q, and R points.

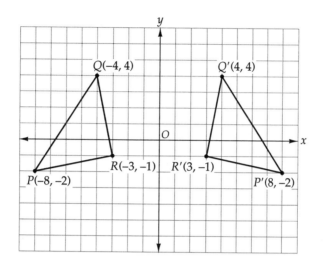

3 Find the reflection across the $y = x$ line of $\triangle ABC$ with coordinates $A(2, 1)$, $B(9, 6)$, and $C(5, -4)$.

SOLUTION

Using our mapping rule, the image points are $A'(1, 2)$, $B'(6, 9)$, and $C'(-4, 5)$.

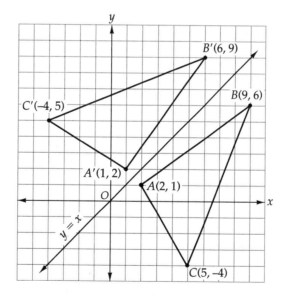

4 Find the reflection in the $y = -x$ line of $\triangle PQR$ with the coordinates $P(2, 2)$, $Q(5, 3)$, and $R(3, -1)$.

SOLUTION

Using our mapping rule, the image points are $P'(-2, -2)$, $Q'(-3, -5)$, and $R'(1, -3)$.

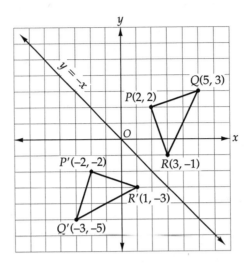

For reflections across any vertical or horizontal line, the easiest way to find the image is to use the **counting method**. Count the distance from each point to the line of reflection and then use that distance to find the image point on the other side of the line. In horizontal and vertical reflections, either the x or the y will change, not both.

 MODEL PROBLEMS

1 Find the reflection of the figure whose coordinates are $A(-1, 3)$, $B(4, 6)$, $C(7, 2)$ across the line represented by $x = 2$.

SOLUTION

The line $x = 2$ is the perpendicular bisector of $\overline{AA'}$, $\overline{BB'}$, and $\overline{CC'}$. Count to find the distance between each point A, B, and C and the line $x = 2$. Then use the distance to find points A', B', and C'. Since the y-values remain the same, the image points are $A'(5, 3)$, $B'(0, 6)$, and $C'(-3, 2)$.

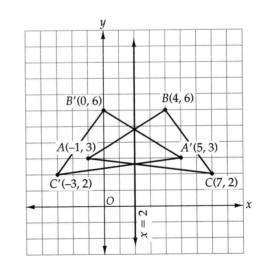

2 Find the reflection of the figure whose coordinates are $A(-3, -7)$, $B(3, -4)$, and $C(9, -6)$ across the line represented by $y = -3$.

SOLUTION

The line $y = -3$ is the perpendicular bisector of $\overline{AA'}$, $\overline{BB'}$, and $\overline{CC'}$. Count to find the distance between each point A, B, and C, and the line $y = -3$. Then use that distance to find points A', B', and C'. Since the x-values remain the same, the image points are $A'(-3, 1)$, $B'(3, -2)$, and $C'(9, 0)$.

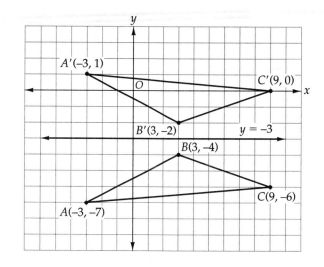

If a figure has **line symmetry**, a line can be drawn through the figure such that both sides of the figure are "mirror images" of each other. Such a line is also called the **axis of symmetry**. There can be more than one line of symmetry in a figure, or there may be none.

One line of symmetry	M, E, DOCK, WOW
Two lines of symmetry	Ellipse
Four lines of symmetry	Square

Infinite number of lines of symmetry	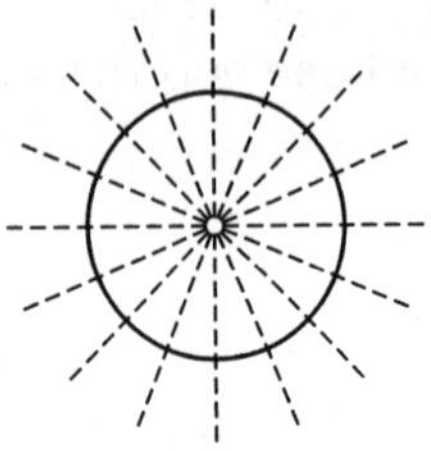
No lines of symmetry	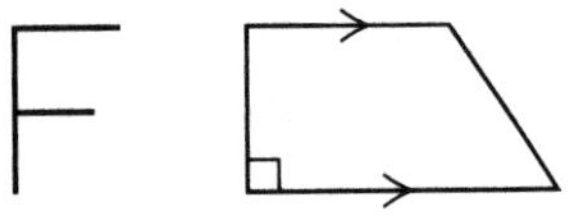 F

There are many real objects that exhibit symmetry, including butterflies, people's faces, and some works of art and architecture.

→ MODEL PROBLEM

Draw all the lines of symmetry for this figure.

SOLUTION

There are only two lines of symmetry.

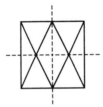

Practice

1 Which letter has vertical line symmetry?

  (1) S
  (2) N
  (3) A
  (4) B

2 Which letter has vertical but not horizontal line symmetry?

  (1) X
  (2) O
  (3) V
  (4) E

3 What kind of symmetry does the name OTTO have?

(1) only vertical line symmetry
(2) only horizontal line symmetry
(3) both vertical and horizontal line symmetry
(4) neither horizontal nor vertical line symmetry

4 What is the total number of lines of symmetry in a rectangle that is not a square?

(1) 1
(2) 2
(3) 3
(4) 4

5 When point $(-2, 7)$ is reflected in the line $x = 1$, the image is:

(1) $(7, 2)$
(2) $(-2, -5)$
(3) $(4, 7)$
(4) $(0, 7)$

Exercises 6–9: Determine whether each figure is symmetric over the x-axis, the y-axis, both, or neither.

6

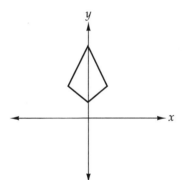

7

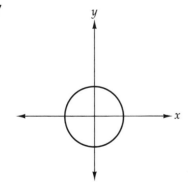

8

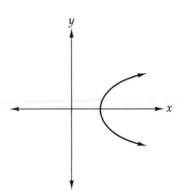

9

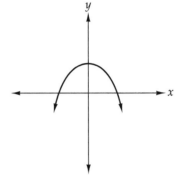

Exercises 10–12: Plot the point and find its image when reflected in the line $y = -2$.

10 $(1, 4)$

11 $(-3, 3)$

12 $(4, -5)$

Exercises 13–15: State the coordinates of the point $(-2, 5)$ under the reflection.

13 in the line $y = x$

14 in the line $y = 4$

15 in the line $x = -2$

Exercises 16–19: The coordinates of the vertices of a polygon are given. Graph and label the polygon and its reflection in the given line.

16 $A(2, 1), B(3, 4), C(-4, 5), r_{x\text{-axis}}$

17 $G(0, 0), H(4, 3), I(1, 4), J(-5, 2), r_{y\text{-axis}}$

18 $A(3, 3), B(8, 5), C(5, 1), r_{y = x}$

19 $Q(-4, -2), Z(-4, 3), D(-2, -1), r_{y = -x}$

20 Using the domain $-3 \leq x \leq 3$, graph and label the parabola $y = x^2$. On the same set of axes, sketch the graph of the image of the parabola under reflection in the line $y = x$. Label the image $x = y^2$.

6-4 Point Reflection and Symmetry

If a figure is reflected in or through point P, then P is the *midpoint* of the line segment joining each point to its corresponding image. In the diagram below, $\triangle ABC$ is reflected through point P to $\triangle A'B'C'$. In the diagram, $AP = PA'$, $BP = PB'$, and $CP = PC'$. The notation is $r_p(\triangle ABC) = \triangle A'B'C'$.

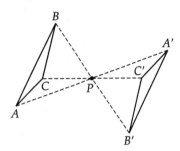

One way to visualize a point reflection is as two line reflections. The first reflection is over a horizontal line through point P. The second is over a vertical line through P. The image after both line reflections is the same as after a single point reflection. Since the only property of a shape changed by a line reflection is the clockwise order of the points, the two line reflections cancel each other out, and the image has all the properties of the original figure. Under a point reflection, distance, angle measure, collinearity, betweenness, parallelism, and orientation are preserved.

Point Reflection Mapping Rule A reflection through the origin is written $r_{\text{origin}}(x, y) = (-x, -y)$ or $r_O(x, y) = (-x, -y)$, where point O is the origin.

In coordinate geometry, the usual point of reflection is the origin. In the figure below, $\triangle BUG$ with vertices $B(2, 1)$, $U(3, 5)$, and $G(6, 3)$ is reflected through the origin onto the image $\triangle B'U'G'$ with coordinates $B'(-2, -1)$, $U'(-3, -5)$, and $G'(-6, -3)$.

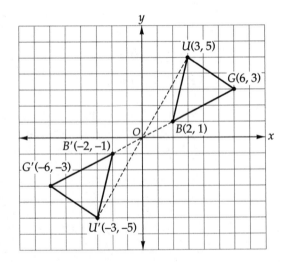

A figure is said to have **point symmetry** if the figure coincides with itself when reflected through a point or when rotated in either direction 180° about a point. The point that is the center of the reflection or rotation is called the **point of symmetry**.

Shapes without point symmetry	F, G, 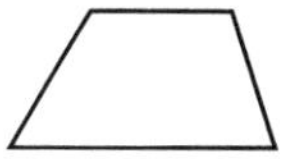 △
Shapes with point symmetry	Z, N, S, 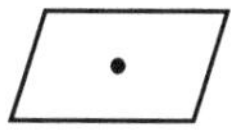 ▱

Practice

1 What letter has both point symmetry and line symmetry?

   (1) A
   (2) H
   (3) E
   (4) S

2 *All* isosceles trapezoid have:

   (1) only line symmetry
   (2) only point symmetry
   (3) both point and line symmetry
   (4) neither point nor line symmetry

3 What kind of symmetry does a rhombus have?

   (1) only point symmetry
   (2) only line symmetry
   (3) both point and line symmetry
   (4) neither point nor line symmetry

4 What is the image of $(k, 2k)$ after a reflection through the origin?

   (1) $(2k, k)$
   (2) $(k, -2k)$
   (3) $(-k, -2k)$
   (4) $(-2k, -k)$

Exercises 5–8: Identify whether the figure has point symmetry, line symmetry, or both.

5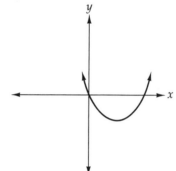

Parabola

6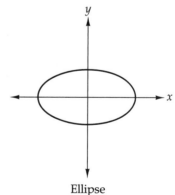

Ellipse

7

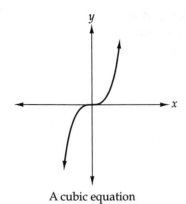

A cubic equation

8

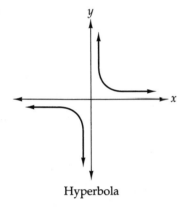

Hyperbola

Exercises 9–13: Find the image of each point under a point reflection in the origin.

9 $(1, 3)$

10 $(3, -1)$

11 $(-9, 0)$

12 $(-2, -6)$

13 $(-4, -4)$

Exercises 14–17: Find the image of $(-4, 2)$ under the reflection in the given point.

14 $(2, 2)$

15 $(-1, -1)$

16 $(-1, 5)$

17 $(3, -4)$

18 What is the difference between point reflection and point symmetry? Illustrate your answer.

6-5 Rotations

A **rotation** is a transformation in which a figure is turned around a point called the **point of rotation**. In the coordinate plane, this point is typically the origin. The image of the rotated figure has all the attributes of the preimage, differing only in location. Under a rotation, distance, angle measure, collinearity, betweenness, parallelism, and orientation are preserved. Rotations that are counterclockwise are rotations of positive degree measure. Rotations that are clockwise are rotations of negative degree measure. The two rotated right triangles below illustrate counterclockwise positive 90° rotation and clockwise −90° rotation.

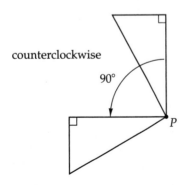
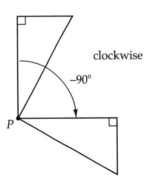

A figure has rotational symmetry if the figure is its own image under a rotation of more than 0° but less than 360°. Rotational symmetry of exactly 180° is the same as point symmetry.

Using the letters of the alphabet with point symmetry (Z, X, S, O, N, I, H), it is easy to see—by turning the page upside down—that they have rotational symmetry. However, the converse is *not* true. For example, equilateral triangle *ABC* has rotational symmetry of 120°, but it does not have point symmetry.

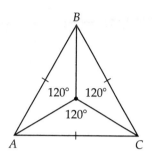

All rotations are assumed to be counterclockwise about the origin unless stated otherwise.

Rotation Mapping Rules

Rotation of 90°	$R_{90°}(x, y) = (-y, x)$	
Rotation of 180°	$R_{180°}(x, y) = (-x, -y)$	

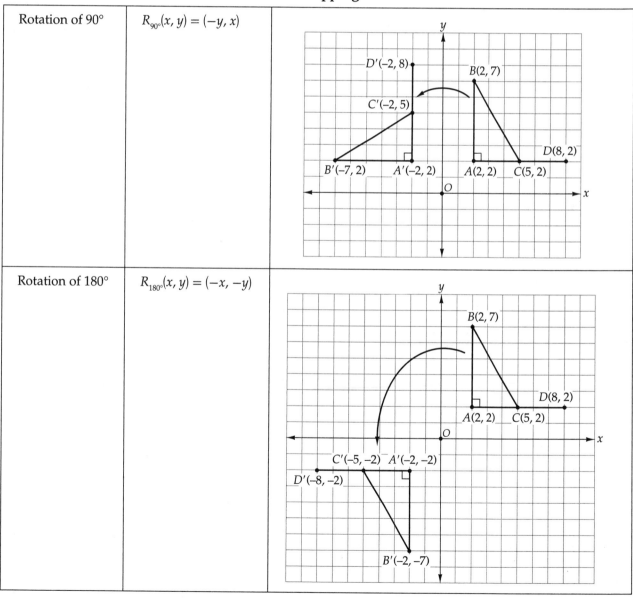

Rotation of 270°	$R_{270°}(x, y) = (y, -x)$	

Rotation of 360°	$R_{360°}(x, y) = (x, y)$	

MODEL PROBLEM

What is the image of $(-2, 3)$ under a rotation of 90°? 180°? 360°?

SOLUTION

To find each image, simply substitute -2 for x and 3 for y in the equation above.

$R_{90°}(x, y) = (-y, x)$ $R_{90°}(-2, 3) = (-3, -2)$

$R_{180°}(x, y) = (-x, -y)$ $R_{180°}(-2, 3) = (2, -3)$

$R_{360°}(x, y) = (x, y)$ $R_{360°}(-2, 3) = (-2, 3)$

 **Practice**

1 Which of the following figures does *not* have rotational symmetry?

(1) square
(2) trapezoid
(3) equilateral triangle
(4) regular pentagon

2 Which figure has 60° rotational symmetry?

(1) regular hexagon
(2) regular pentagon
(3) square
(4) equilateral triangle

3 Which geometric figure has 72° rotational symmetry?

(1) regular hexagon
(2) regular pentagon
(3) square
(4) rhombus

4 Which polygon has rotational symmetry of 90°?

(1) equilateral triangle
(2) rectangle
(3) regular pentagon
(4) regular hexagon

5 Which figure has 120° rotational symmetry?

(1) equilateral triangle
(2) square
(3) regular pentagon
(4) regular hexagon

6 If the letter F is rotated 180°, which is the resulting figure?

(1)

(2)

(3)

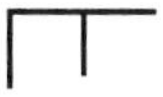

(4)

Exercises 7–10: In the accompanying figure, point P is the center of the square. Find the image of each of the indicated letters under the given rotation.

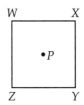

7 $R_{P, 90°}(W)$

8 $R_{P, 180°}(Z)$

9 $R_{P, 270°}(X)$

10 $R_{P, -90°}(Y)$

Exercises 11–13: Name the coordinates of the image of each point under a counterclockwise rotation of 90°.

11 $(5, 1)$

12 $(-3, 3)$

13 $(8, -2)$

Exercises 14–16: Name the coordinates of the image of each point under a clockwise rotation of 90°.

14 $(-3, 2)$

15 $(-2, -2)$

16 $(4, 4)$

Exercises 17–19: Name the coordinates of the image of each point under a counterclockwise rotation of 270°.

17 $(-3, 6)$

18 $(-6, -2)$

19 $(5, 5)$

20 If the coordinates of $\triangle WHY$ are $W(3, 2)$, $H(8, 2)$, and $Y(5, 10)$, what are the coordinates of $\triangle W'H'Y'$, the image of $\triangle WHY$ after a half turn or $R_{180°}$?

6-6 Dilations

A **dilation** is a transformation in which the size of a figure is changed and the figure is moved. In the physical world, enlarging and reducing photographs is a typical size transformation. All the angle measures of the image are the same as the measures of the corresponding angles of the original.

Dilation Mapping Rule In a dilation of constant k, where the center of dilation is the origin, the x-values and y-values of each point in the figure are multiplied by the constant to generate the coordinates of its image. The dilation is written $D_k(x, y) = (kx, ky)$. For example:

$$D_3(x, y) = (3x, 3y) \qquad \text{and} \qquad D_{\frac{1}{2}}(x, y) = \left(\tfrac{1}{2}x, \tfrac{1}{2}y\right)$$

In the figure below, the image of $\triangle ABC$ under the dilation D_2 results in the larger triangle $A'B'C'$. The image of $\triangle ABC$ under the dilation D_{-1} results in the smaller triangle $A''B''C''$, which is also a point reflection.

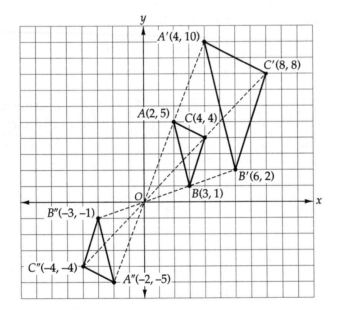

Under a dilation, angle measure, collinearity, betweenness, and parallelism are preserved. If the constant of dilation, k, is positive, orientation is preserved. If the constant of dilation, k, is negative, orientation is reversed. Size is preserved only if $|k| = 1$.

Note: If $k = 1$, then the image is congruent and is identical to the original.

If $k = -1$, then the image is congruent and is the same as a point reflection.

If $|k| > 1$, then the image is similar and is larger.

If $|k| < 1$, then the image is similar and is smaller.

MODEL PROBLEMS

1 What are the coordinates of the image of point $(2, -4)$ under the dilation D_{-2}?

SOLUTION

Multiply each coordinate by -2. Thus, $(-2 \times 2, -2 \times -4) = (-4, 8)$.

ANSWER: $(-4, 8)$

2 Find the constant or scale factor, k, for the dilation that maps $(-4, 6)$ onto $(-10, 15)$.

SOLUTION

Solve either equation.

$$k(-4) = -10 \qquad \text{or} \qquad k(6) = 15$$
$$k = \frac{-10}{-4} \qquad\qquad\qquad k = \frac{15}{6}$$
$$k = 2.5 \qquad\qquad\qquad\quad k = 2.5$$

ANSWER: $k = 2.5$

3 $\triangle EAT$ has vertices $E(1, 1)$, $A(1, 4)$, and $T(5, 1)$. (a) What is the image of $\triangle EAT$ under the dilation D_3? (b) What is the ratio of the area of $\triangle EAT$ to the area of $\triangle E'A'T'$?

SOLUTION

a Using the mapping rule $D_3(x, y) = (3x, 3y)$, the coordinates of the image are found by multiplying each x-value and y-value by 3: $D_3 E(1, 1) = E'(3, 3)$, $D_3 A(1, 4) = A'(3, 12)$, and $D_3 T(5, 1) = T'(15, 3)$.

ANSWER: Image $\triangle E'A'T'$ is $E'(3, 3)$, $A'(3, 12)$, and $T'(15, 3)$.

b The ratio of the area of $\triangle EAT$ to the area of $\triangle E'A'T'$ is the ratio of any corresponding segments squared or the ratio of corresponding dilations squared.

$$\frac{\text{Area } \triangle EAT}{\text{Area } \triangle E'A'T'} = \frac{1^2}{3^2} = \frac{1}{9}$$

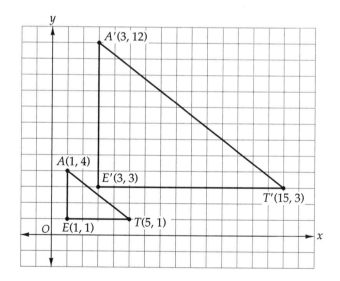

ANSWER: $\frac{1}{9}$

1 What are the coordinates of the image of point $(2, -5)$ under the dilation D_{-2}?

(1) $(-10, 4)$
(2) $(4, -10)$
(3) $(-4, 10)$
(4) $(10, -4)$

2 If the dilation $D_k(2, -4) = (-1, 2)$, the scale factor k is equal to:

(1) -2

(2) $-\frac{1}{2}$

(3) $\frac{1}{2}$

(4) 2

3 Which mapping represents a dilation?

(1) $(x, y) \rightarrow (y, x)$
(2) $(x, y) \rightarrow (-y, -x)$
(3) $(x, y) \rightarrow (x + 3, y + 3)$
(4) $(x, y) \rightarrow (2x, 2y)$

4 If the area of $\triangle ANT$ is 5 square inches, the area of its image, $\triangle A'N'T'$, under the dilation D_{-2} would be:

(1) $\frac{5}{2}$ square inches

(2) 3 square inches
(3) 10 square inches
(4) 20 square inches

Exercises 5–7: Find the image of $(6, -9)$ under the dilation.

5 D_{-1}

6 $D_{-\frac{1}{2}}$

7 $D_{\frac{2}{3}}$

Exercises 8–11: $\triangle ABC$ has vertices whose coordinates are $A(0, 4)$, $B(-1, 1)$, and $C(-3, 2)$. Graph $\triangle ABC$ and find its image under each dilation.

8 D_2

9 $D_{-\frac{3}{4}}$

10 D_{-3}

11 D_{-2}

Exercises 12–14: Find the coordinates (x, y).

12 $D_2\left(\frac{1}{2}, \frac{\sqrt{3}}{2}\right) \rightarrow (x, y)$

13 $D_4(x, y) \rightarrow \left(2\sqrt{2}, 2\sqrt{2}\right)$

14 $D_3(a, b) \rightarrow (x, y)$

15 Transformation D_k maps $(-3, 6)$ to $(-1, 2)$. What is the value of k? What is the image of $(-6, -12)$ under the same transformation?

16 Transformation D_k maps $(4, -12)$ to $(-2, 6)$. What is the value of k? What is the image of $(2, 4)$ under the same transformation?

17 Complete this transformation. If $D_k(2, -3) \rightarrow (6, -9)$, then $D_k(-1, 4) \rightarrow (?)$.

18 Rectangle $GNAT$ has the following vertices: $G(-2, 2)$, $N(8, 2)$, $A(8, -2)$, and $T(-2, -2)$. What is the image of rectangle $GNAT$ under the dilation $D_{\frac{1}{2}}$?

6-7 Properties Under Transformations

Every geometric shape has intrinsic properties, some of which are changed by the transformations in this chapter, and others that are **preserved**, or not changed. There are six properties to be considered:

- **Angle measures** are preserved when each angle and its image are equal in measure. Example: If $\angle ABC$ is a right angle, then $\angle A'B'C'$ is also a right angle.
- **Betweenness** is preserved when the transformation of a segment and its midpoint results in a segment image that includes the corresponding midpoint image. Example: If $\overline{AD}$ had midpoint M, then $\overline{A'D'}$ has the midpoint M'.

- **Collinearity** is preserved when three or more points lie on a straight line and their transformed images also lie on a straight line. Example: If A, G, and E are collinear, then their images A', G', and E' are also collinear.
- **Distance** is preserved when each segment and its transformed image are equal in length. Example: If $QR = 7$, then $Q'R'$ must equal 7.
- **Parallelism** is preserved when images of parallel lines are also parallel. Example: If $\overline{AB} \parallel \overline{DC}$, then the transformed image $\overline{A'B'} \parallel \overline{D'C'}$.
- **Orientation** is preserved when the clockwise or counterclockwise reading of points in a given figure is the same as the image of that figure. Example: If a quadrilateral has clockwise vertices of A, B, C, and D, then the clockwise order of the image's vertices must also read A', B', C', and D'.

Properties Preserved Under Transformations

	Translation	Line Reflection	Point Reflection	Dilation	Rotation
Angle measure	✔	✔	✔	✔	✔
Betweenness	✔	✔	✔	✔	✔
Collinearlity	✔	✔	✔	✔	✔
Distance	✔	✔	✔	✗	✔
Parallelism	✔	✔	✔	✔	✔
Orientation	✔	✗	✔	✔	✔

A transformation that preserves distance is called an **isometry**. A **direct isometry** preserves orientation. Translations, point reflections, and rotations are direct isometries. An **opposite isometry** reverses orientation. A line reflection is an opposite isometry. A dilation is a direct isometry only when the constant of dilation is 1 or −1.

 Practice

1 Under which transformation is the area of a triangle *not* equal to the area of its image?

   (1) rotation
   (2) dilation
   (3) line reflection
   (4) translation

2 Which transformation is *not* an example of an isometry?

   (1) line reflection
   (2) translation
   (3) rotation
   (4) dilation

3 △ABC with coordinates $A(4, 0)$, $B(8, 1)$, and $C(8, 4)$ is mapped onto △$A'B'C'$ with coordinates $A'(4, -8)$, $B'(8, -7)$, and $C'(8, -4)$. Which of the following transformations is responsible for this mapping?

   (1) reflection
   (2) translation
   (3) rotation
   (4) dilation

4 Which transformation does *not* preserve orientation?

(1) $T_{3, -5}$

(2) $r_{y = x}$

(3) D_4

(4) $R_{90°}$

5 A transformation that maps $(2, 3)$ onto $(-2, -3)$ is equivalent to

(1) rotation $R_{90°}$

(2) rotation $R_{-90°}$

(3) dilation D_{-1}

(4) translation $T_{-2, -3}$

Exercises 6–9: Describe the transformation that maps figure *A* to figure *B*.

6

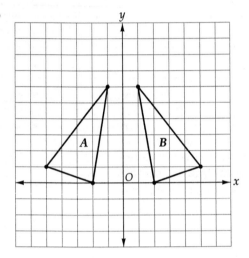

7

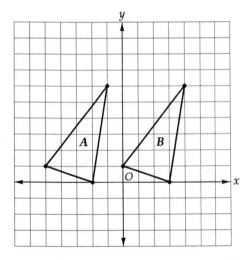

8

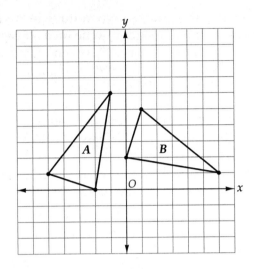

9

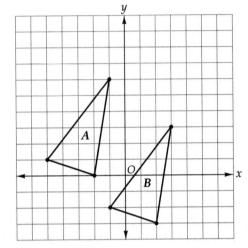

Exercises 10–12: The coordinates of the vertices of $\triangle KMZ$ are $K(2, -2)$, $M(5, -2)$, and $Z(3, -4)$. Graph and label $\triangle KMZ$ and its image under the transformation. State whether the transformation is an isometry or whether it preserves orientation.

10 $A(x, y) \rightarrow (-x, y)$

11 $B(x, y) \rightarrow (x - 3, y + 3)$

12 $C(x, y) \rightarrow (2x, 2y)$

13 The coordinates of the vertices of $\triangle CAR$ are $C(-1, -2)$, $A(0, -4)$ and $R(3, -1)$. Graph and label $\triangle CAR$. State the coordinates of the vertices for each new image.

a Graph and label $\triangle C'A'R'$, the image of $\triangle CAR$ after the translation $T_{4, -3}$.

b Graph and label $\triangle C''A''R''$, the image of $\triangle C'A'R'$ after a reflection in the origin.

c Graph and label $\triangle C'''A'''R'''$, the image of $\triangle C''A''R''$ after a reflection in the line $y = -x$.

d Which transformation does *not* preserve orientation: **a**, **b**, or **c**?

14 The coordinates of the vertices of $\triangle KID$ are $K(1, 6)$, $I(2, 9)$, and $D(7, 10)$. Graph and label $\triangle KID$.

   a Graph and state the coordinates of $\triangle K'I'D'$, the image of $\triangle KID$ after a reflection over the line $y = x$.

   b Graph and state the coordinates of $\triangle K''I''D''$, the image of $\triangle K'I'D'$ after a reflection over the y-axis.

   c Graph and state the coordinates of $\triangle K'''I'''D'''$, the image of $\triangle K''I''D''$ after the transformation $(x, y) \rightarrow (x + 5, y - 3)$.

15 Graph and label clearly $\triangle JAR$, whose vertices have the coordinates $J(2, 0)$, $A(6, -2)$, and $R(4, -4)$.

   a Graph and state the coordinates of $\triangle J'A'R'$, the image of $\triangle JAR$ after the transformation $(x, y) \rightarrow \left(\frac{1}{2}x, \frac{1}{2}y\right)$.

   b Graph and state the coordinates of $\triangle J''A''R''$, the image of $\triangle JAR$ after a counterclockwise rotation of 90° about the origin.

   c Graph and state the coordinates of $\triangle J'''A'''R'''$, the image of $\triangle JAR$ after a reflection in the origin.

6-8 Composition of Transformations

Compositions of transformations occur when two or more transformations are performed one after another. The first transformation produces an image, then the second transformation is performed on that image. The symbol for a composition of transformations is the same as for a composition of functions. For example, a rotation of 90° followed by a rotation of 180° would be indicated by $R_{180°} \circ R_{90°}$. Just as with functions, it is important to realize which transformation is performed first. $R_{180°} \circ R_{90°}$ is read as "a rotation of 180° following a rotation of 90°." In this particular case, we would get the same result regardless of which rotation was performed first, but this is not always the case.

Note: To remember which transformation to perform first, replace the composition symbol and what follows it inside parentheses. Then work from the inside out. For example, when you are given $R_{180°} \circ R_{90°}$, replace the $\circ$ with parentheses around $R_{90°}$ as shown.

$$R_{180°} \circ R_{90°} \rightarrow R_{180°}(R_{90°})$$

Now it is clear that the 90° rotation must be done first.

 MODEL PROBLEM

The coordinates of triangle FUN are $F(-5, 1)$, $U(-1, 1)$, and $N(-1, 7)$.

   a On a coordinate plane draw and label $\triangle FUN$.

   b Draw and label $\triangle F'U'N'$, the image of $\triangle FUN$ after $r_{x\text{-axis}}$.

   c Draw and label $\triangle F''U''N''$, the image of $\triangle F'U'N'$ after $r_{y\text{-axis}}$.

   d What single transformation is equivalent to $r_{y\text{-axis}} \circ r_{x\text{-axis}}$?

SOLUTION

   a $\triangle FUN$ is shown on the graph.

   b When we reflect in the x-axis, we negate all of the y-values. Thus, the coordinates of $\triangle F'U'N'$ are $F'(-5, -1)$, $U'(-1, -1)$, and $N'(-1, -7)$, as shown in the graph.

c Be sure to use $\triangle F'U'N'$ to obtain $\triangle F''U''N''$. Since we are reflecting in the y-axis, we negate all of the x-values. The coordinates of $\triangle F''U''N''$ are $F''(5, -1)$, $U''(1, -1)$, $N''(1, -7)$, as shown in the figure.

d To decide what single transformation is equivalent to $r_{y\text{-axis}} \circ r_{x\text{-axis}}$, look at $\triangle FUN$ and at $\triangle F''U''N''$. Ask yourself the question, "How can I get from $\triangle FUN$ to $\triangle F''U''N''$ in only one step?" $\triangle F''U''N''$ is a point reflection of $\triangle FUN$ through the origin (O). Thus, our answer is R_O. Since a 180° rotation is equivalent to R_O, an alternative answer would be $R_{180°}$.

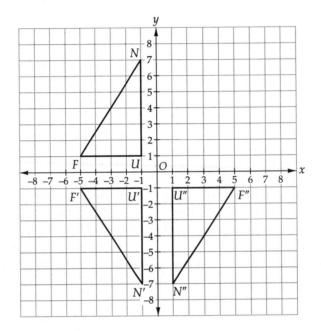

A **glide reflection** is a composition of a line reflection and a translation that is parallel to the line of reflection, or vice versa.

 MODEL PROBLEM

The coordinates of triangle GLD are $G(1, -5)$, $L(6, -4)$, and $D(3, -1)$.

a Draw and label $\triangle GLD$.

b Draw and label $\triangle G'L'D'$, the image of $\triangle GLD$ after $T_{-8, 0}$.

c Draw and label $\triangle G''L''D''$, the image of $\triangle G'L'D'$ after $r_{x\text{-axis}}$.

d Draw and label $\triangle G'''L'''D'''$, the image of $\triangle GLD$ after $T_{-8, 0} \circ r_{x\text{-axis}}$. How does this image compare to $\triangle G''L''D''$?

e What single transformation maps $\triangle GLD$ onto $\triangle G''L''D''$?

SOLUTION

a   △GLD is drawn below.

b   The translation slides the triangle 8 units to the left. The new coordinates are $G'(-7, -5)$, $L'(-2, -4)$, and $D'(-5, -1)$.

c   A reflection over the x-axis produces the triangle as shown. The new coordinates are $G''(-7, 5)$, $L''(-2, 4)$, and $D''(-5, 1)$.

d   The new coordinates are $G'''(-7, 5)$, $L'''(-2, 4)$, and $D'''(-5, 1)$. The two images are the same.

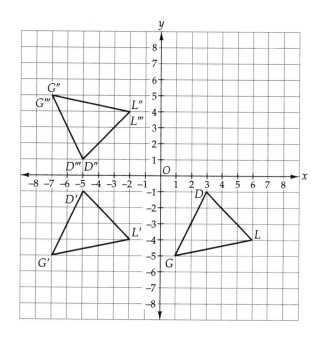

e   The translation $T_{-8, 0}$ is parallel to the x-axis, which is the line of reflection. This composition is a glide reflection.

Note: A glide reflection is a special composition since it is commutative.

Since a line reflection can be thought of as "flip," and a translation can be thought of as a "slide," "a flip and a slide" make a glide.

Model problems 1 and 2 below illustrate how we combine symmetry with our study of composition of transformations.

1 In the figure below, l and m are lines of symmetry for pentagon $ABCDE$. Find $r_1 \circ r_m(E)$.

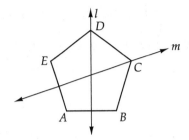

SOLUTION

Determine which transformation to perform first.

$$r_1 \circ r_m(E) \rightarrow r_1(r_m(E))$$

Imagine folding the paper on line m to see that $r_m(E) = A$.

Now imagine folding the paper on line l to see that $r_1(A) = B$. Thus, $r_1 \circ r_m(E) = B$.

2 In the figure below, line n is a line of symmetry in square $MATH$. Find $R_{90°} \circ r_n(A)$.

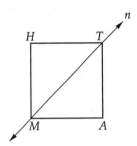

SOLUTION

Determine which transformation to perform first.

$$R_{90°} \circ r_n(A) \rightarrow R_{90°}(r_n(A))$$

Imagine folding the paper on line n to see that $r_n(A) = H$. Now turn your paper 90° in a counter-clockwise direction. Point H is now in the bottom left-hand corner of the figure. Remember that position. Turn your paper right side up to see that M is now in the bottom left-hand corner. Thus, $R_{90°}(H) = M$.

Putting this together, we get $R_{90°} \circ r_n(A) = M$.

3 Given triangle TRY, with coordinates $T(-2, 3)$, $R(3, 6)$, and $Y(1, -1)$.

   a Find the coordinates of $\triangle T'R'Y'$, the image of $\triangle TRY$ after $R_{90°}$.
   b Find the coordinates of $\triangle T''R''Y''$, the image of $\triangle T'R'Y'$ after $r_{x\text{-axis}}$.
   c What kind of isometry is $R_{90°}$?
   d What kind of isometry is $r_{x\text{-axis}}$?
   e What kind of isometry is $r_{x\text{-axis}} \circ R_{90°}$?

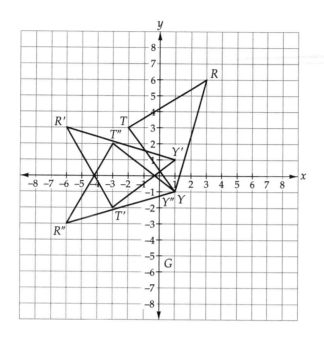

a As shown in the figure, the coordinates are $T'(-3, -2)$, $R'(-6, 3)$, and $Y'(1, 1)$.

b The coordinates are $T''(-3, 2)$, $R''(-6, -3)$, and $Y''(1, -1)$.

c Since the orientation of the points is the same, $R_{90°}$ is a direct isometry.

d Since the orientation of the points is different, $r_{x\text{-axis}}$ is an opposite isometry.

e The composition produces an opposite isometry.

Note: The composition of a direct isometry and an opposite isometry is always an opposite isometry.

 ## Practice

1 $R_{240°} \circ R_{-40}$ is equivalent to which of the following?

(1) $R_{360°}$

(2) $R_{280°}$

(3) $R_{200°}$

(4) $R_{40°}$

2 In the figure below l and m are symmetrys. What is $r_l \circ r_m(\overline{MA})$?

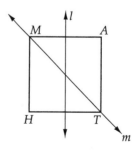

(1) $\overline{MA}$

(2) $\overline{AT}$

(3) $\overline{TH}$

(4) $\overline{HM}$

3 $R_O \circ R_O(x, y)$ would result in a point whose coordinates are:

(1) (x, y)
(2) $(-x, y)$
(3) $(x, -y)$
(4) (y, x)

4 Which composition would produce an image triangle whose area is *not* equal to the area of the original triangle?

(1) $r_{y\text{-axis}} \circ r_{x\text{-axis}}$
(2) $T_{2, -3} \circ r_{y = x}$
(3) $r_{y = -x} \circ D_3$
(4) $R_O \circ R_O$

5 $r_{y = x} \circ r_{x\text{-axis}}$ produces a transformation that is:

(1) a direct isometry
(2) an opposite isometry
(3) an isometry that is both direct and opposite
(4) not an isometry

6 $D_2 \circ D_{\frac{1}{2}}(x, y) =$

(1) $(2x, 2y)$

(2) (x, y)

(3) $\left(\frac{1}{2}x, \frac{1}{2}y\right)$

(4) $\left(\frac{1}{4}x, \frac{1}{4}y\right)$

7 What is $r_{y = 2} \circ r_{x\text{-axis}}(-3, 4)$?

(1) $(-3, 0)$
(2) $(-3, 2)$
(3) $(-3, 4)$
(4) $(-3, 8)$

8 Given square $ABCD$ labeled counterclockwise. What is $R_{90°} \circ R_{180°}(A)$?

(1) A
(2) B
(3) C
(4) D

9 Which of the following is equivalent to $T_{2, 4} \circ T_{2, -4}$?

(1) $T_{4, 8}$
(2) $T_{4, -16}$
(3) $T_{4, 0}$
(4) $T_{0, -8}$

10 $r_{y = x} \circ r_{y = x}(x, y) =$

(1) (x, y)
(2) $(-x, y)$
(3) $(x, -y)$
(4) (y, x)

11 Which property is *not* preserved under a glide reflection?

(1) distance
(2) angle measure
(3) orientation
(4) parallelism

12 In the given figure, p and q are lines of symmetry for regular hexagon $HEXAGN$. Find $r_q \circ r_p(X)$.

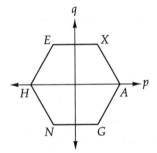

13 In the given figure, r and s are lines of symmetry for regular octagon $REOCTAGN$. Find $r_s \circ r_r(O)$.

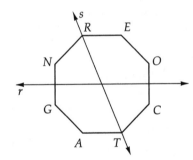

14 What single rotation is equivalent to $R_{40°} \circ R_{60°} \circ R_{-10°}$?

15 Write a composition of three rotations that will produce a rotation equivalent to $R_{100°}$.

16 Write a composition of two rotations that will produce a rotation equivalent to R_O.

17 What single transformation is equivalent to the composition of a line reflection and a translation that is parallel to the line reflection?

18 What are the coordinates of $r_{x\,=\,4} \circ r_{y\,=\,3}(2, 5)$?

19 Given circle O, with its center at the origin and a radius of 5. Find the center of circle O', the image of circle O after the composition $r_{x\text{-axis}} \circ T_{2,3}(O)$.

20 Find $r_{y\,=\,x} \circ r_{y\,=\,x}(2, 7)$.

21 Triangle CMP has vertices $C(1, 2)$, $M(5, 7)$, and $P(8, 4)$.

   a On a coordinate plane, draw and label triangle CMP.
   b On the same set of axes, draw and label two images leading to $R_{180°} \circ r_{y\,=\,x}(\triangle CMP)$. Label the first image $\triangle C'M'P'$ and the second image $\triangle C''M''P''$.
   c Find the coordinates of $\triangle C''M''P''$, the image of $\triangle CMP$ $R_{180°} \circ r_{y\,=\,x}(\triangle CMP)$.
   d What single transformation would produce the same results as $R_{180°} \circ r_{y\,=\,x}(\triangle CMP)$?

22 a On a coordinate plane, graph and label triangle XYZ whose coordinates are $X(-5, 3)$, $Y(2, 6)$, and $Z(7, 1)$.
   b Graph and label triangle $X'Y'Z'$, the image of triangle XYZ after $r_{y\text{-axis}}$.
   c Graph and label triangle $X''Y''Z''$, the image of triangle $X'Y'Z'$ after $r_{y\,=\,x}$.
   d The composition $r_{y\,=\,x} \circ r_{y\text{-axis}}(\triangle XYZ) = \triangle X''Y''Z''$ is a:
      (1) rotation
      (2) dilation
      (3) translation
      (4) glide reflection

CHAPTER REVIEW

1 After the mapping $M:(x, y) \rightarrow (-x, y)$, the image of a point that lies in the second quadrant would now lie in quadrant:
   (1) I
   (2) II
   (3) III
   (4) IV

2 Which word has vertical line symmetry?
   (1) WOW
   (2) EVE
   (3) DAD
   (4) BOB

3 If point $(0, 6)$ is mapped onto point $(2, 6)$ by some line reflection, how would you describe the line of reflection?
   (1) y-axis
   (2) parallel to the x-axis
   (3) parallel to the y-axis
   (4) line $y = x$

4 If the coordinates of Q are $(-2, 5)$, what are the coordinates of $(r_{y\text{-axis}} \circ R_{90°})(Q)$?
   (1) $(-2, -5)$
   (2) $(-5, 2)$
   (3) $(5, -2)$
   (4) $(2, -5)$

5 Which of the following is *not* an isometry?
   (1) $(x, y) \rightarrow (-y, x)$
   (2) $(x, y) \rightarrow (-4 + x, y + 3)$
   (3) $(x, y) \rightarrow (x, 2y)$
   (4) $(x, y) \rightarrow (-x, y)$

6 If line a is parallel to line b, then $r_a \circ r_b(\triangle CTH)$ is equivalent to a:
   (1) translation
   (2) rotation
   (3) dilation
   (4) reflection in $y = x$

7 The transformation that moves every point in the plane under the rule $(x, y) \rightarrow (-y, x)$ is a:

(1) rotation
(2) reflection in the x-axis
(3) dilation
(4) point reflection

8 Using the diagram of a regular polygon below, find $R_{-120°} \circ R_{180°} \circ R_{240°}(B)$.

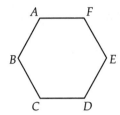

(1) A
(2) B
(3) E
(4) F

9 In this figure, p, m, and n are lines of reflection. Find $r_p \circ r_n \circ r_m(D)$.

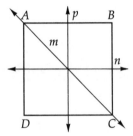

(1) A
(2) B
(3) C
(4) D

10 If point $M(-5, 8)$ is reflected in the line $y = 2$, what are the coordinates of M'?

(1) $(-5, 10)$
(2) $(-5, -4)$
(3) $(9, -4)$
(4) $(-3, 10)$

11 A transformation maps $(1, 3)$ onto $(-3, -1)$. This transformation is equivalent to a:

(1) rotation of 90°
(2) reflection in the origin
(3) reflection in the line $y = -x$
(4) translation of $-3, -1$

12 Which of these transformations would alter the perimeter of a triangle?

(1) $(x, y) \rightarrow (x + 2, y - 3)$
(2) $(x, y) \rightarrow (4x, 2y)$
(3) $(x, y) \rightarrow (x, -y)$
(4) $(x, y) \rightarrow (y, -x)$

13 If the point $(0, -4)$ is rotated 90° *clockwise* about the origin, its image is on the line:

(1) $y = x$
(2) $y = -x$
(3) $x = 0$
(4) $y = 0$

14 Which of the following compositions is a direct isometry?

(1) $R_{90°} \circ r_{x\text{-axis}}$
(2) $r_{y = x} \circ T_{-3, 4}$
(3) $r_{x = 1} \circ r_{y\text{-axis}}$
(4) $D_2 \circ r_{y = x}$

15 If the dilation D_k of point $A(4, -8)$ is $A'(-2, 4)$, the dilation factor k equals:

(1) $-\frac{1}{2}$

(2) $\frac{1}{2}$

(3) 2

(4) 4

16 Look at the figure below.

If the figure is rotated 90° counterclockwise and then reflected in the y-axis, its image would be which of the following?

(1)   (3)

(2)   (4)

17 Use the diagram provided to evaluate $(r_c \circ r_d)(K)$.

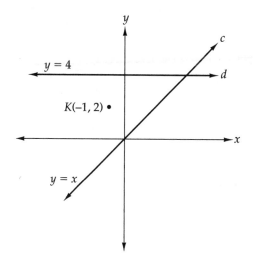

(1) $(1, 2)$
(2) $(2, 9)$
(3) $(6, -1)$
(4) $(-1, 6)$

Exercises 18–22: Find the distance between each pair of points. Answers that are not integers should be left in simplest radical form.

18 $(1, 3)$ and $(-2, 7)$

19 $(0, 5)$ and $(12, 0)$

20 $(-6, 3)$ and $(-4, -3)$

21 $(8, -1)$ and $(-4, 4)$

22 $(-10, -11)$ and $(-7, -20)$

23 If M is the transformation $(x, y) \rightarrow (-x, y - 3)$, then what is the image of $(-1, 4)$ after the transformation M?

24 What is the image of point $(-3, 9)$ under the mapping $M{:}(x, y) \rightarrow \left(\frac{2}{3}x, \frac{2}{3}y\right)$?

25 If translation T is defined as $(x, y) \rightarrow (x + 2, y - 1)$, then what is the image of $(-5, 1)$ under translation T?

26 Find the coordinates of the image of $N(-1, 4)$ after a reflection over the line $y = -x$.

27 Write an equation of the line of reflection that maps $A(1, 8)$ onto $A'(8, 1)$.

28 What is the image of point $(9, -4)$ under the rotation $R_{90°}$ about the origin?

29 Given: Pentagon *FRANK* with coordinates $F(2, 2)$, $R(4, 0)$, $A(2, -2)$, $N(-2, -2)$, $K(-4, 0)$. Write the coordinates of the images of the given point after the transformation described.

   a the image of point F after a reflection in the line $y = x$

   b the image of point R after a reflection in the y-axis

   c the image of point A after a reflection in the origin

   d the image of point N after a rotation of $-90°$ about the origin

   e the image of point K after the transformation $(x, y) \rightarrow (x + 7, y - 2)$

30 Triangle *CTH* has coordinates $C(-3, 4)$, $T(1, 9)$, and $H(-3, 10)$.

   a Graph and state the coordinates of $\triangle C'T'H'$, the image of $\triangle CTH$ under the composition $R_{90°} \circ r_{x\text{-axis}}$.

   b State the single transformation equivalent to $R_{90°} \circ r_{x\text{-axis}}$.

   c Graph and state the coordinates of $\triangle C''T''H''$, the image of $\triangle C'T'H'$ after $D_2 \circ T_{-5, -2}$.

Polygon Sides and Angles

7-1 Basic Inequality Postulates

In an *inequality*, the left-hand and right-hand members are not equal. Several postulates of equality and inequality help us complete proofs involving *geometric inequalities*, the comparison of unequal lengths and angle measures.

- **Postulate of equality.** A whole is equal to the sum of its parts.

  Example: $\overline{AMB} = \overline{AM} + \overline{MB}$

- **Postulate of inequality.** A whole is greater than any of its parts.

  Example: $\overline{AMB} = \overline{AM} + \overline{MB}$; thus, $\overline{AMB} > \overline{AM}$ and $\overline{AMB} > \overline{MB}$.

- **Transitive postulate of equality.** If quantities are equal to the same quantity, they are equal to each other.

  Example: If $AB = CD$ and $CD = EF$, then $AB = EF$.

- **Transitive postulate of inequality.** If the first of three quantities is greater than the second and the second is greater than the third, then the first is greater than the third.

  Example: If $m\angle a > m\angle b$ and $m\angle b > m\angle c$, then $m\angle a > m\angle c$.

- **Substitution postulate of equality.** A quantity may be substituted for its equal in any equality.

  Example: If $m\angle a = m\angle b$, then $m\angle a + m\angle c = m\angle b + m\angle c$.

- **Substitution postulate of inequality.** A quantity may be substituted for its equal in any inequality.

  Example: If $AB > CD$ and $AB = XY$, then $XY > CD$.

- **Trichotomy postulate.** Given any two quantities, exactly one of the following relations is true:

    1   The first quantity is less than the second quantity.

    2   The first quantity is equal to the second quantity.

    3   The first quantity is greater than the second quantity.

- **Addition postulate of equality.** If equals are added to equals, the sums are equal.

    Example: If $m\angle a = m\angle b$ and $m\angle c = m\angle d$, then $m\angle a + m\angle c = m\angle b + m\angle d$.

- **Addition postulate of inequality.**

    1   If equals are added to unequals, the sums are unequal in the same order. And if unequals are added to equals, the results are unequal in the same order.

        Example: If $a > b$ and $c = d$, then $a + c > b + d$.

    2   If unequals are added to unequals of the same order, the sums are unequal in the same order.

        Example: If $a < b$ and $c < d$ then $a + c < b + d$.

- **Subtraction postulate of equality.** If equals are subtracted from equals, the differences are equal.

    Example: If $m\angle a = m\angle b$ and $m\angle c = m\angle d$, then $m\angle a - m\angle c = m\angle b - m\angle d$.

- **Subtraction postulate of inequality.** If equals are subtracted from unequals, the differences are unequal in the same order, and if unequals are subtracted from equals, the differences are unequal in the opposite order.

    Example: If $a > b$, then $a - c > b - c$ and $c - a < c - b$.

    Note: If unequals are subtracted from unequals, the results may be equal or unequal.

- **Multiplication postulate of equality.** If equals are multiplied by equals, the products are equal.

    Example: If $a = b$ and $c = d$, then $ac = bd$.

- **Multiplication postulate of inequality.**

    1   If unequals are multiplied by positive equals, the products are unequal in the same order.

        Example: If $a > b$ and $c > 0$, then $ac > bc$.

    2   If unequals are multiplied by negative equals, the products are unequal in the opposite order.

        Example: If $a > b$ and $c < 0$, then $ac < bc$.

- **Division postulate of equality.** If equals are divided by equals, the quotients are equal.

    Example: If $a = b$ and $c = d$, then $a \div c = b \div d$.

- **Division postulate of inequality.**

    1   If unequals are divided by positive equals, the quotients are unequal in the same order.

        Example: If $a > b$ and $c > 0$, then $a \div c > b \div c$ or $\frac{a}{c} > \frac{b}{c}$.

    2   If unequals are divided by negative equals, the quotients are unequal in the opposite order.

        Example: If $a > b$ and $c < 0$, then $a \div c < b \div c$ or $\frac{a}{c} < \frac{b}{c}$.

Note: The last two postulates above have special cases that are used very often:

- Postulate. Doubles of unequal quantities are unequal in the same order.
- Postulate. Halves of unequal quantities are unequal in the same order.

 MODEL PROBLEMS

1   Given: In $\triangle ABC$, $AC = BC$ and $m\angle 1 < m\angle 3$.

    Prove: $m\angle 2 < m\angle 3$

Statements	Reasons
1. $AC = BC$	1. Given.
2. $\angle 1 \cong \angle 2$	2. If two sides of a triangle are congruent, the angles opposite them are congruent.
3. $m\angle 1 = m\angle 2$	3. If two angles are congruent, they have the same measure.
4. $m\angle 1 < m\angle 3$	4. Given.
5. $m\angle 2 < m\angle 3$	5. Substitution postulate for inequalities.

2   Given: In $\triangle ABC$, $AB > AC$ and M is the midpoint of $\overline{AC}$.

    Prove: $AB > AM$

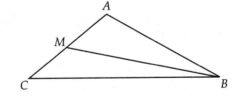

Statements	Reasons
1. $AB > AC$	1. Given.
2. M is the midpoint of $\overline{AC}$.	2. Given.
3. $AC = AM + MC$	3. Definition of midpoint.
4. $AC > AM$	4. A whole is greater than any of its parts.
5. $AB > AM$	5. Transitive property of inequality.

3

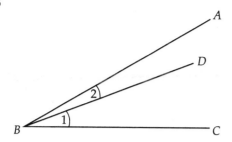

Given: m∠ABC < m∠EFG, ∠1 ≅ ∠3

Prove: m∠2 < m∠4

Proof: Since ∠1 ≅ ∠3, we know that m∠1 = m∠3 because congruent angles have the same measure. Using the Subtraction postulate of inequality, m∠ABC − m∠1 < m∠EFG − m∠3, and using the substitution postulate for inequality, m∠2 < m∠4.

4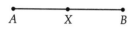

Given: $AB < CD$, X is the midpoint of $\overline{AB}$, Y is the midpoint of $\overline{CD}$.

Prove: $AX < CY$

Statements	Reasons
1. $AB < CD$	1. Given.
2. $\frac{1}{2}AB < \frac{1}{2}CD$	2. Halves of unequals are unequal in the same order.
3. X is the midpoint of $\overline{AB}$.	3. Given.
4. Y is the midpoint of $\overline{CD}$.	4. Given.
5. $AX = \frac{1}{2}AB$ $CY = \frac{1}{2}CD$	5. Definition of midpoint.
6. $AX < CY$	6. Substitution postulate for inequalities.

 Practice

1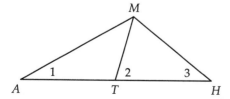

If m∠1 < m∠2 and m∠2 < m∠3, prove that m∠1 < m∠3.

2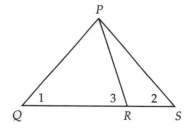

Given: △QPS; PQ = PS; m∠1 < m∠3
Prove: m∠2 < m∠3

3

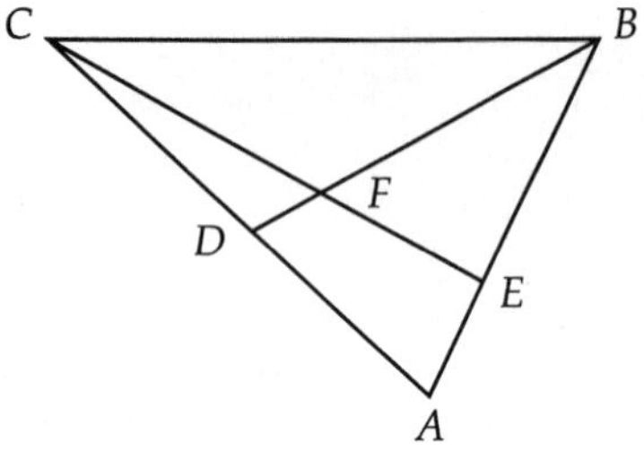

Given: $CE > BD$; $CF = BF$
Prove: $FE > FD$

4

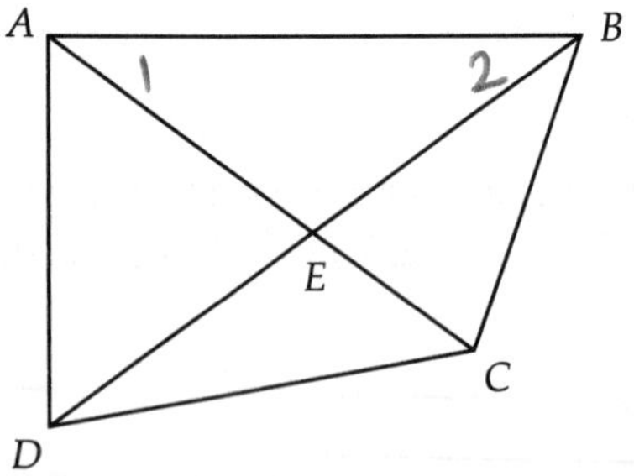

Given: m$\angle DAB$ > m$\angle CBA$; $\overline{AE} \cong \overline{EB}$
Prove: m$\angle CAD$ > m$\angle DBC$

5

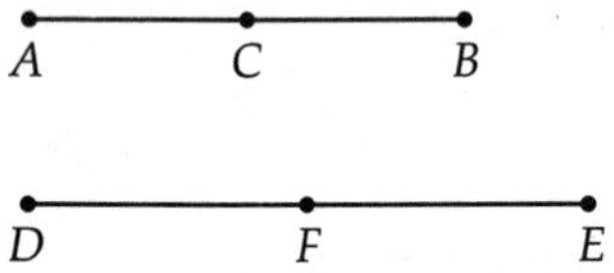

Given: $AC < DF$, C is the midpoint of $\overline{AB}$, F is the midpoint of $\overline{DE}$.
Prove: $AB < DE$

6

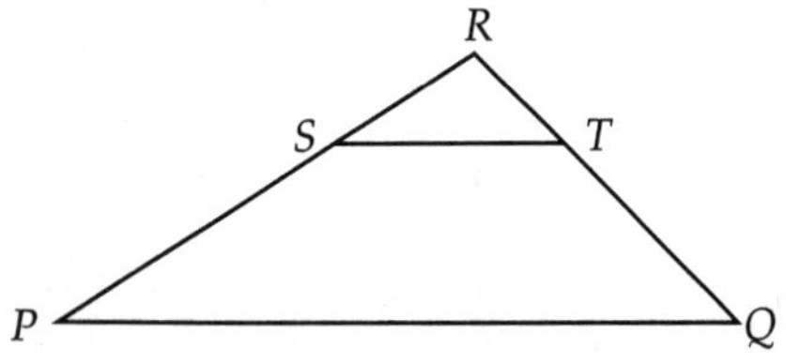

Given: $RS > RT$; $RP = 3RS$; $RQ = 3RT$
Prove: $RP > RQ$

7

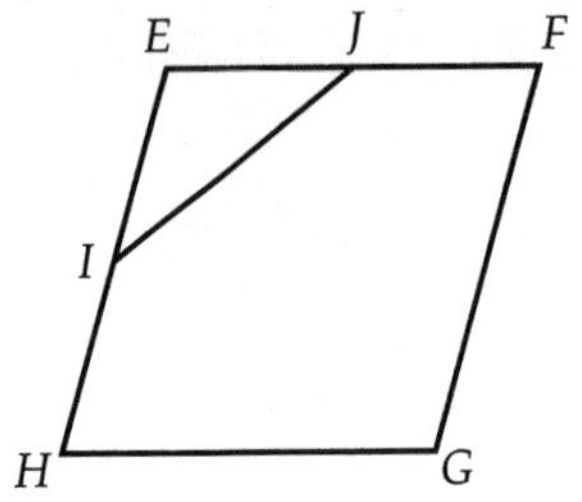

Given: $EH > EF$; I is the midpoint of $\overline{EH}$; J is the midpoint of $\overline{EF}$.
Prove: $EI > EJ$

8

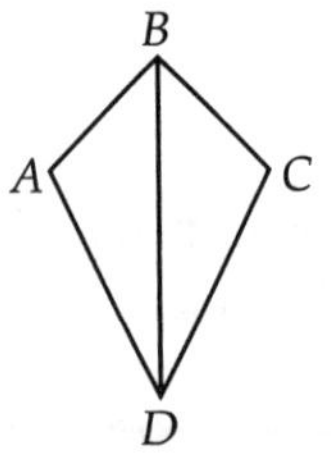

Given: m$\angle ABC$ > m$\angle ADC$; $\overline{BD}$ bisects $\angle ABC$; $\overline{BD}$ bisects $\angle ADC$.
Prove: m$\angle ABD$ > m$\angle ADB$

9

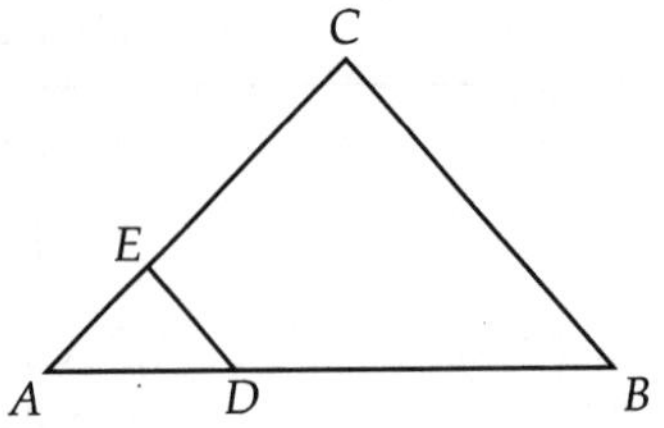

Given: $AC < AB$; $AE = \frac{1}{3}AC$; $AD = \frac{1}{3}AB$
Prove: $AE < AD$

10

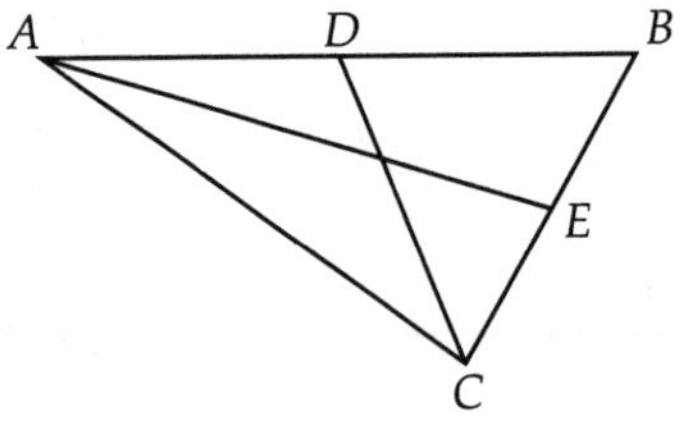

Given: $AB > BC$, $\overline{AE}$ is the median from A to $\overline{BC}$, $\overline{CD}$ is the median from C to $\overline{AB}$.
Prove: $AD > BE$

7-2 The Triangle Inequality Theorem

- Theorem 7.1 (**The Triangle Inequality Theorem**). The length of one side of a triangle is less than the sum of the lengths of the other two sides.

Proof: An earlier postulate states that the shortest distance between two points is a straight line. Given any $\triangle ABC$, C is *not* a point on $\overline{AB}$. Since AB is the shortest distance from A to B, $AB < AC + CB$.

The Triangle Inequality Theorem leads to an important rule. To show that three given line segments can be the sides of a triangle, it is necessary to show that the length of each side is less than the sum of the lengths of the two other sides.

In $\triangle ABC$ below, we see that AB is the longest side.

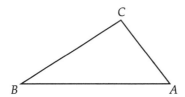

Once we determine the longest side, we need to show only that the measure of the longest side, AB in our triangle, is less than the sum of the measures of the other two sides, $AC + CB$.

Sometimes we are given the lengths of two sides of a triangle and are asked to find the range of possible lengths for the third side. Assume that the lengths of the three sides of a triangle are a, b, and c. Using the Triangle Inequality Theorem, we know that $a < b + c$. Subtracting c from each side of the inequality, we find that $a - c < b$. From the Triangle Inequality Theorem, we can also say that $b < a + c$. Combining the two inequalities results in the compound inequality $a - c > b > a + c$. This means that *any third side, b, is greater than the difference of the other two sides and is less than the sum of the other two sides.*

 MODEL PROBLEMS

1 Which of the following may be the lengths of the sides of a triangle?

   (1)   3, 5, 8
   (2)   4, 4, 9
   (3)   6, 9, 4
   (4)   3, 7, 2

SOLUTION

   (1) $8 = 3 + 5$ Not a triangle
   (2) $9 > 4 + 4$ Not a triangle
   (3) $9 < 6 + 4$ Yes, is a triangle
   (4) $7 > 3 + 2$ Not a triangle

ANSWER: Choice (3)

2 Two sides of a triangle have lengths 7 and 11. Find the range of possible lengths of the third side.

SOLUTION

Call the length of the third side S.
$11 - 7 < S < 11 + 7$

ANSWER: $4 < S < 18$

Exercises 1–10: Determine whether the given lengths can be the measures of the sides of a triangle.

1 3, 3, 3

2 5, 7, 12

3 4, 2, 4

4 2, 4, 6

5 10, 8, 6

6 1, 2, 3

7 5, 7, 4

8 12, 9, 6

9 10, 10, 1

10 15, 10, 6

Exercises 11–15: The lengths of two sides of a triangle are given. Determine the range for the length of the third side of the triangle.

11 4, 5

12 2, 8

13 1.5, 4

14 6, 6

15 $\frac{5}{2}$, 1

7-3 The Exterior Angles of a Triangle

A **polygon** is a closed figure that is the union of three or more line segments in a plane. The line segments are the **sides** of the polygon and the endpoints are the **vertices**. The vertices in order are called **consecutive vertices** or **adjacent vertices** as in points A, B, C, D, E, F, G, and H in the octagon below. These consecutive vertices mark the **consecutive angles**.

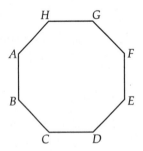

An **exterior angle** of a polygon is an angle that forms a linear pair with one of the interior angles of the polygon. An exterior angle is formed by extending one of the sides of the polygon. There are two exterior angles at each vertex.

The relationships between the exterior and interior angles of triangles are important enough to be stated as theorems. The figure below shows $\triangle ABC$ and the two exterior angles at C.

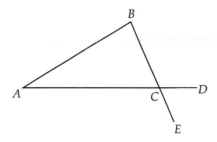

Angles *BCD* and angle *ACE* are exterior angles at C.

Each exterior angle of a triangle is associated with one *adjacent* interior angle and two *nonadjacent* interior angles.

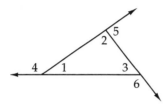

Exterior Angle	Adjacent Interior Angle	Nonadjacent Interior Angles
$\angle 4$	$\angle 1$	$\angle 2$ and $\angle 3$
$\angle 5$	$\angle 2$	$\angle 1$ and $\angle 3$
$\angle 6$	$\angle 3$	$\angle 1$ and $\angle 2$

- **Theorem 7.2 (the Exterior Angle Theorem).** The measure of an exterior angle of a triangle is greater than the measure of either nonadjacent interior angle.

Given: $\angle CBD$ is an exterior angle of $\triangle ABC$.

Prove: $\angle CBD$ is greater than $\angle A$ and $\angle CBD$ is greater than $\angle C$.

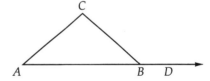

A sketch of the proof will be presented for $\angle C$.

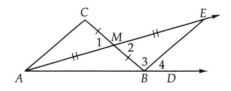

Extend the median $\overline{AM}$ to point E so that $AM = ME$. Since $CM = BM$ ($\overline{AM}$ is a median, M is the midpoint of $\overline{BC}$) and m$\angle 1$ = m$\angle 2$ (vertical angles are congruent), $\triangle ACM$ and $\triangle EBM$ are congruent by ASA and m$\angle 3$ = m$\angle C$ (corresponding parts of congruent triangles are congruent). But m$\angle CBD$ > m$\angle 3$ (a whole is greater than any of its parts), so m$\angle CBD$ > m$\angle C$.

- Theorem 7.3. The measure of an exterior angle of a triangle is equal to the sum of the measures of its two nonadjacent interior angles.

Proof:

If the measure of an exterior angle of a triangle is x, the measure of the interior angle at the same vertex is $180 - x$ because these angles are linear pairs. Since the sum of the measures of the interior angles of a triangle is 180,

$$y + z + 180 - x = 180$$
$$\underline{-180 = -180}$$
$$y + z - x = 0$$
$$\underline{+x = +x}$$
$$y + z = x$$

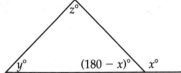

MODEL PROBLEM

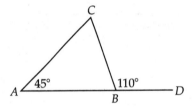

In $\triangle ABC$, m$\angle CAB = 45$ and m$\angle CBD = 110$. Find m$\angle ACB$.

SOLUTION Since the measure of an exterior angle of a triangle is equal to the sum of the measures of its two nonadjacent interior angles, m$\angle CAB$ + m$\angle ACB$ = m$\angle CBD$.

$45 + \text{m}\angle ACB = 110$
$\text{m}\angle ACB = 65$

ANSWER: 65°

Practice

1 In $\triangle ABC$, an exterior angle at C measures 110° and m$\angle A = 40$. The triangle must be:

(1) equiangular
(2) isosceles
(3) obtuse
(4) right

2 In $\triangle DEF$, m$\angle D$, $= x + 10$ and m$\angle F = 3x$. An exterior angle at E measures $5x - 20$. The triangle must be:

(1) equiangular
(2) acute
(3) obtuse
(4) right

3

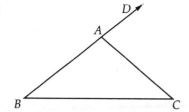

   a In the figure above, name the exterior angle shown.

   b With respect to that angle, name two nonadjacent interior angles.

   c Using the Exterior Angle Theorem, write two inequalities for this triangle.

4 Determine which of the following statements are true. You should draw an obtuse triangle, an acute triangle, and a right triangle and all six exterior angles for each triangle to help you.

   a All exterior angles of a triangle may have different measures.

   b All six exterior angles of a triangle may be obtuse.

   c An exterior angle of a triangle may be congruent to one of the interior angles.

   d An obtuse triangle has four obtuse exterior angles.

Exercises 5–7: Refer to the figure below.

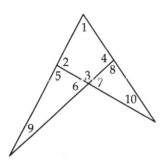

5 Which angles must be smaller than ∠2?

6 Which angles must be smaller than ∠3?

7 Which angles must be smaller than ∠4?

8

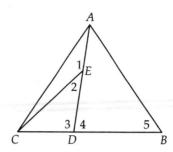

Given: $\overline{AED}, \overline{CDB}$
Prove: m∠1 > m∠5

9

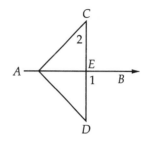

Given: $\overline{AB} \perp \overline{CD}$ and $\overline{AB}$ bisects $\overline{CD}$.
Prove: m∠1 > m∠2.

10

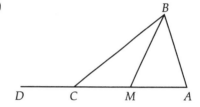

Given: △ABC, $\overline{AC}$ extended through C to D, $\overline{BM}$ is a median of △ABC.
Prove: m∠DCB > m∠MBA.

11

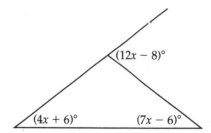

Find the value of x.

12

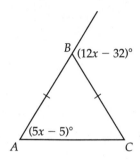

Find the value of x.

13 In $\triangle ABC$, $m\angle A$ is three times larger than $m\angle B$. An exterior angle at C measures $104°$. Find $m\angle A$.

14 Find the measure of either of the exterior angles formed by extending the base angles of an isosceles triangle if the vertex angle of the triangle measures $130°$.

7-4 Inequalities Involving Sides and Angles of Triangles

In our discussion of isosceles triangles, we learned that if the lengths of two sides of a triangle are equal, the measures of the angles opposite these sides are also equal. We also learned that the converse is true. If the measures of two angles of a triangle are equal, the lengths of the sides opposite these angles are also equal. We will now examine relationships when sides and angles are not equal.

- Theorem 7.4. If the lengths of two sides of a triangle are unequal, the measures of the angles opposite these sides are unequal and the larger side lies opposite the larger angle.

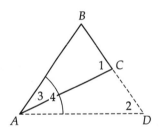

Proof: Draw triangle ABC, $AB > BC$. Extend $\overline{BC}$ to D so that $BD = BA$. Mark $\angle 1$, $\angle 2$, $\angle 3$, and $\angle 4$ as shown. Then $m\angle 1 > m\angle 2$ (Exterior Angle Theorem), and since $m\angle 2 = m\angle 4$ (Isosceles Triangle Theorem), $m\angle 1 > m\angle 4$ (substitution postulate). Then, $m\angle 4 > m\angle 3$ (a whole is greater than any of its parts) and $m\angle 1 > m\angle 3$ (transitive property of inequality).

- Theorem 7.5 (converse of theorem 7.4). If the measures of the angles of two opposite sides of a triangle are unequal, the lengths of these two sides are unequal and the greater side lies opposite the greater angle.

Practice

1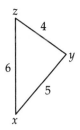

Name the smallest angle of △XYZ.

2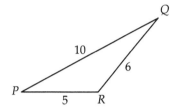

Name the largest angle of △PQR.

3 In △ABC, m∠A = 65, m∠B = 75, m∠C = 40. Name the longest side.

4 In △FGH, FG = 10, GH = 13, HF = 9. Name the largest angle.

5 In △JKL, m∠K = 50 and the measure of an exterior angle at J is 110°. Name the shortest side.

6 In △ABC, AB = 4BC and AB = 6CA. Which is the largest interior angle in △ABC?

7 In △XYZ, an exterior angle at X measures 70°. Name the longest side of the triangle.

8 Given: Isosceles triangle DEF, DE = EF, G is any point lying between D and F on $\overline{DF}$, $\overline{EG}$ is drawn.
Prove: $\overline{DE} > \overline{EG}$

9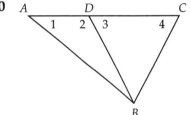

Given: △PQS ≅ △RSQ and PQ ≠ SP.
Prove: $\overline{QS}$ does not bisect ∠Q.

10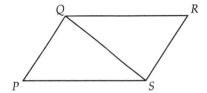

Given: △ABC; $\overline{BD}$ drawn to $\overline{AC}$; BD = CB
Prove: m∠4 > m∠1

CHAPTER REVIEW

1 If m < n and p is a positive number, which of the following is *not* true?

(1) pm < pn
(2) m + p < n + p
(3) p − m < p − n
(4) m − p < n − p

2 If the lengths of two sides of a triangle are 12 and 17, which of the following may be the length of the third side?

(1) 4
(2) 5
(3) 28
(4) 29

3 In triangle *FGH*, m∠*H* = 40 and *FG* > *GH*. Angle *G* is:

(1) an acute angle
(2) an obtuse angle
(3) a right angle
(4) a straight angle

Exercises 4 and 5: State whether the conclusion is correct. If the conclusion is correct, state the property of inequality that justifies the conclusion.

4 If Eric is older than Wendy and Wendy is older than Andrew, then Eric is older than Andrew.

5 If Harry weighs more than Carol and Len weighs more than Barbara, then together Harry and Len weigh more than Carol and Barbara weigh together.

Exercises 6 and 7: Refer to the diagram below. State whether the conclusion is correct. If it is correct, state the property of inequality that justifies the conclusion.

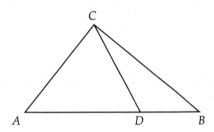

6 m∠*ACD* < m∠*ACB*.

7 *AD* > *DB*.

8

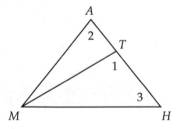

Given: m∠2 > m∠3
Prove: m∠1 > m∠3

9

Given: *BEST* is a parallelogram and *BT* > *BE*.
Prove: *ES* > *BE*

10

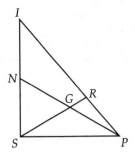

Given: m∠*ISR* > m∠*IPN* and $\overline{GS} \cong \overline{GP}$
Prove: m∠*ISP* > m∠*IPS*

11

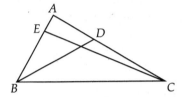

If m∠*BCE* > m∠*DBC* and m∠*ACE* > m∠*ABD*, prove that m∠*ACB* > m∠*ABC*.

12

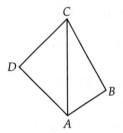

If m∠*DAB* > m∠*DCB* and $\overline{AD} \cong \overline{DC}$, prove that m∠*CAB* > m∠*ACB*.

13

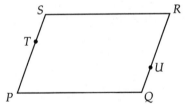

Given: *PQRS* is a parallelogram and *TP* > *QU*.
Prove: *ST* < *RU*

14 In △*RST* m∠*R* = 40 and m∠*S* = 80. Which is the shortest side of the triangle?

15 In right triangle *ABC*, $\overline{BC}$ is the hypotenuse. If m∠*B* = 60, name the shortest side of the triangle.

16 An exterior angle at *A* in △*ABC* measures 120°. If m∠*B* < m∠*C*, name the longest side of the triangle.

17 In △*ABC*, m∠*A* = 80 and an exterior angle at *B* measures 130°. Which is the longest side of the triangle?

18 In △*DEF*, m∠*D* = 45 and angle *E* is an obtuse angle. Name the shortest side of the triangle.

19 In △*ABC*, m∠*A* < m∠*B* and the bisectors of ∠*A* and ∠*B* meet at *D*. What conclusion can be made about the relationship between $\overline{AD}$ and $\overline{BD}$?

20 In △*ABC*, an exterior angle at *A* measures 120°. What conclusion can be made about the measure of angle *B*?

21

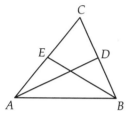

If $\overline{AD}$ bisects ∠*CAB*, $\overline{BE}$ bisects ∠*CBA*, and m∠*DAB* < m∠*EBA*, prove that m∠*CAB* < m∠*CBA*.

22

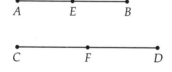

Given: $\overline{CF} > \overline{AE}$; *E* is the midpoint of $\overline{AB}$, *F* is the midpoint of $\overline{CD}$.
Prove: $\overline{CD} > \overline{AB}$.

23

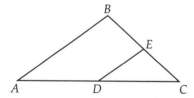

If $\overline{AC} > \overline{CB}$, *D* is the midpoint of $\overline{AC}$, and *E* is the midpoint of $\overline{BC}$, prove $\overline{AD} > \overline{BE}$.

24 Prove that the supplement of an acute angle is an obtuse angle.

25 Given: m∠*A* > m∠*B*.
Prove: The measure of the complement of ∠*A* is less than the measure of the complement of ∠*B*.

26

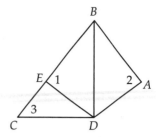

If m∠1 = m∠2, and *C*, *E*, and *B* are collinear, prove that m∠2 > m∠3.

27 Given: In △*ABC*; $\overline{CA} \cong \overline{CB}$, *D* is a point on $\overline{CA}$ between *A* and *C*.
Prove: *DB* > *DA*.

28 Given: In isosceles triangle *ABC*, $\overline{AB} \cong \overline{BC}$ and *D* is the midpoint of $\overline{BC}$.
Prove: *AB* > *AD*.

29 Given: In quadrilateral *ABCD*, $\overline{AB} \cong \overline{BC}$, and *AD* > *CD*.
Prove: m∠*BCD* > m∠*BAD*.

30 Given: In acute △*DEF*, the altitude from *E* meets $\overline{DF}$ at *G* and m∠*DEG* > m∠*FEG*.
Prove: *DE* > *EF*.

31

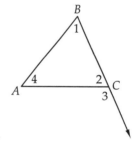

In △*ABC*, if m∠4 = 50 and m∠3 = 114, find m∠1 and m∠2.

32

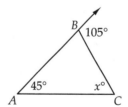

Find the measure of ∠*x*.

33

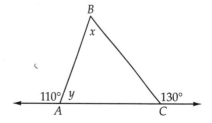

Find the measures of ∠*x* and ∠*y*.

Exercises 34–38: Mark each statement as **True** or **False**.

34 An equilateral triangle has congruent exterior angles.

35 Every exterior angle of a triangle is obtuse.

36 The measure of each exterior angle of an equilateral triangle is 120°.

37 The exterior angles at the base of an isosceles triangle are acute.

38 One of the exterior angles of a right triangle must be an acute angle.

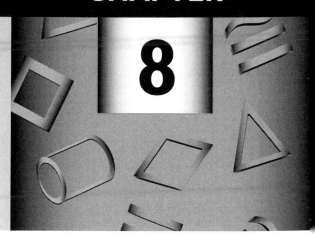

CHAPTER 8

Slopes and Equations of Lines

8-1 The Slope of a Line

Coordinate geometry examines geometric concepts and theorems from an algebraic point of view. Essential to coordinate geometry analytical proofs is the notion of the slope of a line.

The **slope** of a line is the ratio of the difference in y-values to the difference in x-values between any two points on the line. Thus,

$$\text{slope} = \frac{\text{difference in } y\text{-values}}{\text{difference in } x\text{-values}} \text{ or } \frac{\text{vertical change}}{\text{horizontal change}}$$

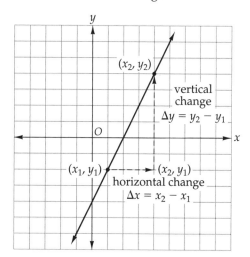

Mathematicians use the Greek letter Δ (delta) as a symbol for difference. Slope is usually symbolized by the letter m. Therefore, the formula for the slope of the line connecting points (x_1, y_1) and (x_2, y_2) is

$$m = \frac{\Delta y}{\Delta x} \text{ or } m = \frac{y_2 - y_1}{x_2 - x_1}$$

It makes no difference which points are labeled (x_1, y_1) and (x_2, y_2); the value of m will always be the same.

To Find the Slope of a Line

- Choose any two points (x_1, y_1) and (x_2, y_2) on the line.
- Find the difference in y-values by subtracting y_1 from y_2.
- Find the difference in x-values by subtracting x_1 from x_2.
- Write the ratio: slope $= \dfrac{\text{difference in } y\text{-values}}{\text{difference in } x\text{-values}}$ as $m = \dfrac{y_2 - y_1}{x_2 - x_1}$ or $m = \dfrac{\Delta y}{\Delta x}$.

Possible Values of m

Value of m	Values of Δy and Δx	Appearance of Graph
Positive	Δy and Δx have the same sign.	Line rises from left to right. /
Negative	Δy and Δx have opposite signs.	Line falls from left to right. \
Zero	$\Delta y = 0$	Line is horizontal. —
Undefined	$\Delta x = 0$	Line is vertical.	

The *fundamental property of a straight line* is that the slope is constant. Thus, since all segments of a line have the same slope, any two points on a line may be used to compute the slope of that line.

 MODEL PROBLEMS

1   For each of the following pairs of points, (i) graph the points, (ii) draw the line that joins these points, (iii) find the slope of the line, and (iv) describe the graph as positive or negative.

   a $A(-1, 5)$ and $B(3, -1)$
   b $C(-2, -6)$ and $D(4, 2)$

SOLUTION

Graph the two pairs.

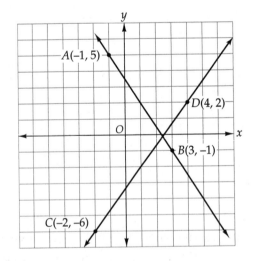

The slope of $\overleftrightarrow{AB}$ is $\dfrac{\Delta y}{\Delta x} = \dfrac{5 - (-1)}{-1 - 3} = \dfrac{6}{-4} = \dfrac{3}{-2}$ or $-\dfrac{3}{2}$.

The slope of $\overleftrightarrow{CD}$ is $\dfrac{\Delta y}{\Delta x} = \dfrac{-6 - 2}{-2 - 4} = \dfrac{-8}{-6} = \dfrac{4}{3}$.

The graph of $\overleftrightarrow{AB}$ is negative and the slope is downhill. The graph of $\overleftrightarrow{CD}$ is positive and the slope is uphill.

2 Determine if the following three points $A(1, 4)$, $B(3, 9)$, and $C(5, 14)$ are collinear.

SOLUTION

To be collinear (i.e. all points lie on the same line) any pairs of points must result in the same slope. The slopes of $\overline{AB}$, $\overline{AC}$, and $\overline{BC}$ must be the same. Although we will compute the slopes of three segments, we need to check only any two of these slopes, since any two will include the points A, B, and C.

$$m_{AB} = \frac{4-9}{1-3} = \frac{-5}{-2} = \frac{5}{2}$$

$$m_{BC}\, \frac{9-14}{3-5} = \frac{-5}{-2} = \frac{5}{2}$$

$$m_{AC} = \frac{4-14}{1-5} = \frac{-10}{-4} = \frac{5}{2}$$

ANSWER: Since all the slopes, m, are the same, $\frac{5}{2}$, the points are collinear.

3 Which of the following points does NOT lie in the shaded triangular region in the figure below?

(1) $(7, 3)$
(2) $(7, 2.5)$
(3) $(5, 2.5)$
(4) $(4, 2.5)$

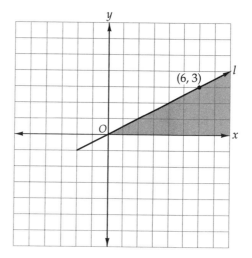

SOLUTION

Since line l passes through the origin $(0, 0)$ and point $(6, 3)$, the slope is $\frac{0-3}{0-6} = \frac{-3}{-6}$ or $\frac{1}{2}$.

We could also have taken the coordinates $(6, 3)$ and simply written $\frac{3}{6} = \frac{1}{2}$. This always works when the line passes through the origin. Furthermore, any point that lies in the shaded region must lie on a line that passes through the origin and whose slope is less than or equal to $\frac{1}{2}$.

Thus, we can check the given points by simply writing the fraction $\frac{y\text{-value}}{x\text{-value}}$. If the fraction's value is more than 0.5, then that point does NOT lie in the shaded region. Only the fraction $\frac{2.5}{4}$, which equals 0.625, is more than 0.5.

ANSWER: Choice (4), the point $(4, 2.5)$ does not lie in the shaded region.

Horizontal Lines and Vertical Lines

For horizontal lines, the y-coordinate of each point on the line is the same. For example, consider these four points: $(-4, 2), (1, 2), (0, 2),$ and $(3, 2)$. The line that passes through these points is $y = 2$.

The slope of the horizontal line $y = 2$ is *zero*. Since $\frac{\Delta y}{\Delta x} = \frac{2-2}{-4-(-1)} = \frac{0}{-3} = 0.$

- In general, an equation of the form $y = b$ is parallel to the x-axis, with the y-intercept equal to b.

Similarly, for vertical lines, the x-coordinate of each point on the line is the same. For example, consider these four points: $(-1, 4), (-1, 0), (-1, -2), (-1, -4)$. The line that passes through these points is $x = -1$.

The slope of the vertical line $x = -1$ is *undefined*. $\frac{\Delta y}{\Delta x} = \frac{4-0}{-1-(-1)} = \frac{4}{0}$, and there is no division by zero.

- In general, an equation of the form $x = a$ is parallel to the y-axis, with the x-intercept equal to a.

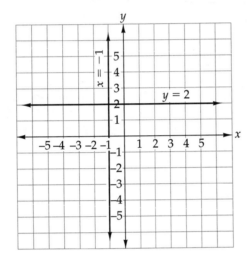

Keep in Mind

- Horizontal lines have a *zero* (0) slope.
- Vertical lines have *no* slope, or the slope is *undefined*.
- A vertical line and a horizontal line always intersect and are perpendicular.

Note: Having no slope is **not** the same as having a slope equal to zero.

MODEL PROBLEMS

1   Find the value of k so that the line joining the point $(-3, 7)$ and $(4, k)$ is horizontal.

SOLUTION

If the line is horizontal, then the slope is zero, which means that the numerator (or change in y) is zero. Thus, $\frac{\Delta y}{\Delta x} = \frac{7-k}{-3-4} = \frac{7-k}{-7} = 0$. By cross-multiplying, $7 - k = 0$, and $7 = k$.

ANSWER: $k = 7$

2   Find the value of k so that the line joining the points $(k, 5)$ and $(2, -3)$ is vertical.

SOLUTION

If the line is vertical, then the slope is undefined, which means that the denominator (or change in x) is zero.

Thus, $\frac{\Delta y}{\Delta x} = \frac{5-(-3)}{k-2} = \frac{8}{k-2}$, where $k - 2 = 0$. Solving for the variable, $k = 2$.

ANSWER: $k = 2$

3   Which is true of the graph of the equation $y = -3$?

　(1) It has a slope of -3.
　(2) It is parallel to the y-axis.
　(3) It is parallel to the x-axis.
　(4) It passes through the point $(-3, 0)$.

SOLUTION

The equation $y = -3$ indicates that the line is horizontal. Thus, the line $y = -3$ is parallel to the x-axis, its slope is zero, and it intersects the y-axis only at $(0, -3)$.

ANSWER: Choice (3) It is parallel to the x-axis.

 Practice

1   The graph of the equation $y = 4$ passes through the point:

　(1) $(4, 0)$
　(2) $(0, 4)$
　(3) $(0, 0)$
　(4) $(4, -4)$

2   Which is true of the graph of $x = -2$?

　(1) It has a slope of -2.
　(2) It has an x-intercept of -2.
　(3) It is parallel to the x-axis.
　(4) It has a y-intercept of -2.

3   Which of the following is the equation of a line parallel to the x-axis and passing through the point $(2, -3)$?

　(1) $x = 2$
　(2) $x = -3$
　(3) $y = 2$
　(4) $y = -3$

4   The graph of $y = -5$ is a line that has:

　(1) a slope of -5
　(2) a negative slope
　(3) a y-intercept of -5
　(4) an x-intercept of -5

5 Which of the following graphs illustrates a linear function with negative slope and a positive *y*-intercept?

(1)

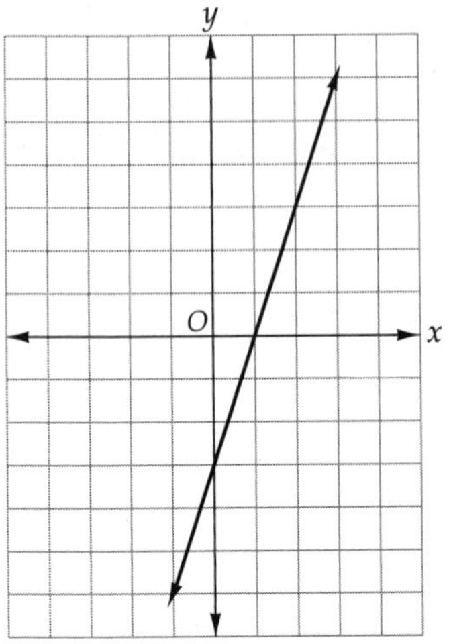

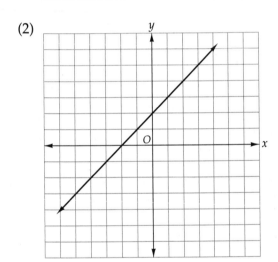

(2)

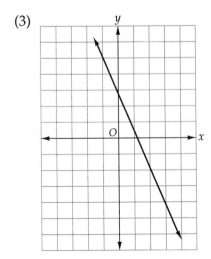

(3)

(4)

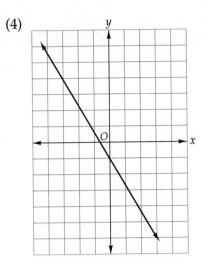

6 Which of the following is the equation of a line parallel to the *y*-axis and passing through the point $(-1, 6)$?

(1) $x = 6$
(2) $x = -1$
(3) $y = 6$
(4) $y = -1$

Exercises 7–15: In each case, (a) plot the points and draw the line determined by these points. (b) Find the slope of the line. (c) State whether the slope of the line that passes through these points is positive, negative, zero, or undefined.

7 $(5, 3)$ and $(8, -2)$

8 $(1, 1)$ and $(5, 9)$

9 $(-1, 1)$ and $(3, 4)$

10 $(3, -2)$ and $(3, 2)$

11 $(-3, 10)$ and $(4, -4)$

12 $(-5, -7)$ and $(3, 5)$

13 $(1, 2)$ and $(6, 2)$

14 $(-8, -7)$ and $(-2, -4)$

15 $(-13, -2)$ and $(-7, 16)$

16 For each of the following, state the equation of the line with the given characteristics.

    a Has a slope of 0 and pass through the point $(8, -5)$.
    b Is parallel to the x-axis and 1 unit above it.
    c Is perpendicular to the x-axis and passes through the point $(-2, 3)$.
    d Is parallel to the y-axis and is 10 units to the left of it.
    e Is perpendicular to the y-axis and is 4.5 units below the x-axis.

17 Find the slope of a line containing the given points.

    a (d, e) and (f, g)
    b $((h - k), 3)$ and $((h - k), n)$
    c (a, b) and $((a - b), (b - a))$
    d $((r + w), (r - w))$ and $((r - w), (r + w))$

18 In the figure below, if a point on line l is $(4, 6)$, what is the slope of line l?

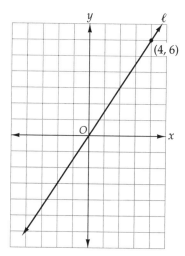

19 In the figure below, if the slope of line n is $\frac{-7}{10}$, what is the value of y?

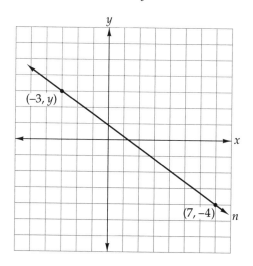

Exercises 20–25: Find the missing coordinate.

20 Points $(0, 6)$ and $(-4, y)$ lie on the line with a slope of 5.

21 Points $(-6, 8)$ and $(0, y)$ lie on a line with a slope of -2.

22 Points $(-5, -1)$ and $(x, 9)$ lie on a line with a slope of 2.

23 Points $(13, 2)$ and $(x, -5)$ lie on the line with a slope of $\frac{-7}{2}$.

24 Points $(5, 3)$ and $(x, 6)$ lie on a line with a slope of 1.

25 Points $(-4, 8)$ and $(x, -2)$ lie on a line that has no slope.

26 Find the slope of the line represented by each table of values.

a

x	y
-3	0
0	-3
3	-6

b

x	y
-2	-2
0	0
3	3

27 Determine if the following sets of points are collinear.

    a $\{(-2, 4), (-1, 0), (0, -2)\}$
    b $\{(-8, -1), (1, 8), (8, 1)\}$
    c $\{(4, -3), (2, -3), (2, 5)\}$

28 In the figure below, if line m passes through the origin and point $(-1, 4)$, what is the value of $\frac{q}{p}$?

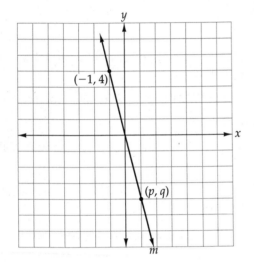

29 The foundation of a new house being built extends 3 feet aboveground. The ramp needed to carry up the floor beams for framing must rest on top of the foundation and have a slope of $\frac{1}{5}$. How many feet from the base of the house should the ramp be?

30 Given the points $A(-3, 1)$, $B(0, 0)$, $C(2, -1)$, and $D(8, -3)$.

   a State the slope of $\overline{AB}$, $\overline{CD}$, and $\overline{AD}$.
   b Are the points A, B, C, and D collinear?

31 Points $A(-3, -2)$, $B(3, 2)$, and $C(3, -2)$ are the vertices of $\triangle ABC$. Find the slope of each side of $\triangle ABC$. What type of triangle could this be? Explain your answer.

8-2 The Equation of a Line

Recall that the equation of a line can describe the points that lie on the line. Theorems 8.1 and 8.2 describe the *slope-intercept* form of the equation, while Theorem 8.3 describes the *point-slope* form of the equation.

- Theorem 8.1 (Slope-Intercept Form). If the equation of a line is in the form $y = mx + b$, then m is the slope and b is the y-intercept.

   Example:

   If the equation of the line AB is $y = 4x - 5$, then $m = 4$ and $b = -5$.

- Theorem 8.2 (Slope-Intercept Form). If a line has the slope, m, and y-intercept, b, then its equation is $y = mx + b$.

   Example:

   If the given slope is $\frac{4}{3}$ and the y-intercept is -2, then we can find the equation of the line by substituting $\frac{4}{3}$ for m and -2 for b into the slope-intercept form $y = mx + b$. Thus, $y = \frac{4}{3}x - 2$.

- Theorem 8.3 (Point-Slope Form). If $P(x_1, y_1)$ lies on the line q and the slope of line q is m, then an equation of line q is: $y - y_1 = m(x - x_1)$.

   Example:

   If the slope of a line is -7 and passes through the point $(2, -3)$, we can find the equation of the line by substituting -7 for m and $(2, -3)$ for (x_1, y_1) into the point-slope form, $y - y_1 = m(x - x_1)$. Thus,

   $$y - y_1 = m(x - x_1)$$
   $$y - (-3) = -7(x - 2)$$
   $$y + 3 = -7x + 14$$
   $$y = -7x + 11$$

Note: This same equation can also be found using the slope-intercept method when $m = -7$ and $(x, y) = (2, -3)$. The object is to first find the y-intercept or b. Thus,

$$y = mx + b$$
$$-3 = -7(2) + b$$
$$-3 = -14 + b$$
$$b = 11$$

Now substitute -7 for m and 11 for b. The equation is $y = -7x + 11$.

There are two other conditions that need to be addressed in finding an equation of a line:

(1) If we are given a point (x, y) and the y-intercept, b.

Example:

Find the equation of a line when given the point $(x, y) = (-3, 4)$ and y-intercept $= 8$. Using $y = mx + b$ and substituting

$$4 = m(-3) + 8$$
$$3m = 4$$
$$m = \frac{4}{3}$$

ANSWER: The equation of a line that passes through the point $(-3, 4)$ and y-intercept $= 8$ is $y = \frac{4}{3}x + 8$.

(2) If we are given two points, (x_1, y_1) and (x_2, y_2).

Example:

Find the equation of a line when given two points, say $(3, -2)$ and $(4, 1)$. The slope $m = \frac{-2 - 1}{3 - 4} = \frac{-3}{-1} = 3$. Now substitute one point, say $(4, 1)$ for (x, y), and $m = 3$ in the equation $y = mx + b$ so that

$$1 = 3(4) + b$$
$$b = -11$$

ANSWER: The equation of a line that pass through the points $(3, -2)$ and $(4, 1)$ is $y = 3x - 11$.

Keep in Mind

The equation of a line describes all the points on a line such that

- if a point is on a line, then its coordinates satisfy the equation of the line.
- if the coordinates of a point satisfy the equation of a line, then the point is *on the line.*

We can determine the equation of a line if we are given

- the slope, m, and the y-intercept, b.
- the slope, m, and a point (x, y).
- the y-intercept, b, and a point (x, y).
- two points (x_1, y_1) and (x_2, y_2).

MODEL PROBLEMS

1 The point $P(-5, -2)$ lies on the graph of which equation?

    (1) $3x - 2y = 4$
    (2) $-2x + y = 12$
    (3) $x - 3y = 1$
    (4) $y = x - 3$

SOLUTION

Test the coordinates in each equation until one of them works.

Choice (1)
$3x - 2y = 4$
$3(-5) - 2(-2) = 4$
$-15 + 4 = 4$
$-11 \neq 4$

Choice (2)
$-2x + y = 12$
$-2(-5) + (-2) = 12$
$10 - 2 = 12$
$8 \neq 12$

Choice (3)
$x - 3y = 1$
$(-5) - 3(-2) = 1$
$-5 + 6 = 1$
$1 = 1$

Choice (4)
$y = x - 3$
$-2 = (-5) - 3$
$-2 \neq -8$

ANSWER: Choice (3) point P lies on the graph of the equation $x - 3y = 1$.

2 Find the x-intercept and the y-intercept of the graph of the equation $x - 2y = -10$.

SOLUTION

The x-intercept of a line means that the y-value is 0. By substituting 0 for y, we have $x - 2(0) = -10$ and $x = -10$.
The y-intercept of a line means that the x-value is 0. By substituting 0 for x, we have $0 - 2y = -10$ and $y = 5$.

ANSWER: The x-intercept is $(-10, 0)$ and the y-intercept is $(0, 5)$.

3 Write the equation of a line with y-intercept $= -4$ and x-intercept $= 3$.

SOLUTION

If the y-intercept is -4, this means that $b = -4$. If the x-intercept is 3, then the coordinate point is $(3, 0)$. Substituting in the slope-intercept equation $y = mx + b$, we have $0 = m(3) - 4$. Solve for m, we have $4 = 3m$ and $m = \frac{4}{3}$.

ANSWER: The equation of the line is $y = \frac{4}{3}x - 4$.

Practice

1. For each of the following, determine whether the given point lies on the line with the given equation.

   a. $(8, -7); y = -\frac{1}{4}x - 3$

   b. $(-5, 3); y = -3x - 12$

   c. $(6, 1); y = -\frac{2}{3}x + 5$

2. Write each equation in the form $y = mx + b$. Identify the slope and y-intercept of each equation.

   a. $x + y = 6$
   b. $5 + y = 3x$
   c. $3x + y = 0$
   d. $4x - 2y = 8$
   e. $2x + 3y - 12 = 0$
   f. $2y + 6 = 3x$
   g. $-3x - y = 5$
   h. $x + 2y - 9 = 0$

3. Determine the x-intercept and y-intercept of each of the following.

   a. $y = x + 7$
   b. $2x + y = 8$
   c. $6 + y = 2x$
   d. $y = 2x - 4$
   e. $2y = x$
   f. $2x - 3y - 12 = 0$

4. State the equation of the line with the given slope, m, and y-intercept.

   a. $m = 2$; y-intercept $= 5$

   b. $m = \frac{1}{2}$; y-intercept $= -2$

   c. $m = 0$; y-intercept $= -3$
   d. $m = -1$; y-intercept $= 4$

5. Determine the equation of the line with the given slope, m, and passing through point P.

   a. $m = 1; P(1, 4)$
   b. $m = 0; P(6, 2)$

   c. $m = \frac{1}{2}; P(4, -3)$

   d. $m = \frac{5}{2}; P(0, 3)$

   e. $m = -\frac{3}{2}; P(-2, 5)$

   f. $m = -\frac{3}{5}; P(10, -1)$

6. State the equation of the line with the given y-intercept, b, and passing through point P.

   a. $b = 5; P(2, -2)$
   b. $b = -2; P(3, 4)$
   c. $b = -10; P(-1, -5)$
   d. $b = 3; P(-2, 6)$
   e. $b = 13; P(-3, 1)$
   f. $b = 6; P(-5, 0)$

7. Determine the equation of the line containing the following pairs of points.

   a. $(3, 2)$ and $(6, 5)$
   b. $(-3, 4)$ and $(0, 2)$
   c. $(-7, 5)$ and $(-3, 5)$
   d. $(-1, 3)$ and $(1, -1)$
   e. $(6, -1)$ and $(7, -3)$
   f. $(-5, 2)$ and $(1, 0)$

8-3 The Slopes of Parallel and Perpendicular Lines

- Theorem 8.4. Two nonvertical lines are *parallel* if and only if they have the same slope.

   Examples:

   1 The lines $y = \frac{2}{3}x + 7$ and $y = \frac{2}{3}x - 5$ are parallel since their slopes are the same, $\frac{2}{3}$.

   2 The graphs of the linear equations $y = 2x + 4$ and $y = 2x - 2$, show these lines to be parallel. The slope for both lines is 2 and the y-intercepts are 4 and -2.

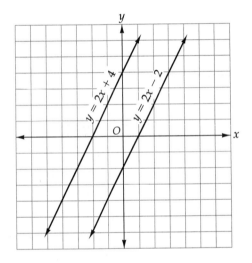

- Theorem 8.5. Two nonvertical lines are *perpendicular* if the product of their slopes is -1. Their slopes are negative reciprocals of each other.

   Example

   The lines $y = 4x + 1$ and $y = -\frac{1}{4}x + 2$ have slopes of 4 and $-\frac{1}{4}$. Since they are negative reciprocals of each other, their product is $4 \times \left(-\frac{1}{4}\right) = -1$.

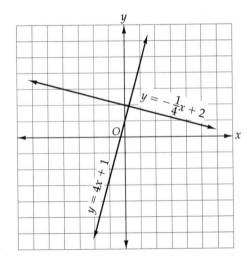

MODEL PROBLEMS

1 Find the value of x such that line r that passes through $(x, 2)$ and $(1, 6)$ is perpendicular to line k that passes through $(16, 6)$ and $(4, -3)$.

SOLUTION

First find the slope of line k passing through $(16, 6)$ and $(4, -3)$.

$$\frac{\Delta y}{\Delta x} = \frac{6 - (-3)}{16 - 4} = \frac{9}{12} = \frac{3}{4}$$

A line perpendicular to k must have a slope of $-\frac{4}{3}$, that is, the negative reciprocal of $\frac{3}{4}$. Thus, we set the slope of line $r = \frac{(-2) - 6}{x - 1} = -\frac{4}{3}$ or $\frac{-8}{x - 1} = -\frac{4}{3}$.

By cross multiplying, $4(x - 1) = (-3)(-8)$

$$4x - 4 = 24$$
$$4x = 28$$
$$x = 7$$

ANSWER: $x = 7$

2 If the line whose equation is $3x + 2y = 8$ is parallel to the line whose equation is $y = ax - 5$, then what is the value of a?

SOLUTION

Lines that have the same slope are parallel. Solve the given equation for y in the form $y = mx + b$ and determine the slope.

$$3x + 2y = 8$$
$$2y = -3x + 8$$
$$y = \frac{-3}{2}x + 4$$

The variable a is the coefficient of x and the value of the slope, or $\frac{-3}{2}$.

ANSWER: $a = \frac{-3}{2}$

3 Write the equation of a line passing through $(1, 9)$ and perpendicular to the line $y = \frac{1}{2}x - 7$.

SOLUTION

The slope of the line perpendicular to $y = \frac{1}{2}x - 7$ is the negative reciprocal of $\frac{1}{2}$. Thus, $m = -2$. Sub-in for x, y, and m, and solve for b.

$$9 = (-2)(1) + b$$
$$b = 11$$

ANSWER: The equation is $y = -2x + 11$.

Practice

1 Line p has a positive slope and passes through the origin. If line l is perpendicular to line p, which of the following must be true?

   (1) Line l has a positive x-intercept.
   (2) Line l has a positive y-intercept.
   (3) Line l passes through the point $(0, 0)$.
   (4) Line l has a negative slope.

2 If a square is plotted on the coordinate plane so that its sides are not parallel to the x-axis or y-axis, what is the product of the slopes of all four sides of the square?

   (1) -5
   (2) -1
   (3) 1
   (4) 5

3 For each line that passes through the following pairs of points, (i) find the slope of a parallel line, (ii) find the slope of a perpendicular line.

   a $(-3, 7)$ and $(4, -2)$
   b $(0, 5)$ and $(3, 5)$
   c $(-3, -1)$ and $(5, -8)$
   d $(6, -2)$ and $(1, -4)$
   e $(9, -3)$ and $(-1, 6)$
   f $(1, -5)$ and $(0, 8)$

4 Determine whether theses pairs of lines are parallel, perpendicular, or neither. Explain your answer.

   a $3x + 5y = 2$
     $3y - 7 = 5x$
   b $y - x = 14$
     $x + y = 8$

   c $y = \frac{1}{2}x + 3$
     $x + 2y = -6$
   d $y = 5x - 3$
     $5x + y = 7$
   e $y = -2$
     $x = 10$
   f $3y - 2x = 15$
     $\frac{3}{2}y = x - \frac{9}{2}$

5 Determine if the line passing through points A and B is perpendicular to the line passing through points C and D.

   a $A(5, 5), B(-3, -11)$
     $C(3, -2), D(-7, 3)$
   b $A(7, 5), B(-14, -9)$
     $C(0, 1), D(4, -5)$
   c $A(7, 19), B(0, 5)$
     $C(1, 2), D(-5, 0)$

6 Write the equation of a line passing through the given point and perpendicular to the given line.

   a $(5, 3); y = 4x + 2$
   b $(-4, 1); y = \frac{1}{2}x - 5$
   c $(10, 6); 5x + y = 4$

7 Determine whether one, both, or neither of the triangles with the given vertices are right triangles.

   a $A(6, 2), B(-3, 4)$, and $C(-1, 13)$
   b $A(1, 2), B(2, 3)$, and $C(4, 5)$

8-4 The Midpoint of a Line Segment

The midpoint of a line segment can be used to show that a line segment is bisected by another line, to find the center of a circle, to aid in finding congruent segments, and to find the endpoint of a median.

The **midpoint formula** states that for any two points $A(x_1, y_1)$ and $B(x_2, y_2)$ the midpoint of $\overline{AB}$ has coordinates $\left(\dfrac{x_1 + x_2}{2}, \dfrac{y_1 + y_2}{2}\right)$.

Since the midpoint of $\overline{AB}$ lies halfway between the endpoints A and B, the midpoint is the average of the x-values and the average of the y-values.

MODEL PROBLEMS

1 Find the coordinates of M, the midpoint of the segment joining $A(1, 3)$ and $B(9, 5)$.

SOLUTION

Substitute the coordinates of the points in the midpoint formula.

$$M = \left(\frac{x_1 + x_2}{2}, \frac{y_1 + y_2}{2}\right)$$

$$M = \left(\frac{1+9}{2}, \frac{3+5}{2}\right) = (5, 4)$$

ANSWER: M (midpoint) $= (5, 4)$

2 If $A(-5, 4)$ and $B(x, y)$ are the endpoints of segment AB and $M(-2, 1)$ is the midpoint of $\overline{AB}$, what are the coordinates of B?

SOLUTION

Substitute the known values in the midpoint formula.

$$M = \left(\frac{x_1 + x_2}{2}, \frac{y_1 + y_2}{2}\right)$$

$M = (-2, 1) = \left(\frac{-5 + x}{2}, \frac{4 + y}{2}\right)$, so the x-coordinate of $M = -2 = \frac{-5 + x}{2}$ and the y-coordinate of

$M = 1 = \frac{4 + y}{2}$.

Solve for x: $-4 = -5 + x$ Solve for y: $2 = 4 + y$
              $x = 1$ $y = -2$

ANSWER: The coordinates of B are $(1, -2)$.

ALTERNATIVE SOLUTION

To find the missing endpoint of a line segment if the midpoint and one endpoint are known, use the LOOP method.

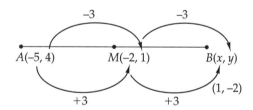

The distance from -5 to -2 is the same as the distance from -2 to x, so add 3 to -2. Thus, $x = -2 + 3 = 1$.

The distance from 4 to 1 is the same as the distance from 1 to y, so add -3 to 1. Thus, $y = 1 + (-3) = -2$.

The coordinates of $B(x, y) = (1, -2)$.

3 $\overline{QS}$ is the diameter of a circle whose center is $R(-1, 5)$. If point Q has coordinates $(-3, 2)$, what are the coordinates of point S?

SOLUTION

Draw a diagram and use the LOOP method.

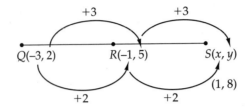

ANSWER: The coordinates of point S are $(1, 8)$.

4 If $\triangle ABC$ has vertices $A(7, -3)$, $B(-1, 5)$, and $C(4, 8)$, what are the coordinates of M if the median is drawn from C to $\overline{AB}$?

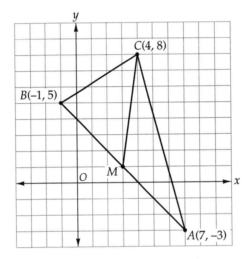

SOLUTION

Use the midpoint formula to find the coordinates of the midpoint of $\overline{AB}$.

$$M = \left(\frac{x_1 + x_2}{2}, \frac{y_1 + y_2}{2}\right)$$

$$M = \left(\frac{7 + (-1)}{2}, \frac{-3 + 5}{2}\right) = (3, 1)$$

ANSWER: $M = (3, 1)$

5 Find the equation of a line that is the perpendicular bisector of $\overline{PQ}$ with coordinates $P(-5, 3)$ and $Q(3, 7)$.

SOLUTION

Find the slope of the line passing through points P and Q.

Slope $= \dfrac{3-7}{-5-3} = \dfrac{-4}{-8} = \dfrac{1}{2}$.

The slope of the perpendicular bisector is the negative reciprocal, -2.

The bisector must also pass through the midpoint $\left(\dfrac{-5+3}{2}, \dfrac{3+7}{2}\right) = (-1, 5)$.

Substituting $m = -2$ and $(x, y) = (-1, 5)$ in the equation $y = mx + b$, we have $5 = -2(-1) + b$, so $5 = 2 + b$ and $b = 3$.

ANSWER: The equation of the perpendicular bisector is $y = -2x + 3$.

 Practice

Exercises 1–3: Find the midpoint of the line segment that connects each pair of points.

1 $(-2, 7)$ and $(5, -9)$

(1) $(-3.5, 8)$
(2) $(1.5, -1)$
(3) $(2.5, 2)$
(4) $(3.5, 6)$

2 $(-1, 0.5)$ and $(-4, 3.5)$

(1) $(-0.25, -0.25)$
(2) $(0.25, 1.75)$
(3) $(1.25, -1.75)$
(4) $(-2.5, 2)$

3 $(-2.7, -5.3)$ and $(-1.3, 5.5)$

(1) $(-4, 2.1)$
(2) $(-2, 0.1)$
(3) $(0.7, 5.4)$
(4) $(1.4, -3.3)$

Exercises 4–6: Find the coordinates of the endpoint B when midpoint M of $\overline{AB}$ and endpoint A are given.

4 $A(4, -2)$ and $M(-2, -1)$

(1) $(-8, 0)$
(2) $(-6, 1)$
(3) $(0, -4)$
(4) $(1, -1.5)$

5 $A(-3, 2)$ and $M(7, 11)$

(1) $(2, 6.5)$
(2) $(10, 9)$
(3) $(11, 22)$
(4) $(17, 20)$

6 $A(-5, 1)$ and $M(4, -6)$

(1) $\left(-\dfrac{1}{2}, -\dfrac{5}{2}\right)$
(2) $(3, 13)$
(3) $(9, -7)$
(4) $(13, -13)$

7 Find the midpoint of the line segment that connects points $(3a, 7r)$ and $(7a, 3r)$.

8 Find endpoint B of the segment AB where M, the midpoint of $\overline{AB}$, has coordinates $(2x, 3y)$ and endpoint A has coordinates (x, y).

9 $\overline{AB}$ is the diameter of a circle whose center is $C(4, 7)$. If point A has coordinates $(-2, 3)$, what are the coordinates of point B?

10 The vertices of rhombus $GLAD$ are $G(-1, 1)$, $L(1, -3)$, $A(3, 1)$, and $D(1, 5)$. Draw the graph of the rhombus, find the midpoint of each side, and connect the midpoints in order. What kind of quadrilateral is formed?

11 If $\triangle SAD$ has vertices $S(-4, -3)$, $A(4, -1)$, and $D(-2, 3)$, find the coordinates of M (the midpoint of $\overline{SA}$).

12 The vertices of triangles BAD are $B(1, 3)$, $A(7, 5)$, and $D(9, -3)$. If E is the midpoint of $\overline{BA}$ and F is the midpoint of $\overline{AD}$, show that

  a $\overline{EF}$ is parallel to $\overline{BD}$.

  b $EF = \frac{1}{2}BD$.

13 If the coordinates of the vertices of $\triangle DAN$ are $D(-3, 0)$, $A(-5, -5)$, and $N(-7, 0)$, find

  a the slope of side $\overline{DA}$.

  b the slope of the altitude from N to side $\overline{DA}$.

  c the midpoint of $\overline{DA}$.

  d the equation of the line drawn from N to the midpoint of $\overline{DA}$.

14 If the coordinates of $\overline{AB}$ are $A(-1, 4)$ and $B(7, 2)$, what is the equation of the line that is the perpendicular bisector of $\overline{AB}$?

15 Find the equation of a line that is the perpendicular bisector of $\overline{JB}$ with coordinates $J(3, -9)$ and $B(-1, 11)$.

8-5 Coordinate Proof

Direct analytical proofs require the use of specific coordinates along with our theorems and formulas.

    Coordinate geometry proofs should be arranged in an orderly step-by-step format with reasoned conclusions clearly stated at the end of the algebraic or arithmetic procedures. Of course, many of the problems can be proved by more than one method.

General Methods of Proof and Formulas

To Prove	Formula to Use
that line segments are congruent, show that the lengths are equal.	Distance formula $d = \sqrt{(x_2 - x_1)^2 + (y_2 - y_1)^2}$
that line segments bisect each other, show that the midpoints are the same.	Midpoint formula $M = \left(\dfrac{x_1 + x_2}{2}, \dfrac{y_1 + y_2}{2}\right)$
that lines are parallel, show that the slopes are equal.	Slope formula $m = \dfrac{y_2 - y_1}{x_2 - x_1}$ $m_1 = m_2$
that lines are perpendicular, show that the slopes are negative reciprocals.	Products of slopes $= -1$ $m_1 \bullet m_2 = -1$ or $m_1 = -\dfrac{1}{m_2}$

The table below gives methods that can be used to prove that a quadrilateral belongs to a specific category.

To Prove a Figure is a(n)	Methods
Parallelogram	Show *one* of the following: • The diagonals bisect each other. • Both pairs of opposite sides are parallel. • Both pairs of opposite sides are congruent. • One pair of opposite sides is congruent and parallel.
Rectangle	Show that the figure is a parallelogram using any one of the four methods above AND *one* of the following: • The figure has one right angle. • The diagonals are congruent.
Rhombus	Show that the figure is a parallelogram using any one of the four methods above AND *one* of the following: • The diagonals are perpendicular. • Two adjacent sides are congruent.
Square	Show that the figure is a rectangle AND two adjacent sides are congruent. OR Show that the figure is a rhombus AND one angle is a right angle.
Trapezoid	Show that the quadrilateral has only one pair of opposite sides parallel.
Isosceles trapezoid	Show that the figure is a trapezoid AND *one* of the following: • The diagonals are congruent. • The legs are congruent.
Right trapezoid	Show that the figure is a trapezoid AND one of the legs is perpendicular to a base of the trapezoid.

⟶ MODEL PROBLEMS

1   In right triangle PAC, the vertices are $P(-2, -1)$, $A(4, 7)$, and $C(-4, 3)$. Prove that the median to the hypotenuse, $\overline{CM}$, is equal to one-half of the hypotenuse.

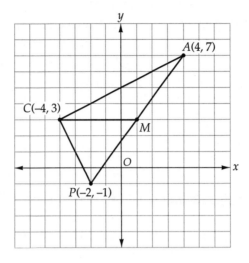

SOLUTION

Plan: Step 1: Find the midpoint M of hypotenuse $\overline{AP}$. Step 2: Find the length of the median $\overline{CM}$. Step 3: Find the length of hypotenuse $\overline{AP}$ and take half of it. Then compare the lengths.

Step 1: Use the midpoint formula to find the midpoint of hypotenuse $\overline{AP}$.

$$M = \left(\frac{x_1 + x_2}{2}, \frac{y_1 + y_2}{2}\right)$$
$$M = \left(\frac{4 + (-2)}{2}, \frac{7 + (-1)}{2}\right) = (1, 3)$$

Step 2: Use the distance formula to find the length of the median.

$$d = \sqrt{(x_2 - x_1)^2 + (y_2 - y_1)^2}$$
$$CM = \sqrt{(1 - (-4))^2 + (3 - 3)^2} = \sqrt{25 + 0} = 5$$

Step 3: Use the distance formula to find the length of the hypotenuse.

$$d = \sqrt{(x_2 - x_1)^2 + (y_2 - y_1)^2}$$
$$AP = \sqrt{(-2 - 4)^2 + (-1 - 7)^2} = \sqrt{36 + 64} = \sqrt{100} = 10$$

Thus, half the hypotenuse = 5

ANSWER: Median $CM = 5 = \frac{1}{2} \times$ (hypotenuse)

Theorem 8.6. The midpoint of the hypotenuse is equidistant from the vertices.

2 The vertices of triangle ABC are $A(-3, 1)$, $B(4, 2)$, and $C(-2, -1)$.

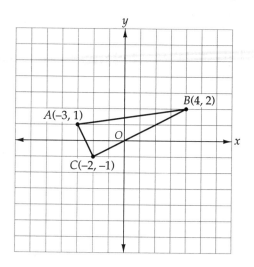

   a Prove that $\triangle ABC$ is a right triangle.
   b Using the information found in **a**, find the area of triangle ABC.

SOLUTION

Plan: (a) Find the length of each side of $\triangle ABC$ and test the measures in the Pythagorean theorem, and (b) apply the formula for the area of any triangle.

   a Use the distance formula to find the lengths of the sides of $\triangle ABC$.

$$d = \sqrt{(x_2 - x_1)^2 + (y_2 - y_1)^2}$$
$$d_{AB} = \sqrt{(4 - (-3))^2 + (2 - 1)^2} = \sqrt{49 + 1} = \sqrt{50}$$
$$d_{BC} = \sqrt{((-2) - 4)^2 + ((-1) - 2)^2} = \sqrt{36 + 9} = \sqrt{45}$$
$$d_{CA} = \sqrt{((-3) - (-2))^2 + (1 - (-1))^2} = \sqrt{1 + 4} = \sqrt{5}$$

Is it true that $(AB)^2 = (BC)^2 + (CA)^2$? By substitution:

$$(\sqrt{50})^2 = (\sqrt{45})^2 + (\sqrt{5})^2$$
$$50 = 45 + 5$$

ANSWER: Since the Pythagorean theorem is true, $\triangle ABC$ is a right triangle.

   b Area of $\triangle ABC = \frac{1}{2}\sqrt{45} \times \sqrt{5} = \frac{1}{2}\sqrt{225} = \frac{1}{2}(15) = 7.5$

ANSWER: The area of $\triangle ABC = 7.5$ sq units.

3 If the coordinates of the vertices of quadrilateral *CARD* are *C*(−4, 1), *A*(−2, 3), *R*(1, 0), and *D*(−1, −2), prove that *CARD* is a rectangle.

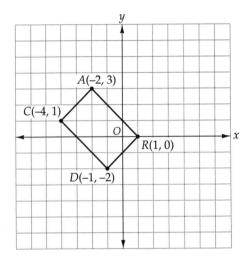

SOLUTION

Plan: Step 1: Find the midpoints of the diagonals to show that they bisect each other. Step 2: Find the length of the diagonals to show that they are congruent.

Step 1: Use the midpoint formula to find the midpoint M_{CR} of diagonal $\overline{CR}$ and the midpoint M_{AD} of diagonal $\overline{AD}$.

$$M = \left(\frac{x_1 + x_2}{2}, \frac{y_1 + y_2}{2} \right)$$

$$M_{CR} = \left(\frac{-4 + 1}{2}, \frac{1 + 0}{2} \right) = \left(\frac{-3}{2}, \frac{1}{2} \right)$$

$$M_{AD} = \left(\frac{-2 + (-1)}{2}, \frac{3 + (-2)}{2} \right) = \left(\frac{-3}{2}, \frac{1}{2} \right)$$

Since midpoints *M* and *N* are the same, the diagonals bisect each other, and quadrilateral *CARD* is a parallelogram.

Step 2: Use the distance formula to find the lengths of the diagonals.

$$d = \sqrt{\left(x_2 - x_1 \right)^2 + \left(y_2 - y_1 \right)^2}$$

$$d_{CR} = \sqrt{(1 - (-4))^2 + (0 - 1)^2} = \sqrt{25 + 1} = \sqrt{26}$$

$$d_{AD} = \sqrt{((-1) - (-2))^2 + ((-2) - 3)^2} = \sqrt{1 + 25} = \sqrt{26}$$

ANSWER: Since the diagonals $\overline{CR}$ and $\overline{AD}$ are congruent, parallelogram *CARD* is a rectangle.

4 If the vertices of quadrilateral *PEAR* are $P(-3, 0)$, $E(0, 4)$, $A(5, -6)$, and $R(-1, -4)$, show, using coordinate geometry, that quadrilateral *PEAR* is *not* an isosceles trapezoid.

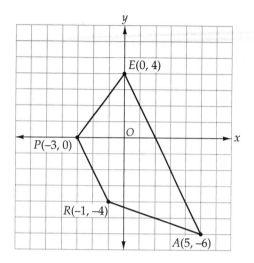

SOLUTION

Plan: Step 1: Find the slopes of all the sides of the quadrilateral and show that it is a trapezoid. Step 2: If quadrilateral *PEAR* is a trapezoid, then find the lengths of the two nonparallel sides and compare them.

Step 1:

$$\text{Slope}_{PE} = \frac{0 - 4}{-3 - 0} = \frac{-4}{-3} = \frac{4}{3}$$

$$\text{Slope}_{EA} = \frac{4 - (-6)}{0 - 5} = \frac{10}{-5} = -2$$

$$\text{Slope}_{AR} = \frac{-6 - (-4)}{5 - (-1)} = \frac{-2}{6} = \frac{-1}{3}$$

$$\text{Slope}_{RP} = \frac{-4 - 0}{1 - (-3)} = \frac{-4}{2} = -2$$

Since only the slopes of $\overline{EA}$ and $\overline{RP}$ are the same, only one pair of sides (or bases) are parallel. Thus, quadrilateral *PEAR* is a trapezoid.

Step 2: Use the distance formula to find the lengths of nonparallel sides.

$$d = \sqrt{(x_2 - x_1)^2 + (y_2 - y_1)^2}$$
$$d_{PE} = \sqrt{(0 - (-3))^2 + (4 - 0)^2} = \sqrt{9 + 16} = \sqrt{25} = 5$$
$$d_{RA} = \sqrt{(5 - (-1))^2 + ((-6) - (-4))^2} = \sqrt{36 + 4} = \sqrt{40}$$

Since the nonparallel sides (or legs) $\overline{PE}$ and $\overline{RA}$ do not have the same lengths, the trapezoid is not an isosceles trapezoid.

Using General Coordinates

Instead of using specific constant values for coordinates, we also use variables such as *a*, *b*, *c*, etc., to represent points in the coordinate plane. Then we can either avoid plotting the points and work algebraically, or we can analyze the relationships and attempt to position the points in the coordinate plane.

When placing generic geometric figures on a coordinate plane:

1   Use the origin $(0, 0)$ as a starting vertex.
2   Place at least one side of the polygon on the *x*- or *y*-axis.
3   If possible, keep the figure within the first quadrant.
4   Use easy and obvious coordinates so that computations are easy.

The following examples are typical illustrations of this procedure.

1   Placing the Right Triangle

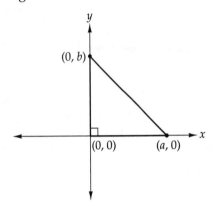

2   Placing the Isosceles Triangle

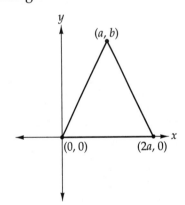

3   Placing the Rectangle

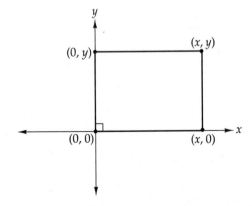

4 Placing the Parallelogram

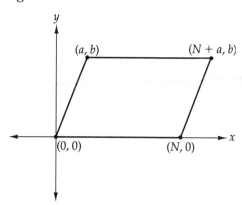

5 Placing the Isosceles Trapezoid

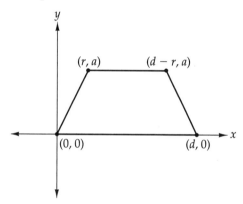

Now carefully study the two model problems below.

→ MODEL PROBLEMS

1 Given: $\triangle ELF$ with vertices $E(0, 0)$, $L(4a, 0)$, and $F(4b, 4c)$.

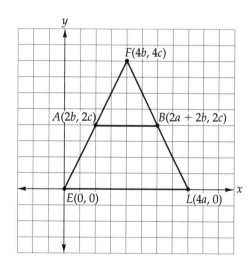

a Find point A, the midpoint of $\overline{EF}$, and point B, the midpoint of $\overline{LF}$.
b Show that $\overline{AB} \parallel \overline{EL}$ and show your reasoning.
c Show that $AB = \frac{1}{2}EL$.

SOLUTION

a Even without using the suggested figure given, we can use the midpoint formula to find points A and B.

Point $A = \left(\frac{0+4b}{2}, \frac{0+4c}{2}\right) = (2b, 2c)$

Point $B = \left(\frac{4a+4b}{2}, \frac{0+4c}{2}\right) = (2a+2b, 2c)$

b $\text{Slope}_{AB} = \frac{2c-2c}{2b-(2a+2b)} = \frac{0}{-2a} = 0$

$\text{Slope}_{EL} = \frac{0-0}{0-4a} = \frac{0}{-4a} = 0$

Since the slope of $\overline{AB}$ is equal to the slope of $\overline{EL}$, which is 0, we have shown $\overline{AB} \parallel \overline{EL}$.

c $d_{AB} = \sqrt{(2a+2b-2b)^2 + (2c-2c)^2} = \sqrt{(2a)^2+0} = \sqrt{4a^2} = 2a$

$d_{EL} = \sqrt{(4a-0)^2 + (0-0)^2} = \sqrt{(4a)^2} = 4a$

Hence, $2a = \frac{1}{2}(4a)$ or $AB = \frac{1}{2}EL$.

2 Given: The vertices of quadrilateral $MATH$ are $M(0,0)$, $A(b, c)$, $T(a+b, c)$, and $H(a, 0)$.

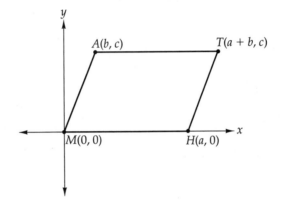

Using coordinate geometry, prove that

a diagonals $\overline{MT}$ and $\overline{AH}$ bisect each other.
b $\overline{MH} \cong \overline{AT}$.

SOLUTION

a The midpoint of $\overline{MT} = \left(\frac{0+(a+b)}{2}, \frac{0+c}{2}\right) = \left(\frac{a+b}{2}, \frac{c}{2}\right)$

The midpoint of $\overline{AH} = \left(\frac{b+a}{2}, \frac{c+0}{2}\right) = \left(\frac{a+b}{2}, \frac{c}{2}\right)$

ANSWER: Since the midpoint of $\overline{MT}$ and $\overline{AH}$ is the same, they bisect each other.

b The length of diagonal $\overline{MH} = \sqrt{(a-0)^2 + (0+0)^2} = \sqrt{a^2} = a$

The length of diagonal $\overline{AT} = \sqrt{((a+b)-b)^2 + (c-c)^2} = \sqrt{a^2} = a$

ANSWER: Since $MH = AT = a$, then $\overline{MH} \cong \overline{AT}$.

Practice

1 The vertices of triangle WIN are $W(2, 1)$, $I(4, 7)$, and $N(8, 3)$. Using coordinate geometry, show that $\triangle WIN$ is an isosceles triangle and state the reasons for your conclusion.

2 Triangle NAQ has coordinates $N(2, 3)$, $A(6, 0)$, and $Q(12, 8)$. Show, by means of coordinate geometry, that $\triangle NAQ$ is a right triangle and state the reasons for your conclusion.

3 If the vertices of right triangle ABC are $A(-1, 2)$, $B(3, 8)$, and $C(5, -2)$, use coordinate geometry to prove that point M, the midpoint of the hypotenuse, is equidistant from all three vertices of the triangle.

4 The coordinates of the vertices of triangle KEN are $K(2, 1)$, $E(9, 4)$, and $N(5, 8)$. Show that the median from K to $\overline{EN}$ is perpendicular to $\overline{EN}$.

5 The vertices of $\triangle BIG$ are $B(-4, 3)$, $I(1, 8)$, and $G(6, 3)$. Show that $\triangle BIG$ is an isosceles right triangle. Explain your reasoning.

6 If the vertices of quadrilateral $PQRS$ are $P(1, 1)$, $Q(2, 4)$, $R(5, 6)$, and $S(4, 3)$, use slopes to show that $PQRS$ is a parallelogram.

7 If the vertices of quadrilateral $SAND$ are $S(-2, -2)$, $A(-1, 2)$, $N(5, 3)$, and $D(4, -1)$, use the midpoint formula to show that $SAND$ is a parallelogram.

8 If the vertices of quadrilateral $LEAP$ are $L(-3, 1)$, $E(2, 6)$, $A(9, 5)$, and $P(4, 0)$, use the distance formula to show that $LEAP$ is a parallelogram.

9 The vertices of quadrilateral $PQRS$ are $P(-2, 1)$, $Q(2, 5)$, $R(6, -1)$, and $S(4, -7)$. If points, A, B, C, and D are the midpoints of sides $\overline{PQ}$, $\overline{QR}$, $\overline{RS}$, and $\overline{SP}$, respectively, show that $ABCD$ is a parallelogram. Explain your reasoning.

10 The coordinates of the vertices of quadrilateral $BETH$ are $B(-4, -1)$, $E(5, -2)$, $T(2, 3)$, and $H(-7, 4)$. Using coordinate geometry:

- a find the length of the diagonals.
- b show that the diagonals *do* or *do not* bisect each other.
- c give a reason to show whether $BETH$ *is* or *is not* a parallelogram.
- d give a reason to show whether $BETH$ *is* or *is not* a rectangle.

11 The coordinates of the vertices of quadrilateral $NICK$ are $N(-3, -1)$, $I(3, 1)$, $C(7, 5)$, and $K(1, 3)$. Use slopes only to show:

- a that $NICK$ is a parallelogram.
- b that $NICK$ is or is not a rhombus.

12 The coordinates of the vertices of parallelogram $KATE$ are $K(-1, 0)$, $A(3, 3)$, $T(6, -1)$, and $E(2, -4)$. Use coordinate geometry to show that $KATE$ is a square. Give reasons for your conclusion.

13 The vertices of isosceles trapezoid $PLAY$ are $P(0, 0)$, $L(10, 0)$, $A(6, 8)$, and $Y(4, 8)$. If points A, B, C, and D are the midpoints of sides $\overline{PL}$, $\overline{LA}$, $\overline{AY}$, and $\overline{YP}$, respectively, prove that quadrilateral $ABCD$ is a rhombus. Give clear reasons for your conclusion.

14 The coordinates of the vertices of triangle SUE are $S(-2, -4)$, $U(2, -1)$, and $E(8, -9)$. Using coordinate geometry, prove that:

- a triangle SUE is a right triangle.
- b triangle SUE is *not* an isosceles right triangle.

15 Quadrilateral $NORA$ has vertices $N(3, 2)$, $O(7, -3)$, $R(11, 2)$, and $A(7, 7)$. Use coordinate geometry to prove that:

- a quadrilateral $NORA$ is a rhombus.
- b quadrilateral $NORA$ is *not* a square.

16 Quadrilateral $JACK$ has vertices $J(1, -7)$, $A(10, 2)$, $C(8, 5)$, and $K(2, -1)$. Use coordinate geometry to prove that:

- a quadrilateral $JACK$ is a trapezoid.
- b quadrilateral $JACK$ is *not* isosceles.

17 The vertices of quadrilateral $MARY$ are $M(-3, 3)$, $A(7, 3)$, $R(3, 6)$, and $Y(1, 6)$. Use coordinate geometry to prove that quadrilateral $MARY$ is an isosceles trapezoid.

Exercises 18–24: Find the missing coordinates in terms of the given variables.

18 △ABC is isosceles triangle.

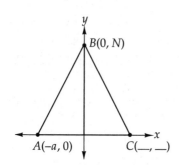

19 Quadrilateral *SPIN* is a parallelogram.

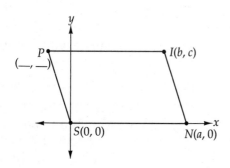

20 Quadrilateral *EFGH* is a square.

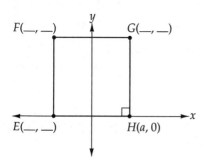

21 Quadrilateral *ABCD* is a parallelogram.

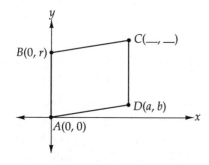

22 Quadrilateral *KLMN* is a parallelogram.

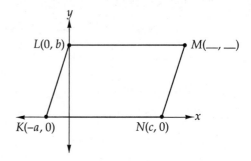

23 △*NTH* is a right isosceles triangle.

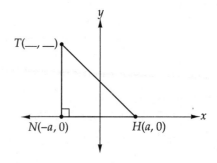

24 Quadrilateral *TRAP* is an isosceles trapezoid.

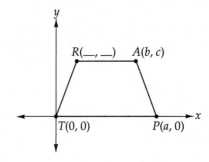

25 Is the line determined by $P(0, 0)$ and $Q(a, r)$ parallel to the line determined by $J(b, 0)$ and $K(a + b, r)$?

26 The coordinates of square *ABCD* are $A(0, 0)$, $B(a, 0)$, $C(a, a)$, and $D(0, a)$. Place the figure on the coordinate system and prove that $\overline{AC} \perp \overline{BD}$.

27 Given: $\triangle ABC$ is a right triangle with coordinates $A(0, 0)$, $B(0, 2b)$, and $C(2a, 0)$.

    a Find the coordinates of M, the midpoint of the hypotenuse.

    b Prove that M is equidistant from A, B, and C.

28 Given: The vertices of $\triangle TEQ$ are $T(0, 0)$, $E(2x, 2y)$, and $Q(4x, 0)$. The midpoints of $\overline{TE}$, $\overline{EQ}$, and $\overline{QT}$ are A, B, and C, respectively.

    a Plot the points and draw the figure.

    b Express the coordinates of points A, B, and C in terms of x and y.

    c Express the lengths of the medians from T, E, and Q.

    d Is $\triangle TEQ$ an isosceles, right, equilateral, or scalene?

29 Triangle ART has vertices $A(a, b)$, $R(a + c, b)$, and $T\left(a + \frac{c}{2}, b + d\right)$. Use coordinate geometry to prove that $\triangle ART$ is isosceles.

30 The vertices of quadrilateral $JANE$ are $J(0, 0)$, $A(a, 0)$, $N(a + b, c)$, and $E(b, c)$. Use coordinate geometry to prove that quadrilateral $JANE$ is a parallelogram.

31

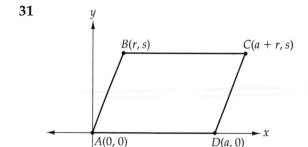

Given the figure above, prove that diagonals $\overline{AC}$ and $\overline{BD}$ of parallelogram $ABCD$ bisect each other.

32

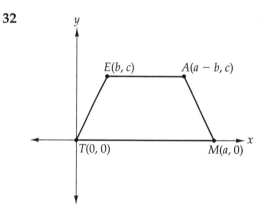

Given the figure above, the coordinates of isosceles trapezoid $TEAM$ are $T(0, 0)$, $E(b, c)$, $A(a - b, c)$, and $M(a, 0)$. Prove that diagonals $\overline{TA}$ and $\overline{EM}$ are congruent.

8-6 Concurrence of the Altitudes of a Triangle (the Orthocenter)

The **altitude of a triangle** is a line segment drawn from the vertex and perpendicular to the opposite side.

• Theorem 8.7. The three altitudes (or the lines containing the altitudes) meet in a common point. This point is called the *point of concurrency*, or the *orthocenter*.

Depending on the triangle, the point of intersection, the *orthocenter*, can be found *inside* the triangle, *on* the side of a triangle (specifically, at the vertex of a right triangle), or *outside* the triangle. The figures below illustrate the possible concurrences. In each of these illustrations, the lines are concurrent at point *P*.

Concurrence *Inside* the Triangle

Acute Triangle

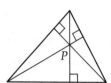

Equilateral Triangle

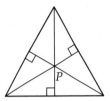

Concurrence *on* the Triangle

Right Triangle

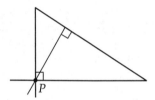

Right Isosceles Triangle

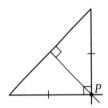

Concurrence *Outside* the Triangle

Obtuse Triangle

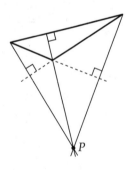

Obtuse Isosceles Triangle

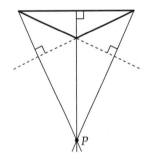

The preceding notes and illustrations provide an informal way of looking at the point of concurrency. However, we can use coordinate geometry to locate the exact coordinates of the orthocenter.

MODEL PROBLEMS

1 Find the coordinates of the point of intersection of the altitudes of $\triangle PQR$, if the vertices are $P(-2, -2)$, $Q(0, 4)$, and $R(3, -2)$.

SOLUTION

The altitude from point Q to side $\overline{PR}$ is on the y-axis. The equation of the altitude from Q is $x = 0$. The slope of $\overline{QR} = \frac{4 - (-2)}{0 - 3} = \frac{6}{-3} = -2$. The slope of the altitude from point P to $\overline{QR}$ will be the negative reciprocal of -2, which is $\frac{1}{2}$. The equation for the perpendicular line (or altitude) from point P to $\overline{QR}$ will pass through point $P(-2, -2)$. Thus, using the slope-intercept form of a line, $y = mx + b$, and substituting, $-2 = \frac{1}{2}(-2) + b$ or $-2 = -1 + b$ and $b = -1$. The equation for the altitude from point P is $y = \frac{1}{2}x - 1$.

The point of concurrency is the intersection of the altitude from Q and the altitude from P. To find the intersection of $x = 0$ and $y = \frac{1}{2}x - 1$, we only need to substitute 0 for x and solve for y. Thus, $y = \frac{1}{2}(0) - 1$ or $y = -1$ when $x = 0$.

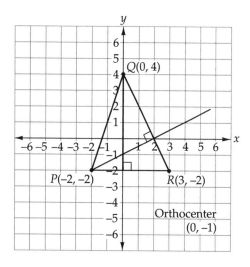

ANSWER: The point of concurrency (the orthocenter) is $(0, -1)$.

2 Find the orthocenter for the altitudes drawn from the vertices of $\triangle ABC$ where the coordinates are $A(0, 1)$, $B(-2, 7)$, and $C(4, 1)$.

SOLUTION

By extending the horizontal base $\overline{AC}$, it is clear that the vertical altitude from point B intersects $\overline{AC}$, extended at coordinates $(-2, 1)$. The equation for this altitude from B is $x = -2$.

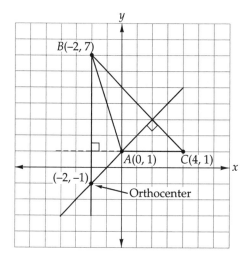

Thus, we know the x-coordinate of the orthocenter is $x = -2$. The slope of side $\overline{BC} = \frac{7 - 1}{-2 - 4} = \frac{6}{-6} = -1$. Hence, the altitude or perpendicular from A to $\overline{BC}$ has a slope of 1 (the negative reciprocal of -1). We know that the y-intercept for the line that passes through point $A(0, 1)$ is also 1 because A is on the y-axis.

The equation for the altitude from A to $\overline{BC}$ is $y = x + 1$. Since we know that the orthocenter has an x-value of -2, sub-in the value and solve for y. $y = -2 + 1$ or $y = -1$.

ANSWER: The orthocenter is $(-2, -1)$.

Practice

1   If two altitudes of a triangle fall outside the triangle, the triangle is:

(1) acute
(2) equilateral
(3) right
(4) obtuse

2   The altitudes drawn from the vertices of a right triangle intersect:

(1) in the interior of the triangle
(2) in the exterior of the triangle
(3) at the midpoint of the base of the triangle
(4) at one of the vertices of the triangle

Exercises 3–9: In each of the following, (a) plot the given points, (b) graph the figure, and (c) determine the coordinates of the point of intersection of the altitudes of the triangle.

3   $A(-1, 2)$, $B(7, 0)$, and $C(1, -6)$

4   $D(-3, 8)$, $E(-3, 0)$, and $F(9, 4)$

5   $P(-3, 0)$, $Q(3, 2)$, and $R(3, -6)$

6   $A(-6, -6)$, $B(-1, 4)$, and $C(3, 4)$

7   $D(-6, 2)$, $G(2, 8)$, and $H(6, 2)$

8   $W(-3, -3)$, $E(0, 7)$, and $T(5, -3)$

9   $P(-5, 3)$, $E(4, 3)$, and $N(-1, -5)$

10 The vertices of a triangle are $A(3, 5)$, $B(6, 9)$, and $C(10, 6)$.

a   Show that triangle ABC is a right triangle.

b   Show that B is the point of intersection of the altitudes of the triangle.

CHAPTER REVIEW

1

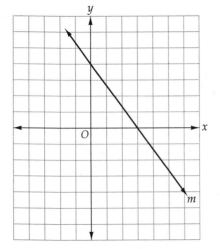

What is the equation of line m in the figure above?

(1) $y = -\frac{4}{3}x + 3$

(2) $y = -\frac{4}{3}x + 4$

(3) $y = -\frac{3}{4}x + 4$

(4) $y = \frac{3}{4}x + 4$

2   Which point is *not* on the line $x = -3$?

(1) $(-3, -3)$
(2) $(0, -3)$
(3) $(-3, 0)$
(4) $(-3, 3)$

3   Which ordered pair is in the solution set of $x - y = 8$?

(1) $(-8, 0)$
(2) $(0, 8)$
(3) $(-1, 9)$
(4) $(-1, -9)$

4   If the slope of a line is 5 and the y-intercept is 1, which of the following is the equation of that line?

(1) $y + 5x = 1$
(2) $y - 5x = 1$
(3) $x + 5y = 1$
(4) $x - 5y = 1$

5 If the graph of $y = \frac{1}{3}x + 1$ is rotated 90° clockwise about the origin, the equation of the new line is

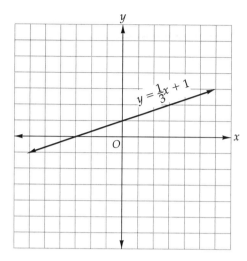

$y = \frac{1}{3}x + 1$

(1) $y = -3x + 3$
(2) $y = -3x + 1$
(3) $y = -3x - 3$
(4) $y = -\frac{1}{3}x + 1$

6 Does the equation $3x - 4y = 0$ pass through the point $(5, -2)$? Explain.

7 To the simplest radical form, what is the distance between the x-intercept and the y-intercept of $2y = 6 + 3x$?

8 To the nearest tenth, what is the distance between the x-intercept and the y-intercept of $5y = 15 - x$?

9 If $ay = 4x + 14$ and $2x - 5y = 12$, for what value of a will the two equations have *no solution*?

10 Given the midpoint $M(4, 9)$ of $\overline{AB}$ and endpoint $A(-2, 8)$, what are the coordinates of point B?

11 If the given figure is a rhombus, use slopes to show that the diagonals $\overline{AC}$ and $\overline{OB}$ are perpendicular to each other. (Hint: Show that the product of the slopes is -1.)

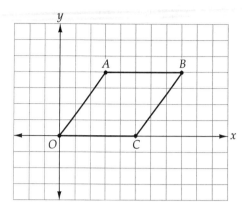

12 At what point does the graph of $3x - 4y = 12$ cross:

a the y-axis?
b the x-axis?
c the line whose equation is $y = 3$?

13 Using the equation $3x - y = 12$, determine the following:

a the slope of the line
b the x-intercept
c the y-intercept
d whether the point $(-3, -3)$ lies on the given line

14 Determine whether $\overleftrightarrow{AB}$ is vertical, horizontal, or neither when the coordinates are:

a $A(-2, 3)$ and $B(3, -2)$
b $A(-3, 1)$ and $B(-3, 2)$
c $A(-5, 1)$ and $B(-5, 3)$
d $A(1, -4)$ and $B(-4, 1)$
e $A(5, 0)$ and $B(-3, 0)$
f $A(0, -2)$ and $B(0, 3)$

15 Determine the slope in each of the following equations.

a $2y = -x + 1$
b $y = 3 - 2x$
c $3x - 4y = 7$
d $2x - 3y = 4$
e $2x + 3y = 9$
f $ax + dy = b$

16 Find the slope of the line joining the two given points.

    a $(-4, 1)$ and $(-4, 7)$
    b $(8, -2)$ and $(5, -2)$
    c $(-2, -3)$ and $(-5, 0)$
    d $(1, 0)$ and $(3, 7)$
    e (a, b) and (c, d)
    f $(x + h, y)$ and $(x, y - k)$

17 In each of the following, find the value of k if:

    a the line joining $(3, 3)$ and $(-8, -8)$ is parallel to the line joining $(3, 6)$ and $(4, k)$
    b the line joining $(3, -2)$ and $(5, k)$ is horizontal
    c the slope of the line joining $(3, k)$ and $(6, 5)$ is -3
    d the line joining $(-2, -2)$ and $(k, 1)$ is vertical
    e the point $(k, 3)$ lies on the line $2x + 3y = 21$
    f the graph of the equation $2x + 3y = k$ passes through the point $(4, -1)$
    g the line through $(k, 5)$ and $(1, 7)$ is perpendicular to the line that passes through $(-4, 8)$ and $(-6, 5)$

18 Determine whether or not the three given points are collinear.

    a $(-2, 2)$; $(2, -2)$; $(-2, -2)$
    b $(-3, -1)$; $(-3, 1)$; $(-3, 5)$
    c $(6, 1)$; $(6, 0)$; $(6, 4)$
    d $(4, -5)$; $(1, -5)$; $(-3, -5)$
    e $(0, -1)$; $(4, 3)$; $(6, 5)$
    f $(7, 7)$; $(3, 1)$; $(1, -2)$

19 In each of the following, use the given information to write the equation of a line that:

    a is parallel to the x-axis and three units below it
    b passes through the point $(-2, 3)$ and has a slope of $\frac{3}{4}$
    c passes through the points $(-4, 3)$ and $(2, 1)$
    d passes through the origin and is parallel to the graph of $2x - 3y = 4$
    e passes through the point $(3, 5)$ and is perpendicular to the graph of $y = \frac{2}{3}x + 3$

20 The vertices of $\triangle ABC$ are $A(-2, 3)$, $B(0, -3)$, and $C(4, 1)$. Prove by means of coordinate geometry that:

    a $\triangle ABC$ is isosceles
    b the median to side $\overline{BC}$ is also the altitude to side $\overline{BC}$

21 The following are endpoints of the diameter $\overline{AB}$ of a circle. In each case, find the center of the circle.

    a $A(-2, 6)$ and $B(8, -2)$
    b $A(-1, 7)$ and $B(-3, -1)$
    c $A(8, 11)$ and $B(5, 6)$

22 Quadrilateral $DRAW$ have vertices $D(-3, 6)$, $R(6, 3)$, $A(6, -2)$, and $W(-6, 2)$. By means of coordinate geometry, prove quadrilateral $DRAW$ is an isosceles trapezoid.

23 Quadrilateral $NOPE$ has coordinates $N(0, -6)$, $O(5, -1)$, $P(3, 3)$, and $E(-1, 1)$. Using coordinate geometry, prove that:

    a at least two sides are not congruent
    b the diagonals $\overline{EO}$ and $\overline{PN}$ are perpendicular

24 The points $W(-2, 1)$, $X(2, 5)$, $Y(6, -1)$, and $Z(4, -7)$ form a quadrilateral. The points A, B, C, and D are the midpoints of sides $\overline{WX}$, $\overline{XY}$, $\overline{YZ}$, and $\overline{ZW}$, respectively. Using coordinate geometry, prove that $ABCD$ is a parallelogram. (Hint: Keep in mind that both pairs of the opposite sides of a quadrilateral must be parallel.)

25 Quadrilateral $QRST$ has vertices $Q(a, b)$, $R(0, 0)$, $S(c, 0)$, and $T(a + c, b)$. Using coordinate geometry, prove that $QRST$ is a parallelogram. (Hint: Keep in mind that both pairs of the opposite sides of a quadrilateral must be parallel.)

26 The vertices of $\triangle BUG$ are $B(-5, 3)$, $U(4, 0)$, and $G(0, 4)$.

    a Plot the given points.
    b Graph the figure.
    c Determine the coordinates of the point of intersection of the three altitudes drawn from the three vertices of the triangle.

27 The vertices of $\triangle KAT$ are $K(3, -1)$, $A(7, 3)$, and $T(1, 3)$.

    a Find the coordinates of the midpoint of each side of the triangle.

    b Find the slope of each side.

    c Find the slope of the lines that would be perpendicular to each side of the triangle.

    d Write an equation of the perpendicular bisector of each side of $\triangle KAT$.

    e Show that the three perpendicular bisectors intersect in a common point and name the coordinates of that point.

28 $\triangle ABC$ is a right triangle with the right angle at point $A(0, 5)$. If the coordinates of point C are $(3, -1)$ and the equation of the line through B and C is $3x - y - 10 = 0$, find:

    a the equation of the line through A and C

    b the coordinates of point B

    c the equation of the line through A and B

9

Parallel Lines

9-1 Proving Lines Perpendicular

Recall that a *right angle* is an angle that measures 90°.

If two line segments, or a line and a segment, intersect to form an angle that measures 90°, then the angles formed are right angles and the lines or segments are said to be perpendicular to each other.

For example, $\angle DBC$ is a right angle, so $\overleftrightarrow{CA} \perp \overleftrightarrow{DE}$ at point B.

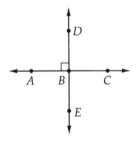

Conversely, if $\overleftrightarrow{AB} \perp \overleftrightarrow{CD}$, then $\angle 1$, $\angle 2$, $\angle 3$, and $\angle 4$ are each right angles.

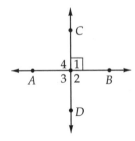

Review of previous theorems:

- All right angles are congruent.
- If two angles are congruent and supplementary, then each angle is a right angle.

Although an infinite number of perpendicular lines can be drawn to a line, there is one and only one perpendicular to a line *at a given point **on** that line*.

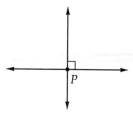

Also, there is one and only one line that can be drawn perpendicular to a line *through a given point **not** on the line*.

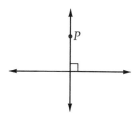

Furthermore, the shortest distance from a point (not on a line) to a line is the length of the perpendicular segment drawn from the point to the line.

To prove that lines are perpendicular

- Show that they intersect to form right angles or an angle that measures 90°.
- Show that they intersect to form congruent adjacent angles.

9-2 Proving Lines Parallel

Points and lines that lie in the same plane are said to be **coplanar**. *Parallel lines* are coplanar lines that have no points in common (they do not intersect), or have all points in common and, therefore, coincide. The following are two examples of $\overleftrightarrow{AB} \parallel \overleftrightarrow{CD}$.

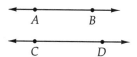

Both lines extend infinitely and never intersect.

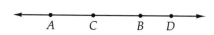

These lines have all points in common and are really different names for the same line.

Conversely, coplanar lines that have no points in common or all points in common are parallel lines.

Transversals

A **transversal** is a line that intersects two other distinct coplanar lines. When a transversal cuts two coplanar lines, 8 angles are formed. These 8 angles, numbered in the figure below, can be *classified* as follows.

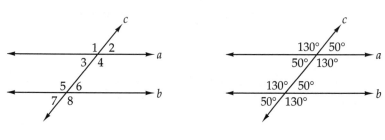

Interior angles (4): ∠3, ∠4, ∠5, ∠6

Alternate interior angles (2 pairs): ∠3 and ∠6, ∠4 and ∠5

Exterior angles (4): ∠1, ∠2, ∠7, ∠8

Alternate exterior angles (2 pairs): ∠1 and ∠8, ∠2 and ∠7

Corresponding angles (4 pairs): ∠1 and ∠5, ∠3 and ∠7, ∠2 and ∠6, ∠4 and ∠8

Interior angles on the same side of the transversal (2 pairs): ∠3 and ∠5, ∠4 and ∠6

Exterior angles on the same side of the transversal (2 pairs): ∠1 and ∠7, ∠2 and ∠8

However, if the lines cut by the transversal are *parallel*, several key relationships are formed. In Figure 1, lines *a* and *b* are parallel, line *c* is the transversal, and all the angles are numbered from 1 to 8. In Figure 2, with *a* parallel to *b* and line *c* is the transversal, the measure of each angle is indicated.

Figure 1   Figure 2

The following table summarizes the key relationships using the figures above as examples.

Type and Relationship	Examples	
Alternate interior angles are congruent.	∠3 ≅ ∠6	∠4 ≅ ∠5
Alternate exterior angles are congruent.	∠2 ≅ ∠7	∠1 ≅ ∠8

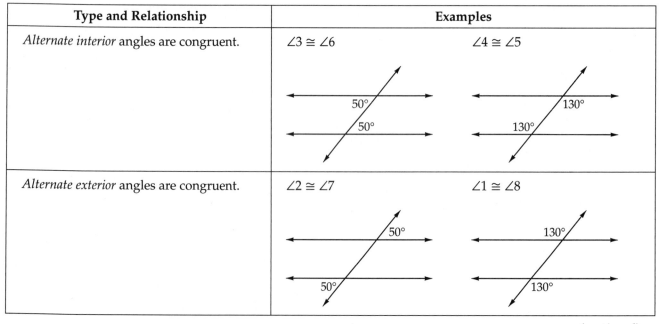

(continued)

Corresponding angles are congruent. **Note:** all stated pairs are on the same side of the transversal, with one angle in the interior and the other angles in the exterior.	$\angle 2 \cong \angle 6$ and $\angle 3 \cong \angle 7$ 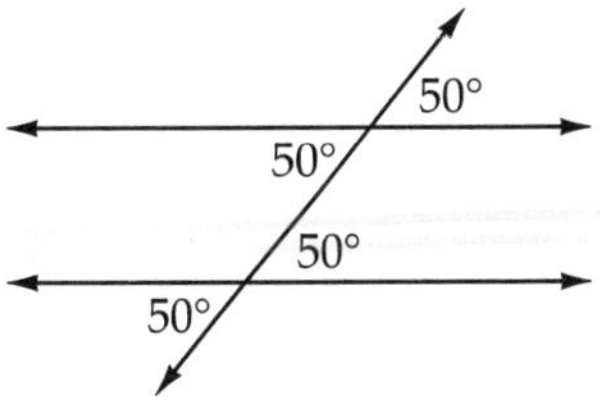 $\angle 1 \cong \angle 5$ and $\angle 4 \cong \angle 8$ 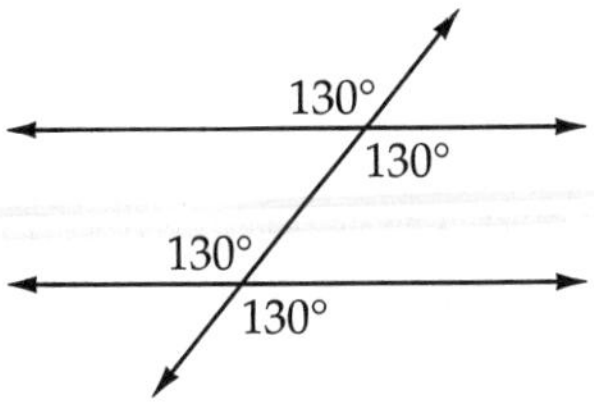 50° 50° 50° 50° 130° 130° 130° 130°
Interior angles on the same side of the transversal are supplementary.	$\angle 4 + \angle 6 = 180°$ and $\angle 3 + \angle 5 = 180°$ 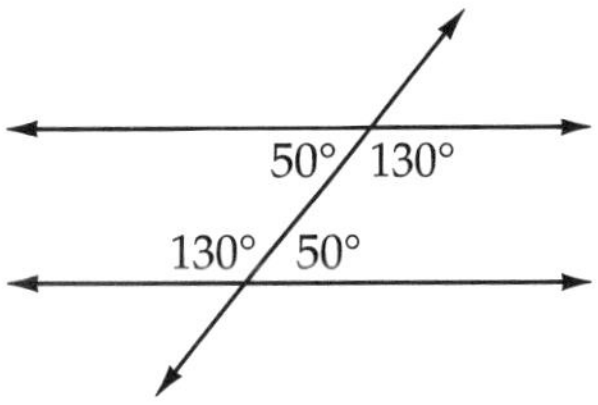 50° 130° 130° 50°

Four Important Reminders:

1 All pairs of vertical angles are congruent.
2 Any pair of consecutive angles are supplementary.
3 Any pair of angles chosen will be either congruent or supplementary.
4 When parallel lines are cut by a perpendicular transversal, all angles formed are right angles.

Methods of Proving Lines Parallel

Two lines are parallel

- if they are coplanar and do not intersect.
- if, cut by a transversal, alternate interior angles are congruent.
- if, cut by a transversal, corresponding angles are congruent.
- if, cut by a transversal, alternate exterior angles are congruent.
- if, cut by a transversal, the consecutive interior angles are supplementary.
- if they are both perpendicular to the same line.
  For example, if $a \perp m$ and $b \perp m$, then, $a \parallel b$.

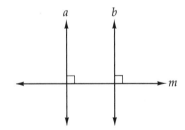

- if they are both parallel to the same line.
  For example, if $a \parallel n$ and $b \parallel n$, then, $a \parallel b$.

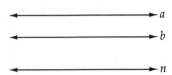

If a line is perpendicular to one of two parallel lines, it is perpendicular to the other line. For example, if $l \parallel m$ and $n \perp l$, then, $n \perp m$.

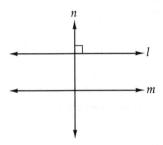

→ MODEL PROBLEMS

1   Given: $\angle 1 \cong \angle 3$, and $\angle 2 \cong \angle 1$
    Prove: $\overleftrightarrow{BF} \parallel \overleftrightarrow{GH}$

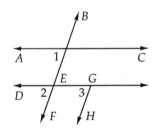

Statements	Reasons
1. $\angle 1 \cong \angle 3$	1. Given.
2. $\angle 2 \cong \angle 1$	2. Given.
3. $\angle 2 \cong \angle 3$	3. Transitive Property of Congruence.
4. $\overleftrightarrow{BF} \parallel \overleftrightarrow{GH}$	4. If two lines are cut by a transversal forming a pair of congruent corresponding angles, the two lines are parallel.

2 Given: $\overline{AC}$ bisects $\angle BAD$, and $\overline{AB} \cong \overline{BC}$
Prove: $\overline{AD} \parallel \overline{BC}$

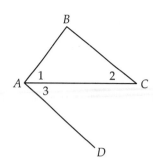

Statements	Reasons
1. $\overline{AC}$ bisects $\angle BAD$.	1. Given.
2. $\angle 1 \cong \angle 3$	2. Definition of an angle bisector
3. $\overline{AB} \cong \overline{BC}$	3. Given.
4. $\angle 1 \cong \angle 2$	4. If two sides of a triangle are congruent, then the angles opposite those sides are congruent.
5. $\angle 2 \cong \angle 3$	5. Transitive Property of Congruence
6. $\overline{AD} \parallel \overline{BC}$	6. If two lines are cut by a transversal forming a pair of congruent alternate interior angles, the two lines are parallel.

 Practice

Exercises 1–8: In each figure, identify where, if possible, the lines that are parallel.

1

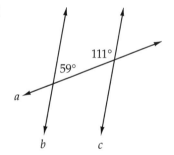

2

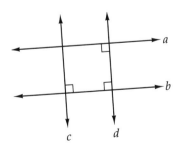

3

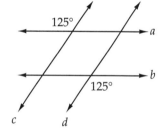

4

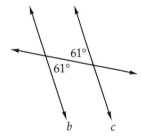

5

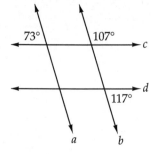

6

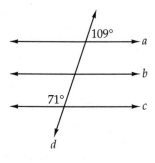

7

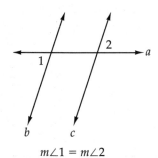

$m\angle 1 = m\angle 2$

8

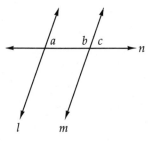

$m\angle a = 70, m\angle b = 110$

Exercises 9–11: Given the angle measures for the figure below, identify which lines cannot be parallel. Explain your reasoning.

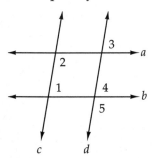

9 $m\angle 2 = 126$ and $m\angle 1 = 64$

178 Chapter 9: Parallel Lines

10 $m\angle 1 = 79$ and $m\angle 4 = 82$

11 $m\angle 3 = 75$ and $m\angle 5 = 115$

12

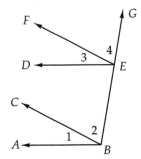

Given: $\angle 1 \cong \angle 3$ and $\angle 2 \cong \angle 4$
Prove: $\overrightarrow{ED} \parallel \overrightarrow{BA}$

13

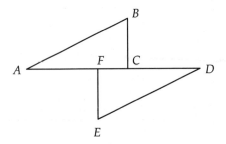

Given: $\overline{BC} \perp \overline{AD}, \overline{EF} \perp \overline{AD}, \overline{BC} \cong \overline{EF}, \overline{CD} \cong \overline{AF}$
Prove: $\overline{ED} \parallel \overline{AB}$

14

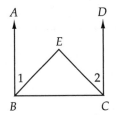

Given: $\overline{BE}$ bisects $\angle ABC$, $\overline{CE}$ bisects $\angle DCB$,
and $m\angle 1 + m\angle 2 = 90$.
Prove: $\overrightarrow{BA} \parallel \overrightarrow{CD}$

15

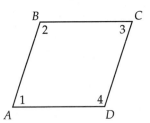

Given: $m\angle 1 + m\angle 2 + m\angle 3 + m\angle 4 = 360$;
$\angle 1 \cong \angle 3$ and $\angle 2 \cong \angle 4$
Prove: $\overline{AB} \parallel \overline{CD}$ and $\overline{AD} \parallel \overline{BC}$

16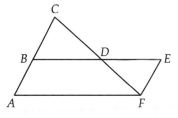

Given: D is the midpoint of $\overline{CF}$ and of $\overline{BE}$
Prove: $\overline{AC} \parallel \overline{FE}$

17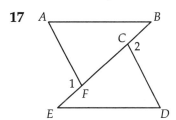

Given: $\angle 1 \cong \angle 2$, $\overline{EF} \cong \overline{CB}$, $\overline{AF} \cong \overline{CD}$
Prove: $\overline{AB} \parallel \overline{ED}$

18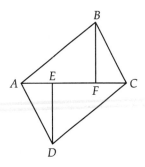

Given: $\overline{AEFC}$; $\overline{BF} \perp \overline{AC}$, $\overline{DE} \perp \overline{AC}$; $\overline{DE} \cong \overline{BF}$,
and $\overline{AE} \cong \overline{FC}$
Prove: $\overline{AB} \parallel \overline{DC}$

9-3 Properties of Parallel Lines

The following table states and illustrates the properties of parallel lines.

Postulate	Example
There is exactly *one* line that can be drawn through a given point that is *not* on a given line and is parallel to the given lines. (See Chapter 14 for construction.)	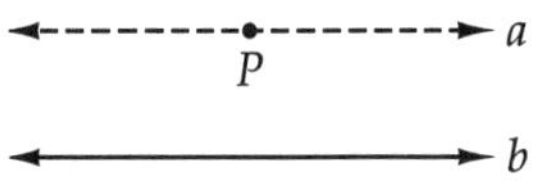 Line a is drawn through point P and $a \parallel b$.
Theorems	**Example**
9.1 If two parallel lines are cut by a transversal, then the *alternate interior angles are congruent*.	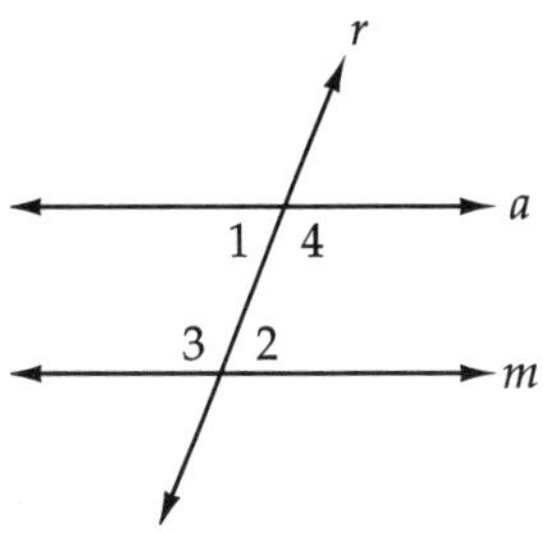 $a \parallel m$ $\angle 1 \cong \angle 2$ $\angle 3 \cong \angle 4$

(continued)

9.2 If two parallel lines are cut by a transversal, then the *corresponding angles are congruent*.	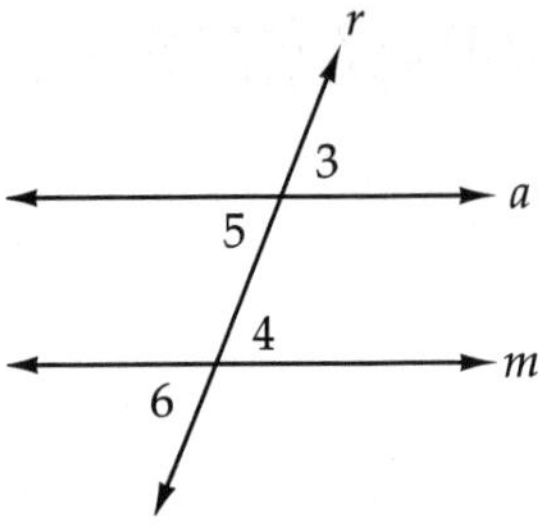 $a \parallel m$ $\angle 3 \cong \angle 4$ $\angle 5 \cong \angle 6$
9.3 If two parallel lines are cut by a transversal, then *two interior angles on the same side of the transversal are supplementary*.	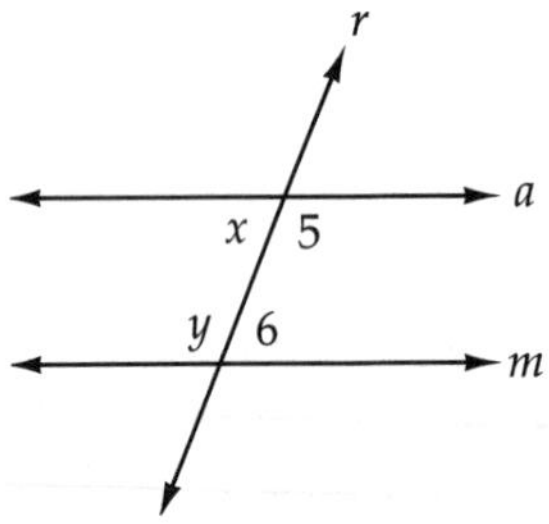 $a \parallel m$ $\angle 5 + \angle 6 = 180°$ $\angle x + \angle y = 180°$
9.4 If a line is perpendicular to one of two parallel lines, it is also perpendicular to the other.	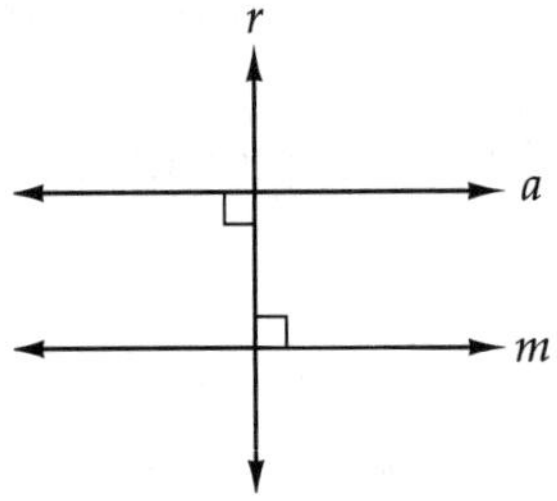 $a \parallel m$ $r \perp a$ $\therefore r \perp m$
9.5 If a line is parallel to one of two parallel lines, it is also parallel to the other.	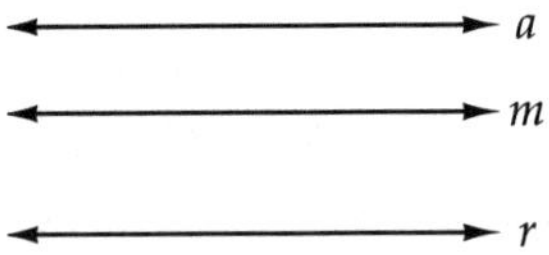 $a \parallel m$ $r \parallel m$ $\therefore r \parallel a$
9.6 If two lines are parallel, the distance from any point on the first line to the second line is always the same. **9.7** Perpendiculars drawn between parallel lines are congruent.	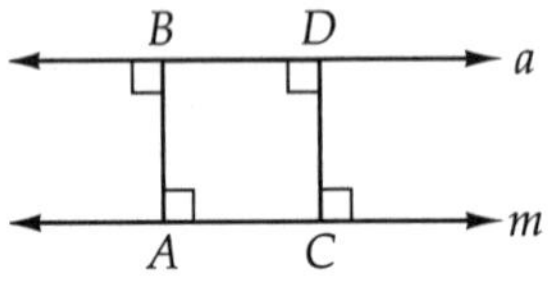 $a \parallel m$ $\overline{AB} \perp a, \overline{AB} \perp m, \overline{CD} \perp a, \overline{CD} \perp m$ $\therefore \overline{AB} \cong \overline{CD}$

→ MODEL PROBLEMS

1 If $\overleftrightarrow{AB} \parallel \overleftrightarrow{CD}$ and t is not perpendicular to them, which pair of angles are NOT congruent?

(1) $\angle 1$ and $\angle 4$
(2) $\angle 2$ and $\angle 7$
(3) $\angle 6$ and $\angle 3$
(4) $\angle 3$ and $\angle 5$

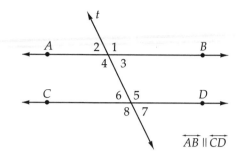

$\overrightarrow{AB} \parallel \overrightarrow{CD}$

SOLUTION

Consider each pair.

Choice (1): $\angle 1 \cong \angle 4$ because they are vertical angles.

Choice (2): $\angle 2 \cong \angle 7$ because they are alternate exterior angles.

Choice (3): $\angle 6 \cong \angle 3$ because they are alternate interior angles.

Choice (4): $\angle 3$ and $\angle 5$ are same-side interior angles, so they are supplementary. Two supplementary angles are congruent only if each measures 90°, and that is not possible here, because t is not perpendicular to lines AB and CD.

ANSWER: Choice (4)

2

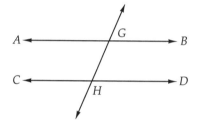

Transversal $\overline{GH}$ intersects parallel lines $\overleftrightarrow{AB}$ and $\overleftrightarrow{CD}$. If $m\angle BGH = 3x - 25$ and $m\angle GHC = 2x + 15$

a Find the value of x.
b Find $m\angle GHC$.
c Find $m\angle GHD$.

SOLUTION

a Since the parallel lines are cut by transversal $\overleftrightarrow{GH}$, the alternate interior angles are congruent.
$m\angle BGH = m\angle GHC$
$3x - 25 = 2x + 15$
$3x - 2x = 15 + 25$
$x = 40$

ANSWER: $x = 40$

b $m\angle GHC = 2x + 15 = 2(40) + 15 = 95$

ANSWER: $m\angle GHC = 95$

c Since, $m\angle GHC$ and $m\angle GHD$ form a linear pair and are supplementary, $m\angle GHD = 180 - m\angle GHC = 180 - 95 = 85$.

ANSWER: $m\angle GHD = 85$

3

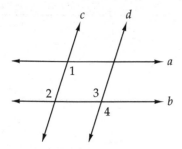

Given: $a \parallel b, c \parallel d$
Prove: $\angle 1 \cong \angle 4$

Statements	Reasons
1. $a \parallel b, c \parallel d$	1. Given.
2. $\angle 1 \cong \angle 2$	2. Alternate interior angles are congruent.
3. $\angle 2 \cong \angle 3$	3. Corresponding angles are congruent.
4. $\angle 1 \cong \angle 3$	4. Transitive Property of Congruence.
5. $\angle 3 \cong \angle 4$	5. Vertical angles are congruent.
6. $\angle 1 \cong \angle 4$	6. Transitive Property of Congruence.

 Practice

1 Two parallel lines are cut by a nonperpendicular transversal. Which are *not* congruent?

    (1) same-side exterior angles
    (2) corresponding angles
    (3) alternate interior angles
    (4) alternate exterior angles

2 Which choice lists all the angles that are supplementary to $\angle 13$ in the figure below?

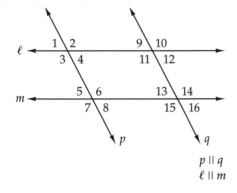

    (1) $\angle 1, \angle 4, \angle 5, \angle 8, \angle 16$
    (2) $\angle 2, \angle 3, \angle 6, \angle 7, \angle 10, \angle 11, \angle 14, \angle 15$
    (3) $\angle 1, \angle 4, \angle 5, \angle 8, \angle 9, \angle 12, \angle 16$
    (4) $\angle 1, \angle 2, \angle 3, \angle 4, \angle 5, \angle 6, \angle 7, \angle 8$

3 In the figure below, with $\overline{AB} \parallel \overline{CD}$, if $m\angle 8 = 120$, what are the values of the other angles?

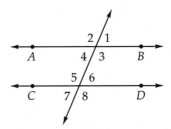

4 In the figure below, if $m\angle 6 = 45$, and $\overline{AB} \parallel \overline{CD}$, what are the values of the other angles?

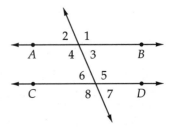

5 In the figure below, $l_1 \parallel l_2$. Fill in the missing angle values.

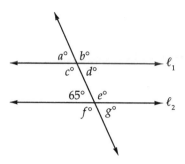

6 In the figure below, $l_1 \parallel l_2$ and $l_3 \parallel l_4$. What are the values of w, x, y, and z?

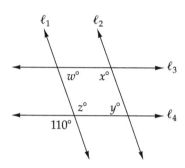

7 In the diagram, $\overleftrightarrow{AB} \parallel \overleftrightarrow{CD}$, and $\overleftrightarrow{EF}$ is a transversal.

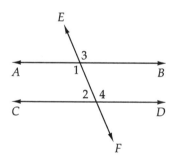

   a $m\angle 1 = 8x$ and $m\angle 2 = 6x - 30$. Find the value of x.

   b $m\angle 3 = 2x + 10$ and $m\angle 4 = 5x - 47$. Find $m\angle 3$.

8 In the figure below, $\overline{DA} \parallel \overline{BC}$. Find $m\angle 1$.

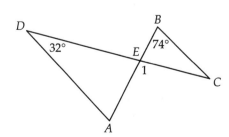

9 In the figure below, $\overline{AC} \parallel \overline{BD}$. Find $m\angle A$ and $m\angle C$.

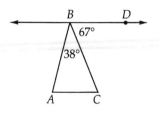

10 In the figure below, $\overline{AB} \parallel \overline{CD}$. What is $m\angle CAD$?

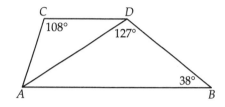

11 In the figure below, $\overline{QR} \parallel \overline{PS}$, $\overline{QP} \parallel \overline{RS}$, and $m\angle 1 = m\angle 2$. Find $m\angle 3$.

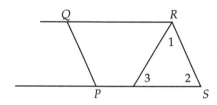

12 Fill in the missing reasons.

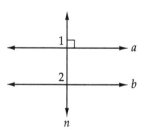

Given: $a \parallel b$; n is the transversal; $n \perp a$.
Prove: $n \perp b$ (In other words, prove that if a line is perpendicular to one of two parallel lines, then it is perpendicular to the other.)

Statements	Reasons
1. $a \parallel b$, and $n \perp a$	1. Given.
2. $\angle 1$ is a right angle.	2.
3. $m\angle 1 = 90$	3.
4. $\angle 1 \cong \angle 2$	4.
5. $m\angle 1 = m\angle 2$	5.
6. $m\angle 2 = 90$	6.
7. $\angle 2$ is a right angle.	7.
8. $n \perp b$	8.

13

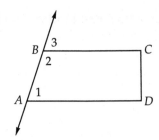

Given: $\overleftrightarrow{AB}$, ∠2 is supplementary to ∠1.
Prove: $\overleftrightarrow{BC} \parallel \overleftrightarrow{AD}$

14

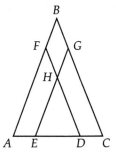

Given: △ABC; $\overline{AB} \cong \overline{BC}$; $\overline{EHG} \parallel \overline{AB}$, $\overline{FHD} \parallel \overline{BC}$
Prove: △EHD is an isosceles triangle.

15

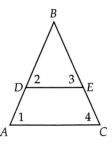

Given: $\overline{DE} \parallel \overline{AC}$; ∠2 ≅ ∠3
Prove: ∠1 ≅ ∠4

16

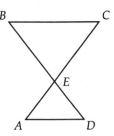

Given: $\overline{AC}$ intersects $\overline{BD}$ at E; $\overline{AE} \cong \overline{ED}$, $\overline{AD} \parallel \overline{BC}$.
Prove: $\overline{AC} \cong \overline{BD}$

17

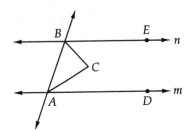

Given: $n \parallel m$, $\overline{BC}$ bisects ∠ABE, $\overline{AC}$ bisects ∠BAD.
Prove: $\overline{BC} \perp \overline{AC}$

18 Use the given figure below and write a proof for each of the following.

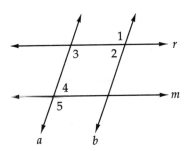

Given: $r \parallel m$ and $a \parallel b$
Prove:

a ∠4 ≅ ∠2
b ∠5 ≅ ∠1

19 In the figures below, lines l and m are parallel and cut by transversal k. Find the value for x and the measure of each of the eight angles.

a

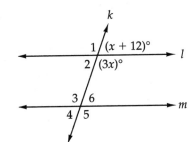

b

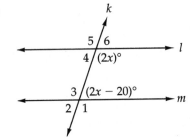

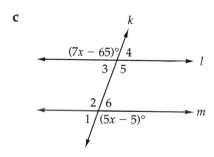

a Name an angle congruent to ∠3.
b Name an angle congruent to ∠1.
c Find two angles congruent to ∠2.
d If m∠2 = 70 and m∠4 = 50, find m∠5.
e If m∠7 = 125, m∠3 = 35, find m∠4.

20 In the figure below, $\overleftrightarrow{AB} \parallel \overleftrightarrow{CD}$.

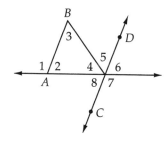

21 Prove: If two parallel lines are cut by a transversal, the bisectors of a pair of corresponding angles are parallel.

22 Prove: If two opposite sides of a quadrilateral are both congruent and parallel, the other two sides are both congruent and parallel.

9-4 Parallel Lines in the Coordinate Plane

In the graph at on the right, certain properties can be seen.

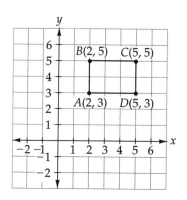

- Points *A* and *B* have the same *y*-value (abscissa), 2. Therefore, $\overleftrightarrow{AB} \parallel$ *y*-axis and, similarly, $\overleftrightarrow{DC} \parallel$ *y*-axis.
- Points *A* and *D* have the same *x*-value (ordinate), 3. Therefore $\overleftrightarrow{AD} \parallel$ *x*-axis, and, similarly, $\overleftrightarrow{BC} \parallel$ *x*-axis.
- $\overleftrightarrow{AD} \parallel \overleftrightarrow{BC}$ since each is parallel to the same line, the *x*-axis. And $\overleftrightarrow{AB} \parallel \overleftrightarrow{DC}$ since each is parallel to the same line, the *y*-axis.
- In the *xy*-coordinate plane, every horizontal line is perpendicular to every vertical line. Thus, $\overleftrightarrow{AD} \perp \overleftrightarrow{AB}, \overleftrightarrow{AD} \perp \overleftrightarrow{CD}$, and $\overleftrightarrow{BC} \perp \overleftrightarrow{AB}$, $\overleftrightarrow{BC} \perp \overleftrightarrow{CD}$.
- ∠A, ∠B, ∠C, and ∠D are all right angles.

Thus, in the coordinate plane, we can generalize as follows:

1 If two lines are horizontal, then they are parallel. Furthermore, all horizontal lines have the *same slope*, 0.
2 If two lines are vertical, then they are parallel. Furthermore, vertical lines have *no slope*.
3 If two nonvertical lines in the coordinate plane are parallel, they have the same slope. *Conversely*, if two nonvertical lines in the coordinate plane have the same slope, then the lines are parallel.

Refer back to Chapter 8 for a review of positive, negative, zero, and undefined slopes.

Remember

- If two nonvertical lines are perpendicular, then the slope of one line is the negative reciprocal of the slope of the other line.
- *Conversely*, if the slope of one line is the negative reciprocal of the slope of the other, then the lines are perpendicular.
- One number is the negative reciprocal of a second number if the product of the two numbers is -1.

Examples: $-\frac{2}{3}$ is the negative reciprocal of $\frac{3}{2}$, since $\frac{3}{2}\left(-\frac{2}{3}\right) = -\frac{6}{6} = -1$.

$-\frac{1}{4}$ is the negative reciprocal of 4, since $4\left(-\frac{1}{4}\right) = -\frac{4}{4} = -1$.

To find the negative reciprocal of any fraction, simply invert the given fraction and change the sign.

 MODEL PROBLEMS

1 The vertices of quadrilateral *MATH* are $M(3, -1)$, $A(4, 2)$, $T(7, 1)$, and $H(9, -3)$.

   a Show that only two sides of the quadrilateral are parallel.
   b Show that the quadrilateral has two right angles.
   c What kind of quadrilateral is this?

SOLUTION

   a Plot the points and find the slope of each side of the quadrilateral.

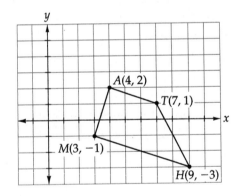

$$\text{Slope}_{MA} = \frac{-1-2}{3-4} = \frac{-3}{-1} = 3 \qquad \text{Slope}_{AT} = \frac{2-1}{4-7} = \frac{1}{-3}$$

$$\text{Slope}_{TH} = \frac{1-(-3)}{7-9} = \frac{4}{-2} = -2 \qquad \text{Slope}_{HM} = \frac{-3-(-1)}{9-3} = \frac{-2}{6} = \frac{-1}{3}$$

Since only the slopes of sides *AT* and *HM* are the same, $-\frac{1}{3}$, $\overline{AT} \parallel \overline{HM}$.

   b Since the slopes of sides *MA* and *AT* are negative reciprocals, and so are the slopes of sides *MA* and *HM*, $\overline{MA} \perp \overline{AT}$ and $\overline{MA} \perp \overline{HM}$.

   c A quadrilateral with only two sides parallel and one leg perpendicular to the parallel sides is a right trapezoid.

2 Write an equation for the line parallel to $2x + y = 10$ and that passes through the point $(-3, 5)$.

SOLUTION

Rewrite $2x + y = 10$ in $y = mx + b$ form, so that $y = -2x + 10$.

The new line must have the same slope, -2. If (x, y) and $(-3, 5)$ are two points on the line, substitute the values for m and (x_1, y_1) using the point-slope method.

$$y_1 - y_2 = m(x_1 - x_2)$$
$$5 - y = -2(-3 - x)$$
$$5 - y = 6 + 2x$$
$$-y = 1 + 2x$$
$$y = -2x - 1$$

ANSWER: $y = -2x - 1$ or $2x + y = -1$

3 If the line joining $A(3, 5)$ and $B(1, 2)$ is parallel to the line joining $Q(7, k)$ and $R(5, 6)$, then what is the value of k?

SOLUTION

Find the slopes of $\overline{AB}$ and $\overline{QR}$, because the slopes of parallel lines are equal.

$\text{Slope}_{AB} = \frac{5 - 2}{3 - 1} = \frac{3}{2}$ and $\text{slope}_{QR} = \frac{k - 6}{7 - 5} = \frac{k - 6}{2}$

Set the slopes equal to each other: $\frac{3}{2} = \frac{k - 6}{2}$ and cross multiply; $6 = 2k - 12$.

Solve: $2k = 12 + 6$
$\quad\quad\quad 2k = 18$
$\quad\quad\quad\; k = 9$

ANSWER: The value of k is 9.

 Practice

1 Find the negative reciprocal of each of the following.

   a $\frac{1}{4}$

   b $-\frac{3}{7}$

   c $\frac{5}{2}$

   d $-\frac{a}{x}$

2 Find the slope of a line parallel to each of the following lines.

   a $y - x = -3$
   b $5y + 3x = 1$
   c $2x - 5y + 10 = 0$

3 Find the slope of a line perpendicular to each line with the given equation.

   a $y = -4x + 7$
   b $y = \frac{1}{7}x - 4$
   c $x + y = 9$
   d $3y = 2x$

4 Are the following pairs of lines parallel, perpendicular, or neither?

  a $x + y = 8$
     $x - y = 5$
  b $x = 3$
     $x = 7$
  c $x = 2$
     $y = -5$
  d $2x - y = 6$
     $y = 2x - 2$
  e $x = -y + 3$
     $y = x - 2$
  f $3x + y = 6$
     $3x - y = 3$

5 Find the slope of a line parallel to $\overleftrightarrow{RM}$, if R and M are the points given.

  a $R(1, 6), M(2, 5)$
  b $R(4, -5), M(6, 0)$
  c $R(-3, 2), M(7, -1)$
  d $R(-3, -1), M(6, -8)$
  e $R(-4, 3), M(-7, -1)$
  f $R(0, 0), M(-2, -3)$

6 Find the slope of a line perpendicular to $\overleftrightarrow{AB}$, if A and B are the points given.

  a $A(-3, 1), B(4, 2)$
  b $A(8, 5), B(-1, -4)$
  c $A(6, -2), B(-5, -3)$
  d $A(0, 4), B(-6, 4)$
  e $A(4, -7), B(4, -2)$
  f $A(-1, -2), B(0, 0)$

7 For each of the following, use slopes to show whether or not $\overleftrightarrow{AB} \parallel \overleftrightarrow{CD}$.

  a $A(2, -1), B(1, 6), C(5, 3),$ and $D(-2, 2)$
  b $A(-3, -3), B(0, 3), C(2, -1),$ and $D(-6, 3)$

Exercises 8–14: Write an equation of the line that satisfies the given conditions.

8 Parallel to $y = -5x + 1$ with y-intercept 3

9 Perpendicular to $y = -5x + 1$ with y-intercept 3.

10 Perpendicular to $y = \frac{2}{3}x - 4$ and passing through the point $(-3, 1)$

11 Parallel to $x - 3y = -12$ and passing through the point $(6, 5)$

12 Parallel to and 4 units below the x-axis

13 Perpendicular to $3x + 6y = 15$ and passing through the point $(0, 6)$

14 Perpendicular to $3x + 2y = -7$ and passing through the point $(-6, 5)$

15 If the line joining $R(2, 3)$ and $S(7, 9)$ is perpendicular to the line joining $A(8, k)$ and $B(2, 4)$, find the value of k.

16 The vertices of rectangle $PQRS$ are the points $P(0, 0), Q(7, 0), R(7, k),$ and $S(0, 5)$. Find the value of k.

17 If $\triangle ABC$ has vertices $A(3, 4), B(0, 0),$ and $C(12, -9),$ show that $\triangle ABC$ is a right triangle. Explain your reasoning.

18 If the coordinates of quadrilateral $PQRS$ are $P(-5, -4), Q(1, -2), R(2, 3),$ and $S(-4, 1),$ show that both pairs of opposite sides are parallel.

19 $PATH$ is a rectangle with the coordinates $P(5, 0), A(0, 0),$ and $T(0, -6)$. What are the coordinates of point H?

20 Three of the vertices of quadrilateral $ABCD$ have coordinates $A(2, 7), B(-1, 1),$ and $C(3, -1)$. If both pairs of opposite sides are parallel,

  a find the coordinates of point D.
  b show that $ABCD$ is a rectangle. Explain your reasoning.

9-5 The Sum of the Measures of the Angles of a Triangle

Since the property of parallel lines cut by a transversal produces the congruence of alternate interior angles, the following key theorem can be proved:

- Theorem 9.8. The sum of the measures of the interior angles of a triangle is 180°.
  Proof: If line n is constructed or drawn through B and parallel to base $\overline{AC}$, then $m\angle 1 + m\angle B + m\angle 2 = 180$. Since $m\angle A = m\angle 1$ and $m\angle C = m\angle 2$ (using alternate interior angles), then by substitution, $m\angle A + m\angle B + m\angle C = 180$.

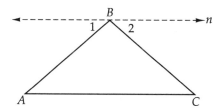

Corollaries can be deduced from the use of theorem 9.8.

- Corollary 9.8.1. If two angles of one triangle are congruent to two angles of another triangle, then the third angles are congruent.

  Example: If $\angle A \cong \angle F$, $\angle B \cong \angle E$; $m\angle 1 = 2x - 35$, and $m\angle 2 = x + 5$, find $m\angle 1$.

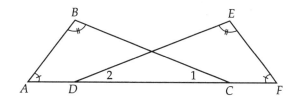

  SOLUTION
  $m\angle 1 = m\angle 2$ (Corollary 9.8.1)
  $2x - 35 = x + 5$
  $\qquad x = 40$
  Thus, $m\angle 1 = 2x - 35$
  $\qquad\qquad = 2(40) - 35$
  $\qquad\qquad = 45$
  ANSWER: $m\angle 1 = 45$

- Corollary 9.8.2. The acute angles of a right triangle are complementary.

  For right triangle ABC, $m\angle A + m\angle B = 90$
  $\qquad\qquad\qquad x + (90 - x) = 90$
  $\qquad\qquad\qquad\qquad\quad 90 = 90$

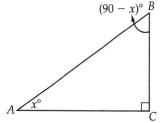

- Corollary 9.8.3. In a triangle there can be no more than one right angle or one obtuse angle.

- Corollary 9.8.4. Each acute angle of an isosceles right triangle measures 45°.

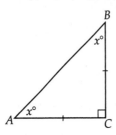

For isosceles right triangle ABC, $m\angle A + m\angle B = 90$.
Since $\overline{AC} \cong \overline{BC}$, $m\angle A = m\angle B$. By substitution, $m\angle A + m\angle A = 2m\angle A = 90$.
Thus, $m\angle A = 45$ and $m\angle B = 45$.

- Corollary 9.8.5. Each angle of an equilateral triangle measures 60°.

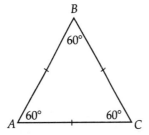

For equilateral triangle ABC, $\overline{AB} \cong \overline{BC} \cong \overline{CA}$, so that $m\angle A = m\angle B = m\angle C$. Since $m\angle A + m\angle B + m\angle C = 180$, then by substitution, $m\angle A + m\angle A + m\angle A = 3m\angle A = 180$. Thus, $m\angle A = 60$, $m\angle B = 60$, and $m\angle C = 60$.

- Corollary 9.8.6. The sum of the measures of the angles of a quadrilateral is 360°. For quadrilateral $PQRS$, draw a segment $\overline{PR}$ that divides $PQRS$ into two triangles, $\triangle PQR$ and $\triangle PRS$.

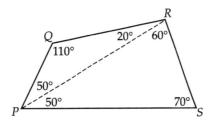

The sum of the measures of the two triangles, $180° + 180°$, equals the sum of the angles of the quadrilateral, $360°$.

The **exterior angle** of a triangle is an angle that is adjacent and supplementary to an angle of the triangle. An exterior angle is formed when a side of the triangle is extended. Consider the following illustrations.

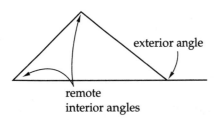

remote
interior angles

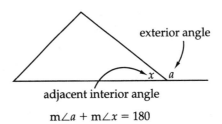

adjacent interior angle

$m\angle a + m\angle x = 180$

- Corollary 9.8.7. The measure of an exterior angle of a triangle is equal to the sum of the measures of the two nonadjacent (or remote) interior angles.

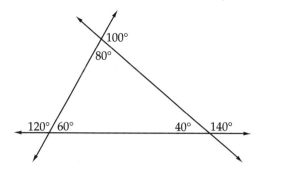

$$140 = 80 + 60$$
$$120 = 40 + 80$$
$$100 = 40 + 60$$

A triangle has six exterior angles. The two exterior angles at each vertex are congruent.

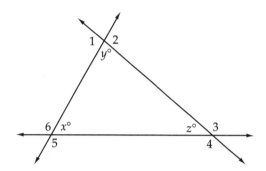

Exterior Angle		Nonadjacent Interior Angles
m∠1	=	m∠x + m∠z
m∠2	=	m∠x + m∠z
m∠3	=	m∠x + m∠y
m∠4	=	m∠x + m∠y
m∠5	=	m∠y + m∠z
m∠6	=	m∠y + m∠z

- Corollary 9.8.8. The measure of an exterior angle is greater than either non-adjacent interior angle.

Using the figure above:

m∠1 > m∠x or m∠z	m∠2 > m∠x or m∠z
m∠3 > m∠x or m∠y	m∠4 > m∠x or m∠y
m∠5 > m∠y or m∠z	m∠6 > m∠y or m∠z

1   If $m\angle B = 43$ and $m\angle C = 115$, what is the measure of exterior $\angle BAD$?

SOLUTION

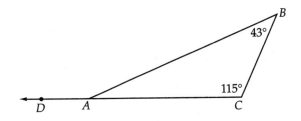

$m\angle B + m\angle C + m\angle BAC = 180$
$m\angle B + m\angle C = 43 + 115 = 158$
By substitution, $158 + m\angle BAC = 180$
$m\angle BAC = 22$
$m\angle BAD + m\angle BAC = 180$ (straight angle)
$\quad\quad m\angle BAD + 22 = 180$
$\quad\quad\quad\quad m\angle BAD = 158$

ANSWER: exterior $\angle BAD = 158$

ALTERNATE SOLUTION

Corollary 9.8.7 states that the measure of an exterior angle of a triangle is equal to the sum of the measures of two nonadjacent interior angles. Therefore,

$m\angle BAD = m\angle B + m\angle C$
$m\angle BAD = 43 + 115$
$m\angle BAD = 158$

2   If $m\angle C = x + 10$, $m\angle D = 3x - 7$, and $m\angle ABD = 2x + 25$, find the measure of $\angle ABD$.

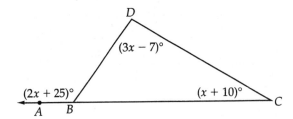

SOLUTION

$m\angle ABD = m\angle D + m\angle C$
$\ 2x + 25 = 3x - 7 + x + 10$
$\ 2x + 25 = 4x + 3$
$\quad\quad 22 = 2x$
$\quad\quad 11 = x$
Therefore, $m\angle ABD = 2x + 25 = 2(11) + 25 = 47$

ANSWER: $m\angle ABD = 47$

3 In isosceles $\triangle ABC$, $\overline{AB} \cong \overline{BC}$, and $\overline{AC}$ is extended through C to D. If $m\angle A = x$ and $m\angle BCD = 3x + 30$, find the value of x.

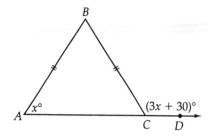

SOLUTION

Since base angles of an isosceles triangle are congruent, $m\angle BCA = x$. Exterior $\angle BCD$ is supplementary to $\angle BCA$, so that

$$m\angle BCD + m\angle BCA = 180$$
$$(3x + 30) + x = 180$$
$$4x = 150$$
$$x = 37.5$$

ANSWER: $x = 37.5°$

 Practice

1 If the degree measures of three angles of a triangle are represented by $x + 40$, $4x + 30$, and $10x - 40$, the triangle must be:

(1) right
(2) obtuse
(3) isosceles
(4) scalene

2 An exterior angle at the base of an isosceles triangle is always:

(1) acute
(2) right
(3) obtuse
(4) cannot be determined

3 In equilateral triangle ABC, the bisectors of angles A and C intersect at point P. What is the measure of $\angle APC$?

(1) 60
(2) 90
(3) 120
(4) 150

4 If the measure of one angle of a triangle is equal to the sum of the measures of the other two angles, then the triangle is always:

(1) acute
(2) right
(3) obtuse
(4) isosceles

5 In the figure, $\overline{RA} \cong \overline{AB}$, $m\angle 1 = 44$. What is $m\angle ABT$?

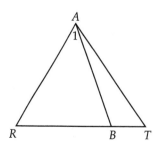

(1) 46°
(2) 68°
(3) 112°
(4) 136°

6 Given the figure below.

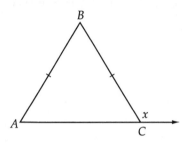

Find the measure of the base angles A and C, and the vertex $\angle B$ of an isosceles triangle, if the exterior angle x is

a 150°
b 120°
c 128°
d 144°
e 160°

7 In the diagram, $\triangle BCD$ is isosceles.

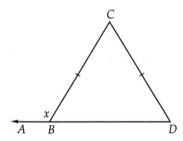

Find the measure of the base angles and the exterior angle x when the vertex $\angle C$ is

a 80°
b 100°
c 72°
d 60°
e 20°

8 If the measure of each base angle of an isosceles triangle is 42° more than the measure of the vertex angle, find the measure of all three angles.

9 In $\triangle PQR$, the measures of $\angle P$ and $\angle Q$ are in the ratio 3:5 and the measure of $\angle R$ is 81° more than the measure of $\angle P$. Find the measure of each angle.

10 The measure of the vertex angle of an isosceles triangle is 40° more than three times the measure of a base angle. Find the measure of each angle.

11

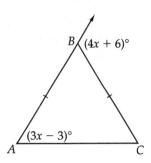

In the figure, the measure of an exterior angle at $\angle B$, the vertex angle of isosceles $\triangle ABC$, is $4x + 6$. If the base angle measure is $3x - 3$, what is the measure of the exterior angle and of the interior angles?

12 If three angles of a triangle are in the ratio 1:3:6, what is the degree measure of each angle?

13 The measure of the exterior angle of a triangle is $4x + 12$. The measures of the remote interior angles are $3x$ and 45°. Find the measure of each angle of the triangle.

14 In the figure, $l \parallel m$, $m\angle a = 75$ and $m\angle b = 110$. Find $m\angle c$.

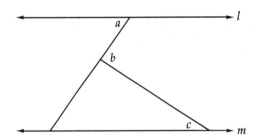

15 In $\triangle BCD$, the measure of $\angle B$ is twice the measure of $\angle C$, and an exterior angle at vertex D measures 117°. Find the measure of $\angle B$.

16 In the figure, $\overline{RST}$, $\overline{PR} \cong \overline{RS}$, and $m\angle 1 = 60$. Find $m\angle x$.

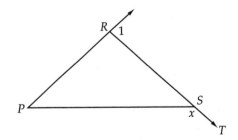

17 In the figure, $\overline{DE} \perp \overline{BC}$, m$\angle ADB = 70$ and, m$\angle EDC = 50$. Find m$\angle x$.

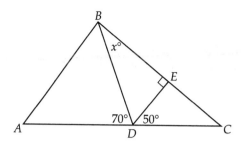

18 In the diagram, $\overline{RT} \perp \overline{QS}$, $\overline{SW} \perp \overline{QR}$. If m$\angle Q = 50$, find m$\angle 1$.

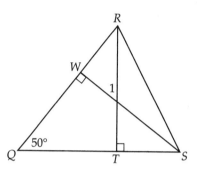

19 In triangle ABC, $\overline{BE}$ bisects $\angle ABC$, $\overline{AC}$ bisects $\angle BAD$, m$\angle BAC = 30$, and m$\angle BEC = 80$. Find m$\angle D$.

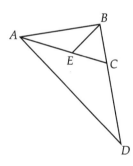

20 In the diagram, $r \parallel l$, m$\angle a = 45 - 3x$, m$\angle b = 10x + 75$, and m$\angle c = x + 20$. Find m$\angle d$.

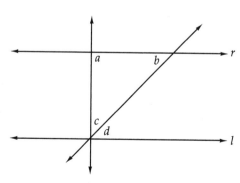

21

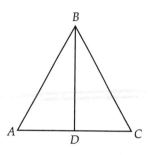

Given: $\angle A \cong \angle C$, $\overline{BD}$ bisects $\angle ABC$.
Prove: $\overline{BD} \perp \overline{AC}$

22

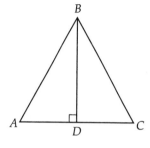

Given: $\angle A \cong \angle C$, $\overline{BD} \perp \overline{AC}$
Prove: $\overline{BD}$ bisects $\angle ABC$.

23

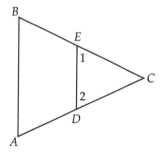

Given: $\angle 1 \cong \angle 2$, $\angle A \cong \angle B$
Prove: $\overline{BA} \parallel \overline{ED}$

24

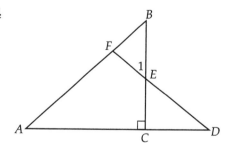

Given: $\overline{BC} \perp \overline{AD}$, $\angle A \cong \angle D$
Prove: $\angle B \cong \angle 1$

9-6 Proving Triangles Congruent by Angle, Angle, Side

- Theorem 9.9. If two angles and a side opposite one of the angles in one triangle are congruent to the corresponding angles and side in another triangle, then the triangles are congruent. (AAS)

Given: $\triangle ABC$ and $\triangle XYZ$ with $\angle A \cong \angle X$,
   $\angle C \cong \angle Z$, and $\overline{BC} \cong \overline{YZ}$
Prove: $\triangle ABC \cong \triangle XYZ$

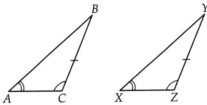

Proof: Using Corollary 9.8.1 (if two angles of one triangle are congruent to two angles of another triangle, then the third angles are congruent) leads to the ASA theorem and the proof for Theorem 9.9. See the diagrams above.

Note: When *two angles and any side* in one triangle are congruent to the corresponding two angles and side of a second triangle, we conclude that the triangles are congruent by ASA or AAS.

Recall the special case of the ASA Theorem for the right triangle:

- The Leg-Angle Theorem. If a leg and an acute angle of one right triangle are congruent to the corresponding leg and acute angle of a second right triangle, then the triangles are congruent. That congruence could involve any of these four cases.

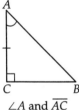
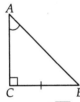
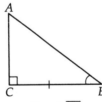
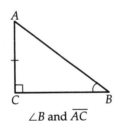

$\angle A$ and $\overline{AC}$ $\angle A$ and $\overline{BC}$ $\angle B$ and $\overline{BC}$ $\angle B$ and $\overline{AC}$

Similarly, there is a special case of the AAS Theorem for right triangles in Corollary 9.9.1.

- Corollary 9.9.1 (Hypotenuse-Angle). If the hypotenuse and an acute angle of one right triangle are congruent to the hypotenuse and an acute angle of a second right triangle, then the triangles are congruent.

Note: Since right triangles already have one pair of right angles congruent, $A \cong A$, adding another angle (A) and the hypotenuse (S) results in AAS $\cong$ AAS.

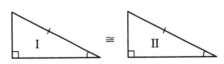

Statement: $\triangle I \cong \triangle II$ **Reason:** AAS $\cong$ AAS

- Corollary 9.9.2. If a point lies on the bisector of an angle, it is equidistant from the sides of an angle.

Given: $\overline{DB} \perp \overline{AB}$, $\overline{DC} \perp \overline{AC}$, $\overrightarrow{AD}$ bisects $\angle BAC$.
Prove: $\overline{DB} \cong \overline{DC}$

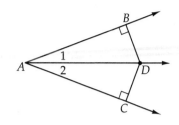

Statements	Reasons
1. $\overline{DB} \perp \overline{AB}$, $\overline{DC} \perp \overline{AC}$	1. Given.
2. $\angle ABD$ and $\angle ACD$ are right angles.	2. Perpendicular lines form right angles.
3. $\angle ABD \cong \angle ACD$ (A $\cong$ A)	3. Right angles are congruent angles.
4. $\overrightarrow{AD}$ bisects $\angle BAC$.	4. Given.
5. $\angle 1 \cong \angle 2$ (A $\cong$ A)	5. Definition of angle bisector.
6. $\overline{AD} \cong \overline{AD}$ (S $\cong$ S)	6. Reflexive property.
7. $\triangle ABD \cong \triangle ACD$	7. AAS $\cong$ AAS.
8. $\overline{DB} \cong \overline{DC}$	8. Congruent parts of congruent triangles are congruent.

While it is possible for two triangles with AAA $\cong$ AAA to be congruent, we cannot *always* prove them congruent. For example, consider the two triangles below. While all the corresponding angles in $\triangle ABC$ and $\triangle DEF$ are congruent, the corresponding sides are obviously not congruent.

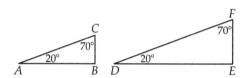

Similarly, while it is possible that two triangles can be congruent with SSA $\cong$ SSA, it is again *not always* true. Consider the three triangles below. $\triangle ABC$ and $\triangle DEF$ are congruent by having all pairs of corresponding sides congruent and, obviously, all pairs of corresponding angles congruent. But $\triangle ABC$ is not congruent to $\triangle GHI$ despite having two corresponding sides and an angle. Not all corresponding sides are congruent.

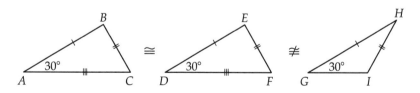

Two triangles are not always congruent when we have AAA $\cong$ AAA or SSA $\cong$ SSA.

Therefore, two triangles are not always congruent when two sides and an opposite angle of one triangle are congruent, respectively, to two sides and an opposite angle of the other.

MODEL PROBLEM

Given: $\overleftrightarrow{AC}$ and $\overline{QR}$ intersect at D; $\overline{PQ} \cong \overline{RS}$, $\angle 1 \cong \angle 2$
Prove: $\triangle I \cong \triangle II$

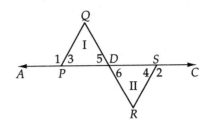

Statements	Reasons
1. $\overleftrightarrow{AC}$ and $\overline{QR}$ intersect at D.	1. Given.
2. $\angle 3$ is supplementary to $\angle 1$.	2. Definition of a linear pair.
$\angle 4$ is supplementary to $\angle 2$.	
3. $\angle 1 \cong \angle 2$	3. Given.
4. $\angle 3 \cong \angle 4$ (A $\cong$ A)	4. Supplements of congruent angles are congruent.
5. $\angle 5 \cong \angle 6$ (A $\cong$ A)	5. Vertical angles are congruent.
6. $\overline{PQ} \cong \overline{RS}$ (S $\cong$ S)	6. Given.
7. $\triangle I \cong \triangle II$	7. AAS $\cong$ AAS.

Practice

1 Which sets of letters indicating congruence would not be sufficient to guarantee congruence?

a SSS
b SSA
c SAS
d ASA
e AAS
f AAA

2 In each of the following figures, the congruent parts have been marked. State whether the marked parts are sufficient to prove that the triangles are congruent. If they are not sufficient (i) name the third pair of parts that must be congruent and (ii) name the method that can be used to prove the triangles congruent.

a

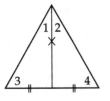

b

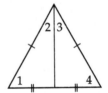

c

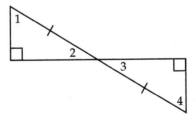

d

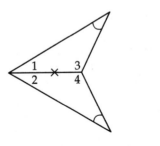

e

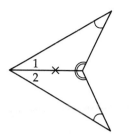

f

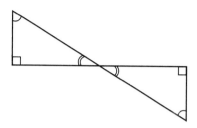

g

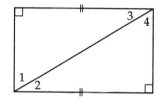

h

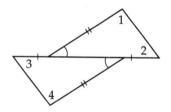

i

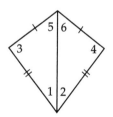

j

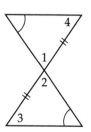

3

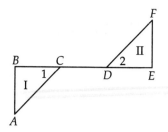

Given: $\overline{AB} \cong \overline{EF}, \overline{BC} \cong \overline{DE}, \angle 1 \cong \angle 2, \overline{AB} \perp \overline{BE}$, and $\overline{FE} \perp \overline{BE}$

Prove: $\triangle \text{I} \cong \triangle \text{II}$

4

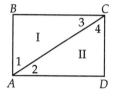

Given: $\angle 1 \cong \angle 4, \angle B \cong \angle D$

Prove: $\triangle \text{I} \cong \triangle \text{II}$

5

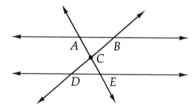

Given: $\overleftrightarrow{AB} \parallel \overleftrightarrow{DE}$, point C is the midpoint of $\overline{BD}$.

Prove: $\triangle ABC \cong \triangle DCE$

6

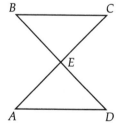

Given: $\angle B \cong \angle D, \overline{BC} \cong \overline{AD}$

Prove: $\overline{AE} \cong \overline{CE}$

7

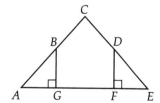

Given: $\angle A \cong \angle E, \overline{BC} \cong \overline{DC}; \overline{BG} \perp \overline{AE}, \overline{DF} \perp \overline{AE}$

Prove: $\overline{BG} \cong \overline{DF}$

8

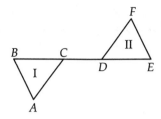

Given: $\overline{AB} \parallel \overline{EF}$; $\angle A \cong \angle F$, $\overline{AC} \cong \overline{DF}$
Prove: $\triangle I \cong \triangle II$

9

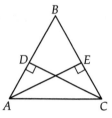

Given: Isosceles triangle with $\overline{AB} \cong \overline{CB}$;
$\overline{CD} \perp \overline{AB}$, $\overline{AE} \perp \overline{CB}$
Prove: $\overline{CD} \cong \overline{AE}$

10

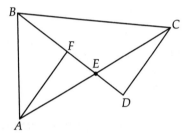

Given: E is the midpoint of $\overline{AC}$; $\overline{AF} \perp \overline{BD}$,
$\overline{CD} \perp \overline{BD}$
Prove: $\overline{AF} \cong \overline{CD}$

11

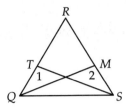

Given: $\overline{QR} \cong \overline{SR}$, $\angle 1 \cong \angle 2$
Prove: $\overline{QM} \cong \overline{ST}$

12

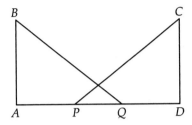

Given: $\overline{BA} \perp \overline{AD}$, $\overline{BA} \parallel \overline{CD}$, $\overline{AP} \cong \overline{QD}$,
$\angle B \cong \angle C$
Prove: $\overline{BA} \cong \overline{CD}$

9-7 The Converse of the Isosceles Triangle Theorem

The Isosceles Triangle Theorem in Chapter 5 states:

If two sides of a triangle are congruent, then the angles opposite those sides are congruent.

The converse of theorem is

- Theorem 9.10. If two angles of a triangle are congruent, then the sides opposite these angles are congruent.

In biconditional form, the statement of the Isosceles Triangle Theorem reads as follows:

Two angles of a triangle are congruent if and only if the sides opposite these angles are congruent.

- Corollary 9.10.1. If a triangle is equiangular, then it is equilateral.

MODEL PROBLEMS

1 In $\triangle ABC$, $\angle A \cong \angle C$. If $AB = 7x - 9$ and $BC = 5x + 13$, find

  a the value of x.
  b side AB.
  c side BC.

SOLUTION

Since $\angle A$ and $\angle C$ are equal, the two sides opposite these angles, AB and BC, are also equal. Therefore, $\triangle ABC$ is isosceles.

  a $7x - 9 = 5x + 13$
  $2x = 22$
  $x = 11$

ANSWER: $x = 11$

  b side $AB = 7x - 9$
  $ = 7(11) - 9$
  $ = 77 - 9$
  $ = 68$

ANSWER: $AB = 68$

  c side $BC = 5x + 13$
  $ = 5(11) + 13$
  $ = 55 + 13$
  $ = 68$

ANSWER: $BC = 68$

2 The degree measures of three angles of $\triangle ABC$ are $4x - 2$, $3x + 6$, and $4x - 11$. Describe $\triangle ABC$ as

  a acute, right, or obtuse.
  b scalene, isosceles, or equilateral.

SOLUTION

$(4x - 2) + (3x + 6) + (4x - 11) = 180$
$ 11x - 7 = 180$
$ 11x = 187$
$ x = 17$

$4x - 2 = 4(17) - 2 = 66°$
$3x + 6 = 3(17) + 6 = 57°$
$4x - 11 = 4(17) - 11 = 57°$

ANSWER: a Since all the angles are less than 90°, the triangle is acute.
  b Since two angles are equal, the triangle is isosceles.

3

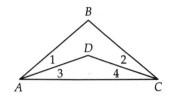

Given: $\overline{AB} \cong \overline{BC}$, $\angle 1 \cong \angle 2$
Prove: $\triangle ADC$ is an isosceles triangle.

Statements	Reasons
1. $\overline{AB} \cong \overline{BC}$	1. Given.
2. $\angle 1 \cong \angle 2$	2. Given.
3. $\angle BAC \cong \angle BCA$	3. If two sides of a triangle are congruent, the angles opposite those sides are congruent.
4. $\angle BAC - \angle 1 \cong \angle BCA - \angle 2$ or $\angle 3 \cong \angle 4$	4. Subtraction postulate.
5. $\overline{AD} \cong \overline{DC}$	5. If two angles of a triangle are congruent, then the sides opposite those angles are congruent.
6. $\triangle ADC$ is an isosceles triangle.	6. If a triangle has two congruent sides, it is an isosceles triangle.

 Practice

1 In isosceles $\triangle ABC$, $\overline{AB} \cong \overline{BC}$. Find the measure of each angle if m$\angle A = 3x + 4$ and m$\angle B = 2x - 4$.

2 In isosceles $\triangle ABC$, $\overline{AB} \cong \overline{BC}$. Find the measure of each angle if m$\angle C = 3x + 3$ and m$\angle B = 4x - 16$.

3 In isosceles $\triangle ABC$, $\overline{AB} \cong \overline{BC}$. If m$\angle A = 82$ and m$\angle B = 2x$, find the value of x.

4 If the degree measures of $\triangle ADC$ are $2x + 14$, $3x - 2$, and $5x + 8$, show that $\triangle ADC$ is isosceles.

5 Find the measures of the marked angles x, y, and z if $\overline{AC} \cong \overline{CB}$ and m$\angle B = 49$.

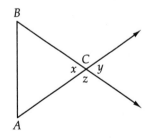

6 Find the measure of angles Q, x, y, and z if $\overline{SR} \cong \overline{SQ}$ and m$\angle R = 58$.

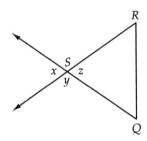

7

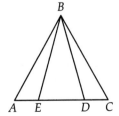

Given: $\angle A \cong \angle C$ and $\overline{AD} \cong \overline{EC}$
Prove: $\triangle ABD \cong \triangle CBE$

8

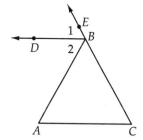

Given: $\overrightarrow{BD} \parallel \overline{AC}$ and $\angle 1 \cong \angle 2$
Prove: $\triangle ABC$ is isosceles.

9

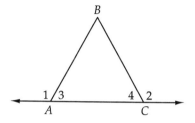

Given: $\angle 1 \cong \angle 2$
Prove: $\triangle ABC$ is isosceles.

10

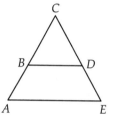

Given: $\overline{BD} \parallel \overline{AE}$, $\overline{AC} \cong \overline{CE}$
Prove: $\overline{BC} \cong \overline{DC}$

11

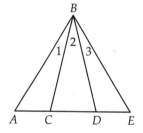

Given: $\overline{BC} \cong \overline{BD}$, $\angle 1 \cong \angle 3$
Prove: $\overline{AB} \cong \overline{BE}$

12

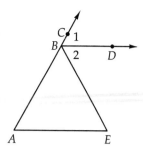

Given: $\overrightarrow{BD} \parallel \overline{AE}$, $\overline{AB} \cong \overline{EB}$
Prove: $\angle 1 \cong \angle 2$

13

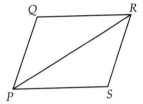

Given: Quadrilateral $PQRS$ with $\overline{PQ} \parallel \overline{SR}$, $\overline{PQ} \cong \overline{SR}$, and $\overline{PR}$ bisects $\angle QPS$
Prove: $\overline{PS} \cong \overline{SR}$

14

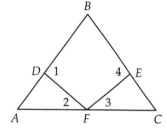

Given: $\angle 2 \cong \angle 3$, $\angle 1 \cong \angle 4$, and $\overline{DF} \cong \overline{FE}$
Prove: $\triangle ABC$ is an isosceles triangle.

15

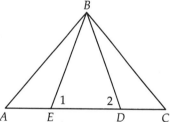

Given: $\overleftrightarrow{AEDC}$, $\overline{AE} \cong \overline{DC}$, $\angle 1 \cong \angle 2$
Prove: $\triangle ABC$ is an isosceles triangle.

9-8 Proving Right Triangles Congruent by Hypotenuse-Leg; Concurrence of Angle Bisectors of a Triangle

For triangles that are not right triangles, the SSA rule does not work. However, when two triangles are right triangles and *two sides* and *one angle* (namely, the right angle) are congruent, we can prove the triangles are congruent. In this case SSA ≅ SSA does work.

- Theorem 9.11 (Hypotenuse-Leg Theorem). Two right triangles are congruent if the hypotenuse and leg of one triangle are congruent, respectively, to the hypotenuse and corresponding leg of the other triangle. (HL ≅ HL)

Note: The Hypotenuse-Leg Theorem is the one congruence theorem for triangles that is not a special case of a more general theorem for triangles.

Right triangles can be proved congruent by any one of the following:

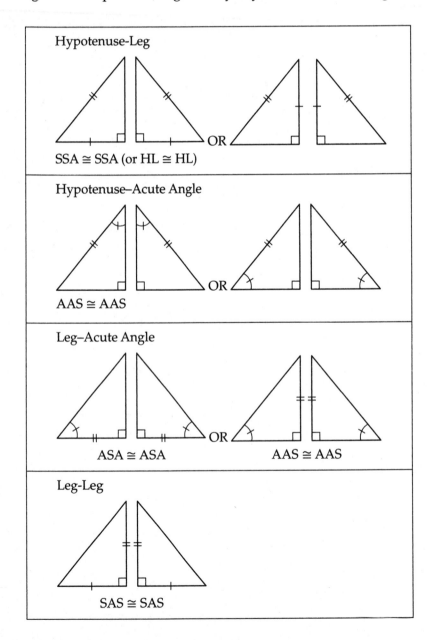

Hypotenuse-Leg

SSA ≅ SSA (or HL ≅ HL)

Hypotenuse–Acute Angle

AAS ≅ AAS

Leg–Acute Angle

ASA ≅ ASA   AAS ≅ AAS

Leg-Leg

SAS ≅ SAS

Given: D is the midpoint of $\overline{AC}$.
$\overline{DR} \perp \overline{AB}$, $\overline{DQ} \perp \overline{BC}$, and $\overline{DR} \cong \overline{DQ}$
Prove: $\angle A \cong \angle C$

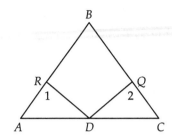

Statements	Reasons
1. $\overline{DR} \perp \overline{AB}$ and $\overline{DQ} \perp \overline{BC}$.	1. Given.
2. $\angle 1$ and $\angle 2$ are right angles.	2. Perpendicular lines form right angles.
3. $\triangle ARD$ and $\triangle CQD$ are right triangles.	3. A triangle with a right angle is a right triangle.
4. D is the midpoint of $\overline{AC}$.	4. Given.
5. $\overline{AD} \cong \overline{DC}$ (H $\cong$ H)	5. Definition of a midpoint.
6. $\overline{DR} \cong \overline{DQ}$ (Leg $\cong$ Leg)	6. Given.
7. $\triangle ARD$ and $\triangle CQD$ are congruent.	7. HL $\cong$ HL.
8. $\angle A \cong \angle C$	8. Congruent parts of congruent triangles are congruent.

The following corollary is the converse of the earlier Corollary 9.9.2.

- Corollary 9.11.1. If a point is equidistant from the sides of an angle, then it lies on the bisector of the angle.

Given: $\triangle ABC$; $\overline{PD} \perp \overline{AB}$, $\overline{PE} \perp \overline{BC}$; $\overline{PD} \cong \overline{PE}$
Prove: $\overline{BP}$ is the bisector of $\angle ABC$.

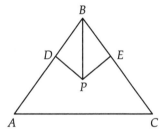

Statements	Reasons
1. $\triangle ABC$; $\overline{PD} \perp \overline{AB}$, $\overline{PE} \perp \overline{BC}$	1. Given.
2. $\angle PDB$ and $\angle PEB$ are right angles.	2. Perpendicular lines form right angles.
3. $\triangle PDB$ and $\triangle PEB$ are right triangles.	3. A triangle with a right angle is a right triangle.
4. $\overline{PB} \cong \overline{PB}$ (H $\cong$ H).	4. Reflexive Property.
5. $\overline{PD} \cong \overline{PE}$ (Leg $\cong$ Leg).	5. Given.
6. $\triangle PDB$ and $\triangle PEB$ are congruent.	6. HL $\cong$ HL.
7. $\angle DBP \cong \angle EBP$	7. Congruent parts of congruent triangles are congruent.
8. $\overline{BP}$ is the bisector of $\angle ABC$.	8. Definition of an angle bisector.

Keep in Mind

There are sets of conditions on triangles that allow us to deduce congruence.

For Triangles in General	For Right Triangles
Side-Side-Side (SSS)	Leg-Leg
Side-Angle-Side (SAS)	Leg–Acute Angle
Angle-Side-Angle (ASA)	Hypotenuse–Acute Angle
Angle-Angle-Side (AAS)	Hypotenuse-Leg

Concurrence: Three or more lines are *concurrent* if and only if their intersection is exactly one point. Concurrent points have been seen earlier in discussions of the perpendicular bisectors of the sides of a triangle as well as the altitudes of a triangle.

> Chapter 14 will introduce constructions and analysis of points of concurrency.

- Theorem 9.12. The bisectors of the interior angles of a triangle are concurrent. That point of concurrency is called the *incenter* of the triangle.

 MODEL PROBLEM

In $\triangle ABC$, the angle bisectors intersect at P. If $m\angle ABC = 80$ and $m\angle CAB = 60$, find the measures of the numbered angles 1 through 9.

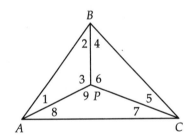

SOLUTION

Bisecting $m\angle ABC$ means $\frac{1}{2}m\angle ABC = m\angle 2 = m\angle 4 = \frac{1}{2}(80) = 40$.

Bisecting $m\angle CAB$ means $\frac{1}{2}m\angle CAB = m\angle 1 = m\angle 8 = \frac{1}{2}(60) = 30$.

$m\angle 3 = 180 - (m\angle 1 + m\angle 2) = 180 - (30 + 40) = 110$

$m\angle ACB = 180 - (m\angle CAB + m\angle ABC) = 180 - (60 + 80) = 40$

Thus, bisecting $\angle ACB$ means $\frac{1}{2}m\angle ACB = m\angle 7 = m\angle 5 = \frac{1}{2}(40) = 20$.

$m\angle 9 = 180 - (m\angle 8 + m\angle 7) = 180 - (30 + 20) = 130$

$m\angle 6 = 180 - (m\angle 4 + m\angle 5) = 180 - (40 + 20) = 120$

ANSWERS: $m\angle 1 = 30$, $m\angle 2 = 40$, $m\angle 3 = 110$, $m\angle 4 = 40$, $m\angle 5 = 20$, $m\angle 6 = 120$, $m\angle 7 = 20$, $m\angle 8 = 30$, $m\angle 9 = 130$

Practice

Exercises 1–5: Refer to the diagram. Using only the given information for right triangles *ABC* and *RST*, state which congruent correspondence makes the triangle congruent: (a) Hypotenuse-Leg, (b) Hypotenuse–Acute Angle, (c) Leg–Acute Angle, or (d) Leg-Leg.

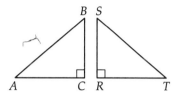

1 $\overline{AC} \cong \overline{RT}$ and $\overline{AB} \cong \overline{ST}$

2 $\overline{AC} \cong \overline{RT}$ and $\overline{BC} \cong \overline{RS}$

3 $\angle A \cong \angle T$ and $\overline{AC} \cong \overline{RT}$

4 $\overline{AB} \cong \overline{ST}$ and $\angle B \cong \angle S$

5 $\overline{BC} \cong \overline{SR}$ and $\overline{AB} \cong \overline{ST}$

6 If m$\angle C = 28$, m$\angle A = 48$, and the angle bisectors intersect at *P*, find the measures of the numbered angles 1 through 9.

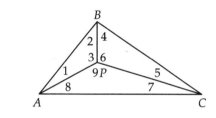

7

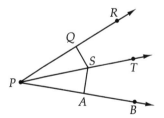

Given: $\overline{SQ} \perp \overrightarrow{PR}$, $\overline{SA} \perp \overrightarrow{PB}$, and $\overline{SQ} \cong \overline{SA}$
Prove: $\overrightarrow{PT}$ bisects $\angle RPB$.

8

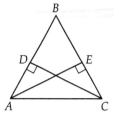

Given: $\overline{AE} \perp \overline{BC}$, $\overline{CD} \perp \overline{AB}$, and $\overline{AE} \cong \overline{CD}$
Prove: $\triangle ACE \cong \triangle CAD$

9

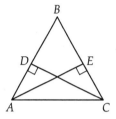

Given: $\overline{AE} \perp \overline{BC}$, $\overline{CD} \perp \overline{AB}$, and $\overline{DB} \cong \overline{EB}$
Prove: $\overline{AE} \cong \overline{CD}$

10

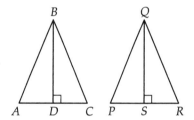

Given: $\triangle ABC \cong \triangle PQR$; $\overline{BD} \perp \overline{AC}$, $\overline{QS} \perp \overline{PR}$, and $\overline{BD}$ bisects $\angle ABC$.
Prove: $\overline{QS}$ bisects $\angle PQR$.

11

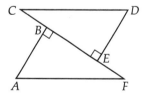

Given: $\overline{AB} \perp \overline{CF}$, $\overline{DE} \perp \overline{CF}$; $\overline{CB} \cong \overline{FE}$, $\overline{CD} \cong \overline{AF}$
Prove: $\overline{AB} \cong \overline{DE}$

12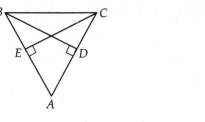

Given: $\overline{CE} \perp \overline{BA}$, $\overline{BD} \perp \overline{AC}$, $\overline{AB} \cong \overline{AC}$
Prove: $\overline{CE} \cong \overline{BD}$

13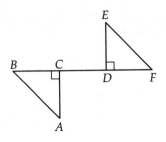

Given: $\overline{AC} \perp \overline{BF}$, $\overline{ED} \perp \overline{BF}$, $\overline{AC} \cong \overline{ED}$, and
$\overline{BA} \cong \overline{EF}$
Prove: $\angle A \cong \angle E$

9-9 Interior and Exterior Angles of Polygons

A **polygon** is a closed figure that is the union of three or more line segments in a plane. The segments are **sides** of a polygon, and the endpoints are the **vertices**.

A **convex polygon** is a polygon in which each interior angle measures less than 180°. The convex polygons we are most familiar with are the triangle and the family of quadrilaterals (4 sides). Some other common convex polygons are the **pentagon** (5 sides), the **hexagon** (6 sides), the **octagon** (8 sides), and the **decagon** (10 sides).

A **diagonal** of a polygon is a line segment connecting one vertex to any other nonconsecutive vertex. Examine the quadrilateral below.

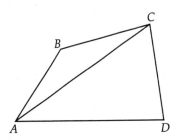

By drawing a diagonal through any two nonconsecutive vertex, two triangles are formed. Since the sum of the measures of each triangle is 180°, the sum of the measures of both triangles is 2 × 180° = 360°. Therefore, the sum of the measures of the interior angles of a quadrilateral is 360°.

In the convex polygons drawn below, a pentagon and a hexagon, diagonals are drawn from one vertex to every nonadjacent vertex, forming triangles.

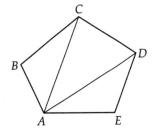
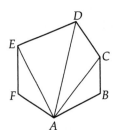

The results for quadrilaterals, pentagons, and hexagons are shown in the table below:

Polygon	Number of Sides	Number of Triangles	Sum of the Measures of the Interior Angles
Quadrilateral	4	2	360°
Pentagon	5	3	540°
Hexagon	6	4	720°
Heptagon	7	5	900°

This pattern can be extended. The number of triangles formed by the diagonals is two less than the number of sides. Therefore, a convex polygon with n sides contains $n - 2$ triangles.

- Theorem 9.13. The sum of the measures of the interior angles of a polygon of n sides is $180(n - 2)$.

A **regular polygon** is both equilateral and equiangular; all of its sides are congruent and all of its angles are congruent.

- Corollary 9.13.1. The measure of each interior angle of a regular polygon of n sides is $\frac{180(n - 2)}{n}$.

- Theorem 9.14. The sum of the measures of the exterior angles of a polygon of n sides, taking one angle at each vertex, is 360°.

    Proof: A polygon of n sides has n pairs of interior angles and exterior angles drawn at the same vertex. Each pair is a *linear pair*, with a combined measure of 180°. The sum of the measures of the n pairs of interior and exterior angles is $180n$. From theorem 9.13, the sum of the measures of the interior angles of a polygon of n sides is $180(n - 2)$. Therefore, the sum of the measures of the exterior angles of a polygon of n sides, taking one angle at each vertex, is $180n - 180(n - 2) = 180n - 180n + 360 = 360°$.

- Corollary 9.14.1. The measure of each exterior angle of a regular polygon of n sides is $\frac{360}{n}$.

Summary of Angle Measures in a Polygon With n Sides

1 The sum of the interior angle measures is $180(n - 2)$.
2 For a regular polygon, each interior angle measures $\frac{180(n - 2)}{n}$.
3 The sum of the exterior angles is 360°.
4 For a regular polygon, each exterior angle measures $\frac{360}{n}$.
5 The sum of the measures of all the interior and exterior angles of a polygon is $180n$.

1   How many sides does a regular polygon have if the measure of an exterior angle is 15°?

SOLUTION

Use the formula: the measure of each angle is $\frac{360}{n}$.

$15 = \frac{360}{n}$

$15n = 360$

$n = \frac{360}{15} = 24$

ANSWER: 24 sides

2   If the sum of the measures of the interior angles of a regular polygon is 1,080°, what is the measure of one exterior angle?

SOLUTION

Use the formula to find the number of sides: $180(n - 2) = 1,080$.

$\frac{180(n - 2)}{180} = \frac{1,080}{180}$

$n - 2 = 6$

$n = 8$ sides

The formula for finding an exterior angle is

$\frac{360}{n} = \frac{360}{8} = 45$

ANSWER: 45°

 Practice

1   Copy and complete this table.

Polygon	Number of Sides	Number of Triangles	Sum of Interior Angles $180(n - 2)$	Measure of Each Interior Angle $\frac{180(n - 2)}{n}$	Measure of Each Exterior Angle
Triangle	3	1	$180(1) = 180°$	$\frac{180}{3} = 60°$	$\frac{360}{3} = 120°$
Quadrilateral	4	2	$180(2) = 360°$	$\frac{360}{4} = 90°$	$\frac{360}{4} = 90°$
Pentagon	5	3	$180(3) = 540°$	$\frac{540}{5} = 108°$	$\frac{360}{5} = 72°$
Hexagon	6				
Heptagon	7				
Octagon	8				
Nonagon	9				
Decagon	10				
24-gon	24				
n-gon	n				

2 If the sum of the measures of the interior angles of a polygon is 18,000°, how many sides does the polygon have?

3 How many diagonals can be drawn from one vertex of a convex polygon having

 a 3 sides?
 b 4 sides?
 c 5 sides?
 d 7 sides?
 e 11 sides?

4 How many triangles can be drawn from diagonals drawn from one vertex of a convex polygon having

 a 9 sides?
 b 12 sides?
 c 17 sides?
 d 100 sides?

5 How many degrees are in the sum of the interior and exterior angles of a polygon having

 a 4 sides?
 b 5 sides?
 c 7 sides?
 d 19 sides?

6 How many sides does a polygon have if the sum of its interior and exterior angles is

 a 1,000 straight angles?
 b 200 right angles?

7 How many degrees are in each exterior angle of an equiangular polygon of

 a 9 sides?
 b 10 sides?
 c 36 sides?
 d 72 sides?

8 How many sides does a regular polygon have if each exterior angles equals

 a 30°?
 b 36°?
 c 60°?
 d 45°?

9 How many sides does a regular polygon have if each interior angle equals

 a 160°?
 b 179°?
 c 135°?
 d $\frac{4}{3}$ of a right angle?

10 How many sides are there in the polygon whose sum of its interior angles equals

 a 1,800°?
 b 3,960°?
 c 8,640°?
 d 179,640°?

11 If three of the exterior angles of an equiangular polygon total 90°, how many sides does it have?

12 If the sum of the interior angles of a regular polygon equals twice the sum of its exterior angles, how many sides does it have?

13 If each interior angle of a regular polygon equals eight times the adjacent exterior angle, how many sides does it have?

Exercises 14–16: Find the measures of each numbered angle.

14

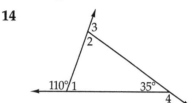

15

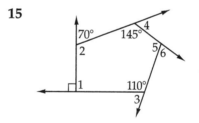

16

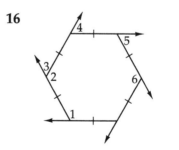

17 The sum of the measures of the interior angles of a polygon is five times the sum of the measures of the exterior angles. How many sides does the polygon have?

18 Find the value for x and the measure of each interior angle.

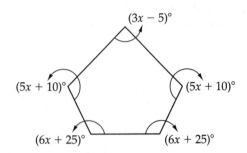

$(3x - 5)°$

$(5x + 10)°$ $(5x + 10)°$

$(6x + 25)°$ $(6x + 25)°$

19 The measures of the five exterior angles of a pentagon are x, $3x$, $4x$, $4x$, and $6x$. Find the measure of each exterior angle. Find the measure of each interior angle.

20 The measures of the six exterior angles of a hexagon are $3x + 4$, $7x + 7$, $6x - 5$, $5x + 8$, $3x - 2$, and $5x$. Find the measure of each exterior angle. Find the measure of each interior angle.

 # CHAPTER REVIEW

1 Given the coordinates of two points on $\overleftrightarrow{AB}$, find the slope of a line parallel to $\overleftrightarrow{AB}$.

   a $A(2, 6)$, $B(2, -1)$
   b $A(-3, 4)$, $B(1, 5)$
   c $A(5, 7)$, $B(-2, -8)$
   d $A(3, -8)$, $B(-3, 7)$
   e $A(2, 1)$, $B(-3, 4)$
   f $A(-3, 6)$, $B(3, 6)$

2 Given the coordinates of two points on $\overleftrightarrow{CD}$, find the slope of a line perpendicular to $\overleftrightarrow{CD}$.

   a $C(2, 5)$, $D(-2, 3)$
   b $C(4, -6)$, $D(-3, 1)$
   c $C(-5, 0)$, $D(3, 0)$
   d $C(2, -6)$, $D(2, -2)$
   e $C(3, 7)$, $D(-4, 2)$
   f $C(5, 2)$, $D(-3, 2)$

3 If the coordinates of $\triangle ABC$ are $A(-4, -1)$, $B(-2, 7)$, and $C(1, 2)$, show that $\triangle ABC$ is a right triangle.

4 Using the coordinates $S(-2, -6)$, $L(3, -1)$, $A(1, 1)$, and $P(-4, -4)$, show that quadrilateral $SLAP$ is a rectangle.

5 Show that quadrilateral $PLAN$, with coordinates $P(5, -8)$, $L(10, -3)$, $A(9, 1)$, and $N(4, -4)$, is a parallelogram.

6 In the figure, $m \parallel n$, $m\angle 6 = 2y$, $m\angle 10 = 3y - 10$, $m\angle 4 = 2y + 15$, and $m\angle 12 = 3y - 7$. Find the measure of angles 1 through 16.

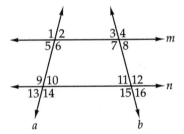

7 In the figure, $a \parallel b$, $\overline{AB} \parallel \overline{CD}$; $\overline{CB} \perp \overleftrightarrow{BD}$, and $m\angle 1 = 42$. Find $m\angle 2$, $m\angle 3$, and $m\angle 4$.

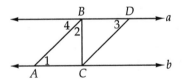

Exercises 8–10: Use the given information to find the degree measure of $\angle x$.

8 $a \parallel b \parallel c$

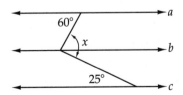

$60°$

x

$25°$

9 $a \parallel b$ and $m \parallel n$

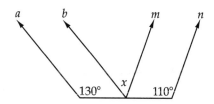

10 $m \parallel r$, $m\angle 1 = 42$, and $m\angle 2 = 110$

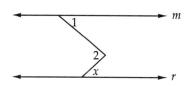

11 If two angles of a triangle are 60° and 40°, what is the measure of the angle formed by the intersection of the bisectors of these angles?

12 In each of the following, find the measure of $\angle x$ and $\angle y$.

a

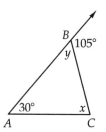

b

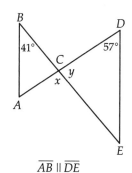

$\overline{AB} \parallel \overline{DE}$

c

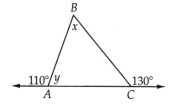

d

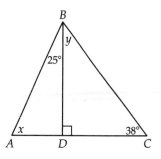

e

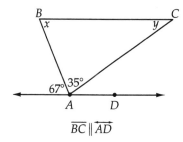

$\overline{BC} \parallel \overrightarrow{AD}$

f

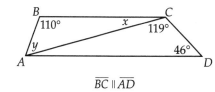

$\overline{BC} \parallel \overline{AD}$

g

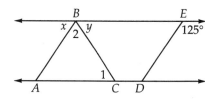

$\overrightarrow{BE} \parallel \overrightarrow{AD}$, $\overline{AB} \parallel \overline{DE}$, $m\angle 1 = m\angle 2$

13 Find the number diagonals in a polygon of

a 5 sides
b 8 sides
c 10 sides
d 36 sides
e n sides

14 If the sum of the measures of the angles of a polygon is 18,000°, how many sides does the polygon have?

15 How many sides does a polygon have if the sum of its interior angles equals three times the sum of the exterior angles?

16 How many sides does a polygon have if the sum of its interior angles equals to three times the sum of the interior angles of a hexagon?

17 How many sides does an equilateral polygon have, whose exterior angle is equal to the interior angle of an equilateral triangle?

18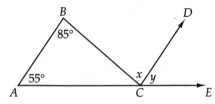

Given $\overrightarrow{AE}$, $\overline{AB} \parallel \overline{CD}$; m∠A = 55 and m∠B = 85, find

a m∠x.
b m∠y.

19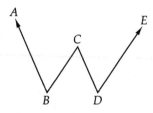

If $\overline{AB} \parallel \overline{CD}$, $\overline{BC} \parallel \overline{DE}$, and m∠B = 45, find m∠D.

20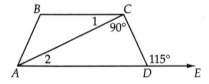

If $\overline{BC} \parallel \overline{AE}$, find m∠1 and m∠2.

21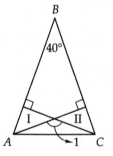

In the figure, △I ≅ △II, $\overline{AB} \cong \overline{CB}$, and m∠B = 40. Find m∠1.

22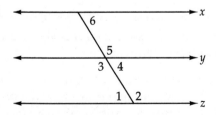

Given: x ∥ z; ∠6 ≅ ∠4
Prove: y ∥ z

23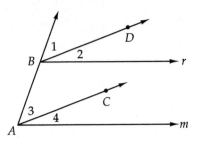

Given: ∠2 ≅ ∠4, ∠1 ≅ ∠3
Prove: m ∥ r

24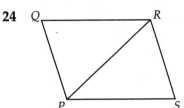

Given: $\overline{QR} \parallel \overline{PS}$, ∠QPS ≅ ∠QRS
Prove: $\overline{QP} \parallel \overline{RS}$

25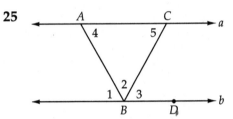

Given: $\overline{BC}$ bisects ∠ABD; ∠1 ≅ ∠2, ∠5 ≅ ∠1.
Prove: a ∥ b

26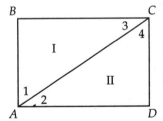

Given: $\overline{AC}$ bisects ∠BCD; $\overline{AB} \perp \overline{BC}$, $CD \perp \overline{AD}$.
Prove: △I ≅ △II

27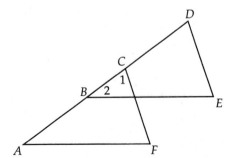

Given: $\overleftrightarrow{ABCD}$, $\overline{AB} \cong \overline{CD}$, $\overline{CF} \cong \overline{DE}$; $\overline{CF} \parallel \overline{DE}$
Prove: $\overline{AF} \cong \overline{BE}$

28

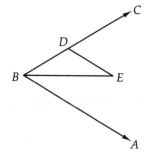

If $\overrightarrow{BE}$ bisects $\angle ABC$, and $\overline{DE} \parallel \overrightarrow{BA}$, prove $\triangle BDE$ is an isosceles triangle.

29

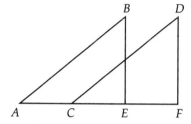

If AF is a line; $\overline{AC} \cong \overline{EF}$, $\overline{AB} \cong \overline{CD}$; and $\overline{AB} \parallel \overline{CD}$, prove $\overline{BE} \cong \overline{DF}$.

30

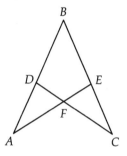

Given: $\overline{AB} \cong \overline{BC}$ and $\angle A \cong \angle C$
Prove: $\overline{AE} \cong \overline{CD}$

31

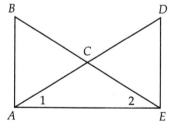

Given: $\overline{BA} \perp \overline{AE}$; $\angle 1 \cong \angle 2$, and $\angle B \cong \angle D$
Prove: $\overline{DE} \perp \overline{AE}$

32

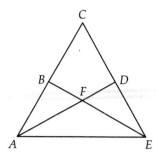

Given: $\angle CAE \cong \angle CEA$, $\overline{BA} \cong \overline{DE}$
Prove: $\angle BEA \cong \angle DAE$

33

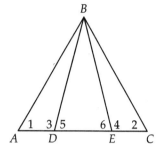

Given: $\angle 1 \cong \angle 2$, $\angle 3 \cong \angle 4$, and $\overline{AD} \cong \overline{EC}$
Prove: $\angle ABE \cong \angle CBD$

34

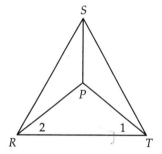

Given: $\overline{RS} \cong \overline{ST} \cong \overline{TR}$ and $\angle 1 \cong \angle 2$
Prove: $\overline{SP}$ bisects $\angle RST$

35

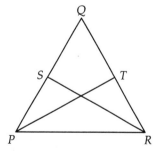

Given: $\overline{PT} \perp \overline{QR}$, $\overline{RS} \perp \overline{PQ}$, and $\overline{PT} \cong \overline{RS}$
Prove: $\triangle PQR$ is an isosceles triangle.

36

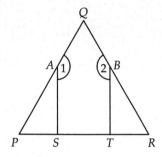

Given: $\overline{AS} \perp \overline{PR}$, $\overline{BT} \perp \overline{PR}$; $\overline{AS} \cong \overline{BT}$, $\angle 1 \cong \angle 2$
Prove: $\triangle PQR$ is isosceles.

Exercises 37–50: State **True** or **False**.

37 Coplanar lines that do not intersect are parallel.

38 Coplanar lines parallel to the same line are parallel to each other.

39 All angles of an isosceles triangle are congruent.

40 An equilateral triangle is isosceles.

41 Base angles of an isosceles triangle are congruent.

42 All sides of an isosceles triangle are congruent.

43 An equiangular triangle is isosceles.

44 A right triangle cannot be isosceles.

45 A transversal perpendicular to one of three parallel lines is perpendicular to each of the other parallel lines.

46 If two lines have the same slope, then they are perpendicular to each other.

47 A line parallel to one of two perpendicular lines is parallel to the other line.

48 A point that lies on the bisector of an angle is equidistant from the sides of the angle.

49 The median to the hypotenuse of a right triangle always divides the right triangle into two isosceles triangles.

50 If the slopes of the diagonals of a quadrilateral are perpendicular to each other, the quadrilateral is a rhombus.

Quadrilaterals

10-1 The General Quadrilateral

A **quadrilateral** is a polygon with four sides. Figure *ABCD* is an example of a quadrilateral. Refer to *ABCD* as the parts of a quadrilateral are defined below.

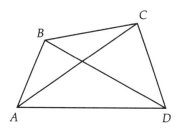

Parts of a Quadrilateral

- **Opposite sides** are sides that do not share a common endpoint (or vertex). $\overline{AB}$ and $\overline{CD}$ are opposite sides. $\overline{AD}$ and $\overline{BC}$ are opposite sides.
- **Consecutive (or adjacent) sides** share a common vertex. $\overline{DA}$ and $\overline{AB}$ are consecutive sides sharing the common vertex *A*. Likewise, $\overline{AB}$ and $\overline{BC}$ share vertex *B*, $\overline{BC}$ and $\overline{CD}$ share vertex *C*, and $\overline{CD}$ and $\overline{DA}$ share vertex *D*.
- **Opposite vertices** are vertices not connected by a side. *A* and *C* are opposite vertices, and *B* and *D* are opposite vertices.
- **Consecutive (or adjacent) vertices** are vertices that are the endpoints of the same side. *A* and *B*, *B* and *C*, *C* and *D*, as well as *D* and *A* are called consecutive vertices.
- **Consecutive (or adjacent) angles** are angles whose vertices are consecutive. That is, their vertices are next to each other, either clockwise or counterclockwise. In our example, consecutive angles are $\angle ABC$ and $\angle BCD$, $\angle BCD$ and $\angle CDA$, $\angle CDA$ and $\angle DAB$, $\angle DAB$ and $\angle ABC$.
- **Opposite angles** are angles whose vertices are not consecutive. $\angle ABC$ and $\angle CDA$ are opposite angles. $\angle BCD$ and $\angle DAB$ are opposite angles.
- **Diagonals** of a quadrilateral are line segments whose endpoints are pairs of opposite vertices. In our example, $\overline{AC}$ and $\overline{BD}$ are the diagonals.

The following sections will focus on special quadrilaterals and their properties. These quadrilaterals include parallelograms, rectangles, rhombuses, squares, trapezoids, and kites. As a preview to understanding the relationship of these special quadrilaterals, study the following diagram.

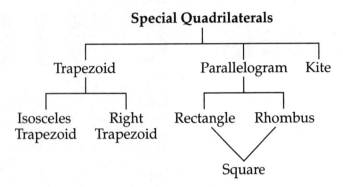

Note: The square contains all the properties of both rectangle and rhombus.

10-2 The Parallelogram

A **parallelogram** is a quadrilateral in which both pairs of opposite sides are parallel.

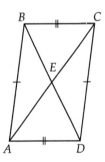

Opposite sides of a parallelogram are parallel. For example, referring to the figure above, $\overline{AB} \parallel \overline{CD}$ and $\overline{BC} \parallel \overline{AD}$.

- Theorem 10.1. Each diagonal divides a parallelogram into two congruent triangles; $\triangle ABC \cong \triangle CDA$ and $\triangle DAB \cong \triangle BCD$.
- Corollary 10.1.1. Opposite sides of a parallelogram are congruent; $\overline{AB} \cong \overline{CD}$ and $\overline{BC} \cong \overline{AD}$.
- Corollary 10.1.2. Opposite angles of a parallelogram are congruent; $\angle ABC \cong \angle CDA$ and $\angle BCD \cong \angle DAB$.
- Theorem 10.2. Consecutive angles of a parallelogram are supplementary; $m\angle ABC + m\angle BCD = 180$ and $m\angle BCD + m\angle CDA = 180$.
- Theorem 10.3. Diagonals of a parallelogram bisect each other; $\overline{AE} \cong \overline{EC}$ and $\overline{BE} \cong \overline{ED}$.

The **distance between two parallel lines** is the length of the perpendicular segment drawn from any point on one line to the other line.

MODEL PROBLEMS

1 Given: *PQRS* is a parallelogram.
$\overline{YQ}$ bisects ∠*PQR*.
$\overline{XS}$ bisects ∠*PSR*.
Prove: $\overline{SY} \cong \overline{XQ}$

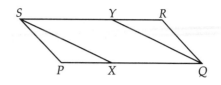

Statements	Reasons
1. *PQRS* is a parallelogram.	1. Given.
2. $\overline{PQ} \cong \overline{SR}$; $\overline{SP} \cong \overline{RQ}$	2. Opposite sides of a parallelogram are congruent.
3. ∠*PQR* ≅ ∠*PRS*; ∠*SPQ* ≅ ∠*SRQ*	3. Opposite angles of a parallelogram are congruent.
4. $\overline{YQ}$ bisects ∠*PQR*. $\overline{XS}$ bisects ∠*PSR*.	4. Given.
5. ∠*PSX* is one half ∠*PSR*. ∠*YQP* is one half ∠*PQR*.	5. An angle bisector divides an angle in half.
6. ∠*PSX* ≅ ∠*RQY*	6. Halves of equals are equal.
7. △*PXS* ≅ △*YQR*	7. ASA ≅ ASA.
8. $\overline{PX} \cong \overline{RY}$	8. Congruent parts of congruent triangles are congruent.
9. $\overline{SY} \cong \overline{XQ}$	9. Subtraction Postulate (When equals are subtracted from equals, the results are equal.)

2 In parallelogram *ABCD*, m∠*A* = 3*x* − 60 and m∠*C* = 40 − *x*. Find the value of *x* and the measures of each of the angles.

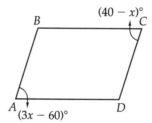

SOLUTION

Since opposite angles of a parallelogram are equal, m∠*A* = m∠*C*.

$3x - 60 = 40 - x$
$4x = 100$
$x = 25$

m∠*A* = 3*x* − 60 = 3(25) − 60 = 15
m∠*C* = 40 − *x* = 40 − 25 = 15
m∠*B* = m∠*D* = 180 − 15 = 165

ANSWER: m∠*A* = 15, m∠*B* = 165, m∠*C* = 15, and m∠*D* = 165

3 In parallelogram $ABCD$, m$\angle ABC = 80$, $BD = 12$, and $AC = 9$.

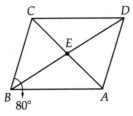

Find each of the following:

    a   m$\angle BAD$
    b   m$\angle ADC$
    c   m$\angle DCB$
    d AE
    e DE

SOLUTION

    a   Since consecutive angles are supplementary,
$$\text{m}\angle BAD + \text{m}\angle ABC = 180$$
$$\text{m}\angle BAD + 80 = 180$$
$$\text{m}\angle BAD = 100$$

    b m$\angle ADC = $ m$\angle ABC = 80$

    c m$\angle DCB = $ m$\angle BAD = 100$

    d $AE = \frac{1}{2}AC = \frac{1}{2}(9) = 4.5$

    e $DE = \frac{1}{2}BD = \frac{1}{2}(12) = 6$

Note: A surprising property of *all* quadrilaterals (including even nonconvex quadrilaterals) was discovered by Pierre Varignon, a French mathematician (1654–1722). His theorem states that *"If the midpoints of consecutive sides of ANY quadrilateral are connected, the resulting quadrilateral is a parallelogram."*

Example 1

In the figure below, the midpoints (A, B, C, and D) of the sides of the general quadrilateral $WXYZ$ are joined so that quadrilateral $ABCD$ is a parallelogram with $\overline{AB} \parallel \overline{CD}$ and $\overline{BC} \parallel \overline{AD}$.

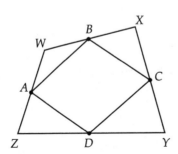

Example 2

In the figure below, the midpoints (A, B, C, and D) of the sides of the concave quadrilateral PQRS are joined to form parallelogram ABCD with $\overline{AB} \parallel \overline{CD}$ and $\overline{BC} \parallel \overline{AD}$.

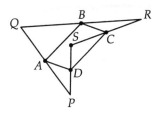

Varignon's theorem follows from an earlier theorem that says, "The segment that joins the midpoints of two sides of a triangle is parallel to the third side and one-half the length of the third side."

 Practice

Exercises 1–6: Use the given figure of parallelogram PQRS.

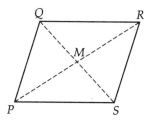

1 If m∠R = 48, find the measure of each of the other angles.

2 If m∠P = 30, find the measure of each of the other angles.

3 If m∠Q = 3x − 5 and m∠R = 4x − 25, find m∠S and m∠P.

4 If m∠P = 7x − 12 and m∠Q = 2x + 3, find m∠R and m∠S.

5 If diagonals PR and QS are drawn and intersect at point M so that diagonal PR = 5x − 3 and QS = 3x − 5, and QS = $\frac{1}{2}$PR, what are the lengths of the diagonals?

6 With the diagonals drawn in problem 5, name four pairs of congruent triangles.

7 One angle of a parallelogram is 6 less than five times the measure of the adjacent angle. What are the measures of these angles?

8 If one angle of a parallelogram is 24° more than three times the measure of the adjacent angle, find the measure of the angles of the parallelogram.

9 If the coordinates of the vertices of parallelogram ABCD are A(0, 0), B(5, 0), C(8, 1), and D(x, 1), what is the numerical value of x?

10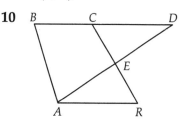

Given: Parallelogram ABCR and $\overline{CE} \cong \overline{ER}$. If AB = 12 and AR = 4, what is the length of CD?

11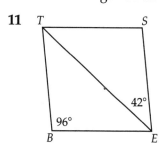

In parallelogram BEST, find m∠ETS, BTE, and m∠TEB.

12

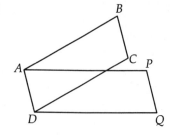

Given: Parallelogram *ABCD* and parallelogram *DAPQ*
Prove: $\overline{BC} \cong \overline{PQ}$

13

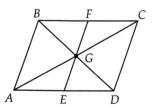

Given: Parallelogram *ABCD*
Prove: Point *G* is the midpoint of $\overline{FE}$.

14

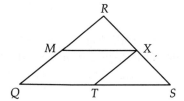

Given: *M* is the midpoint of $\overline{QR}$; $\overline{MX} \parallel \overline{QS}$, $\overline{TX} \parallel \overline{QM}$.
Prove: $\triangle MRX \cong \triangle TXS$

15

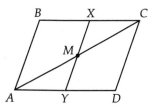

Given: Parallelogram *ABCD*, *X* is the midpoint of $\overline{BC}$, *Y* is the midpoint of $\overline{AD}$.
Prove: (a) *M* is the midpoint of $\overline{XY}$. (b) *M* is the midpoint of $\overline{AC}$.

16

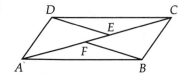

Given: $\overline{AC}$ is a diagonal in parallelogram *ABCD*, $\overline{AF} \cong \overline{CE}$
Prove: $\overline{DE} \parallel \overline{BF}$

17

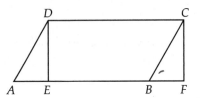

Given: *ABCD* is a parallelogram. $\overline{DE} \perp \overline{AF}$, $\overline{CF} \perp \overline{AF}$.
Prove: $\overline{DE} \cong \overline{CF}$

18

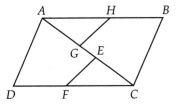

Given: Parallelogram *ABCD* with *H* and *F* the midpoints of $\overline{AB}$ and $\overline{DC}$, respectively. $\overline{HG} \perp \overline{AC}$, $\overline{FE} \perp \overline{AC}$.
Prove: $\overline{HG} \cong \overline{FE}$

19

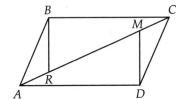

Given: Parallelogram *ABCD*, $\overline{AR} \cong \overline{CM}$
Prove: $\overline{BR} \cong \overline{DM}$

20

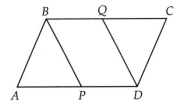

Given: Parallelogram *ABCD*, $\overline{QD}$ bisects $\angle D$, $\overline{PB}$ bisects $\angle B$.
Prove: (a) $\overline{AP} \cong \overline{CQ}$. (b) $\overline{PD} \cong \overline{BQ}$.

21

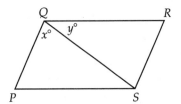

Given: Parallelogram *PQRS*, diagonal $\overline{QS}$, *PS* > *PQ*
Prove: m$\angle x$ > m$\angle y$

22

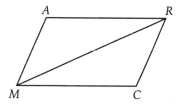

Given: Parallelogram *MARC* with *AR* > *MA*
and diagonal $\overline{MR}$
Prove: ∠*AMR* is *not congruent* to ∠*CMR*.

10-3 Proving That a Quadrilateral Is a Parallelogram

To prove that a quadrilateral is a parallelogram, you may use *any one* of these methods:

- Prove that both pairs of opposite sides are parallel. (Definition)
- Prove that both pairs of opposite sides are congruent. (Theorem 10.4)
- Prove that one pair of opposite sides is both congruent and parallel. (Theorem 10.5)
- Prove that both pairs of opposite angles are congruent. (Theorem 10.6)
- Prove that the diagonals of the figure bisect each other. (Theorem 10.7)

 MODEL PROBLEM

Given: Quadrilateral *MATH*. $\overline{AH}$ bisects $\overline{MT}$ at *Q*,
∠*TMA* ≅ ∠*MTH*.
Prove: *MATH* is a parallelogram.

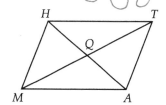

Statements	Reasons
1. $\overline{AH}$ bisects $\overline{MT}$ at *Q*.	1. Given.
2. $\overline{MQ} \cong \overline{QT}$	2. A bisector forms two equal line segments.
3. ∠*TMA* ≅ ∠*MTH*	3. Given.
4. $\overline{MA} \parallel \overline{HT}$	4. If alternate interior angles are congruent when lines are cut by a transversal, the lines are parallel.
5. ∠*MQA* ≅ ∠*HQT*	5. Vertical angles are congruent.
6. △*MQA* ≅ △*TQH*	6. ASA ≅ ASA.
7. $\overline{MA} \cong \overline{HT}$	7. Congruent parts of congruent triangles are congruent.
8. *MATH* is a parallelogram.	8. If one pair of opposite sides of a quadrilateral is both parallel and congruent, the quadrilateral is a parallelogram.

1 The vertices of quadrilateral *ABCD* are *A*(0, −3), *B*(1, 0), *C*(4, 0), and *D*(3,−3). Using coordinate geometry, show that *ABCD* is a parallelogram and state a clear reason for that conclusion.

2 The coordinates of two of the vertices of parallelogram *PQRS* are *P*(2, 6) and *R*(5, 10).

  a What is the length of diagonal *PR*?
  b What are the coordinates the intersection point of the diagonals?

3 The coordinates of the vertices of quadrilateral *DRAB* are *D*(−4, 0), *R*(6, 0), *A*(8, 5), and *B*(−2, 5).

  a Using coordinate geometry, show that quadrilateral *DRAB* is a parallelogram and state a reason for your conclusion.
  b Find the length of the altitude from *B* to $\overline{DR}$.

4

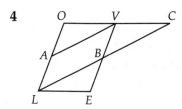

Given: Parallelogram *LOVE*; ∠*OAV* ≅ ∠*EBL*
Prove: △*OAV* ≅ △*EBL*

5

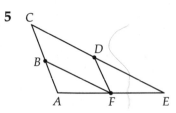

Given: *D*, *F*, and *B* are the midpoints of $\overline{CE}$, $\overline{AE}$, and $\overline{AC}$, respectively.
Prove: *BCDF* is a parallelogram.

6

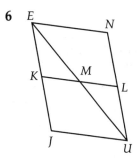

Given: *JUNE* is a quadrilateral. *K* is the midpoint of $\overline{JE}$. *L* is the midpoint of $\overline{UN}$. $\overline{KL}$ and $\overline{EU}$ bisect each other at *M*.
Prove: *JUNE* is a parallelogram.

7

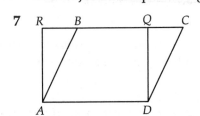

Given: *ABCD* is a parallelogram. $\overline{RC}$ is a line segment, $\overline{DQ} \perp \overline{RC}$, $\overline{AR} \perp \overline{RC}$.
Prove: *ARQD* is a parallelogram.

8

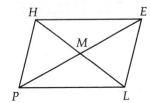

Given: Quadrilateral *HELP*. $\overline{PE}$ bisects $\overline{HL}$ at *M*. ∠*EPL* ≅ ∠*PEH*.
Prove: *HELP* is a parallelogram.

9

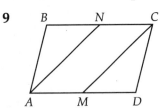

Given: *ABCD* is a parallelogram. *M* is the midpoint of $\overline{AD}$. *N* is the midpoint of $\overline{BC}$.
Prove: *ANCM* is a parallelogram.

10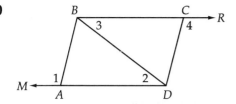

Given: $\overrightarrow{BR}$ and $\overrightarrow{DM}$; $\angle 1 \cong \angle 4$, $\angle 2 \cong \angle 3$
Prove: $ABCD$ is a parallelogram.

11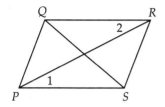

Given: $\overline{QS}$ bisects $\overline{PR}$, $\angle 1 \cong \angle 2$.
Prove: $PQRS$ is a parallelogram.

12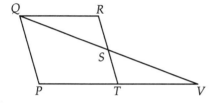

Given: Quadrilateral $PQRT$. $\overline{QSV}$, $\overline{RST}$, $\overline{PTV}$.
$\overline{QV}$ bisects $\overline{RT}$. $\overline{QR} \parallel \overline{PV}$; $\overline{PT} \cong \overline{TV}$.
Prove: $PQRT$ is a parallelogram.

13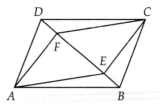

Given: Parallelogram $ABCD$. $\overline{DFEB}$, $\overline{DF} \cong \overline{BE}$.
Prove: $AECF$ is a parallelogram.

14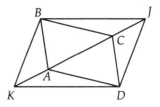

Given: $\overline{KJ}$ is a diagonal in parallelogram $KBJD$. $\overline{KA} \cong \overline{JC}$.
Prove: $ABCD$ is a parallelogram.

15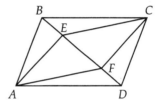

Given: $\overline{BD}$ is a diagonal in parallelogram $ABCD$. $\angle BEC \cong \angle AFD$.
Prove: $AECF$ is a parallelogram.

10-4 Rectangles

A **rectangle** is a parallelogram one of whose angles is a right angle.

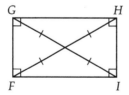

The following are theorems that define the properties of a rectangle.

- Theorem 10.8. A parallelogram in which all angles are right angles. In the figure above, m$\angle FGH$ = m$\angle GHI$ = m$\angle HIF$ = m$\angle IFG$ = 90.
- Theorem 10.9. The diagonals of a rectangle are congruent. In the figure above, $\overline{FH} \cong \overline{GI}$.
- Theorem 10.10. A rectangle is equiangular.
  Proof: Since *adjacent angles* of a parallelogram are *supplementary*, and since the *opposite angles* of a parallelogram are *congruent*, a rectangle has four right angles. Thus, a rectangle is equiangular.

To prove a quadrilateral is a rectangle, use *any one* of these methods:

- Prove it is a parallelogram with one right angle.
- Prove it is a parallelogram with congruent diagonals.
- Prove it is equiangular (that all angles are right angles).

 MODEL PROBLEMS

1   Prove Theorem 10.9.
      Given: Right triangle ABC with right angle ABC.
      $\overline{BE}$ is a median; $\overline{BE} \cong \overline{ED}$.
      Prove: $ABCD$ is a rectangle.

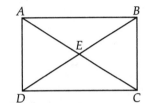

Statements	Reasons
1. Right triangle ABC with right angle ABC. $\overline{BE}$ is a median; $\overline{BE} \cong \overline{ED}$.	1. Given.
2. $\overline{AE} \cong \overline{EC}$	2. A median divides a line segment into two congruent line segments.
3. $ABCD$ is a parallelogram.	3. If the diagonals of a quadrilateral bisects each other, the quadrilateral is a parallelogram.
4. $ABCD$ is a rectangle.	4. A rectangle is a parallelogram with one right angle.

2   Given: Parallelogram $ABCD$, with $\overline{AC} \cong \overline{BD}$
      Prove: $ABCD$ is a rectangle.

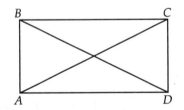

Statements	Reasons
1. $\overline{AB} \cong \overline{CD}$	1. Opposite sides of a parallelogram are congruent.
2. $\overline{AC} \cong \overline{BD}$	2. Given.
3. $\overline{AD} \cong \overline{AD}$	3. Reflexive Property.
4. $\triangle BAD \cong \triangle CDA$	4. SSS $\cong$ SSS.
5. $\angle BAD \cong \angle CDA$	5. Congruent parts of congruent triangles are congruent.
6. $\angle BAD$ and $\angle CDA$ are supplementary.	6. Consecutive angles of a parallelogram are supplementary.
7. $\angle BAD$ is a right angle.	7. Congruent supplementary angles are right angles.
8. $ABCD$ is a rectangle.	8. A parallelogram with a right angle is a rectangle.

Practice

1   A parallelogram must be a rectangle if the diagonals:

 (1) are congruent
 (2) are perpendicular
 (3) bisect the angles
 (4) bisect each other

Exercises 2–5: Refer to rectangle $ABCD$ below, with diagonals $\overline{AC}$ and $\overline{BD}$ intersecting at point R.

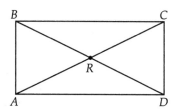

2   If $AR = 3(4x - 3)$ and $DR = 10x + 1$; find AR, CR, DR, and BR.

3   If $AR = 2(x - 6)$ and $BR = 3x - 20$, find x, AR, CR, and BD.

4   If $DR = 4(3x - 10)$ and $CR = 3(x - 2) + 12$, find x, AR, AC, and BD.

5   If $AC = 3(2x + 5) - \frac{1}{4}(4x + 4)$ and $BD = \frac{2}{3}(12x - 3) + 5x$, find x, AC, and DR.

6   In rectangle $ABCD$, diagonals $\overline{AC}$ and $\overline{BD}$ intersect at point E. If $AE = 18$ and $BD = 2x + 30$, find x.

7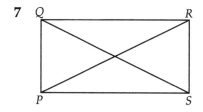

In the figure above, $PQRS$ is a rectangle with $PR = 4x + 3$ and $QS = 6x - 7$. Find the square root of the product of the diagonals.

8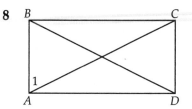

In rectangle $ABCD$, $\overline{AC}$ and $\overline{BD}$ are diagonals. If $m\angle 1 = 49$, find $m\angle ADB$.

9   Quadrilateral $ABCD$ is a rectangle. What are the coordinates of point D, if the coordinates of A, B, and C are $A(5, 0)$, $B(0, 0)$, and $C(0, -6)$?

10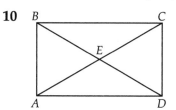

Given: Rectangle $ABCD$
Prove: $\angle CAD \cong \angle BDA$

11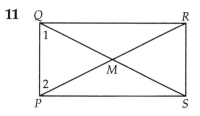

Given: Rectangle $PQRS$
Prove: $\angle 1 \cong \angle 2$

12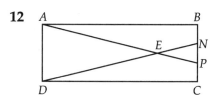

Given: Rectangle $ABCD$, $\overline{BNPC}$, $\overline{AEP}$, $\overline{DEN}$. $\overline{AP} \cong \overline{DN}$.
Prove: $\triangle ABP \cong \triangle DCN$ and $\overline{AE} \cong \overline{DE}$

13

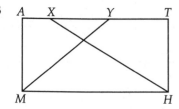

Given: *MATH* is a rectangle with $YT \neq AX$.
Prove: $MY \neq HX$

14

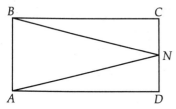

Given: Rectangle *ABCD*, with *N* the midpoint of $\overline{CD}$
Prove: $\overline{BN} \cong \overline{AN}$

15

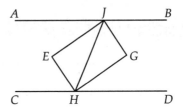

Given: $\overline{AB} \parallel \overline{CD}$, $\overline{JG}$ bisects $\angle BJH$, $\overline{HG}$ bisects $\angle JHD$, $\overline{EJ}$ bisects $\angle AJH$, and $\overline{EH}$ bisects $\angle CHJ$.
Prove: Quadrilateral *EJGH* is a rectangle.

16

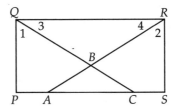

Given: Rectangle *PQRS*, and $\overline{PA} \cong \overline{CS}$
Prove:

a $\angle 1 \cong \angle 2$
b $\angle 3 \cong \angle 4$
c $\overline{QB} \cong \overline{BR}$

10-5 Rhombuses

A **rhombus** is a parallelogram that has two congruent consecutive sides.

Note: Since opposite sides of a parallelogram are congruent, the rhombus must be an *equilateral quadrilateral.*

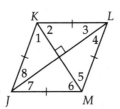

The following are theorems that define the properties of a rhombus.

- Theorem 10.11. All sides of a rhombus are congruent; $\overline{JK} \cong \overline{KL} \cong \overline{LM} \cong \overline{MJ}$.
- Theorem 10.12. The diagonals of a rhombus are perpendicular; $\overline{JL} \perp \overline{KM}$.
- Theorem 10.13. The diagonals bisect the angles of the rhombus; $\angle 1 \cong \angle 2$, $\angle 3 \cong \angle 4$, $\angle 5 \cong \angle 6$, $\angle 7 \cong \angle 8$.

To prove a quadrilateral is a rhombus, use *any one* of these methods:

- Prove it is a parallelogram with two congruent consecutive sides.
- Prove it is a parallelogram with perpendicular diagonals. (Theorem 10.12)
- Prove it is a parallelogram with one diagonal that bisects the opposite angles through which it is drawn.
- Prove it is equilateral.

1

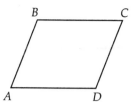

If $ABCD$ is a parallelogram, with $AB = 2x + 1$, $DC = 3x - 10$, and $AD = x + 12$, show that $ABCD$ is a rhombus.

SOLUTION

Since opposite sides are congruent, they are equal in length, so $DC = AB$.

$3x - 10 = 2x + 1$

$\quad x = 11$

$AB = 2x + 1 = 2(11) + 1 = 23$
$AD = x + 12 = 11 + 12 = 23$

Therefore, $AB = AD$ and $\overline{AB} \cong \overline{AD}$.

ANSWER: $ABCD$ is a rhombus, since it is a parallelogram in which two consecutive sides are congruent.

2 In rhombus $PINK$, the diagonals measure 6 units and 8 units. What is the length of a side?

SOLUTION

Diagonals of a rhombus are perpendicular to each other. Thus, they form four right triangles within the rhombus, and for each of these triangles the hypotenuse is a side of the rhombus:

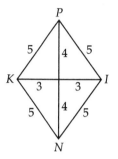

Since diagonals of a rhombus bisect each other, the legs of each right triangle are 3 units and 4 units.

Substitute the values in the Pythagorean theorem, where c is the hypotenuse, and a and b are the legs:

$c^2 = a^2 + b^2$
$c^2 = 3^2 + 4^2 = 9 + 16 = 25$
$c = \sqrt{25} = 5$

ANSWER: The length of a side of rhombus $PINK$ is 5 units.

 Practice

1

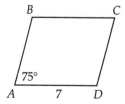

If $ABCD$ is a rhombus, find m$\angle B$, m$\angle C$, m$\angle D$, and the length of sides AB and BC.

2

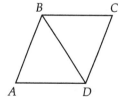

In rhombus $ABCD$, diagonal BD is drawn and m$\angle C = 48$. Find m$\angle ADB$.

3 In rhombus *RSTV*, *RS* = 4*x* − 2 and *ST* = 3*x* + 3. Find the value of *x* and the length of *RS*.

4

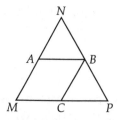

△*MNP* is an equilateral triangle and *MABC* is a rhombus. If *A* is midpoint of $\overline{MN}$ and the perimeter of △*MNP* is 12, what is the perimeter of *MABC*?

5

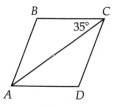

In rhombus *ABCD* with diagonal $\overline{AC}$, the measure of ∠*ACB* is 35°. Find m∠*ADC*.

6 In rhombus *ABCD*, *BC* = 2*x* − 2 and *CD* = *x* + 8. Find the length of side *CD*.

7

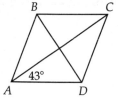

In rhombus *ABCD*, m∠*CAD* = 43. Find m∠*ADC*.

8 The vertices of quadrilateral *ABCD* are *A*(3, 2), *B*(5, 6), *C*(9, 8), and *D*(7, 4). Show by means of coordinate geometry that

a $\overline{AC}$ and $\overline{BD}$ bisect each other.
b *ABCD* is a rhombus.

9 The coordinates of the vertices of rhombus *PQRS* are *P*(−3, 1), *Q*(2, 6), *R*(*x*, *y*), and *S*(4, 0).

a Find the numerical coordinates of point *R*.
b Show by means of coordinate geometry that *PQ* = *PS*.
c Show by means of coordinate geometry that diagonals $\overline{PR}$ and $\overline{QS}$ are perpendicular to each other.

10 The vertices of quadrilateral *ABCD* are *A*(0, 0), *B*(*k*, 0), *C*(*x* + *k*, *k*), and *D*(*x*, *k*). If *k* > 0 and *x* > 0, show by means of coordinate geometry that

a *ABCD* is a parallelogram
b *ABCD* is *not* a rhombus.

11

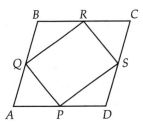

Given: Rhombus *ABCD* with *P*, *Q*, *R*, and *S* as midpoints of $\overline{AD}$, $\overline{AB}$, $\overline{BC}$, and $\overline{CD}$, respectively
Prove: *PQRS* is a rectangle.

12

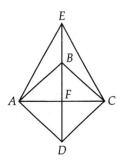

Given: Rhombus *ABCD*
Prove: △*ACE* is isosceles.

13

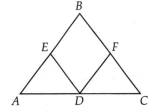

Given: $\overline{AB} \cong \overline{BC}$, and *E*, *F*, and *D* are midpoints of $\overline{AB}$, $\overline{BC}$, and $\overline{AC}$, respectively.
Prove: *EBFD* is a rhombus.

14

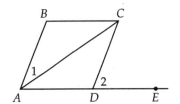

Given: Parallelogram *ABCD*, diagonal $\overline{AC}$ and $\overline{ADE}$
Prove: m∠2 > m∠1

15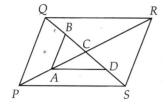

Given: *PQRS* is a rhombus, *B* is the midpoint of $\overline{QC}$, *D* is the midpoint of $\overline{SC}$, and *A* is the midpoint of $\overline{PC}$.

Prove: △*BAD* is an isosceles triangle.

16 Prove: If a quadrilateral is equilateral, it is a rhombus.

17 Prove: If the diagonal of a parallelogram bisects the angles whose vertices it joins, then the parallelogram is a rhombus.

18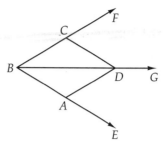

Given: $\overrightarrow{BG}$ bisects ∠*FBE*, $\overline{CD} \parallel \overrightarrow{BE}$, and $\overline{AD} \parallel \overrightarrow{BF}$.

Prove: *ABCD* is a rhombus.

10-6 Squares

A **square** is a rectangle that has two congruent consecutive sides.

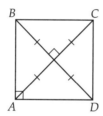

The following are properties of a square.

- A square is a rectangle in which all sides are congruent; $\overline{AB} \cong \overline{BC} \cong \overline{CD} \cong \overline{DA}$.
- Theorem 10.14. A square is a rhombus in which all angles are right angles; m∠*ABC* = m∠*BCD* = m∠*CDA* = m∠*DAB* = 90.
- Diagonals of a square are equal and perpendicular; $\overline{AC} \cong \overline{BD}$ and $\overline{AC} \perp \overline{BD}$.
- Diagonals of a square bisect the angles of the square.

Note: Since a square is a special kind of rectangle and also a special kind of rhombus, a square has all the properties of a rectangle and all the properties of a rhombus. Thus, a square is an *equilateral equiangular quadrilateral*.

To prove a quadrilateral is a square, use *any one* of these methods:

- Prove the quadrilateral is a rectangle in which two consecutive (or adjacent) sides are congruent. (Definition)
- Prove the quadrilateral is a rhombus one of whose angles is a right angle. (Theorem 10.14)

 **MODEL PROBLEM**

Given: △BAD is an isosceles right triangle, with ∠BAD a right angle and $\overline{BA} \cong \overline{AD}$. $\overline{AC}$ bisects $\overline{BD}$ at E, and $\overline{AE} \cong \overline{EC}$.

Prove: ABCD is a square.

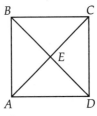

Statements	Reasons
1. $\overline{AE} \cong \overline{EC}$	1. Given.
2. $\overline{AC}$ bisects $\overline{BD}$ at E.	2. Given.
3. $\overline{BE} \cong \overline{ED}$	3. Definition of a bisector.
4. Quadrilateral ABCD is a parallelogram.	4. If the diagonals of a quadrilateral bisect each other, the quadrilateral is a parallelogram.
5. ∠BAD is a right angle.	5. Given.
6. ABCD is a rectangle.	6. A parallelogram with a right angle is a rectangle.
7. $\overline{BA} \cong \overline{AD}$	7. Given.
8. ABCD is a square.	8. If a rectangle has two congruent consecutive sides, the rectangle is a square.

 Practice

1 Which statement is *false*?

   (1) A parallelogram is a quadrilateral.
   (2) A rectangle is a parallelogram.
   (3) A square is a rhombus.
   (4) A rectangle is a square.

2 A quadrilateral *must* be a square if its:

   (1) opposite sides and opposite angles are congruent
   (2) diagonals are congruent
   (3) sides and angles are congruent
   (4) diagonals bisect each other and are perpendicular to each other

3 Which statement is *not always true*?

   (1) A square is a rhombus.
   (2) A square is a rectangle.
   (3) A parallelogram is a polygon.
   (4) A trapezoid is a parallelogram.

4

Quadrilateral ABCD is a square with diagonal $\overline{AC}$. Which is *not* true?

   (1) ∠2 ≅ ∠3
   (2) ∠1 ≅ ∠3
   (3) $\overline{AC} \cong \overline{DC}$
   (4) ∠1 ≅ ∠2

5 A parallelogram *must* be a square if the diagonals are:

  (1) congruent and bisect the angles to which they are drawn
  (2) congruent and do not bisect the angles to which they are drawn
  (3) not congruent and bisect the angles to which they are drawn
  (4) not congruent and do not bisect the angles to which they are drawn

6 If the length of a side of a square is represented by x, then the length of the diagonal of the square in terms of x is

  (1) $x\sqrt{3}$ (3) $\dfrac{x\sqrt{3}}{2}$

  (2) $x\sqrt{2}$ (4) $\dfrac{x\sqrt{2}}{2}$

7 The coordinates of the vertices of quadrilateral *DAVE* are $D(-2, -1)$, $A(2, 2)$, $V(5, -2)$, and $E(1, -5)$. Prove that quadrilateral *DAVE* is a square.

8 If the coordinates of quadrilateral *MATH* are $M(5, 0)$, $A(2, 4)$, $T(-2, 1)$, and $H(1, -3)$, prove that the quadrilateral is a square.

9 Prove: Diagonals of a square are perpendicular to each other.

10 Points $P(-x, 0)$, $Q(x, 0)$, $R(x, y)$, and $S(-x, y)$ form a quadrilateral.

  a Prove that quadrilateral *PQRS* is a rectangle
  b If $x = 10$ and $y = 7$, prove that *PQRS* is *not* a square.

11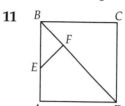

Given: *ABCD* is a square. $\overline{AD} \cong \overline{FD}$ and $\overline{EF} \perp \overline{BD}$.
Prove: (a) $\overline{BF} \cong \overline{EF}$ and (b) $\overline{EF} \cong \overline{EA}$.

12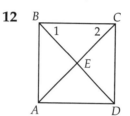

Given: Rhombus *ABCD* with diagonals $\overline{AC}$ and $\overline{BD}$ intersecting at *E*. $\angle 1 \cong \angle 2$.
Prove: *ABCD* is a square.

10-7 Trapezoids

A **trapezoid** is a quadrilateral having two, and only two, sides parallel.

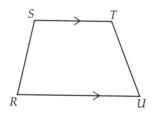

The following are properties of a trapezoid.

- A trapezoid has only one pair of parallel sides. These are called the **bases** of a trapezoid. Referring to the figure above, $\overline{ST} \parallel \overline{RU}$.
- The nonparallel sides of a trapezoid are the **legs**. In the figure above, $\overline{RS}$ and $\overline{UT}$ are legs of trapezoid *RSTU*.

- If one leg is perpendicular to the bases, then the figure is a **right trapezoid**. In the figure below, $\overline{RS} \perp \overline{RU}$ and $\overline{RS} \perp \overline{ST}$.

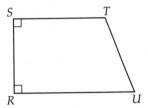

An **isosceles trapezoid** is a trapezoid in which the nonparallel sides are congruent.

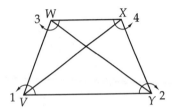

The following are properties of a isosceles trapezoid.

- Trapezoid with congruent legs. In the figure above, $\overline{VW} \cong \overline{YX}$.
- The diagonals are congruent. In the figure above, $\overline{VX} \cong \overline{YW}$.
- The **base angles** are congruent. In the figure above, $\angle 1 \cong \angle 2$ and $\angle 3 \cong \angle 4$.

To prove a quadrilateral is a trapezoid, prove that there is only one pair of parallel sides.

To prove a quadrilateral is an isosceles trapezoid, prove that there is only one pair of parallel sides, and that the nonparallel sides are congruent.

The **median** of a trapezoid is the line segment that joins the midpoints of the nonparallel sides. The median is also parallel to the bases and its measure is one-half the sum of the bases. For example:

In the trapezoid below, the bases are 8 and 20 and the median $\overline{AB}$ has a measure that is $\frac{1}{2}(8 + 20) = 14$.

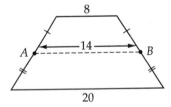

1 The bases of an isosceles trapezoid $ABCD$ measure 10 cm and 20 cm. The height (altitude) is 12 cm. How long are the legs AB and CD?

SOLUTION

In the figure, the shorter base is centered over the larger base. The altitudes drawn from the upper vertices form a rectangle with sides 10 cm and 12 cm.

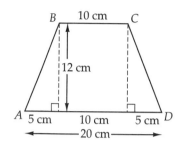

The lower base is evenly divided to the left and right of the rectangle, so that each remaining segment is 5 cm.

The two right triangles are formed with legs 5 cm and 12 cm, and hypotenuse $\overline{AB}$ is a leg of the trapezoid.

Substituting the values in the Pythagorean theorem:
$a^2 + b^2 = c^2$
$5^2 + 12^2 = 25 + 144 = 169 = c^2$
$c = \sqrt{169} = 13$

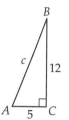

ANSWER: 13 cm

2 Given: Isosceles trapezoid $ABCD$ with $\overline{BC} \parallel \overline{AD}$

If $m\angle A = 4(x + 5)$ and $m\angle D = 2(x + 15) + 8$, find $m\angle A$, $m\angle B$, $m\angle C$, and $m\angle D$.

SOLUTION

In an isosceles trapezoid, the base angles are equal. Thus, we can use the fact that $m\angle A = m\angle D$ to solve for x.
$4(x + 5) = 2(x + 15) + 8$
$4x + 20 = 2x + 30 + 8$
$\quad\quad 2x = 18$
$\quad\quad\ x = 9$

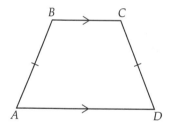

Substitute 9 for the value of x into the equations for the measures of angles A and D.
$m\angle A = 4(x + 5) = 4(9 + 5) = 56$
$m\angle D = 2(x + 15) + 8 = 2(9 + 15) + 8 = 56$

Angles A and B are supplementary.
$m\angle A + m\angle B = 180$
$\quad 56 + m\angle B = 180$
$\quad\quad\quad m\angle B = 124$

Since base angles B and C are equal, $m\angle C = 124$.

ANSWERS: $m\angle A = 56$, $m\angle B = 124$, $m\angle C = 124$, $m\angle D = 56$

3 The coordinates of the vertices of quadrilateral $ABCD$ are $A(3, 1)$, $B(11, -3)$, $C(10, 3)$, and $D(6, 5)$.

a Show, by means of coordinate geometry, that $ABCD$ is a trapezoid and state a reason for the conclusion.

b Show, by means of coordinate geometry, that $ABCD$ is *not* an isosceles trapezoid.

SOLUTION

a Find the slope of each side to determine if any sides are parallel.

$$\text{Slope}_{AB} = \frac{1 - (-3)}{3 - 11} = \frac{4}{-8} = -\frac{1}{2}$$

$$\text{Slope}_{BC} = \frac{-3 - 3}{11 - 10} = \frac{-6}{1} = -6$$

$$\text{Slope}_{CD} = \frac{3 - 5}{10 - 6} = \frac{-2}{4} = -\frac{1}{2}$$

$$\text{Slope}_{DA} = \frac{5 - 1}{6 - 3} = \frac{4}{3}$$

Since only two sides, $\overline{AB}$ and $\overline{CD}$, have the same slope, then only two sides are parallel: $\overline{AB} \parallel \overline{CD}$. Therefore, quadrilateral $ABCD$ is a trapezoid.

b Find the length of the legs.

$$\text{Distance}_{BC} = \sqrt{(11 - 10)^2 + (-3 - 3)^2} = \sqrt{1 + 36} = \sqrt{37}$$

$$\text{Distance}_{DA} = \sqrt{(6 - 3)^2 + (5 - 1)^2} = \sqrt{9 + 16} = \sqrt{25}$$

Since the length of the legs are not equal, $\sqrt{37} \neq \sqrt{25}$, the trapezoid is *not* isosceles.

 Practice

---

1 Which of the following statements about the diagonals of an isosceles trapezoid is *always* true?

(1) They bisect each other.
(2) They are congruent.
(3) They are perpendicular to each other.
(4) They divide the trapezoid into four congruent triangles.

2

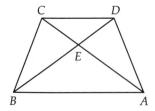

Given: Isosceles trapezoid $ABCD$, with $\overline{AB} \parallel \overline{DC}$ and diagonal $\overline{DB}$ intersects $\overline{AC}$ at E. Which statement is *not* true?

(1) $\overline{AC} \cong \overline{BD}$
(2) $\angle CDB \cong \angle DBA$
(3) $\angle ADC \cong \angle ABC$
(4) $\angle CBA \cong \angle DAB$

3 Find the missing angle measures for x, y, and z in each of the isosceles trapezoids.

a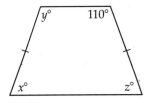

b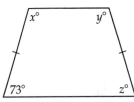

c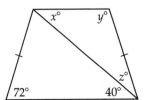

d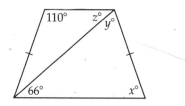

e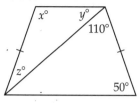

f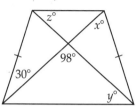

4 Given: Quadrilateral *MATH* has vertices *M*(−8, 2), *A*(0, 6), *T*(8, 0), and *H*(−8, −8).
Prove: Quadrilateral *MATH* is an isosceles trapezoid.

5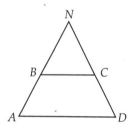

Given: *ABCD* is an isosceles trapezoid with $\overline{BC} \parallel \overline{AD}$.
Prove: △*NBC* is isosceles.

6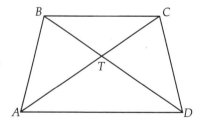

Given: Isosceles trapezoid *ABCD*, with $\overline{AB} \cong \overline{DC}$ and $\overline{BC} \parallel \overline{AD}$
Prove: △*ADB* ≅ △*DAC*

7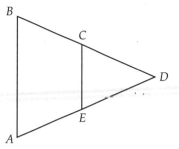

Given: Triangle *ABD* and trapezoid *ABCE*. $\overline{BD} \cong \overline{AD}$ and $\overline{AB} \parallel \overline{CE}$.
Prove: *ABCE* is an isosceles trapezoid.

8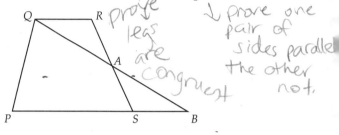

prove legs are congruent

↓ *prove one pair of sides parallel the other not.*

Given: Quadrilateral *PQRS*, $\overline{QAB}$, $\overline{RAS}$, and $\overline{PSB}$. $\overline{QB}$ bisects $\overline{RS}$, and $\overline{PSB} \parallel \overline{QR}$.
Prove: $\overline{QA} \cong \overline{AB}$

9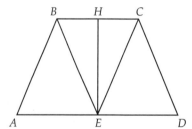

Given: Isosceles trapezoid *ABCD* with ∠*A* ≅ ∠*D*, $\overline{AD} \parallel \overline{BC}$, and *E* and *H* are midpoints of $\overline{AD}$ and $\overline{BC}$, respectively.
Prove: (a) $\overline{BE} \cong \overline{CE}$ (b) $\overline{EH} \perp \overline{BC}$

10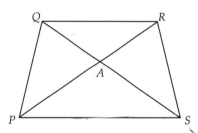

Given: Isosceles trapezoid *PQRS* with $\overline{PQ} \cong \overline{RS}$ and $\overline{QR} \parallel \overline{PS}$
Prove: △*PAQ* ≅ △*SAR*

11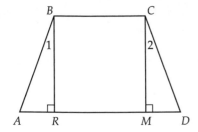

Given: Trapezoid $ABCD$ with $\overline{AB} \cong \overline{CD}$;
$\overline{BR} \perp \overline{AD}, \overline{CM} \perp \overline{AD}$
Prove: $\angle 1 \cong \angle 2$

12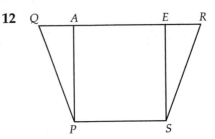

Given: Trapezoid $PQRS$, with $\angle Q \cong \angle R$;
$\overline{PA} \perp \overline{QR}, \overline{SE} \perp \overline{QR}$
Prove: $\overline{QP} \cong \overline{RS}$

10-8 Kites

The **kite** is a quadrilateral with two distinct pairs of adjacent sides congruent.

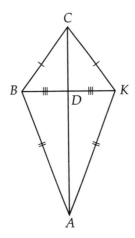

The following are properties of a kite.

- A kite is formed by the union of two distinct isosceles triangles with the same base; isosceles $\triangle BCK$ and isosceles $\triangle BAK$ with base $\overline{BK}$.
- Only two pairs of adjacent sides are congruent; $\overline{BC} \cong \overline{CK}$ and $\overline{AB} \cong \overline{AK}$.
- A kite has only one line of symmetry (the **symmetry diagonal**), which joins the common endpoints of the congruent sides. Diagonal $\overline{AC}$ joins common endpoints A and C.
- The symmetry diagonal is the perpendicular bisector of the other diagonal; $\overline{AC}$ bisects $\overline{BK}$ such that $\overline{BD} \cong \overline{DK}$.
- The symmetry diagonal bisects the angles whose vertices are its endpoints; $\overline{AC}$ bisects $\angle C$ and $\angle A$.
- Opposite angles not joined by the symmetry diagonal are congruent; $\angle CBA \cong \angle CKA$.

Practice

1 Define a kite. Explain why a kite is not the same as a rhombus.

Exercises 2–9: Using the figure of a kite below, state whether each of the following is *True* or *False*.

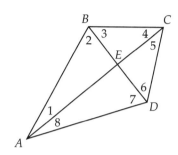

2 $\overline{BD} \perp \overline{CA}$

3 $\angle 5 \cong \angle 4$

4 $\angle 5 \cong \angle 6$

5 $\overline{ED} \cong \overline{BE}$

6 $\angle 3 \cong \angle 6$

7 $\overline{BD}$ is the perpendicular bisector of $\overline{CA}$.

8 $\angle 3 \cong \angle 2$

9 $\overline{CA}$ is the perpendicular bisector of $\overline{BD}$.

10 Referring to the figure for exercises 2–9, find

    a the symmetric diagonal.
    b all the pairs of congruent angles.

11
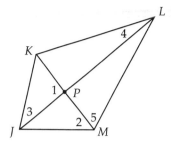

If *JKLM* is a kite with symmetry line $\overline{JL}$, find the value for each of the following:

    a m∠1
    b m∠2 if m∠3 = 45
    c length of $\overline{KM}$ if *KP* = 8.5
    d m∠4 and m∠KLM if m∠5 = 65

12
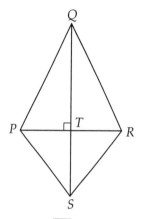

Given: $\overline{QS}$ is the perpendicular bisector of $\overline{PR}$, with $\overline{QT} > \overline{ST}$.
Prove: *PQRS* is a kite.

10-9 Areas of Polygons

The *area* of a polygonal region is the number of area units contained within the region. The table below presents the formulas used to find the area of common polygons.

Area Formulas

Polygon	Formula	
Triangle	$A = \frac{1}{2}(\text{base} \times \text{height}) = \frac{1}{2}bh$ 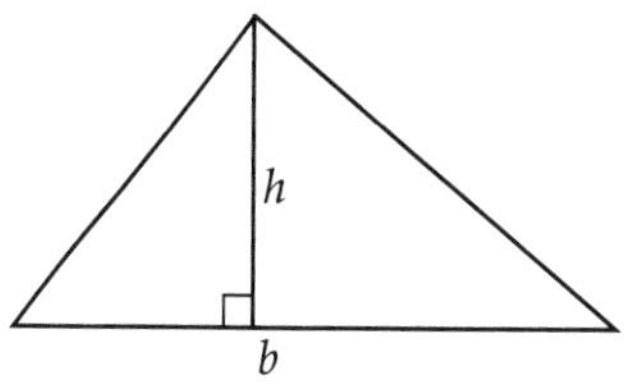	

(continued)

Polygon	Formula
Equilateral triangle	$A = \frac{s^2\sqrt{3}}{4}$, where s = side 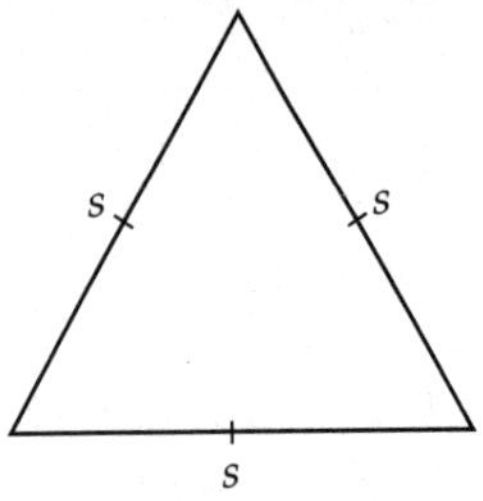
Parallelogram	$A = \text{base} \times \text{height} = bh$ 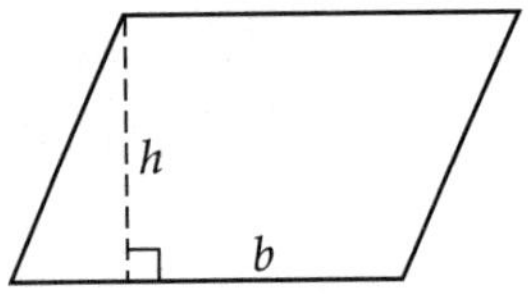
Rectangle	$A = \text{base} \times \text{height} = bh$ 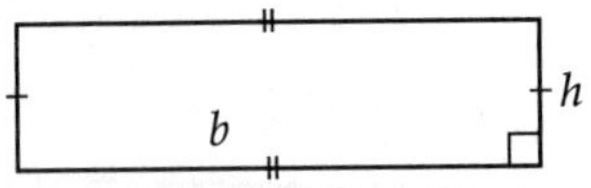
Square	$A = \text{base} \times \text{height or (side)}^2 = bh = s^2$ 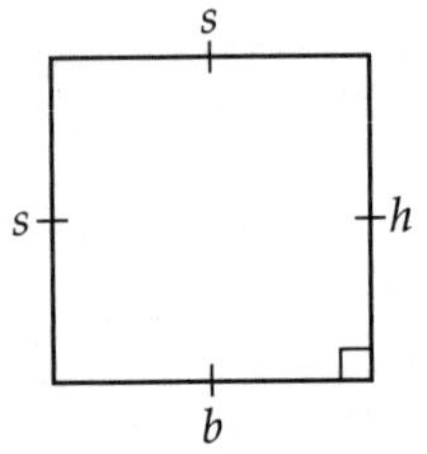 OR $A = \frac{1}{2}(\text{diagonal} \times \text{diagonal}) = \frac{1}{2}(\text{diagonal})^2$ 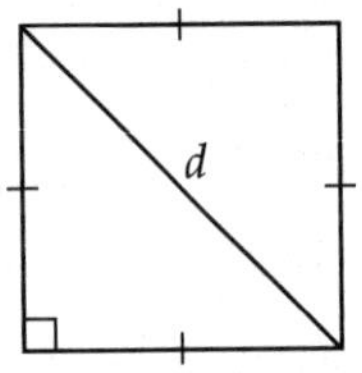
Rhombus	$A = \text{base} \times \text{height} = bh$ OR $A = \frac{1}{2}(\text{diagonal}_1 \times \text{diagonal}_2)$ 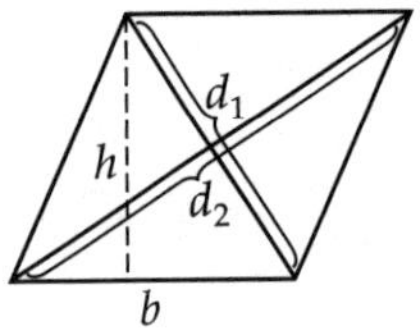
Trapezoid	$A = \frac{1}{2}(\text{height}) \times (\text{base}_1 + \text{base}_2) = \frac{1}{2}h(b_1 + b_2)$ 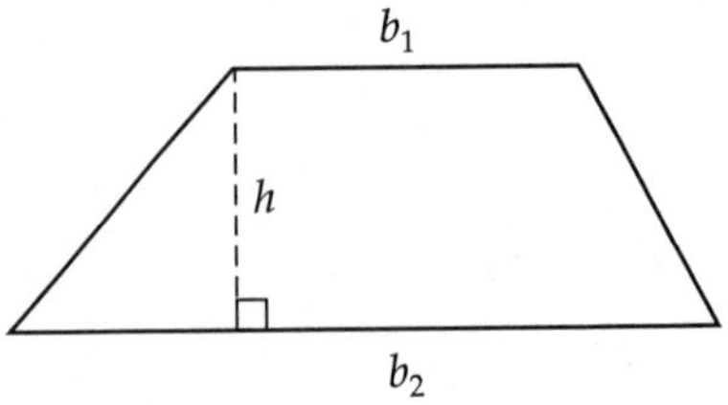 OR $A = \text{height} \times \text{median} = hm$ 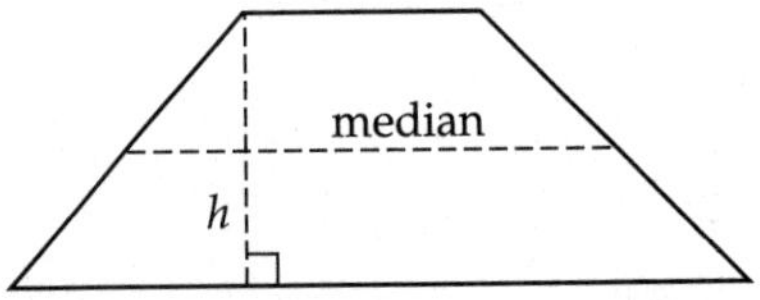

MODEL PROBLEMS

1 The vertices of $\triangle BEN$ are $B(2, 1)$, $E(4, 7)$, and $N(8, 3)$.

    a Show that it is an isosceles triangle. State your reasons.
    b Find the area of $\triangle BEN$.

SOLUTION

    a To determine whether or not $\triangle BEN$ is isosceles, find the distance, d, of each side.

$$d_{BE} = \sqrt{(2-4)^2 + (1-7)^2} = \sqrt{4+36} = \sqrt{40}$$
$$d_{EN} = \sqrt{(4-8)^2 + (7-3)^2} = \sqrt{16+16} = \sqrt{32}$$
$$d_{BN} = \sqrt{(2-8)^2 + (1-3)^2} = \sqrt{36+4} = \sqrt{40}$$

    Since two of the sides are equal, BE and BN, $\triangle BEN$ is isosceles.

    b To find the area, we need to find the altitude to the base, $\overline{EN}$. Since the altitude of an isosceles triangle is perpendicular to the base at its midpoint, we need to find the midpoint and the length of that altitude drawn to the midpoint.

    Midpoint of $\overline{EN}$ is $\left(\frac{4+8}{2}, \frac{7+3}{2}\right) = (6, 5)$. Call that point $P(6, 5)$.

$$d_{BP} = \sqrt{(2-6)^2 + (1-5)^2} = \sqrt{16+16} = \sqrt{32} = \text{length of altitude}$$
$$\text{Area} = \tfrac{1}{2}(\text{base} \times \text{altitude}) = \tfrac{1}{2}(\sqrt{32} \times \sqrt{32}) = \tfrac{1}{2} \times 32 = 16 \text{ square units}$$

ALTERNATE SOLUTION: THE BOX METHOD

Plot the coordinates of $\triangle BEN$ and *box-in* the figure as illustrated.

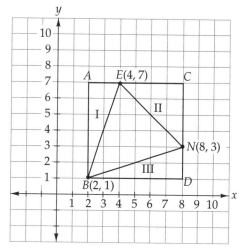

Find the area of the rectangle formed and subtract the areas of the triangles formed that are not part of the given figure, $\triangle BEN$. In the diagram, rectangle $BACD$ has an area $6 \times 6 = 36$.

The areas of each of the three triangles formed are:

$\triangle\text{I} = 6$, $\triangle\text{II} = 8$, and $\triangle\text{III} = 6$

Thus, area of $\triangle BEN$ = area $BACD - (\triangle\text{I} + \triangle\text{II} + \triangle\text{III})$
= $36 - (6 + 8 + 6)$
= $36 - 20$
= 16 square units

2 Quadrilateral *JANE* has vertices $J(-4, -2)$, $A(0, 5)$, $N(9, 3)$, and $E(7, -4)$. On graph paper, plot and draw quadrilateral *JANE* and find its area.

SOLUTION

When the polygon does not have sides parallel to either axis, we can find the area by *boxing in* the figure, which means drawing lines parallel to the axes and through the given vertices, forming rectangles and triangles, as in the previous model problem.

The area of the larger figure, the box *WXYZ*, equals $9 \times 13 = 117$ square units.

As illustrated, the area of each triangle is:

$\triangle I = 11$, $\triangle II = 14$, $\triangle III = 9$, and $\triangle IV = 7$

The area of JANE =
area $WXYZ - (\triangle I + \triangle II + \triangle III + \triangle IV) =$
$117 - (11 + 14 + 9 + 7) = 117 - 41 = 76$ square units

ANSWER: The area of *JANE* is 76 square units.

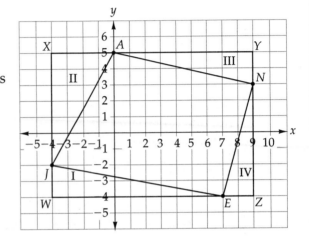

3 If the perimeter of a rhombus is 52, and one of its diagonals measures 10, what is the area of the rhombus?

SOLUTION

Since all sides of a rhombus are equal, $52 \div 4 = 13$. The given diagonal is 10. The second diagonal is perpendicular to and bisects the original diagonal. A 5-12-13 right triangle is formed.

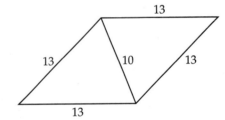

Thus, the longer diagonal is 24,
and the area $= \frac{1}{2}(10)(24) = 120$.

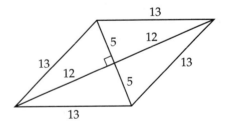

ALTERNATE SOLUTION

$4 \times$ area of one triangle $= 4\left(\frac{1}{2}(5)(12)\right) = 4(30) = 120$

ANSWER: The area of the rhombus is 120 square units.

Practice

1   A side of a triangle measures 12 and the altitude to this side measures 5. A second side of the triangle measures 15. Find the altitude drawn to this side.

2   A triangle is equal in area to a square whose sides measure 12. If the base of the triangle has a length of 18, find the length of the altitude drawn to this side of the triangle.

3   The measures of the legs of a right triangle are in the ratio 3:4. If the area of the triangle is 54, what are the lengths of the three sides of the triangle?

4   What are the dimensions of a rectangle whose area is 20 ft^2 and whose perimeter is 18 ft?

5   The base of a rectangle is given as x and the perimeter is 20.

   a   Represent the height in terms of x.
   b   Represent the area of the rectangle in terms of x.

6   Find, in terms of x, the area of a square with a side that measures

   a x
   b $3x$
   c $x + 2$
   d $x - 2$
   e $2x + 1$

7   Find the area of a square whose diagonal is

   a   5
   b   6
   c   7
   d $\sqrt{2}$
   e $3\sqrt{2}$

8   If each side of a square is doubled, the area of the new square is increased by 363 cm^2. What is the length of a side of the original square?

9   Find the area of a rhombus if the diagonals are

   a   4 and 6
   b   6 and 15
   c   5 and 8
   d   6 and $6\sqrt{3}$
   e   5 and 9

10   If the area of a rhombus is 144 square inches and one diagonal is 24 inches, what is the length of a side of the rhombus?

11   Given rhombus $ABCD$ with diagonals $\overline{BD}$ and $\overline{AC}$. If $AB = 13$ and $AC = 24$, find

   a   the length of BD.
   b   the area of rhombus $ABCD$.

12   Find the area of a rhombus if one angle measures 60° and the longer diagonal measures 12.

13   If the area of a square equals the area of a rhombus with diagonals 9 and 8, find a side of the square.

14   If the diagonals of a rhombus are 10 and 24,

   a   find the side of the rhombus.
   b   find the area of the rhombus.
   c   find the length of the altitude of the rhombus.

15   Determine, in terms of x, the area of the parallelograms whose base (b) and height (h) are

   a $b = 3x, h = 7$
   b $b = 2x, h = 5x$
   c $b = x + 3, h = 4$
   d $b = 6, h = 3x - 2$
   e $b = x - 3, h = 2x$

16   In a parallelogram whose area is 60, a side is represented by $4x - 4$ and the height drawn to that side is 5.

   a   Find the value of x.
   b   Find the length of the side represented by $4x - 4$.

17   In a parallelogram with area of 40, a side is 3 less than the altitude drawn to that side. Find the altitude of the parallelogram.

18   Find the area of a parallelogram if one base angle is 60° and the measures of the sides including the angle are 6 and 9.

19   Find the area of a parallelogram if one base angle measures 45° and the measures of the sides including this angle are 6 and 10.

20 The diagonals of a rhombus measure 15 and 20 and the rhombus is equal in area to a trapezoid whose height is 10. If one base of the trapezoid is twice the second base, find the bases of the trapezoid.

21 Using the given information, find the area of the trapezoid.

    a height = 8 and median = 12
    b height = 13 and median = 20
    c height = 6 and bases are 8 and 12

22 In the isosceles trapezoid *SIGN*, the bases are 20 and 28 and the legs are 5. Find the area of the trapezoid.

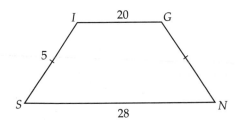

23 In trapezoid *PRAT*, the length of the bases $\overline{RA}$ and $\overline{PT}$ are 20 and 30. If m∠P = 30 and PR = 8, what is the area of trapezoid *PRAT*?

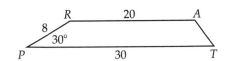

24

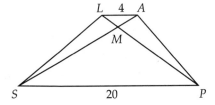

Quadrilateral *SLAP* is a trapezoid with bases $\overline{LA}$ and $\overline{SP}$, and diagonals $\overline{SA}$ and $\overline{LP}$ intersect at *M*. If SP = 20 and LA = 4, and the area of the trapezoid is 72,

    a find the altitude of trapezoid *SLAP*.
    b find the length of the perpendicular drawn from point *M* to $\overline{SP}$.

25 In trapezoid *QRST*, RS = 10, QT = 20, and height AB = 12.

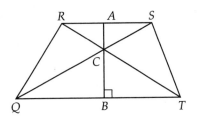

If *x* represents the length of *AC*,

    a write an equation that can be used to find *AC*.
    b solve for *x*.
    c find the area of △*RCS* and △*QCT*.

26 Trapezoid *ABCD* has vertices $A(3, -1)$, $B(7, -1)$, $C(7, 10)$, and $D(3, 7)$.

    a Find the area of the trapezoid.
    b Find the coordinates of the midpoint of the diagonal $\overline{AC}$.

27 △*JEN* has coordinates $J(2, 3)$, $E(6, 0)$, and $N(12, 8)$.

    a Show by means of coordinate geometry that △*JEN* is a right triangle. State clearly a reason for your conclusion.
    b Find the area of △*JEN*.

28 The vertices of △*PAT* are $P(0, 0)$, $A(6, 2)$, and $T(12, 10)$.

    a Find the area of △*PAT*.
    b Find the length of $\overline{AT}$.
    c Find the length of the altitude drawn from *P* to $\overline{AT}$.

29 The vertices of △*SAM* are $S(-1, 2)$, $A(3, 8)$, and $M(5, -2)$.

    a Prove, using coordinate geometry, that △*SAM* is an isosceles right triangle.
    b Find the area of △*SAM*.
    c Find the length of the altitude from *S* to the hypotenuse. (Leave the answer in simplest radical form.)

30 Find the area of a pentagon *SIMON* whose vertices are $S(-2, -5)$, $I(-2, 2)$, $M(2, 4)$, $O(5, 2)$, and $N(4, -2)$.

31 Find the area of pentagon *JANET* with vertices at coordinates $J(-5, 6)$, $A(1, -7)$, $N(6, 0)$, $E(1, 3)$, and $T(1, 6)$.

32 Find the area of quadrilateral *RYAN* with coordinate vertices $R(-1, 1)$, $Y(3, 4)$, $A(8, 5)$, and $N(5, -3)$.

33 Quadrilateral *NICK* has coordinates $N(0, 3m)$, $I(3m, 3m)$, $C(4m, 0)$, and $K(-m, 0)$. Prove by coordinate geometry that quadrilateral *NICK* is an isosceles trapezoid.

34 If the coordinates of quadrilateral *JOHN* are $J(-3, -2)$, $O(9, 2)$, $H(1, 6)$, and $N(-5, 4)$, using coordinate geometry, prove that quadrilateral *JOHN* is a right trapezoid.

35 The coordinates of trapezoid *ABCD* are $A(3, 0)$, $B(7, 0)$, $C(7, 11)$, and $D(3, 8)$.

   a Find the area of the trapezoid.
   b Find the perimeter of the trapezoid.
   c Find the slope of diagonal $\overline{BD}$.
   d Find the coordinates of the midpoint of diagonal $\overline{BD}$.

CHAPTER REVIEW

1 Which statement is *always* true?

   (1) The diagonals of a parallelogram are perpendicular.
   (2) The diagonals of a parallelogram bisect the angles of the parallelogram.
   (3) The diagonals of a parallelogram are congruent.
   (4) The diagonals of a parallelogram bisect each other.

2 Given *any* parallelogram *ABCD*, which statement is *never* true?

   (1) $\overline{AB} \cong \overline{DC}$
   (2) $\angle A \cong \angle C$
   (3) $\overline{AC} \perp \overline{DB}$
   (4) $m\angle B + m\angle C = 360$

3 Which quadrilateral does *not always* have congruent diagonals?

   (1) rhombus
   (2) square
   (3) rectangle
   (4) isosceles trapezoid

4 If the diagonals of a quadrilateral are perpendicular and *not congruent*, the quadrilateral could be:

   (1) a rhombus
   (2) a rectangle
   (3) an isosceles trapezoid
   (4) a square

5 Which statement is *not* true?

   (1) A square is a rectangle.
   (2) A square is a rhombus.
   (3) A rhombus is a square.
   (4) A rectangle is a parallelogram.

6 If the midpoints of the sides of a quadrilateral are joined consecutively, the resulting figure will always be a:

   (1) rhombus
   (2) square
   (3) rectangle
   (4) parallelogram

7 The coordinates of the vertices of parallelogram *FISH* are *F*(0, 0), *I*(5, 0), *S*(8, 1), and *H*(*x*, 1). The numerical value of *x* is:

(1) 1
(2) 2
(3) 3
(4) 4

8 If quadrilateral *PQRS* is parallelogram, which statement is true?

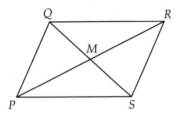

(1) $\overline{QS} \perp \overline{PR}$
(2) $\overline{QS} \cong \overline{PR}$
(3) $\overline{QS}$ bisects ∠*PQR* and ∠*PSR*.
(4) $\overline{QS}$ and $\overline{PR}$ bisect each other.

9 To prove that a parallelogram is a rectangle, you *must* show that:

(1) the diagonals are congruent
(2) the diagonals are perpendicular to each other
(3) opposite sides are congruent
(4) adjacent sides are congruent

10 Name the special quadrilateral that corresponds to each set of marked diagonals.

a

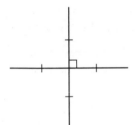

b

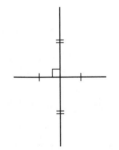

c

d

11 If the measures of two opposite angles of a parallelogram are represented by $3x + 40$ and $x + 50$, what is the value of *x*?

12 If the diagonals of a rhombus have lengths of 8 and 6, find the length of a side of the rhombus.

13

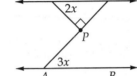

In the figure, $\overleftrightarrow{CD} \parallel \overleftrightarrow{AB}$, $\overline{CP} \perp \overline{AD}$, m∠*DAB* = 3*x*, and m∠*DCP* = 2*x*. Find the value of *x*.

14 Two consecutive angles of a parallelogram measure $3x + 20$ and $7x - 40$. Find the value of *x*.

15 If the length of a side of a square is $\sqrt{2}$, what is the length of the diagonal of the square?

16

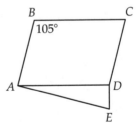

In the figure above, *ABCD* is a parallelogram. $\overline{ED} \perp \overline{AD}$, ∠*C* ≅ ∠*E*, and m∠*B* = 105. Find m∠*DAE*.

17 The coordinates of two of the vertices of parallelogram *MARK* are *A*(2, 5) and *K*(6, 1). What are the coordinates of the point of intersection of the diagonals?

18 In rectangle *ABCD* with diagonals $\overline{AC}$ and $\overline{BD}$, if $AC = 3x - 15$ and $BD = 7x - 55$, what is the value of *x*?

19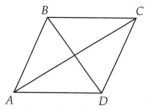

In parallelogram *ABCD*, if m∠*ACD* = 4*x* − 2 and m∠*CAB* = 3*x* + 6,

a find m∠*ACD* and m∠*CAB*.
b If m∠*CAD* = 2*x* + 44, find m∠*CAD*. What kind of parallelogram is *ABCD*?

20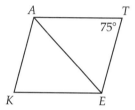

In rhombus *KATE*, with diagonal $\overline{AE}$ and m∠*ATE* = 75, find the measure of ∠*AEK*.

21 What is the length of a rectangle with an area of 20 sq ft and a width of 4 ft?

22 If the coordinates of the vertices of rectangle *VERA* are *V*(−1, 5), *E*(3, 5), and *R*(3, 1), what are the coordinates of vertex *A*?

23 If the length of a side of a square is 3, what is the length of the diagonal?

24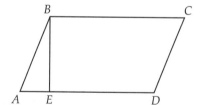

In parallelogram *ABCD*, if the altitude $\overline{BE}$ is drawn to side *AD*, and *BE* = *AE*, what is m∠*A*?

25 The shorter base of an isosceles trapezoid is 8 units, the longer base is 20 units, and each nonparallel side is 10 units. Find the height of the trapezoid.

26 Two congruent isosceles triangles are joined at their bases. Which special parallelogram is formed? Explain.

27 In parallelogram *PQRS*, if *QR* = *x* + 2, *PQ* = 3*x* − 8, and *PS* = 2*x* − 3, what is the value of *x*? What kind of figure is *PQRS*?

28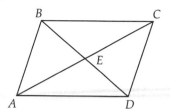

ABCD is a parallelogram. If m∠*DAB* = 2*x* + 8 and m∠*ABC* = 3(*x* + 34),

a find the measures of ∠*ABC*, ∠*BCD*, ∠*CDA*, and ∠*DAB*.
b If *AE* = 4*y*, *EC* = 6*y* − 36, *BE* = 3*x* − 1, and *ED* = *x* + 13, find the length of *AC* and *BD*.

29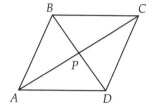

Diagonals of rhombus *ABCD* intersect at *P*. If m∠*ABP* = 5*x* + 10 and m∠*BAP* = 2*x* − 4, find m∠*DCB* and m∠*APB*.

30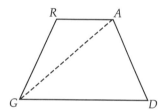

Trapezoid *GRAD* is an isosceles trapezoid with $\overline{GR} \cong \overline{DA}$ and diagonal $\overline{GA}$ bisects ∠*RGD*. If m∠*GAR* = 15, find

a m∠*R*
b m∠*RAD*
c m∠*GAD*
d m∠*D*

31 In rhombus *QRST*, diagonals $\overline{QS}$ and $\overline{RT}$ are drawn. Each side measures 20 and the measure of ∠*TQR* is 60°.

a Find the length of diagonal *QS* to the nearest integer.
b Find the length of the diagonal *RT* to the nearest integer.
c Using the results from parts **a** and **b**, find the area of the rhombus.

32 The vertices of △*ABC* are *A*(−3, 4), *B*(2, 9), and *C*(7, 4).

    a Show that △*ABC* is isosceles and state a reason for your conclusion.
    b Show that △*ABC* is also a right triangle and state a reason for your conclusion.
    c Find the area of △*ABC*.

33 Quadrilateral *DAVE* has vertices *D*(0, 0), *A*(0, 5), *V*(9, 8), and *E*(12, 4). Prove by coordinate geometry that quadrilateral *DAVE* is an isosceles trapezoid.

34 Quadrilateral *PQRS* has vertices *P*(−1, 0), *Q*(3, 3), *R*(6, −1), and *S*(2, −4). Prove that quadrilateral *PQRS* is a square.

35 Quadrilateral *ABCD* has vertices *A*(2, 3), *B*(7, 3), *C*(4, 7), and *D*(−1, 7). Using coordinate geometry, prove that *ABCD* is a rhombus.

36 Quadrilateral *LEAF* has vertices *L*(2, 5), *E*(7, 1), *A*(2, −3), and *F*(−3, 1). By means of coordinate geometry, prove that *LEAF* is a rhombus.

37

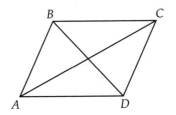

Given: Quadrilateral *TRIP*, with $\overline{TR} \cong \overline{RI}$, diagonals $\overline{TAI}$ and $\overline{RAP}$, and m∠1 = m∠2
Prove: (a) △*RAT* ≅ △*RAI* and (b) ∠3 ≅ ∠4

38

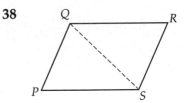

Given: Parallelogram *PQRS*. Diagonal $\overline{QS}$ bisects ∠*PQR*.
Prove: *PQRS* is a rhombus.

39

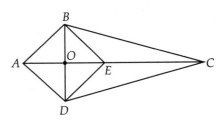

Given: *ABED* is a rhombus, and diagonal $\overline{BD}$ and $\overline{AOEC}$ intersect at *O*.
Prove: (a) $\overline{BC} \cong \overline{DC}$ and (b) ∠*ABC* ≅ ∠*ADC*

40

Given: Parallelogram *ABCD* with diagonals $\overline{AC}$ and $\overline{BD}$, and *AC* > *BD*
Prove: m∠*ADC* > m∠*DCB*

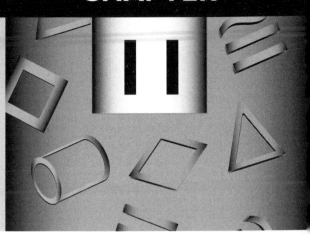

Geometry of Three Dimensions

In plane geometry we have learned about points, lines, angles, polygons, and circles. These figures have all of their points lying in the same plane. *Solid geometry* involves figures that require a third dimension; thickness (height or depth).

In solid geometry, we study pyramids, cones, spheres, cylinders, as well as other solid figures. These are figures whose parts *do not* all lie in the same plane. The study of space geometry or 3-dimensional geometry deals with real-world figures. We see objects representing these figures everywhere. Baseballs and basketballs are *spheres*, we eat ice-cream *cones*, farm silos and soup cans are *cylinders*, and of course we have seen pictures of Egyptian *pyramids*. However, in solid geometry we must think of these solids in a new way. If we picture in our minds the portion of space that a material solid occupies, rather than the object itself, we will be thinking of a geometric solid. Thus, a **geometric solid** is a three-dimensional figure.

11-1 Points, Lines, and Planes

A **plane** is an infinite set of points generating a flat unbounded surface with no thickness. An unbounded surface ia a plane surface that extends infinitely in all directions. A plane is also defined as a surface such that a straight line joining any two points in it lies entirely in that surface.

Coplanar points: A set of points all lying in the same plane. Any three points are coplanar. In the figure, points *A*, *B*, and *C* are coplanar.

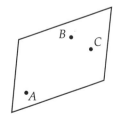

Coplanar lines: Lines that lie in the same plane.

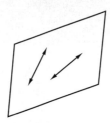

Skew lines are lines that do not lie in the same plane.

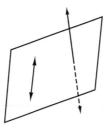

Note: As illustrated below, a line is either in a given plane, intersects it at one point, or does not intersect it at all and is parallel to the plane.

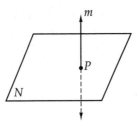

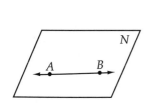

Two distinct points determine
a unique line in a plane.

Line *m* intersects plane *N*
at one point. Point *P*
belongs to both the line
and the plane.

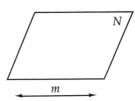

Line *m* is below plane *N*
and parallel to the plane.

A plane is determined by

(a) three noncollinear points

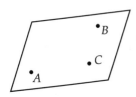

(b) a line and a point not on the line

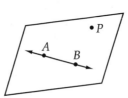

(c) two distinct intersecting lines

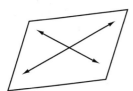

(d) two distinct parallel lines

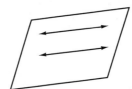

However, if two lines are *skew*, that is, neither parallel nor intersecting, there is no plane that will contain those lines. To illustrate skew lines, consider the cube below and skew lines *AB* and *CD*.

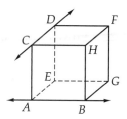

You should be able to find at least two more pairs of skew lines.

Planes that do not intersect are called **parallel**, as in the ceiling and floor of a room. See the planes *M* and *N* below. If two distinct planes intersect, then their intersection is a line, *m*, as in the planes *X* and *Y* below.

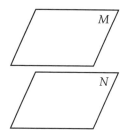

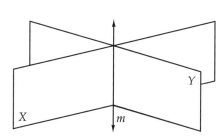

 Practice

Exercises 1–10: State whether each of the following is *True* or *False*.

1 There is exactly one plane containing two nonintersecting lines.

2 There is exactly one plane containing two nonparallel lines.

3 There is exactly one plane containing two lines with exactly one point in common.

4 There is exactly one plane containing a line and a point not on a line.

5 There is exactly one plane containing three noncollinear points.

6 Every triangle is a plane figure.

7 Two parallel lines must be coplanar.

8 Three parallel lines must be coplanar.

9 Two perpendicular lines must always be coplanar.

10 If each of two parallel lines is parallel to a plane, then the plane determined by the two lines is parallel to the given plane.

Exercises 11–19: Use the figure below and identify *one* other point in the plane determined by the given lines and points.

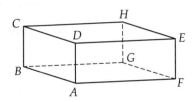

11 A, D, and E

12 $\overleftrightarrow{CD}$ and E

13 $\overleftrightarrow{DA}$ and $\overleftrightarrow{AF}$

14 $\overleftrightarrow{DH}$ and E

15 $\overleftrightarrow{DA}$ and $\overleftrightarrow{DH}$

16 $\overleftrightarrow{HG}$ and $\overleftrightarrow{BG}$

17 D, B, and E

18 A, B, and H

19 G, F, and C

20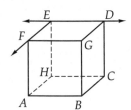

Using the lettered vertices in the cube above, name as many of these kinds of lines as possible:

a sets of parallel lines
b pairs of skew lines

Exercises 21–35: For each of the following, state none, one, or infinitely many.

21 How many lines can pass through a point in a plane?

22 How many lines can pass through a point in space?

23 How many planes can pass through a given point?

24 How many lines can be passed through two points in a plane?

25 How many lines can be passed through two points in space?

26 How many planes can be passed through two points in space?

27 How many planes can contain a given line in space?

28 In how many points can a line intersect a plane when the line does not lie in the plane?

29 How many lines can intersect plane M at point P?

30 How many planes can intersect line k at one of its points P?

31 When two planes intersect, how many lines are formed?

32 How many planes can be passed through a line and a point *not* on that line?

33 How many planes can be passed through a pair of parallel lines?

34 How many planes can be passed through a pair of skew lines?

35 How many lines are parallel to a line through a point *not* on the line?

11-2 Perpendicular Lines, Planes, and Dihedral Angles

- Postulate. If a line, n, is perpendicular to a plane, M, then it is perpendicular to every line in M containing the intersection of n and M.

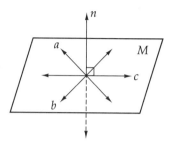

- Postulate. If a line is perpendicular to each of two intersecting lines at their point of intersection, as in a and b above, then it is perpendicular to the plane determined by those lines.
- Postulate. There is *one and only one* line perpendicular to a plane at a point in the plane. In the figure below, $\overleftrightarrow{BP}$ is perpendicular to plane M at point P.

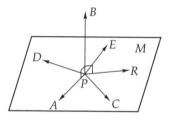

- Postulate. All the perpendiculars to a line, at a point on the line, lie in a plane that is perpendicular to the line at that point. In the figure above, all the lines $\overleftrightarrow{AP}$, $\overleftrightarrow{CP}$, $\overleftrightarrow{DP}$, $\overleftrightarrow{EP}$, and $\overleftrightarrow{RP}$ are perpendicular to $\overleftrightarrow{BP}$ at point P.
- Postulate. There is one and only one line perpendicular to a plane and passing through a point not in the plane. In the figure below, point P, not in plane Q, lies on the single line n, which is perpendicular to plane Q.

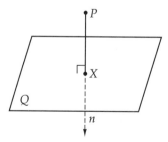

The **distance from a point to a plane** is the length of the perpendicular from the point to that plane. More specifically, in the figure above, the distance from point P (not in plane Q) to plane Q is the length of the perpendicular segment $\overline{PX}$, where X is in plane Q.

A straight line in a plane separates the plane into three parts: the line and two regions on either side of the line each, of which is called a **half plane**.

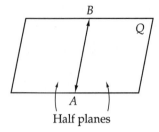

Half planes

However, if we consider the plane a flat piece of paper and fold the plane along the straight line, creasing the paper, we create a dihedral angle.

A **dihedral angle** is a set of points consisting of the union of two intersecting half planes and their common edge. Alternately, a dihedral angle is the union of two half planes with a common edge, as shown in the figure below.

The half planes that form the dihedral angle are called the *faces* of the dihedral angle. The line of intersection of the faces of the angle is called the *edge* of the dihedral angle, as in $\overline{BC}$.

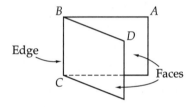

A dihedral angle is indicated by naming a point in one face, the edge, and a point in the other face, for example, the dihedral angle A–BC–D above. When there is no doubt as to the meaning, a dihedral angle may be indicated by naming only its edge: for example, ∠BC.

The **plane angle of a dihedral angle** is the angle formed by two rays, one in each face, and each perpendicular to the edge at the same point.

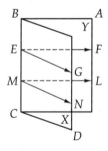

For example, in the dihedral angle A–BC–D, $\overrightarrow{EF}$ in face Y is perpendicular to $\overline{BC}$ at E, and $\overrightarrow{EG}$ in face X is perpendicular to $\overline{BC}$ at E. Thus, is ∠FEG is the plane angle of the dihedral angle.

• Theorem 11.1. The plane angles of a dihedral angle are congruent.

  In the figure above, if ∠FEG and ∠LMN are plane angles of dihedral angle A–BC–D, then ∠FEG ≅ ∠LMN.

The *measure of a dihedral angle* is the measure of its plane angle. Therefore, the number of degrees contained in dihedral angle A–BC–D is equal to the degrees contained in its plane angle FEG.

Following the analogy of the corresponding definitions in plane geometry, we can define *adjacent*, *vertical*, *supplementary*, and *complementary* dihedral angles.

Adjacent dihedral angles are two dihedral angles that have the same edge and a common face between them. In the figure below, dihedral angles *A–BC–D* and *E–BC–D* are adjacent dihedral angles. The plane determined by points *B*, *C*, and *D* is the common face between them.

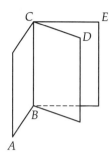

Congruent dihedral angles are dihedral angles that have the same measure.

- Theorem 11.2. Two dihedral angles are congruent if their plane angles are congruent.
- Theorem 11.3. If two dihedral angles are congruent, their plane angles are congruent.
- Theorem 11.4. If two planes intersect, the vertical dihedral angles formed are congruent.
  In the figure below, the vertical dihedral angles *A–BE–F* and *R–BE–D* are congruent.

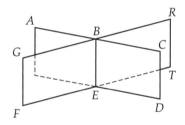

A dihedral angle is called *acute, right, obtuse,* or *straight* if its plane angle is acute, right, obtuse, or straight.

Two dihedral angles are called *complementary* or *supplementary* if their plane angles are correspondingly complementary or supplementary.

Two planes are *perpendicular* if they intersect and form right dihedral angles. In the figure below, dihedral angles *A–BC–D* and *G–BC–D* are right dihedral angles, such that plane *N* is perpendicular to plane *M*.

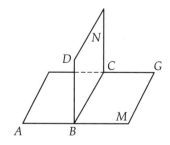

- Theorem 11.5. If a straight line is perpendicular to a plane, then every plane that contains the line is perpendicular to the plane. In the figure below, plane Q contains $\overleftrightarrow{RS}$, which is perpendicular to plane X, so that plane Q is perpendicular to plane X.

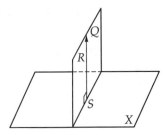

- Theorem 11.6. If each of two intersecting planes is perpendicular to a third plane, their intersection is also perpendicular to that plane. In the figure below, planes Q and R intersect in $\overleftrightarrow{AB}$; plane $Q \perp$ plane M and plane $R \perp$ plane M, such that $\overleftrightarrow{AB} \perp$ plane M.

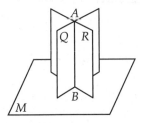

Note: To prove two planes are perpendicular to each other:
(1) Show that they form a dihedral angle whose plane angle is a right angle.
(2) Show that one plane contains a line that is perpendicular to the other plane.

 MODEL PROBLEM

Given: $PEST$ is a square.
      $PQRT$ is a square.
      $\overleftrightarrow{ST}$ and $\overleftrightarrow{TR}$ lie in plane M.
Prove: $\overleftrightarrow{PT} \perp$ plane M

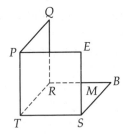

Statements	Reasons
1. $PEST$ is a square.	1. Given.
2. $\overleftrightarrow{PT} \perp \overleftrightarrow{ST}$	2. Adjacent sides of a square are perpendicular to each other.
3. $PQRT$ is a square.	3. Given.
4. $\overleftrightarrow{PT} \perp \overleftrightarrow{TR}$	4. Adjacent sides of a square are perpendicular to each other.
5. $\overleftrightarrow{ST}$ and $\overleftrightarrow{TR}$ lie in plane M.	5. Given.
6. $\overleftrightarrow{PT} \perp$ plane M	6. If a line is perpendicular to each of two intersecting lines at their point of intersection, then the line is perpendicular to the plane determined by these two intersecting lines.

Exercises 1–8: For each of the following, state *True* or *False*.

1 A line perpendicular to a plane is perpendicular to every line in the plane.

2 Two planes that are perpendicular to the same line are parallel.

3 A line perpendicular to each of two intersecting lines at their intersection is perpendicular to the plane they determine.

4 If a line is perpendicular to another line at a given point in the plane, then it is perpendicular to the plane.

5 In space, an infinite number of lines can be drawn perpendicular to a given line at a given point on the line.

6 All plane angles of a dihedral angle are congruent.

7 Through a point outside a plane, one and only one plane can be drawn perpendicular to the plane.

8 If two rays form a plane angle of a dihedral angle, then these rays lie in the same plane.

Exercises 9–14: For each of the following, state none, one, infinitely many, or state the number.

9 How many lines in a plane are perpendicular to a line at a point on the line?

10 How many lines in space are perpendicular to a line at a point on the line?

11 How many planes are determined by four points that *do not all lie* in the same plane?

12 If a line is perpendicular to a plane, how many planes containing this line are perpendicular to the plane?

13 If a line that is not perpendicular to a plane intersects the plane, how many planes containing this line are perpendicular to the plane?

14 If a line lies in a plane, how many planes containing this line are perpendicular to the plane?

15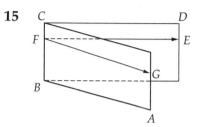

In the figure above,

a name the dihedral angle.
b name the plane angle of each dihedral angle.

16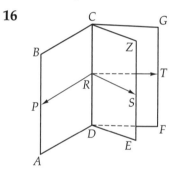

In the figure above, plane Z bisects dihedral angle B–DC–F.

a Name the congruent dihedral angles
b Name the congruent plane angles.

17 What is the set of all points equidistant from the faces of a dihedral angle?

18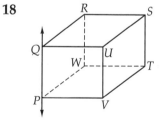

In the figure above, a rectangular prism or "box," name all the lines that are perpendicular to $\overleftrightarrow{QP}$.

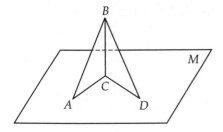

Given: $\overleftrightarrow{BC} \perp$ plane M; $\overline{AB} \cong \overline{DB}$.
$\overleftrightarrow{AC}$ and $\overleftrightarrow{DC}$ lie in plane M.
Prove: $\angle BAC \cong \angle BDC$

11-3 Parallel Lines and Planes

• Theorem 11.7. If two or more lines are perpendicular to the same plane, these lines are parallel.

In the figure below, line $r \perp$ plane M, and line $s \perp$ plane M, such that $r \parallel s$.

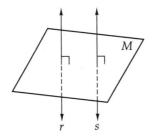

• Corollary 11.7.1. Two lines perpendicular to the same plane are coplanar. In the figure above, lines r and s lie in the same plane.
• Theorem 11.8. If each of two lines is parallel to a third line, then the lines are parallel to each other.

In the figure below, $a \parallel c$ and $b \parallel c$, therefore, $a \parallel b$.

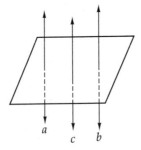

Parallel planes are planes that have no points in common. Thus, if two planes do not intersect, they are parallel. Two parallel planes are everywhere equidistant. Likewise, a line and a plane are parallel if they do not intersect.

- Theorem 11.9. Two planes perpendicular to the same line are parallel to each other.

  In the figure below, plane $M \perp \overleftrightarrow{AB}$ at point X, and plane $R \perp \overleftrightarrow{AB}$ at point Y, such that plane M is parallel to plane R.

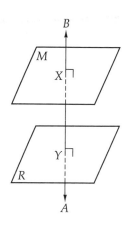

- Theorem 11.10. If two parallel planes are intersected by a third plane, the lines of intersection formed are parallel.

  In the figure below, plane M is parallel to plane N, and plane R intersects planes M and N, so that $a \parallel b$.

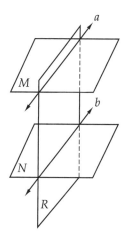

Note: Two lines are parallel if they are coplanar (such as a and b) and do not intersect.

 Practice

Exercises 1–7: Use *parallel* or *perpendicular* to complete each sentence.

1 Two planes that are perpendicular to the same line are _____ to each other.

2 Two lines _____ to the same plane are parallel.

3 If $\overleftrightarrow{AB}$ and $\overleftrightarrow{CD}$ are parallel lines and plane P is perpendicular to $\overleftrightarrow{AB}$, plane P must be _____ to $\overleftrightarrow{CD}$

4 If each of two lines is _____ to a third line, the lines are parallel to each other.

5 If a line outside a plane is parallel to a line in the plane, the line is _____ to the plane.

6 If lines $\overleftrightarrow{AB}$ and $\overleftrightarrow{CD}$, which intersect at E, are both parallel to plane P, then plane P is _____ to the plane determined by lines $\overleftrightarrow{AB}$ and $\overleftrightarrow{CD}$.

7 A straight line _____ to one of two parallel lines is parallel to the other.

Exercises 8–10: Choose *none*, *one*, or *infinitely many*, to answer each question.

8 If point P lies outside plane M, how many lines parallel to plane M can be drawn through point P?

9 If $\overleftrightarrow{XY}$ intersects plane M, how many planes containing $\overleftrightarrow{XY}$ can be drawn parallel to plane M?

10 If line $\overleftrightarrow{MK}$ is parallel to plane N, how many planes that contain $\overleftrightarrow{MK}$ can be drawn parallel to plane N?

11

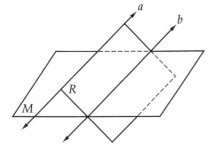

Given: a is a line in plane R, line a is parallel to plane M, plane R intersects plane M at line b.
Prove: $a \parallel b$

Exercises 12–30: State *True* or *False*.

12 If two planes are parallel to a third plane, then they are parallel to each other.

13 If a plane intersects one of two parallel planes, then it intersects the other.

14 If a line intersects one of two parallel planes, then it intersects the other.

15 Two planes parallel to the same line are parallel to each other.

16 If two planes are parallel, any line in one is parallel to any line in the other.

17 A line parallel to the intersection of two planes is parallel to each of the planes.

18 Any two planes parallel to the same plane are perpendicular to each other.

19 A line parallel to a plane is parallel to each line contained in the plane.

20 Two planes perpendicular to the same line are parallel to each other.

21 Given a plane and a point not in the plane, there is exactly one plane that contains the point and is parallel to the given plane.

22 If a plane intersects two parallel planes, then the intersections are parallel lines.

23 The set of points at a given distance from a plane is two planes parallel to the given plane.

24 If each of two intersecting lines is parallel to a plane, the plane determined by the lines is parallel to the given plane.

25 If a plane is parallel to one of two intersecting planes, then it intersects the other plane.

26 Two skew lines intersect in a point.

27 If any two parallel lines are parallel to a plane, then the plane determined by the parallel lines is perpendicular to the given plane.

28 If a line is parallel to a second line, then it is parallel to any plane containing the second line.

29 If a line is perpendicular to a plane, then there is at least one plane containing this line that is parallel to the plane.

30 If a line lies in a plane, there is one and only one plane containing this line that is perpendicular to the plane.

11-4 Surface Area of a Prism

As introduced at the beginning of this chapter, a *geometric solid* (3-dimensional figure) is a region in space enclosed by planes and curved surfaces. Some of these solids are prisms, cubes, cylinders, pyramids, cones, and spheres. A figure in space must have at least four points that are not all in the same plane.

A **polyhedron** is a solid enclosed by plane polygons. The *faces* of the polyhedron are the bounding polygons; the *edges* are the intersections of the faces; the *vertices* (or corner points) are the intersections of the edges. A *diagonal* through a solid is a straight line joining any two vertices not in the same face. For example, $\overline{AB}$ is one of four possible diagonals.

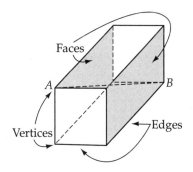

A **regular polyhedron** is a polyhedron whose faces are congruent regular polygons and that has the same number of faces intersecting at each vertex. There are only *five regular polyhedrons*, each of which is shown below with its name and number of faces. They are also called the *Platonic solids*, named after Plato, who felt that these solids symbolized the four ancient elements (earth, air, fire, and water) and the universe.

The table below shows the relationship among the figures and the faces.

Polyhedron	Number of Faces	Figure and Geometric Net
Tetrahedron	4	
Hexahedron (cube)	6	

(continued)

Polyhedron	Number of Faces	Figure and Geometric Net
Octahedron	8	
Dodecahedron	12	
Icosahedron	20	

Note: The faces are either *equilateral triangles* (for the tetrahedron, octahedron, and icosahedron), *squares* (for the hexahedron or cube), or *regular pentagons* (for the dodecahedron).

Prisms

A **prism** is a polyhedron of which two faces (called the *bases*) are congruent polygons in parallel planes and the other faces (called *lateral faces*) are parallelograms intersecting in parallel lines. These intersecting lines of the lateral faces are called *lateral edges*.

For example, in the prism shown, the parallel polygons, pentagons $ABCDE$ and $PQRST$, are the *bases*. The vertical parallelograms that link the bases are the *lateral faces* or *lateral sides*—parallelograms $PQAE$, $QRBA$, $RSCB$, $STDC$, and $TPED$.

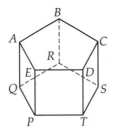

The lines of intersection of the lateral faces ($\overline{PE}$, $\overline{QA}$, $\overline{RB}$, $\overline{SC}$, and $\overline{TD}$) are called the *lateral edges*. These edges are both congruent and parallel. The *altitude* (or height) of a prism is the length of a line segment perpendicular to each of the bases, with an endpoint on each base.

A **right prism** is a prism whose lateral edges are perpendicular to the bases. All the lateral faces of a right prism are rectangles. If their bases are triangles, quadrilaterals, or hexagons, the prisms are **triangular**, **quadrangular**, or **hexagonal**, as illustrated.

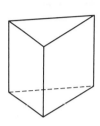 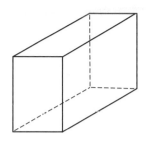 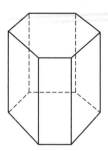

Triangular Prism   Quadrangular Prism   Hexagonal Prism
(Rectangular Solid)

A **regular prism** is a right prism having *regular polygons* for its bases.

A **parallelepiped** is a prism whose bases are parallelograms.

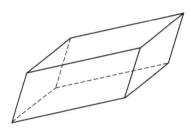

A **right parallelepiped** is a parallelepiped whose lateral edges are perpendicular to the bases, as in the quadrangular prism or rectangular solid above. A **cube** is a rectangular solid with all its edges equal.

Characteristics of parallelepipeds:

(a) All the faces of a parallelepipeds are parallelograms.
(b) The lateral faces of a rectangular solid (or right parallelepiped) are rectangles.
(c) All the faces of a rectangular solid are rectangles.
(d) All the faces of a cube are squares.
(e) The opposite faces of a parallelepiped are congruent.

The following *formulas* are used to find the *lateral area* and *total surface area* of a prism.

- The **lateral area** of a prism is the sum of the areas of the lateral faces.
- The **lateral area** of a prism is also equal to the product of the height and the perimeter of a base.
- The **total surface area** of a prism is the sum of the lateral area and the area of the bases.

1 The base of a right prism is equilateral triangle ABC and the length of one edge of the base is 6 inches. If the height of the prism, CD, is 10 inches, find the lateral area and the total surface area.

SOLUTION

We must find the sum of the lateral area and the area of the two bases.

The lateral area of the triangular prism = perimeter × height.

The perimeter of the triangle is $3(6) = 18$ in. and the height = 10 in.

Thus, lateral area is $18(10) = 180$ sq in.

The total area = lateral area $(180 \text{ sq in.}) + 2 \times (\text{area of the base})$.

The area of the equilateral triangular base = $\frac{s^2\sqrt{3}}{4}$, where s is the length of a side.

Thus, if $s = 6$, then $\frac{6^2\sqrt{3}}{4} = \frac{36\sqrt{3}}{4} = 9\sqrt{3}$, the area of one base of the prism.

The sum of the two bases = $18\sqrt{3}$.

Therefore, the total surface area = $180 + 18\sqrt{3}$ sq in.

ANSWER: The lateral area is 180 sq in. The total surface area is $180 + 18\sqrt{3}$ sq in.

2 Find the altitude of a right prism if its lateral area equals 190 sq in., and its base is a quadrilateral whose sides are 7 in., 8 in., 11 in., and 12 in.

SOLUTION

The lateral area equals the perimeter of the base × altitude.

The perimeter = $7 + 8 + 11 + 12 = 38$ in.

Thus, $38 \times \text{altitude} = 190$ and the altitude = $\frac{190 \text{ in.}^2}{38 \text{ in.}} = 5$ in.

ANSWER: The altitude of the right prism is 5 inches.

 Practice

1 The number of square inches in the total surface area of the rectangular prism with dimensions 4, 4, and 3 is:

(1) 48
(2) 56
(3) 80
(4) 88

2 Find the lateral area of each right prism.

a

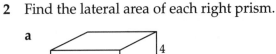

b

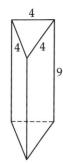

c

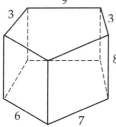

3 What is the least number of faces that a polyhedron can have? The least number of edges? The least number of vertices?

4 What is the least number of faces that a prism can have?

5 If the lateral edge of a prism is an altitude, what kind of prism is it?

6 Find the total surface area of a rectangular solid with the following dimensions:

    a 6.0 cm by 8.0 cm by 11 cm
    b 3.5 ft by 4.0 ft by 13.0 ft

7 If the base of rectangular solid is 6 by 4 and the lateral edge is 8, find the total surface area.

8 If the length of an edge of a cube is 6.35 inches. What is the total surface area of the cube to the nearest square inch?

9 A prism with a pentagon base has a perimeter of 42 and a lateral edge of 14. Find the lateral area of the prism.

10 Find the lateral area of a right prism if its altitude is 15 in., and its base is a triangle with sides 8 in., 10 in., and 11 in.

11 Find the lateral area and the total area of a right prism whose altitude is 17 cm and whose base is an equilateral triangle with a side of 5 cm.

12 If the base of a prism is an equilateral triangle with side 3 cm, and each lateral edge measures 5 cm, what is the lateral area of the prism? What is the total area of the prism?

13 Find the total area of a right triangular prism with altitude that measures 6 cm and whose bases are equilateral triangles with sides measuring 8 cm.

14 The base of a right prism 50 inches high is a rhombus with diagonals 30 and 16. Find the total surface area of the prism.

15 The base of a regular hexagonal prism has a side of 2 and lateral edge of 6. Find the lateral area of the prism. Find the total area. (Hint: There are six equilateral triangles in a hexagon.)

16 Find the lateral area and the total area of a right prism whose altitude is 17 inches and whose base is a regular hexagon with a side of 5 inches.

17 Find the altitude of a right prism if its base is an equilateral triangle inscribed in a circle of radius 5 in., and its lateral area is 135 sq in.

18 Prove that the square of a diagonal of any rectangular solid is equal to the sum of the squares of its three dimensions. (In other words, prove that $d^2 = l^2 + w^2 + h^2$.)

11-5 Symmetry Planes

We recall that the line of symmetry presents a figure that coincides with its reflection image over the line, as the figure below illustrates. Line *m* is the line of symmetry.

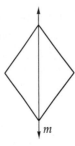

Similarly, a plane of symmetry is a reflection plane. A plane that intersects a three-dimensional figure so that one half is the reflected image of the other half is called a **symmetry plane**.

The following figures present six illustrations of the symmetry plane *P* that slices through each figure to produce the reflected image of the other half.

Cylinders and a Symmetry Plane *P*   Cone and a Symmetry Plane *P*

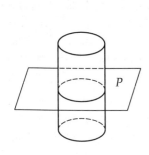
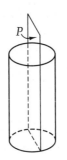
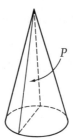

Triangular Prism and Cubes with Symmetry Planes *P*

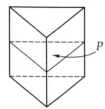
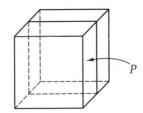
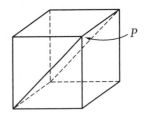

 **Practice**

Exercises 1–3: Refer to the cube below.

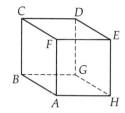

1 Which of the following points can be found in the symmetry plane determined by the vertices *F*, *D*, and *G*?

(1) *A*
(2) *C*
(3) *E*
(4) *H*

2 Which of the following points can be found in the symmetry plane determined by the vertices *C*, *B*, and *H*?

(1) *D*
(2) *E*
(3) *F*
(4) *A*

3 Which of the following points can be found in the symmetry plane determined by the vertices *B*, *G*, and *E*?

(1) *F*
(2) *A*
(3) *H*
(4) *E*

Exercises 4–7: The number of symmetry planes that could be drawn through the given solid figure is identified. For each figure, describe the location of all symmetry planes and (where possible) sketch in your answer.

4 Five symmetry planes

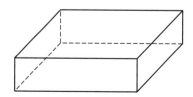

Rectangular Prism

5 Six symmetry planes

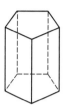

Regular Pentagonal Prism

6 Four symmetry planes

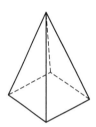

Square Pyramid

7 Infinite number of symmetry planes

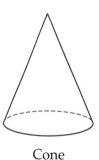

Cone

8 Identify the number of symmetry planes that can be drawn through the hexagonal prism. Sketch them in, if you can.

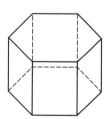

9 Identify the nine symmetry planes that can be drawn through the cube.

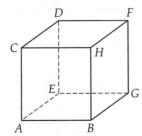

10 Points A, B, C, and D are the midpoints of the edges shown; $\angle ABC$ measures $60°$; and $\overline{CE} \perp \overline{AB}$. What is the area of the trapezoid formed by the intersection of plane P with the right triangular prism?

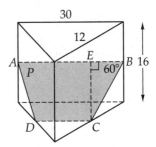

11-6 Volume of a Prism

Formula statements

The **volume of a rectangular prism** (or rectangular solid) is equal to the product of its three dimensions.
Stated as a formula: $V = l \cdot w \cdot h$

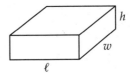

The **volume of a triangular prism** equals the product of the base (B) and the altitude (or height) h.
Stated as a formula: $V = B \cdot h$

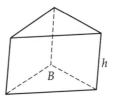

The **volume of a cube** equals the cube of its edges.
Stated as a formula: $V = e^3$

More generally, the volume of *any* prism equals $B \cdot h$, where B = the area of the base and h = the altitude of the prism.

Other useful theorems:

- Theorem 11.11. The ratio of the volumes of two similar polyhedrons is the same as the ratio of the cubes of any two corresponding edges.
- Theorem 11.12. The ratio of the volumes of two rectangular solids having equal bases is the same as the ratio of their altitudes.
- Theorem 11.13. In general, if two rectangular solids have two dimensions in common, they are to each other as the ratio of the third dimension.

MODEL PROBLEMS

1 Find the volume of a right triangular prism with sides of 3, 4, and 5, and an altitude of 8.

SOLUTION

Since the dimensions are 3, 4, and 5, the triangular base B must be a right triangle (recall the Pythagorean triple 3, 4, 5).

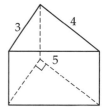

Thus, the triangular base has an area of $\frac{3 \cdot 4}{2} = 6$.

Since $B = 6$ and $h = 8$, the volume $= B \cdot h = 6 \cdot 8 = 48$ cubic inches.

ANSWER: The volume is 48 cubic inches.

2 If the total surface area of a cube is 450 square inches, find the volume. (Leave your answer in simplest radical form.) Find the length of the longest diagonal rod that would fit in this cube.

SOLUTION

First, we need to find the length of the edge of the cube.

Surface area of a cube $= 6e^2$, where $e =$ the cube's edge.

Thus, $6e^2 = 450$, so $e^2 = 75$ and $e = 5\sqrt{3}$.

The volume of the cube is $e^3 = (5\sqrt{3})^3 = 375\sqrt{3}$.

The longest diagonal can be determined by using the formula:

diagonal $= \sqrt{l^2 + w^2 + h^2} = \sqrt{(5\sqrt{3})^2 + (5\sqrt{3})^2 + (5\sqrt{3})^2} = \sqrt{75 + 75 + 75} = \sqrt{225} = 15$

ANSWER: The volume of the cube is $225\sqrt{3}$ cubic inches. The longest diagonal rod that would fit in this cube is 15 inches.

3 The height of a parallelepiped is 6. Find the volume if the longest side of the base is 20 and the altitude to that side is 10.

SOLUTION

The area of the base of the parallelepiped is base × height.

Thus, base × height $= 20 \times 10 = 200$.

The volume of the parallelepiped is $B \times h = 200 \times 6 = 1,200$.

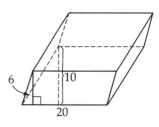

ANSWER: The volume is 1,200 cubic units.

 Practice

1 Find the volume of a right prism with a 4-by-6 rectangle as a base and an altitude of 12.

2 Find the volume of a cube with edges 25 meters in length.

3 Find the volume and surface area of a rectangular solid with dimensions

  a 3 cm, 7 cm, and 5 cm.
  b 10 in., 15 in., and 24 in.
  c 2 ft by 4 ft by 6 ft.

4 Find the volume of a prism if the base is a square with sides measuring 7 and an altitude of 3.

5 Find the edge of a cube with the following volumes

    a   8
    b   216
    c   64
    d   125
    e   27

6 Find the area of the base of a prism if the volume is 42 and the height is 3.

7 Find the height of a prism if the volume is 9 and the area of the base is 18.

8 A right prism has a rhombus for its base. If the diagonals of the rhombus are 12 ft and 16 ft, and the height of the prism is 20 ft, what is the total surface area and volume of this prism?

9 If the base of a right prism is a rhombus with diagonals 10 in. and 12 in. and the volume of the prism is 60 cu in., find the height of the prism.

10 The entire surface of a cube is 1,014 sq ft. Find the volume of the cube and the length of one diagonal.

11 Anna has a fish tank in the shape of a rectangular solid and she plans to put 8 fish in the tank. If each fish requires 6,480 cubic inches of space, and the dimensions of the base of the tank are 24 inches by 72 inches, what should be the minimum height of the fish tank?

12 If the edges of the base of a rectangular prism are 8 cm and 6 cm, and the diagonal is $10\sqrt{2}$, what is the volume of the solid?

13 Find the length of the longest diagonal of a box that is 3 by 6 by 6. (Hint: The formula for the length of a diagonal $= \sqrt{l^2 + w^2 + h^2}$.)

14 Find, to the nearest tenth of a foot, the length of the longest rod that will fit in a box 2 ft by 18 in. by 1 ft.

15 What is the length of a diagonal of a cube with side x?

16 The diagonal of a cube is 9 inches. Find the volume of the cube.

17 The diagonal of a cube is $7\sqrt{3}$. Find its volume and its surface area.

18 An equilateral triangular prism has a side of 4 inches and a lateral edge of 6 inches. What is the volume of the prism? (Hint: Area of an equilateral triangle $= \frac{s^2\sqrt{3}}{4}$.)

19 If the area of the base of a prism is multiplied by 10 while the height is kept constant, what is the effect on the volume?

20 Two regular prisms, one with a triangular base and the other with an hexagonal base, each have a base area of $36\sqrt{3}$ square units. If the lateral edge of each prism is 10 units,

    a   what is the volume of each solid?
    b   what is the lateral area of each solid? (Hint: The hexagon contains six equilateral triangles.)

21 Prove: The sum of the squares of the lengths of the four diagonals of a rectangular prism is equal to the sum of the squares of the lengths of the twelve edges.

11-7 Cylinders

A **cylinder** is a solid bounded by a closed cylindrical surface and two parallel planes.

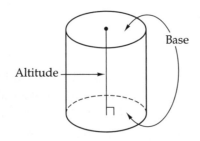

The *bases* of a cylinder are the two parallel planes. The bases are also congruent. The *altitude* is the perpendicular drawn between the planes of the bases. The *lateral surface* is the cylindrical surface included between the bases.

A typical view of the lateral surface is the label on a can which, when removed and flattened out, forms a rectangle.

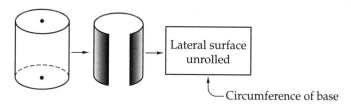

A **right circular cylinder** is a cylinder whose lateral surface is perpendicular to the planes of the bases.

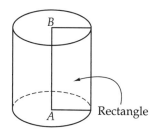

Since a right circular cylinder is generated by revolving a rectangle about one of its sides as an axis, such as $\overline{AB}$, this right circular cylinder is also called a **cylinder of revolution**.

Intersections With a Plane

1 Every section of a right circular cylinder made by a plane passing through the cylinder and perpendicular to the bases is a rectangle.

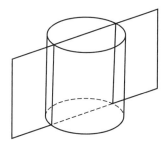

2 A plane parallel to the bases and intersecting the lateral surface forms a circle congruent to the bases.

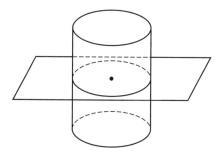

Since the lateral area of a prism is the product of the perimeter and the altitude, by analogy, the lateral area of a right circular cylinder equals the product of the circumference of its base and its altitude. Stated as a formula, the *lateral area of a right circular cylinder* is $2\pi rh$.

The *total area of a right circular cylinder* equals the sum of its lateral area and the areas of its bases. Total area $= 2\pi rh + 2(\pi r^2)$ or $2\pi r(h + r)$.

The *volume of a circular cylinder* is equal to the product of its base and its altitude or $V = \pi r^2 h$.

 MODEL PROBLEMS

1 The lateral surface area of a right circular cylinder equals 440 sq in. and the altitude equals 7 in.

    a Find the radius of the base of the cylinder.
    b Find the total surface area of the cylinder (to the nearest tenth).
    c Find the volume of the cylinder. Use $\pi = \frac{22}{7}$.

SOLUTION

    a The formula for the lateral surface area $= 2\pi rh$. Since the surface area is 440 sq in., then $2\pi rh = 440$.

    By substitution,
$$2 \times \tfrac{22}{7} \times r \times 7 = 440$$
$$44r = 440$$
$$r = 10 \text{ in.}$$

ANSWER: The radius of the base of the cylinder is 10 in.

    b To find the total surface area, use the formula:
Total area $= 2\pi r(h + r)$
$$= 2 \times \tfrac{22}{7} \times 10(7 + 10)$$
$$= \tfrac{440}{7}(17) = 1{,}068.57 \text{ or } 1{,}068.6 \text{ sq in. (to the nearest tenth)}$$

ANSWER: The total surface area of the cylinder is 1,068.6 sq in.

    c To find the volume, substitute the known values in the formula for volume.
Volume $= \pi r^2 h$
$$= \tfrac{22}{7} \times 10^2 \times 7 = 22 \times 100 = 2{,}200 \text{ in.}^3$$

ANSWER: The volume of the cylinder is 2,200 in.^{3}.

2 A right circular cylinder is inscribed in a cube whose edge is 2 inches.

    a Find the radius of the cylinder.
    b Find the lateral surface area of the cylinder in terms of π square inches.
    c Find the volume of the cylinder.

SOLUTION

    a If the edge of the cube is 2 inches, then the diameter of the cylinder is 2 inches and the radius is 1 inch.

ANSWER: The radius of the cylinder is 1 inch.

    b The lateral area = $2\pi rh = 2\pi(1)(2) = 4\pi$ in.².

    c The volume $= \pi r^2 h = \pi(1)^2(2) = 2\pi$ in.³.

Practice

1 If a cylinder is opened (as in the figure) to form a rectangle, and the area of the circular base is $\frac{9}{\pi}$ in.², then the length of the rectangle is:

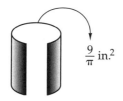

$\frac{9}{\pi}$ in.²

    (1) $\frac{6}{\pi}$ in.
    (2) 3 in.
    (3) 6 in.
    (4) 6π in.

Exercises 2–5: Given a right circular cylinder. Solve for the indicated variable. Leave answers in terms of π. Let V = volume, h = altitude, and r = radius of the base.

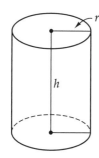

r

h

2 Find h when $V = 44\pi$ in.³ and $r = 2$ in.

3 Find V when $h = \frac{1}{4}$ in. and $r = \frac{2}{3}$ in.

4 Find r when $V = \pi$ in.³ and $h = 16$ in.

5 Find h when $V = \pi^2$ in.³ and $r = \pi$ in.

Exercises 6–9: In the following right circular cylinder problems, let V = volume, h = altitude, and r = radius. Leave the answers in terms of π. For each cylinder, find (a) the lateral surface area, (b) the total surface area, and (c) the volume.

6 $r = 3.5$ cm and $h = 16$ cm

7 $r = 6$ in. and $h = 8$ in.

8 $r = 1$ in. and $h = 1$ ft

9 $r = 2$ m and $h = 150$ cm

10 Find the radius of the base of a right circular cylinder if

    a the lateral area is 30π sq ft and the height is 5 ft.

    b the lateral area is 24π sq in. and the height is 3 in.

11 Two different right circular cylinders are generated by the revolution of a rectangle about one of its sides, depending on whether it revolves about the longer or the shorter side. If a rectangle has dimensions 8 by 12 and two cylinders are created, find the volume of each and explain the difference (if there is any).

12 A cylindrical iron pipe is 2 inches in diameter and 4 feet long. If a cubic inch of iron weighs 0.25 pound, what is the weight of the pipe (to the nearest pound)?

13 If the volume of a right circular cylinder is 297.8 cu cm and the height is 8.2 cm, what is the radius of the base (to the nearest tenth)?

14 A cylindrical container 10 inches in diameter is required to hold 10 gallons of water. Find the height to the nearest tenth of an inch, if one gallon of water occupies 231 cubic inches of space.

15 The radius and height of a right circular cylinder are each 4. (Leave all answers in terms of π.)

   a Find the volume of the cylinder.
   b If the radius is doubled and the height decreased by half, what can be said about the two volumes?
   c Find the lateral area of the cylinder.
   d Again, if the radius is doubled and the height decreased by half, what is the difference in the lateral areas? What conclusion can be drawn?

16 For each of the following, draw a conclusion.

   a If the height of a right circular cylinder is doubled and the base is unchanged, what is the effect on the volume of the cylinder?
   b If the radius of a right circular cylinder is halved and the height is unchanged, how does this change the volume of the cylinder?

17 Two cylindrical glasses have the same height. If the diameters of the glasses are 2.4 and 3.4, can the second glass hold twice as much water as the first glass?

Exercises 18 and 19: State whether each is *True* or *False*.

18 The volume of a right circular cylinder is doubled if its altitude is doubled and its radius halved.

19 If a right circular cylinder is circumscribed about a cube, the diameter of the base of the cylinder is equal to a diagonal of one of the faces of the cube.

20 Find the lateral surface area and volume of a cylindrical hot-water tank 60 inches high and 16 inches in diameter.

21 The diameter of a cylindrical water tank is 12 inches and the tank holds 30 gallons. If we allow 231 cubic inches to a gallon, what is the height of the tank?

22 In the figure below, a right circular cylinder is inscribed in a cube with an edge of 4 cm. What is the ratio of the volume of the cylinder to the volume of the cube?

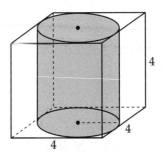

23 A right circular cylinder with a radius of $4\sqrt{2}$ inches is circumscribed about a cube.

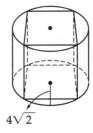

$4\sqrt{2}$

   a Find the volume of the cylinder. (Leave your answer in terms of π.)
   b Find the volume of the cube.
   c If the cube is an ancient artifact that must be shipped carefully, what is the volume of soft packing, to the nearest integer, that can be placed around the box for protection?

11-8 Pyramids

A **pyramid** is a solid figure (a polyhedron) with a base that is a polygon and lateral faces that are triangles having the sides of the polygon as bases and all having a common vertex.

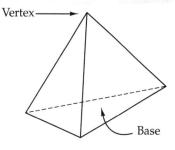

The *base* of the pyramid is the polygon.

The *lateral faces* are the triangles.

The *lateral edges* are the intersections of the lateral faces.

The *vertex* is the common vertex of the triangles.

The *altitude* is the perpendicular from the vertex to the plane of the base.

Pyramids are classified by the number of sides in their bases. For example, a triangular pyramid has a triangle for its base. This pyramid has four faces and is called a *tetrahedron*. A quadrilateral pyramid has a quadrilateral for its base, a pentagonal pyramid has a pentagon for its base, a hexagonal pyramid has a hexagon for its base, and so on. Below are illustrations of three pyramids.

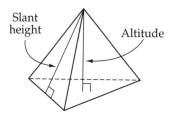

Triangular Pyramid

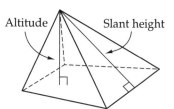

Quadrilateral Pyramid

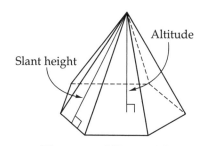

Hexagonal Pyramid

A **regular pyramid** is a pyramid whose base is a regular polygon, whose altitude is the perpendicular from the vertex to the center of the base, and whose lateral faces are congruent isosceles triangles.

The lateral faces of a regular pyramid are congruent, and the *slant height* of a regular pyramid is the altitude to the base of any one of the lateral faces. In the case of a *regular tetrahedron*, all of its faces are equilateral triangles.

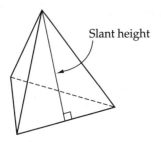

Regular Triangular Pyramid

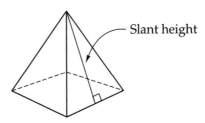

Regular Square Pyramid

The *lateral surface area of a pyramid* is the sum of the areas of its lateral faces. The *lateral area of a regular pyramid* is equal to half the product of its slant height (l) and the perimeter of the base (p). Stated as a formula: Lateral area $= \frac{1}{2}lp$.

Using the diagram below, lateral area $= \frac{1}{2}VM(AB + BC + CD + DE + EA)$

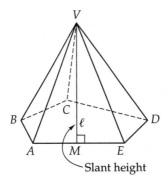

The *total surface area of a pyramid* is the sum of the area of the base (B) and the lateral area.

The *volume of any pyramid* is equal to one-third the product of the base and the altitude. Stated as a formula: Volume $= \frac{1}{3}Bh$.

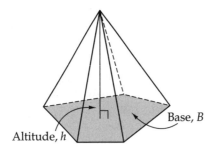

MODEL PROBLEMS

1 Find the altitude of a pyramid with a rhombus as a base and diagonals of 4 in. and 6 in. and a volume of 3 in.³.

SOLUTION

Use the volume formula: $V = \frac{1}{3}Bh$

The base B = area of rhombus = $\frac{1}{2}$(product of diagonals)

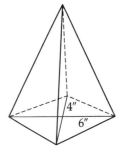

$B = \frac{1}{2}(4)(6) = 12$

$V = \frac{1}{3}Bh$

$3 = \frac{1}{3}(12)h$ Substitute 3 for V and 12 for B in the equation.

$3 = 4h$

$h = \frac{3}{4}$

ANSWER: Altitude, h, = $\frac{3}{4}$ in.

2 A regular square pyramid has 12 as the measure of each edge of the base and the height of the pyramid is 8. Find

a the lateral area.
b the total area.
c the volume.

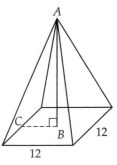

SOLUTION

a To find the lateral area, we need to know both the slant height and the perimeter. To find the slant height, l, we need to look inside the pyramid and complete the right $\triangle ABC$ as drawn in the figure above.

$\overline{AC}$, the hypotenuse, will be the *slant height*, and the leg, $\overline{CB}$, will be half of 12.

$(AC)^2 = (AB)^2 + (CB)^2$
$(AC)^2 = 8^2 + 6^2$
$\quad\quad = 64 + 36$
$\quad\quad = 100$
$AC = \sqrt{100} = 10$

The slant height is 10. The perimeter, p, is $4 \times 12 = 48$.

Lateral area = $\frac{1}{2}lp = \frac{1}{2}(10)(48) = 240$ square units.

ANSWER: The lateral area is 240 square units

b The total area = B(area of the base) + lateral area
The base of the square pyramid is a square, therefore the area of the base, B, is $12^2 = 144$. The total area = $144 + 240 = 384$ square units.

ANSWER: The total area is 384 square units.

c The volume of the pyramid is $V = \frac{1}{3}Bh = \frac{1}{3}(144)(8) = 384$ cubic units.

ANSWER: The volume is 384 cubic units.

3 What is (a) the lateral area and (b) the total surface area of a regular square pyramid with the length of each edge equal to 6? Leave the answers in simplest radical form.

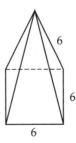

SOLUTION

a We first need to find the area of one lateral face. Since each lateral face is an equilateral triangle, we use the special area formula for an equilateral triangle, $\frac{s^2\sqrt{3}}{4}$, where s represents a side of the triangle. Substitute 6 for s and $\frac{s^2\sqrt{3}}{4} = \frac{6^2\sqrt{3}}{4} = \frac{36\sqrt{3}}{4} = 9\sqrt{3}$. Since the lateral faces are four congruent triangles, the lateral area of the square pyramid is $4(9\sqrt{3}) = 36\sqrt{3}$.

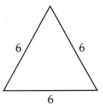

One Lateral Face

ANSWER: The lateral area is $36\sqrt{3}$ square units.

b The area of the base (B) of the pyramid is $6^2 = 36$. The total area $= B +$ lateral area $= 36 + 36\sqrt{3}$.

ANSWER: The total area is $36 + 36\sqrt{3}$ square units.

 Practice

Exercises 1–3: Find the lateral area of each of the following regular pyramids.

1 a square base having an edge of 13 cm and a slant height of 9 cm

2 a triangular base, an edge of 10 cm, and a slant height of 16 cm

3 a hexagonal base, an edge of 24 in., and a slant height of 16 in

Exercises 4–7: Find the volume of each regular pyramid.

4 The area of the base is 1,212 sq cm and the altitude is 12 cm.

5 The area of the base is 28.6 sq in. and the altitude is 6.0 in.

6 The base is a square with edge 3 ft and height 2.5 ft.

7 The base is an equilateral triangle with a side of 8 and an altitude of 9.

8 The volume of a pyramid is 1,000 cu ft and the area of the base is 10 sq ft. What is the height of the pyramid?

9 What is the length of the altitude of a pyramid whose base is a square, if the volume equals 72, and the side of the base equals 6?

10 If the volume of a pyramid is 1,674 cu ft and the height is 18 ft, what is the area of the pyramid's base?

11 Find the volume of a pyramid if the base is a rectangle with sides 9 inches and 4 inches and an altitude of 6 feet.

12 The base of a pyramid is a rhombus whose diagonals are 10 and 12. What is the volume if the altitude is 6?

13 Find the total surface area of a regular pyramid having each side of the base 10 and the lateral edge 13, if the base is a

   a triangle.
   b square.
   c hexagon.

14 What is the total surface area of a regular tetrahedron, if a side of the base is 2 and the slant height is $\sqrt{3}$? Leave the answer in simplest radical form.

15 A pyramid and a prism have bases that are triangles with sides of 5, 12, and 13. If each has an altitude of 8, find the volume of each.

16 Find the lateral area of a regular square pyramid where each edge of the base is 12 and the height of the pyramid is 8.

17 Find the total surface area of a regular tetrahedron if an edge is 12 cm.

18 If the base of a regular pyramid 24 feet high is a hexagon whose side is 6 feet, what is the volume of the pyramid? (Hint: A hexagon is formed by six equilateral triangles.)

11-9 Cones

A **cone** is a solid bounded by a conical surface and a plane cutting all its elements and forming the base of the figure.

The *lateral surface* of the cone is the curved or conical surface.

The *base* of the cone is the plane surface that forms a circle.

The *axis* of a circular cone is a line from the vertex to the center of the base.

The *slant height* is the shortest line segment that can be drawn from the vertex to the circumference of the circle that forms the base.

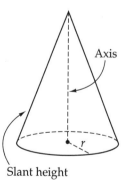

A **right circular cone** is a cone whose axis is perpendicular to the base. The axis in this case is the altitude. A right circular cone is also called a **cone of revolution** because it can be generated by revolving a right triangle about one of its legs as an axis. For example, right triangle AOB is rotated around leg $\overline{AO}$ and generates the cone. Line segment AB is the slant height.

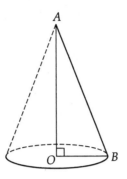

Just as the theorems about the lateral area and volume of the cylinder are developed from the corresponding theorems for the prism, so too, a cone is comparable to a regular pyramid with a circular base. Thus, the same formulas apply to both regular pyramids and right circular cones, with the perimeter replaced by the circumference of the base of the cone. Where the lateral area of the pyramid is $\frac{1}{2}lp$, we have the following:

- The *lateral area of a cone of revolution* is equal to half the product of its slant height and the circumference of its base. Stated as a formula: Lateral area $= \frac{1}{2}l(2\pi r)$ or $\pi r l$.
- The *total area of a cone of revolution* is equal to the sum of its lateral area and the area of its base. Stated as a formula: Total Area $= \pi r l + \pi r^2$ or $\pi r(l + r)$.
- The *volume of a circular cone* is equal to one-third the product of the area of the base, B, and the altitude, h. Stated as a formula: Volume $= \frac{1}{3}Bh = \frac{1}{3}\pi r^2 h$.

Note: A pyramid and a cone with equal altitudes and bases of equal area have the same volume. That is, if B, the base of the pyramid, equals πr^2, and the altitudes are both h, then it is clear that the volumes of pyramid and cone must be the same.

Some observations about planes and cones

- Every section of a cone made by a plane passing through the vertex and the lateral surface (but not tangent to the cone's lateral surface) is a triangle. In the figure, plane S passes through vertex B and generates $\triangle ABC$.

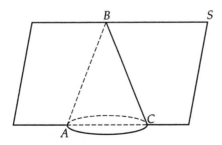

- If a plane (not passing through the vertex) intersects the cone and is parallel to the base, then the figure generated is a circle. In the figure below, plane S is parallel to the base of the cone, intersects the cone, and forms a circle O.

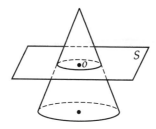

The **frustum** of a cone is the portion of the cone included between its base and a plane parallel to the base. The *lower base* of the frustum is the base of the cone, and the *upper base* is the section made by the plane.

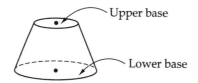

 MODEL PROBLEMS

1 If the lateral area of a right circular cone is 60π and its slant height is 10, what is the volume of the cone? Leave the answer in terms of π.

SOLUTION

To find the volume, we need to know both the area of the base and the altitude of the cone. Use the lateral area formula with $l = 10$. Set the formula equal to 60π and solve for the radius, r.

$\pi r l = \pi r(10) = 60\pi$, and $r = 6$

Area of the base is $\pi r^2 = \pi(6^2) = 36\pi$

The altitude, $\overline{AB}$, can be found by using the Pythagorean theorem and the right triangle ABC. Substitute 10 for the slant height $\overline{AC}$ and 6 for the radius $\overline{BC}$.

$AB^2 + BC^2 = AC^2$
$AB^2 + 6^2 = 10^2$
$\qquad AB^2 = 64$
$\qquad AB = 8$

Volume $= \frac{1}{3}Bh = \frac{1}{3}(36\pi)(8) = 96\pi$

ANSWER: The volume of the right circular cone is 96π.

2 The volume of a right circular cone is 100π and the axis of the cone is 12. Leave the answers in terms of π.

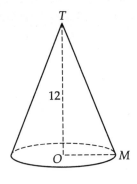

    a Find the radius of the base.
    b Find the slant height.
    c Find the lateral area.
    d Find the total surface area.

SOLUTION

    a Volume $= \frac{1}{3}Bh = \frac{1}{3}\pi r^2 h = \frac{1}{3}\pi r^2 (12) = 4\pi r^2$

       Set $4\pi r^2 = 100\pi$

              $r^2 = 25$

               $r = 5$

ANSWER: The radius of the base is 5.

    b Using the figure drawn, right triangle *TOM* has two legs, 5 and 12, and recalling the Pythagorean triple 5, 12, 13, the slant height or hypotenuse is 13.

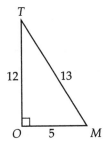

ANSWER: The slant height is 13.

    c The lateral area $= \pi r l$ and, by substitution, $\pi(5)(13) = 65\pi$.

ANSWER: The lateral area is 65π.

    d Total surface area $=$ lateral area $+$ area of the base

       $= 65\pi + \pi r^2$

       $= 65\pi + \pi(5)^2$

       $= 65\pi + 25\pi$

       $= 90\pi$

ANSWER: The total surface area is 90π.

3 A cone with a height of 12 inches and a base with a radius of 8 inches is cut, parallel to the base, into two parts. If the upper cone has a height of 9 inches, what is the volume of the lower part, the frustum, of the cone? Leave answers in terms of π.

SOLUTION

To find the volume of the frustum, find the difference between the volumes of the large cone and the small cone.

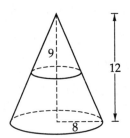

The volume of the large cone is $\frac{1}{3}\pi(8)^2(12) = 256\pi$.

To find the volume of the small cone, we need to know the radius of that cone's base. Since the two cones are similar figures, we can set up a proportion:

$\dfrac{\text{height of small cone}}{\text{height of large cone}} = \dfrac{\text{radius of small cone}}{\text{radius of large cone}}$ or $\dfrac{9}{12} = \dfrac{r}{8}$

Cross multiply and solve: $12r = 72$ and $r = 6$

The volume of the small cone is $\frac{1}{3}\pi(6)^2(9) = 108\pi$.

Volume of the frustum of the cone $= 256\pi - 108\pi = 148\pi$

ANSWER: The volume of the frustum of the cone is 148π.

Exercises 1–3: In the right circular cones below, find the lateral area, total area, and volume. Leave answers in terms of π.

1

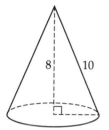

2

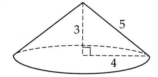

3

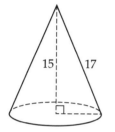

4 In a certain medieval castle, the slant height of a cone-shaped room in the tower is 16 feet and the diameter of the base measures 10 feet. What is the lateral area and total area of the room?

5 The slant height of a cone is 15 cm and the radius of the base measures 9 cm. Find the lateral area and the volume.

6 What is the lateral area, total area, and volume of a right circular cone if the altitude measures 24 in. and the slant height is 26 in.?

Exercises 7–11: Given a right circular cone, find the value for the indicated variable. Let V = volume, h = altitude, and r = radius of the base of a cone.

7 If $V = 127.5\pi$ cu in. and $h = 42.5$ in., find the value of r.

8 Find V if $h = 12$ and $r = 3$.

9 Find V if $r = 4$ and the slant height of the cone is 5.

10 Find V if $h = 9$ and the area of the base is 4.

11 If $V = 314$ and $h = 3$, find the value of r. (Let $\pi = 3.14$)

Exercises 12–15: Complete each sentence.

12 The formula for the volume of a cone or pyramid is _____.

13 If two pyramids have bases of equal area and equal altitudes, then their volumes are _____.

14 If a right prism and a pyramid have congruent altitudes and congruent bases, then the volume of the prism is _____ the volume of the pyramid.

15 If a cylinder and a cone have the same base and same altitude, then the volume of the cone is _____ the volume of the cylinder.

16 Is it possible for the lateral area of a cone to be equal to the area of the base? Explain.

17 Cone A and cone B have the same height, 10. If the diameter of cone B equals the radius of cone A, which is 8, then what is the ratio of the volume of cone A to the volume of cone B?

18 The diameter of the base of a right circular cone in 12 feet and its altitude is 18 feet. Find the altitude of a right circular cylinder of equivalent volume, the diameter of whose base is 18 feet.

19 A cone 6 inches high is cut by a plane parallel to the base and 2 inches from the base. If the radius of the upper base of the frustum is 3 inches, what is the volume of the frustum? Leave the answer in terms of π.

20 A cone of revolution 12 in. high and 32 in. in diameter at the base is cut by a plane parallel to the base and 9 in. from it. Find the volume and lateral area of the frustum formed.

21 The sides in quadrilateral *ABCD*, below, are each 12 inches and diameter *AC* is 12 inches. Find the volume of the solid generated by revolving triangle *BCD* about diagonal $\overline{BD}$.

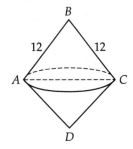

22 A right circular cone 12 cm in height and a right cylinder stand on the same circular base with a radius of 9 cm. If the altitude of the cylinder is 4 cm, what is the lateral surface area of that part of the cone that is above the cylinder? Leave the answer in terms of π.

11-10 Spheres

The **sphere** is a closed surface all points of which are equidistant from a fixed point called the *center*. The *radius* of the sphere is the length of the line segment from the center to any point on the sphere.

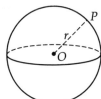

The sphere on the right is the set of points at a distance *r* from point *O*, the center of the sphere. Segment *OP* is the radius of the sphere with distance *r*.

A sphere may be generated by revolving a semicircle about its diameter as an axis.

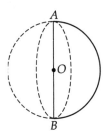

Some informally proved theorems include the following:

- All radii of a sphere (or equal spheres) are equal. Similarly, all diameters of a sphere are equal.
- A point is outside, on, or inside a sphere, if its distance from the center is, respectively, greater than, equal to, or less than a radius of the sphere.

Similarly,

(a) If the distance of a plane from the center of a sphere is *greater than* the radius, the plane will have *no points* in common with the sphere.

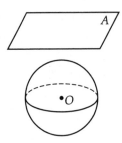

(b) If the distance of a plane from the center of a sphere is *equal* to the radius, the plane will have *one point* in common with the sphere. The plane is considered *tangent* to the sphere at this point.

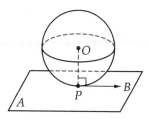

(c) If the distance of a plane from the center of a sphere is *less than* the radius, the plane will have an *infinite number of points* in common with the sphere. The set of infinite points forms a circle.

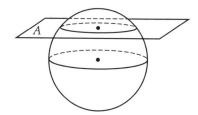

In figure (b) above, with plane *A* tangent to sphere *O* at point *P*, the radius $\overline{OP}$ is perpendicular to plane *A* at point *P*. Also, any line in the plane, such as $\overleftrightarrow{BP}$, which is perpendicular to the radius of the sphere at the tangent point, is said to be *tangent to the sphere*.

- Theorem 11.14. The intersection of a sphere and a plane not tangent to the sphere is a circle.

The intersection of a sphere with a plane that passes through its center is called a **great circle of the sphere**. In the figure below, plane *M* intersects sphere *O* and passes through the center. Circle *O* is the great circle.

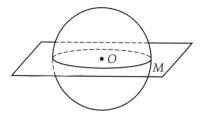

- Corollary 11.14.1. A great circle is the largest circle that can be drawn in a sphere.
- Corollary 11.14.2. All great circles of a sphere bisect the sphere.
- Corollary 11.14.3. The center of the great circle of a sphere is the center of the sphere.
- Corollary 11.14.4. All great circles of a sphere are congruent.
- Corollary 11.14.5. Any two great circles of a sphere bisect each other.
- Theorem 11.15. If two planes are equidistant from the center of a sphere and intersect the sphere, then the intersections are congruent circles.

Some additional informally proved theorems include the following:

- Through any three points on a sphere, one and only one circle may be drawn.
- Circles of a sphere equidistant from the center are congruent.
- Conversely, if circles of a sphere are congruent, then they are equidistant from the center of the sphere.
- Circles of a sphere unequally distant from the center are unequal, and the circle nearest to the center is the greatest. Alternatively, the smaller the circle, the farther it lies from the center.

Note: Since any two spheres are similar, the *ratio of the surface areas* of two spheres is the ratio of any two corresponding parts *squared*, and the *ratio of their volumes* is any two corresponding parts *cubed*.

> Ratios are covered more thoroughly in Chapter 12.

The following are the formulas for the surface area (S) and volume (V) of a sphere.

- The *surface area of a sphere* is the product of its radius, r, and the area of four great circles. Therefore, $S = 4\pi r^2$.
- The *volume of a sphere* is equal to the product of its surface area and one-third the measure of its radius: $V = S\left(\frac{1}{3}r\right)$.

  However, since $S = 4\pi r^2$, by substitution, $V = (4\pi r^2)\frac{1}{3}r$ or $\frac{4}{3}\pi r^3$.

 MODEL PROBLEMS

1 To the nearest tenth, find the surface area and the volume of a sphere whose radius is 4.5 inches.

SOLUTION

$S = 4\pi r^2 = 4(\pi)(4.5)^2 = 254.46 \approx 254.5$ in.^{2}

$V = \frac{4}{3}\pi r^3 = \frac{4}{3}(\pi)(4.5)^3 = 381.70 \approx 381.7$ in.^{3}

ANSWER: The surface area of a sphere whose radius is 4.5 in. is 254.5 in^2., and its volume is 381.7 in.^{3}.

2 If the surface area of a sphere is 36π ft^2, find the volume in terms of π.

SOLUTION

Use the surface area formula to solve for r.

$S = 4\pi r^2 = 36\pi$ (divide by π)
$4r^2 = 36$
$r^2 = 9$
$r = 3$

Substitute r into the volume formula:

$V = \frac{4}{3}\pi r^3 = \frac{4}{3}\pi(3)^3 = \frac{4}{3}(27)\pi = 36\pi$ ft^3

ANSWER: The volume of the sphere is 36π ft^3.

3 If the ratio of the volumes of two spheres is $\frac{125}{216}$, find the ratio of their surface areas.

SOLUTION

The ratio of the volumes of two spheres, is ratio of the cubes of any two corresponding parts. Therefore, $\frac{125}{216} = \frac{5^3}{6^3}$, so $\frac{5^3}{6^3} = \frac{(\text{radius of small sphere})^3}{(\text{radius of large sphere})^3} = \frac{r^3}{R^3}$.

By taking the cube root of both sides, $\frac{5^3}{6^3} = \frac{r^3}{R^3}$, we have $\frac{r}{R} = \frac{5}{6}$.

Thus, $r = 5$ and $R = 6$, and the ratio $\frac{\text{surface area of small sphere}}{\text{surface area of large sphere}} = \frac{r^2}{R^2} = \frac{5^2}{6^2} = \frac{25}{36}$.

ANSWER: The ratio of the surface areas of the two spheres is $\frac{25}{36}$.

4 If the radius of sphere A is 10, what is the area of a circle in terms of π, formed by the intersection of a plane 6 inches from the center?

SOLUTION

In the figure, a right triangle ABC is formed by the following segments: (a) the radius $r = AC = 10$; (b) the distance from the center of the sphere to the center of the circle is $AB = 6$; and (c) the unknown radius of the circle, BC.

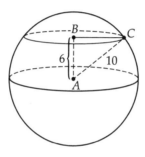

Using the Pythagorean theorem

$(BC)^2 + 6^2 = 10^2$

$(BC)^2 = 100 - 36 = 64$

$BC = \sqrt{64} = 8$

The area of the circle $= \pi r^2 = \pi(8)^2 = 64\pi$.

ANSWER: The area of the circle is 64π.

 Practice

1 Using $\pi = \frac{22}{7}$, to the nearest tenth, find the radius of spheres whose volumes are

    a   4,851 ft³
    b   1,000 ft³
    c   100 ft³

2 To the nearest tenth, find the radius of a sphere whose surface area is

    a 100π mi²
    b 80π mi²
    c 64π mi²
    d 10π mi²

3 Find the volume of a sphere, in terms of π, whose radius is

    a 6 inches
    b 3 feet
    c 90 miles
    d 0.5 yard
    e $\frac{1}{3}$ meter

4 If the surface area of a sphere is 196π in.^{2}, find the length of the radius of the sphere.

5 If the area of a great circle of a sphere is 25π sq cm, what are the surface area and volume of the sphere?

6 If the area of a great circle of a sphere is 48π sq in., what are the surface area and volume of the sphere?

7 If the diameter of the moon is 2,160 miles, find its volume and surface area.

8 If we assume Earth to be a perfect sphere with a radius of approximately 3,980 miles, to the nearest square mile, what is the surface area of Earth?

9 If the diameter of the sun is approximately 100 times that of Earth, then the volume of the sun is how many times that of Earth?

10 Find the radius of a sphere whose surface area is equal to the sum of the surfaces of two spheres whose radii are 3 and 4.

11 If the number of square inches in the surface area of a sphere is equal to the number of cubic inches in its volume, what is the measure of the radius of the sphere?

12 If two spheres have radii of 3 in. and 5 in., what is the ratio of their surface areas?

13 The ratio of the volumes of two spheres is 8 to 125. Find the ratio of their

    a radii.
    b surface areas.

14 If the ratio of the volumes of two spheres is $\frac{8}{27}$, find the ratio of their

    a radii.
    b surface areas.

15 If two spheres have radii in the ratio $m:n$, what is the ratio of their

    a surface areas?
    b volumes?

16 If the ratio of the surface areas of two spheres is $\frac{16}{9}$, what is the ratio of their volumes?

17 A sphere whose radius is 2 inches weighs 32 ounces. Find the weight of a sphere of the same material whose radius is 3 inches.

18 If the diameter of a metal wrecking ball is 36 inches and 16 cubic inches of the metal weigh 3 pounds, how much does the wrecking ball weigh?

19 Find the radius of a sphere if the surface area of the sphere is equal to the volume of a cube with

    a an edge equal to 2.
    b an edge equal to 4.

20 Find the radius of a sphere if the surface area is equal to the surface area of a cube whose edge is 4.

21 What is the volume of the largest ball that can be packed into a cubic cardboard box whose edges have length

    a 1 foot?
    b 2 feet?
    c 3 feet?

22 If a sphere of radius 10 inches is cut by a plane at a point 6 inches from the center of the sphere, what is the area, in terms of π, of the circle formed?

23 A cone and a sphere have the same volume. If the radius of the base of the cone equals the radius of the sphere, what is the height of the cone?

24 A spherical holiday ornament with radius r is to be packaged in a cubical box so that all sides touch the sphere. What is the ratio of the volume of the sphere to the volume of the cube?

25 If the same ornament in problem 24 is to be packaged in a cylinder so that all surfaces touch the sphere, what is the ratio of the volume of the sphere to the volume of the cylinder?

26 A cylinder has a base congruent to a great circle of a sphere and a height equal to the diameter of the sphere. If the radius of the sphere equals 2 inches, compare the lateral area of the cylinder to the surface area of the sphere.

1 If the edges of a cube are 6 in. long, what is the total surface area?

    (1) 12 in.²
    (2) 36 in.²
    (3) 72 in.²
    (4) 216 in.²

Exercises 2–11: State whether each of the following is *True* or *False*.

2 If a line is parallel to a plane it is parallel to any line in the plane.

3 If a line is perpendicular to a line in a plane, the line is perpendicular to the plane.

4 If one plane is perpendicular to a line in another plane, the two planes are perpendicular to each other.

5 A line is parallel to a plane if it is parallel to a line in the plane.

6 Three planes can have only one common point.

7 Two planes perpendicular to the same plane are parallel.

8 Through a given point, only one plane can be drawn perpendicular to a given plane.

9 Through a point outside a plane, only one line can be drawn parallel to the plane.

10 Through a point outside a plane, only one line can be drawn perpendicular to the plane.

11 If a plane and a line not in the plane are perpendicular to the same plane, they are parallel.

12 How many vertices, faces, and edges do each of these figures have?

    a parallelepiped
    b a right triangular prism
    c a cube
    d a right pentagonal prism

13 Find the total surface area and volume of each solid in terms of π.

a

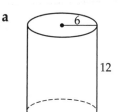

b

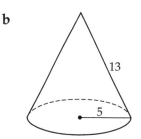

c

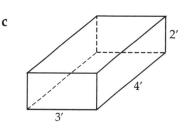

14 What is the total area, in terms of π, of a sheet of metal needed to make a soup can with a radius of 2.5 in. and a height of 7 in.?

15 If the volume of a right circular cylinder is 314 in.³ and the base has a diameter of 10 in., what is the height of the cylinder? (Let $\pi = 3.14$.)

16 If the lateral area of a right circular cylinder is 20π cm² and its altitude is 4 cm, what is the volume?

17 A rectangle has sides 6 cm and 8 cm. If the rectangle is spun about one of the longer sides, forming a cylinder, what is the volume, in terms of π, of this cylinder? If the rectangle is spun about the shorter side, how much more is the volume of this cylinder?

18 A regular triangular pyramid has each lateral edge equal to 5 in. and each base edge equal to 6 in. Find the total surface area.

19 Find the volume of a regular square pyramid with the length of each edge equal to 6 in.

20 Find the volume of a regular hexagonal pyramid if a side of the base is 6 cm and the altitude is 8 cm. (Hint: The area of a regular hexagon is formed by six equilateral triangles.)

21 Find the lateral area of a regular octagonal pyramid if a lateral edge equals 13 cm and a side of the base is 10 cm.

22 Find the lateral area of a cone of revolution whose radius is 12 in. and whose altitude is 5 in.

23 Find the altitude of a right circular cone if the lateral area is 36π in.^{2} and radius is 4 in.

24 Find the volume of a right circular cone with radius 5 ft and slant height 13 ft.

25 Find the lateral area of a right circular cone whose base is a circle of radius 6 ft and whose altitude is 8 ft.

26 A right circular cone has a diameter of 6 in. and the altitude equal to 4 in. Find the lateral area and the volume of the cone.

27 If a sphere has a surface area of 36π in.^{2}, what is the radius of the sphere? Find the volume of the sphere.

28 If the radius of a sphere is 100 cm, find the surface area and volume of the sphere.

29 Find the surface area and volume, in terms of π, of a sphere with radius of 1 foot.

30 A cone and a pyramid have equal volumes and equal heights. Each side of the square base of the pyramid measures 8 meters. What is the radius of the base of the cone? Leave the answer in terms of π.

31 Two prisms with square bases have equal volumes and the height of one prism is one-fourth the height of the other. If the measure of the side of the prism with the shorter height is 5 inches, find the measure of the side of the base of the other prism.

32 A large container of ice cream is a right circular cylinder. The base of that cylinder has a diameter of 6 inches and a height of 8 inches. If a scoop of ice cream is a sphere with a diameter of 2.2 inches, how many scoops of ice cream are in the container? Round to the nearest integer.

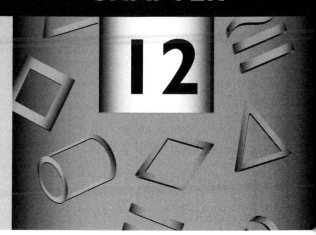

CHAPTER 12

Ratios, Proportion, and Similarity

In our earlier study of congruent triangles we were working with triangles that had the same size and the same shape. However, triangles and other polygons that have the same shape but *not* the same size are called similar figures. To grasp the relationship of similar figures, we need to have a clear understanding of *ratio* and *proportion*.

12-1 Ratio and Proportion

Ratio

A **ratio** is a comparison between two numbers by division. Ratios can be written as 3 to 4, or 3:4, or $\frac{3}{4}$. The forms 3:4 or $\frac{3}{4}$ can also be written as $\frac{3x}{4x}$, where x is the *common ratio factor* so that $\frac{3x}{4x}$ can equal $\frac{3}{4}, \frac{6}{8}, \frac{9}{12}, \frac{15}{20}$, etc.

Of course, a ratio can be extended to represent more than two numbers. If the angle measures in a triangle are 30, 60, and 90, the ratio of these measures can be written as 30:60:90 or, in lowest terms, 1:2:3. Also, if we have the ratio 3:4:7 this means the ratio of the first to the second is 3:4, the ratio of the second to the third is 4:7, and the ratio of the first to the third is 3:7. Again, the numbers do not have to be 3, 4, and 7, but can be represented as $3x$, $4x$, and $7x$, where $x \neq 0$.

Ratios are used to compare numbers with the same units (which then cancel, like common factors). For example: $\frac{6 \text{ quarts}}{10 \text{ quarts}} = \frac{\overset{3}{\cancel{6 \text{ quarts}}}}{\underset{5}{\cancel{10 \text{ quarts}}}} = \frac{3}{5} = \frac{3}{5}$.

In some comparisons the ratio needs to be changed into the same unit of measure: For example: $\frac{3 \text{ in.}}{2 \text{ ft}} = \frac{3 \text{ in.}}{24 \text{ in.}} = \frac{1}{8}$ or 1:8.

Lastly, ratios can also be used to compare numbers in different units. These comparisons are called **rates**. For example: If a car travels 60 miles in 1 hour, it travels at the rate of 60 miles per hour, or $\frac{60 \text{ miles}}{1 \text{ hour}}$.

Proportion

A **proportion** is an equation that states that two ratios are equal.

$$\frac{1}{4} = \frac{2}{8} \text{ or } \frac{1}{3} = \frac{4}{12}$$

Of course, proportions can be extended and involve more than two ratios, as with $\frac{1}{4} = \frac{2}{8} = \frac{3}{12} = \frac{5}{20}$, etc. And, in general, writing $\frac{a}{b} = \frac{c}{d} = \frac{m}{n} = \frac{x}{y}$ means the four ratios represent the same number.

The proportion $\frac{a}{x} = \frac{y}{b}$ can be written as $a{:}x = y{:}b$ where a, x, y, and b are the **terms** of the proposition. The first and fourth terms, a and b, are the *extremes* of the proportion, while x and y, the second and third terms, are the *means*.

- Theorem 12.1. In a proportion, the product of the extremes is equal to the product of the means.

  Example: $\frac{\text{extreme}}{\text{mean}} = \frac{\text{mean}}{\text{extreme}}$ or $\frac{a}{x} = \frac{y}{b}$ is a proportion, if and only if, ab(product of the extremes) $= xy$(product of the means), and where $x \neq 0$ and $b \neq 0$.

  Theorem 12.1 is also known as solving proportions by *cross multiplication*. If $\frac{2}{x} = \frac{3}{12}$, then $3x = (2)(12)$, or $3x = 24$, and $x = 8$.

- Corollary 12.1.1. In a proportion, the means can be interchanged and, similarly, the extremes can be interchanged.

  Example: In $\frac{2}{x} = \frac{3}{12}$, the means can be interchanged and the proportion is equivalent to $\frac{2}{3} = \frac{x}{12}$.

  Similarly, the extremes can be interchanged and the proportion is equivalent to $\frac{12}{x} = \frac{3}{2}$. More generally, $\frac{a}{x} = \frac{y}{b}$ equals $\frac{b}{x} = \frac{y}{a}$ or $\frac{a}{y} = \frac{x}{b}$ or $\frac{b}{y} = \frac{x}{a}$.

- Corollary 12.1.2. If the product of two nonzero numbers is equal to the product of two other nonzero numbers, as with $ab = jk$, then either factor pair can be the means or the extremes. Thus, the following proportions can be formed.

  Example: If $ab = jk$, then $\frac{a}{j} = \frac{k}{b}$ or $\frac{j}{a} = \frac{b}{k}$ or $\frac{b}{j} = \frac{k}{a}$ or $\frac{j}{b} = \frac{a}{k}$, where $a, b, j, k \neq 0$. Each proportion must have the same cross product: $ab = jk$.

  If the two *means* of a proportion are equal, as in $\frac{3}{x} = \frac{x}{12}$, then x is called the **mean proportional**.

  Example: $\frac{3}{x} = \frac{x}{12}$ means that $x^2 = (3)(12) = 36$ and $x = \pm\sqrt{36} = \pm 6$. However, unless otherwise indicated, the *mean proportional*, x, is always considered to be positive. Therefore, $x = 6$.

The following are five properties of proportions. These relationships come in handy when discussing areas and volumes.

1 **Denominator-Addition Property**

   If four quantities are in proportion, they are in proportion by addition; that is, the sum of the first two terms is to the second term as the sum of the last two terms is to the fourth term. Illustration:

   If $\frac{a}{b} = \frac{c}{d}$, then $\frac{a+b}{b} = \frac{c+d}{d}$.

   Using numbers: if $\frac{3}{4} = \frac{6}{8}$, then $\frac{3+4}{4} = \frac{6+8}{8}$ or $\frac{7}{4} = \frac{14}{8}$.

2 Denominator-Subtraction Property

If four quantities are in proportion, they are in proportion by subtraction; that is, the difference of the first two terms is to the second term as the difference between the last two terms is to the fourth term. Illustration:

If $\frac{a}{b} = \frac{c}{d}$, then $\frac{a-b}{b} = \frac{c-d}{d}$.

Using numbers: if $\frac{3}{4} = \frac{6}{8}$, then $\frac{3-4}{4} = \frac{6-8}{8}$ or $\frac{-1}{4} = \frac{-2}{8}$.

3 Addition-Subtraction Property

If four quantities are in proportion, they are in proportion by addition and subtraction. Illustration:

If $\frac{a}{b} = \frac{c}{d}$, then $\frac{a+b}{a-b} = \frac{c+d}{c-d}$.

Using numbers: if $\frac{1}{2} = \frac{3}{6}$, then $\frac{1+2}{1-2} = \frac{3+6}{3-6}$ or $\frac{3}{-1} = \frac{9}{-3}$ or $-3 = -3$.

4 Summation Property

If $\frac{a}{b} = \frac{c}{d} = \frac{e}{f} = \ldots = \frac{w}{x}$, then $\frac{a+c+e+\ldots+w}{b+d+f+\ldots+x} = \frac{a}{b}$.

5 Powers and Roots Property

If four quantities are in proportion, then like powers and like roots are in proportion. Illustration:

If $\frac{a}{b} = \frac{c}{d}$, then $\frac{a^n}{b^n} = \frac{c^n}{d^n}$ and $\frac{\sqrt[n]{a}}{\sqrt[n]{b}} = \frac{\sqrt[n]{c}}{\sqrt[n]{d}}$.

Using numbers: if $\frac{2}{3} = \frac{4}{6}$, then $\frac{2^2}{3^2} = \frac{4^2}{6^2}$ or $\frac{4}{9} = \frac{16}{36}$. Also, if $\frac{4}{9} = \frac{16}{36}$, then $\frac{\sqrt{4}}{\sqrt{9}} = \frac{\sqrt{16}}{\sqrt{36}}$ or $\frac{2}{3} = \frac{4}{6}$.

→ MODEL PROBLEMS

1 Solve the following proportion and check:

$\frac{9}{x+1} = \frac{3}{4}$

SOLUTION

Cross multiply

$3x + 3 = 36$

$3x = 33$

$x = 11$

Check: $\frac{9}{x+1} = \frac{3}{4}$

Substitute 11 for x: $\frac{9}{11+1} = \frac{3}{4}$ and $\frac{9}{12} = \frac{3}{4}$.

And the cross products are equal: $9 \times 4 = 12 \times 3$ or $36 = 36$.

2 Find the mean proportional between the given numbers:

a 5 and 20
b 6 and 30

SOLUTION

a $\frac{5}{x} = \frac{x}{20}$

$x^2 = 100$

$x = 10$

b $\frac{6}{x} = \frac{x}{30}$

$x^2 = 180$

$x = \sqrt{180} = \sqrt{36 \cdot 5} = 6\sqrt{5}$

 **Practice**

Exercises 1–4: Identify which statements are proportions.

1 $\dfrac{3}{5} = \dfrac{9}{12}$

2 $\dfrac{3}{4} = \dfrac{75}{100}$

3 $\dfrac{8}{3} = \dfrac{14}{6}$

4 $\dfrac{6}{7} = \dfrac{9}{10.5}$

5 If $\overline{AB}$ has a point X such that $\dfrac{AX}{XB} = \dfrac{2}{3}$, state the numerical value for each of the following ratios:

   a $\dfrac{XB}{AX}$

   b $\dfrac{AX}{AB}$

   c $\dfrac{XB}{AB}$

   d $\dfrac{AB}{XB}$

Exercises 6–13: Solve the proportions for x.

6 $\dfrac{x}{7} = \dfrac{11}{1}$

7 $\dfrac{3}{x} = \dfrac{5}{25}$

8 $\dfrac{8}{3} = \dfrac{6}{n}$

9 $\dfrac{12}{x+1} = \dfrac{3}{4}$

10 $\dfrac{5}{15} = \dfrac{x}{10+x}$

11 $\dfrac{x+11}{x} = \dfrac{12}{16}$

12 $5{:}x = 7{:}21$

13 $x{:}6 = 65{:}10$

14 $a{:}t = m{:}x$

15 $2m{:}r = x{:}a$

16 $2r{:}3t = x{:}6a$

Exercises 17–26: Find the mean proportional between the given numbers. Express answers in simplest radical form, where necessary.

17 3 and 27

18 4 and 16

19 5 and 45

20 3 and 16

21 3 and 33

22 3 and 25

23 6 and 12

24 6 and 16

25 $\dfrac{1}{5}$ and $\dfrac{1}{20}$

26 $\dfrac{1}{3}$ and $\dfrac{1}{9}$

27 The measure of an angle and the measure of its complement are in the ratio 5:4. Find the number of degrees in the angle and its complement.

28 If the measures of two supplementary angles are in the ratio 11:7, find the number of degrees in the measure of each angle.

29 A line segment is divided into two segments that are in the ratio 4:7. The measure of one segment is 15 inches longer than the measure of the other. Find the measure of each segment.

30 The measures of the sides of a triangle are in the ratio 4:5:6. Find the measure of each side if the perimeter of the triangle is 60 inches.

31 The length and width of a rectangle are in the ratio 4:7. If the perimeter of the rectangle is 154 feet, what is the length and width of the rectangle?

32 The measures of two consecutive angles of a parallelogram are in the ratio 3:9. Find the measure of each angle.

33 In the given figure, the segments of $\triangle ABC$ are in the proportion, $\frac{BD}{DA} = \frac{BE}{EC}$.

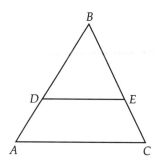

a If $EC = 24$, $DA = 15$, and $BD = 5$, find BE.

b If $BE = 12$, $BC = 36$, and $BD = 3$, find DA.

c If $EC = 18$, $BC = 30$, and $AB = 25$, find BD.

34

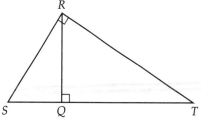

a In $\triangle SRT$, $\frac{SQ}{RQ} = \frac{RQ}{QT}$. If $RQ = 10$ and $SQ = 5$, find QT.

b In $\triangle SRT$, $\frac{SQ}{SR} = \frac{SR}{ST}$. If $SQ = 3$ and $ST = 27$, find SR.

12-2 Proportions Involving Line Segments

- Theorem 12.2. If a line is parallel to one side of a triangle then it divides the other two sides proportionally.

For example:

In the figure, $\overleftrightarrow{AB} \parallel \overline{CD}$, and $\overleftrightarrow{AB}$ intersects $\overline{EC}$ at F and $\overline{ED}$ at G.

Therefore, the following proportions are made:

$\frac{EF}{EC} = \frac{EG}{ED} = \frac{FG}{CD}$ and $\frac{EF}{FC} = \frac{EG}{GD}$.

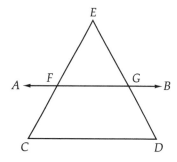

- Theorem 12.3. If a line divides two sides of a triangle proportionally, it is parallel to the third side.

For example:

In $\triangle WXY$, line m intersects $\overline{WX}$ and $\overline{XY}$ at A and B so that

$\frac{XA}{XW} = \frac{XB}{XY}$ and $\frac{XA}{AW} = \frac{XB}{BY}$. Thus, line $m \parallel \overline{WY}$ or $\overline{AB} \parallel \overline{WY}$.

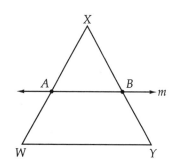

From these two theorems, the next, and more specific, theorem (which we have actually seen previously in coordinate geometry and Chapter 10) can be derived.

- Theorem 12.4. If a line segment joins the midpoints of two sides of a triangle, then it is parallel to the third side and its length is $\frac{1}{2}$ the length of the third side. (The converse is also true.)

  For example, in $\triangle ACE$, points A, B, and C are equally spaced and points E, D, and C are equally spaced. If $AC = 10$, $EC = 6$, and $BD = 6$, we can find the perimeter of quadrilateral $ABDE$.

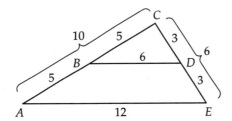

  $AB = BC = 5$, $ED = DC = 3$, and since $BD = 6$, by Theorem 12.4, $AE = 12$. The perimeter of quadrilateral $ABDE = 5 + 6 + 3 + 12 = 26$.

- Theorem 12.5. If two parallel lines are cut by three or more transversals passing through a common point, the corresponding segments are proportional.

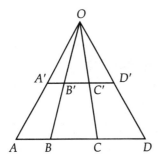

  In the figure, $\overline{A'D'} \parallel \overline{AD}$, so that $\frac{AB}{A'B'} = \frac{BC}{B'C'} = \frac{CD}{C'D'}$

Special Notes

1 Connecting, in order, the midpoints of the sides of a parallelogram results in another parallelogram.

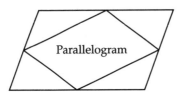

Parallelogram

2 Connecting, in order, the midpoints of the sides of a rectangle results in a rhombus.

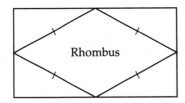

Rhombus

3 Connecting, in order, the midpoints of the sides of a rhombus results in a rectangle.

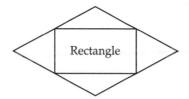

4 Connecting, in order, the midpoints of the sides of a square results in another square.

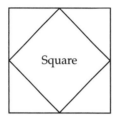

 MODEL PROBLEMS

1 In $\triangle ABC$, points D, E, and F are the midpoints of the sides with the measures shown. Find the measure of the perimeter of $\triangle DEF$.

SOLUTION

$\overline{DE}$, $\overline{EF}$, and $\overline{FD}$ join the midpoints of the sides $\overline{AB}$, $\overline{BC}$, and $\overline{AC}$, respectively.

Thus, $DE = \frac{1}{2}AC = 10$

$EF = \frac{1}{2}AB = 12$

$FD = \frac{1}{2}BC = 11$

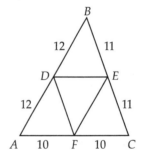

ANSWER: The measure of the perimeter of $\triangle DEF = 10 + 12 + 11 = 33$.

2 In $\triangle AEC$, if $AB = 12$, $BC = 16$, $AD = 15$, and $DE = 20$, is $\overline{BD} \parallel \overline{CE}$?

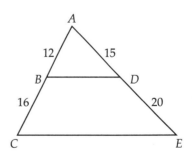

SOLUTION

Check the proportions. If $\overline{BD} \parallel \overline{CE}$, then the following statement should be true:

$\frac{12}{16} = \frac{15}{20}$ or, by reducing, $\frac{3}{4} = \frac{3}{4}$.

ANSWER: Since the ratios are equal, $\overline{BD} \parallel \overline{CE}$.

3 In $\triangle ABC$, R is the midpoint of $\overline{AB}$, and D is the midpoint of $\overline{BC}$.

If $AC = 5x - 8$, $RD = 2x - 1$, $DC = 3x + 2$, and $AB = 10x - 1$, find the lengths of AB, AC, DC, and RD.

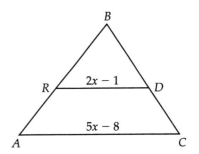

SOLUTION

The base $AC = 2(RD)$ so that
$5x - 8 = 2(2x - 1)$
$5x - 8 = 4x - 2$
$\quad x = 6$

Substitute 6 for x in each relevant measure.

$AB = 10x - 1$
$AB = 10(6) - 1 = 59$

$AC = 5x - 8$
$AC = 5(6) - 8 = 22$

$DC = 3x + 2$
$DC = 3(6) + 2 = 20$

$RD = 2x - 1$
$RD = 2(6) - 1 = 11$

 Practice

---

1 In $\triangle ABC$, if $\overline{DE} \parallel \overline{AC}$, which of the following are true?

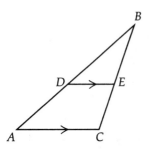

a $\dfrac{BD}{BA} = \dfrac{BE}{BC}$

b $\dfrac{BD}{DA} = \dfrac{BE}{EC}$

c $\dfrac{BA}{DA} = \dfrac{BC}{EC}$

d $\dfrac{BD}{BA} = \dfrac{DE}{AC}$

2

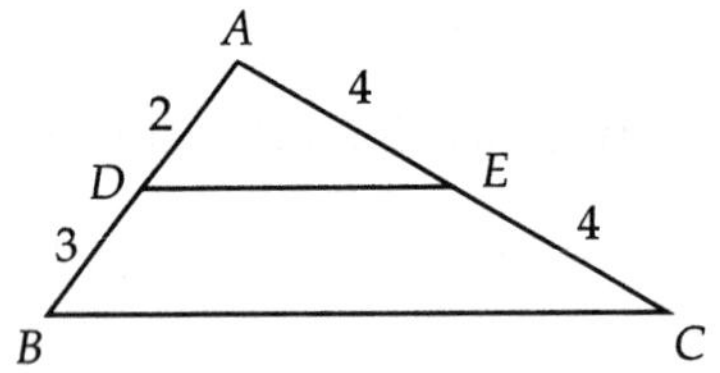

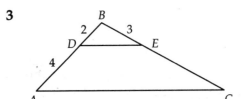

Given $\triangle ABC$ and segment DE, if $AD = 2$, $DB = 3$, $AE = 4$, and $EC = 4$, is $\overline{DE} \parallel \overline{BC}$? State your reason.

3

In $\triangle ABC$, $\overline{DE} \parallel \overline{AC}$. Using the given measures, what is the length of EC?

4

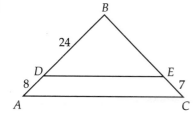

In $\triangle ABC$, $\overline{DE} \parallel \overline{AC}$. Using the given measures, find the length of BC.

Exercises 5–13: In $\triangle ABC$, $\overline{DE} \parallel \overline{AC}$.

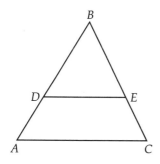

5 Find EB, if $AD = 10$, $DB = 6$, and $CE = 9$.

6 Find DB, if $AC = 12$, $DE = 8$, and $AD = 3$.

7 Find CB, if $CE = 6$, $AC = 20$, and $DE = 15$.

8 Find DE, if $BE = 5$, $CE = 1$, and $AC = 6$.

9 Find DA, if $BD = a$, $BE = b$, and $EC = c$.

10 Find BE, if $AB = m$, $BD = n$, and $BC = p$.

11 Find BD, if $BD = EC$, $DA = 4$, and $BE = 9$.

12 Find BE, if $BE = 2(DA)$, $BD = 10$, and $EC = 20$.

13 Find EC, if $AB = a$, $BD = b$, and $BC = c$.

Exercises 14–18: Examine the given conditions and determine whether they imply that $\overline{DE} \parallel \overline{AB}$.

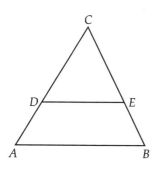

14 $CD = 3$, $DA = 9$, $CE = 5$, and $CB = 15$

15 $CD = 6$, $CA = 15$, $CE = 10$, and $EB = 25$

16 $CD = 30$, $DA = 20$, $CE = 44$, and $EB = 6$

17 $\dfrac{CD}{CA} = \dfrac{CE}{CB}$

18 $\dfrac{CD}{DA} = \dfrac{CE}{EB}$

19 In $\triangle ABC$, points D and E are the midpoints of $\overline{AB}$ and $\overline{BC}$. If the perimeter of $\triangle ABC$ is 24, what is the perimeter of $\triangle BDE$?

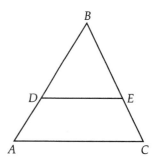

20 In the figure, $\overline{KT} \parallel \overline{AC}$, $KT = 24$, and $RT = 18$. What is the ratio of AD to DC?

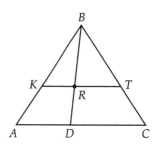

21 The length of the diagonal of a rectangle is 22 cm. What is the measure of a line segment that joins the midpoints of two consecutive sides of the rectangle?

22

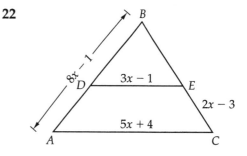

In $\triangle ABC$, $\overline{DE}$ joins midpoints D on side $\overline{AB}$ and E on side $\overline{BC}$. If $AB = 8x - 1$, $DE = 3x - 1$, $AC = 5x + 4$, and $EC = 2x - 3$, find the value of x and the measures of AB, DE, AC, EC, BE, AD, and DB.

23 In the figure, the midpoints of the sides of △*ABC* are *P*, *Q*, and *R*.

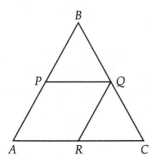

a Prove that quadrilateral *PQRA* is a parallelogram.

b If *AB* = 14, *BC* = 10, and *AC* = 16, what is the perimeter of quadrilateral *PQRA*?

24 The midpoints of the sides of quadrilateral *ABCD* are *w*, *x*, *y*, and *z*. Prove that quadrilateral *wxyz* is a parallelogram. (Hint: Draw diagonal $\overline{AC}$ or $\overline{BD}$.)

25

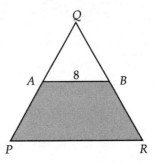

In the figure, △*PQR* is an equilateral triangle. If *A* and *B* are the midpoints of sides $\overline{PQ}$ and $\overline{QR}$, respectively, what is the area of the shaded region? State the answer in the simplest radical form.

12-3 Similar Polygons

Two polygons are similar if there is a *one-to-one* correspondence between their vertices such that both conditions, stated below, must be true.

1   All pairs of corresponding angles are congruent.
2   The ratio of the measures of all the pairs of corresponding sides are equal.

Note:

• All equilateral triangles are similar.
• All squares are similar.
• All regular polygons with the same number of sides are similar.

Example: Regular Pentagon *ABCDE* ~ Regular Pentagon *A′B′C′D′E′*

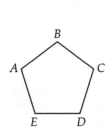
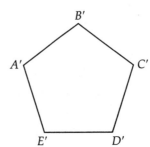

Corresponding Angles Are Congruent: ∠*A* ≅ ∠*A′*, ∠*B* ≅ ∠*B′*, ∠*C* ≅ ∠*C′*, ∠*D* ≅ ∠*D′*, ∠*E* ≅ ∠*E′*

Corresponding Sides Are in Proportion: $\dfrac{AB}{A'B'} = \dfrac{BC}{B'C'} = \dfrac{CD}{C'D'} = \dfrac{DE}{D'E'} = \dfrac{EA}{E'A'}$

In the following examples, polygons I, II, and III are *not similar*.

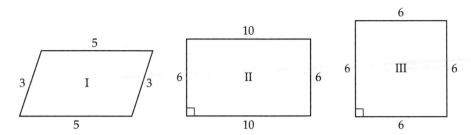

1. Polygon I, the parallelogram, has corresponding sides in proportion to Polygon II, the rectangle, but the corresponding angles are not congruent.
2. In Polygon III, the square, the corresponding angles are all congruent to Polygon II, but the corresponding sides are not in proportion.

- Theorem 12.6. A line parallel to one side of a triangle cuts off a triangle that is similar to the original triangle.

Recall that theorem 12.2 states that a line parallel to one side of a triangle divides the other two sides proportionally.

For example; in $\triangle RST$, if $\overline{AB} \parallel \overline{RT}$, then

1. $\triangle ASB \sim \triangle RST$
2. Corresponding angles are congruent: $\angle R \cong \angle SAB$, $\angle S \cong \angle S$, and $\angle T \cong \angle SBA$.
3. Corresponding sides of the triangles are in proportion: $\frac{AS}{RS} = \frac{SB}{ST} = \frac{AB}{RT}$.
4. (By Theorem 12.7) $\frac{SA}{AR} = \frac{SB}{BT}$

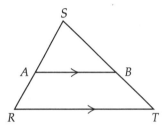

The ratio of the lengths of corresponding segments (or sides) is called the **ratio of similitude**. When working with the transformation called a *dilation*, the ratio of similitude is often called the scale factor.

Section 12-5 will cover dilations more thoroughly.

For example: The image of $\triangle PCL$, with sides 3, 4, and 5, is enlarged to $\triangle RTS$, with corresponding sides, 9, 12, and 15. The scale factor is 3 and the ratio of similitude is 3:1.

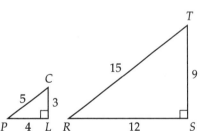

A good mathematical definition is reversible. Thus, if two polygons have corresponding congruent angles and corresponding sides that are in proportion, then the polygons are similar.

Recall that relations that retain the *reflexive, symmetric,* and *transitive* properties such as "equal to" and "congruent to" and "parallel to" are called **equivalence relations**. The concept of "is similar to" is also an equivalence relationship such that

1. Reflexive Property: Polygon $ABCD \sim$ Polygon $ABCD$
2. Symmetric Property: If Polygon $ABCD \sim$ Polygon $PQRS$, then Polygon $PQRS \sim$ Polygon $ABCD$.
3. Transitive Property: If Polygon $ABCD \sim$ Polygon $PQRS$ and Polygon $PQRS \sim$ Polygon $WXYZ$, then Polygon $ABCD \sim$ Polygon $WXYZ$.

→ MODEL PROBLEM

The sides of a quadrilateral are 15, 20, 25, and 30, and the shortest side of a similar quadrilateral measures 6.

    a   Find the ratio of similitude.
    b   Find each corresponding side of the smaller quadrilateral.
    c   Find the perimeter of the smaller quadrilateral.

SOLUTION

    a   To find the ratio of similitude, compare the image to the original. In this case, we have 6:15 or 2:5.

ANSWER: The ratio of similitude is 2:5.

    b   To find the missing sides, take $\frac{2}{5}$ of each of the given sides.

$$\frac{2}{5}(20) = 8$$
$$\frac{2}{5}(25) = 10$$
$$\frac{2}{5}(30) = 12$$

ANSWER: Each corresponding side of the smaller quadrilateral is 8, 10, and 12.

    c   To find the perimeter, add the sides: $6 + 8 + 10 + 12 = 36$

ANSWER: The perimeter is 36.

Practice

1   If two similar polygons are also congruent, what is the ratio of similitude?

2   The sides of a quadrilateral measure 12, 18, 20, and 16. If the shortest side of a similar quadrilateral measures 3, find the measures of the remaining sides of this quadrilateral.

3   In two similar triangles, two corresponding sides measure 6 inches and 2 feet. What is the ratio of similitude of the two triangles?

4   If the sides of a triangle measure 4, 9, and 11, and the shortest side of a similar triangle measures 20, find the measures of the remaining sides of this triangle.

5   In the figures, $\triangle ABC \sim \triangle DEF$.

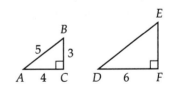

    a   Find the ratio of similitude.

    b   Find the lengths of EF and DE.

    c   Find the perimeter of $\triangle DEF$.

6 $\triangle ABC \sim \triangle A'B'C'$ and the ratio of similitude is 2:3. If the measures of the sides of $\triangle ABC$ are 6, 9, and 12, find the measures of the sides of $\triangle A'B'C'$.

7 △ABC ~ △PQR and the ratio of similitude is 1:5. If the measures of the sides of △ABC are represented by a, b, and c, find the measures of the sides of △PQR in terms of a, b, and c.

8 Rhombus PQRS has a 50° angle and a side of 7 inches, and rhombus ABCD has a 130° angle and a side of 14 inches. Use a narrative proof to show that rhombus PQRS is similar to rhombus ABCD.

9 The ratio of similitude of two similar quadrilaterals is 3:1. If the measures of the sides of the larger quadrilateral are represented by w, x, y, and z, what are the measures of the lengths of the sides of the smaller quadrilateral?

10 If 3, 8, and 10 are the sides of a triangle and the shortest side of a similar triangle measures 12, what are the measures of the remaining sides?

11 Parallelogram ABCD is similar to parallelogram PRNQ. If m∠A = 70, find m∠R and m∠Q.

12 Quadrilateral ABCD is similar to quadrilateral HIJK. If m∠A = 48, m∠B = 40, and m∠C = 112, find the measures of ∠I and ∠K.

13 Pentagon ABCDE ~ pentagon TRWQX.

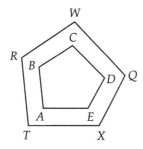

If TR = 12, TX = 16, and AB = 9, find the length of AE.

14 Polygon ABCDE ~ polygon PQRST.

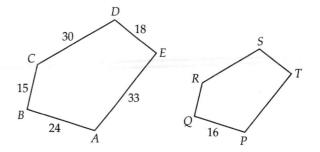

a Find the ratio of similitude.
b Find the missing lengths of the sides of polygon PQRST.

15 State whether each of the following statements is *True* or *False*.

a Two congruent polygons are always similar.
b Two similar polygons are never congruent.
c The ratio of similitude for similar and congruent polygons is 1:1.
d All squares are similar.
e All rectangles are similar.
f All circles are similar.
g All rhombi are similar.
h Quadrilaterals are sometimes similar to pentagons.

16 Prove that two isosceles triangles are similar if an angle of one is equal to the corresponding angle of another.

12-4 Proving Triangles Similar

Since triangles are polygons, we can prove two triangles are similar if we can show that they satisfy the two necessary conditions required of similar polygons.

1   All pairs of corresponding angles are congruent.
2   The corresponding sides are in proportion.

However, there are other shorter methods to proving triangles similar.

Theorems and Corollaries to Prove Triangles Similar

• Theorem 12.7 (AAA ≅ AAA). Two triangles are similar if three angles of one triangle are congruent to three corresponding angles of the other.
• Corollary 12.7.1 (AA ~). Two triangles are similar if two angles of one triangle are congruent to two corresponding angles of the other.

Example:

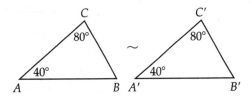

△ABC ~ △A′B′C′ because each has a 40° angle and an 80° angle. For the sum of the angles to equal 180°, the third angle in each triangle is 60°. Thus, all three pairs of angles are congruent.

• Corollary 12.7.2 (AA ~). Two right triangles are similar if an acute angle of one triangle is congruent to an acute angle of the other.

Example:

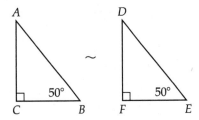

Right triangles ABC and DEF each have 90° and 50° angles, so that the third angle for each must be 40°. (This is another version of AAA ≅ AAA.)

• Theorem 12.8 (SSS ~). Two triangles are similar if the three ratios of corresponding sides are equal.

Example:

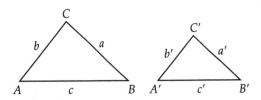

△ABC ~ △A′B′C′ because $\frac{a}{a'} = \frac{b}{b'} = \frac{c}{c'}$.

- Theorem 12.9 (SAS ~). Two triangles are similar if the ratios of two pairs of corresponding sides are equal and the corresponding angles included between these sides are congruent.

  Example:

  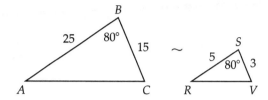

  $\angle B \cong \angle S$ and $\frac{AB}{RS} = \frac{BC}{SV}$ or $\frac{25}{5} = \frac{15}{3}$, so $\triangle ABC \sim \triangle RSV$.

Overlapping Triangles

- Theorem 12.10. If a line is parallel to one side of a triangle and intersects the other two sides, it divides the sides proportionally and cuts off a triangle similar to the given triangle.

  Example:

  If $\overline{DE} \parallel \overline{AC}$, then $\triangle ABC \sim \triangle DBE$.

  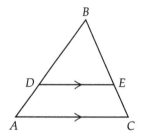

  All corresponding angles are congruent: $\angle A \cong \angle BDE$, $\angle B \cong \angle B$, and $\angle C \cong \angle BED$.

  Corresponding sides are in proportion: $\frac{AB}{DB} = \frac{BC}{BE} = \frac{AC}{DE}$.

  Segments of intersected sides are in proportion: $\frac{BD}{DA} = \frac{BE}{EC}$.

- Theorem 12.11 (Converse of theorem 12.10). If the points at which a line intersects two sides of a triangle divides those sides proportionally, then the line is parallel to the third side and the triangles formed are similar.
- Corollary 12.11.1. If a line segment joins the *midpoints* of two sides of a triangle, that segment is parallel to the third side and its length is half the length of the third side.

  Example:

  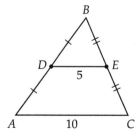

  In $\triangle ABC$, points D and E are midpoints, $\overline{DE} \parallel \overline{AC}$, $\triangle ABC \sim \triangle DBE$, and $DE = \frac{1}{2}AC$.

1 In the figure, $AD = 5$, $DB = 3$, $DE = 4$, $EC = 4.5$, and $AC = 12$.

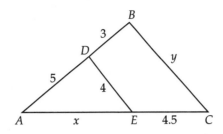

a Prove that $\triangle DEA \sim \triangle BCA$.
b Find the value for x and y.

SOLUTION

a Set up proportions to determine whether the sides are in proportion.

$AE = 12 - 4.5 = 7.5$

$\dfrac{AB}{AC} = \dfrac{AD}{AE}$ or $\dfrac{8}{12} = \dfrac{5}{7.5}$

Cross multiply: $8(7.5) = 12(5)$ or $60 = 60$

Since the sides are in proportion and the corresponding angles between the sides are congruent, the two triangles are similar.

b $AE = x = 7.5$

To find y, set up another proportion: $\dfrac{5}{4} = \dfrac{8}{y}$

$5y = 32$ and $y = 6.4$

ANSWER: $x = 7.5$ and $y = 6.4$

2 Given: $\overline{AB} \perp \overline{CB}$, $\overline{BD} \perp \overline{AC}$
   Prove: $\triangle I \sim \triangle II$

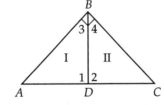

Statements	Reasons
1. $\overline{AB} \perp \overline{CB}$, $\overline{BD} \perp \overline{AC}$	1. Given.
2. $\angle 1 \cong \angle 2$ (A $\cong$ A)	2. Perpendicular lines form congruent right angles.
3. $\angle ABC$ is a right angle.	3. Perpendicular lines form right angles.
4. $\angle 3$ and $\angle 4$ are complements.	4. Two adjacent angles that form a right angle are complementary.
5. $\angle 3$ and $\angle A$ are complements.	5. Acute angles of a right triangle are complementary.
6. $\angle 4 \cong \angle A$ (A $\cong$ A)	6. Complements of congruent angles are congruent.
7. $\triangle I \sim \triangle II$	7. If two angles of a triangle are congruent to two angles of another triangle, the triangles are similar.

1 If the vertex angles of two isosceles triangles are congruent, then the two triangles must be:

(1) congruent
(2) similar
(3) right
(4) obtuse

2

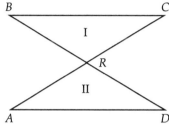

In the figure, m∠A = 20, m∠B = 20.
Prove △I ∼ △II.

3

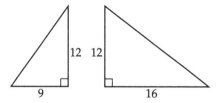

With the given measures of the two right triangles, determine whether the triangles are similar.

4

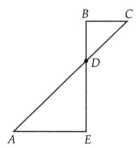

Given: $\overline{AE} \parallel \overline{BC}$, $\overleftrightarrow{AC}$ and $\overleftrightarrow{BE}$ intersect at D.

a Show △ADE ∼ △CDB.
b If BD = 10, ED = 15, and CD = 20, what is the measure of AD?

5

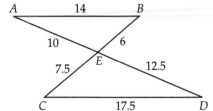

Given: $\overline{CB}$ and $\overline{AD}$ intersect at E, and the lengths are as given.
Prove: △ABE ∼ △DCE

6

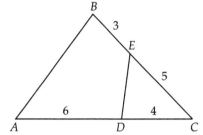

Using the measure of segments in the figure, determine whether △ABC ∼ △EDC.

7

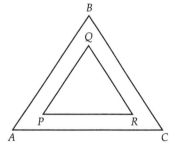

If AB = 12, BC = 14, AC = 16, PQ = 8, and QR = 10, determine whether △ABC ∼ △PQR.

8

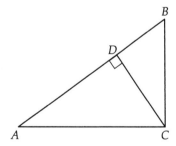

Given: $\overline{CD} \perp \overline{AB}$ and ∠CAD ≅ ∠BCD.
Prove: △CDA ∼ △BDC

9

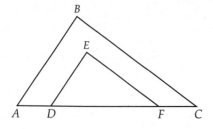

Given: $\overline{AB} \parallel \overline{DE}$ and $\overline{BC} \parallel \overline{EF}$
Prove: $\triangle ABC \sim \triangle DEF$

10

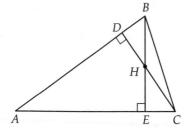

Given: $\overline{BE} \perp \overline{AC}$ and $\overline{CD} \perp \overline{AB}$
Prove: $\triangle EHC \sim \triangle DHB$

11

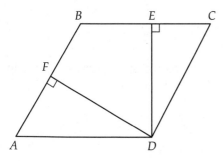

Given: Parallelogram $ABCD$; $\overline{DE} \perp \overline{BC}$, and $\overline{DF} \perp \overline{AB}$
Prove: $\triangle AFD \sim \triangle CED$

12

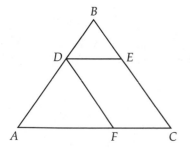

Given: $\triangle DBE \sim \triangle ADF$
Prove: $\triangle DBE \sim \triangle ABC$

13

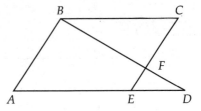

Given: Parallelogram $ABCE$, $\overline{AED}$
Prove: $\triangle BAD \sim \triangle FCB$

14

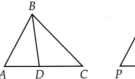

Given: $\triangle ABC \sim \triangle PQR$, $\overline{BD}$ bisects $\angle ABC$, $\overline{QS}$ bisects $\angle PQR$.
Prove: $\triangle ABD \sim \triangle PQS$

15

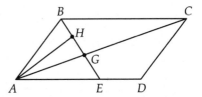

Given: Parallelogram $ABCD$; diagonal $\overline{AC}$ bisects $\angle HAE$; $\overline{AE} \cong \overline{AH}$.
Prove: $\triangle HAG \sim \triangle BCG$

12-5 Dilations

A **dilation** is a size-change transformation that transforms a figure into a similar figure. Typically, as shown in the figure below, beginning at point O, the *center of dilation*, rays are drawn through each of the vertices of $\triangle ABC$ so that other images of $\triangle ABC$ can be formed. These rays can be used as guides to the expansion or contraction of a figure. The figures in this case show that $\triangle A'B'C'$ is the contraction of $\triangle ABC$ and $\triangle A'B'C'$ is the expansion of $\triangle ABC$ and $\triangle A'B'C' \sim \triangle ABC \sim \triangle A''B''C''$.

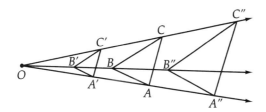

The ratio of any length in the transformed figure to the corresponding length in the original figure is called the **scale factor (k)** or the **constant of dilation**. Essentially, the scale factor, $k = \dfrac{\text{image}}{\text{orignal}}$.

If, for example, $AC = 5$ and $A'C' = 3$, then the ratio of $A'C':AC$ is 3:5 or $k = \frac{3}{5}$. If $AC = 5$ and $A''C''$ is 10, then the ratio of $A''C'':AC$ is 10:5 or $k = 2$.

In the more familiar arrangement below, if $\triangle PQR$ has a line $P'R'$ drawn parallel to $\overline{PR}$, such that segment $P'R' = 12$ and segment $PR = 15$, then point $Q = Q'$ and is the center of dilation.

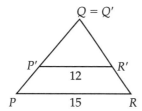

The scale factor is $k = \dfrac{P'R'}{PR} = \dfrac{12}{15}$ or 4:5. And, $\triangle P'Q'R' \sim \triangle PQR$.

Recall that in coordinate geometry, under the *dilation of k* (a positive scale factor) whose center of dilation is the origin, the rule for dilation is $D_k(x, y) = (kx, ky)$. The scale factor, k, is the factor of *expansion* if $k > 0$ or the factor of *contraction* if $0 < k < 1$. If k is the scale factor of the identity transformation, then $k = 1$. Recall that, dilation preserves angle measures, betweenness, and collinearity.

 MODEL PROBLEMS

1 Find the coordinates of $M(-3, 5)$ under the composition of transformations, $r_{y\text{-axis}} \circ D_3$.

SOLUTION

Perform the transformations from right to left. Thus, $D_3(-3, 5) = (-9, 15)$. Then perform the next transformation, $r_{y\text{-axis}}$. Thus, $r_{y\text{-axis}}(-9, 15) = (9, 15)$.

ANSWER: $r_{y\text{-axis}} \circ D_3(-3, 5) = (9, 15)$

2 The vertices of rectangle *PQRS* are *P*(1, −2), *Q*(3, −2), *R*(3, 2), and *S*(1, 2).

    a Find the coordinates of the vertices of *P′Q′R′S′*, the image of *PQRS*, under D_4.

    b Show that *P′Q′R′S′* is a rectangle.

    c Prove that *PQRS* ~ *P′Q′R′S′*.

SOLUTION

    a To find the coordinates of the vertices of *P′Q′R′S′*, simply multiply each of the coordinates of *PQRS* by the scale factor, *k* = 4. The coordinates are *P′*(4, −8), *Q′*(12, −8), *R′*(12, 8), and *S′*(4, 8).

    b To show that *P′Q′R′S′* is a rectangle, find the slopes of the sides.

$$\text{Slope}_{P'Q'} = \frac{-8-(-8)}{4-12} = \frac{0}{-8} = 0 \text{ (horizontal line)}$$

$$\text{Slope}_{Q'R'} = \frac{-8-8}{12-12} = \frac{-16}{0} = \text{undefined (vertical line)}$$

$$\text{Slope}_{R'S'} = \frac{8-8}{12-4} = \frac{0}{8} = 0 \text{ (horizontal line)}$$

$$\text{Slope}_{S'P'} = \frac{8-(-8)}{4-4} = \frac{16}{0} = \text{undefined (vertical line)}$$

Since the slopes of opposite sides are equal, the opposite sides are parallel, and *P′Q′R′S′* is a parallelogram. Since adjacent sides are perpendicular to each other (one horizontal, one vertical), the angles formed are right angles. A parallelogram with all right angles is a rectangle.

    c Since all the corresponding angles are right angles and the lengths of each pair of corresponding sides have been increased by a scale factor of 4, the corresponding sides are in proportion. As a check, use the distance formula to verify that the length of *PQ* = 2 and *P′Q′* = 8, while *QR* = 4 and *Q′R′* = 16. Similarly, the other corresponding sides have a ratio of 1:4.

Practice

1 In the figure, with *O* as the center, △*A′B′C′* is the expansion of △*ABC*.

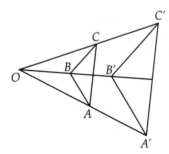

If *AB* = 6, *BC* = 8, *A′B′* = 20, and *A′C′* = 30, find

    a *k*, the scale factor

    b *B′C′*

    c *AC*

2

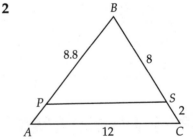

Given: △*ABC* ~ △*PBS*, with *BS* = 8, *SC* = 2, *AC* = 12, and *BP* = 8.8

    a Find the lengths of segments *BC*, *PA*, *BA*, and *PS*.

    b Find *k*, the constant of dilation.

Exercises 3–6: Using the rule $D_3(x, y) = (3x, 3y)$, find the coordinates of the image of each given point.

3 $(7, 3)$

4 $(-2, 4)$

5 $(3, 0)$

6 $(-9, -1)$

Exercises 7–10: Find the coordinates of the image of each point under D_4.

7 $(3, 3)$

8 $(2.5, 9)$

9 $(-5, 3)$

10 $\left(\frac{5}{8}, -\frac{1}{4}\right)$

Exercises 11–14: Each given point is the image under D_2. Find the coordinates of each preimage.

11 $(8, -4)$

12 $(6, 0)$

13 $(-6, 7)$

14 $(4\sqrt{2}, 5)$

Exercises 15–20: Find the coordinates of the image of each given point under the given composition of transformations.

15 $r_{y\text{-axis}} \circ D_4(4, -2)$

16 $R_{90} \circ D_2(1, 5)$

17 $D_3 \circ T_{2,1}(-7, -1)$

18 $r_{x\text{-axis}} \circ D_3(-1, 5)$

19 $D_{\frac{1}{2}} \circ T_{1,-1}(5, -3)$

20 $r_{y = x} \circ D_2(-4, 2)$

Exercises 21–24: Each transformation is the composition of a dilation and a reflection in either the x-axis or the y-axis. In each case, write a rule for the composition of transformations for which the image of A is A′.

21 $A(5, 2)$ is transformed to $A'(10, -4)$.

22 $A(-1, 3)$ is transformed to $A'(3, 9)$.

23 $A(8, 2)$ is transformed to $A'(4, -1)$.

24 $A(-10, 4)$ is transformed to $A'(-2.5, -1)$.

25 The coordinates of parallelogram $ABCD$ are $A(0, 0)$, $B(4, 0)$, $C(5, 2)$, and $D(1, 2)$. Under D_3, the image of $ABCD$ is $A'B'C'D'$.

a Find the coordinates of the vertices of $A'B'C'D'$.

b Show that $A'B'C'D'$ is a parallelogram.

c Let M be the midpoint of diagonal AC and M' the midpoint of $A'C'$. Find the coordinates of M and M'. Is M' the image result of D_3 operating on point M? Can we say that midpoints are preserved under a dilation?

12-6 Proving Proportional Relationships Among Segments Related to Triangles

We know already that if two triangles are similar, their corresponding sides are in proportion. A logical extension is that any other corresponding segments (such as, *altitudes, medians,* and *angle bisectors*) are also in proportion.

- **Theorem 12.12.** If two triangles are similar, the lengths of corresponding altitudes have the same ratio as the lengths of any two corresponding sides.

  Example:

  $\triangle ABC \sim \triangle PQR$, such that $\frac{\text{altitude } BD}{\text{altitude } QS} = \frac{AB}{PQ}$ (or any other pair of corresponding sides).

  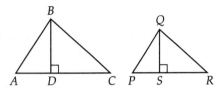

- **Theorem 12.13.** If two triangles are similar, the lengths of corresponding medians have the same ratio as the lengths of any two corresponding sides.

  Example:

  $\triangle ABC \sim \triangle PQR$, such that $\frac{\text{median } BW}{\text{median } QT} = \frac{BC}{QR}$ (or any other pair of corresponding sides).

  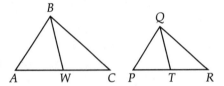

- **Theorem 12.14.** If two triangles are similar, the lengths of corresponding angle bisectors have the same ratio as the lengths of any two corresponding sides.

  Example:

  $\triangle ABC \sim \triangle PQR$, such that $\frac{\text{angle bisector } AD}{\text{angle bisector } PS} = \frac{AB}{PQ}$ (or any other pair of corresponding sides).

  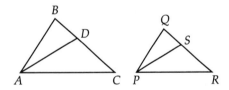

- **Corollary 12.14.1.** The bisector of an angle of a triangle divides the opposite side into segments proportional to the two sides of the bisected angle.

  Example:

  $\overline{BW}$ bisects $\angle ABC$ such that $\frac{AW}{WC} = \frac{AB}{BC}$.

  Substituting the values given, $\frac{10}{4} = \frac{15}{6}$

  or $\frac{5}{2} = \frac{5}{2}$.

  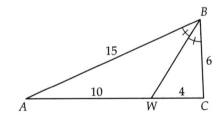

The Medial Triangle

In Theorem 12.4 we learned that the line segment that joins the midpoint of two sides of a triangle equals $\frac{1}{2}$ the length of the third side. However, if all the midpoints are joined, the triangle formed is called the **medial triangle**.

For example, in $\triangle ABC$, if P, Q, and R, the midpoints of the sides, are joined, and $\triangle PQR$ is the *medial triangle*.

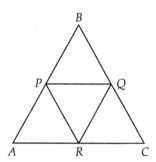

Furthermore, $\triangle PQR \sim \triangle ABC$, and the ratio of similitude is 1:2.

 MODEL PROBLEMS

1 Two triangles are similar and the sides of the larger triangle have lengths of 10 cm, 12 cm, and 18 cm. The perimeter of the smaller triangle is 25 cm.

   a Find the ratio of similitude.
   b Find the lengths of each side of the smaller triangle.

SOLUTION

   a In similar triangles, the ratio of corresponding sides is the same as the ratio of corresponding perimeters. The ratio of perimeters is also called the **ratio of similitude**:

$$\frac{\text{perimeter of smaller triangle}}{\text{perimeter of larger triangle}} = \frac{25}{10 + 12 + 18} = \frac{25}{40} = \frac{5}{8}$$

ANSWER: The ratio of similitude is $\frac{5}{8}$.

   b Represented the sides of the smaller triangle, from smallest to largest, as a, b, and c.

$\frac{5}{8} = \frac{a}{10}$, so $8a = 50$ and $a = 6.25$

$\frac{5}{8} = \frac{b}{12}$, so $8b = 60$ and $b = 7.5$

$\frac{5}{8} = \frac{c}{18}$, so $8c = 90$ and $c = 11.25$

ANSWER: $a = 6.25$, $b = 7.5$, $c = 11.25$

2 $\triangle ABC \sim \triangle RST$ with medians $\overline{AD}$ and $\overline{RM}$

If $AC = 12$, $RT = 9$, and $RM = 6$, what is the length of AD?

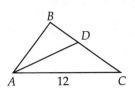

SOLUTION

$$\frac{AD \text{ (median)}}{RM \text{ (median)}} = \frac{AC \text{ (side)}}{RT \text{ (side)}}$$

$$\frac{AD}{6} = \frac{12}{9}$$

$$9(AD) = 72$$

$$AD = 8$$

ANSWER: $AD = 8$

3 In triangle ABC, $m\angle 1 = m\angle 2$, $AB = 9$, $BC = 11$, and $AC = 15$. Find the lengths of AD and DC.

SOLUTION

Split the base AC into two parts: x and $15 - x$.

According to Corollary 12.15.1, since $\overline{BD}$ bisects $\angle ABC$, we can set up a proportion.

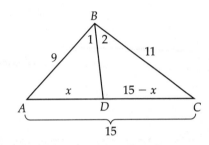

$$\frac{x}{15 - x} = \frac{9}{11}$$

$$9(15 - x) = 11x$$

$$135 - 9x = 11x$$

$$135 = 20x$$

$$x = 6.75$$

ANSWER: $AD = 6.75$ and $DC = 15 - 6.75 = 8.25$

4 If $\triangle ABC$ has sides 15, 28, and 38, then what is the perimeter of the medial triangle?

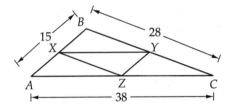

SOLUTION

Mark the midpoints of each side X, Y, and Z, and join them to form $\triangle XYZ$. Since each side of $\triangle XYZ$ is half the corresponding side of the larger $\triangle ABC$, the perimeter of $\triangle XYZ$ is half the perimeter of $\triangle ABC$.

The perimeter of $\triangle ABC = 15 + 28 + 38 = 81$ and the perimeter of $\triangle XYZ = 40.5$.

ANSWER: The perimeter of the medial triangle, $\triangle XYZ$, is 40.5.

1 If the lengths of the sides of two similar triangles are in the ratio 3:4, what is the ratio of the lengths of a pair of corresponding altitudes? What is the ratio of their perimeters?

2 The ratio of similitude in two similar triangles is 6:1. If a side of the larger triangle measures 30 centimeters, what is the measure of the corresponding side in the smaller triangle?

3 If two triangles are similar and the ratio of two corresponding altitudes is 4:9, what is the ratio of two corresponding medians?

4 The lengths of two corresponding sides of two similar triangles are 22 inches and 12 inches. If an altitude of the smaller triangle has a length of 6 inches, find the length of the corresponding altitude of the larger triangle.

5 In $\triangle ABC$, $m\angle 1 = m\angle 2$, $AB = 9$, $BC = 12$, and $AC = 14$.

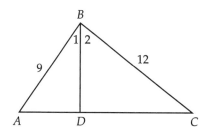

Find the lengths of AD and DC.

6

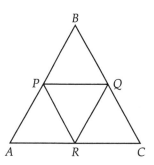

If $\overline{BD}$ bisects $\angle ABC$, $AD = 6$, $DC = 4$, and $BC = 12$, what is the measure of AB?

7 The ratio of similitude in two similar triangles is 5:6. If the length of a median in the larger triangle is 18 inches, find the length of the corresponding median in the smaller triangle.

8 The ratio of the lengths of the corresponding sides of two similar triangles is 4:7. What is the ratio of the angle bisectors of the corresponding angles?

Exercises 9–13: Refer to the figure, where $\triangle PQR$ is the medial triangle of $\triangle ABC$.

9 If P, Q, and R are the midpoints of the sides of $\triangle ABC$, $PQ = 11.5$ and $BQ = 8$, what are the lengths of AC and PR?

10 If $AB = 12$, $PR = 6.1$, and $PQ = 10.3$, find the lengths of RQ, BC, and AC.

11 If $AB = 3x - 4$ and $QR = 2x - 7$, find the length of QR.

12 If $BC = 2x + 3$ and $PR = 3x - 5$, find the length of PR.

13 If $AC = 8x + 4$ and $PQ = 6x - 8$, find the length of PQ.

14 Corresponding altitudes of two similar triangles have lengths of 11 inches and 8 inches. If the length of the median of the larger triangle is 16.5 inches, then what is the length of a corresponding median of the smaller triangle?

15 The sides of a triangle measure 21, 28, and 35. The length of the shortest side of a similar triangle is 12.

    a What is the ratio of similitude?
    b What are the lengths of the other two sides of the smaller triangle?
    c Find the perimeter of each triangle.
    d Verify that the ratio of the perimeters equals the ratio of similitude.

16 Triangle PQR is the medial triangle of isosceles $\triangle ABC$. $BC = 16$ and $AC = 10$.

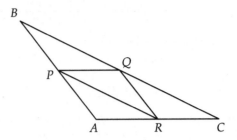

    a Find the length of segments BQ, QR, and PR.
    b Find the area of trapezoid $PRCB$.

12-7 Using Similar Triangles to Prove Proportions or to Prove a Product

Using Similar Triangles to Prove Proportions

To prove whether or not a stated proportion is a true proportion, we can sometimes use similar triangles and show that the proportion involves their corresponding sides. The key is to look at each ratio and match the sides with the given diagram to see if an actual pair of triangles exist and if that pair of triangles can be proved similar. For example, in the figure below, $\overline{PQ} \parallel \overline{SR}$ and we would like to prove the truth of $\frac{QP}{RS} = \frac{PA}{RA}$.

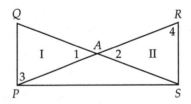

    If we examine the figure, we see that the numerators QP and PA belong to $\triangle I$ and the denominators RS and RA belong to $\triangle II$. Therefore, $\triangle I$ and $\triangle II$ are the two triangles under discussion and not triangles QPS, PAS, or PRS.

The steps to proving similarity here:

1 Vertical angles, $\angle 1$ and $\angle 2$, are congruent.
2 The alternate interior angles, $\angle 3$ and $\angle 4$, are also congruent because they are alternate interior angles of parallel lines, $\overline{PQ}$ and $\overline{SR}$, cut by the transversal, $\overline{PAR}$.
3 Therefore, $\triangle I \sim \triangle II$ (AA $\cong$ AA), and the original given proportion, $\frac{QP}{RS} = \frac{PA}{RA}$, is true.

Using Similar Triangles to Prove a Product

To prove that the product of the means equals the product of the extremes in a geometric proportion, use the following easy method. Then study the first three model problems.

1 Rewrite the products as a proportion, using one pair as the means and the other pair as the extremes. If we have $AG \times GF = AD \times GC$, split the first pair as the extremes: $\frac{AG}{[\ ]} = \frac{[\ ]}{GF}$. Then write in the other pair as the means: $\frac{AG}{AD} = \frac{GC}{GF}$.

2 Determine the triangles to be proved similar by reading the proportions and marking the figures given.

3 If, however, one of the given products is a square, as in $MS \times ST = (AB)^2$ or $MS \times ST = AB \times AB$, write that product as a mean proportional: $\frac{MS}{AB} = \frac{AB}{ST}$.

 MODEL PROBLEMS

1

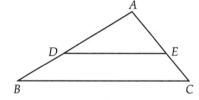

Given: $\triangle ABC$; D is a point on $\overline{AB}$ and E is a point on $\overline{AC}$ such that $\overline{DE} \parallel \overline{BC}$.
Prove: **a** $\triangle ADE \sim \triangle ABC$
      b $AD \times AC = AB \times AE$

Statements	Reasons
1. $\triangle ABC$ with $\overline{DE} \parallel \overline{BC}$	1. Given.
2. $\angle ADE \cong \angle ABC$ and $\angle AED \cong \angle ACD$	2. If two parallel lines are cut by a transversal, the corresponding angles are congruent.
3. $\triangle ADE \sim \triangle ABC$	3. AA Theorem.
4. $\frac{AD}{AB} = \frac{AE}{AC}$	4. Corresponding sides of similar triangles are in proportion.
5. $AD \times AC = AB \times AE$	5. In a proportion, the product of the means equals the product of the extremes.

2

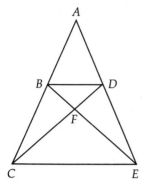

Given: $\triangle ACE$, B is a point on $\overline{AC}$, D is a point on $\overline{AE}$. $\overline{BE}$ and $\overline{DC}$ intersect at F. $\angle ABE \cong \angle ADC$.
Prove: $AB \times AC = AD \times AE$

Statements	Reasons
1. $\angle ABE \cong \angle ADC$	1. Given.
2. $\angle A \cong \angle A$	2. Reflective Postulate.
3. $\triangle ABE \sim \triangle ADC$	3. AA Theorem.
4. $\dfrac{AB}{AD} = \dfrac{AE}{AC}$	4. Corresponding sides of similar triangles are in proportion.
5. $AB \times AC = AD \times AE$	5. In a proportion, the product of the means equals the product of the extremes.

3

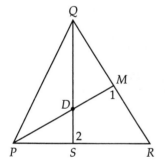

Given: Acute triangle PQR with altitudes $\overline{QS}$ and $\overline{PM}$ intersecting at D
Prove: **a** $\dfrac{QS}{PM} = \dfrac{QR}{PR}$
     b $\quad QS \times PR = PM \times QR$

Statements	Reasons
1. $\triangle PQR$, with altitudes $\overline{QS}$ and $\overline{PM}$	1. Given.
2. $\overline{QS} \perp \overline{PR}$, $\overline{PM} \perp \overline{QR}$	2. Definition of altitudes.
3. $\angle 1$ and $\angle 2$ are right angles.	3. Perpendicular lines form right angles.
4. $\angle 1 \cong \angle 2$ (A $\cong$ A)	4. All right angles are congruent.
5. $\angle R \cong \angle R$ (A $\cong$ A)	5. Reflexive property.
6. $\triangle QSR \sim \triangle PMR$	6. AA Theorem.
7. (a) $\dfrac{QS}{PM} = \dfrac{QR}{PR}$	7. Corresponding sides of similar triangles are in proportion.
8. (b) $QS \times PR = PM \times QR$	8. In a proportion, the product of the means equals the product of the extremes.

4

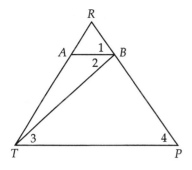

Given: $\triangle TRP$, $\overline{TAR}$, $\overline{RBP}$, $\overline{AB}$ bisects $\angle RBT$, and $\overline{AB} \parallel \overline{TP}$

Prove: **a** $\dfrac{RA}{AT} = \dfrac{RB}{BP}$

   b $\dfrac{RA}{AT} = \dfrac{RB}{BT}$

Statements	Reasons
1. $\overline{AB}$ bisects $\angle RBT$, and $\overline{AB} \parallel \overline{TP}$.	1. Given.
2. (a) $\dfrac{RA}{AT} = \dfrac{RB}{BP}$	2. A line joining two sides of triangle and parallel to the third side divides those sides proportionally.
3. $\angle 1 \cong \angle 2$	3. Definition of an angle bisector.
4. $\angle 2 \cong \angle 3$	4. Alternate interior angles are congruent.
5. $\angle 1 \cong \angle 3$	5. Transitive Property.
6. $\angle 1 \cong \angle 4$	6. Corresponding angles are congruent.
7. $\angle 3 \cong \angle 4$	7. Transitive Property.
8. $\overline{BT} \cong \overline{BP}$	8. Sides opposite congruent angles are congruent.
9. (b) $\dfrac{RA}{AT} = \dfrac{RB}{BT}$	9. Substitution Postulate.

 Practice

Exercises 1–3: Using the data given, (a) establish a proportion and (b) find the indicated product.

1

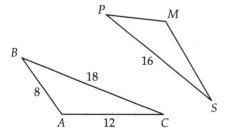

Given: $\triangle ABC \sim \triangle MPS$. Find $PM \times BC$.

2

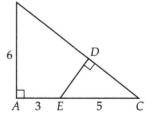

Given: $\overline{BA} \perp \overline{CA}$, $\overline{ED} \perp \overline{BC}$. Find $DC \times BC$.

3

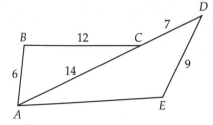

Given: $\triangle ABC \sim \triangle DEA$. Find $AB \times AE$.

4

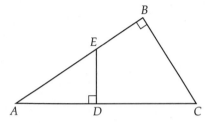

Given: $\overline{AB} \perp \overline{CB}, \overline{ED} \perp \overline{AC}$

a   Prove $\triangle ADE \sim \triangle ABC$

b   Write a proportion to be used in finding the product $AB \times AE$.

c   Find the product $AB \times AE$ if $AD = 4$, $AC = 8$, and $BC = 6$.

5

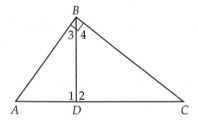

Given: $\overline{AB} \perp \overline{CB}$, altitude $\overline{BD}$ drawn to side $\overline{AC}$

a   Prove $\triangle ADB \sim \triangle BDC$.

b   Prove $\dfrac{AD}{BD} = \dfrac{BD}{DC}$.

c   Prove $AD \times DC = (BD)^2$.

d   If $AD = 4$ and $DC = 9$, find the altitude BD.

6

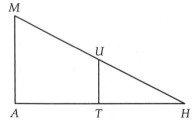

Given: Right triangle MAH with $\angle A$ a right angle, $\overline{UT} \perp \overline{AH}$

Prove: $\dfrac{MA}{UT} = \dfrac{AH}{TH}$

7

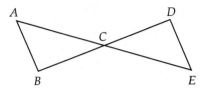

Given: $\overline{AB} \parallel \overline{DE}$

Prove: $\dfrac{AB}{ED} = \dfrac{AC}{EC}$

8

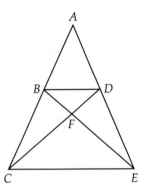

Given: Isosceles triangle ACE with $\overline{AC} \cong \overline{AE}$. $\angle EBA \cong \angle CDA$.

Prove: $BC \times DC = DE \times BE$

9

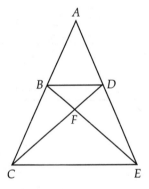

Given: $\triangle ACE$, B is a point on $\overline{AC}$, D is a point on $\overline{AE}$, $\angle EBC \cong \angle CDE$.

Prove: $\dfrac{FB}{FD} = \dfrac{FC}{FE}$

10

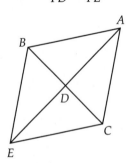

Given: $\overline{AE} \perp \overline{BC}$, $\angle DAC \cong \angle DEC$

Prove: $AD \times EC = AC \times ED$

11

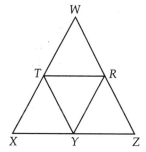

Given: Isosceles triangle WXZ with $\overline{WX} \cong \overline{WZ}$, and $\angle YTW \cong \angle YRW$

Prove: $\dfrac{YT}{YR} = \dfrac{XY}{ZY}$

12

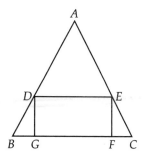

Given: Isosceles triangle ADE with $\overline{AD} \cong \overline{AE}$. Rectangle $DEFG$, $\overline{ADB}$, $\overline{AEC}$, $\overline{BGFC}$.

Prove: $\dfrac{DG}{EF} = \dfrac{BG}{CF}$

12–8 Proportions in a Right Triangle

If an altitude is drawn to the hypotenuse of a right triangle, the following three theorems are essential.

Right Triangle Proportions

• Theorem 12.15. The two interior triangles formed are similar to each other and to the original triangle.	*(figure: right triangle ABC with altitude CD; regions I and II)*	$\triangle\text{I} \sim \triangle\text{II}$ $\triangle\text{I} \sim \triangle ABC$ $\triangle\text{II} \sim \triangle ABC$
• Theorem 12.16. The altitude is the *mean proportional* between the measures of the segments of the hypotenuse.	*(figure: right triangle ABC with altitude m, segments x and y)*	$\dfrac{x}{m} = \dfrac{m}{y}$ or $m^2 = xy$
• Theorem 12.17. The measure of each leg of the original triangle is the *mean proportional* between the hypotenuse and the segment of the hypotenuse that is adjacent to that leg.	*(figure: right triangle ABC with legs b, a, segments x, y, hypotenuse h)*	$\dfrac{h}{b} = \dfrac{b}{x}$ or $b^2 = hx$ and $\dfrac{h}{a} = \dfrac{a}{y}$ or $a^2 = hy$

Note: If x is the *mean proportional between a and b*, the proportion is true: $\dfrac{a}{x} = \dfrac{x}{b}$.

MODEL PROBLEMS

1 In right triangle ABC, altitude CD is drawn to the hypotenuse AB. If $AD = 4$ and $DB = 9$, find the lengths of (a) CD, (b) AC, and (c) CB.

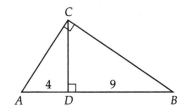

SOLUTION

	Use a proportion.	Substitute.	Cross multiply.	Find the positive square root of each side.
a	$\dfrac{\text{left segment}}{\text{altitude}} = \dfrac{\text{altitude}}{\text{right segment}}$	$\dfrac{4}{CD} = \dfrac{CD}{9}$	$(CD)^2 = 36$	$CD = 6$
b	$\dfrac{\text{hypotenuse}}{\text{leg}} = \dfrac{\text{leg}}{\text{adjacent segment}}$	$\dfrac{13}{AC} = \dfrac{AC}{4}$	$(AC)^2 = 4 \times 13$	$AC = 2\sqrt{13}$
c	$\dfrac{\text{hypotenuse}}{\text{leg}} = \dfrac{\text{leg}}{\text{adjacent segment}}$	$\dfrac{13}{CB} = \dfrac{CB}{4}$	$(CB)^2 = 9 \times 13$	$CB = 3\sqrt{13}$

ANSWER: $CD = 6$, $AC = 2\sqrt{13}$, $CB = 3\sqrt{13}$

2 In right $\triangle ABC$, altitude $CD = 10$, and DB exceeds AD by 15.

   a If $AD = x$, express DB in terms of x.
   b Write an equation in terms of x to find AD.
   c Find AD.

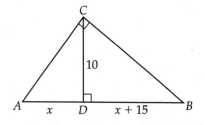

SOLUTION

   a If $AD = x$, then $DB = x + 15$.

   b State a proportion: $\dfrac{AD}{CD} = \dfrac{CD}{DB}$ or $\dfrac{x}{10} = \dfrac{10}{x + 15}$.

   c Cross multiply. $x(x + 15) = (10)(10)$

$x^2 + 15x = 100$
$x^2 + 15x - 100 = 0$
$(x + 20)(x - 5) = 0$
$x + 20 = 0$ or $x - 5 = 0$
$x = -20$ (reject since lengths are positive) or $x = 5$

ANSWER: $AD = 5$

Practice

1 Find the mean proportional between 4 and 25.

(1) 10
(2) 14.5
(3) 15
(4) 20

Exercises 2–4: Use the diagram below.

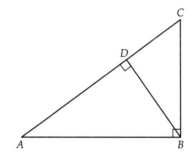

2 If $AD = 7$ and $DC = 3$, find DB.

(1) $\sqrt{10}$
(2) 4
(3) $\sqrt{21}$
(4) 5

3 If $CB = 6$ and $AC = 9$, find DC.

(1) $3\sqrt{6}$
(2) 7.5
(3) 4
(4) $3\sqrt{2}$

4 If $AD = 7$ and $DC = 4$, find AB.

(1) $\sqrt{77}$
(2) $2\sqrt{11}$
(3) $2\sqrt{7}$
(4) $\sqrt{11}$

5 If the lengths of the sides are represented by the letters a, b, c, d, x, and y, which of the following statements are true?

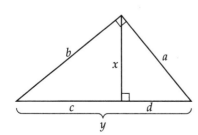

a $a^2 = cd$
b $a^2 = dy$

c $b^2 = cd$
d $b^2 = cx$
e $x^2 = cd$
f $b^2 = cy$
g $\frac{c}{x} = \frac{x}{d}$
h $\frac{a}{y} = \frac{y}{b}$

Exercises 6–9: Use the diagram below.

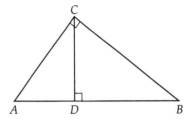

6 If $AD = 5$ and $DB = 12$, what is the value of CD?

7 If $CD = 3\sqrt{5}$ and $DB = 9$, what is the value of AD?

8 If $BC = 3\sqrt{2}$ and $DB = 3$, what is the value of AB?

9 If $AD = 5$ and $DB = 6$, what is the value of AC?

Exercises 10–19: Find the values of x, y, and z. Any radical answer should be left in simplest radical form.

10

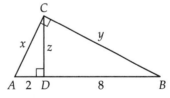

11

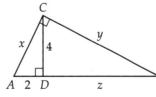

12

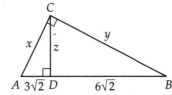

Proportions in a Right Triangle **323**

13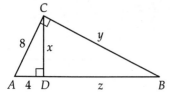

14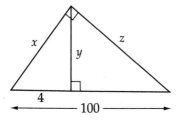

15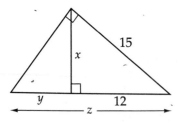

16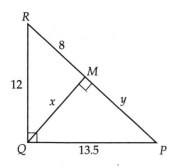

17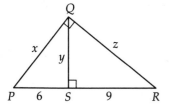

18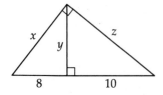

19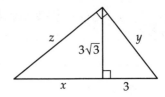

Exercises 20 and 21: Find the values of x, y, and z to the nearest tenth.

20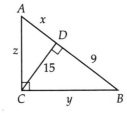

21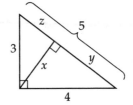

22 In right $\triangle PQR$, altitude QS is drawn to hypotenuse PR. $QS = 10$ and SR exceeds PS by 21.

   a If $PS = x$, express SR in terms of x.
   b Write an equation in terms of x to find PS.
   c Solve for PS.

23 If an altitude of 6 inches is drawn to the hypotenuse of a right triangle and divides that hypotenuse into segments x and $x + 5$, find the length of the hypotenuse.

24 In right triangle LTM, $\overline{TR}$ is the altitude to hypotenuse $\overline{LM}$, $TR = 5$, and RM is 2 more than LR.

   a Find the values of LR and LM.
   b Between which two consecutive integers does the value of LR lie?

12-9 Pythagorean Theorem and Special Triangles

The **Pythagorean theorem** expresses the relationship among the sides of a right triangle. The first proof of this theorem is usually attributed to the Pythagoreans (a mathematics study group founded by Pythagoras in the 6th century B.C.)

- Theorem 12.18. In a right triangle, the square of the hypotenuse is equal to the sum of the squares of the other two sides (or legs).

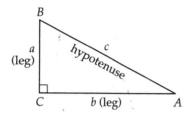

Thus, if any two sides of the right triangle are known, the third side can be found by using one of the following formulas:

$$c^2 = a^2 + b^2 \qquad c = \sqrt{a^2 + b^2} \qquad a = \sqrt{c^2 - b^2} \qquad b = \sqrt{c^2 - a^2}$$

- Theorem 12.19. Conversely, if a triangle has sides a, b, and c that satisfy the Pythagorean theorem, such that $a^2 + b^2 = c^2$, then the triangle is a right triangle.

Pythagorean Triples

Any three integers that satisfy the equation $c^2 = a^2 + b^2$ form a **Pythagorean triple**. The most well-known triples are {3, 4, 5}, {5, 12, 13}, {7, 24, 25}, and {8, 15, 17}. Furthermore, any multiples of any of these sets of triples are also Pythagorean triples. For example: {3, 4, 5} × 2 = {6, 8, 10} and {3, 4, 5} × 5 = {15, 20, 25}, etc.

 MODEL PROBLEMS

1 In right triangle ABC, find hypotenuse AB, if side $AC = 15$, and side $BC = 8$.

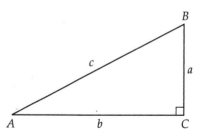

SOLUTION

Using $a = 8$ and $b = 15$ and $c = \sqrt{a^2 + b^2}$
$c = \sqrt{8^2 + 15^2}$
$c = \sqrt{64 + 225} = \sqrt{289}$
$c = 17$

ANSWER: hypotenuse $AB = 17$

2 In right triangle *DEF*, find side *a* if side *c* = 40 in. and side *b* = 24 in.

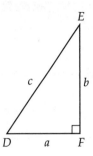

SOLUTION

Using $a = \sqrt{c^2 - b^2}$

$a = \sqrt{40^2 - 24^2}$

$a = \sqrt{1,600 - 576} = \sqrt{1,024}$

$a = 32$

ANSWER: $a = 32$ inches

3 The shape of a pocket park in the city is a rhombus. If the diagonals are 10 yards and 24 yards, find the length of a side of the park.

SOLUTION

The diagonals of a rhombus are the perpendicular bisectors of each other.

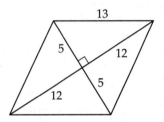

In the figure, the rhombus is divided into four right triangles, each of which has legs 5 and 12. As part of a Pythagorean triple, the hypotenuse is 13.

ANSWER: A side of the park is 13 yards.

4 If the hypotenuse of a right triangle is 4 inches more than one leg and 2 inches more than another, what is the perimeter of the triangle?

SOLUTION

Let *x* represent the hypotenuse. Then the legs can be represented by $x - 2$ and $x - 4$.

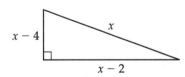

The Pythagorean theorem can help us find *x*.

Write the Pythagorean theorem.	$a^2 + b^2 = c^2$
Substitute.	$(x - 4)^2 + (x - 2)^2 = x^2$
Square each binomial.	$(x^2 - 8x + 16) + (x^2 - 4x + 4) = x^2$
Combine like terms.	$2x^2 - 12x + 20 = x^2$
Subtract x^2 from each side.	$x^2 - 12x + 20 = 0$
Factor.	$(x - 10)(x - 2) = 0$
Set each factor equal to zero and solve.	$(x - 10) = 0$ or $(x - 2) = 0$
	$x = 10$ or $x = 2$

Check: If $x = 2$, then $x - 4 = -2$. Since a length can never be negative, we must reject this value. If $x = 10$, then $x - 2 = 8$ and $x - 4 = 6$.

Add the sides. $10 + 8 + 6 = 24$

ANSWER: The perimeter is 24 inches.

Practice

1 The hypotenuse of a right triangle has length 15 and one leg that measures 5. What is the length of the other leg?

   (1) 10
   (2) $10\sqrt{2}$
   (3) $\sqrt{250}$
   (4) 100

2 The legs of a right triangle have a ratio of 5:12. If the hypotenuse is 65 feet in length, what is the length of the shorter leg?

   (1) 63.88 feet
   (2) 60 feet
   (3) 25 feet
   (4) 13 feet

3 If the diagonals of a rhombus are 6 and 4, which of the following is a measure of a side?

   (1) $\sqrt{13}$
   (2) 4
   (3) 5
   (4) $\sqrt{52}$

4 Two college roommates, Harry and Nicholas, leave college at the same time. Harry travels south at 30 mph and Nicholas travels west at 40 mph. How far apart are they at the end of one hour?

   (1) 50 miles
   (2) 60 miles
   (3) 70 miles
   (4) 80 miles

5 In circle C, $\overline{CD}$ is the perpendicular bisector of $\overline{AB}$.

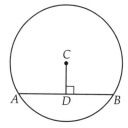

If $CD = 4$ and $AB = 10$, what is the length of the radius of the circle?

   (1) 3
   (2) 5
   (3) 6
   (4) $\sqrt{41}$

6 A ladder 26 feet long leans against a building and reaches the bottom ledge of a window. If the foot of the ladder is 10 feet from the foot of the building, how high is the window ledge above the ground?

   (1) 24 feet
   (2) 24.2 feet
   (3) 36 feet
   (4) 41.8 feet

7 If the center of a circle is the origin and the circle passes through the point (5, 12), what is the radius of the circle?

   (1) 12
   (2) 13
   (3) 15
   (4) 169

8 Which set of numbers could represent the lengths of the sides of a right triangle?

   (1) {4, 5, 6}
   (2) {5, 5, 10}
   (3) {6, 8, 12}
   (4) {10, 24, 26}

9 In $\triangle DEF$, altitude $\overline{EG}$ is drawn to base $\overline{DF}$.

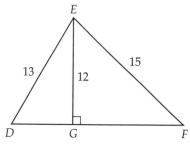

If $EG = 12$, $EF = 15$, and $DE = 13$, what is the measure of DF?

10 Which of the following are the lengths of the sides of a right triangle?

   a $\sqrt{3}, \sqrt{4}, \sqrt{5}$
   b 15, 20, 25
   c 300, 400, 500
   d $2, 2, 2\sqrt{2}$
   e $\sqrt{3}, \sqrt{4}, \sqrt{7}$
   f 20, 21, 29
   g $2\sqrt{3}, 3\sqrt{2}, \sqrt{30}$

11 Find the length of the third side of each right triangle. If the answer is not an integer, leave the answer in simplest radical form.

a

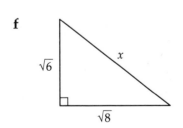

b

c

d

e

f

12 If a right triangle has legs that measure $\sqrt{15}$ and $\sqrt{21}$, what is the length of the hypotenuse?

13 Isosceles $\triangle ABC$ has a base of 12 and legs 10 each. Find the altitude to the base.

14 In an isosceles triangle, each of the equal sides is 26 cm long and the base is 20 cm long. Find the area. (Hint: First, draw the altitude to the base.)

15 If the base of an isosceles triangle is 12 in. and the altitude is 8 in., what is the perimeter of the triangle?

16 In the right triangle below, the hypotenuse equals 50 and the legs are x and $2x$.

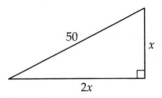

In simplest radical form, find the lengths of the legs.

17 In right triangle PQR, m$\angle Q = 90$, $RQ = 6$, and $RP = 10$. Find the perimeter of $\triangle PQR$.

18 In the right triangle below, the legs are x and $2x$, and the hypotenuse is 5.

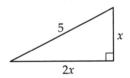

What is the area of the triangle?

19 To the nearest tenth of an inch, find the base of a rectangle whose diagonal is 25 inches and whose height is 16 inches.

20 If a rectangle has a diagonal of 20 feet and a side of 12 feet, find the perimeter and area of the rectangle.

21 If a right triangle has sides of lengths $x + 9$, $x + 2$, and $x + 10$, find the value of x.

22 If the diagonals of a rhombus are 12 and 16, find the length of a side of the rhombus.

23 If the diagonals of a rhombus are 6 and $6\sqrt{2}$, what is the length of a side of the rhombus?

24 In $\triangle ABC$, $\overline{BD}$ is the altitude to side $\overline{AC}$.

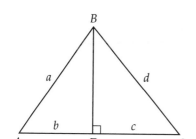

Show that $a^2 - d^2 = b^2 - c^2$.

25 Right triangles ADC and ACB have side $\overline{AC}$ in common.

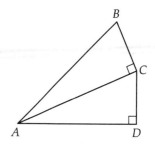

Show that $(AB)^2 = (BC)^2 + (AD)^2 + (CD)^2$.

Special Triangles

The sides of a special right triangle have a fixed relationship. If one side is known, then the other sides can be found.

45°–45°–90° Isosceles Right Triangle

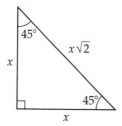

- Condition 1: If a leg is known, then the hypotenuse = leg $\times \sqrt{2}$, as in x, x, $x\sqrt{2}$.

Example 1

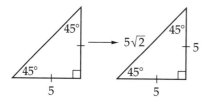

Legs = 5 each
Hypotenuse = $5 \times \sqrt{2}$

Example 2

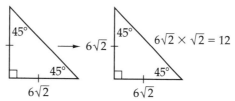

Legs = $6\sqrt{2}$ each
Hypotenuse = $6\sqrt{2} \times \sqrt{2} = 12$

- Condition 2: If the hypotenuse is known, then each leg = $\frac{1}{2} \times$ hypotenuse $\times \sqrt{2}$.

Example 3

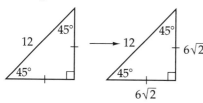

Hypotenuse = 12
Legs = $\frac{1}{2}(12)\sqrt{2}$

Example 4

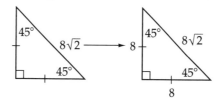

Hypotenuse = $8\sqrt{2}$
Legs = $\frac{1}{2}(8)(8\sqrt{2})(\sqrt{2}) = 8$

→ MODEL PROBLEMS

1 To the nearest tenth, find the distance from second base to home plate on a baseball diamond where the bases are 90 feet apart.

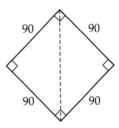

SOLUTION

The line from second base to home plate splits the field into two isosceles right triangles, with legs 90 feet long. The distance is $90 \times \sqrt{2}$ or approximately 127.3 feet.

2 If the hypotenuse of a right isosceles triangle is 10, find the exact length of the legs.

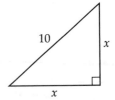

SOLUTION

To find the legs, divide 10 by $\sqrt{2}$.

$$\frac{10}{\sqrt{2}} = \frac{10}{\sqrt{2}} \bullet \frac{\sqrt{2}}{\sqrt{2}} = \frac{10\sqrt{2}}{2} = 5\sqrt{2}$$

30°–60°–90° Right Triangle

If the hypotenuse is known, then

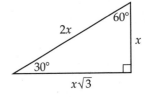

    a the leg opposite the 30° angle $= \frac{1}{2} \times$ hypotenuse

    b the leg opposite the 60° angle $= \frac{1}{2} \times$ hypotenuse $\times \sqrt{3}$

The following are some typical problems and answers

Example 1	**Example 2**	**Example 3**	**Example 4**

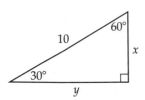 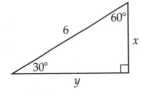 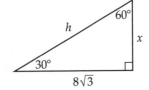 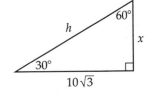

$x = 5$	$x = 3$	$x = 8$	$x = 10$
$y = 5\sqrt{3}$	$y = 3\sqrt{3}$	$h = 16$	$h = 20$

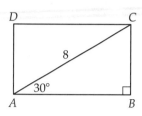

MODEL PROBLEMS

1 The diagonal of a rectangle is 8 and the smaller acute angle of the triangle formed is 30°.

a Find the dimensions of the rectangle
b Find the area of the rectangle.

SOLUTION

a $\triangle ABC$ is a right triangle. The measure of angle ACB is 60°.

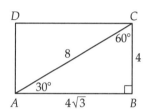

Side $\overline{BC}$, opposite the 30° angle, is $\frac{1}{2}$ × hypotenuse or $\frac{1}{2}(8) = 4$.

Side $\overline{AB}$, opposite the 60° angle, is $\frac{1}{2}$ × hypotenuse × $\sqrt{3}$ or $4\sqrt{3}$.

ANSWER: $\overline{BC} = 4$ and $\overline{AB} = 4\sqrt{3}$

b Since the dimensions of the rectangle are 4 (height) and $4\sqrt{3}$ (base), the area = $4 \times (4\sqrt{3}) = 16\sqrt{3}$.

ANSWER: area = $16\sqrt{3}$

2 In the figure at the right, $AB = 2$, $\angle A = 45$, and $\angle C = 30$. Find the lengths of altitude $\overline{BD}$ and side $\overline{BC}$.

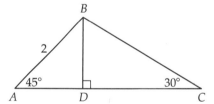

SOLUTION

$\triangle ABD$ is a 45°–45°–90° triangle, so side $\overline{BD}$ opposite $\angle A = \frac{1}{2}$ × hypotenuse × $\sqrt{2}$ or $\frac{1}{2}(2)\sqrt{2} = 1\sqrt{2}$.

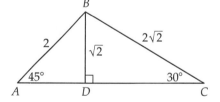

$\triangle BDC$ is a 30°–60°–90° triangle, so $\overline{BD}$ is the side opposite the 30° angle. So the measure of $\overline{BD}$ is half the hypotenuse.

Side $\overline{BC}$, the hypotenuse, is $2 \times \overline{BD}$ or $2(\sqrt{2}) = 2\sqrt{2}$.

ANSWER: $\overline{BD} = \sqrt{2}$ and $\overline{BC} = 2\sqrt{2}$

1   If the longest side of an isosceles right triangle is 12 ft long, how long are the other sides?

(1) $6\sqrt{2}$ ft and $6\sqrt{2}$ ft
(2) 6 ft and $6\sqrt{3}$ ft
(3) 6 ft and $6\sqrt{2}$ ft
(4) $4\sqrt{3}$ ft and $4\sqrt{3}$ ft

2   If the ratio of measures of the angles of a certain triangle is 1:2:3, what is the ratio of the lengths of the sides?

(1) 1:2:3
(2) $1:\sqrt{2}:\sqrt{3}$
(3) $1:\sqrt{3}:2$
(4) 1:2:4

3   If an isosceles right triangle has an area of 18, what is the length of the hypotenuse?

(1) 3
(2) $3\sqrt{2}$
(3) 6
(4) $6\sqrt{2}$

4   If the hypotenuse of an isosceles right triangle is 2, what is the area of the triangle?

(1) 1
(2) 2
(3) $2\sqrt{2}$
(4) 4

5   In the figure below, what is the length of PQ?

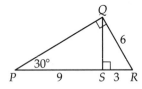

(1) $6\sqrt{2}$
(2) $6\sqrt{3}$
(3) $9\sqrt{2}$
(4) $9\sqrt{3}$

6   If the exterior angle of a parallelogram is 30°, and the sides of the parallelogram measure 5 and 12, what is the area?

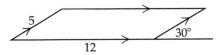

(1) 30
(2) 36
(3) 48
(4) 60

7   If $x^2 = 2.5$, and right triangle ABC has sides x, $3x$, and 5, what is the area?

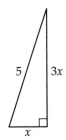

(1) 1.25
(2) 2.50
(3) 3.75
(4) 7.50

8   In right triangle KAT, $KT = 2\sqrt{3}$. What is the measure of hypotenuse $\overline{AT}$?

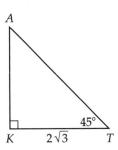

(1) $2\sqrt{3}$
(2) $2\sqrt{6}$
(3) $4\sqrt{3}$
(4) $4\sqrt{6}$

9 If the altitude of an equilateral triangle is $10\sqrt{3}$ inches, what is the perimeter of the triangle?

    (1) 30
    (2) $30\sqrt{3}$
    (3) 60
    (4) $60\sqrt{3}$

10 $\triangle ABC$ is a 30°–60°–90° triangle. The length of one side is given. Find the lengths of the other two sides. Leave any noninteger answer in simplest radical form.

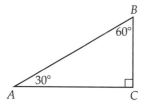

    a $AB = 14$
    b $AB = 5$
    c $AB = 6\sqrt{3}$
    d $BC = 9$
    e $BC = 4\sqrt{3}$
    f $AC = 7\sqrt{3}$
    g $AB = 5.5\sqrt{3}$
    h $AC = 12$

11 $\triangle ABC$ is a 45°–45°–90° triangle. The length of one side is given. Find the lengths of the other two sides. Leave any noninteger answer in simplest radical form.

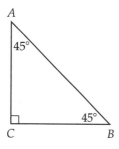

    a $BC = 4$
    b $AC = 10$
    c $AB = 8\sqrt{2}$
    d $AB = 1.5\sqrt{2}$
    e $AB = 12$
    f $AC = 3\sqrt{2}$
    g $AC = 10\sqrt{2}$
    h $AB = 15$
    i $AC = 4\sqrt{3}$
    j $AB = 8\sqrt{3}$

12 What is the length of the diagonal of a square whose perimeter is 28?

13 If the perimeter of a square is $8\sqrt{2}$, what is the length of the diagonal?

14 If the perimeter of equilateral $\triangle ABC$ is 30, find the length of the altitude from B to side $\overline{AC}$.

15 In the figure below, with altitude 6, find the measures of x, y, and z.

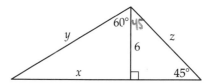

16 The diagonals of a rectangle intersect and form vertical angles of 60° and 120°. If the length of the diagonals is 12,

    a   find the dimensions of the rectangle.
    b   find the perimeter of the rectangle.
    c   find the area of the rectangle.

Leave all answers in simplest radical form.

17 In the figure, $DB = 4$ and $BE = 5$.

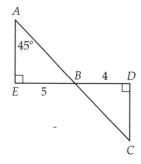

In simplest radical form, find the length of $\overline{ABC}$.

18 If the area of parallelogram $ABCD$ is 66 sq units, $\angle A = 30°$, and $AD = 11$, what is the perimeter of the parallelogram?

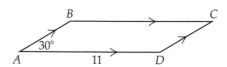

19 In right triangle ACB, $\angle A = 30$, $BC = 8\sqrt{3}$, and $\overline{BD}$ is drawn such that $\overline{AD} \cong \overline{DB}$.

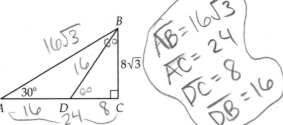

Find the lengths of AB, AC, DC, and DB.

20 Square $PQRS$ is inscribed in circle O.

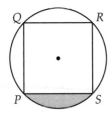

If the area of the square is 16, find, to the nearest hundredth, the area of the shaded region.

21 In the figure below, lines l and m intersect.

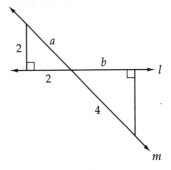

The two right triangles have sides as indicated.

a   Find the product ab.
b   If $ab = N^3$, what is the value of N?

12-10 Perimeters, Areas, and Volumes of Similar Figures (Polygons and Solids)

The Fundamental Theorem of Similarity

If two similar figures have a ratio of similitude $\frac{a}{b}$, then

- corresponding angle measures are equal.
- corresponding lengths (whether altitudes, medians, or angle bisectors) are in the ratio $\frac{a}{b}$.
- the ratio of corresponding volumes is $\frac{V'}{V} = \frac{a^3}{b^3}$.
- the ratio of corresponding perimeters is $\frac{P'}{P} = \frac{a}{b}$.
- the ratio of corresponding areas is $\frac{A'}{A} = \frac{a^2}{b^2}$.

MODEL PROBLEMS

1 The perimeters of two similar polygons are in the ratio 9:16.

    a Find the ratio of the lengths of corresponding diagonals.
    b Find the ratio of their areas.

SOLUTION

    a The ratio of corresponding diagonals equals the ratio of perimeters: 9:16.

ANSWER: 9:16

    b The ratio of their areas is $9^2:16^2$ or 81:256.

ANSWER: $9^2:16^2$

2 Pentagons *ABCDE* and *PQRST* are similar with a ratio of similitude 3:4.

    If pentagon *ABCDE* has an area of 36 sq units, find the area of *PQRST*.

SOLUTION

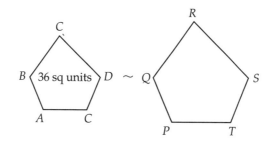

Since the ratio of similitude is 3:4, the ratio of their areas must be $3^2:4^2$ or 9:16. Set up a proportion.

$\frac{9}{16} = \frac{36}{x}$

$9x = (16)(36)$

$9x = 576$

$x = 64$

ANSWER: The area of *PQRST* is 64 square units.

3 The surface areas of two spheres are in the ratio 4:25.

    a Find the ratio of their radii.
    b Find the ratio of their volumes.

SOLUTION

    a Set up a proportion: $\frac{\text{radius of smaller sphere}}{\text{radius of larger sphere}} = \frac{r^2}{R^2} = \frac{4}{25}$

       Take the square root of both sides of the equation: $\frac{r}{R} = \frac{2}{5}$.

ANSWER: The ratio of their radii is $\frac{2}{5}$.

    b The ratio of their volumes equals the ratio of their radii cubed.

       $\frac{\text{volume of smaller sphere}}{\text{volume of larger sphere}} = \frac{2^3}{5^3}$ or $\frac{8}{125}$

ANSWER: The ratio of their volumes is $\frac{8}{125}$.

1 In rectangle $ABCD$, $BC = 6$.

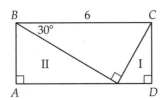

What is the ratio of the area of $\triangle$I to the area of $\triangle$II?

(1) 1:3
(2) $\sqrt{3}$:3
(3) $\sqrt{3}$:2
(4) $2\sqrt{3}$:2

2 Two squares have areas of 9 sq cm and 25 sq cm. What is the ratio of the perimeter of the smaller square to the perimeter of the larger square?

(1) 9:25
(2) 81:625
(3) 3:5
(4) $\sqrt{3}$:$\sqrt{5}$

3 In the figure below, $\overline{AB} \parallel \overline{PR}$.

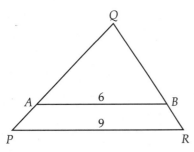

If $PR = 9$, $AB = 6$, and the area of $\triangle PQR$ is 63, what is the area of $\triangle AQB$?

(1) 28
(2) 36
(3) 42
(4) 54

4 Find the ratio of the areas of two similar triangles if each of the following gives the ratio of a pair of corresponding altitudes.

a 3:1
b 4:9
c 9:2
d 5:1
e $\sqrt{2}$:$\sqrt{3}$

5 Find the ratio of the lengths of a pair of corresponding sides in two similar triangles if each of the following gives the ratio of their areas.

a 4:9
b 36:25
c 1:49
d 4:25
e 81:121

6 Since all circles are similar figures, and if circle A has a radius of length r and circle B has a radius of length $3r$, what is the ratio of the area of circle A to the area of circle B?

7 If the area of each face of a cube is 49 square in., what is the volume of the cube in cubic in.?

8 The areas of two similar triangles are in the ratio 4:9. The length of one side of the smaller triangle is 9. What is the length of the corresponding side of the other triangle?

9 If $\triangle ABC \sim \triangle A'B'C'$ and the ratio of similitude is 5:1, find the ratio of their areas.

10 The corresponding altitudes of two similar triangles are 6 and 14. If the area of the first triangle is 99, how many square feet are there in the area of the second triangle?

11 In the figure below, $\overline{DE} \parallel \overline{AC}$ and $\frac{DE}{AC} = 0.2$.

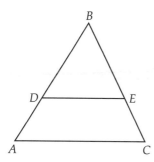

What is the ratio of the area of $\triangle DBE$ to the area of $\triangle ABC$?

12 If two similar coffee mugs have heights of 3 in. and 4 in., what is the ratio of their volumes?

13 Two triangles are similar and the area of one is 9 times the area of the other. The length of one side of the smaller triangle is 16. Find the length of the corresponding side of the larger triangle.

14 A pyramid has a volume of 729 ft³. If a similar pyramid is $\frac{1}{3}$ as high, what is the volume of this pyramid?

15 In inches squared, the areas of two similar triangles are 72 and 216. If the length of the median of the smaller triangle is 16 in., find the length of the corresponding median of the larger triangle (to the nearest tenth).

16 A sphere with diameter 2 meters has a mass of 150 kilograms. What is the mass, in kilograms, of a sphere of the same material with a diameter of 3 meters?

17 The ratio of the volumes of two similar solids is 1:27.

    a What is the ratio of their surface areas?
    b What is the ratio of any two corresponding edges?

18 The rectangular prisms have dimensions as shown.

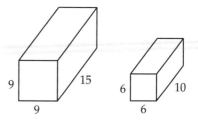

    a Are the two figures similar?
    b What is the ratio of their corresponding edges?
    c What is the ratio of their surface areas?
    d What is the ratio of their volumes?
    e Justify your answers for **c** and **d**.

19 The ratio of the areas of two squares is 9:1. If the perimeter of the smaller square is 24, what is the perimeter of the larger square?

20

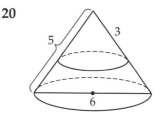

In the figure above, a circular cone with a base of diameter 6 is intersected by a plane parallel to the base, creating a smaller cone. The slant height of the larger cone is 5 and of the smaller cone is 3.

    a What is the altitude of the smaller cone?
    b What is the ratio of the volume of the smaller cone to the larger?

1 If $\frac{5}{2}x = \frac{2}{5}y$ and $y \neq 0$, what is the ratio of x to y?

(1) 4:25
(2) 1:1
(3) 5:2
(4) 25:4

2 If the ratio of m to r is 5 to 7, and the ratio of r to s is 14 to 17, then the ratio of m to s is:

(1) 5:17
(2) 5:14
(3) 7:17
(4) 10:17

3 The ratio of two corresponding sides of two similar triangles is 2:3 and the altitude of the smaller triangle is 10. What is the corresponding altitude of the greater triangle?

(1) $6\frac{2}{3}$
(2) 12
(3) 15
(4) 30

4 In the figure below, if $\overline{PR} \parallel \overline{DF}$, $PR = x$, and $QR = a$, then $\frac{DS}{SF} =$

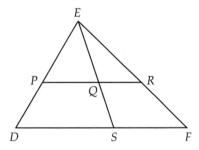

(1) $\frac{a}{x}$

(2) $\frac{x-a}{a}$

(3) $\frac{a}{x-a}$

(4) $\frac{a-x}{x}$

5 Two right triangles ABD and BDC have a common side between them. If $AD = BC = 1$, what is the length of AB?

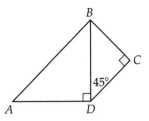

(1) 1
(2) $\sqrt{2}$
(3) $\sqrt{3}$
(4) $\sqrt{5}$

6 A sphere whose radius is 2 inches weighs 8 pounds. What is the weight of a sphere of the same material with a radius of 4 inches?

(1) 8 pounds
(2) 16 pounds
(3) 32 pounds
(4) 64 pounds

7 Determine the value of x if

a $3:x = 4:8$
b $112:42 = 16:x$
c $a:m = x:n$

8 Find the ratio of $x:y$ if

a $6x = 5y$
b $9x = 2y$
c $mx = ny$
d $(a + b)x = cy$
e $mx + nx = py$
f $ax + bx = my + ny$
g $ax + by = mx + ny$

9 Find the mean proportional of

a 2 and 18
b $2a$ and $32a$
c $\frac{4}{3}$ and $\frac{25}{3}$

10 A wooden beam is cut into three pieces whose lengths are in the ratio of 3:4:5. If the middle board is 10 feet long, what is the length in feet of the original board?

11 A rectangular picture measures 4.5 inches by 6.75 inches. If the picture is proportionally enlarged so that the shorter side is now 7.5 inches, what will be the length of the longer side? Translate into an equation, solve, and check your answer.

12 If the ratio of x to y is 6 to 7 and the ratio of y to z is 1 to 5, what is the ratio of x to z?

Exercises 13–16: Given $\triangle ABC$ with $\overline{DE} \parallel \overline{AC}$.

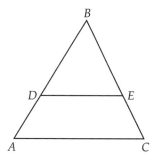

13 Find EC if $BD = 4$, $DA = 8$, and $BE = 3$.

14 Find BE if $AB = 12$, $BD = 8$, and $BC = 9$.

15 Find AD if $BD = 6$, $AC = 10$, and $DE = 3$.

16 Find EC if $AB = a$, $BD = b$, and $BC = c$.

17 Given $\triangle ABC$ with $BE = 8$, $EC = x$, $DE = 5$, and $AC = x + 4$.

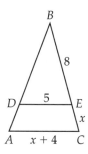

Write an equation to solve for x and find the values for EC and AC.

18 A' is the image of A under a dilation and B' is the image of B under a dilation. $AB = 5$ in. and $A'B' = 15$ in.

  a What is the value of k, the scale factor?

  b Is the dilation an expansion or a contraction?

19 $\triangle ABC$ is transformed under a dilation to $\triangle A'B'C'$. If $A'B' = 18$ in. and the constant of dilation is $\frac{1}{3}$, what is the length of AB?

20 If P, Q, and R are the midpoints of the sides of $\triangle ABC$, with the given measures, find the perimeter of $\triangle ABC$.

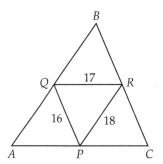

21 Use the distance formula to determine whether $\triangle ABC$ is similar to $\triangle A'B'C'$ if the coordinates of the vertices are $A(0, 4)$, $B(-2,0)$, $C(1, -1)$ and $A'(1,4)$, $B'(-2,-2)$, $C'(2.5,-3.5)$.

22 Use the distance formula to show that $\triangle PQR$ is similar to $\triangle ABC$ if the coordinates of the vertices are $P(-4, 1)$, $Q(-1, 1)$, $R(-1, 5)$ and $A(1, -2)$, $B(1, 4)$, $C(9, 4)$.

23 Given $\triangle ABC \sim \triangle PQR$ with ratio of similitude 5:2. If $AB = 3$, $BC = 5$, and $m\angle B = 125$, find the measure of $\angle Q$ and sides PQ and QR.

24 $\overline{BD}$ is the altitude to the hypotenuse of right $\triangle ABC$. If $AB = 4$ and $DC = 6$, find AD.

25 The altitude $\overline{BD}$ is drawn to the hypotenuse $\overline{AC}$ of right $\triangle ABC$ and divides that hypotenuse into segments x and $x + 5$. If $BD = 6$ in., what is the length of the hypotenuse?

26 In right $\triangle ABC$, altitude $\overline{BD}$ is drawn to the hypotenuse. If $AD = 8$ and $DC = 18$, find the lengths of $\overline{AB}$, $\overline{BC}$, and $\overline{BD}$.

27 The legs of a right triangle are consecutive integers and the hypotenuse is 9 inches longer than the smaller of the two legs. Find the lengths of the sides of the triangle.

28 The diagonal of a square measures 10 feet.

    a Find the exact measure of a side of the square.

    b Find the area of the square.

29 What is the slant height of a cone if the altitude is 30 and the diameter is 32?

Exercises 30–32: In each 30°–60°–90° triangle, use the given data to solve for the measure of sides x and y.

30

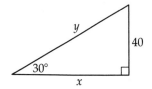

31

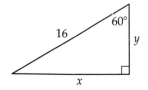

32

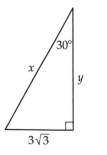

33 In an isosceles right triangle, if the length of a leg is 1, what is the length of the hypotenuse?

34 If the altitude of an equilateral triangle is $21\sqrt{3}$, what is the perimeter of the triangle?

35 The lengths of two corresponding altitudes of a pair of similar polygons are in the ratio 3:5. If the area of the smaller polygon is 27 sq ft, find the area of the larger polygon.

36 If the ratio of the radii of two similar cones is 2:3, then what is the ratio of their volumes?

37 The ratio of the surface area of two similar polyhedrons is 4:1. The volume of the smaller polyhedron is 10 cubic inches. Find the volume of the larger polyhedron.

38 In the figure below, $\overline{DE} \parallel \overline{AC}$, $AC = 9$, and $DE = 6$.

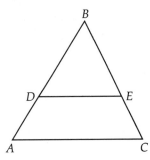

If the area of $\triangle DBE$ is 36, what is the area of $\triangle ABC$?

39 If the pentagon below is formed by a square and a triangle and the side of the square is 6, what is the area of the pentagon?

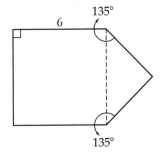

40 If $SR = \frac{1}{2}PS$ and $QR = QS$, what is the length of PQ?

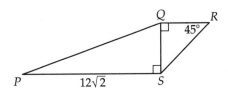

41 The side of rhombus $ABCD$ measures 12 inches and the measure of angle A is 60°. Find the area of the rhombus. (Hint: Draw a perpendicular from B to side $\overline{AD}$.

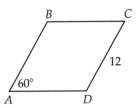

42 The lengths of the bases in an isosceles trapezoid are 7 and 17 and the measure of each of the base angles is 45°.

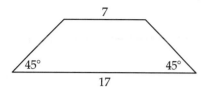

Find the area and perimeter of the trapezoid. Leave any noninteger answer in simplest radical form.

43

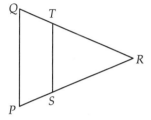

Given: △PQR with $\overline{TS} \parallel \overline{QP}$
Prove: △PQR ~ △STR

44

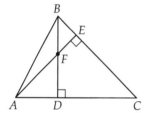

Given: $\overline{AE} \perp \overline{BC}$ and $\overline{BD} \perp \overline{AC}$
Prove: △BFE ~ △BCD

45

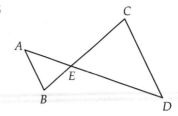

Given: $\overline{AB} \parallel \overline{CD}$
Prove: **a** △ABE ~ △DCE
     b $\frac{BE}{EC} = \frac{AE}{ED}$
     c $BE \times ED = EC \times AE$

46

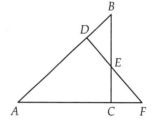

Given: $\overline{BC} \perp \overline{AF}$ and $\overline{FD} \perp \overline{AB}$
Prove: $BA \times DF = AF \times BC$

Geometry of the Circle

13-1 Arcs and Angles

A **circle** is the set of all points in a plane that are equidistant from a fixed point called the **center** of the circle. The **radius** of a circle (plural, *radii*) is a line segment from the center to any point *on* the circle.

• Theorem 13.1. All radii of the same circle are congruent.

A **chord** is a line segment that joins any two points on the circle. The **diameter** of a circle is a chord that passes through the center of the circle. The diameter is the longest chord. The diameter (*d*) is also twice the length of the radius (*r*) of the circle: $d = 2r$.

In the circle below, $\overline{AOC}$ is the diameter, $\overline{OB}$ is a radius, and both $\overline{FC}$ and $\overline{ED}$ are chords.

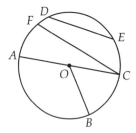

A circle divides a plane, *M*, into three sets of points:

• The boundary or circle itself
• The interior points of the circle
• The exterior points of the circle

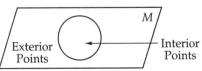

The **interior points** of a circle are the set of all points whose distance from the center is less than the length of the radius of the circle. The **exterior points** of a circle are the set of all points whose distance from the center is greater than the length of the radius of the circle.

An **arc** of a circle is any curved portion of the circle. Its measure is between 0° and 360°. Because a circle contains 360°, the sum of all the nonoverlapping arcs around the circle must total 360°. There are three kinds of arcs: *semicircle, minor arc,* and *major arc.* Arcs are classified by their degree measure and are named with two or three letters.

The **semicircle** is an arc that represents half the circle and measures 180°. The diameter of a circle divides the circle into two semicircles. In circle O, with diameter $\overline{AB}$, $m\overarc{ACB} = m\overarc{BHA} = 180°$

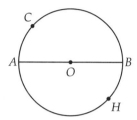

A **minor arc** is an arc whose measure is less than 180°. In circle O, arc PN is a minor arc.

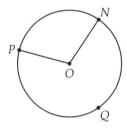

A **major arc** is an arc that is greater than a semicircle and its measure is between 180° and 360°. A major arc is named with three letters to distinguish it from the minor arc having the same endpoints. In circle O, $\overarc{NQP}$ is the major arc with endpoints N and P.

Central Angles

A **central angle** of a circle is an angle whose vertex is the center of the circle and whose sides are radii.

The **degree measure of an arc** is equal to the measure of the central angle that intercepts the arc.

Note: The degree measure of an arc is *never* the measure of the length of the arc.

For example, in the three concentric circles to the right, the measure of central angle $AOB = 75°$ so that, by definition, $m\overarc{AB} = m\overarc{CD} = m\overarc{EF} = 75$. However, it is obvious that $\overarc{AB}$, $\overarc{CD}$, and $\overarc{EF}$ do not have the same lengths.

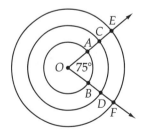

Congruent circles are circles with congruent radii. **Congruent arcs** are arcs in the same circle or in congruent circles that have the same degree measure. For example, in circle O, the central angles $\angle AOB$ and $\angle TOP$ each measure 70°. Since $m\angle AOB = m\angle TOP$, then $m\overset{\frown}{AB} = m\overset{\frown}{TP} = 70$.

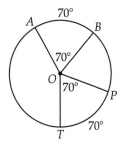

- **Arc Addition Postulate.** If $\overset{\frown}{AB}$ and $\overset{\frown}{BP}$ are arcs of the same circle having a common endpoint and no other points in common (as in circle O), then $\overset{\frown}{AB} + \overset{\frown}{BP} = \overset{\frown}{ABP}$ and $m\overset{\frown}{AB} + m\overset{\frown}{BP} = m\overset{\frown}{ABP}$.
- **Theorem 13.2.** In a circle or congruent circles, congruent central angles intercept congruent arcs, and, *conversely*, congruent arcs are intercepted by congruent central angles.

 MODEL PROBLEM

In circle O, $\overline{AC}$ and $\overline{BE}$ are diameters, $m\angle DOC = 40$, and $m\overset{\frown}{AE} = 80$. Find:

a $m\overset{\frown}{ED}$
b $m\angle EOD$
c $m\angle BOC$
d $m\angle AOB$
e $m\overset{\frown}{AB}$
f $m\overset{\frown}{BAD}$
g $m\overset{\frown}{DBE}$

SOLUTION

Fill in all the missing arcs and angles.

Since $\overset{\frown}{AE} = 80$, $\angle AOE = 80$. Since $\angle DOC = 40$, $\overset{\frown}{DC} = 40$.
Arc $AEDC$ is a semicircle, so all the arcs in the half circle should add up to 180°:

a $\overset{\frown}{AE} + \overset{\frown}{ED} + \overset{\frown}{DC} = 180$, so $80 + \overset{\frown}{ED} + 40 = 180$, and $\overset{\frown}{ED} = 60$.
b   Since $\overset{\frown}{ED} = 60$, $m\angle EOD = 60$ also.
c $\angle AOE$ and $\angle BOC$ are vertical angles and congruent. Since $\overset{\frown}{AE} = 80$, $\angle AOE = 80$ and $\angle BOC = 80$.
d $\angle BOC$ is the supplement of $\angle AOB$, so $\angle AOB = 100$.
e   Since $\angle AOB = 100$, $\overset{\frown}{AB} = 100$.
f $\overset{\frown}{BAD} = \overset{\frown}{AB} + \overset{\frown}{AE} + \overset{\frown}{ED} = 100 + 80 + 60 = 240$
g $\overset{\frown}{DBE} = \overset{\frown}{DC} + \overset{\frown}{CB} + \overset{\frown}{AB} + \overset{\frown}{AE} = 40 + 80 + 100 + 80 = 300$

 **Practice**

1. If an arc has the given degree measure, what is the measure of the central angle that intercepts that arc?

    a   36°
    b   51°
    c   90°
    d   180°
    e $(2r)°$

2. In circle O, $\overline{AC}$ is the diameter and $\overline{BD}$ is a chord.

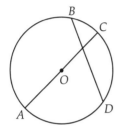

    Identify all

    a   the minor arcs.
    b   the semicircles.
    c   the major arcs.

3. $\overline{AB}$ and $\overline{RS}$ are diameters of circle O. If $m\angle ROB = 105$, find the measures of all the minor arcs.

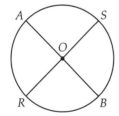

4. In circle O, $\overline{CA}$ is the diameter and $m\angle AOB = 25$.

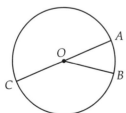

    Find:

    a $m\angle COB$
    b $m\widehat{AB}$
    c $m\widehat{BC}$
    d $m\widehat{ACB}$

5. If $\overline{PR}$ and $\overline{QS}$ are diameters of circle O and $m\angle QOR = 64$, find the measure of each of the following major arcs.

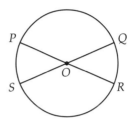

    a $\widehat{PQS}$
    b $\widehat{PSQ}$
    c $\widehat{QPR}$
    d $\widehat{RPS}$

6. In circle O, $\overline{AOC}$ is the diameter, $m\angle AOD = 107$, and $m\angle AOB = 48$.

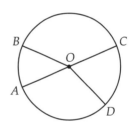

    Find the measure of each of the following.

    a $\angle DOC$
    b $\angle BOC$
    c $\angle BOD$
    d $\widehat{ABC}$
    e $\widehat{BAD}$
    f $\widehat{BDC}$
    g $\widehat{ACD}$
    h $\widehat{DCB}$
    i $\widehat{DBC}$

7 In circle O, $\angle POQ$ and $\angle SOR$ are supplementary.

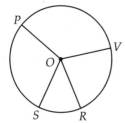

If $m\angle SOR = 3x$, $m\angle POV = 2x + 80$, and $m\angle POS = 5x + 10$, find the measures of each of the following.

a x
b $\angle SOR$
c $\angle POV$
d $\angle POS$
e $\angle VOR$
f $\overset{\frown}{SR}$
g $\overset{\frown}{RV}$
h $\overset{\frown}{PV}$
i $\overset{\frown}{PS}$
j $\overset{\frown}{SPV}$
k $\overset{\frown}{VSP}$
l $\overset{\frown}{RPV}$

13-2 Arcs and Chords

The endpoints of any chord (other than the diameter) determine two different arcs of a circle, a minor arc and a major arc.

• Theorem 13.3. In a circle or in congruent circles, congruent central angles have congruent chords. *Conversely*, congruent chords have congruent central angles.

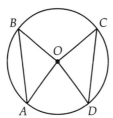

For example, in circle O, $\angle BOA \cong \angle COD$, such that $\overline{AB} \cong \overline{CD}$; and, *conversely*, if $\overline{AB} \cong \overline{CD}$, then $\angle BOA \cong \angle COD$.

Since central angles and their intercepted arcs have equal degree measures, we can state the following theorem.

• Theorem 13.4. In a circle or congruent circles, congruent arcs have congruent chords. *Conversely*, congruent chords have congruent arcs.

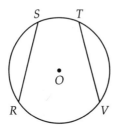

For example, in circle O, $\overset{\frown}{RS} \cong \overset{\frown}{TV}$, such that $\overline{RS} \cong \overline{TV}$, and, *conversely*, if $\overline{RS} \cong \overline{TV}$, then $\overset{\frown}{RS} \cong \overset{\frown}{TV}$.

The **distance from a point to a line** is the length of the perpendicular from that point to the line. Furthermore, the perpendicular is the shortest line segment that can be drawn from a point to a line.

- Theorem 13.5. A diameter perpendicular to a chord bisects the chord and its arcs.

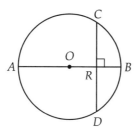

In circle O, $\overline{AB} \perp \overline{CD}$, such that $\overline{CR} \cong \overline{DR}$ and $\overarc{CB} \cong \overarc{BD}$. Furthermore, if $CD = 10$ and $m\overarc{CBD} = 62$, then $CR = DR = 5$, and $m\overarc{CB} = m\overarc{BD} = 31$.

- Corollary 13.5.1. The perpendicular bisector of the chord of a circle passes through the center of the circle. In circle O above, diameter $\overline{AB}$ passes through the center O.
- Theorem 13.6. If two chords of a circle are congruent, then they are equidistant from the center of the circle. *Conversely*, if two chords are equidistant from the center of a circle, then the chords are congruent.

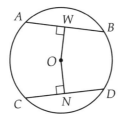

In circle O, $\overline{AB} \cong \overline{CD}$, with $\overline{OW} \perp \overline{AB}$ and $\overline{ON} \perp \overline{CD}$ such that $\overline{OW} \cong \overline{ON}$.

It is obvious that the diameter, the longest chord, passes through the center, which suggests the following theorem: that the shorter the chord, the farther from the center it must be.

- Theorem 13.7. If two chords are unequal in length, then the shorter chord is farther from the center.

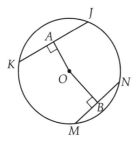

In circle O, $KJ > MN$ such that $OA < OB$.

Inscribing Polygons in a Circle

Recall that the perpendicular bisectors of the sides of a triangle meet at a common point—the point of concurrency—that is equidistant from the vertices of the triangle. If this triangle is inscribed in a circle, any line drawn from the point of concurrency to a vertex of the triangle is a radius of the circle. The center in this case is also called the *circumcenter*. The figure below illustrates this concept.

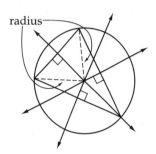

Chapter 14 includes further discussion of points of concurrency.

- Theorem 13.8. Three points *not* in a straight line determine a circle.

The logical proof of this theorem requires that we connect the three noncollinear points, which would form a triangle. Then the perpendicular bisectors of the sides of the triangle would meet at the circumcenter, and from there the triangle is inscribed in the circle.

If all of the vertices of a polygon are points on a circle, then the polygon is said to be inscribed in the circle or the circle is circumscribed about the polygon. Although every triangle can be inscribed in a circle, not all polygons have this property. However, any *regular* polygon can be inscribed in a circle. Furthermore, if a regular polygon is inscribed in a circle, then all its vertices lie on the circle and its sides are chords of the circle. Consider the inscribed polygons below.

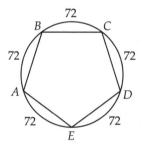

Regular Pentagon

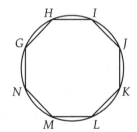

Regular Octagon

Given the regular pentagon *ABCDE* and the regular octagon *GHIJKLMN* inscribed in the circles, above, we can find the measure of each arc intercepted by the sides of these polygons. Divide 360° by the number of sides of the regular polygon. For the pentagon, 360° ÷ 5 means each arc measures 72°, and for the octagon, 360° ÷ 8 means each arc measures 45°.

1 In circle O, if $\overline{AB} \cong \overline{CD}$, name three pairs of congruent arcs.

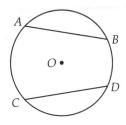

SOLUTION

Since congruent chords divides congruent arcs, one congruent arc pair is $\overset{\frown}{AB}$ and $\overset{\frown}{CD}$. Since $\overset{\frown}{AC} \cong \overset{\frown}{AC}$, by arc addition, $\overset{\frown}{ACD} \cong \overset{\frown}{CAB}$. Since $\overset{\frown}{BD} \cong \overset{\frown}{BD}$, again by arc addition, $\overset{\frown}{CDB} \cong \overset{\frown}{ABD}$.

2 If circle O has a radius of 6, what is the length of a chord $\overline{CD}$ that intercepts an arc of 90°?

SOLUTION

Draw radii $\overline{OC}$ and $\overline{OD}$ so that the measure of the central angle, $\angle COD$, is 90° and $\triangle COD$ is an isosceles right triangle.

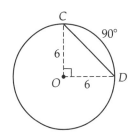

As a special 45°–45°–90° triangle, the sides are $6, 6, 6\sqrt{2}$.

ANSWER: Chord $CD = 6\sqrt{2}$.

3 Given: Circle $O \cong$ circle P, the radii are 8.
$\quad\quad$ m$\overset{\frown}{AB} = 120$, m$\overset{\frown}{QS} = 120$.
$\quad$ Find the measure of chords $\overline{AB}$ and $\overline{QS}$.

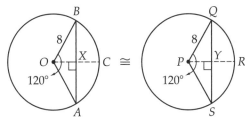

SOLUTION

Since arcs $\overset{\frown}{AB}$ and $\overset{\frown}{QS}$ have the same degree measure, their chords AB and QS are equal. $\triangle AOB$ and $\triangle SPQ$ are isosceles triangles. Let X be the midpoint of AB and Y the midpoint of QS. Then $\overline{OX}$ bisects $\angle AOB$ and $\overline{OX} \perp \overline{AB}$. So too, $\overline{PY}$ bisects $\angle QPS$ and $\overline{PY} \perp \overline{QS}$. The radii bisect both the central angle and the chords, so that m$\angle BOC = 60$ and m$\angle QPR = 60$. $\triangle BOX$ and $\triangle QPY$ are each 30°–60°–90° special triangles. In circle O, side BX opposite 60° is $4\sqrt{3}$, as is side QY. If we double that measure, then $AB = QS = 8\sqrt{3}$.

ANSWER: Chords $AB = QS = 8\sqrt{3}$.

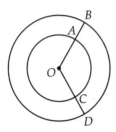
1 Find the radius, if each of the following is the diameter of a circle.

   a 32

   b 15

   c m

   d $6\sqrt{6}$

   e $\sqrt{200}$

2 If concentric circles with center O have radii as marked, determine whether the statements given are *True* or *False*.

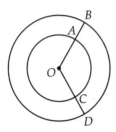

   a $m\angle BOD = m\angle AOC$

   b $m\overarc{AC} = m\overarc{BD}$

   c $\overarc{AC} \cong \overarc{BD}$

3 In circle O, $\overarc{TM} \cong \overarc{CB}$. If $m\overarc{TM} = 4x - 11$ and $m\overarc{CB} = 3x + 19$, what is the measure of $\overarc{TM}$?

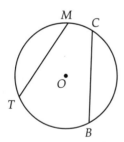

4 Find the measure of the minor arc determined by one of the sides of the following regular polygons.

   a square

   b pentagon

   c hexagon

   d decagon

5 If a regular polygon with the given number of sides is inscribed in a circle, what is the measure of each intercepted arc?

   a 15 sides

   b 16 sides

   c 18 sides

   d 20 sides

   e 24 sides

6 In circle O, the length of the chord $\overline{AB}$ is 10. Find the length of the radius if the measure of the arc is

   a 60°

   b 90°

   c 180°

7 If a circle has a radius of 6, what is the length of a chord determined by an arc of

   a 60°

   b 90°

   c 180°

   d 270°

8 In circle O with a radius of 5 inches, chord $\overline{AB}$ is 4 inches from the center.

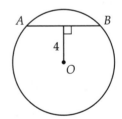

   Find the length of chord $\overline{AB}$.

Exercises 9 and 10: In circle O, $\overline{MB}$ and $\overline{CD}$ are diameters.

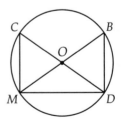

9 If $MO = 3x + 8$ and $CD = 10x + 4$, find the length of the radius of the circle.

10 Angle *CMD* is a right angle. *CM* = 9 and *MD* = 12.

    a Find *CD*, the diameter of the circle.
    b Find the length of *OM*.

11 If a regular hexagon is inscribed in a circle with a radius of 1, what is the perimeter of the hexagon?

12 What is the perimeter of a square inscribed in a circle if the radius of the circle is 2?

13 If a square is inscribed in a circle of radius *x*, what is a length of a side of the square in terms of *x*?

Exercises 14–17: $\overline{RT}$ is the diameter of circle *O*, $\overline{RT} \perp$ chord $\overline{SM}$ at point *A*.

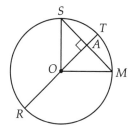

14 If *SM* = 8 and *OA* = 3, find *OM*.

15 If *SM* = 48 and *OA* = 7, find *OM*.

16 If m∠*SOR* = 150, find

    a m∠*SOA*
    b m∠*OSA*
    c m∠*AMO*
    d m∠*SOM*
    e m$\widehat{SM}$
    f m$\widehat{SRM}$
    g m$\widehat{MR}$

17 If m∠*SOM* = 60 and *SO* = 10, find

    a m∠*SOA*
    b m∠*SMO*
    c *SM*
    d *SA*
    e *OA*

18

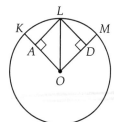

Given: Radii $\overline{OK}$ and $\overline{OM}$, $\overline{LA} \perp \overline{OK}$, $\overline{LD} \perp \overline{OM}$, and $\widehat{KL} \cong \widehat{ML}$
Prove: △*LAO* ≅ △*LDO*

19

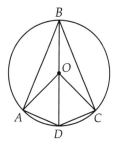

Given: $\overline{DB}$ is the diameter of circle *O*, ∠*ABD* ≅ ∠*CBD*.
Prove: $\widehat{AD} \cong \widehat{CD}$

20

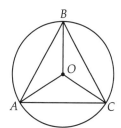

Given: $\overline{OA}$, $\overline{OB}$, and $\overline{OC}$ are radii of circle *O*. ∠*BAC* ≅ ∠*BCA*.
Prove: ∠*AOB* ≅ ∠*COB*

13-3 Inscribed Angles and Their Measure

An **inscribed angle** of a circle is an angle whose vertex is *on* the circle and whose sides contain chords of the circle. There are three cases to consider. In each case, Theorem 13.9 (below) holds true.

Case I	Case II	Case III
The center of the circle lies *on* one ray of ∠ABC.	The center of the circle is in the *interior* of ∠ABC.	The center of the circle is in the *exterior* of ∠ABC.
B 30° C A 60°	B 40° A C 80°	B 20° C A 40°

- Theorem 13.9. The measure of an inscribed angle of a circle equals one-half the measure of its intercepted arc. (The three figures above are examples of this.)
- Corollary 13.9.1. An angle inscribed in a semicircle is always a right angle.

   For example, in the circle below, all three inscribed angles intercept $\overset{\frown}{AMC}$, which is a semicircle and measures 180°. Therefore, m∠ABC = m∠ADC = m∠AEC = 90.

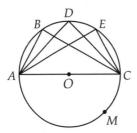

- Corollary 13.9.2. Inscribed angles that intercept the same arc are congruent.

   For example, in circle O, all three inscribed angles, ∠DAE, ∠DBE, and ∠DCE, intercept $\overset{\frown}{DE}$, and each angle equals $\frac{1}{2}m\overset{\frown}{DE}$, so ∠DAE ≅ ∠DBE ≅ ∠DCE.

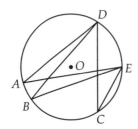

- Corollary 13.9.3. In a circle, the opposite angles of an inscribed quadrilateral are supplementary.

  For example, in circle O, quadrilateral $PQRS$ is inscribed. Therefore, m$\angle P$ + m$\angle R = 180$ and m$\angle Q$ + m$\angle S = 180$.

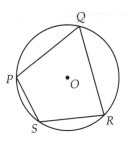

- Corollary 13.9.4. Parallel lines that intersect a circle intercept equal arcs.

  For example, in circle O, $\overline{AR}$ and $\overline{MT}$ are parallel, so m$\widehat{AM}$ = m$\widehat{RT}$.

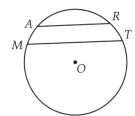

 MODEL PROBLEMS

1 Triangle ART is inscribed in circle O with m$\widehat{RT} = 86$.

   Find:

   a m$\angle A$
   b m$\angle R$
   c m$\angle T$
   d m$\widehat{AR}$

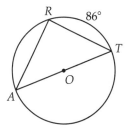

SOLUTION

   a m$\angle A = \frac{1}{2}$m$\widehat{RT} = \frac{1}{2}(86) = 43$

   b m$\angle R = 90$, since the intercepted arc is the semicircle $\widehat{AT}$.

   c m$\angle T = 180 - (90 + 43) = 47$

   d m$\widehat{AR}$ is twice m$\angle T$, so m$\widehat{AR} = 2(47) = 94$.

2 Triangle PQR is inscribed in circle O so that $m\overarc{PQ}:m\overarc{QR}:m\overarc{RP} = 2:3:4$. Find:

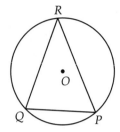

   a $m\overarc{PQ}$
   b $m\overarc{QR}$
   c $m\overarc{RP}$
   d $m\angle P$
   e $m\angle Q$
   f $m\angle R$

SOLUTION

Since the sum of the arcs of a circle is $360°$,
$2x + 3x + 4x = 360$
$\qquad\quad 9x = 360$
$\qquad\qquad x = 40$

Substitute 40 for the value of x.

   a $m\overarc{PQ} = 2x = 2(40) = 80$

   b $m\overarc{QR} = 3x = 3(40) = 120$

   c $m\overarc{RP} = 4x = 4(40) = 160$

   d $m\angle P = \frac{1}{2}\overarc{QR} = \frac{1}{2}(120) = 60$

   e $m\angle Q = \frac{1}{2}\overarc{RP} = \frac{1}{2}(160) = 80$

   f $m\angle R = \frac{1}{2}\overarc{PQ} = \frac{1}{2}(80) = 40$

Practice

1 What is the degree measure of an inscribed angle that intercepts an arc with the following degree measures?

   a $50°$
   b $110°$
   c $250°$
   d $120.8°$
   e $(8x)°$

2 If an inscribed angle has the following measure, what is the degree measure of the intercepted arc?

   a $26°$
   b $62°$
   c $7.5°$
   d $90°$
   e $(8x)°$

3

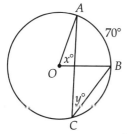

In circle O, if $m\widehat{AB} = 70$, find the sum of $x + y$.

4

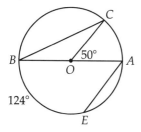

Given: Circle O with diameter $\overline{AOB}$, radius $\overline{OC}$, chords $\overline{BE}$ and $\overline{AC}$, and $m\widehat{BE} = 124$, $m\angle COB = 50$. Find:

a $m\widehat{CB}$
b $m\widehat{AC}$
c $m\widehat{AE}$
d $m\angle A$
e $m\angle B$
f $m\angle C$

Exercises 5–9: $\overline{AB} \parallel \overline{FG}$ in circle O. Find the degree measure of x.

5

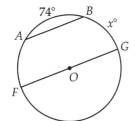

6

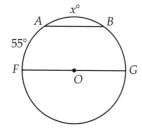

7

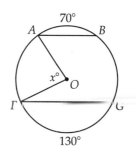

8

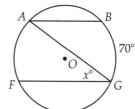

9

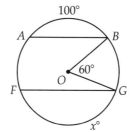

10 If quadrilateral $MADC$ is inscribed in a circle and $m\angle A = 105$, $m\angle D = 98$, and $m\widehat{MC} = 100$, find the measures of $\angle C$ and $\angle M$.

11 Quadrilateral $TRAP$ is inscribed in a circle. If $m\widehat{TR} = 118$, $m\widehat{RA} = 71$, and $m\widehat{AP} = 65$, what is the measure of $\angle TRA$?

Exercises 12–14: Find the measures of the four missing angles and/or arcs, as indicated by the numbers 1–4.

12

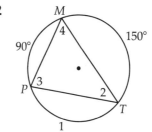

13

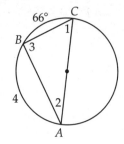

14

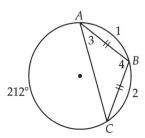

15

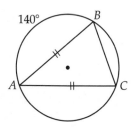

Triangle *ABC* is inscribed in circle *O*, with $\overline{AB} \cong \overline{AC}$ and m$\widehat{AB}$ = 140. Find:

a   m$\widehat{AC}$
b   m$\widehat{BC}$
c   m∠*A*
d   m∠*B*
e   m∠*C*

16

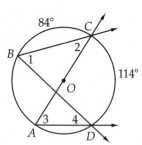

In circle *O*, m$\widehat{CD}$ = 114, and m$\widehat{BC}$ = 84. Find m∠1, m∠2, m∠3, and m∠4.

17   In circle *O*, m∠*X* = 40, m∠*W* = 94, and $\overline{XW} \cong \overline{YZ}$.

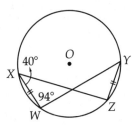

Find:

a   m$\widehat{WZ}$
b   m$\widehat{XY}$
c   m$\widehat{XW}$
d   m∠*Z*

18   In the circle below, m∠*A* = 86, m∠*BDC* = 32, and m$\widehat{AD}$ = 48.

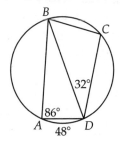

Find:

a   m$\widehat{BC}$
b   m$\widehat{CD}$
c   m$\widehat{AB}$
d   m∠*ADB*
e   m∠*ABD*
f   m∠*DBC*
g   m∠*BCD*

19   In circle *O*, m∠*C* = 94, m∠*B* = 78, and m$\widehat{AD}$ = 100.

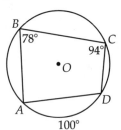

Find:

a   m∠*A*
b   m∠*D*
c   m$\widehat{AB}$
d   m$\widehat{DC}$
e   m$\widehat{BC}$

20 In the circle below, $\overline{KA} \cong \overline{TE}$ and m∠K = 44.

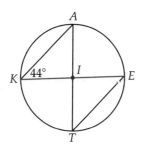

Find:

a m∠E
b m$\widehat{KT}$
c m∠A
d m∠T
e m∠KIA
f m$\widehat{AE}$

21 In circle O, $\overline{AC}$ is the diameter, m∠COD = 120, and $\overline{BD}$ bisects ∠ADO.

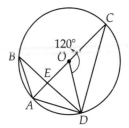

Find:

a m∠AOD
b m∠OAD
c m∠ODA
d m∠OCD
e m$\widehat{AD}$
f m$\widehat{DC}$
g m∠BDA
h m$\widehat{BA}$
i m$\widehat{BC}$
j m∠BAC
k m∠BEC

22 Prove that the opposite angles of a quadrilateral inscribed in a circle are supplementary.

23 Prove that if a parallelogram is inscribed in a circle, then the parallelogram is a rectangle.

13-4 Tangents and Secants

There are other angles that fall inside and outside the circle. These angles are formed by combinations of lines, rays, and segments that intersect the circle. When talking about the intersection of a circle and a line, there are three possibilities to consider:

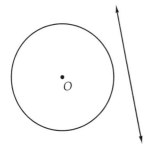

(a) No intersection.
Circle and line disjoint.

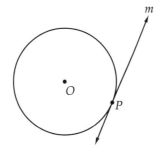

(b) One intersection point.
Tangent line m.

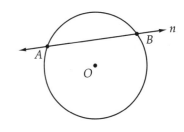

(c) Two intersection points.
Secant line n.

A **tangent to a circle** is a line in the plane of the circle that intersects the circle at one and only one point (the *point of tangency*). In figure (b) above, tangent line *m* intersects the circle at *P*, the point of tangency.

A **secant of a circle** is a line in the plane of the circle that intersects the circle at two points. In figure (c) above, secant line *n* intersects the circle at points *A* and *B*.

- Postulate. At any given point on a circle, one and only one line can be drawn that is tangent to the circle.
- Theorem 13.10. If a line is perpendicular to a radius at a point on the circle, then the line is tangent to the circle. *Conversely*, if a line is tangent to a circle then it is perpendicular to the radius at that point.

In circle *O*, radius $\overline{OP}$ is perpendicular to tangent line *m* at point *P*.

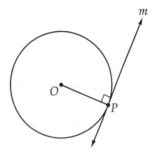

Line of Centers for Two Circles

The **line of centers for two circles** is the line segment that joins the centers of the circles. In the circles below, $\overline{OO'}$ is the line of centers.

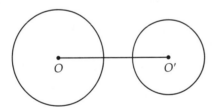

- Theorem 13.11. If two circles intersect in two points, their line of centers is the perpendicular bisector of their common chord.

In circles *O* and *O'*, their line of centers $\overline{OO'}$ is the perpendicular bisector of common chord $\overline{AB}$.

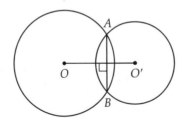

Common Tangents

A **common tangent** is a line that is tangent to each of two circles. Common tangents can be *internal* or *external*.

A **common internal tangent** intersects the line segment that joins the centers of the circle. Line *m* is the common internal tangent to circles *A* and *B*.

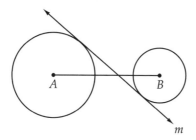

A **common external tangent** does *not* intersect the line segment that joins the centers of the circles. Line *l* is the common external tangent to circles *A* and *B*.

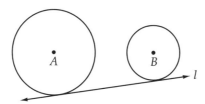

The diagrams below illustrate how two circles can have zero, one, two, three, or four common tangents.

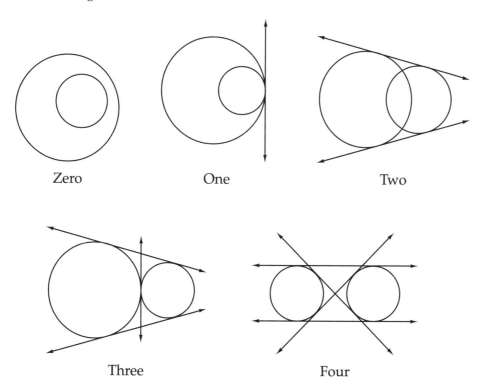

Relationship of Circles in the Same Plane

The six pairs of circles below illustrate zero, one, and two intersections.

Disjoint Circles

Concentric Circles

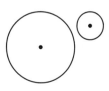 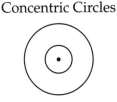

Tangent Circles

Two circles are *tangent* to each other if they are tangent to the same line at the same point. Circles can be tangent either *internally* or *externally*. Refer to the illustrations below.

Internally
Tangent Circles

Externally
Tangent Circles

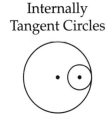 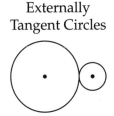

Intersecting Circles

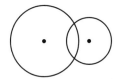

Tangent Segments

A **tangent segment** is a segment of a tangent line, one of whose endpoints is at the point of tangency. In circle O, $\overline{AP}$ and $\overline{BP}$ are tangent segments.

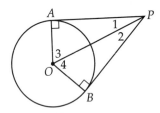

- Theorem 13.12. Two tangent segments drawn to a circle from an external point are congruent. In circle O, tangent segments $\overline{AP}$ and $\overline{BP}$ are congruent.
- Corollary 13.12.1. If two tangents are drawn to a circle from an external point, then the line passing through that point and the center of the circle bisects the angle formed by the tangents. In circle O, $\overline{PO}$ bisects $\angle APB$ such that $\angle 1 \cong \angle 2$.
- Corollary 13.12.2. If two tangents are drawn to a circle from an external point, then the line passing through that point and the center of the circle bisects the angle whose vertex is the center of the circle and whose rays are the two radii drawn to the points of tangency. In circle O, $\overline{PO}$ bisects central angle $\angle AOB$ such that $\angle 3 \cong \angle 4$. Furthermore, for any of these reasons, SSS, SAS, ASA, $\triangle PAO \cong \triangle PBO$.

Polygons Circumscribed About a Circle

A polygon circumscribes a circle when all the sides of the polygon are tangent to the circle. We may also say that the *circle is inscribed in the polygon*. For example, circle O is inscribed in square $ABCD$.

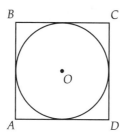

In general, a regular polygon with n sides can be circumscribed about a circle by drawing tangents at all the points on a circle that form n arcs of equal measure. Consider the tangents that are drawn at the six points on circle O that divide the circle into six equal arcs of 60°. The figure formed is a regular hexagon.

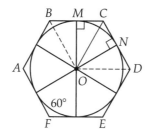

Furthermore, if we label two of the points of tangency M and N in hexagon $ABCDEF$, we can prove that $\triangle MOC \cong \triangle NOC$, and $\triangle BOC \cong \triangle DOC$, and $m\angle MOC = m\angle NOC$.

The **semiperimeter**, s, of a polygon is half the perimeter.

- Theorem 13.13. The area of any circumscribed polygon equals the product of the radius (r) of the inscribed circle and the semiperimeter (s) (Area = rs). For example, in the given figure, the radius is 4, the sum of the sides is 38, and the semiperimeter is 19. The area is $rs = 4(19) = 76$.

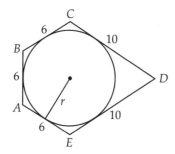

Note: As the number of sides of a regular polygon increases, its area approaches that of the inscribed circle.

MODEL PROBLEMS

1   Circle O is inscribed in $\triangle MNP$ with tangent points A, B, and C. If $MN = 12$, $MP = 14$, and $NB = 7$, find the perimeter of the triangle.

SOLUTION

Since tangents from the same point are equal, $NB = NA = 7$.
$MA = MN - NA$
$MA = 12 - 7$
$MA = 5$
If $MA = 5$, then $MC = 5$.

$CP = MP - MC$
$CP = 14 - 5$
$CP = 9$
If $CP = 9$, then $BP = 9$.

The perimeter of $\triangle MNP = 12 + 14 + 7 + 9 = 42$.

ANSWER: Perimeter of $\triangle MNP$ is 42.

2   Circle O is inscribed in regular pentagon $ABCDE$. $\overline{OP}$ is the radius drawn to the point of tangency on side $\overline{AE}$. Segments $\overline{OA}$ and $\overline{OE}$ are drawn.

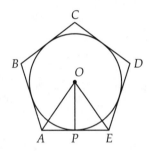

a   Find m$\angle AOE$, m$\angle POE$, m$\angle PEO$, and m$\angle AED$.
b   Find the area of the pentagon if a side of the pentagon is 8 and the radius of the circle is 5.5.

SOLUTION

a   To find m$\angle AOE$, the central angle, divide 360 by 5: m$\angle AOE = 72$.

m$\angle POE = \frac{1}{2}(m\angle AOE) = \frac{1}{2}(72) = 36$

m$\angle PEO$ is the other acute angle in right triangle OPE: m$\angle PEO = 90 - 36 = 54$.

m$\angle AED$ is twice the measure of $\angle PEO = 2 \times 54 = 108$

ANSWER: m$\angle AOE = 72$, m$\angle POE = 36$, m$\angle PEO = 54$, and m$\angle AED = 108$.

b   The perimeter of the pentagon is $5(8) = 40$. The semiperimeter is 20.
The area $= rs = 5.5 \times 20 = 110$.

ANSWER: The area of the pentagon is 110.

 **Practice**

1 Draw a picture of the two circles as described.

   a Intersecting but not tangent
   b Internally disjoint but not concentric
   c Internally tangent
   d Externally tangent

2 Draw *externally* tangent circles with centers A and B such that circle A has radius 5 and circle B has radius 7.

   a What is the length of $\overline{AB}$?
   b How many lines can be drawn tangent to both circles at the same time?

3 Draw *internally* tangent circles with centers M and P such that circle M has radius 6 and circle P has radius 2.75.

   a What is the length of $\overline{MP}$?
   b How many lines can be drawn tangent to both circles at the same time?

4 What are the relative positions of two circles if the line of centers is

   a greater than the sum of the radii.
   b equal to the sum of the radii.
   c less than the sum but greater than the difference of the radii.
   d equal to the difference of the radii.
   e less than the difference of the radii.
   f equal to zero.

5 Draw two circles whose radii are 4 and 5 if the length of the line of centers is

   a 11
   b 7
   c 9
   d 1

6 State the number of common tangents that can be drawn to

   a two circles internally tangent.
   b two circles externally tangent.
   c two circles that intersect in two points.
   d two circles that are disjoint.

7 In circle O, $\overline{PA}$ and $\overline{PB}$ are tangents. $\overline{OA}$ and $\overline{OB}$ are radii.

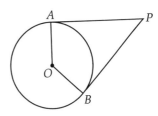

Find m∠P if m∠AOB is

   a 20
   b 50
   c 90
   d 140
   e x

Exercises 8 and 9: Use circle O, with $\overline{CA}$ and $\overline{CB}$ as tangents.

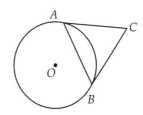

8 Find the measure of ∠A if the degree measure of ∠C is

   a 60°
   b 90°
   c 110°
   d 78°
   e 45°

9 Find the measure of ∠B if m∠C is represented by

   a n
   b 4n
   c 180 − n
   d 90 − 2n
   e m + n

10 Circle X and circle Y are tangent to each other at point P. Line l is tangent to circle X at A and to circle Y at B.

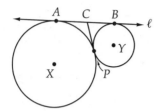

If the length of PC is 8, find the length of AB.

11 Circle O is inscribed in $\triangle STV$. $ST = 20$, $TV = 32$, and $SC = 8$.

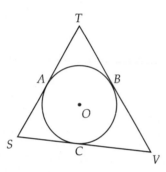

Find the perimeter of the triangle.

12 Circle O is inscribed in $\triangle ABC$ with the given lengths and the tangent points P, Q, and R.

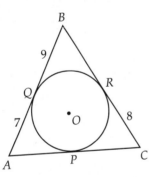

Find the perimeter of $\triangle ABC$.

13

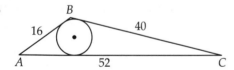

If the radius of the inscribed circle is $4\frac{1}{3}$, use the given lengths and find the area of $\triangle ABC$.

14 The figure shows a portion of circle P with radius $PR = 3$ in. inscribed in a decagon. $\overline{QT}$ is a side of the decagon.

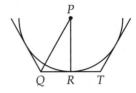

a   Find m$\angle QPR$.
b   Find m$\angle PQR$.
c   If the length of $QT = 1.95$, what is the area of the polygon?

Exercises 15–18: Circle O is inscribed in $\triangle ABC$ with D, E, and F the points of tangency.

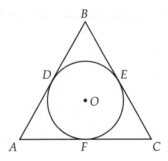

15 If $AD = 6$, $EB = 5$, and $CF = 12$,

   a   find the lengths of the sides of the triangle.
   b   show that the triangle is scalene.

16 If $AF = 8$, $CE = 12$, and $BD = 4$,

   a   find the lengths of the sides of $\triangle ABC$.
   b   show that $\triangle ABC$ is a right triangle.

17 If $AD = 5$, $BE = 5$, and $FC = 10$,

   a   find the lengths of the sides of the triangle
   b   show that $\triangle ABC$ is isosceles.

18 If $DB = 4$, $BC = 9$, and the perimeter of the triangle is 30, find BE, EC, CF, AF, AC, and AB.

Exercises 19–24: $\overline{BA}$ and $\overline{BC}$ are tangents, and $\overline{DB}$ intersects circle O at points R and D.

27

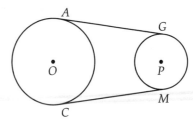

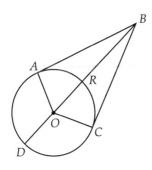

19 If $OA = 15$ and $OB = 25$, find AB, CB, and RB.

20 If $OB = 25$ and $OA = 7$, find AB, DR, and DB.

21 If $OA = 10$ and $AB = 24$, find OB, DB, and RB.

22 If $OA = 6$ and $RB = 14$, find OB, AB, and CB.

23 If $OC = 10$ and $DB = 32$, find OB, CB, and AB.

24 If $AB = 4x$, $CB = 6x - 10$, and $OC = 2x + 5$, find AB, CB, OC, and OB.

Given: Common external tangents $\overline{AG}$ and $\overline{CM}$ of circles O and P
Prove: $\overline{AG} \cong \overline{CM}$

28

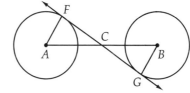

Given: Circle A is congruent to Circle B. $\overleftrightarrow{FG}$ is the common internal tangent, and line of centers $\overline{AB}$ intersects $\overleftrightarrow{FG}$ at point C.
Prove: $\overline{AC} \cong \overline{BC}$

25

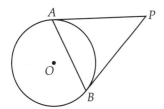

Given: Tangents $\overline{PA}$ and $\overline{PB}$ with m$\angle P = 60$
Prove: $\triangle APB$ is an equilateral triangle.

29

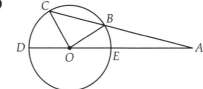

Given: Secants $\overline{AD}$ and $\overline{AC}$, and radii $\overline{OC}$ and $\overline{OB}$. $\triangle OBA$ is isosceles with $\overline{OB} \cong \overline{AB}$, and $\overline{CO} \perp \overline{DOE}$.
Prove: m$\angle COD = 3$(m$\angle A$)

26

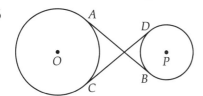

30 Given: Two concentric circles with two chords $\overline{AB}$ and $\overline{CD}$ drawn in the larger circle and tangent to the smaller circle.
Prove: $\overline{AB} \cong \overline{CD}$

Given: Common internal tangents $\overline{AB}$ and $\overline{CD}$ of circles O and P
Prove: $\overline{AB} \cong \overline{CD}$

13-5 Angles Formed by Tangents, Chords, and Secants

The angle between a tangent and a chord is derived to the measure of an inscribed angle.

- Theorem 13.14. The measure of an angle formed by a tangent and a chord is equal to one-half the measure of its intercepted arc.

  In circle O, the measure of $\angle ABC$, formed by tangent $\overleftrightarrow{DBC}$ and chord $\overline{BA}$, is equal to one-half the measure of the intercepted arc $\overparen{BA}$. That is, $m\angle ABC = \frac{1}{2}(110) = 55$.

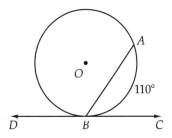

- Theorem 13.15. The measure of an angle formed by two chords intersecting within a circle is equal to one-half the sum of the measures of the intercepted arcs.

  In circle O, chords $\overline{AB}$ and $\overline{CD}$ intersect at point P. If $m\overparen{DB} = 80$ and $m\overparen{AC} = 38$, then the measure of $\angle DPB = \frac{1}{2}(m\overparen{DB} + m\overparen{AC}) = \frac{1}{2}(80 + 38) = \frac{1}{2}(118) = 59$.

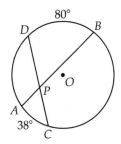

Up to this point we have studied angles whose vertex has been *in* or *on* the circle. We will now study angles formed by two secants, a tangent and a secant, or two tangents. All of these angles have vertices *outside* the circle and have measures that again are related to their intercepted arcs.

- Theorem 13.16. The measure of an angle formed by two secants, a tangent and a secant, or two tangents intersecting outside the circle is equal to one-half the difference of the measures of the intercepted arcs.

The table on the next page illustrates the three cases presented in theorem 13.16.

| Case I
Two Secants	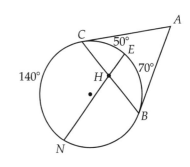	$m\angle A = \frac{1}{2}\left(m\widehat{CG} - m\widehat{BF}\right)$ $m\angle A = \frac{1}{2}(70 - 20)$ $m\angle A = \frac{1}{2}(50) = 25$
Case II
Tangent and
Secant | | $m\angle A = \frac{1}{2}\left(m\widehat{BD} - m\widehat{BC}\right)$
 $m\angle A = \frac{1}{2}(220 - 30)$
 $m\angle A = \frac{1}{2}(190) = 95$ |
| Case III
Two Tangents | | $m\angle P = \frac{1}{2}\left(m\widehat{AXB} - m\widehat{AB}\right)$
 $m\angle P = \frac{1}{2}(260 - 100)$
 $m\angle P = \frac{1}{2}(160) = 80$ |

→ MODEL PROBLEMS

1 Given: $\overline{AB}$ and $\overline{AC}$ are tangents to the circle. Chords
$\overline{NE}$ and $\overline{BC}$ intersect at point H, $m\widehat{CN} = 140$,
$m\widehat{CE} = 50$, and $m\widehat{EB} = 70$.
Find: (a) $m\widehat{NB}$, (b) $m\angle A$, (c) $m\angle NHB$, (d) $m\angle ABC$

SOLUTION

  a   The sum of the arcs equals 360°.
$$140 + 50 + 70 + m\widehat{NB} = 360$$
$$260 + m\widehat{NB} = 360$$
$$m\widehat{NB} = 100$$

  b $m\angle A = \frac{1}{2}m\widehat{CNB} - m\widehat{CB} = \frac{1}{2}(240 - 120)$
$$= \frac{1}{2}(120) = 60$$

  c $m\angle NHB = \frac{1}{2}\left(m\widehat{CE} + m\widehat{NB}\right) = \frac{1}{2}(50 + 100) = 75$

  d   Angle ABC is formed by tangent $\overline{AB}$ and chord $\overline{BC}$. Therefore,
$$m\angle ABC = \frac{1}{2}\left(\text{intercepted } \widehat{CEB}\right)$$
$$m\angle ABC = \frac{1}{2}(120) = 60$$

2 Given: Circle O with tangent $\overrightarrow{PAD}$, secants $\overrightarrow{PHB}$ and
   $\overrightarrow{PVCF}$, and chord $\overline{AEC}$. $\text{m}\widehat{AB} = 70$, $\text{m}\widehat{CB} = 160$,
   $\text{m}\widehat{CV} = 60$, and $\text{m}\widehat{VH} = 50$.

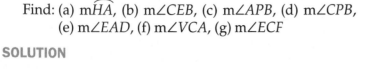

   Find: (a) $\text{m}\widehat{HA}$, (b) $\text{m}\angle CEB$, (c) $\text{m}\angle APB$, (d) $\text{m}\angle CPB$,
   (e) $\text{m}\angle EAD$, (f) $\text{m}\angle VCA$, (g) $\text{m}\angle ECF$

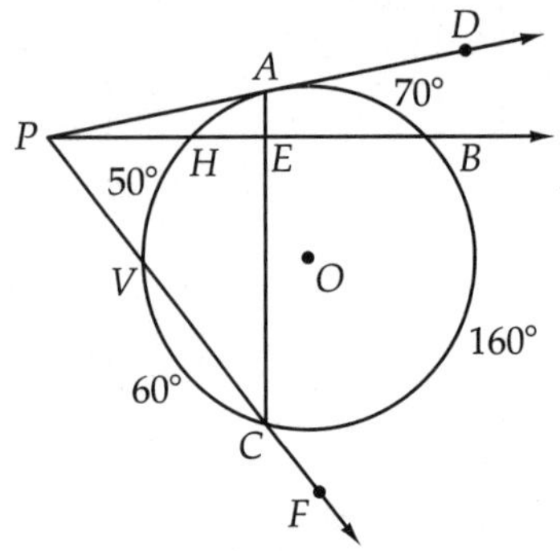

SOLUTION

a The sum of the arcs is $360°$.

$$70 + 160 + 60 + 50 + \text{m}\widehat{HA} = 360.$$
$$340 + \text{m}\widehat{HA} = 360$$
$$\text{m}\widehat{HA} = 20$$

b $\text{m}\angle CEB = \frac{1}{2}\left(\text{m}\widehat{CB} + \text{m}\widehat{HA}\right) = \frac{1}{2}(160 + 20) = 90$

c $\text{m}\angle APB = \frac{1}{2}\left(\text{m}\widehat{AB} - \text{m}\widehat{HA}\right) = \frac{1}{2}(70 - 20) = 25$

d $\text{m}\angle CPB = \frac{1}{2}\left(\text{m}\widehat{CB} - \text{m}\widehat{VH}\right) = \frac{1}{2}(160 - 50) = 55$

e $\text{m}\angle EAD = \frac{1}{2}\left(\text{m}\widehat{ABC}\right) = \frac{1}{2}(70 + 160) = 115$

f $\text{m}\angle VCA = \frac{1}{2}\left(\text{m}\widehat{VHA}\right) = \frac{1}{2}(50 + 20) = 35$

g The measure of $\angle ECF$ is equal to the supplement of $\angle VCA$.

$$\text{m}\angle ECF = 180 - \text{m}\angle VCA$$
$$\text{m}\angle ECF = 180 - 35$$
$$\text{m}\angle ECF = 145$$

 Practice

1 Chords $\overline{MN}$ and $\overline{PQ}$ intersect at point R in circle O. If $\text{m}\widehat{MQ} = 112$ and $\text{m}\widehat{PN} = 80$, what is the measure of $\angle MRQ$?

(1) 32
(2) 96
(3) 112
(4) 192

2 From an external point, two tangents are drawn to a circle. If the tangent intercepts a major arc of $204°$, the measure of the angle formed by the tangents is:

(1) 24
(2) 48
(3) 102
(4) 156

3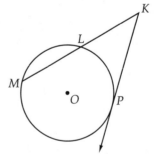

In the diagram above, secant $\overline{KLM}$ and tangent $\overline{KP}$ are drawn to circle O. If the measure of $\widehat{LP}$ is $50°$ and the measure of $\angle PKM$ is $47°$, the measure of $\widehat{MP}$ is:

(1) 94
(2) 144
(3) 188
(4) 310

4

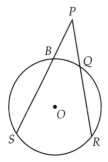

In circle O, secants $\overline{PBS}$ and $\overline{PQR}$ are drawn. If the measure of $\angle SPR$ is $65°$ and the measure of $\overparen{BQ}$ is $43°$, the measure of $\overparen{SR}$ is:

(1) $87°$
(2) $107°$
(3) $130°$
(4) $173°$

5 In circle O, chords $\overline{CH}$ and $\overline{AD}$ intersect at point Q inside the circle. If $m\angle AQH = 51$ and $m\overparen{CD} = 64$, then $m\overparen{AH}$ is:

(1) 38
(2) 51
(3) 102
(4) 115

6 In circle O, tangent $\overline{PB}$ intersects radius $\overline{OB}$. The measure of $\angle OBP$ is:

(1) $90°$
(2) $45°$
(3) equal to the intercept arc
(4) unable to be determined

7 For each of the following, find the degree measure of each arc or angle as indicated by x.

a

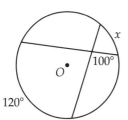

b

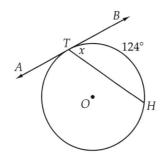

c

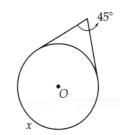

d

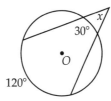

e

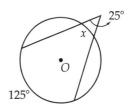

f

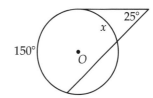

g

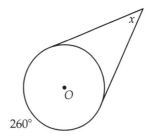

h

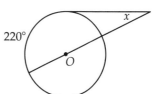

Angles Formed by Tangents, Chords, and Secants **369**

8 For each of the following figures, find the measure of each arc or angle indicted by $x, y,$ and z.

a

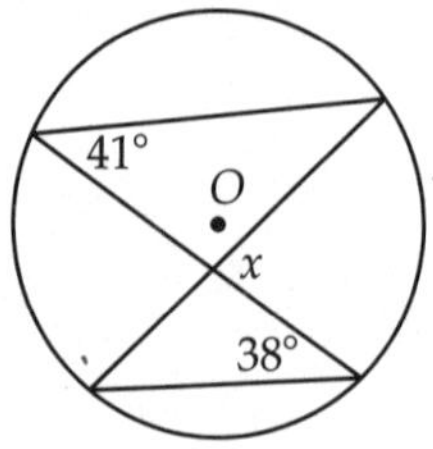

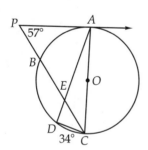

b

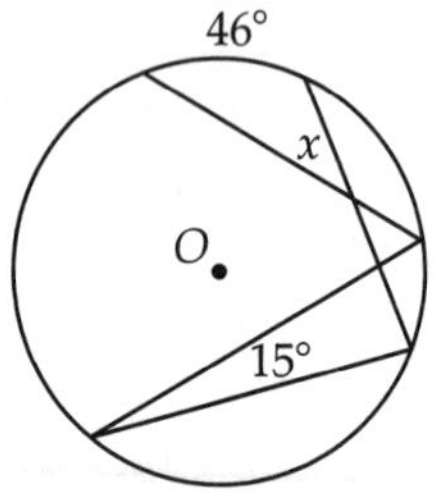

c

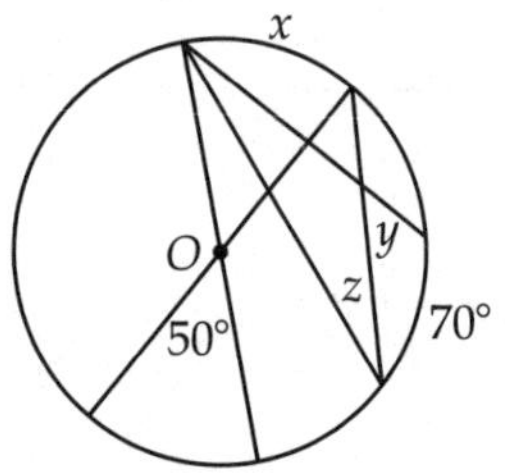

9 In circle O, tangent $\overline{PA}$, secant $\overline{PBC}$, diameter $\overline{AOC}$, and chords $\overline{AD}$ and $\overline{DC}$ are drawn. $m\angle APC = 57$, $m\widehat{DC} = 34$.

Find:

a $m\widehat{BA}$
b $m\widehat{BD}$
c $m\angle ACD$
d $m\angle BED$
e $m\angle PCA$
f $m\angle PAD$

10 In circle O, $\overrightarrow{PAB}$ and $\overrightarrow{PDC}$ are secants with chords $\overline{AC}$ and $\overline{DB}$ intersecting at point G.

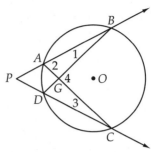

If $m\widehat{DA}:m\widehat{AB}:m\widehat{BC} = 2:3:4$ and $\widehat{AB} \cong \widehat{DC}$, find:

a $m\widehat{AB}$ **e** $m\angle 1$
b $m\widehat{BC}$ **f** $m\angle 2$
c $m\widehat{CD}$ **g** $m\angle 3$
d $m\widehat{DA}$ **h** $m\angle 4$

11 In circle O, $\overline{PA}$ is tangent at point A, $\overline{PA} \parallel \overline{DB}$, $\overline{PDC}$ is a secant, $\overline{AD}$ and $\overline{AB}$ are chords, $\widehat{AB} \cong \widehat{BC}$, and $m\widehat{DA} = 80$.

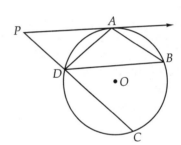

Find:

a $m\widehat{DC}$
b $m\angle CDB$
c $m\angle CDA$
d $m\angle CPA$
e $m\angle PAB$
f $m\angle PDA$

12

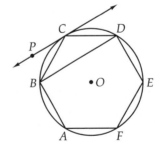

Given: Regular hexagon $ABCDEF$ inscribed in circle O with $\overleftrightarrow{CP}$ tangent to the circle at point C.
Prove: $\overleftrightarrow{PC} \parallel \overline{BD}$

13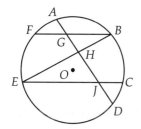

Given: Circle O with chords $\overline{FB} \parallel \overline{EC}$ and chord $\overline{BE}$ drawn. Chord $\overline{AD}$ intersects $\overline{FB}$, $\overline{BE}$, and $\overline{EC}$ at points G, H, and J, respectively.

Prove: $BH \times JH = HE \times HG$

14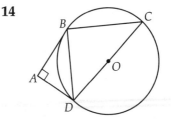

Given: $\overline{AB}$ is tangent to circle O at B, $\overline{DC}$ is the diameter, $\overline{BD}$ and $\overline{BC}$ are chords, and $\overline{DA} \perp \overline{BA}$.

Prove: $(BD)^2 = DC \times DA$

13-6 Measures of Tangent Segments, Chords and Secant Segments

The next theorems refer to the relationships of line segments and the circle. The proofs of these theorems is the result of working with similar triangles and the essential concept reviewed in Chapter 12: When two polygons are similar, the ratio of all pairs of corresponding sides are equal.

As shown below, in a circle with intersecting chords, two secants, or a secant and a tangent,

- similar triangles can be drawn.
- corresponding sides can be set up in a proportion.
- formulas can be derived from setting the product of the means equal to the product of the extremes.

Case 1 Intersecting Chords

- Theorem 13.17. If two chords intersect within a circle, the product of the measures of the segments of one chord equals the product of the measures of the segments of the other.

Example:

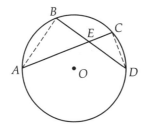

Given: Chords $\overline{AC}$ and $\overline{BD}$ intersect at E, an interior point of circle O.

It can be proved that

a $\quad \triangle AEB \sim \triangle DEC$

b $\quad \dfrac{BE}{CE} = \dfrac{EA}{ED}$

c $\quad BE \times ED = CE \times EA$

Case 2 Two Secants

- Theorem 13.18. If two secants intersect outside a circle, then the product of the measures of the whole secant and external segment is equal to the product of the measures of the other whole secant and its external segment.

  Example:

  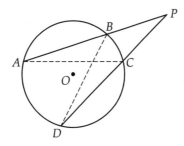

  Given: Secants $\overline{PBA}$ and $\overline{PCD}$ intersect at point P outside circle O.

  It can be proved that

    a $\triangle PAC \sim \triangle PDB$

    b $\dfrac{PA}{PD} = \dfrac{PC}{PB}$

    c $PA \times PB = PD \times PC$

Case 3 A Tangent and a Secant

- Theorem 13.19. If a tangent and a secant are drawn to a circle from an external point, then the square of the measure of the tangent segment is equal to the product of the measures of the whole secant and its external segment.

  Example:

  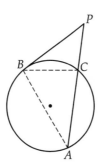

  Given: Tangent $\overline{PB}$ and secant $\overline{PCA}$ intersect at point P, outside circle O.

  It can be proved that

    a $\triangle PBC \sim \triangle PAB$

    b $\dfrac{PC}{PB} = \dfrac{PB}{PA}$

    c $(PB)^2 = PC \times PA$

Note: Theorem 13.19 can be restated this way:

If a tangent and a secant are drawn to a circle from an external point, then the measure of the tangent is the *mean proportional* between the whole segment and its eternal segment.

1 In circle O, chords $\overline{AB}$ and $\overline{CD}$ intersect at point E.

If $AE = 6$, $EB = 8$, and $CE = 4$, find the length of ED.

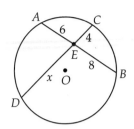

SOLUTION

$AE \times EB = CE \times ED$

Let $ED = x$.

$6 \times 8 = 4x$

$48 = 4x$

$x = 12$

ANSWER: The length of ED is 12.

2 In circle O, chords $\overline{RN}$ and $\overline{AB}$ intersect at point E.

If $AB = 16$, $RE = 6$, and $EN = 8$, find the length of AE given that $AE < EB$.

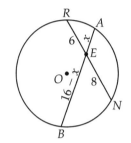

SOLUTION

Let $AE = x$ and let $EB = 16 - x$.

Then $AE \times EB = RE \times EN$ and by substitution,

$x(16 - x) = (6)(8)$

$16x - x^2 = 48$

$0 = x^2 - 16x + 48$

$0 = (x - 4)(x - 12)$

$x - 4 = 0$ or $x - 12 = 0$

$x = 4$ or $x = 12$

$EB = 16 - 4 = 12$ or $EB = 16 - 12 = 4$

Since $AE < EB$, $AE = 4$.

ANSWER: $AE = 4$

3 Find the length of a chord 4 cm from the center of a circle whose radius measures 5 cm.

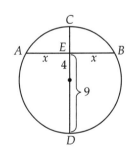

SOLUTION

Let $AE = EB = x$. The length of ED is 4 more than the length of the radius. Then,

$ED = 5 + 4 = 9$ and $CE = 1$

$AE \times EB = CE \times ED$

By substitution, $(x)(x) = (1)(9)$.

$x^2 = 9$

$x = \pm 3$

Since the length cannot be negative, $x = 3$ and $AE = EB = 3$.

Chord $AB = x + x = 3 + 3 = 6$

ANSWER: The length of a chord 4 cm from the center of a circle is 6 cm.

4 In the circle, secants $\overline{PBA}$ and $\overline{PCD}$, with $PA = 12$, $PB = 5$, and $PD = 15$. Find the length of PC.

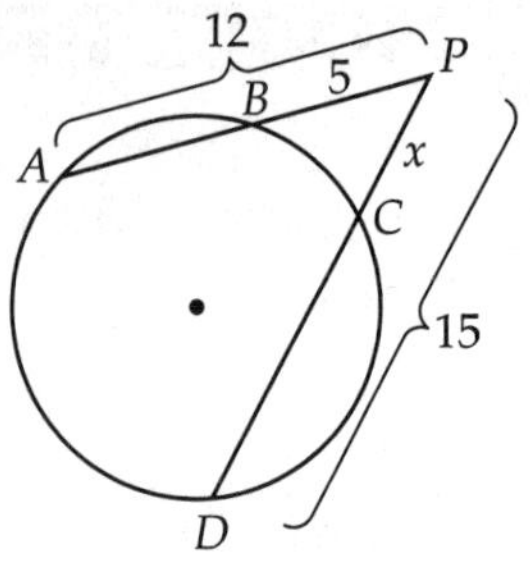

SOLUTION

Let $PC = x$.
$PB \times PA = PC \times PD$

$(5)(12) = x(15)$
$\quad 60 = 15x$
$\quad\quad x = 4$

ANSWER: The length of PC is 4.

5 Given: Tangent $\overline{PA}$ and secant $\overline{PBC}$, with $PA = 8$ and $CB = 12$. Find the length of PC.

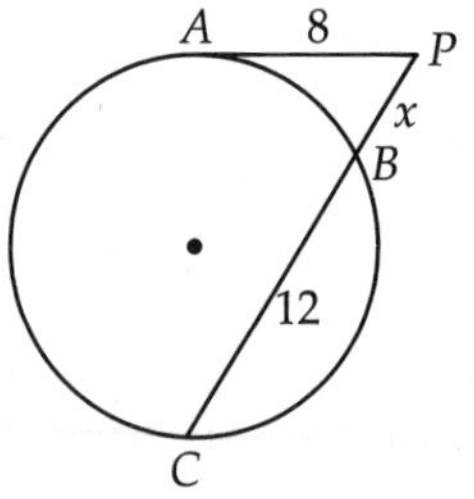

SOLUTION

Let $PB = x$ and $PC = x + 12$.
$(PA)^2 = PB \times PC$
$8^2 = x(x + 12)$
$64 = x^2 + 12x$
$0 = x^2 + 12x - 64$
$0 = (x + 16)(x - 4)$
$x = -16$ (rejected) and $x = 4$
$PC = x + 12 = 4 + 12 = 16$

ANSWER: The length of PC is 16.

Practice

1 In circle O, chords $\overline{AB}$ and $\overline{CD}$ intersect at E. If $AE = 6$, $BE = 16$, and $CE = 12$, which of the following is the length of $\overline{CD}$?

(1) 8
(2) 12
(3) 18
(4) 20

2 In the diagram below, circle O is inscribed in triangle ABC so that the circle is tangent to $\overline{AB}$ at F, to $\overline{BC}$ at E, and to $\overline{AC}$ at D.

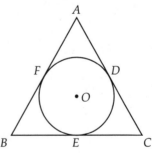

If $AD = 6$, $BF = 7$, and $CE = 10$, what is the perimeter of triangle ABC?

(1) 23
(2) 46
(3) 69
(4) 23π

3 In circle O, the length of $\overline{OE}$ is 8 and the length of chord $\overline{AB}$ is 30.

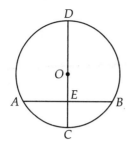

If $\overline{CD}$ is perpendicular to $\overline{AB}$ at E, which of the following is the length of $\overline{CO}$?

(1) 17
(2) 16
(3) 12
(4) 8

4 Secant $\overline{ADC}$ and tangent $\overline{AB}$ are drawn to circle O from external point A. If $AB = 12$ and $AD = 6$, the length of AC is:

(1) 12
(2) 18
(3) 24
(4) 30

5 Secants $\overline{PAB}$ and $\overline{PCD}$ are drawn to a circle from an external point P. If $PA = 4$, $AB = 16$, and $PC = 8$, the length of $\overline{PCD}$ is which of the following?

(1) 8
(2) 10
(3) 20
(4) 80

6 In a circle, a chord of 30 centimeters bisects a chord of 18 centimeters. The length of the shorter segment of the 30-centimeter chord is:

(1) 3
(2) 10
(3) 12
(4) 27

7 $\overline{PC}$ is tangent to circle O at C and $\overline{PAB}$ is a secant.

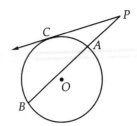

If $PC = 10$ and $PA = 4$, the length of $\overline{PAB}$ equals:

(1) 6
(2) 21
(3) 25
(4) 29

8 In circle O, chords $\overline{CH}$ and $\overline{AD}$ intersect at Z. If $AZ = a$, $ZH = z$, and $CZ = c$, what is the length of $\overline{DZ}$ in terms of a, z, and c?

(1) azc
(2) $\frac{az}{c}$
(3) $\frac{cz}{a}$
(4) $\frac{ac}{z}$

9 In circle O, chords $\overline{AB}$ and $\overline{CD}$ intersect at E. If $AE = 6$, $BE = 12$, and $CE = 8$, CD measures:

(1) 4
(2) 9
(3) 17
(4) 18

10 $\overline{PA}$ and $\overline{PB}$ are tangents drawn to circle O from external point P. If $PA = 8r - 7$ and $PB = 4r + 13$, PA equals:

(1) 5
(2) 7
(3) 33
(4) 41

11   In circle O below, the length of the radius is 41 and the length of chord $\overline{AEB}$ is 80.

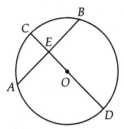

If $\overline{CO}$ is perpendicular to $\overline{AEB}$ at E, what is the length of $\overline{EO}$?

(1) 9
(2) 20
(3) 20.5
(4) 39

12   Secant $\overline{XYZ}$ and tangent $\overline{XA}$ are drawn to circle O from external point X. If $XA = 16$ and $XY = 8$, find the length of $\overline{YZ}$.

13   Secant $\overline{PAB}$ and $\overline{PCD}$ are drawn to a circle from an external point P. If $PA = 5$, $AB = 25$, and $PC = 6$, find the length of $\overline{CD}$.

14   In a circle, a chord of 50 centimeters bisects a chord of 40 centimeters. Find the length of the longer segment of the 50-centimeter chord.

15   Quadrilateral $PADB$ circumscribes circle O. If $PM = 4$, $AC = 7$, $DN = 6$, and $BQ = 5$, find the perimeter of $PADB$.

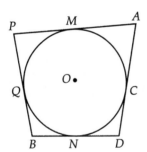

16   Tangent $\overline{PA}$ and secant $\overline{PBC}$ are drawn to circle O from external point P. If $PC = 24$ and $PB = 6$, find the length of $\overline{PA}$.

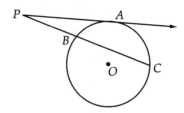

17   In circle O, diameter $\overline{AOB}$ is perpendicular to chord $\overline{CD}$ at E. If $AOB = 40$ and $ED = 12$, find the length of $\overline{OE}$.

18   In circle O, chords $\overline{LM}$ and $\overline{NP}$ intersect at Q. If $LQ = 12$, $QM = 8$, and $NP = 22$, find the lengths of $\overline{NQ}$ and $\overline{QP}$ given that $NQ < QP$.

19   Chords $\overline{GH}$ and $\overline{JK}$ in circle O intersect at W. If $GW = x$, $WH = x + 8$, $JW = 6$, and $KW = 8$, find the value of x and the length of $\overline{GH}$.

20   In circle O, diameter $\overline{AOB}$ and chord $\overline{WZ}$ intersect at X. If $AX = 20$, $XB = 5$, $XW = 10$, and $XZ = 10$, determine whether or not $\overline{AOB} \perp \overline{WZ}$. Explain your reasoning.

13-7 Circle Proofs

Follow the steps below to find the measure of an angle in a circle:

Step 1: Locate the angle.
Step 2: Identify the line segments that form the angle.
Step 3: Find the measure(s) of the arc(s) intercepted by the sides of the angle.
Step 4: Determine which formula is needed to find the measure of the angle.

Formulas for Determining Angle Measures				
Type of Angle	**Identifying Elements**	**Diagram**	**Formula**	**Example**
Central angle	Its vertex is the center of the circle and its sides are radii.	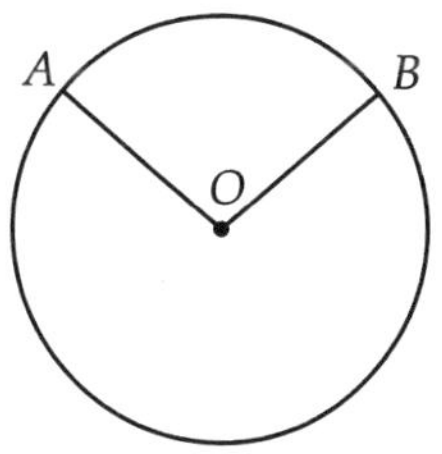	Measure of a central angle is equal to the degree measure of the intercepted arc. $m\angle AOB = m\overset{\frown}{AB}$	If $m\overset{\frown}{AB} = 74$, then $m\angle AOB = 74$.
Inscribed angle	Its vertex is on the circle; its sides are chords	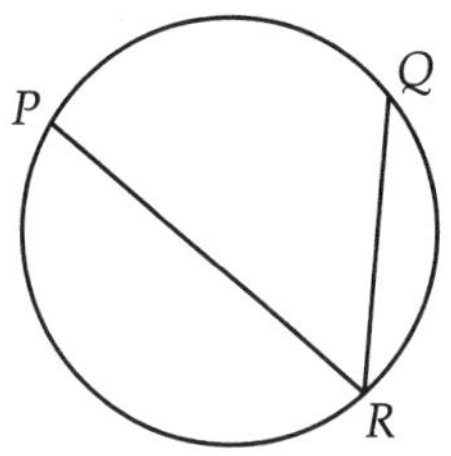	Measure of an inscribed angle is one-half the measure of the intercepted arc. $m\angle PRQ = \frac{1}{2}m\overset{\frown}{PQ}$	If $m\overset{\frown}{PQ} = 74$, then $m\angle PRQ = \frac{1}{2}(74) = 37$.
Angle formed by a tangent and a chord	The vertex is on the circle at the point of tangency; one side is a chord; one side is a tangent.	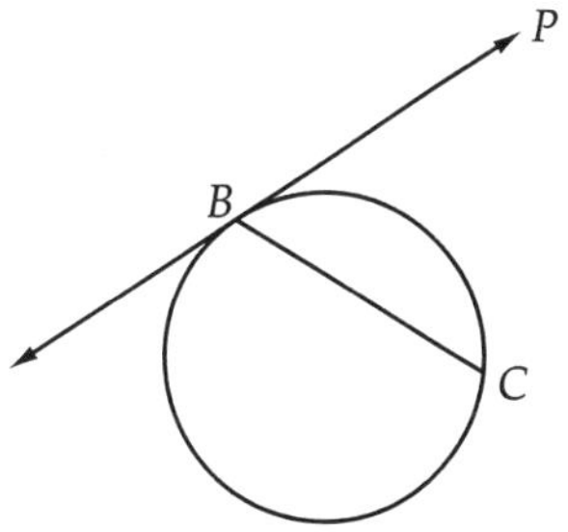	Measure of the angle is one-half the intercepted arc. $m\angle PBC = \frac{1}{2}m\overset{\frown}{BC}$	If $m\overset{\frown}{BC} = 110$, then $m\angle PBC = \frac{1}{2}(110) = 55$.
Angle formed by a secant and a chord	The vertex is on the circle but one side of the angle lies inside the circle and one side lies outside. Angle formulas cannot be used.	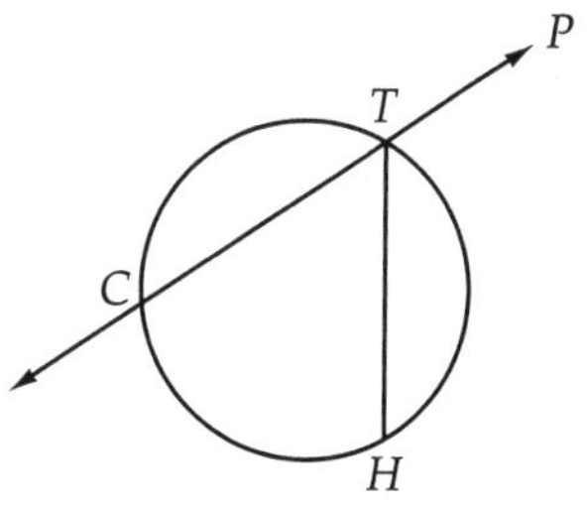	Measure of the angle equals 180 − the measure of the adjacent inscribed angle. $\angle CTP$ is a straight angle, therefore, $m\angle PTH = 180 − m\angle CTH$.	If $m\overset{\frown}{CH} = 116$, then $m\angle CTH = \frac{1}{2}\overset{\frown}{CH} = \frac{1}{2}(116) = 58$. $m\angle PTH = 180 − m\angle CTH = 180 − 58 = 122$

(continued)

Type of Angle	Identifying Elements	Diagram	Formula	Example
Angle formed by two chords intersecting within a circle	Its vertex is inside the circle, and its sides are parts of chords. The chords form vertical angles.		Measure of an angle formed by two intersecting chords equals one-half the sum of the measures of the intercepted arcs of the angle and its vertical angle. $m\angle MEJ = \frac{1}{2}\left(m\widehat{MJ} + m\widehat{KN}\right)$	If $m\widehat{MJ} = 56$ and $m\widehat{KN} = 164$, then $m\angle MEJ = \frac{56 + 164}{2} = \frac{1}{2}(220) = 110$.
Angle formed by a tangent and a radius	The vertex is on the circle at the point of tangency.		Angle formed is always a right angle. $m\angle OAB = 90$	$m\angle OAB = 90$
Angle formed by two tangents intersecting outside the circle	The vertex is outside the circle and the sides of the angle are tangents. The tangents divide the circle's 360° into two arcs.		Measure of the angle formed by two tangents equals one-half the difference of the measure of the intercepted arcs. $m\angle QPR = \frac{1}{2}\left(m\widehat{QTR} - m\widehat{QR}\right)$ OR The angle formed by two tangents outside the circle is supplementary to the measure of the minor arc of the circle. $m\angle P + m\widehat{QR} = 180$	If $m\widehat{QR} = 114$, then $m\widehat{QTR} = 360 - 114 = 246$. $m\angle QPR = \frac{246 - 114}{2} = \frac{1}{2}(132) = 66$. If $m\widehat{QR} = 114$, then $m\angle QRP = 180 - 114 = 66$. **Note:** The results are the same. Either approach can be used.
Angle formed by two secants intersecting outside the circle	The vertex is outside the circle and the sides of the angle are secants.		The measure of an angle formed by two secants equals one-half the difference of the measures of the intercepted arcs. $m\angle RPS = \frac{1}{2}\left(m\widehat{SR} - m\widehat{QV}\right)$	If $m\widehat{SR} = 128$ and $m\widehat{QV} = 32$, then $m\angle RPS = \frac{128 - 32}{2} = \frac{1}{2}(96) = 48$.

(continued)

Type of Angle	Identifying Elements	Diagram	Formula	Example
Angle formed by a secant and a tangent intersecting outside the circle	The vertex is outside the circle. One ray of the angle is a secant and one is a tangent.		The measure of the angle formed by a secant and a tangent equals one-half the difference of the measures of the intercepted arcs. $m\angle APC = \frac{1}{2}(m\overset{\frown}{CA} - m\overset{\frown}{AB})$	If $m\overset{\frown}{CA} = 140$ and $m\overset{\frown}{AB} = 52$, then $m\angle APC = \frac{140-52}{2} = \frac{1}{2}(88) = 44$.

Theorems Used in Circle Proofs

Triangles within circles have the same properties and applicable theorems as triangles outside circles. In addition to the theorems for congruence and similarities covered in earlier chapters, as well as the summary set of theorems on angles and arcs, the following is a list of theorems and corollaries that are often used in circle proofs.

- Theorem 13.1. All radii of a circle are congruent.
- Theorem 13.3. In a circle, congruent central angles have congruent arcs.
- Theorem 13.4. In a circle, congruent arcs have congruent chords. *Conversely*, congruent chords have congruent arcs.
- Theorem 13.5. A diameter perpendicular to a chord bisects the chord and its arcs.
- Theorem 13.6. Congruent chords in the same circle are equidistant from the center of the circle.
- Theorem 13.7. In a circle, if two chords are unequal, the shorter chord is farther from the center.
- Corollary 13.9.1. An angle inscribed in a semicircle is a right angle.
- Corollary 13.9.2. In a circle, inscribed angles that intercept the same arc are congruent.
- Corollary 13.9.4. Parallel lines intercept congruent arcs.
- Theorem 13.10. If a line is tangent to a circle then it is perpendicular to the radius at that point.
- Theorem 13.12. Two tangent segments drawn to a circle from an external point are congruent.

MODEL PROBLEMS

1 Given: Circle O with diameters $\overline{AOB}$ and
  $\overline{COD}$, and chords $\overline{AC}$ and $\overline{DB}$

  Prove: $\overline{AC} \cong \overline{DB}$

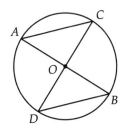

Statements	Reasons
1. Circle O with diameters $\overline{AOB}$ and $\overline{COD}$, and chords $\overline{AC}$ and $\overline{DB}$	1. Given.
2. $\overline{OA} \cong \overline{OB} \cong \overline{OC} \cong \overline{OD}$	2. All radii of a circle are congruent.
3. $\angle AOC \cong \angle DOB$	3. Vertical angles are congruent.
4. $\triangle AOC \cong \triangle BOD$	4. SAS $\cong$ SAS.
5. $\overline{AC} \cong \overline{DB}$	5. Corresponding parts of congruent triangles are congruent.

2 Given: Circle O with diameter $\overline{AOD}$,
  tangent $\overrightarrow{CA}$; $m\overarc{AB} = 2m\overarc{AE}$

  Prove: **a** $\triangle OAC \sim \triangle DBA$
  b $AD \times AC = OC \times BD$

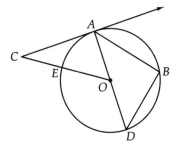

Statements	Reasons
1. Circle O with diameter $\overline{AOD}$, tangent $\overrightarrow{CA}$; $m\overarc{AB} = 2m\overarc{AE}$	1. Given.
2. $m\angle AOC = m\overarc{AE}$	2. The measure of a central angle equals the measure of its intercepted arc.
3. $m\overarc{AE} = \frac{1}{2}m\overarc{AB}$	3. Equals divided by equals are equals.
4. $m\angle AOC = \frac{1}{2}m\overarc{AB}$	4. Transitive postulate.
5. $m\angle BDA = \frac{1}{2}m\overarc{AB}$	5. The measure of an inscribed angle equals half the measure of its intercepted arc.
6. $m\angle AOC = m\angle BDA$	6. Quantities equal to equal quantities are equal.
7. $\overline{DA} \perp \overrightarrow{CA}$	7. A tangent is perpendicular to a diameter at point of tangency.
8. $\angle OAC$ is a right angle.	8. Perpendiculars form right angles.
9. $\angle DBA$ is a right angle.	9. An angle inscribed in a semicircle is a right angle.
10. $\angle OAC \cong \angle DBA$	10. All right angles are congruent.
11. (a) $\triangle OAC \sim \triangle DBA$	11. AA $\cong$ AA.
12. $\dfrac{CO}{DA} = \dfrac{AC}{AB}$	12. Corresponding sides of similar triangles are proportional.
13. (b) $AD \times AC = OC \times BD$	13. In a proportion, the product of the means equals the product of the extremes.

1

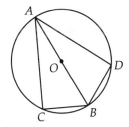

Given: A is the midpoint of $\overset{\frown}{CD}$; $\overline{AOB}$ is a diameter.
Prove: $\overline{CB} \cong \overline{DB}$

2

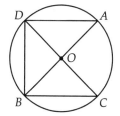

Given: Circle O, with chords $\overline{DA}$, $\overline{AB}$, $\overline{DC}$, $\overline{DB}$, and $\overline{BC}$; $\overline{AD} \cong \overline{CB}$
Prove: $\overline{AB} \cong \overline{CD}$

3

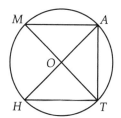

Given: Circle O with diameters $\overline{MOT}$ and $\overline{AOH}$
Prove: $\overline{MA} \cong \overline{HT}$

4

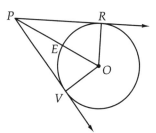

Given: Circle O, tangents $\overrightarrow{PR}$, $\overrightarrow{PV}$
Prove: $\angle RPO \cong \angle VPO$

5

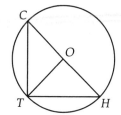

Given: Circle O with T the midpoint of $\overset{\frown}{CH}$
Prove: $\dfrac{CT}{CH} = \dfrac{TO}{TH}$

6

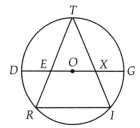

Given: Circle O, with diameter $\overline{DOG}$; $\overset{\frown}{DR} \cong \overset{\frown}{GI}$
Prove: $TX \times RI = EX \times TI$

7

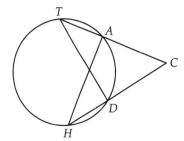

Given: $CT \neq CH$
Prove: $HA \neq TD$

8

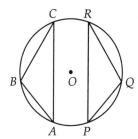

Given: $\triangle ABC$ and $\triangle PQR$ are inscribed in circle O. $\overline{BC} \cong \overline{QR}$ and $\overline{BA} \cong \overline{QP}$.
Prove: $\overline{AC} \cong \overline{PR}$

9

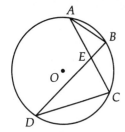

Given: Circle O with chords $\overline{AB}$, $\overline{AC}$, $\overline{DB}$, and $\overline{DC}$. $\triangle ABE$ and $\triangle DCE$ have a common vertex E.

Prove: **a** $\triangle ABE \sim \triangle DCE$

  b If $BE = 4$ and $CE = 5$, find the numerical value of

  (i) $AB:DC$

  (ii) $\dfrac{\text{area of } \triangle ABE}{\text{area of } \triangle DCE}$

10

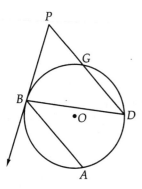

Given: $\overrightarrow{PB}$ is tangent to circle O at point B. Chord $\overline{BA}$ is parallel to secant $\overline{PGD}$.

Prove: $\dfrac{PD}{BD} = \dfrac{BD}{BA}$

11

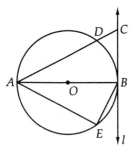

Given: Line l is tangent to circle O at point B, $\overline{AB}$ is the diameter, and chord $\overline{AD}$ is extended to meet the tangent at point C. $\triangle AEB$ is inscribed in circle O.

Prove: $\dfrac{AC}{AB} = \dfrac{AB}{AE}$

12

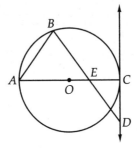

Given: $\triangle ABE$ is inscribed in circle O, $\overline{AC}$ is the diameter, and $\overleftrightarrow{CD}$ is tangent to circle O at point C. Segment $\overline{BD}$ intersects the diameter at point E, and $\overline{AB} \cong \overline{BE}$.

Prove: $AC \times EC = ED \times AB$

13

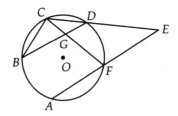

Given: Circle O with secant $\overline{EDC}$, and chords $\overline{BC}$ and $\overline{CGF}$. Chord $\overline{BGD}$ is parallel to secant $\overline{AFE}$, and point D is the midpoint of $\overset{\frown}{CF}$.

Prove: $\dfrac{EF}{CD} = \dfrac{EC}{DB}$

14

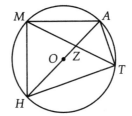

Given: Circle O with diameter $\overline{AOH}$, and chords $\overline{MA}$, $\overline{AT}$, $\overline{TH}$, $\overline{HM}$, and $\overline{MT}$

Prove: $\dfrac{MZ}{ZH} = \dfrac{AZ}{ZT}$

15

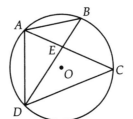

Given: Circle O with chords $\overline{AC}$ and $\overline{BD}$ intersecting at point E. Point C is the midpoint of $\overset{\frown}{BD}$. Chords $\overline{AD}$, $\overline{AB}$, and $\overline{DC}$.

a Prove: $\triangle ACD \sim \triangle ABE$

b If $AE = 7$, $EC = 9$, $DC = 12$, and $AB = 8$, find the measure of BE.

13-8 Circles in the Coordinate Plane

The circle is defined as the locus (or set) of all points *equidistant* from a fixed point called the center. So distance and the distance formula play an important part in understanding and working with circles. In fact, the equation of a circle and the distance formula are inseparable. Consider these two cases:

Case 1: A circle with center at the origin, $(0, 0)$, and radius r

To write an equation that describes all the points $P(x, y)$ in the xy-coordinate plane that lie a distance r from $(0, 0)$, we substitute into the distance formula, $d = \sqrt{(x_1 - x_2)^2 + (y_1 - y_2)^2}$, as follows:

Let $d = r$, and $(x_2, y_2) = (0, 0)$. Then

$$r = \sqrt{(x - 0)^2 + (y - 0)^2} = \sqrt{x^2 + y^2}$$

If we square both sides of the equation, then $r^2 = x^2 + y^2$ is the standard equation for a circle with center at the origin. Also, we can see that this equation is another version of the Pythagorean theorem: that is, $a^2 + b^2 = c^2$, where $c^2 = r^2$.

Case 2: A circle with center (h, k) **not** at the origin

Once again we let $d = r$, and $(x_2, y_2) = (h, k)$, so that $r = \sqrt{(x - h)^2 + (y - k)^2}$ and $r^2 = (x - h)^2 + (y - k)^2$. This is the general equation for any circle. Furthermore, the circle described by the equation $(x - h)^2 + (y - k^2) = r^2$ is simply a translation of the circle $x^2 + y^2 = r^2$ by h horizontal units and k vertical units.

The Geometric Interpretations

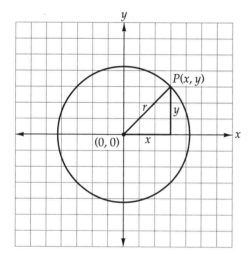
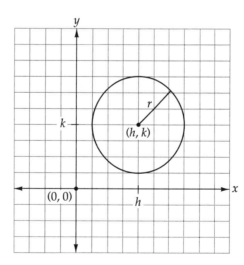

MODEL PROBLEMS

1 Which of the following is the equation of a circle whose center has coordinates $(5, -3)$ and whose radius has length of 6?

(1) $(x + 5)^2 + (y - 3)^2 = 36$
(2) $(x - 5)^2 + (y + 3)^2 = 36$
(3) $(x + 5)^2 + (y - 3)^2 = 6$
(4) $(x - 5)^2 + (y + 3)^2 = 6$

SOLUTION

The general equation of the form $(x - h)^2 + (y - k)^2 = r^2$ shows us that $r^2 = 6^2$ or 36, so choices 3 and 4 are wrong.

Since the center is $(5, -3)$, this means $h = 5$ and $k = -3$. By substitution, $(x - 5)^2 + (y - (-3))^2 = 6^2$ is equivalent to $(x - 5)^2 + (y + 3)^2 = 36$ or choice #2.

ANSWER: (2) $(x - 5)^2 + (y + 3)^2 = 36$

2 Which point lies on the circle $x^2 + y^2 = 49$?

(1) $(0, 0)$
(2) $(3, 4)$
(3) $(-4, 3)$
(4) $(0, 7)$

SOLUTION

To determine the correct point, we will simply substitute the (x, y) pairs that are given until we find one that works. Obviously choice 1: $0^2 + 0^2 \neq 49$. Choice 2: $3^2 + 4^2 = 9 + 16 = 25$, not 49. For the same reason, choice 3 is wrong. Thus, choice 4: $0^2 + 7^2 = 49$, is correct.

ANSWER: (4) $(0, 7)$

3 The center of a circle is at the origin and passes through the point $(2, 4)$.

a Write the equation of the circle.
b Find two other points of the circle.

SOLUTION

a First we need to find the radius. Since the center of the circle is at the origin, we use the equation $r^2 = x^2 + y^2$.
Substitute $(2, 4)$ for (x, y), so that $r^2 = 2^2 + 4^2 = 20$ and $r = \sqrt{20}$.
The equation of the circle is $x^2 + y^2 = (\sqrt{20})^2$, so $x^2 + y^2 = 20$.

ANSWER: $x^2 + y^2 = 20$

b Let $x = 0$, substitute, and solve for y.
$0^2 + y^2 = 20$
$y^2 = 20$
$y = \pm 2\sqrt{5}$

ANSWER: Points $(0, 2\sqrt{5})$ and $(0, -2\sqrt{5})$ lie on the circle.

Two more points
can be found by
letting y = 0.

4 The equation of a circle is $(x - 8)^2 + (y + 11)^2 = 25$,

   a Find the length of radius and the coordinates of the center.
   b Find two points on the circle.

SOLUTION

   a The given equation is of the general form $(x - h)^2 + (y - k^2) = r^2$, so matching up the parts should give us the answers.
   Since $r^2 = 25$, the radius, $r = \sqrt{25} = 5$.
   Since $-h = -8, h = 8$.
   Since $-k = 11, k = -11$.

ANSWER: The radius of the circle is 5 and the center is at $(8, -11)$.

   b Let $x = 8$, the x-value of the center of the circle. Substitute into the given equation and solve for y.
   $(8 - 8)^2 + (y + 11)^2 = 25$
   $0^2 + (y + 11)^2 = 25$
   $(y + 11)^2 = 25$ Take the square root of both sides.
   $y + 11 = \pm 5$ Solve for y.
   $y = 5 - 11$ and $y = (-5) - 11$
   $y = 6$ and $y = -16$

ANSWER: Two points on the circle are $(8, -6)$ and $(8, -16)$.

5 The center of a circle is at the point $(-1, 2)$ and the circle passes through the point $(4, -3)$.

   a Find the length of the radius of the circle.
   b Write the equation of the circle.

SOLUTION

   a Use the distance formula: $r = \sqrt{(4 - (-1))^2 + (-3 - 2)^2} = \sqrt{5^2 + (-5)^2} = \sqrt{50} = 5\sqrt{2}$

ANSWER: The length of the radius of the circle is $5\sqrt{2}$.

   b To find the equation for a circle with center *not* at the origin, we can substitute $(-1, 2)$ for (h, k) in the general equation $(x - h)^2 + (y - k)^2 = r^2$. We can also substitute $5\sqrt{2}$ or $\sqrt{50}$ for the radius, r.
   $(x - (-1))^2 + (y - 2)^2 = (\sqrt{50})^2$
   $(x + 1)^2 + (y - 2)^2 = 50$

ANSWER: $(x + 1)^2 + (y - 2)^2 = 50$

6 Write the equation of a circle if the coordinates of the endpoints of the diameter are $(2, 1)$ and $(4, -5)$.

SOLUTION

We first need to find the center or midpoint of the diameter, and then the radius.
We can use the midpoint formula to find the center of the circle.

$M = \left(\frac{x_1 + x_2}{2}, \frac{y_1 + y_2}{2}\right) = \left(\frac{2 + 4}{2}, \frac{1 + -5}{2}\right) = (3, -2)$

To find the radius of the circle, use the center $(3, -2)$ and either one of the endpoints, say $(2, 1)$, and the distance formula.

$r = \sqrt{(3 - 2)^2 + (-2 - 1)^2} = \sqrt{1 + 9} = \sqrt{10}$

Using the general form for the equation of a circle, with the center $(3, -2)$ and radius $\sqrt{10}$, we can write $(x - 3)^2 + (y - (-2))^2 = (\sqrt{10})^2$. Simplifying, $(x - 3)^2 + (y + 2)^2 = 10$.

ANSWER: The equation of the circle is $(x - 3)^2 + (y + 2)^2 = 10$.

1 Which of the following is the equation of a circle whose center has the coordinates $(4, -3)$ and whose radius is 6?

(1) $(x + 4)^2 + (y - 3)^2 = 36$
(2) $(x - 4)^2 + (y + 3)^2 = 36$
(3) $(x + 4)^2 + (y - 3)^2 = 6$
(4) $(x - 4)^2 + (y + 3)^2 = 6$

2 Which of the following points does **not** lie on the circle whose equation is $(x - 3)^2 + (y - 2)^2 = 100$?

(1) $(-7, 2)$
(2) $(3, -8)$
(3) $(3, 12)$
(4) $(13, 1)$

3 Write the equation of a circle with the given center C and radius or diameter.

a $C(1, 4)$, radius = 5
b $C(3, -2)$, radius = 7
c $C(-4, 1)$, radius = 11
d $C(-2, -5)$, diameter = 16
e $C(2, 0)$, diameter = 22
f C is the origin, diameter = 24

4 Write the equation of each of the following circles in the xy-plane.

a

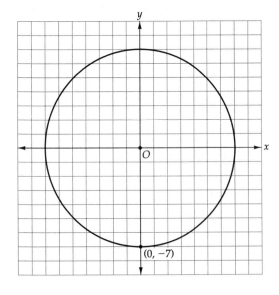

b

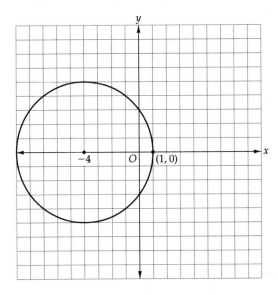

c

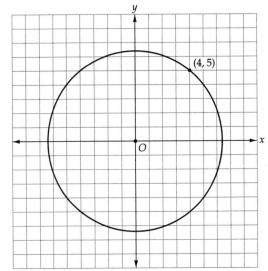

d

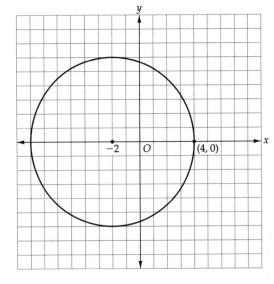

e

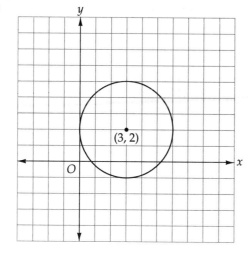

$(3, 2)$

f

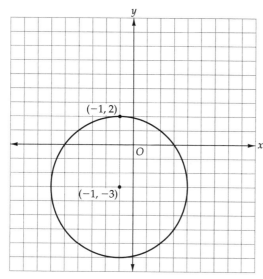

$(-1, 2)$

$(-1, -3)$

5 Sketch the graph of each of the following circles.

    a $(x - 2)^2 + (y - 4)^2 = 9$
    b $(x - 3)^2 + (y + 4)^2 = 25$
    c $x^2 + (y - 2)^2 = 16$
    d $(x + 6)^2 + y^2 = 4$

6 Given the following equations of a circle, identify the center and radius.

    a $x^2 + y^2 = 81$
    b $x^2 + y^2 = 121$
    c $x^2 + y^2 = 400$
    d $x^2 + y^2 = 1$
    e $x^2 + y^2 = 2$

7 Given the equation, identify the center, radius, and two other points on the circle.

    a $(x - 5)^2 + (y - 3)^2 = 64$
    b $(x - 4)^2 + y^2 = 100$
    c $(x + 2)^2 + (y - 5)^2 = 16$
    d $(x + 3)^2 + (y + 7)^2 = 12$

8 Write the equation of a circle with its center at the origin and that passes through the given point P whose coordinates are

    a $(5, 0)$
    b $(2, 0)$
    c $(3, 5)$
    d $(-6, 1)$
    e $(2, -8)$

9 Find the equation of a circle

    a with center $(2, 3)$ and containing the point $(3, 2)$.
    b with center $(-3, -7)$ and containing the point $(1, 1)$.

10 Write an equation of a circle if the endpoints of the diameter of the circle are

    a $(0, 3)$ and $(0, -4)$
    b $(1, 2)$ and $(5, 4)$

11 Find the circumference and area of a circle whose equation is

    a $x^2 + y^2 = 16$
    b $2x^2 + 2y^2 = 72$
    c $(x - 1)^2 + (y - 5) = 13$

12 A circle with center $(3, -1)$ is tangent to the x-axis.

    a What are the coordinates of the point of tangency?
    b Find an equation of the circle.
    c Find the area of the circle.

13 The equation of a circle is $(x - 1)^2 + (y + 3)^2 = 8$.

    a Find the center and the radius of the circle.
    b Find the area and circumference of the circle.

13-9 Tangents, Secants, and the Circle in the Coordinate Plane

When we talk algebraically and graphically about the intersection of tangents or secants with the circle, we are talking about a *linear* equation (for tangents or secants) and a *quadratic* equation (for the circle). The solution to a *quadratic-linear system* involves finding the coordinates of all points of intersection. With the line and circle, there are three intersection possibilities.

1 The circle and line do not intersect and have no common solution.
2 The circle and line intersect only once, where the line is *tangent* to the circle.
3 The circle and the line intersect twice when the line is a *secant*.

The following are three typical graphic illustrations of the three possibilities.

The nonintersection of a circle and a line

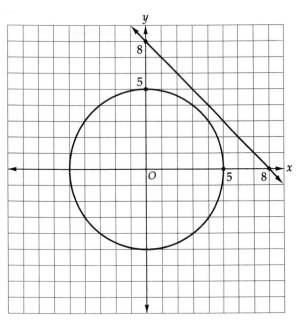

$$x^2 + y^2 = 25$$
$$y = -x + 8$$

The intersection of a tangent and a circle

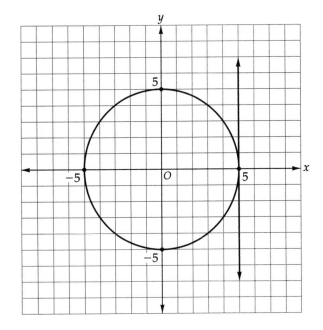

$$x^2 + y^2 = 25$$
$$x = 5$$

The intersection of a secant and a circle

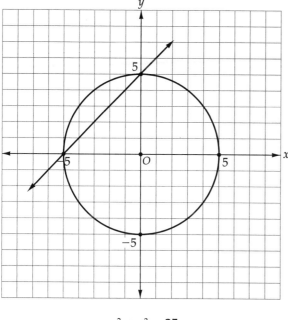

$$x^2 + y^2 = 25$$
$$y = x + 5$$

Every system of equations in two variables in which one is *linear* and the other *quadratic* can be solved algebraically by the substitution method. We recall from previous study that the essential step in the substitution method is to solve the linear equation for one variable in terms of the other and then substitute that fact into the quadratic equation so that only one equation in one variable emerges.

As an example, let us solve the system $x^2 + y^2 = 25$ and $y - 2x = 5$ algebraically. First we solve for y in the linear equation $y - 2x = 5$, so that $y = 2x + 5$. Now, substitute $2x + 5$ for y in the quadratic equation $x^2 + y^2 = 25$, so that $x^2 + (2x + 5)^2 = 25$ and solve for x.

$$x^2 + (2x + 5)(2x + 5) = 25$$
$$x^2 + 4x^2 + 20x + 25 = 25$$
$$5x^2 + 20x = 0$$
$$5(x^2 + 4x) = 0$$
$$x^2 + 4x = 0$$
$$x(x + 4) = 0$$
$$x = 0 \text{ or } x + 4 = 0$$
$$x = -4$$

If $x = 0$, then $y = 2(0) + 5$ and $y = 5$.
If $x = -4$, then $y = 2(-4) + 5$ and $y = -3$.

The solution set is $\{(0, 5), (-4, -3)\}$.

MODEL PROBLEMS

1 Write the equation of a line *tangent* to $x^2 + y^2 = 8$ at $P(2, 2)$.

SOLUTION

To write the tangent equation we need to find (a) the slope, m, and (b) the y-intercept.

a Since the tangent is *perpendicular* to the radius, the slope of the tangent will be the negative reciprocal of the radius line. The slope of the radius, from $(0, 0)$ to $(2, 2)$, is $\frac{2}{2}$ or 1. Therefore, the slope of the tangent is $m = -1$.

b To find the y-intercept, subin $(2, 2)$ for (x, y) and -1 for m in the equation $y = mx + b$.
$$2 = -1(2) + b$$
$$2 = -2 + b$$
$$4 = b \text{ (the } y\text{-intercept)}$$

ANSWER: The tangent equation is $y = -x + 4$.

2 Solve algebraically and graphically for the intersection of $y - x = -4$ and $x^2 + (y + 2)^2 = 4$.

SOLUTION

ALGEBRAIC METHOD

Solve for y in the equation $y - x = -4$.　　$y = x - 4$
Sub into the quadratic.　　　　　　　　　$x^2 + ((x - 4) + 2)^2 = 4$
Simplify.　　　　　　　　　　　　　　　$x^2 + (x - 2)^2 = 4$
　　　　　　　　　　　　　　　　　　　$x^2 + (x^2 - 4x + 4) = 4$
　　　　　　　　　　　　　　　　　　　$2x^2 - 4x = 0$
　　　　　　　　　　　　　　　　　　　$x^2 - 2x = 0$
Factor　　　　　　　　　　　　　　　　$x(x - 2) = 0$
　　　　　　　　　　　　　　　　　　　$x = 0 \text{ or } x = 2$

If $x = 0$, then $y = -4$; if $x = 2$, then $y = -2$.
The set of intersection points is $\{(0, -4), (2, -2)\}$.

Check

For $(0, -4)$
$$\begin{aligned} y - x &= -4 & x^2 + (y + 2)^2 &= 4 \\ (-4) - 0 &= -4 & (0)^2 + (-4 + 2)^2 &= 4 \\ -4 &= -4 & (-2)^2 &= 4 \\ & & 4 &= 4 \end{aligned}$$

For $(2, -2)$
$$\begin{aligned} (-2) - (2) &= -4 & 2^2 + (-2 + 2)^2 &= 4 \\ -4 &= -4 & 4 + 0^2 &= 4 \\ & & 4 &= 4 \end{aligned}$$

GRAPHIC METHOD

For the circle, its center is at $(0, -2)$ and its radius is 2. For the line, m is 1, and y-intercept is -4.

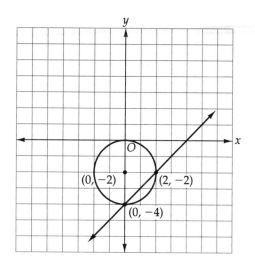

3 The equation of a circle is $x^2 + y^2 = 100$.

a Show that $x = 10$ is a tangent line to the circle.

b Show that the line whose equation is $y = x + 2$ is a secant to the circle.

c Find the coordinates of point P, the intersection of the tangent, $x = 10$, and the secant, $y = x + 2$.

d Show that the line $y = 2x$ contains a diameter of the circle.

SOLUTION

a Sub in 10 for x in the circle equation $x^2 + y^2 = 100$.
$$10^2 + y^2 = 100$$
$$100 + y^2 = 100$$
$$y^2 = 0$$
$$y = 0$$

Since the line $x = 10$ has only one intersection point at $(10, 0)$, $x = 10$ is a tangent line.

b Using the linear equation $y = x + 2$, we can sub in $x + 2$ for y in the quadratic equation $x^2 + y^2 = 100$

$$x^2 + (x + 2)^2 = 100$$
$$x^2 + (x^2 + 4x + 4) = 100$$
$$2x^2 + 4x - 96 = 0$$
$$x^2 + 2x - 48 = 0$$
$$(x + 8)(x - 6) = 0$$
$$x = -8 \text{ or } x = 6$$

Since there are two intersection points, $y = x + 2$ is a secant.

c To find the intersection point P of tangent $x = 10$ and secant $y = x + 2$, sub in 10 for x, so that $y = 10 + 2$ or 12. The intersection point is $(10, 12)$.

d If $y = 2x$ passes through the center of the circle $(0, 0)$, then it contains a diameter of the circle. When we test the coordinates $(0, 0)$, we find that $0 = 2(0)$ or $0 = 0$.

The line $y = 2x$ does contain the diameter.

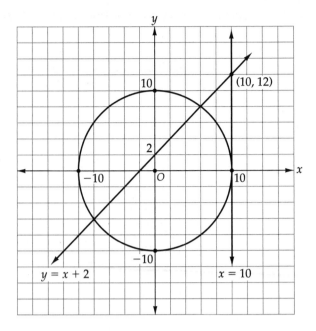

Line $x = 10$ is a tangent and $y = x + 2$ is a secant.

 Practice

1 The graphs of $x^2 + y^2 = 4$ and $y = 4$ have how many points in common?

    (1) 0
    (2) 1
    (3) 2
    (4) 4

2 The circle whose equation is $(x - 3)^2 + (y - 5)^2 = 36$ is intersected by the secant $x = 3$.

    a What are the points of intersection?
    b Which of the following is not a tangent to the circle?

        (1) $y = -1$
        (2) $y = 11$
        (3) $x = -1$
        (4) $x = 9$

3 Write an equation of the secant that intersects $x^2 + y^2 = 36$ at $(6, 0)$ and $(-6, 0)$.

4 Write an equation of the secant that intersects $x^2 + y^2 = 25$ at $(-3, 4)$ and $(5, 0)$.

Exercises 5–8: Write an equation of the line tangent to the given circle at the given point.

5 $x^2 + y^2 = 8$ at $(-2, 2)$

6 $x^2 + y^2 = 9$ at $(0, -3)$

7 $x^2 + y^2 = 16$ at $(0, 4)$

8 $x^2 + y^2 = 20$ at $(-4, 2)$

Exercises 9–16: For each of the following linear-quadratic pairs:

    a Solve algebraically only.
    b Determine whether the line is a tangent or secant to the circle.

9 $x^2 + y^2 = 25$
    $y = x - 1$

10 $x^2 + y^2 = 16$
    $y = x - 4$

11 $x^2 + (y + 1)^2 = 20$
    $y + 1 = 2x$

12 $x^2 + y^2 = 9$
    $y = -3$

13 $x^2 + y^2 = 4$
   $x + y = 2$

14 $x^2 + y^2 = 50$
   $y - x = -10$

15 $x^2 + y^2 = 17$
   $y = 4x$

16 $x^2 + y^2 = 16$
   $y = x$

Exercises 17–21: (a) Find the solution set to each system both algebraically and graphically. (b) Determine whether the line is a tangent or a secant.

17 $x^2 + y^2 = 100$
   $y = 0$

18 $x^2 + y^2 = 98$
   $y = x$

19 $x^2 + y^2 = 36$
   $x = 6$

20 $x^2 + y^2 = 100$
   $x + y = 2$

21 $x^2 + y^2 = 25$
   $y = 2x + 5$

22 **a** Show that points $M(7, -1)$ and $E(0, 6)$ lie on a circle whose radius is 5 and whose center is at $(3, 2)$.

   b What is the distance from the center of the circle to the chord $\overline{ME}$?

23 **a** Write an equation of the tangent to $x^2 + y^2 = 32$ at $A(4, 4)$.

   b Write an equation of the tangent to $x^2 + y^2 = 32$ at $B(-4, 4)$.

   c Find the point P at which the two tangents in parts **a** and **b** intersect.

24 **a** Write an equation of the secant $\overleftrightarrow{AB}$ that intersects $x^2 + y^2 = 100$ at $A(6, 8)$ and $B(0, -10)$.

   b Write an equation of the tangent to $x^2 + y^2 = 100$ at point $M(10, 0)$.

   c Find the coordinates of point P, the intersection of secant $\overleftrightarrow{AB}$ and the tangent line at M.

   d Show that $PA \times PB = PM^2$.

CHAPTER REVIEW

1 Which of the following is an untrue statement about line segments in a circle?

(1) All chords in a circle are congruent.
(2) All radii of a circle are congruent.
(3) If a diameter is perpendicular to a chord, it bisects the chord.
(4) Congruent central angles have congruent arcs.

2 Which of the following is the equation of a circle with center $(4, 2)$ and radius $= 3$?

(1) $(x + 4)^2 + (y + 2)^2 = 9$
(2) $(x - 4)^2 + (y - 2)^2 = 9$
(3) $(x + 4)^2 + (y + 2)^2 = 3$
(4) $(x - 4)^2 + (y - 2)^2 = 3$

3 If the graphs of the equations $x^2 + y^2 = 9$ and $y = 3$ are drawn on the same axes, what is the total number of points common to both figures?

(1) 0
(2) 1
(3) 2
(4) 3

4 In circle O, chords $\overline{CH}$ and $\overline{RD}$ intersect at point S. If S is the midpoint of chord $\overline{CH}$, $RS = 2$, and $SD = 8$, what is the length of chord $\overline{CH}$?

(1) 16
(2) 10
(3) 8
(4) 4

5 Chords $\overline{CH}$ and $\overline{AD}$ intersect in circle O at point T. If $CT = 8$ and $TH = 10$, the lengths of $\overline{AT}$ and $\overline{TD}$ *cannot* be which of the following?

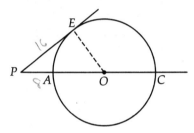

(1) 5 and 16
(2) 4 and 20
(3) 6 and 15
(4) 8 and 10

6 Secants $\overline{PBC}$ and $\overline{PDE}$ are drawn to circle O from point P. If $PB = 9$, $BC = 15$, and $PD = 6$, what is the difference in length between the two secants?

(1) 6
(2) 12
(3) 18
(4) 36

7 Tangent $\overline{PE}$ and secant $\overline{PAC}$ are drawn to circle O from point P. If $PE = 16$ and $PA = 8$, which of the following is the length of the radius of circle O?

(1) 12
(2) 16
(3) 20
(4) 24

8 Tangent $\overline{PA}$ and secant $\overline{PBC}$ are drawn to circle O from point P. If $PB = 4$ and $BC = 5$, then PA is:

(1) 9
(2) 6
(3) 3
(4) $2\sqrt{5}$

9 In circle O, radii $\overline{OA}$ and $\overline{OB}$ are drawn. Central angle AOB measures $68°$. The measure of $\overarc{AB}$ is:

(1) 34°
(2) 68°
(3) 112°
(4) 136°

10 In circle O, radii $\overline{OA}$ and $\overline{OB}$ are drawn. If $\overarc{AB}$ measures $122°$, the measure of $\angle AOB$ is:

(1) 58°
(2) 61°
(3) 122°
(4) 244°

Exercises 11 and 12: In circle O below, radii $\overline{OA}$ and $\overline{OB}$, and chords $\overline{AC}$ and $\overline{BC}$ are drawn.

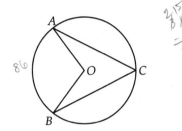

11 If $m\overarc{AB} = 86$, the measure of $\angle ACB$ equals:

(1) 43°
(2) 62°
(3) 86°
(4) 172°

12 If $m\overarc{AB} = 86$, the measure of $\angle AOB$ is:

(1) 43°
(2) 62°
(3) 86°
(4) 172°

13 If a central angle and an inscribed angle intercept the same arc, the ratio of the measure of the central angle to the measure of the inscribed angle is:

(1) 1:1
(2) 2:1
(3) 1:2
(4) 2:2

14 Triangle XYZ is inscribed in circle O. If $m\angle XYZ = 67$ and $m\overarc{XY} = 144$, which of the following is the measure of $\angle ZXY$?

(1) 41°
(2) 82°
(3) 108°
(4) 162°

15 In circle O, chords $\overline{AB}$ and $\overline{CD}$ intersect at E. If AE is 2 inches longer than EB, CE = 8 inches, and ED = 3 inches, what is the length of AB?

(1) 4 inches
(2) 6 inches
(3) 10 inches
(4) 24 inches

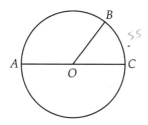

16 In circle O, m$\widehat{BC}$ = 55. Find m∠AOB.

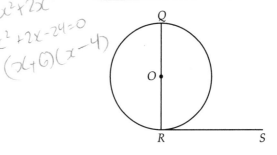

$24 = x^2 + 2x$
$x^2 + 2x - 24 = 0$
$(x+6)(x-4)$

(1) 27.5°
(2) 55°
(3) 125°
(4) 135°

17 In circle O, chords $\overline{AB}$ and $\overline{CD}$ intersect at E. If m$\widehat{AC}$ = 100 and m∠AEC = 70, find m$\widehat{BD}$.

(1) 40°
(2) 70°
(3) 100°
(4) 150°

18 Isosceles triangle ABC is inscribed in circle O. If the measure of the vertex angle ∠ABC is 80, what is the measure of minor arc AB?

(1) 40°
(2) 50°
(3) 80°
(4) 100°

19 Tangents $\overline{PA}$ and $\overline{PB}$ are drawn to circle O. If m∠APB = 50, what is m$\widehat{ACB}$?

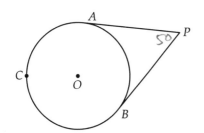

(1) 260°
(2) 230°
(3) 130°
(4) 100°

20 In a circle, diameter $\overline{RS}$ is extended through S to an external point T. Secant $\overline{TUV}$ is then drawn. If RS = 18, ST = 6, and UT = 9, find TV.

21 If $\overline{SR}$ is tangent to circle O at R, find m∠QRS.

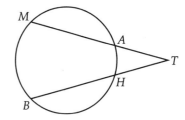

22 If m∠MTB = 23 and m$\widehat{AH}$ = 58, find m$\widehat{MB}$.

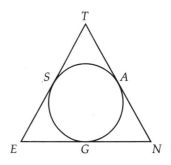

23 Two tangents are drawn to circle O from an external point P. If the major arc has a measure of 200°, find the measure of angle P.

24 If TA = 6, AN = 8, and EG = 10, find the perimeter of triangle TNE.

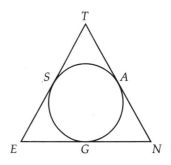

25 In circle O, tangent $\overline{PC}$ and secant $\overline{PAB}$ are drawn from external point P. If PA = 9 and AB = 7, find PC.

26 Given: Circle O with diameter $\overline{FE}$ extended to point C. Secant $\overline{CBA}$, tangent $\overline{CD}$, chord $\overline{FA}$, and diameter $\overline{GOB}$ are drawn. $m\widehat{AF} = 100$, $m\widehat{ED} = 55$, B is the midpoint of $\widehat{AE}$, $\overline{FA} \parallel \overline{GB}$.

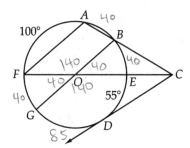

Find:

a $m\widehat{AB}$ $40°$
b $m\widehat{FG}$ $40°$
c $m\angle BOE$ $40°$
d $m\angle AFE$ $40°$
e $m\angle FAC$
f $m\angle GBC$
g $m\angle FCD$

27 Given: Circle O, secants $\overline{MJE}$ and $\overline{MKA}$ are drawn. Chord $\overline{FB}$ intersects secants $\overline{MJE}$ and $\overline{MKA}$ at points G and C, respectively. Chord $\overline{BK}$ and tangent $\overline{KL}$ are drawn. $\overline{EJ} \perp \overline{FB}$, $m\widehat{EF} = 30$, $m\widehat{FJ} = m\widehat{EA}$, $m\angle AKB = 20$, and $m\angle ACB = 65$.

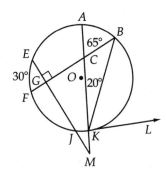

Find:

a $m\widehat{AB}$
b $m\widehat{FJ}$
c $m\widehat{JK}$
d $m\angle FBK$
e $m\angle EMA$
f $m\angle BKL$

28 Given: Circle O, diameter $\overline{AB}$ is extended through B to point C, secant $\overline{CED}$ and chords $\overline{AE}$, $\overline{AF}$, and $\overline{FB}$ are drawn. $m\widehat{EB} = 2 \times m\widehat{DE}$, and $m\widehat{AD} = 3 \times m\widehat{DE}$.

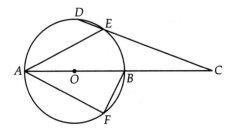

Find:

a $m\widehat{DE}$
b $m\angle DEA$
c $m\angle DCA$
d $m\angle AEC$
e $m\angle AFB$

Exercises 29–32: For each equation of a circle:

a Find the center and the radius.
b Determine the coordinates of two other points on the circle.

29 $x^2 + y^2 = 400$

30 $(x - 7)^2 + (y - 11)^2 = 81$

31 $(x + 3)^2 + (y - 13)^2 = 36$

32 $(x + 3)^2 + (y + 5)^2 = 20$

33 If $x^2 + 6x + 9 + y^2 - 4y + 4 = 16$ is the equation of a circle, identify the center and radius of the circle.

34 Write an equation of the circle satisfying each set of conditions:

a Center $(-4, 2)$, radius 7
b Center $(-5, 0)$, radius $\sqrt{2}$
c Center at the origin, passes through point $(5, -12)$
d Endpoints of the diameter $(-2, 0)$ and $(8, 0)$
e Endpoints of the diameter $(-1, 5)$ and $(-7, 3)$

35 Determine whether the point $(6, 6)$ lies on the circle whose center is at the origin and whose radius is $6\sqrt{2}$.

36 Write the equation of a line tangent to the circle $x^2 + y^2 = 90$ at the point $P(3, 9)$.

Exercises 37–40: For each linear-quadratic pair:

    a Determine the points of intersection.
    b Identify the line as a tangent or secant.

37 $x^2 + y^2 = 25$
     $y = 3$

38 $x^2 + y^2 = 9$
     $y = x - 3$

39 $x^2 + y^2 = 68$
     $y - x = -10$

40 $x^2 + y^2 = 25$
     $3x - y = 5$

41

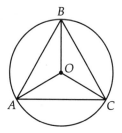

Given: $\overline{OA}$, $\overline{OB}$, and $\overline{OC}$ are radii of circle O.
       $\triangle AOB \cong \triangle COB$.
Prove: $\overparen{AB} \cong \overparen{CB}$

42

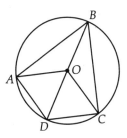

Given: $\overline{DB}$ is the diameter of circle O and
       $\overline{AD} \cong \overline{CD}$.
Prove: $\angle ABD \cong \angle CBD$

43

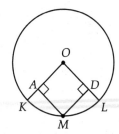

Given: Radii $\overline{OK}$ and $\overline{OL}$, $\overline{MA} \perp \overline{OK}$, $\overline{MD} \perp \overline{OL}$,
      and $\overline{AM} \cong \overline{DM}$.
Prove: $\overparen{MK} \cong \overparen{ML}$

44

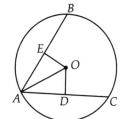

Given: Circle O, with $\overline{AB} \cong \overline{AC}$, $\overline{OE} \perp \overline{AB}$,
      $\overline{OD} \perp \overline{AC}$
Prove: $\triangle AEO \cong \triangle ADO$

45 Prove that any two diagonals of a regular pentagon inscribed in a circle are equal.

14 Locus and Constructions

14-1 Basic Constructions

This chapter will deal with two other applications of geometry on a plane: locus and constructions.

A **locus** is a set of all points, and only those points, that satisfy a given set of conditions. A locus can be described with an equation or a geometric construction. A graph of the points in the solution set of a linear equation is a typical example of a locus.

A **geometric construction** is a process much more constrained than simply drawing an object. When a figure is constructed, only two instruments are allowed: the compass and a straightedge. The *compass* is an adjustable device used for drawing arcs and circles and measuring distances. A *straightedge* is basically an unmarked ruler and is used only for drawing lines.

Remember

• Any arcs made with a certain compass setting will have the same radii.
• All radii of the same circle are congruent.

Let us review the basic constructions that were introduced in Chapter 5. Refer back to Chapter 5 on how to use a compass and straightedge for these constructions.

Construction of Congruent Line Segments

When given line segment *AB*, a congruent line, *CD*, can be constructed.

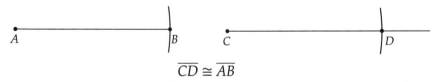

$$\overline{CD} \cong \overline{AB}$$

Justification: $\overline{CD} \cong \overline{AB}$ because $\overline{CD}$ and $\overline{AB}$ are radii of congruent circles.

Construction of Congruent Angles

When given ∠ABC and point E, a congruent angle, ∠FED can be constructed.

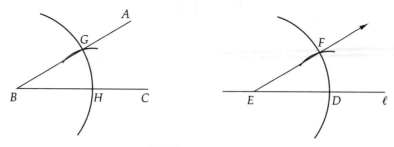

$$\angle ABC \cong \angle FED$$

Justification: If $\overparen{GH}$ and $\overparen{FD}$ are drawn in the angles above, then $\overline{BH} \cong \overline{ED}$, $\overline{BG} \cong \overline{EF}$, and $\overparen{GH} \cong \overparen{FD}$. Thus, $\triangle BGH \cong \triangle EFD$ by SSS $\cong$ SSS, and therefore, $\angle ABC \cong \angle FED$.

Construction of a Perpendicular Bisector of a Line Segment

When given $\overline{AB}$, a perpendicular bisector, $\overline{CD}$, can be constructed.

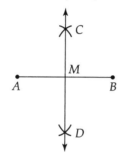

$\overline{CD}$ is the perpendicular bisector of $\overline{AB}$.

Justification: If $\overline{AC}, \overline{AD}, \overline{BC}$, and $\overline{BD}$ are drawn in the construction, then $\overline{AC} \cong \overline{AD}$ and $\overline{BC} \cong \overline{BD}$ because radii of equal circles are congruent. Therefore, $\overline{CD}$ is the perpendicular bisector of $\overline{AB}$ because two points, C and D, each equidistant from the ends of a line segment, determine the perpendicular bisector of a line segment.

Construction of the Bisector of an Angle

When given ∠ABC, an angle bisector, $\overrightarrow{BF}$, can be constructed, such that $\angle ABF \cong \angle CBF$.

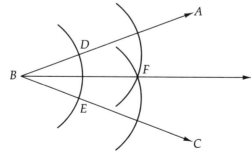

$$\angle ABF \cong \angle CBF$$

Justification: If $\overline{FE}$ and $\overline{FD}$ are drawn in the figure above, then $\overline{BD} \cong \overline{BE}, \overline{FD} \cong \overline{FE}$, and $\overline{BF} \cong \overline{BF}$. Thus, $\triangle BDF \cong \triangle BEF$ by SSS $\cong$ SSS. Therefore, $\angle ABF \cong \angle CBF$ and $\overrightarrow{BF}$ bisects $\angle ABC$.

Construction of a Line Perpendicular to a Line Through a Given Point on the Line

When given point P on $\overleftrightarrow{AB}$, we can construct a line, $\overleftrightarrow{EP}$, such that $\overleftrightarrow{EP} \perp \overleftrightarrow{AB}$.

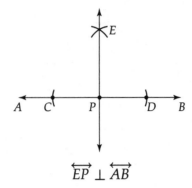

$$\overleftrightarrow{EP} \perp \overleftrightarrow{AB}$$

Justification: The construction bisects straight angle APB such that $\angle APE$ and $\angle BPE$ are congruent and right angles. Therefore, $\overleftrightarrow{EP} \perp \overleftrightarrow{AB}$, because two lines that intersect to form right angles are perpendicular to each other.

Construction of a Line Perpendicular to a Line Through a Given Point *Not* on the Line

When given $\overleftrightarrow{AB}$ and point P *not* on the line, we can construct a line, $\overleftrightarrow{EP}$, that is perpendicular to $\overleftrightarrow{AB}$.

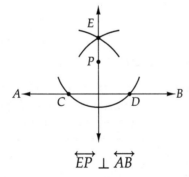

$$\overleftrightarrow{EP} \perp \overleftrightarrow{AB}$$

Justification: If $\overline{PC}$, $\overline{PD}$, $\overline{EC}$, and $\overline{ED}$ are drawn, then $\overline{PC} \cong \overline{PD}$ and $\overline{EC} \cong \overline{ED}$, because radii of congruent circles are congruent. Thus, $\overleftrightarrow{PE}$ is the perpendicular bisector of $\overline{CD}$ since two points, each equidistant from the ends of a line segment, determine the perpendicular bisector of that line segment. Therefore, $\overleftrightarrow{EP} \perp \overleftrightarrow{AB}$.

Note: The same construction is used to construct an **altitude of a triangle** or of any polygon.

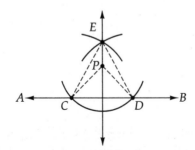

Construction of Parallel Lines and Other Basic Constructions

To Construct a Parallel Line Through a Given Point P, *Not* on the Line

- Using a straightedge, draw line AB.
- Draw any line through P intersecting $\overleftrightarrow{AB}$. Label the point of intersection C. Label a point R on the line on the far side of P.
- Copy angle PCB to point P and label the new angle RPS.
- Draw a line through P and S.

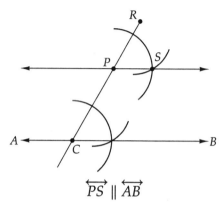

$$\overleftrightarrow{PS} \parallel \overleftrightarrow{AB}$$

Justification: If two lines are cut by a transversal, such that a pair of corresponding angles is congruent, $\angle RPS \cong \angle PCB$, the lines are parallel. Therefore, $\overleftrightarrow{AB}$ is parallel to $\overleftrightarrow{PS}$.

To Construct an Equilateral Triangle

- Using a straightedge, draw segment AB.
- Using point A as the center and a radius whose length equals AB, construct an arc.
- Using point B as the center and a radius whose length equals AB, construct another arc that intersects the first arc. Label the point of intersection C.
- Using a straightedge, construct $\overline{CA}$ and $\overline{CB}$, forming equilateral triangle ABC.

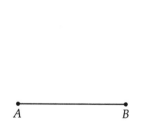
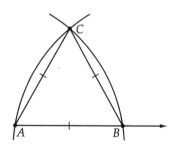

Triangle ABC is an equilateral triangle.

Justification: The construction makes $\triangle ABC$ an equilateral triangle with $\overline{AB} \cong \overline{BC} \cong \overline{CA}$.

Note: Since an equilateral triangle is equiangular, the measure of each angle is $60°$.

To Construct the Median of a Triangle

- Construct $\overleftrightarrow{DE}$, the perpendicular bisector of $\overline{CB}$.
- $\overleftrightarrow{DE}$ intersects $\overline{CB}$ at point M, making M the midpoint.
- Construct line segment AM. This is the median from vertex A to side $\overline{CB}$.

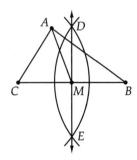

$\overline{AM}$ is the median of $\triangle CAB$.

Justification: Since $\overleftrightarrow{DE}$ is the perpendicular bisector of $\overline{CB}$, point M is the midpoint of $\overline{CB}$. Therefore, $\overline{AM}$ is the median from vertex A to side $\overline{CB}$. A median of a triangle is the line segment that joins a vertex to the midpoint of the opposite side.

To Construct Line Tangent to a Circle at a Point on the Circle

- With point A on circle O, draw $\overrightarrow{OA}$.
- Construct line l perpendicular to $\overrightarrow{OA}$ at A.
- Line l is tangent to circle O at point A.

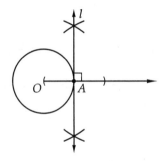

Line l is tangent to circle O.

Justification: By construction, line l is perpendicular to $\overrightarrow{OA}$ at A. Thus, line l is tangent to circle O because a line perpendicular to a radius of a circle at its endpoint is tangent to the circle.

To Construct a Line Tangent to a Given Circle Through a Given Point Outside the Circle

- With point P outside circle O, construct $\overline{OP}$.
- Construct $\overleftrightarrow{AB}$, the perpendicular bisector of $\overline{OP}$, in order to find M, the midpoint of $\overline{OP}$.
- Using M as a center and a radius whose length is $\overline{OM}$, construct a new circle intersecting circle O at points C and D.
- Construct $\overrightarrow{PC}$ and $\overrightarrow{PD}$, which are tangent to circle O at points C and D, respectively.

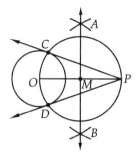

$\overrightarrow{PC}$ and $\overrightarrow{PD}$ are each tangent to circle O.

Justification: Using a straightedge construct radii $\overline{OC}$ and $\overline{OD}$. Since $\overline{OP}$ is a diameter in circle M, the inscribed angles, $\angle OCP$ and $\angle ODP$ are right angles because an angle inscribed in a semicircle is a right angle. Therefore, $\overrightarrow{PC}$ and $\overrightarrow{PD}$ are tangent to circle O because a line perpendicular to a radius of a circle at its extremity is tangent to the circle.

To Locate the Center of a Circle by Construction

- Using any circle, with a straightedge, construct two chords, $\overline{AB}$ and $\overline{BC}$.
- Construct $\overleftrightarrow{DE}$, the perpendicular bisector of $\overline{AB}$, and $\overleftrightarrow{FG}$, the perpendicular bisector of $\overline{BC}$.

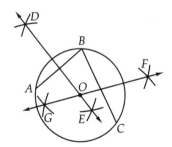

Point O is the center of the circle.

Justification: Since $\overleftrightarrow{DE}$ is the perpendicular bisector of chord $\overline{AB}$, the center of the circle lies on $\overleftrightarrow{DE}$. Recall that the perpendicular bisector of a chord passes through the center of the circle. Similarly, the center of the circle lies on $\overleftrightarrow{FG}$, the perpendicular bisector of chord $\overline{BC}$. Since point O is the only point that lies on both $\overleftrightarrow{DE}$ and $\overleftrightarrow{FG}$, that point must be the center of the circle.

In each of the following, (i) perform the construction and (ii) justify the construction by analysis or by proof.

1 Construct an angle congruent to (a) a given acute angle and (b) a given obtuse angle.

2 Construct a perpendicular to a given point *on* a given line.

3 Construct the bisector of (a) a given acute angle, (b) a given obtuse angle, and (c) a given right angle.

4 Construct a line perpendicular to a given line through a given point *not on* the line.

5 Construct the perpendicular bisector of a given line segment.

6 Construct a line parallel to a given line through a given point *not on* the line.

7 Construct the median to a side of a triangle.

8 Construct the altitude to the side of a triangle.

9 Divide a given line segment into four equal parts.

10 Divide a given obtuse angle into four equal parts.

11 Construct an angle of (a) 90° and (b) 45°.

12 Construct an angle of (a) 60°, (b) 30°, and (c) 15°.

13 Construct the supplement of a given angle *A*.

14 Construct the complement of a given acute angle.

15 Draw two angles *A* and *B*, with *A* being the greater one. Construct an angle equal to

 a $A + B$
 b $2A$
 c $A + 90$
 d $\frac{A}{2}$
 e $\frac{A}{2} + B$

16 Construct an equilateral triangle given a line segment.

17 Given two line segments, with the longer line segment the leg of an isosceles triangle, construct an isosceles triangle.

18 Construct a circle with a given radius tangent to a given line at a given point *on* the line.

19 Construct a circle tangent to a given line at a given point *on* the line and passing through another given point *not on* the line.

20 Draw parallelogram *ABCD* with $\overline{AB}$ the base and longer side. Locate by construction the point on side $\overline{DC}$ that is equidistant from points *A* and *B*.

14-2 Concurrent Lines and Points of Concurrency

Lines are **concurrent** if they pass through the same point. Three or more lines (or rays or segments) are concurrent if there is one common point to all of the lines (or rays or segments). The three lines shown below, *l*, *m*, and *n*, are concurrent at point *P*.

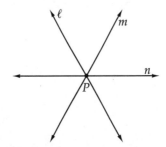

We will examine here the **concurrence** of four sets of line segments (or lines): medians, altitudes, angle bisectors, and perpendicular bisectors of the sides of a triangle.

Medians

If the three medians of a triangle are constructed, they will intersect at the same point in the *interior* of the triangle. This point of concurrency, called the *centroid*, is two-thirds of the distance from that vertex to the midpoint of the opposite side. Therefore, in the figure below, if $\overline{AB}$, $\overline{CD}$, and $\overline{EF}$ are medians in triangle AEC, then P is the *centroid* of triangle AEC. $\overline{AP} = \frac{2}{3}\overline{AB}$; $\overline{EP} = \frac{2}{3}\overline{EF}$, and $\overline{CP} = \frac{2}{3}\overline{CD}$.

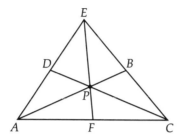

Note: Stated differently, the *centroid* divides each median in the ratio $\frac{2}{1}$, such that, referring to the figure above, $\frac{AP}{PB} = \frac{EP}{PF} = \frac{CP}{PD} = \frac{2}{1}$.

 MODEL PROBLEM

In $\triangle ABC$, medians $\overline{AD}$ and $\overline{BE}$ intersect at P.

If $BE = 3x$ and $BP = 8x - 12$, find BE, BP, and PE.

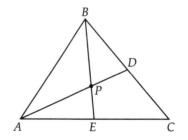

SOLUTION

$BP = \frac{2}{3}BE$

$8x - 12 = \frac{2}{3}(3x)$

$8x - 12 = 2x$

$ 6x = 12$

$ x = 2$

Therefore,
$BE = 3x = 3(2) = 6$
$BP = 8x - 12 = 8(2) - 12 = 4$
$PE = BE - BP = 6 - 4 = 2$

ANSWER: $BE = 6$, $BP = 4$, and $PE = 2$

Altitudes

If the three altitudes of a triangle are constructed, they will all intersect in the same point. This point of concurrency is called the *orthocenter*.

The three altitudes are shown below for acute, right, and obtuse triangles. Note that the *orthocenter* for the right triangle is the *vertex*, point C, and in the obtuse triangle, by extending the sides, the *orthocenter*, point P, falls *outside* the triangle.

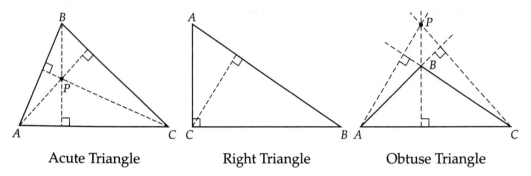

Acute Triangle   Right Triangle   Obtuse Triangle

Angle Bisectors

The angle bisectors of each of the angles of a triangle are concurrent at a point that is equidistant from the sides of the triangle. This point of concurrency is called the *incenter*.

In Figure 1 below, $\overline{AP}$ bisects $\angle A$, $\overline{BP}$ bisects $\angle B$, and $\overline{CP}$ bisects $\angle C$. All three bisectors are concurrent at point P. Since point P is equidistant from all three sides of the triangle, the perpendicular distance to any side, with, $\overline{PX} \perp \overline{AB}$, $\overline{PY} \perp \overline{BC}$, and $\overline{PZ} \perp \overline{AC}$, means $PX = PY = PZ$. Thus, using point P as the *center* of a circle and the perpendicular distance to any side as the *radius*, a circle can be drawn tangent to each side of the triangle. This circle is called the *inscribed circle* of the triangle, which is shown in Figure 2.

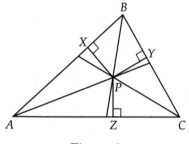
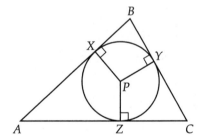

Figure 1   Figure 2

Perpendicular Bisectors

The perpendicular bisectors of the sides of a triangle are concurrent at a point that is equidistant from the vertices of the triangle. This point of concurrency is called the *circumcenter*.

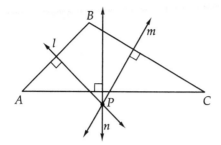

Using this point of concurrency as the *center of a circle* and the distance from this point to any vertex as a *radius*, a circle can be drawn that passes through the three vertices of the triangle. This circle is called the *circumscribed circle* of the triangle.

In the figure below, for $\triangle ABC$, lines l, m, and n are the perpendicular bisectors of sides $\overline{AB}$, $\overline{BC}$, and $\overline{CA}$, respectively. Lines l, m, and n are concurrent at point P. Since any point on the perpendicular bisector of a line segment is equidistant from the ends of the segment, $PA = PB = PC$. Thus, using, $\overline{PA}$, $\overline{PB}$, and $\overline{PC}$ as the radii, a circle can be circumscribed through the three vertices of the triangle, or through any three points that are not collinear.

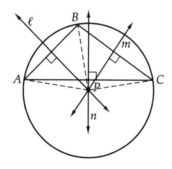

Note: The circumcenter of a right triangle lies on its hypotenuse.

 Practice

---

1 If two altitudes of a given triangle fall outside the triangle, the triangle is:

   (1) acute
   (2) equilateral
   (3) right
   (4) obtuse

2 The altitudes of a right triangle intersect:

   (1) outside triangle
   (2) inside triangle
   (3) at one of the vertices of the triangle
   (4) at the midpoint of the hypotenuse

3 Draw an acute, a right, and an obtuse triangle and locate their centroids by construction.

4 In an isosceles triangle, where do the concurrent points, the centroid, and the orthocenter, appear to lie?

Exercises 5–12: $\triangle QRS$ with medians $\overline{QA}$, $\overline{RB}$, and $\overline{SC}$ concurrent at centroid P.

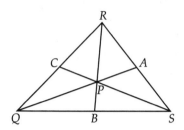

5 If $QA = 15$, find QP.

6 If $RB = 20$, find PB.

7 If $PC = 12$, find SC.

8 If $RP = 11$, find RB.

9 If $QP = 9$, find PA.

10 If $SP = 2x$ and $SC = 5x + 4$, find SP and SC.

11 If $PB = 3x$ and $PR = 7x - 5$, find PB and PR.

12 If $PA = 2x + 6$ and $QA = 10x$, find PA and QA.

Exercises 13–16: $\triangle ABC$, median $\overline{BE}$, centroid Q, and altitude $\overline{BD}$.

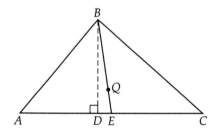

13 If $BD = 12$ and $DE = 5$, find QE.

14 If $BQ = 10$ and $BD = 12$, find DE.

15 If $QE = 2$ and $DE = 3$, find BD.

16 If $BQ = 8$ and $BD = 6\sqrt{3}$, find QE and DE.

Exercises 17–20: State whether the indicated point of concurrency appears on a side of the triangle, in the interior of the triangle, or in the exterior of the triangle. Use quick sketches to serve as a guide.

17 The centroid of

    a an acute triangle
    b a right triangle
    c an obtuse triangle

18 The incenter of

    a an acute triangle
    b a right triangle
    c an obtuse triangle

19 The circumcenter of

    a an acute triangle
    b a right triangle
    c an obtuse triangle

20 The orthocenter of

    a an acute triangle
    b a right triangle
    c an obtuse triangle

Exercises 21–24: For each problem, consider only an equilateral triangle. Find the lengths of the radius of the incenter and the circumcenter.

21 The side of the triangle measures 6 inches.

22 The side of the triangle measures 12 inches.

23 The side of the triangle measures 18 inches.

24 The side of the triangle measures $12\sqrt{3}$.

25 Given: $\triangle ABC$ with median CG

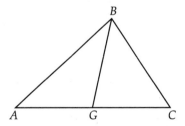

Prove: Area $\triangle ABG$ = Area $\triangle CBG$

14-3 The Meaning of Locus

A **locus** is a set of all points, and only those points, that satisfy a given set of conditions. A locus can be described with a geometric construction or with an equation.

Locus is the Latin name for "place" and the plural of locus is loci.

The figure below is a clear illustration of finding the locus of points 1 inch from a fixed point, P, in a plane. The path of that point, or *locus*, is a circle whose center is P and whose radius is 1 inch in length. While there is an infinite number of these points (and we could draw a solid line to indicate the answer), we use a dotted or dashed line to suggest the answer.

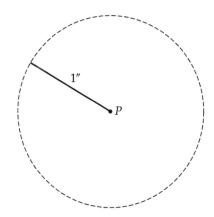

Typical examples of a locus in the coordinate plane are the graph of the points in the solution set of a linear equation or a quadratic equation.

Note:

1   We will assume that all given points, figures, and loci lie in the same plane.
2   Drawing the locus as a dotted line or curve visually separates it from the given information and is especially helpful in diagrams with multiple loci.

Basic Method for Finding the Probable Locus

- Draw a diagram that contains the given data, fixed lines, and/or points.
- Make sure you understand what condition of motion must be satisfied.
- Locate several points that satisfy the given condition. There should be enough of them to indicate the shape of the locus.
- Draw a straight line or curve through these points.
- Accurately describe the geometric figure in words.

In the following section we will examine these six fundamental loci:

- Points at a given distance from a fixed point
- Points equidistant from two points
- Points at a given distance from a given line
- Points equidistant from parallel lines
- Points in the interior of an angle equidistant from the sides of the angle
- Points equidistant from two intersecting lines

14-4 Six Fundamental Loci and the Coordinate Plane

1. Points at a Given Distance From a Fixed Point

The locus of points at a given distance from a given point is a circle whose center is the given point and the length of whose radius is the given distance.

Given: Point P and radius $= d$
Locus Diagram: Circle

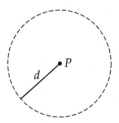

2. Points Equidistant From Two Points

The locus of points equidistant from two points is the perpendicular bisector of the line segment determined by the two points.

Given: Two points A and B
Locus Diagram: Perpendicular bisectors $\overleftrightarrow{RS}$ and $\overline{AB}$

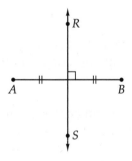

Note: Finding the locus of points equidistant from three fixed points not on the same line means we are finding the *circumcenter* of the triangle formed by joining those three points. Actually, it is sufficient to show the perpendicular bisectors of only two of the sides and that their point of intersection is the center of the circle that can be circumscribed about this triangle.

Given: Three points A, B, and C
Locus Diagram: The circumcenter at point P

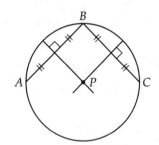

3. Points at a Given Distance From a Given Line

The locus of points at a given distance from a given line is a pair of lines each of which is parallel to the given line and at a given distance from it.

Given: $\overleftrightarrow{AB}$ and the distance d

Locus Diagram: $\overleftrightarrow{CD}$ and $\overleftrightarrow{EF}$ are each parallel to $\overleftrightarrow{AB}$ and at a perpendicular distance d from $\overleftrightarrow{AB}$.

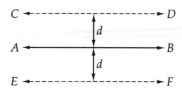

4. Points Equidistant From Parallel Lines

The locus of points equidistant from two parallel lines is a third line parallel to the two lines and midway between them.

Given: $\overleftrightarrow{AB} \parallel \overleftrightarrow{CD}$

Locus Diagram: $\overleftrightarrow{MN}$ is parallel to the two lines and midway between them.

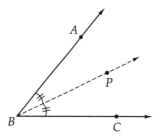

5. Points in the Interior of an Angle Equidistant From the Sides of the Angle

The locus of points in the interior of an angle equidistant from the sides of the angle is the ray that bisects the angle.

Given: $\angle ABC$

Locus Diagram: $\overrightarrow{BP}$ bisecting $\angle ABC$

6. Points Equidistant From Two Intersecting Lines

The locus of points equidistant from two intersecting lines is the pair of lines that bisect the angles formed by the intersecting lines.

Given: $\overleftrightarrow{AB}$ intersecting $\overleftrightarrow{CD}$

Locus Diagram: Perpendicular lines k and m bisecting the angles formed by $\overleftrightarrow{AB}$ and $\overleftrightarrow{CD}$

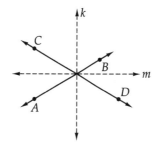

1 Sketch and describe fully the locus of the midpoints of all radii of a given circle.

SOLUTION

Locate the midpoints of some radii of a given circle. Join them in a smooth dashed curve to indicate the complete locus.

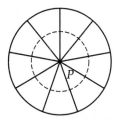

The locus is a circle concentric to the given circle and with a radius one-half the length of the radius of the given circle.

2 Sketch and describe fully the locus of points less than or equal to 1 inch from a given point *Q*.

SOLUTION

Draw a circle 1 inch from the given point and shade the interior as well.

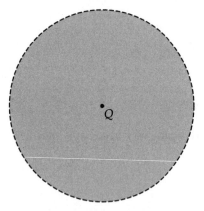

The locus is both the circle itself and all the points in the interior of the circle with center *Q*.

3 Sketch and describe fully the locus of the centers of all circles of the same size that are tangent to a given line.

SOLUTION

Draw circles of the same size tangent to a given line and on both sides of the line. Join the centers in two straight dashed lines.

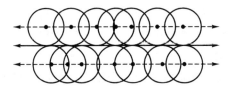

The locus is a pair of lines, each parallel to the given line and at a distance equal to the length of the radius of the given circles.

4 Sketch and describe fully the locus of the midpoints of all chords drawn from a given point on the circle.

SOLUTION

Draw some small chords and some large chords, including the diameter, from the given point on the circle. Mark the midpoints and connect them, forming a circle.

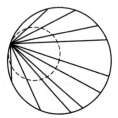

The locus is a circle tangent internally to the given circle at the given point and whose diameter is the radius of the given circle.

412 Chapter 14: Locus and Constructions

5 Sketch and describe fully the locus of points 5 inches from a circle with a 5-inch radius.

SOLUTION

Using the same center, draw a circle 5 inches farther out from the given circle. Also mark the center as a point 5 inches from the given circle.

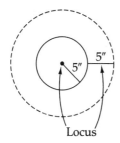

Locus

The locus is a *circle* concentric to the given circle, with a 10-inch radius, and a *point* that is the center of the given circle.

6 Sketch and describe fully the locus of points 3 inches from a circle with a 5-inch radius.

SOLUTION

Using the same center, draw two circles, one 3 inches in from the given circle and the other 3 inches farther out.

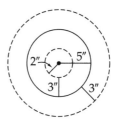

The locus is *two circles* concentric to the given circle, one with an 8-inch radius and one with a 2-inch radius.

 Practice

1 Describe the locus of points equidistant from two concentric circles whose radii are 8 inches and 14 inches.

(1) One concentric circle of radius 6 inches
(2) Two concentric circles of radius 8 inches and radius 14 inches
(3) One concentric circle of radius 11 inches
(4) One concentric circle of radius 22 inches

2 The locus of points equidistant from any two points is:

(1) one point
(2) one line
(3) two points
(4) two lines

3 The locus of points equidistant from the four vertices of a nonsquare rectangle is:

(1) the empty set
(2) a point
(3) a line
(4) a pair of points

4 Point P is on line $\overleftrightarrow{AB}$. The locus of the centers of all circles of radius 4 that pass through point P is:

(1) a circle of radius 4 with center at P
(2) a line passing through P and perpendicular to $\overleftrightarrow{AB}$
(3) two lines, both perpendicular to $\overleftrightarrow{AB}$ and 4 units on either side of P
(4) two lines parallel to $\overleftrightarrow{AB}$, one 4 units above $\overleftrightarrow{AB}$ and the other 4 units below $\overleftrightarrow{AB}$

5 The locus of the midpoints of the radii of a circle is:

(1) a point
(2) two lines
(3) a line
(4) a circle

Exercises 6–17: Sketch and describe fully the locus of points.

6 Three inches from a given point

7 Two inches from a given line

8 Equidistant from two given parallel lines that are 5 inches apart

9 Equidistant from points R and S, which are 2 inches apart

10 Equidistant from two given points A and B

11 Two and a half inches from a given point M

12 Equidistant from the sides of $\angle ABC$

13 Equidistant from two intersecting lines

14 Two inches from a circle with a 7-inch radius

15 Equidistant from two concentric circles

16 Less than 2 inches from a given point

17 Greater than or equal to a distance 3 inches from a given point

18 Describe the locus of the centers of all circles of the same size that are tangent to a given line.

19 Describe the locus of the centers of all circles that are tangent to each of two parallel lines.

20 Describe the locus of the midpoints of all chords parallel to a given chord of a circle.

21 Describe the locus of points within a circle that are equidistant from the endpoints of a given chord.

22 Describe the locus of the centers of all interior circles that are tangent to both sides of a given angle.

23 Describe the locus of the centers of all circles tangent to a given line at a given point.

24 Describe the locus of the centers of all circles that pass through two given points.

Locus in the Coordinate Plane

Let us review the steps to finding the perpendicular bisector of a segment, a third parallel line between two parallel lines, and a circle in the coordinate plane.

To Find the Perpendicular Bisector of a Segment in the Coordinate Plane

- Find the midpoint using the midpoint formula (when necessary).
- Find the slope of the line segment.
- Calculate the negative reciprocal of this slope. This will be the slope of the perpendicular line.
- Use the midpoint and the slope to help find the y-intercept and to write the equation for the perpendicular bisector.

To Find a Third Parallel Line Between Two Parallel Lines in the Coordinate Plane

- Pick one point on each given line and find the midpoint of the segment drawn between them. This point will be on the locus.
- Find the slope of one of the given lines.
- Using the midpoint and the slope, write an equation for the third line.

To Find a Circle in the Coordinate Plane

- A circle can be defined as the set (or *locus*) of all points (x, y) in the plane that are a fixed distance from the center (h, k). Remember that the fixed distance is the radius of the circle. Algebraically, the general equation for a circle with center at (h, k) and radius r is derived from the distance formula. The equation of a circle is $(x - h)^2 + (y - k)^2 = r^2$.
- If the center of the circle is the origin, then $(h, k) = (0, 0)$, and the equation collapses to $x^2 + y^2 = r^2$.
- The x-intercepts are $(-r, 0)$ and $(r, 0)$ and the y-intercepts are $(0, -r)$ and $(0, r)$.

 MODEL PROBLEMS

1 Find the locus of points equidistant from $A(-2, 5)$ and $B(4, 5)$.

SOLUTION

Plot the points. Since the slope is $\frac{5 - 5}{4 - (-2)} = 0$, $\overline{AB}$ is parallel to the x-axis. The locus is the perpendicular bisector of $\overline{AB}$, which is parallel to the y-axis and passes through the midpoint $\left(\frac{-2 + 4}{2}, \frac{5 + 5}{2} \right) = (1, 5)$. The equation of that locus of points is the line $x = 1$.

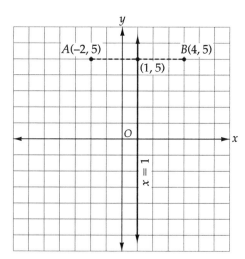

2 Find the locus of points 2 units from the line $x = 3$.

SOLUTION

The line $x = 3$ and the lines parallel to it are vertical. The line $x = 1$ is 2 units to the left and the line $x = 5$ is 2 units to the right.

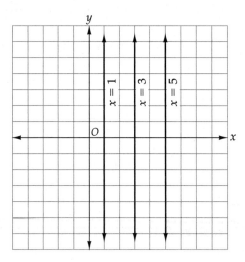

3 Find the locus of points equidistant from the lines $y = 2x + 1$ and $y = 2x - 3$.

SOLUTION

The locus is a line with a slope equal to 2 because it must be parallel to the other two lines. Since it must lie midway between the lines, its y-intercept must be -1, midway between 1 and -3. The required locus is the line $y = 2x - 1$.

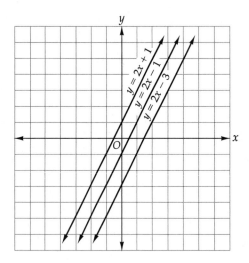

4 Find the locus of points equidistant from the lines $y = 3x + 2$ and $y = -3x + 2$.

SOLUTION

Graph the lines. The lines of symmetry, $x = 0$ and $y = 2$, are the locus.

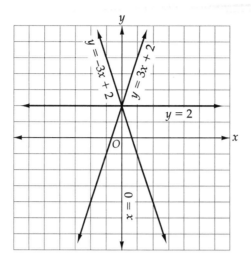

Note: The slope of one of the lines of the locus is the average of the slopes of the two given lines. The slope of the other line must be the negative reciprocal, since the two locus lines are perpendicular.

5 Graph the locus of all points 5 units from the origin. Write an equation for the graph.

SOLUTION

The locus is a circle with its center at $(0, 0)$ and a radius of 5. Every point on the circle is 5 units from the center. Construct the circle by putting the point of the compass at the origin and the pencil at $(5, 0)$.

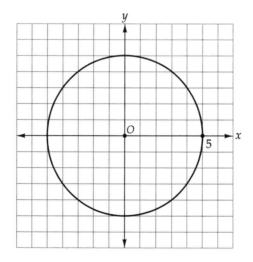

ANSWER: The equation for the circle graph where the radius is 5 is $x^2 + y^2 = 5^2$ or $x^2 + y^2 = 25$.

6 Graph the locus of points 3 units from point $A(1, 2)$ and find the equation for the graph.

SOLUTION

The locus is a circle with its center at $(1, 2)$ and a radius of 3. Every point on the circle is 3 units from the center, so $(1 + 3, 2)$ or $(4, 2)$ is a point on the circle.

Construct the circle by putting the point of the compass at $(1, 2)$ and starting the pencil at $(4, 2)$, which is 3 units from the center.

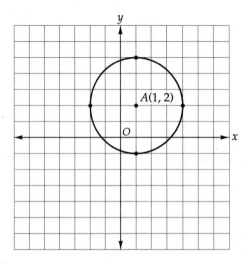

Write the general equation of a circle. $(x - h)^2 + (y - k)^2 = r^2$
Substitute 1 for h, 2 for k, and 3 for r. $(x - 1)^2 + (y - 2)^2 = 3^2$
$(x - 1)^2 + (y - 2)^2 = 9$

ANSWER: The equation for the graph is $(x - 1)^2 + (y - 2)^2 = 9$.

 Practice

---

1 Which statement describes the locus of points 2 units from the x-axis?

  (1) $x = 2$
  (2) $y = -2$
  (3) $x = 2$ or $x = -2$
  (4) $y = 2$ or $y = -2$

2 Which is the equation of the locus of points equidistant from points $(2, 3)$ and $(-6, 3)$?

  (1) $x = -2$
  (2) $y = 3$
  (3) $y - 3 = x + 2$
  (4) $y - 3 = x - 2$

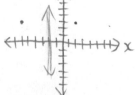

3 An equation that represents the locus of all points 5 units to the left of the y-axis is:

  (1) $x = 5$
  (2) $x = -5$
  (3) $y = 5$
  (4) $y = -5$

4 Which is the equation of the locus of points equidistant from $(3, 2)$ and $(3, -4)$?

  (1) $y = 1$
  (2) $y = -1$
  (3) $x = 3$
  (4) $x = 1$

5 Which equation represents the locus of points 5 units from point $(1, 3)$?

(1) $(x + 1)^2 + (y + 3)^2 = 5$
(2) $(x + 1)^2 + (y + 3)^2 = 25$
(3) $(x - 1)^2 + (y - 3)^2 = 5$
(4) $(x - 1)^2 + (y - 3)^2 = 25$

6 Which of the following is an equation for the locus of points equidistant from the lines $y = x + 3$ and $y = -x + 3$?

(1) $y = 3$
(2) $y = 0$
(3) $y = 3$ and $x = 0$
(4) $x = 3$ and $y = 0$

7 Which are the correct equations for the locus of points equidistant from the lines $y = 3$ and $x = 2$?

(1) $x = 3$ and $y = 2$
(2) $y = x$ and $y = -x$
(3) $y = x + 3$ and $y = -x + 3$
(4) $y = x + 1$ and $y = -x + 5$

8 Write an equation for the locus of points equidistant from the points $A(-1, -3)$ and $B(-1, 5)$.

9 Find an equation for the locus of points 4 units from the line $y = 6$. $(y=2)(y=10)$

10 Write an equation for the locus of points equidistant from the lines $y = 6$ and $y = 2$.

$y = 4$

11 Write an equation for the locus of points equidistant from the lines $y = 0$ and $x = 3$.

12 Find an equation for the locus of points equidistant from the lines $y = -x + 5$ and $y = -x + 1$

13 Write an equation for the locus of points equidistant from the lines $y = 3 - 3x$ and $y = 3x - 3$.

14 Write the equation for the locus of points

a 4 units from the point $(1, -4)$.
b 6 units from the origin.
c 3 units from the point $(0, 1)$.
d 1 unit from the point $(-1, 0)$.
e 2.5 units from the center $(0, 2)$.
f 5.5 units from the center $(-1, 3)$.

15 Marlene is directing renovation of the town swimming center. As shown in the diagram, there are two pools, with the diving board sides of the pool 70 feet apart. Marlene wants to set up outdoor showers at an equal distance from each diving board. Indicate where the showers could be placed. Explain your reasoning.

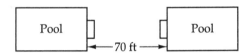

14-5 Compound Locus and the Coordinate Plane

A **compound locus** is a locus that must satisfy two or more conditions.

To Find Points That Satisfy a Compound Locus

- Draw a diagram that contains the given data, fixed lines, and/or points.
- Construct the locus of points for each condition on the same diagram.
- Clearly label each locus.
- Mark the points where the loci intersect. These points will satisfy both sets of conditions.

Note: In cases where the loci do not intersect, there is no point that satisfies the given conditions.

1 Find the locus of points 2 units from line *l and* 3 units from a point on line *l*.

SOLUTION

The locus of points 2 units from line *l* is two lines parallel to line *l*, each 2 units away. Construct the locus meeting the first condition.

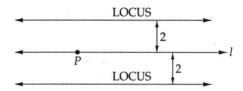

On the same diagram, construct a circle with a radius of 3 units and center at point *P* on line *l*.

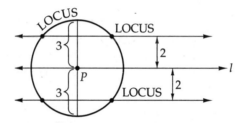

The circle locus intersects each of the two-line loci twice.

2 Two dogs, Archie and Butch, are leashed to stakes that are 4 yards apart. Their leashes allow them to go out to a distance just under 3 yards from their stakes. Janus, the cat, teases the dogs by sitting just outside their reach. Where can Janus sit to tease both dogs at the same time?

SOLUTION

Reword the question so that it includes the word *and*.

Two points *A* and *B* are 4 yards apart. Find the locus of points 3 yards from *A and* 3 yards from *B*.

Construct each locus and label the intersection.

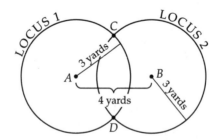

ANSWER: Janus should sit at one of the two points, *C* or *D*, as shown. These locus points lie on the perpendicular bisector of $\overline{AB}$.

3 Sketch and describe the locus of points equidistant from two given points *A* and *B* *and* at a given distance *d* from a third noncollinear point, *G*. Show all possible cases.

SOLUTION

There are three possible cases.

Case 1	Case 2	Case 3
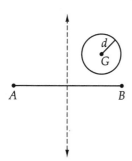	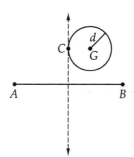	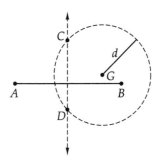
Locus: No points of intersection, { }.	**Locus:** One point of intersection, {*C*}.	**Locus:** Two points of intersection, {*C*, *D*}.

 Practice

---

1 Points *A* and *B* are 10 inches apart. The locus of points 8 inches from *A* and 4 inches from *B* is:

(1) a point
(2) a line
(3) a pair of points
(4) the empty set

2 Points *R* and *G* are 10 inches apart. The locus of points 13 inches from *R* and 2 inches from *G* is:

(1) a point
(2) 2 points
(3) a circle
(4) the empty set

3 Two points *L* and *D* are 8 units apart. How many points are equidistant from *L* and *D* and also 3 units from *L*?

(1) 0
(2) 1
(3) 2
(4) 4

4 Parallel lines *x* and *y* are cut by transversal *t*. What is the locus of points equidistant from *x* and *y* and at a given distance *d* from transversal *t*?

(1) a point
(2) a line
(3) a pair of points
(4) the empty set

5 Two points, *A* and *B*, are 8 inches apart. How many points are equidistant from *A* and *B* and 3 inches from the line passing through *A* and *B*?

(1) 0
(2) 1
(3) 2
(4) 3

6 How many points are equidistant from two given parallel lines and also equidistant from two different points in one of the lines?

(1) 0
(2) 1
(3) 2
(4) 3

7 How many points are 5 centimeters from a line and

a 8 centimeters from point *P* on the line?
b 5 centimeters from point *P* on the line?
c 3 centimeters from point *P* on the line?

8 A heliport must be built equidistant from three university hospitals, not on a straight line. How can planners determine the location of the heliport?

9 Point *W* is 3 inches from line *m*. How many points are 5 inches from point *W* and also 2 inches from line *m*?

10 Two circular riding paths have centers 1,000 feet apart. Both paths have a radius of 600 feet. In how many places do the paths intersect?

11 Given the line *m* and point *R* is 5 inches from the line, sketch and describe the locus of points

a 2 inches from *m* and 3 inches from *R*.
b 2 inches from *m* and 6 inches from *R*.
c 2 inches from *m* and 7 inches from *R*.
d 2 inches from *m* and 9 inches from *R*.

12 Sketch and describe the locus of points

a 3 inches from point *A* and 4 inches from point *B*, where *A* and *B* are 5 inches apart.
b 3 inches from point *A* and 4 inches from point *B*, where *A* and *B* are 7 inches apart.
c 3 inches from point *A* and 3 inches from point *B*, where *A* and *B* are 7 inches apart.

13 Given two intersecting lines *l* and *m*, find the locus of points equidistant from *l* and *m* and 2 inches from the intersection at point *O*.

14 Sketch and describe the locus of points equidistant from two parallel lines *a* and *b* and 3 cm from point *P*, which lies midway between lines *a* and *b*.

15 Sketch and describe the locus of points equidistant from intersecting lines *m* and *n* and *x* units from line *m*.

16 Sketch and describe the locus of points at a given distance, *d*, from a given circle and equidistant from two given lines that intersect at the center of the circle.

17 Sketch and describe the locus of points equidistant from two parallel lines, *m* and *k*, and *d* inches from point *A* on line *m*, where *m* and *k* are *f* feet apart. Show all the cases.

18 Sketch and describe the locus of points equidistant from points *A* and *B* and *x* inches from point *A*, where *A* and *B* are *d* inches apart. Show all the cases.

Compound Loci and the Coordinate Plane

MODEL PROBLEM

The equation of line $\overleftrightarrow{PQ}$ is $x = 3$.

   a Describe fully the locus of points d units from $\overleftrightarrow{PQ}$.
   b Sketch and describe fully the locus of points 2 units from the origin.
   c How many points satisfy the conditions in parts **a** and **b** simultaneously for the following values of d? Illustrate your answers clearly.
      (i) $d = 2$
      (ii) $d = 5$
      (iii) $d = 6$

SOLUTION

   a The locus of points d units from $\overleftrightarrow{PQ}$ is two lines parallel to $x = 3$ where the equations for the two lines are $x_1 = 3 + d$ and $x_2 = 3 - d$.

   b The locus of points 2 units from the origin is a circle whose center is $(0, 0)$ and whose radius is 2.

      The equation of the circle is $x^2 + y^2 = 2^2$.

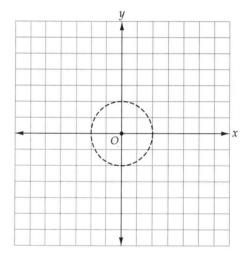

   c (i)   If $d = 2$, then the locus is two points $\{A, B\}$.
      (ii) If $d = 5$, then the locus is one point $\{C\}$.
      (iii) If $d = 6$, then the locus is no points $\{\ \}$.

 Practice

---

1 What is the total number of points that are both 2 units from the x-axis and 3 units from the origin?

    (1) 0
    (2) 1
    (3) 2
    (4) 4

2 What is the total number of points that are both 3 units from the x-axis and 3 units from the origin?

    (1) 0
    (2) 1
    (3) 2
    (4) 4

3 What is the total number of points that are 2 units from the x-axis and also 1 unit from the origin?

(1) 0
(2) 2
(3) 3
(4) 4

4 Find the locus of points 2 units from the origin and 4 units from each given point.

    a $(0, -3)$
    b $(0, 6)$
    c $(7, 0)$

5 Sketch and describe the locus of all points that are 5 units from the graph of $y = 6$ and equidistant from the graphs of $x = 1$ and $x = 7$.

6 Find the locus of points that are 8 units from the origin and that satisfy the equation $y = -x + 8$.

7 Find the locus of points that are 3 units from the graph of $y = 4$ and equidistant from the graphs of $x = 6$ and $x = -2$.

8 Find the locus of all points that satisfy the linear equations $y = -x + 4$ and $x^2 + (y + 1)^2 = 13$.

9 The vertices of $\triangle RST$ are $R(-4, -2)$, $S(2, 6)$, and $T(2, -2)$.

    a Write an equation of the locus of points equidistant from vertex S and vertex T.
    b Write an equation of the line parallel to $\overline{ST}$ and passing through vertex R.
    c Find the coordinates of the point of intersection of the locus in part **a** and the line determined in part **b**.
    d Write an equation of the locus of points that are 4 units from vertex T.
    e What is the total number of points that satisfy the loci described in parts **a** and **d**?

10 The coordinates of point X are $(3, 5)$.

    a Describe fully the locus of points at a distance d units from X.
    b Describe fully the locus of points at a distance of 1 unit from the y-axis.
    c How many points satisfy the condition in parts **a** and **b** simultaneously for the following values of d?

        (i) $d = 2$
        (ii) $d = 4$
        (iii) $d = 5$

14-6 Locus of Points Equidistant From a Point and a Line

A **parabola** is the locus of all points equidistant from a given point, the **focus**, and a given line, the **directrix**.

The following illustrations show the four standard positions of the parabola with line d as the directrix (both vertical and horizontal), and point F as the focus.

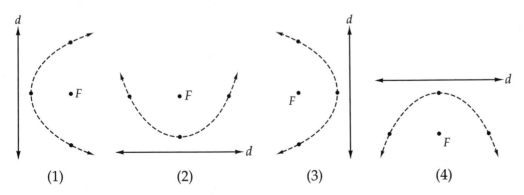

(1)   (2)   (3)   (4)

Some Observations From the Illustrations

- Any line can be the directrix, and any point not on the directrix can be the focus. The focus, F, is never on the directrix.
- No matter which direction the parabola opens, the focus is always inside the parabola.
- The axis of symmetry will pass through the focus as well as the turning point (or *vertex*) of the parabola.
- The axis of symmetry will be perpendicular to the directrix.

Given the directrix, d, and the focus, F, of a parabola, it is possible to construct, by use of a straight edge and compass, as many points of the parabola as desired. The method to how to construct the points of the parabola is shown below.

Note: The first three points are the easiest to construct.

Method

- The first point, P_1, is the midpoint between the focus, F, and the directrix, d. The next points will come in pairs, and the following steps should be repeated as often as you wish depending on how many points you want to have for sketching or plotting a smooth curve.
- Draw a line, l_1, through F and parallel to line d.
- Measure with your compass the distance from F to the d.
- Use that distance as a radius and use F as a center and draw arcs intersecting l_1 at points P_2 and P_3. These two points are equidistant from F and the d and, by definition, are on the parabola.
- Draw lines l_2, l_3, l_4, etc. With the compass, measure the distance from each line to line d. Again, using that distance, make arcs from F that intersect the line.

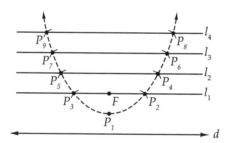

By continuing this process on the xy-coordinate system, the curve can be even more accurately drawn. With the focus $F(5, 3)$ and directrix $y = -1$, the first point on the locus is the vertex of the parabola $(5, 1)$. Two other points are $(9, 3)$ and $(1, 3)$.

Using $R_1(3, 5)$ and $R_2(3, 7)$ as reference points for measuring the distance to the directrix, each of these distances becomes a radius with F as the center and we then make two arcs intersecting the lines $y = 5$ and $y = 7$.

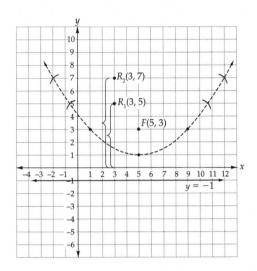

Given the equation of a fixed line and the coordinates of the fixed point, we can find the equation of the locus of points equidistant from the fixed line and fixed point. Study the model problem below.

 MODEL PROBLEM

Given the fixed line $y = 1$ and the fixed point $F(2, 5)$, find

  a the equation for the locus of all points equidistant from the fixed line and the fixed point.
  b the coordinates of three points on the parabola including the turning point.
  c the equation for the axis of symmetry.

SOLUTION

  a The parabola is the locus of points that will satisfy the given conditions. To write an equation for the parabola, let $P(x, y)$ be any point on the parabola. Since segment PF must equal the perpendicular distance from P to the directrix $y = 1$,

$$\sqrt{(x - 2)^2 + (y - 5)^2} = |y - (\text{directrix})|$$
or $|y - 1|$.

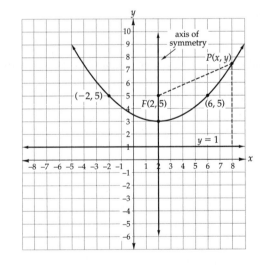

To remove the radical, square both sides of the equation.

$$(x - 2)^2 + (y - 5)^2 = (y - 1)^2$$
$$x^2 - 4x + 4 + y^2 - 10y + 25 = y^2 - 2y + 1$$
$$x^2 - 4x + 29 = 10y - 2y + 1$$
$$x^2 - 4x + 28 = 8y$$
$$\frac{x^2}{8} - \frac{1}{2}x + \frac{7}{2} = y$$

ANSWER: $y = \frac{x^2}{8} - \frac{1}{2}x + \frac{7}{2}$

b The coordinates of three points include the *turning point* or *vertex* of the parabola. The vertex is midway between the focus $F(2, 5)$ and the directrix $y = 1$ or the point $(2, 1)$. So the midpoint is $\left(\frac{2+2}{2}, \frac{5+1}{2}\right)$ or $(2, 3)$.

To find two other points, observe that the vertical distance from $F(2, 5)$ to the directrix $y = 1$ is 4 units. Thus, we can move 4 horizontal units on either side of the focus to obtain two more points that are on the parabola, $(-2, 5)$ and $(6, 5)$.

ANSWER: Three points are $(2, 3)$, $(-2, 5)$, and $(6, 5)$.

c Since the directrix is horizontal, the axis of symmetry for the parabola is vertical and passes through the focus, which is the line $x = 2$.

ANSWER: The axis of symmetry is $x = 2$.

General Comments

When the directrix is on a horizontal or vertical line of the coordinate system, use the method introduced in the model problem to find three points on the parabola. The following is a summary of this method.

- Find the midpoint of the perpendicular segment that joins the focus, F, to the directrix, line d.
- Find the distance from the focus, F, to the directrix, d, and move that distance left and right of the focus (if the directrix is a horizontal line) or up and down from the focus (if the directrix is a vertical line).

 **Practice**

Find the locus of points equidistant from the fixed point and fixed line. For each answer:

  a Sketch the parabola with the given focus and directrix.
  b Find three points on the parabola.
  c Write the equation of the parabola.

1 $F(0, 3)$ and directrix $y = 1$

2 $F(2, 1)$ and directrix $y = -3$

3 $F(2, -2)$ and directrix $y = 2$

4 $F(3, 1)$ and directrix $y = -2$

5 $F(3, 0)$ and directrix $x = -1$

6 $F(-3, 0)$ and directrix $y = 3$

7 $F(-2, -4)$ and directrix $y = 0$

8 $F(4, 4)$ and directrix $x = -2$

9 $F(2, 0)$ and directrix $x = -2$

10 $F(3, 2)$ and directrix $y = -1$

14-7 Solving Other Linear-Quadratic and Quadratic-Quadratic Systems

In addition to finding the locus of points that satisfy the linear-quadratic systems of the line and circle (as seen in Chapter 13), we can determine both algebraically and graphically the solutions to the intersections of a line and a parabola, an ellipse, or a hyperbola. We can also find the common solutions for pairs of quadratic equations.

There is a difference in the number of solutions in quadratic-quadratic systems. While (1) a linear-quadratic system, such as $y = x^2 + 4$ and $x + y = 6$, may have 0, 1, or 2 real solutions, the (2) quadratic-quadratic system, such as $y = -2x^2 + 6x$ and $y = x^2 - 3x$, may have 4, 3, 2, 1, or 0 solutions. Consider the following model problems for all the types.

 MODEL PROBLEMS

1 Solve and graph this system of equations: $y = x^2 + 4$ and $x + y = 6$.

SOLUTION (PARABOLA AND LINE)

Solve the second equation for y, so that $y = 6 - x$.

Since both equations have a common solution at y, substitute $(6 - x)$ for y, so that $6 - x = x^2 + 4$, and solve for x.

$x^2 + 4 - 6 + x = 0$
$\quad x^2 + x - 2 = 0$
$(x + 2)(x - 1) = 0$
$x = -2 \text{ or } x = 1$

Substitute the values for x in either equation and solve for y.

When $x = -2$, $y = 8$, and when $x = 1$, $y = 5$.

ANSWER: $\{(-2, 8), (1, 5)\}$

2 Find the common solutions for $y = -2x^2 + 6x$ and $y = x^2 - 3x$.

SOLUTION (TWO PARABOLAS)

Since they both equal y, we can set the parabola equations equal to each other.
Gather terms on one side and solve for x.
Combine line terms.
Factor.

$x^2 - 3x = -2x^2 + 6x$

$x^2 + 2x^2 - 6x - 3x = 0$
$3x^2 - 9x = 0$
$3x(x - 3) = 0$
$3x = 0 \text{ or } x - 3 = 0$
$x = 0 \text{ or } x = 3$

Substitute the values for x in either equation and solve for y.
When $x = 0$, $y = 0$, and when $x = 3$, $y = 0$.

ANSWER: $\{(0, 0), (3, 0)\}$

3 Find the common solutions for $y + x^2 = 28$ and $y = 3(x - 4)^2$

SOLUTION (TWO PARABOLAS)

Solve $y + x^2 = 28$ for y, so that $y = -x^2 + 28$.
Since they both equal y, set the equations equal to each other.
Foil the expression $3(x - 4)^2$.

$-x^2 + 28 = 3(x - 4)^2$
$-x^2 + 28 = 3(x - 4)(x - 4)$
$-x^2 + 28 = 3(x^2 - 8x + 16)$

Distribute the 3.
Gather terms on one side.
Divide every term by 4.
Factor.

$-x^2 + 28 = 3x^2 - 24x + 48$
$0 = 4x^2 - 24x + 20$
$x^2 - 6x + 5 = 0$
$(x - 5)(x - 1) = 0$
$x - 5 = 0 \text{ or } x - 1 = 0$
$x = 5 \text{ or } x = 1$

Substitute the values for x in either equation and solve for y.
When $x = 5$, $y = 3$, and when $x = 1$, $y = 27$.

ANSWER: $\{(5, 3), (1, 27)\}$

4 Find the common solutions for $x^2 + y^2 = 20$ and $xy = 8$ and sketch the graphs.

SOLUTION (HYPERBOLA AND CIRCLE)

Solve $xy = 8$ for y such that $y = \frac{8}{x}$.

Substitute $\frac{8}{x}$ for y in the circle equation $x^2 + y^2 = 20$.

$x^2 + \left(\frac{8}{x}\right)^2 = 20$

$x^2 + \frac{64}{x^2} = 20$

Multiply each term by x^2.
Gather all terms on one side.
Factor.

$x^4 + 64 = 20x^2$
$x^4 - 20x^2 + 64 = 0$
$(x^2 - 4)(x^2 - 16) = 0$
$x^2 - 4 = 0 \text{ or } x^2 - 16 = 0$
$x^2 = 4 \text{ or } x^2 = 16$
$x = \pm 2 \text{ or } x = \pm 4$

Substitute the values for x in the simpler equation, $xy = 8$.

$x = 2, y = 4; x = -2, y = -4$
$x = 4, y = 2; x = -4, y = -2$

ANSWER: $\{(2, 4), (-2, -4), (4, 2), (-4, -2)\}$

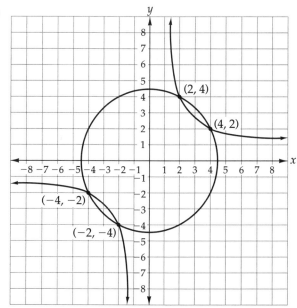

Practice

For each system of equations find all the real solutions. Sketch the graph of each pair.

1 $y = x^2 - 4$
  $y + x^2 = 4$

2 $y = x^2 - 8$
  $y = -x^2 + 8$

3 $x^2 + y^2 = 25$
  $x^2 = 2y + 10$

4 $y = x^2 - 5x + 8$
  $y = -x^2 + 7x - 10$

5 $2x + y = 1$
  $y^2 + 4x = 17$

6 $x^2 + y^2 = 5$
  $x - y = 1$

7 $y = -x^2$
  $y = x^2 - 2$

8 $y = 3x^2 + 10x + 2$
  $y = 2x^2 + 4x - 3$

9 $y = 3x + 1$
  $xy = 10$

10 $x^2 + y^2 = 16$
  $x^2 + 4y^2 = 16$

11 $y = x^2 - 2$
  $y = 2 - x^2$

12 $xy = -6$
  $x + 3y = 3$

13 $x^2 + y^2 = 10$
  $xy = 4$

14 $y = x^2 - 4x + 3$
  $y = \frac{1}{2}x + 1$

15 $y = x^2 - x$
  $y = x - 1$

16 $y = 3x^2$
  $y = -3x^2 + 6$

17 $3x^2 - 4y^2 = 4$
  $x^2 + y^2 = 13$

18 $x^2 + 3y^2 = 7$
  $y^2 = x - 1$

19 $x^2 = 9 + y$
  $y + 1 = (x - 2)^2$

20 $(x - 2)^2 + y^2 = 16$
  $x - y = -2$

CHAPTER REVIEW

1 All the concurrent points; centroid, orthocenter, incenter, and circumcenter, are always found in the interior of:

  (1) isosceles triangles
  (2) acute triangles
  (3) obtuse triangles
  (4) right triangles

2 In the figure below, $\triangle ABC$ is scalene. The construction on this triangle shows that $\overline{BD}$ is the:

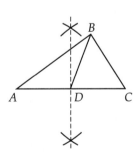

  (1) bisector of angle B
  (2) altitude to side $\overline{AC}$
  (3) perpendicular bisector of side $\overline{AC}$
  (4) median to side $\overline{AC}$

3 In the figure below, $\overrightarrow{PQ}$, the bisector of an angle has been constructed. In proving this construction, which reason is used for the congruence involved?

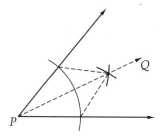

(1) ASA
(2) SSS
(3) AAS
(4) SAS

4 The locus of the midpoints of all radii of two concentric circles is:

(1) a circle
(2) two circles
(3) a line
(4) the empty set

5 $\angle ABC$ is bisected by $\overrightarrow{BD}$. Points R on $\overrightarrow{BA}$ and S on $\overrightarrow{BC}$ are equidistant from point B. If X is a point on $\overrightarrow{BD}$, and not collinear with R and S, then which of the following is always true?

(1) $\triangle SRX$ is an equilateral triangle.
(2) X lies on the locus of points equidistant from R and S.
(3) X is closer to S than to B.
(4) $\triangle SBX$ is an isosceles triangle.

6 Which is the equation of the locus of points whose ordinates are three less than twice their abscissas?

(1) $y = 2x + 3$
(2) $y = 2x - 3$
(3) $x = 2y + 3$
(4) $x = 2y - 3$

7 Which equation describes the locus of points 6 units from point $(3, -4)$?

(1) $(x + 3)^2 + (y - 4)^2 = 6$
(2) $(x - 3)^2 + (y + 4)^2 = 6$
(3) $(x - 3)^2 + (y + 4)^2 = 36$
(4) $(x + 3)^2 + (y - 4)^2 = 36$

8 What is the equation of the locus of points equidistant from points $P(1, 2)$ and $Q(5, 2)$?

(1) $x = 3$
(2) $y = 3$
(3) $x = 2$
(4) $y = 2$

9 What is the equation of the locus of points passing through point $(5, -3)$ and 5 units from the y-axis?

(1) $x = -5$
(2) $y = -5$
(3) $x = 5$
(4) $y = 5$

10 The equation $y = 4$ represents the locus of points that are equidistant from:

(1) $(0, 0)$ and $(0, 8)$
(2) $(4, 0)$ and $(0, 4)$
(3) $(0, 3)$ and $(0, 1)$
(4) $(4, 4)$ and $(-4, 4)$

11

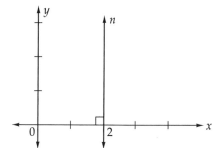

Line n in the figure above, is the locus of all points equidistant from:

(1) $(2, 4)$ and $(2, 2)$
(2) $(3, 1)$ and $(3, 3)$
(3) $(3, 1)$ and $(1, 4)$
(4) $(0, 2)$ and $(4, 2)$

12 The center of the circle that can be circumscribed about a scalene triangle is located by constructing the:

(1) medians of the triangle
(2) altitudes of the triangle
(3) perpendicular bisectors of the sides of the triangle
(4) angle bisectors of the triangle

13 How many points are equidistant from two intersecting lines and also 5 units from the point of intersection?

(1) 0
(2) 2
(3) 4
(4) 5

14 Point P is 3 inches from line k. How many points are 5 inches from point P and also 2 inches from line k?

(1) 1
(2) 2
(3) 3
(4) 4

15 Points A and B lie on line m. Line k intersects line m at A. The number of points equidistant from points A and B are also equidistant from lines m and k is:

(1) 0
(2) 1
(3) 2
(4) 4

16 How many points that are 3 units from the line $y = x$ lie on the circle with equation $x^2 + y^2 = 25$?

(1) 0
(2) 2
(3) 3
(4) 4

17

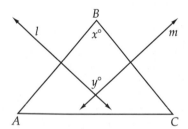

If l is the locus of all points equidistant from A and B and m is the locus of all points equidistant from B and C, then y, in terms of x, equals:

(1) $90 - x$
(2) $180 - x$
(3) $90 + x$
(4) $180 + x$

18

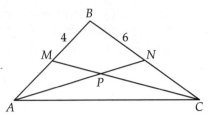

In $\triangle ABC$ with medians $\overline{AN}$ and $\overline{CM}$, what is the length of $\overline{AP}$ when $AN = 12$?

19 In $\triangle RST$, medians $\overline{SE}$ and $\overline{RD}$ are concurrent at point P. If $RP = 8x - 12$ and $PD = 2x$, find x and the lengths of $\overline{PD}$, $\overline{RP}$, and $\overline{RD}$.

20 In $\triangle ABC$, medians $\overline{BE}$ and $\overline{AD}$ intersect at P. If $AP = 2x + y$, $PD = 3x - 2$, $BP = y + 2$, and $PE = x + 1$, find the values for x, y, and the lengths of $\overline{BE}$ and $\overline{AD}$.

Exercises 21–24: Sketch and describe the locus of points.

21 Three inches from a circle with a 4-inch radius

22 Four units from the y-axis and 3 units from the origin

23 Two units from the origin and 2 units from $P(0, -4)$

24 Four centimeters from line m and 2 centimeters from point H, where H is 6 centimeters above line m

Exercises 25–27: Write an equation for the locus of points

25 whose distance from $(4, -2)$ is 1.

26 equidistant from points $A(0, 0)$ and $B(4, 4)$.

27 equidistant from the lines $y = 2$ and $x = 0$.

Exercises 28–31: Find the locus of points equidistant from the fixed point and fixed line. For each answer:

a Sketch the parabola with the given focus and directix.
b Find three points on the parabola.
c Write the equation of the parabola.

28 $F(2, 1)$ and directrix $y = -2$

29 $F(1, 3)$ and directrix $x = -3$

30 $F(2, -2)$ and directrix $y = 2$

31 $F(1, 0)$ and directrix $x = -3$

Exercises 32–37: Find the locus of all points that satisfy each system of equations. Sketch the graph of each set of equations.

32 $x^2 + y^2 = 25$ and $y = x^2 - 5$

33 $y = 2x^2 - 5x + 5$ and $y - x = 5$

34 $y = 2x^2 + 8x - 3$ and $2x - y = 3$

35 $y = x^2 - 3x - 4$ and $y - x = -1$

36 $y = 3x^2 - 5x - 2$ and $y - x = 7$

37 $y = x^2 - 4$ and $x^2 + y^2 = 16$

38 Sketch and describe the locus of points equidistant from points A and B, and x feet from point A, where A and B are f feet apart.

39 What is the locus of points equidistant from two given concentric circles, with radii 1 and 4 units and at a given distance, x, from a given line passing through the center of the circles?

40 Sketch and describe the locus of points d inches from point P and d inches from point Q, where P and Q are x inches apart.

41 Sketch and describe the locus of points d inches from line m and r inches from point A on line m. (Hint: There should be three different illustrations.)

42 An architect is deciding where to install a fountain in a long rectangular courtyard. The fountain should be equidistant from the north and south sides of the courtyard. It should be at least 30 feet from the entrance on the north side. The courtyard is 60 feet across. Create a map showing where the fountain should be installed.

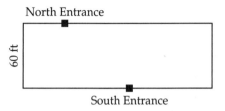

North Entrance

60 ft

South Entrance

43 Draw an acute triangle and construct the three altitudes. Identify the orthocenter.

44 Construct the three perpendicular bisectors of the three sides of a right triangle.

45 Construct a circle that passes through the three vertices of an obtuse triangle.

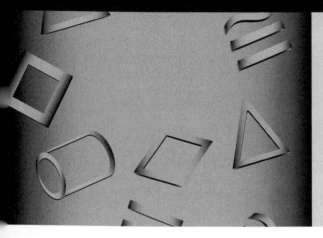

Cumulative Reviews

CUMULATIVE REVIEW
CHAPTERS 1–2

Part I

All questions in this part will receive 2 credits. No partial credit will be allowed.

1 If $a \to b$ and $r \to \sim b$, which statement is a valid conclusion?

   (1) $a \to r$ (3) $b \to r$

   (2) $\sim a \to \sim r$ (4) $a \to \sim r$

2 In the figure given, what is the intersection of $\overrightarrow{AC}$ and $\overrightarrow{BA}$?

   (1) $\overline{AC}$ (3) $\overrightarrow{BA}$

   (2) $\overline{AB}$ (4) $\overleftrightarrow{AC}$

3 Let p represent "x is an odd number" and q represent "x is a prime number." Which is true when $x = 21$?

   (1) $p \to q$ (3) $p \wedge \sim q$

   (2) $\sim p \vee q$ (4) $p \leftrightarrow q$

4 If B is the midpoint of $\overline{AC}$, then which of the following must be true?

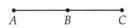

   (1) $AB > BC$ (3) $\frac{1}{2}AC = 2AB$

   (2) $AC < BC$ (4) $2BC = AC$

5 Let s represent "If I play soccer, then I will win a scholarship." The converse of s is:

(1) If I win a scholarship, then I will play soccer.

(2) If I do not win a scholarship, then I will not play soccer.

(3) If I don't play soccer, then I will not win a scholarship.

(4) I will win a scholarship or I don't play soccer.

6 Point G lies on $\overline{AB}$, so that $AG = 2$ and $GB = 1$. What is the probability that a point selected at random from $\overline{AB}$ will lie on $\overline{AG}$?

(1) $\frac{1}{3}$ (3) $\frac{2}{3}$

(2) $\frac{1}{2}$ (4) 1

7 Given an isosceles triangle, which statement is true?

(1) The triangle must be obtuse.

(2) The triangle must be scalene.

(3) The triangle may be acute.

(4) The triangle must be a right triangle.

8 What is the contrapositive of this true statement? "If two angles are right angles, then they are congruent."

(1) If two angles are congruent, then they are right angles.

(2) If two angles are not right angles, then they are not congruent.

(3) If two angles are right angles, then they are not congruent.

(4) If two angles are not congruent, then they are not right angles.

9 If three angles of a triangle are x, y, and $x + y$, then the triangle is:

(1) isosceles   (3) obtuse

(2) right   (4) acute

10 If the measures of the angles of $\triangle PQR$ are represented by $2x$, $x + 10$, and $2x - 30$, then $\triangle PQR$ must be:

(1) isosceles   (3) right

(2) obtuse   (4) scalene

Part II

Each correct answer will receive 2 credits. Clearly indicate the necessary steps, including the appropriate formula substitutions, diagrams, charts, etc. Correct numerical answers without work shown will receive only 1 credit.

11 Use the Chain Rule to create a true statement given that "$AB < CD$" and "$CD < EF$" are both true statements.

12

In segment $\overline{PT}$, L is the midpoint of $\overline{PA}$ and A is the midpoint of $\overline{PN}$. If $PT = 17$ and $LA = 3.5$, what is the length of NT?

13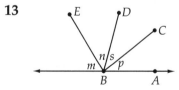

If $m\angle ABD = 75$, $m\angle s = 35$, and $m\angle CBE = 85$, what is the measure of $\angle m$?

14 If $AB = x + 6$, $AC = 5x + 3$, and B is the midpoint of $\overline{AC}$, what is the measure of segment BC?

Each correct answer will receive 4 credits. Partial credit will be allowed. Clearly indicate the necessary steps, including the appropriate formula substitutions, diagrams, charts, etc. Correct numerical answers without work shown will receive only 1 credit.

15 Classify each triangle (i) by sides and (ii) by angles.

a

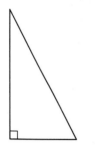

b

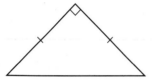

c

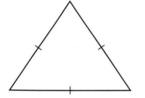

d

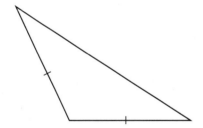

e

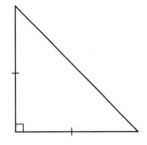

f

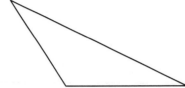

16 Points A, B, C, and D lie on a line in that order and the length of the line is 44. If $\overline{AD}$ is twice as long as $\overline{AC}$ and 4 times as long as $\overline{AB}$, what is the value of $\frac{BD}{AB}$?

17 In the given figure, the angle measures are x, y, and 38. If $x - y = 12$, find the value of x.

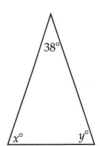

Each correct answer will receive 6 credits. Partial credit will be allowed. Clearly indicate the necessary steps, including the appropriate formula substitutions, diagrams, charts, etc. Correct numerical answers without work shown will receive only 1 credit.

18 Identify the property of real numbers that is used in each of the following algebraic equations.

a $\frac{1}{3}(3x + 5) = \frac{1}{3}(3x) + \frac{1}{3}(5)$

b $\left(2x - \frac{1}{3}\right) + \frac{1}{3} = 2x + \left(-\frac{1}{3} + \frac{1}{3}\right)$

c $5x + 0 = 5x$

d $7\left(2x \cdot \frac{1}{3}\right) = 7\left(\frac{1}{3} \cdot 2x\right)$

19 In the figure given, $\overrightarrow{BC}$ bisects $\angle ABD$, $m\angle 1 = \frac{1}{3}x + 3$, and $m\angle 2 = \frac{5}{6}x - 18$.

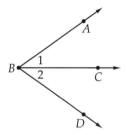

Find $m\angle ABD$.

20 Let p represent "$x < 6$" and q represent "x is not an even number." If the domain for x is $\{0, 1, 2, 3, \ldots, 9, 10\}$, find the solution set for each of the following.

a $\sim p$

b $\sim q$

c $p \wedge q$

d $p \vee q$

Part I

All questions in this part will receive 2 credits. No partial credit will be allowed.

1 In the figure given, what is the value of x?

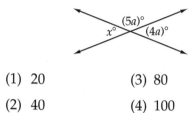

(1) 20   (3) 80

(2) 40   (4) 100

2 If two adjacent angles form a straight line, and the ratio of the larger angle to the smaller is 7 to 3, what is the measure in degrees of the smaller angle?

(1) 18   (3) 72

(2) 54   (4) 126

3

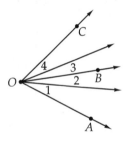

$\overrightarrow{OB}$ bisects $\angle COA$ and $m\angle 1 = m\angle 4$. Which of the following can be used to determine that $m\angle 2 = m\angle 3$?

(1) Subtraction Postulate

(2) Addition Postulate

(3) Transitive Property

(4) Symmetric Property

4 Which of the following is logically equivalent to the true statement "If Cecilia takes AP Calculus, then she is a senior"?

(1) AP Calculus is the only senior math class.

(2) AP Calculus is not a senior class.

(3) If Cecilia does not take AP Calculus, then she is not a senior.

(4) If Cecilia is not a senior, then she does not take AP Calculus.

5

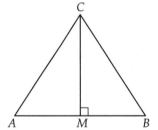

$\overline{CM}$ is the perpendicular bisector of $\overline{AB}$ and intersects $\overline{AB}$ at M. If $CA = CB$, $CA = 2x + 3$, $CB = 3x - 5$, and $AM = x + 3$, then the length of $\overline{AB}$ is:

(1) 8   (3) 16

(2) 11   (4) 22

6 Which of the following statements is not logically equivalent to the other three?

(1) If a triangle is equilateral, then it is isosceles.

(2) An equilateral triangle is also isosceles.

(3) If a triangle is not equilateral, then it is not isosceles.

(4) A triangle is isosceles, if it is equilateral.

7

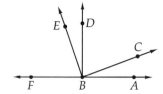

In the figure given, $\overrightarrow{BD} \perp \overleftrightarrow{ABF}$ at point B and $\overrightarrow{BE} \perp \overrightarrow{BC}$ at point B. If m$\angle ABC = 20$, what is m$\angle EBD$?

(1) 20   (3) 90

(2) 70   (4) 110

8 Which of the following can be used for x as a counterexample to prove that the statement "If $x < 0$, then $x^3 \leq x$" is not always true?

(1) -2 (3) $-\frac{1}{2}$

(2) -1 (4) $\frac{1}{2}$

9 On line m, two points A and C are to be placed on opposite sides of point B so that $2BC = AB$. What is the ratio of $\frac{AC}{AB}$?

(1) $\frac{1}{3}$ (3) $\frac{2}{3}$

(2) $\frac{1}{2}$ (4) $\frac{3}{2}$

10 In the given figure, line m intersects vertex P of $\triangle PQR$.

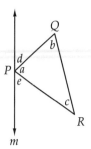

The sum of d and e is equal to which of the following?

(1) $2a$

(2) $b + c$

(3) $b + c - a$

(4) $180 - (b + c)$

Part II

Each correct answer will receive 2 credits. Clearly indicate the necessary steps, including the appropriate formula substitutions, diagrams, charts, etc. Correct numerical answers without work shown will receive only 1 credit.

11

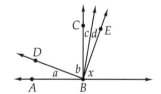

If $\angle ABC$ is a right angle, $\angle DBE$ is a right angle, m$\angle a = 20$, and m$\angle c = 10$, find the measure of $\angle x$.

12 In each of the following, state why the arguments are invalid.

a If $ABCD$ is a square, then it is a quadrilateral.
$ABCD$ is a quadrilateral.
$\therefore ABCD$ is a square.

b If $x > 8$, then x is a positive number.
x is a positive number.
$\therefore x > 8$

13 In the figure given, m∠EBC = 125, m∠w = 35 − x, and m∠t = 2x + 75.

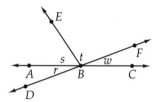

Find the measure of ∠r.

14 In the figure given, C is the midpoint of $\overline{AB}$.

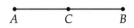

If D (not shown) is the midpoint of $\overline{AC}$ and R (not shown) is a point between C and B so that the length of $\overline{DR}$ is 22 and the length of $\overline{AR}$ is 30, what is the length of $\overline{RB}$?

Part III

Each correct answer will receive 4 credits. Partial credit will be allowed. Clearly indicate the necessary steps, including the appropriate formula substitutions, diagrams, charts, etc. Correct numerical answers without work shown will receive only 1 credit.

15 In △ABC, if ∠A ≅ ∠B, m∠A = 2x + 72, and m∠C = 5x − 9, what is the degree measure of each angle of the triangle?

16

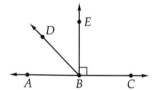

In the figure given:

a Name two acute angles.

b Name two right angles.

c Name an obtuse angle.

d Name a straight angle.

17

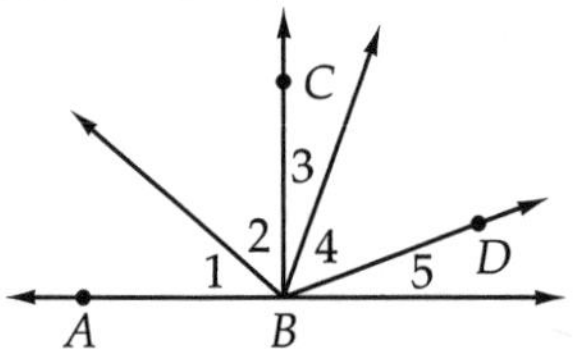

In the given figure, m∠ABC = 90, m∠1 = 40, m∠2 = m∠4, and m∠3 = m∠5. Find m∠4, m∠5, and m∠ABD.

Part IV

Each correct answer will receive 6 credits. Partial credit will be allowed. Clearly indicate the necessary steps, including the appropriate formula substitutions, diagrams, charts, etc. Correct numerical answers without work shown will receive only 1 credit.

18 For the conditional statement "If two acute angles are complementary, then the sum of their measures is 90°," write the

a converse

b inverse

c contrapositive

d biconditional

19 In this formal proof, fill in the missing reasons.

Given: m∠1 = m∠3
Prove: ∠AOC ≅ ∠BOD

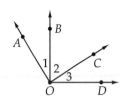

Statements	Reasons
1. m∠1 = m∠3	1. Given.
2. m∠2 = m∠2	2. _____
3. m∠1 + m∠2 = m∠3 + m∠2	3. _____
4. m∠AOC = m∠1 + m∠2 m∠BOD = m∠2 + m∠3	4. _____
5. m∠AOC = m∠BOD	5. _____
6. ∠AOC ≅ ∠BOD	6. Equal angles are congruent angles.

20 In this formal proof, fill in the missing reasons.

Given: $\overline{OE}$ bisects $\overline{AB}$, $\overline{OF}$ bisects $\overline{CD}$, and AE = DF.
Prove: AB = DC

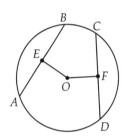

Statements	Reasons
1. $\overline{OE}$ bisects $\overline{AB}$ and $\overline{OF}$ bisects $\overline{CD}$.	1. Given.
2. E is the midpoint of $\overline{AB}$. F is the midpoint of $\overline{DC}$.	2. _____
3. 2AE = AB 2DF = DC	3. _____
4. AE = DF	4. Given.
5. 2AE = 2DF	5. _____
6. AB = DC	6. _____

CUMULATIVE REVIEW
CHAPTERS 1–4

Part I

All questions in this part will receive 2 credits. No partial credit will be allowed.

1

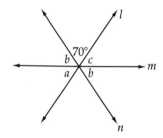

If lines *l*, *m*, and *n* intersect at a common point, what is the sum of *a*, *b*, *c*, and *d*?

(1) 110   (3) 220

(2) 140   (4) 290

2 A line segment joining the vertex of a triangle to the midpoint of the side opposite is called:

(1) an altitude

(2) a median

(3) an angle bisector

(4) a perpendicular bisector

3 If $\overline{AD}$ bisects $\angle A$ in right triangle *ABC*, what is the value of *x*?

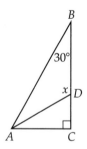

(1) 60°   (3) 100°

(2) 90°   (4) 120°

4 Which statement is logically equivalent to "If a quadrilateral is a rectangle, then the diagonals are congruent"?

(1) If the diagonals of a quadrilateral are congruent, then the quadrilateral is a rectangle.

(2) If a quadrilateral is not a rectangle, then the diagonals of the quadrilateral are not congruent.

(3) If the diagonals of a quadrilateral are not congruent, then the quadrilateral is not a rectangle.

(4) If a quadrilateral is a parallelogram, then the diagonals are congruent.

5 In equilateral triangle *SAM*, the bisectors of angles *S* and *A* intersect at point *P*. What is the measure of $\angle SPA$?

(1) 150   (3) 60

(2) 120   (4) 30

6 In the given figure, which of the following statements is true?

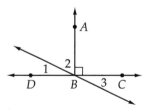

(1) $\angle 3$ and $\angle 2$ are nonadjacent complementary angles.

(2) $\angle 1$ and $\angle 2$ are adjacent and supplementary angles.

(3) $\angle DBA$ and $\angle ABC$ are congruent complementary angles.

(4) $\angle 3$ and $\angle ABC$ are adjacent angles that form a linear pair.

7 In the given figure, which angle has the greatest measure?

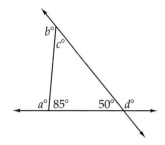

(1) a   (3) c

(2) b   (4) d

8

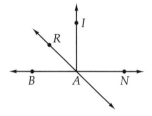

In the given figure, $\overrightarrow{AI} \perp \overleftrightarrow{BN}$ and $\overleftrightarrow{BN}$ intersects $\overleftrightarrow{RA}$. Which of the following statements is true?

(1) $\angle BAR \cong \angle RAI$

(2) Points R, A, and N are collinear.

(3) $\angle BAR$ and $\angle RAI$ are complementary.

(4) $\angle BAR$ and $\angle RAI$ are supplementary.

9 If $\angle x$ is the complement of $\angle D$, and $\angle y$ is the supplement of $\angle D$, then which statement is always true?

(1) $m\angle x < m\angle y$

(2) $m\angle x > m\angle y$

(3) $m\angle x + m\angle y = 180$

(4) $m\angle x + m\angle y = 90$

10 In the given triangle, which of the following must be true?

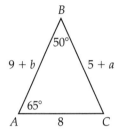

(1) $m\angle A = m\angle B$

(2) $a < b$

(3) $a = b + 4$

(4) $a + 4 = b$

Part II

Each correct answer will receive 2 credits. Clearly indicate the necessary steps, including the appropriate formula substitutions, diagrams, charts, etc. Correct numerical answers without work shown will receive only 1 credit.

11 State whether each of the following is *True* or *False*.

a If two lines intersect, then they intersect in exactly one point.

b Two angles can be both supplements and complements.

c If two angles are complements, then they are also adjacent.

d Complements of congruent angles are congruent.

12

Using the degree measures in the given figure, how much greater is x than the degree measure of $\angle BAD$?

13 The measure of an angle is 44° more than that of its supplement. Find the measures of both angles.

14 Find the measure of an angle if its measure is 40° less than three times the measure of its complement.

Part III

Each correct answer will receive 4 credits. Partial credit will be allowed. Clearly indicate the necessary steps, including the appropriate formula substitutions, diagrams, charts, etc. Correct numerical answers without work shown will receive only 1 credit.

15

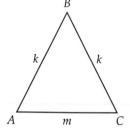

The perimeter of isosceles triangle *ABC* is 44. If the ratio of side *m* to side *k* is 3 to 4, what is length of each side?

16 In the given figure, m$\angle a = 2x + 7$, m$\angle b = 77 - x$, and m$\angle BRF = 3x$.

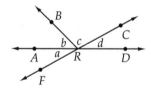

Not drawn to scale

Find the measures of angles *a*, *b*, *c*, and *d*.

17 In the given figure, $\triangle ABC$ is equilateral and $\triangle RPT$ is isosceles with $RP = RT$ and m$\angle PRT = 40$.

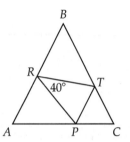

If m$\angle ARP$ is twice the value of m$\angle APR$, what is the measure of $\angle PTC$?

Each correct answer will receive 6 credits. Partial credit will be allowed. Clearly indicate the necessary steps, including the appropriate formula substitutions, diagrams, charts, etc. Correct numerical answers without work shown will receive only 1 credit.

18 For **a** and **b**, use a narrative proof.

a

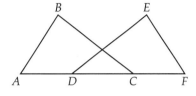

Given: $\overline{AD} \cong \overline{CF}$, $\angle A \cong \angle F$, and $\overline{AB} \cong \overline{EF}$
Prove: $\triangle ABC \cong \triangle DEF$

b

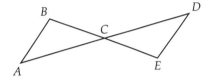

Given: C is the midpoint of $\overline{AD}$, $\angle D \cong \angle A$
Prove: $\triangle ABC \cong \triangle DEC$

Exercises 19 and 20: Write a formal two-column proof for each.

19

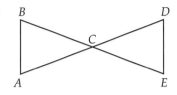

Given: $\angle B \cong \angle D$, $\overline{BC} \cong \overline{DC}$
Prove: $\triangle ACB \cong \triangle ECD$

20

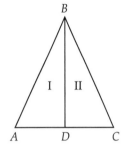

Given: $\overline{BD}$ is the median to side $\overline{AC}$. $\triangle ABC$ is isosceles with $AB = BC$.
Prove: $\triangle \text{I} \cong \triangle \text{II}$

CUMULATIVE REVIEW
CHAPTERS 1–5

Part I

All questions in this part will receive 2 credits. No partial credit will be allowed.

1 In $\triangle PQR$, $\overline{QB} \perp \overline{PR}$, $\angle PQA \cong \angle AQR$, and $\overline{PM} \cong \overline{MR}$.

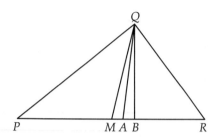

If the segments are listed in correct alphabetical order as altitude, angle bisector, and median, then the same order of segments must be

(1) $\overline{QA}, \overline{QM}, \overline{QB}$

(2) $\overline{QB}, \overline{QM}, \overline{QA}$

(3) $\overline{QA}, \overline{QB}, \overline{QM}$

(4) $\overline{QB}, \overline{QA}, \overline{QM}$

2 What statement is the contrapositive of $p \rightarrow \sim q$?

(1) $q \rightarrow \sim p$ (3) $\sim q \rightarrow p$

(2) $\sim q \rightarrow \sim p$ (4) $q \rightarrow p$

3 In the given figure, lines l, m, and n intersect at a point.

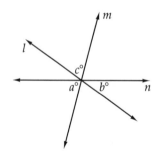

If $a = 75°$ and $b = 35°$, what is the value of c?

(1) 40°   (3) 70°

(2) 65°   (4) 75°

4 Which pair of triangles may not be congruent?

(1)

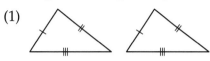

(2)

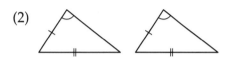

(3)

(4)

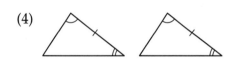

5

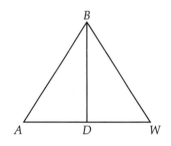

If $\overline{BD}$ is an altitude of $\triangle ABW$, which statement must be true?

(1) $\overline{DA} \cong \overline{DW}$

(2) $\overline{BD}$ bisects $\overline{AW}$.

(3) $\angle ABD \cong \angle WBD$

(4) $\angle ADB \cong \angle WDB$

6 If $5x - 21$, $3x + 9$, and $4x + 12$ represent the measures of the angles of a triangle, then the triangle is:

(1) isosceles   (3) obtuse

(2) right   (4) equilateral

7 In the given figure, $\overline{CD}$ bisects $\angle ACB$.

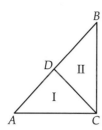

Which of the following facts would not be sufficient to prove that $\triangle I$ is congruent to $\triangle II$?

(1) $\overline{AC} \cong \overline{BC}$

(2) $\angle A \cong \angle B$

(3) $\overline{CD}$ bisects $\overline{AB}$.

(4) $\overline{CD} \perp \overline{AB}$

8

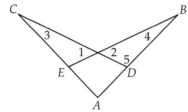

If $\overline{ADB} \cong \overline{AEC}$, which of the following additional information is needed to prove that $\overline{CD} \cong \overline{BE}$?

(1) $\angle 1 \cong \angle 2$ (3) $\angle 3 \cong \angle 5$

(2) $\angle 3 \cong \angle 4$ (4) $\angle 4 \cong \angle 1$

9 $\overrightarrow{PQ}$ is the perpendicular bisector $\overline{AB}$ of at N.

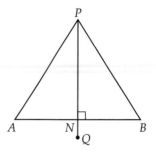

If $PA = 2x + 7$, $PB = 3x - 5$, and $AN = x + 2$, then AB equals:

(1) 14   (3) 28

(2) 16   (4) 35

10

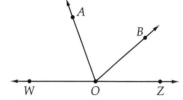

If $\overrightarrow{OA}$ bisects $\angle WOB$ and the measure of $\angle WOB$ is 4 less than 7 times the measure of $\angle BOZ$, find m$\angle AOB$.

(1) 23   (3) 78.5

(2) 75   (4) 157

Part II

Each correct answer will receive 2 credits. Clearly indicate the necessary steps, including the appropriate formula substitutions, diagrams, charts, etc. Correct numerical answers without work shown will receive only 1 credit.

11

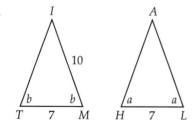

In the two given triangles, if $a = 60°$, how much greater is the perimeter of $\triangle TIM$ than the perimeter of $\triangle HAL$?

12 If $\angle A$ is a supplement of $\angle B$, m$\angle A = 8x + 17$, and m$\angle B = 12x + 3$, find the values of x, m$\angle A$, and m$\angle B$.

13

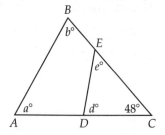

In the given figure, with m∠C = 48, what is the value of $a + b + d + e$?

14 a If two angles are vertical and complementary, what is the measure of each angle?

b What is the measure of the angle formed by the bisectors of any two adjacent, supplementary angles?

Part III

Each correct answer will receive 4 credits. Partial credit will be allowed. Clearly indicate the necessary steps, including the appropriate formula substitutions, diagrams, charts, etc. Correct numerical answers without work shown will receive only 1 credit.

15

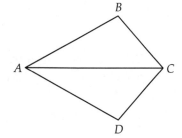

In the given figure, if $\overline{AC}$ bisects ∠BAD, what additional fact would be needed to prove △BAC ≅ △DAC by the

a ASA Postulate?

b SAS Postulate?

16

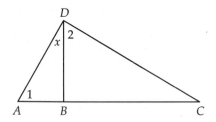

Given: $\overline{DB} \perp \overline{AC}$, $\overline{AD} \perp \overline{DC}$, and ∠1 is the complement of ∠x.
Prove: ∠1 ≅ ∠2

17 Use a narrative proof for each of the following.

a

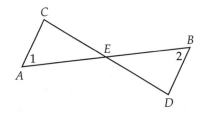

Given: $\overline{CD}$ bisects $\overline{AB}$ at point E,
∠1 ≅ ∠2.
Prove: △ACE ≅ △BDE

b

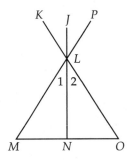

Given: $\overline{MP}, \overline{NJ}$, and $\overline{OK}$ intersect at L,
∠1 ≅ ∠2, $\overline{LN} \perp \overline{MO}$.
Prove: △LMN ≅ △LON

Each correct answer will receive 6 credits. Partial credit will be allowed. Clearly indicate the necessary steps, including the appropriate formula substitutions, diagrams, charts, etc. Correct numerical answers without work shown will receive only 1 credit.

18

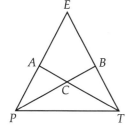

Given: $\triangle PET$, $\overline{PA} \cong \overline{TB}$, $\overline{PCB} \perp \overline{ET}$, and $\overline{TCA} \perp \overline{EP}$.
Prove: $\triangle PCT$ is isosceles.

19

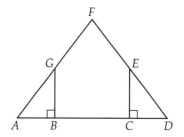

Given: $\triangle AFD$, $\overline{ABCD}$, $\angle AGB \cong \angle DEC$, $\overline{AC} \cong \overline{BD}$, $\overline{GB} \perp \overline{AD}$, and $\overline{EC} \perp \overline{AD}$
Prove: $\overline{AF} \cong \overline{DF}$

20

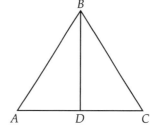

Given: $\overline{BD}$ is a median of $\triangle ABC$, $\overline{BA} \cong \overline{BC}$.
Prove: $\overline{BD}$ is an altitude to side $\overline{AC}$.

CUMULATIVE REVIEW
CHAPTERS 1–6

Part I

All questions in this part will receive 2 credits. No partial credit will be allowed.

1 Simplify: $a - b(a + b)$

(1) $a^2 - b^2$

(2) $a^2 + ab - b^2$

(3) $a - ab - b^2$

(4) $a^2 - ab + b^2$

2 If a translation maps point $G(-3, 1)$ to point $G'(6, 6)$, the translation can be represented by:

(1) $(x + 9, y + 5)$

(2) $(x + 9, y + 7)$

(3) $(x + 3, y + 7)$

(4) $(x + 3, y + 5)$

3 In the given figure, $\overline{AB}$ and $\overline{CD}$ intersect at E. $\angle 1 \cong \angle 2$.

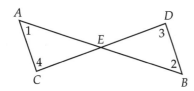

Which additional information is needed to show that $\triangle ACE \cong \triangle BDE$?

(1) $\overline{AB} \cong \overline{CD}$

(2) $\angle 3 \cong \angle 4$

(3) $\overline{AE} \cong \overline{DE}$

(4) $\overline{AE} \cong \overline{BE}$

4 The coordinates of point $(x, -y)$ after a reflection in the origin can be represented by:

(1) (x, y)

(2) $(-x, y)$

(3) $(x, -y)$

(4) $(-x, -y)$

5 If $p \rightarrow q$ and $q \rightarrow r$ are both true statements, then which statement must also be true?

(1) $p \rightarrow {\sim}r$

(2) ${\sim}p \rightarrow r$

(3) $r \rightarrow p$

(4) ${\sim}r \rightarrow {\sim}p$

6 If $2x = 7y$ and $7y = 8z$, then what does x equal in terms of z?

(1) $\frac{7}{8}z$

(2) $\frac{8}{7}z$

(3) $4z$

(4) $56z$

7

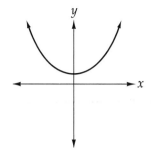

Which of the following represents the rotation of the given graph of the parabola $y = x^2 + 1$ counterclockwise 90° about the origin?

(1)

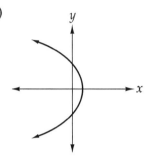

(2)

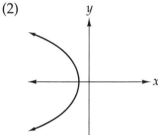

(3)

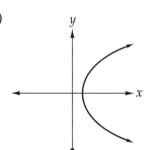

(4)

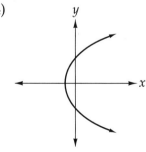

8 Given $\triangle MAX$ with $\overline{XY}$ the angle bisector of $\angle MXA$. Which of the following additional statements would be sufficient to prove $\triangle MYX \cong \triangle AYX$?

(1) Y is the midpoint of $\overline{MA}$.

(2) $\overline{XY} \perp \overline{MA}$

(3) $\overline{XY}$ is the median to $\overline{MA}$.

(4) $\angle AXY \cong \angle MXY$

9

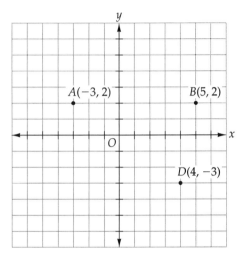

In the given graph, if A is transformed to B by $T_{r,s}$, and D is transformed to E by $T_{s,r}$, then the coordinates of E are:

(1) $(4, 5)$ (3) $(8, 4)$

(2) $(4, 8)$ (4) $(8, 5)$

10 Which of the following is not an isometry?

(1) rotation

(2) dilation

(3) translation

(4) reflection

Each correct answer will receive 2 credits. Clearly indicate the necessary steps, including the appropriate formula substitutions, diagrams, charts, etc. Correct numerical answers without work shown will receive only 1 credit.

11 In the figure given, $\angle 1$ and $\angle 2$ are supplementary.

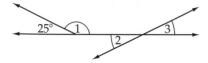

What is m$\angle 3$?

12 In the figure given, $\overline{AB} \cong \overline{BC}$, $\overline{AD} \cong \overline{CD}$, $\overrightarrow{BE}$ bisects $\angle GAD$, and $\overrightarrow{BF}$ bisects $\angle DCH$.

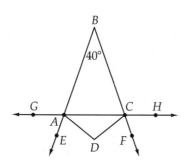

If m$\angle B = 40$, what is the measure of $\angle D$?

13 Find the image of the point whose coordinates are $(3, -4)$ under the given transformations.

  a a reflection in the y-axis

  b a reflection in the x-axis

  c a reflection in the line whose equation is $y = x$

  d a reflection in the line whose equation is $y = -1$

14 The measure of an angle is $27°$ less than twice the measure of its complement. Find the measure of each angle.

Each correct answer will receive 4 credits. Partial credit will be allowed. Clearly indicate the necessary steps, including the appropriate formula substitutions, diagrams, charts, etc. Correct numerical answers without work shown will receive only 1 credit.

15 In $\triangle PQR$, m$\angle P = 4x - 3$, m$\angle Q = 3x + 9$, and m$\angle R = 6x + 18$. Find the measures of the angles and name the kind of triangle.

16

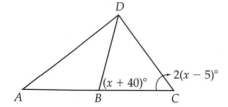

In the given figure, $\overline{AB} \cong \overline{BD} \cong \overline{BC}$. m$\angle C = 2(x - 5)$ and m$\angle DBC = x + 40$. What is the measure of $\angle ADB$?

17

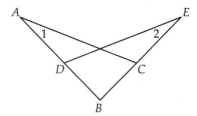

Given: $\overline{AB} \cong \overline{EB}$, $\overline{BC} \cong \overline{BD}$
Prove: $\angle 1 \cong \angle 2$

Each correct answer will receive 6 credits. Partial credit will be allowed. Clearly indicate the necessary steps, including the appropriate formula substitutions, diagrams, charts, etc. Correct numerical answers without work shown will receive only 1 credit.

18 The vertices of △*KAT* are *K*(1, 1), *A*(5, 2), and *T*(3, 5).

    a Find the coordinates of the vertices of △*K'A'T'*, the image of △*KAT* under a reflection in the *y*-axis.

    b Find the coordinates of the vertices of △*K"A"T"*, the image of △*K'A'T'* under a reflection in the origin.

    c Graph △*KAT*, △*K'A'T'*, and △*K"A"T"* on the same set of axes.

    d Under what single transformation is △*K"A"T"* the image of △*KAT*?

19 Prove that the theorem "In an isosceles triangle, the bisector of the vertex angle bisects the base" is valid by constructing a two-column proof for the following.

    Given: Isosceles △*ABC*, with $\overline{AB} \cong \overline{BC}$, $\overline{BD}$ bisects ∠*ABC*
    Prove: $\overline{BD}$ bisects $\overline{AC}$.

20

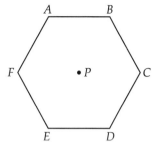

Given: Hexagon *ABCDEF*

    a What is the image of *A* under a reflection in $\overline{BE}$?

    b What is the image of *A* under a reflection in point *P*?

    c What is the image of *D* under a rotation of 120° counterclockwise about *P*?

    d If under a given translation the image of *F* is *E*, what is the image of *B* under the same translation?

CUMULATIVE REVIEW

CHAPTERS 1–7

Part I

All questions in this part will receive 2 credits. No partial credit will be allowed.

1 If the measures of two angles are $4x^2 + 12$ and $-9x + 23$, where $x = -5$, then the angles are:

(1) congruent

(2) complementary

(3) supplementary

(4) vertical

2 At what point does the graph of $3x + 2y = 12$ intersect the y-axis?

(1) $(0, 2)$ (3) $(0, 4)$

(2) $(0, 12)$ (4) $(0, 6)$

3 In $\triangle PQR$, $PQ = 15$ and $QR = 9$. Which of the following could not be the length of $\overline{PR}$?

(1) 6   (3) 8

(2) 7   (4) 23

4

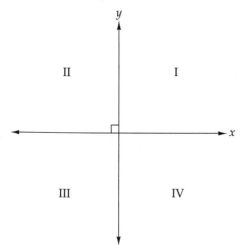

In the figure given, which quadrants contain the coordinate pair (x, y), such that the statement $\frac{y}{x} = 1$ is always true?

(1) I only   (3) I and III only

(2) I and II only   (4) II and IV only

5 If the point $(a, 2a)$ lies on the graph of the equation $2x + y - 8 = 0$, then $a =$

(1) 1   (3) 4

(2) 2   (4) 8

6 Which additional information would not be sufficient to show that $\triangle ABC \cong \triangle MCR$?

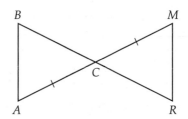

(1) $\overline{BC} \cong \overline{CR}$ (3) $\angle A \cong \angle M$

(2) $\angle B \cong \angle R$ (4) $\overline{AB} \cong \overline{RM}$

7

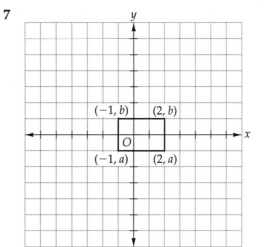

The area of the rectangle in the figure given is

(1) $b - a$

(2) $3(b - a)$

(3) $3(b + a)$

(4) $3(a - b)$

8 In any triangle ABC, if $\overline{AC}$ is the longest side, then which of the following must be true?

(1) $\angle B$ is the largest angle.

(2) $\angle C$ is the smallest angle.

(3) $\overline{AB}$ is the shortest side.

(4) $m\angle A > m\angle B$

9 Isosceles triangle ABC with vertex B and equilateral triangle QRS are shown below.

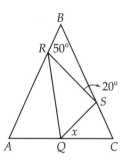

If $m\angle ABC = 50$ and $m\angle BSR = 20$, what is the degree measure of x?

(1) 45   (3) 70

(2) 65   (4) 75

10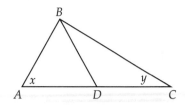

In the figure given, if $AB = BD = DC$, which of the following expresses y in terms of x?

(1) $\frac{x}{2}$

(2) $90 - \frac{x}{2}$

(3) $180 - 2x$

(4) $90 - 2x$

Part II

Each correct answer will receive 2 credits. Clearly indicate the necessary steps, including the appropriate formula substitutions, diagrams, charts, etc. Correct numerical answers without work shown will receive only 1 credit.

11 If each interior angle of a regular polygon contains $120°$, how many sides does the polygon have?

12 The coordinates of A are $(-7, -5)$. If the y-axis is the perpendicular bisector of $\overline{AB}$, what are the coordinates of B?

13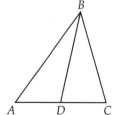

In the given figure, if $\overline{BD}$ is a median, and $AD = 5x + 17$, and $DC = 9x - 27$, what is the length of $\overline{AC}$?

14 Find the coordinates of the point of intersection of the lines whose equations are $y = 3x + 6$ and $x + 3y = -12$.

Each correct answer will receive 4 credits. Partial credit will be allowed. Clearly indicate the necessary steps, including the appropriate formula substitutions, diagrams, charts, etc. Correct numerical answers without work shown will receive only 1 credit.

15 Find the image of the point whose coordinates are $(-6, 3)$ under the given transformations.

   a A translation $T_{(2, -3)}$

   b A dilation whose center is the origin and whose constant of dilation is $\frac{2}{3}$

   c A rotation of $180°$

   d A rotation of $90°$ clockwise

   e A reflection in the line $x = 1$

   f A reflection through the origin

16

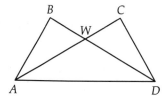

Given: $\overline{AB} \perp \overline{DB}$, $\overline{AC} \perp \overline{DC}$, and $\overline{BW} \cong \overline{CW}$

Using a narrative approach, prove that $\triangle AWD$ is isosceles.

17 Write a formal two-column proof.

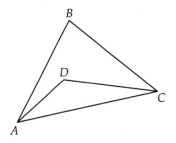

Given: $BC > AB$, $\overline{AD}$ bisects $\angle BAC$, $\overline{CD}$ bisects $\angle BCA$.
Prove: $DC > AD$

Each correct answer will receive 6 credits. Partial credit will be allowed. Clearly indicate the necessary steps, including the appropriate formula substitutions, diagrams, charts, etc. Correct numerical answers without work shown will receive only 1 credit.

18 If $\triangle MAD$ has vertices $M(1, 0)$, $A(3, 4)$, and $D(7, 2)$.

   a Find the coordinate of P, the midpoint of $\overline{MD}$.

   b Find the length of the median from A to $\overline{MD}$

   c Find the equation of the line that contains the points A and P.

   d Determine whether the median is perpendicular to $\overline{MD}$.

19 The coordinates of the vertices of $\triangle CAD$ are $C(3, 0)$, $A(-6, 0)$, and $D(0, -6)$.

   a Write the equation of each altitude of the triangle.

   b Find the coordinates of the point of concurrency of these altitudes.

20

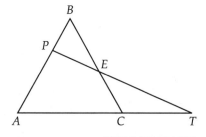

Given: $\triangle ABC$, $\overline{ACT}$, $\overline{PET}$, $\overline{AB} \cong \overline{BC}$
Prove: $PT > AP$

CUMULATIVE REVIEW
CHAPTERS 1–8

Part I

All questions in this part will receive 2 credits. No partial credit will be allowed.

1 Which of the following transformations preserves the slope of a line?

(1) translation

(2) rotation of 90°

(3) rotation of 180°

(4) reflection

2 If the perimeter of a triangle is 12, which of the following could be the length of one side of the triangle?

(1) 5   (3) 7

(2) 6   (4) 8

3 The graph of which equation contains the point $(3, -1)$ and is parallel to the graph of $y = \frac{1}{2}x + 1$?

(1) $x - 2y = 5$

(2) $x + 2y = 1$

(3) $2x - y = 7$

(4) $2x + y = 5$

4 If the supplement of twice a certain angle is 134°, then what is the measure of the angle?

(1) 23°   (3) 67°

(2) 46°   (4) 92°

5 Which set of integers cannot be used as the lengths of the sides of a triangle?

(1) $\{1, 2, 3\}$ (3) $\{3, 4, 5\}$

(2) $\{2, 3, 4\}$ (4) $\{4, 5, 6\}$

6 What is the slope of a line containing the points $(m, 0)$ and $(m + 1, y)$?

(1) y (3) $\frac{1}{y}$

(2) $-y$ (4) $-\frac{1}{y}$

7 If the points $(5, -3)$ and (x, y) are symmetric to each other about the origin, what are the coordinates of (x, y)?

(1) $(-3, 5)$ (3) $(-5, 3)$

(2) $(3, -5)$ (4) $(-5, -3)$

8 In the xy-coordinate system, line m has a positive y-intercept and a negative slope. If line p is parallel to line m and has a negative y-intercept, then the x-intercept of line p must be:

(1) negative and greater than the x-intercept of m

(2) negative and less than the x-intercept of m

(3) positive and greater than the x-intercept of m

(4) positive and less than the x-intercept of m

9 If the linear equation $y = 6x - 12$ crosses the x-axis at the point with coordinates (x, y), what is the value of x?

(1) 0   (3) -2

(2) 2   (4) -12

10

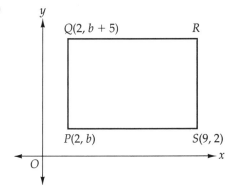

If the rectangle $PQRS$ in the given figure has the indicated coordinates, what are the coordinates of vertex R?

(1) $(2, 7)$ (3) $(9, 5)$

(2) $(7, 9)$ (4) $(9, 7)$

Each correct answer will receive 2 credits. Clearly indicate the necessary steps, including the appropriate formula substitutions, diagrams, charts, etc. Correct numerical answers without work shown will receive only 1 credit.

11

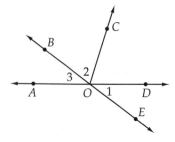

If $\overline{OC}$ bisects $\angle BOD$ and $m\angle COD = 72$, find $m\angle 1$, $m\angle 2$, $m\angle 3$, and $m\angle AOE$.

12 What are the coordinates at which the line $5y + 3 = x - 2$ intersects the y-axis?

13 If $A(0, 0)$, $B(6, -6)$, $C(10, -2)$, and $D(4, 4)$ are the coordinates of the consecutive vertices of rectangle $ABCD$, what are the coordinates for the point of symmetry?

14 In triangle ABC, $\overline{AD}$ and $\overline{BE}$, the bisectors of $\angle A$ and $\angle B$, respectively, intersect at point F. If $m\angle A = 70$ and $m\angle B = 80$, what is the measure of $\angle AFB$?

Each correct answer will receive 4 credits. Partial credit will be allowed. Clearly indicate the necessary steps, including the appropriate formula substitutions, diagrams, charts, etc. Correct numerical answers without work shown will receive only 1 credit.

15 In the given figure, line segment ABC has coordinates; $A(3, 4)$, $B(11, 10)$, and $C(15, 13)$.

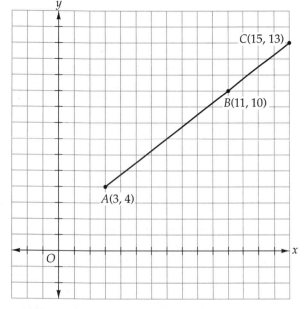

What is the ratio of $\overline{AB}$ to $\overline{AC}$?

16 If angle P is the complement of angle Q, $m\angle P = 8x + 6$, and $m\angle Q = 3x + 7$, find the values of x, $m\angle P$, and $m\angle Q$.

17

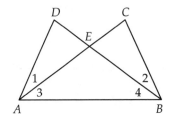

Given: $\overline{AD} \cong \overline{BC}$, $\overline{DE} \cong \overline{CE}$, $\overline{EA} \cong \overline{EB}$
Prove: $\angle DAB \cong \angle CBA$

Each correct answer will receive 6 credits. Partial credit will be allowed. Clearly indicate the necessary steps, including the appropriate formula substitutions, diagrams, charts, etc. Correct numerical answers without work shown will receive only 1 credit.

18 Complete the proof below.

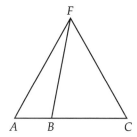

Given: In $\triangle AFC$, $FA = FC$, and B is a point between A and C.
Prove: $FC > FB$

Statements	Reasons
1. In $\triangle AFC$, $FA = FC$, and B is a point between A and C.	1. Given
2. $\triangle AFC$ is an isosceles triangle.	2. _____
3. $m\angle A = m\angle C$	3. _____
4. $m\angle FBC > m\angle A$	4. _____
5. $m\angle FBC > m\angle C$	5. _____
6. $FC > FB$	6. _____

19 Triangle ABC has coordinates $A(2, 2)$, $B(4, 2)$, and $C(2, 5)$.

a Graph $\triangle ABC$ and state the coordinates of its image $\triangle A'B'C'$ after the dilation D_3.

b Graph and state the coordinates of $\triangle A''B''C''$, the image of $\triangle A'B'C'$ after the reflection R: $(x, y) \rightarrow (x, -y)$.

c Graph and state the coordinates of $\triangle A'''B'''C'''$, the image of $\triangle A''B''C''$ after the glide reflection G: $(x, y) \rightarrow (y, x - 2)$.

d Which of the transformations above, D_3, R, or G, is not an isometry?

20 The area of isosceles $\triangle ABC$ is 15. If point B is the vertex of $\triangle ABC$, and the coordinates are $A(-2, -1)$, $B(1, 4)$, and $C(x, -1)$,

    a   Plot the points for A and B.

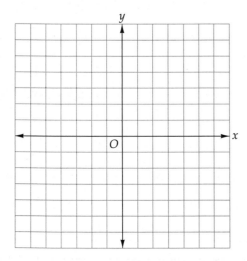

    b   Find the value of x and plot point C.

    c   Find the product of the slopes of AB, BC, and AC.

CUMULATIVE REVIEW
CHAPTERS 1–9

Part I

All questions in this part will receive 2 credits. No partial credit will be allowed.

1 The bisectors of two complementary adjacent angles form what kind of angle?

(1) acute   (3) right

(2) obtuse   (4) straight

2

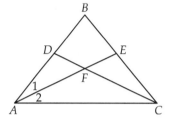

In the figure given, if $\angle 1 \cong \angle 2$, then:

(1) $\angle BAC \cong \angle BCA$

(2) $\overline{AE}$ is a median.

(3) $\overline{AE}$ is an altitude.

(4) $\overline{AE}$ bisects $\angle BAC$.

3 Which of the following could be the lengths of the sides of a triangle?

(1) 3, 4, 1   (3) 4, 11, 6

(2) 3, 7, 10   (4) 4, 5, 6

4

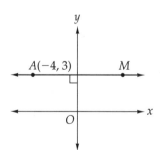

In the figure given, if the distance between points A and M is 9, what are the coordinates of point M?

(1) $(5, 3)$ (3) $(9, 0)$

(2) $(5, -3)$ (4) $(9, 3)$

5 If two angles are supplements of the same angle, then they must be:

(1) adjacent   (3) complementary

(2) congruent   (4) vertical

6 If the base angle of an isosceles triangle measures 73°, then the vertex angle measures:

(1) 34°   (3) 73°

(2) 36.5°   (4) 107°

7 In $\triangle ABC$, $\overline{AB} \cong \overline{BC}$, and $\overline{BD}$ is a median.

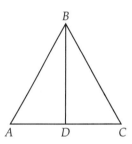

$\triangle ABD$ can be proven congruent to $\triangle CBD$ by means of:

(1) SAS   (3) SSS

(2) ASA   (4) All of these

8

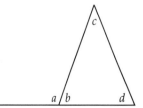

In the given figure, if $c + d = 110°$, what is the sum of the degree measures of a, b, c, and d?

(1) 290°   (3) 250°

(2) 270°   (4) 220°

9 What is the sum of the measures of the interior angles of a 22-sided polygon?

(1) 360°   (3) 3,600°

(2) 1,800°   (4) 6,400°

10 What is the measure of each exterior angle of a regular 12-sided polygon?

(1) 30°   (3) 360°

(2) 150°   (4) 1,800°

Part II

Each correct answer will receive 2 credits. Clearly indicate the necessary steps, including the appropriate formula substitutions, diagrams, charts, etc. Correct numerical answers without work shown will receive only 1 credit.

11 Draw a valid conclusion from the following set of statements.

(i) If an integer is not divisible by 2, then it is not an even number.

(ii) x is an even number.

12 In the given figure, $m \parallel r$, m∠BED = 80, and m∠BDE = 25.

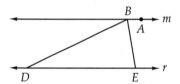

What is the measure of ∠ABD?

13 Under a translation, the image of $(7, -6)$ is $(2, -3)$. What is the image of $(-4, -5)$ under the same translation?

14 What are the coordinates of the midpoint of the segment joining $(-6, -2)$ and $(-2, -2)$?

Part III

Each correct answer will receive 4 credits. Partial credit will be allowed. Clearly indicate the necessary steps, including the appropriate formula substitutions, diagrams, charts, etc. Correct numerical answers without work shown will receive only 1 credit.

15 State whether each of the following is *True* or *False*.

a If an angle is congruent to its supplement, then it is a right angle.

b If two lines intersect, then the bisectors of a pair of adjacent angles are perpendicular to each other.

c If two lines intersect and form congruent angles, then the lines are perpendicular.

d If two lines intersect, then any two adjacent angles are supplementary.

e An exterior angle of a right triangle is always an obtuse angle.

f The median drawn to the base of an isosceles triangle always bisects the vertex angle.

16 The height of a triangle is 8 units more than twice the length of the base. If the area of the triangle is 45, what is the height of the triangle?

17

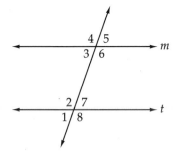

In each case, use the figure and given data to determine whether $m \parallel t$.

a $m\angle 6 = m\angle 2$

b $m\angle 6 + m\angle 7 = 180$

c $m\angle 3 = m\angle 1$

d $m\angle 5 = m\angle 8$

e $m\angle 2 + m\angle 7 = 180$

f $m\angle 2 + m\angle 5 = 180$

Part IV

Each correct answer will receive 6 credits. Partial credit will be allowed. Clearly indicate the necessary steps, including the appropriate formula substitutions, diagrams, charts, etc. Correct numerical answers without work shown will receive only 1 credit.

18 Show that $\triangle ABC$ is an isosceles triangle if the coordinates of the vertices are $A(-3, 5)$, $B(6, 3)$, and $C(-1, -3)$. State your reasons clearly.

19

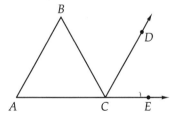

Given: $\triangle ABC$ is equilateral and $\overrightarrow{CD}$ bisects $\angle BCE$.
Prove: $\overrightarrow{CD} \parallel \overline{AB}$

20

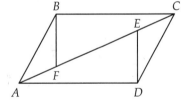

Given: $\overline{BC} \cong \overline{AD}$, $\overline{BC} \parallel \overline{AD}$, and $\overline{BF} \parallel \overline{ED}$
Prove: $\overline{BF} \cong \overline{ED}$

CUMULATIVE REVIEW

CHAPTERS 1–10

Part I

All questions in this part will receive 2 credits. No partial credit will be allowed.

1 What is the sum of the measures of the exterior angles of a pentagon?

(1) 144°   (3) 540°

(2) 360°   (4) 720°

2 Two angles are supplementary. If the measure of the larger angle is 20 degrees less than 4 times the measure of the smaller angle, what is the measure of the larger angle?

(1) 32°   (3) 108°

(2) 40°   (4) 140°

3 The measure of each base angle of an isosceles triangle is 13 more than three times the measure of the vertex angle. The measure of the vertex angle is:

(1) 22°   (3) 29.43°

(2) 23.86°   (4) 79°

4 In the given figure, $\overline{AB} \parallel \overline{DC}$ and $\overline{AC}$ intersects $\overline{BD}$ at E.

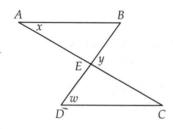

What is the value of w in terms of x and y?

(1) $x + y$ (3) $y - x$

(2) $x - y$ (4) $180 - (x + y)$

5 If each exterior angle of a regular polygon contains 45°, how many sides does the polygon have?

(1) 6   (3) 8

(2) 7   (4) 9

6 If the diagonals of a parallelogram are perpendicular, then the figure must be:

(1) a square

(2) a rectangle

(3) a rhombus

(4) None of these

7 Which of the following is the equation of the line containing the point $(1, -3)$ and perpendicular to the line $y = -3x + 7$?

(1) $y = \frac{1}{3}x - \frac{10}{3}$

(2) $y = \frac{1}{3}x - 10$

(3) $y = -\frac{1}{3}x - \frac{10}{3}$

(4) $y = 3x - 6$

8 Which property is not always true for a parallelogram?

(1) Opposite angles are congruent.

(2) The diagonals bisect each other.

(3) The diagonals form pairs of congruent triangles.

(4) The diagonals bisect the angles of the parallelogram.

9 One way to prove that lines are perpendicular is to show that they form congruent angles that are:

(1) adjacent

(2) complementary

(3) equidistant

(4) vertical

10

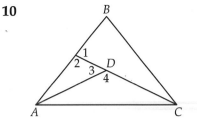

In the given figure, △*ABC* has four angles marked numerically. Which statement is always true?

(1) m∠1 > m∠4   ③ m∠4 > m∠*B*

(2) m∠3 > m∠2   (4) m∠*B* > m∠3

Part II

Each correct answer will receive 2 credits. Clearly indicate the necessary steps, including the appropriate formula substitutions, diagrams, charts, etc. Correct numerical answers without work shown will receive only 1 credit.

11 If the perimeter of a rhombus is 52 and one diagonal is 10, what is the area of the rhombus?

12 In the given figure, *a* ∥ *b*, and the interior angles on the same side of the transversal measure $(3x)°$ and $(4x - 37)°$.

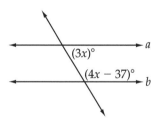

Find the value of *x*.

13

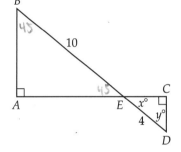

In the given figure, $\overline{BA}$ and $\overline{DC}$ are each perpendicular to $\overline{AEC}$, and *x* = *y*. If *BE* = 10 and *DE* = 4, what is the length of $\overline{AC}$? Leave the answer in simplest radical form.

14 The bases of a trapezoid have lengths of 6 and 12. What is the length of the median of the trapezoid?

Each correct answer will receive 4 credits. Partial credit will be allowed. Clearly indicate the necessary steps, including the appropriate formula substitutions, diagrams, charts, etc. Correct numerical answers without work shown will receive only 1 credit.

15 If the area of a rectangle is 48 and the length is 4 less than twice the width, what is the measure of the width?

16 The vertices of $\triangle ABC$ are $A(-2, 0)$, $B(3, 5)$, and $C(5, -6)$. Find the coordinates of $\triangle A'B'C'$ under the composition $T_{-3, -4} \circ r_{y=x}$.

17 Find the area of polygon $ABCD$ if the coordinates of the vertices are $A(5, -1)$, $B(9, 2)$, $C(9, 9)$, and $D(0, 5)$.

Each correct answer will receive 6 credits. Partial credit will be allowed. Clearly indicate the necessary steps, including the appropriate formula substitutions, diagrams, charts, etc. Correct numerical answers without work shown will receive only 1 credit.

18 Quadrilateral $DART$ has vertices $D(-1, 3)$, $A(5, 5)$, $R(2, 7)$, and $T(-1, 6)$.

    a Prove that $DART$ is a trapezoid.

    b Prove that $DART$ is not isosceles.

19

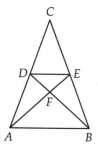

Given: $\triangle ABC$, $\overline{AD} \cong \overline{BE}$, and $\overline{AE} \cong \overline{BD}$

Prove: **a** $\angle BDE \cong \angle AED$

       b $\angle FAB \cong \angle FBA$

20

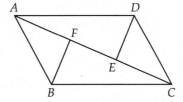

Given: Quadrilateral $ABCD$ and diagonal $\overline{AFEC}$, $\overline{BF} \perp \overline{AC}$, $\overline{DE} \perp \overline{AC}$, $\overline{BF} \cong \overline{DE}$, and $\overline{AE} \cong \overline{CF}$

Prove: $ABCD$ is a parallelogram.

CUMULATIVE REVIEW
CHAPTERS 1–11

Part I

All questions in this part will receive 2 credits. No partial credit will be allowed.

1

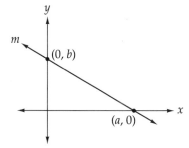

In the given figure, what is the slope of line m?

(1) $\frac{-b}{a}$ (3) $\frac{-a}{b}$

(2) $\frac{b}{a}$ (4) $\frac{a}{b}$

2 If the angles of a triangle measure $3x$, $3x$, and $x + 40$, then the triangle is:

(1) right and isosceles

(2) obtuse and isosceles

(3) equilateral and equiangular

(4) right and scalene

3 In $\triangle ABC$, $\overline{BA} \cong \overline{BC}$. If the measure of the exterior angle at $\angle C$ is $150°$, then $m\angle B =$

(1) 30 (3) 120

(2) 60 (4) 150

4

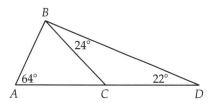

In the given figure, if $m\angle CAB = 64$, $m\angle CBD = 24$, and $m\angle BDC = 22$, what is the longest side of $\triangle ABC$?

(1) $\overline{AC}$ (3) $\overline{AB}$

(2) $\overline{BC}$ (4) $\overline{BD}$

5 If the sum of the measures of the interior angles of a polygon is $1,620°$, how many sides does it have?

(1) 8 (3) 10

(2) 9 (4) 11

6 The base of a prism is a square whose area is 64 square centimeters. The height of the prism is 5 cm. The lateral area of the prism is:

(1) 40 cm² (3) 160 cm²

(2) 80 cm² (4) 288 cm²

7

In the given cube with edge of length 4, if M and N are midpoints, what is the length of segment MN in simplest radical form?

(1) $2\sqrt{6}$ (3) 6

(2) $4\sqrt{6}$ (4) 8

8 In the xy-coordinate plane, line k has a slope of $-\frac{3}{5}$. If line k is the reflection of line m across the x-axis, what is the slope of line m?

(1) $-\frac{5}{3}$ (3) $\frac{3}{5}$

(2) $-\frac{3}{5}$ (4) $\frac{5}{3}$

9 If a cube and a sphere intersect at exactly 6 points, then which of the following is true?

(1) The surface areas of the sphere and the cube are equal.

(2) The cube is inscribed in the sphere.

(3) The sphere is inscribed in the cube.

(4) The diameter of the sphere equals the diagonal of any face of the cube.

10 If the midpoints of the sides of a quadrilateral are joined consecutively, the resulting figure will always be a:

(1) parallelogram

(2) rectangle

(3) rhombus

(4) square

Part II

Each correct answer will receive 2 credits. Clearly indicate the necessary steps, including the appropriate formula substitutions, diagrams, charts, etc. Correct numerical answers without work shown will receive only 1 credit.

11

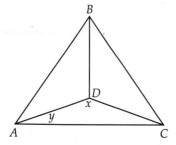

In the given figure, if $\overline{AD} \cong \overline{DB} \cong \overline{DC}$, $\overline{AB} \cong \overline{BC}$, and m$\angle BAD = 29$, what are the degree measures of x and y?

12 If a line passes through the points $(-3, 2n)$ and $(-1, 3n)$, and the slope of the line is $-\frac{1}{2}$, what is the value of n?

13

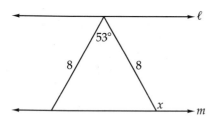

In the given figure, if line l is parallel to line m, what is the measure of angle x?

14

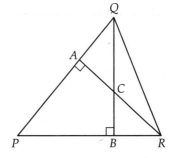

In the given $\triangle PQR$, $\overline{QB} \perp \overline{PBR}$, $\overline{RA} \perp \overline{PAQ}$, and $\overline{RA}$ intersects $\overline{QB}$ at C. If m$\angle APB = 50$, find m$\angle QCA$.

Each correct answer will receive 4 credits. Partial credit will be allowed. Clearly indicate the necessary steps, including the appropriate formula substitutions, diagrams, charts, etc. Correct numerical answers without work shown will receive only 1 credit.

15 What is the distance, in simplest radical form, between the x-intercept and the y-intercept of the line $3y = 9 - x$?

16 If the vertices of $\triangle DNA$ are $D(-2, 8)$, $N(3, -1)$, and $A(12, 4)$, use coordinate geometry to show that $\triangle DNA$ is an isosceles right triangle. State your reasons clearly.

17 A cone and a pyramid have equal volumes and equal heights. Each side of the square base of the pyramid measures 6π meters. What is the radius of the base of the cone? Leave your answer in π form.

Each correct answer will receive 6 credits. Partial credit will be allowed. Clearly indicate the necessary steps, including the appropriate formula substitutions, diagrams, charts, etc. Correct numerical answers without work shown will receive only 1 credit.

18

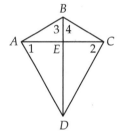

Given: $\overline{DA} \perp \overline{AB}$, $\overline{DC} \perp \overline{CB}$, $\overline{BD} \perp \overline{AC}$ at E,
$\quad\quad\quad \angle 1 \cong \angle 2$
Prove: $\angle 3 \cong \angle 4$

19 Quadrilateral *MIKE* has vertices $M(-1, 0)$, $I(5, -2)$, $K(3, 4)$, and $E(-3, 6)$.

 a Prove *MIKE* is a rhombus.

 b Prove *MIKE* is not a square.

 c Find the area of *MIKE*.

20 a If the volume of a certain sphere is numerically equal to its surface area, what is the radius of the sphere?

 b Using the answer from part **a**, find the volume of the sphere. Leave the answer in π form.

 c If a larger sphere has a radius of 6, what is the ratio of the surface area of the smaller sphere, in part **a**, to that of the larger sphere?

CUMULATIVE REVIEW
CHAPTERS 1–12

Part I

All questions in this part will receive 2 credits. No partial credit will be allowed.

1 Which statement is true of the slope of the line that passes through the points $(5, 2)$ and $(-1, 2)$?

(1) It has no slope.

(2) It has a slope of 3.

(3) It has a slope of 0.

(4) It has a slope of $\frac{2}{3}$.

2 A parallelogram must be a rectangle if the diagonals:

(1) are perpendicular

(2) are congruent

(3) bisect each other

(4) bisect opposite angles

3 If a square is inscribed in a circle whose diameter has length 10, then the area of the square is:

(1) 12.5   (3) 50

(2) 25   (4) 100

4 If a square is rotated 360° around one of its sides as an axis, what kind of solid is generated?

(1) cone   (3) cylinder

(2) cube   (4) sphere

5 In $\triangle ABC$, $\overline{BA} \cong \overline{BC}$. If $m\angle A = 50$, then the measure of the exterior angle at $\angle C$ is:

(1) 50°   (3) 110°

(2) 80°   (4) 130°

6 A sphere has a radius of $2x$. What is the surface area in terms of π and x?

(1) $4\pi x^2$ (3) $16\pi x^2$

(2) $8\pi x^2$ (4) $\frac{32\pi x^3}{3}$

7

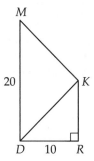

In the figure given, if $m\angle MKR = 135$ and $\overline{DK}$ bisects right angle MDR, what is the length of segment MK?

(1) 10   (3) 12.5

(2) $10\sqrt{2}$ (4) 15

8 If a cylinder and a cone have the same radius and the same height, what is the ratio of the volume of the cone to the volume of the cylinder?

(1) 1:3   (3) 1:$\sqrt{3}$

(2) 1:9   (4) 1:2

9 In the given figure, $m\angle 1 = m\angle 2$, $AD = 6$ and $DB = 4$.

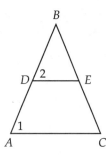

Find the ratio of the area of $\triangle DBE$ to the area of $\triangle ABC$.

(1) $\frac{4}{25}$ (3) $\frac{4}{9}$

(2) $\frac{4}{21}$ (4) $\frac{2}{3}$

10 Select the equation of the line through the point $(0, -2)$ and perpendicular to the line $x + 4y = -3$.

(1) $4x + y = 2$ (3) $4x - y = 2$

(2) $x - 4y = 2$ (4) $4x + y = -2$

Part II

Each correct answer will receive 2 credits. Clearly indicate the necessary steps, including the appropriate formula substitutions, diagrams, charts, etc. Correct numerical answers without work shown will receive only 1 credit.

11

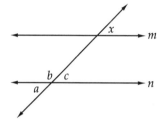

In the given figure, if $m \parallel n$ and $x = 45°$, what is the sum of $a + b + c$?

12 Find the points at which the graph of $2x + 3y = 12$ intersects the x-axis and the y-axis.

13 If the altitudes of two similar cylinders are 9 and 12, respectively, find the ratio, small to large, of:

a their surfaces areas

b their volumes

14 If the sum of the interior angles of a polygon equals 100 straight angles, how many sides does the polygon have?

Part III

Each correct answer will receive 4 credits. Partial credit will be allowed. Clearly indicate the necessary steps, including the appropriate formula substitutions, diagrams, charts, etc. Correct numerical answers without work shown will receive only 1 credit.

15 The measures of the opposite angles, $\angle A$ and $\angle C$, of parallelogram $ABCD$ are $5x - 8$ and $4x + 14$.

a Find the value of x.

b Find the measure of $\angle B$.

16

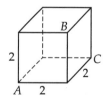

If the vertices A, B, and C in the given cube are joined to form a triangle, and the edge of the cube is 2, what is the area of $\triangle ABC$? (Hint: The formula for the area of an equilateral triangle is $\frac{s^2\sqrt{3}}{4}$.)

17 The coordinates of the center of a circle are $(0, 2)$. If the circle passes through the point $(6, 5)$, what is the length of the diameter of the circle in simplest radical form?

Part IV

Each correct answer will receive 6 credits. Partial credit will be allowed. Clearly indicate the necessary steps, including the appropriate formula substitutions, diagrams, charts, etc. Correct numerical answers without work shown will receive only 1 credit.

18 The coordinates of quadrilateral *MADE* are $M(0, 0)$, $A(a, b)$, $D(a + d, b)$, and $E(d, 0)$.

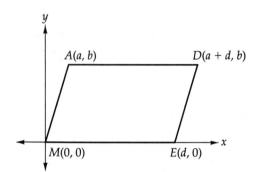

Prove that *MADE* is a parallelogram.

19

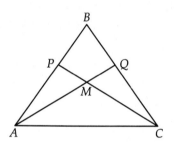

Given: $\triangle ABC$ is isosceles and $\triangle AMC$ is isosceles. $\overline{PM} \cong \overline{QM}$ and $AB = BC$.
Prove: $\triangle ABQ \cong \triangle CBP$

20

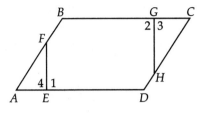

Given: *ABCD* is a parallelogram, $m\angle 1 = m\angle 2$.
Prove: $FE \times CH = GH \times FA$

472 Cumulative Review

CUMULATIVE REVIEW
CHAPTERS 1–13

Part I

All questions in this part will receive 2 credits. No partial credit will be allowed.

1 Which of the following statements is true for every parallelogram *ABCD*?

(1) $\overline{AB} \cong \overline{BC}$

(2) diagonal $\overline{AC} \cong$ diagonal $\overline{BD}$.

(3) $\overline{BD}$ bisects $\angle B$ and $\angle D$.

(4) $\triangle ABD \cong \triangle CDB$

2 In right triangle *DAT*, $\overline{DR}$ is drawn to hypotenuse $\overline{AT}$. If area of $\triangle DAR$ = area of $\triangle DRT$, then $\overline{DR}$ must be:

(1) an altitude

(2) a median

(3) an angle bisector

(4) congruent to $\overline{AD}$

3 In the figure given, right $\triangle EDC$ is similar to right $\triangle BCA$.

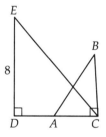

If *A* is the midpoint of $\overline{DC}$, *ED* = 8, and *AC* = 3, what is the perimeter of $\triangle ABC$?

(1) 12   (3) 24

(2) $12\sqrt{2}$ (4) 33

4 If the perimeter of a rectangle is 21, the width is *x*, and the length is 7, what is the ratio of the width to the length?

(1) 1:2   (3) 1:3

(2) 2:3   (4) 1:6

5

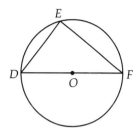

In the given figure, $\overline{DF}$ is the diameter of circle *O*. If $DE = \sqrt{3}$ and $EF = \sqrt{5}$, in terms of π, what is the area of the circle?

(1) 2π (3) 4π

(2) $2\sqrt{2}\pi$ (4) 8π

6 The single transformation that is equivalent to $r_{x\text{-axis}} \circ r_{y=x}$ is:

(1) $r_{y=-x}$ (3) $R_{270°}$

(2) $R_{90°}$ (4) r_{origin}

7 Using the given figure, find the area of parallelogram *ABCD*.

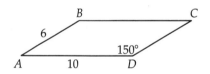

(1) 30   (3) $30\sqrt{3}$

(2) 32   (4) 60

8 If a right circular cone has a radius of 3 and a slant height of 5, what is its volume?

(1) 12π (3) 24π

(2) 15π (4) 36π

9 The graph of $y = -3$ lies in which quadrant?

(1) I and II   (3) III and IV

(2) II and III   (4) II and III

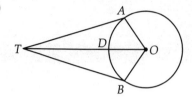

10

In the figure given, if $\overline{TA}$ and $\overline{TB}$ are tangents to circle O at A and B, respectively. Which of the following must be false?

(1) $m\widehat{AD} = m\widehat{DB}$

(2) $m\angle TAO = m\angle TBO$

(3) $m\angle ATB + m\angle AOB = m\angle TAO + m\angle TBO$

(4) $\overline{TA} \cong \overline{TO}$

Part II

Each correct answer will receive 2 credits. Clearly indicate the necessary steps, including the appropriate formula substitutions, diagrams, charts, etc. Correct numerical answers without work shown will receive only 1 credit.

11 Circle O has center $(6, -8)$ and diameter $\overline{AB}$. If the coordinates of A are $(-4, -2)$, find the coordinates of B.

12 In the given figure, $\overline{QR} \parallel \overline{ST}$, $\overline{BC}$ bisects $\angle QCA$.

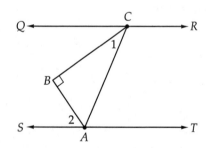

If $m\angle ABC = 90$ and $m\angle 1 = 35$, find $m\angle 2$.

13 The degree measure of the smaller of two complementary angles is 25 more than one-fourth the measure of the larger angle. Find the degree measure of the smaller angle.

14 In circle O, secants $\overline{PAB}$ and $\overline{PCD}$, and chord $\overline{BC}$ are drawn.

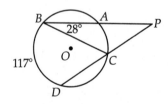

If $m\angle PBC = 28$ and $m\widehat{BD} = 117$, find $m\angle BPD$.

Each correct answer will receive 4 credits. Partial credit will be allowed. Clearly indicate the necessary steps, including the appropriate formula substitutions, diagrams, charts, etc. Correct numerical answers without work shown will receive only 1 credit.

15 Write an equation of the perpendicular bisector of line segment $\overline{AT}$, if the coordinates of the endpoints of $\overline{AT}$ are $A(6, 5)$ and $T(-2, -3)$.

16 In the given figure, $AB = AG$, $CB = CD$, $\triangle ABG \cong \triangle CBD$, $m\angle BAG = 21$, and $m\angle DEG = 114$.

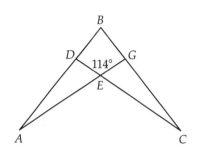

Find the measure of $\angle ADE$, $\angle BGA$, and $\angle ABC$.

17 If the volume of a cube $(V = s^3)$ is equal to the volume of a cylinder $(V = \pi r^2 h)$, and the side of the cube is equal to the radius of the base of the cylinder, represent the height of the cylinder in terms of the radius.

Each correct answer will receive 6 credits. Partial credit will be allowed. Clearly indicate the necessary steps, including the appropriate formula substitutions, diagrams, charts, etc. Correct numerical answers without work shown will receive only 1 credit.

18 A right rectangular prism is 6 inches long and 4 inches wide. The number of cubic inches in its volume is equal to the number of square inches in its total area. What is the height of the prism?

19

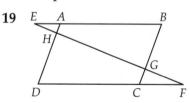

Given: Parallelogram $ABCD$, $\overline{BA}$ is extended through A to E, and $\overline{DC}$ is extended through C to F.

Prove: **a** $\triangle EAH \sim \triangle FCG$

      b $EA \times CG = AH \times FC$

20

Given: Regular pentagon $ABCDE$ is inscribed in circle O. $\overline{RBA}$ is a secant and $\overline{RCG}$ is tangent to circle O at point C. $\overline{AKC}$ and $\overline{BKD}$ are chords.

Find

  a $m\overarc{BC}$

  b $m\angle EDC$

  c $m\angle BCR$

  d $m\angle AKB$

  e $m\angle R$

CUMULATIVE REVIEW
CHAPTERS 1–14

Part I

All questions in this part will receive 2 credits. No partial credit will be allowed.

1 What is the locus of points equidistant from the points $A(2, 5)$ and $B(4, 5)$?

(1) $x = 3$ (3) $x = 5$

(2) $y = 3$ (4) $y = 5$

2 In $\triangle HAT$, $\overline{DE} \parallel \overline{HA}$.

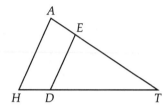

If the ratio of TD to DH is 3:2, then the ratio of DE to HA is

(1) 3:2   (3) 3:5

(2) 2:3   (4) 2:5

3 The volume of a solid wooden cube is 3,375 cubic inches. If no wood is lost in the cutting, how many solid wooden cubes, each with a total surface area of 54 square inches, can be cut from the solid wooden cube?

(1) 50   (3) 125

(2) 62.5   (4) 375

4 In the given figure, $m \parallel n$, and $x = \frac{1}{3}b$.

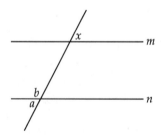

Find the degree measure of a.

(1) 30   (3) 60

(2) 45   (4) 135

5

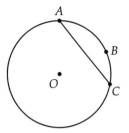

In circle O, if the radius is 2 and the length of arc ABC is π, what is the length of chord AC?

(1) $\sqrt{2}$ (3) $2\sqrt{2}$

(2) 2   (4) π

6 In the given figure, altitude $\overline{BD}$ is drawn in $\triangle ABC$.

If $AC = 8.4$, $AD = 4$, and $m\angle C = 60$, what is the length of $\overline{BC}$?

(1) 8.4   (3) $8.8\sqrt{3}$

(2) 8.8   (4) 16

7 The lengths of the bases of a trapezoid are represented by $x + 3$ and $3x - 9$. In terms of x, the length of the median of the trapezoid is:

(1) $2x - 6$ (3) $4x - 12$

(2) $2x - 3$ (4) $4x - 6$

8

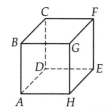

In the given cube, which set of points are the same distance from *A* as they are from *E*?

(1) {*C, D, G, H*}

(2) {*B, C, F, G*}

(3) {*B, F, G, H*}

(4) {*H, G, F, D*}

9 The equation of a line that is perpendicular to the line $x - 3y = 15$ is:

(1) $y = \frac{1}{3}x + 5$

(2) $y = 3x + 5$

(3) $y = -\frac{1}{3}x + 5$

(4) $y = -3x + 5$

10

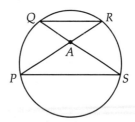

In the given circle, chords $\overline{QR}$, $\overline{PS}$, $\overline{PR}$, and $\overline{QS}$ intersect at point *A*, $\overline{QR} \parallel \overline{PS}$. $\triangle PAS$ and $\triangle QAR$ are always:

(1) right triangles

(2) congruent triangles

(3) equal in area

(4) similar triangles

Part II

Each correct answer will receive 2 credits. Clearly indicate the necessary steps, including the appropriate formula substitutions, diagrams, charts, etc. Correct numerical answers without work shown will receive only 1 credit.

11 Find the sum of the degree measures of all the interior angles of a hexagon.

12

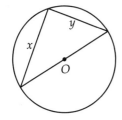

In the given circle *O*, if the circumference of the circle is 12π, what is the value of $x^2 + y^2$?

13 If the lengths of the diagonals of a rhombus are 10 and 24, find the length of one side of the rhombus.

14 Find the lateral area of a square pyramid if the side of the base is 8 and the altitude is 3.

Each correct answer will receive 4 credits. Partial credit will be allowed. Clearly indicate the necessary steps, including the appropriate formula substitutions, diagrams, charts, etc. Correct numerical answers without work shown will receive only 1 credit.

15 Using the given coordinates, show that $\triangle BAT$ is equilateral.

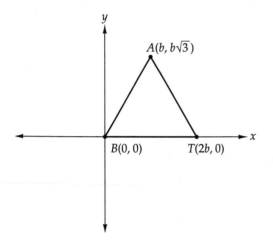

16 In the given diagram, circle A is tangent to the x-axis and y-axis, and circle B is tangent to only the x-axis.

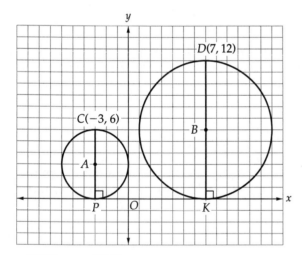

If $\overline{PAC}$ and $\overline{KBD}$ are diameters, what is the slope of the line that passes through the center points A and B?

17 An ice sculpture is in the form of a cone. How many cubic inches of ice does the cone consists of if the circumference of the cone is 90 inches and its height is 10 inches? Round your answer to the nearest tenth of a cubic inch.

Each correct answer will receive 6 credits. Partial credit will be allowed. Clearly indicate the necessary steps, including the appropriate formula substitutions, diagrams, charts, etc. Correct numerical answers without work shown will receive only 1 credit.

18 Use the same set of axes.

    a Graph the following equations:

        (i) $x + y = 7$

        (ii) $3y - 2x = 6$

        (iii) $y = -2$

    b Find the area of the triangle formed by the lines drawn in part **a**.

19 Given: $\triangle MAX$ with coordinates $M(-1, 2)$, $A(7, 0)$, and $X(1, -6)$, and a point $E(4, -3)$ on side $\overline{AX}$.

    Prove: **a** $\overline{ME}$ is the perpendicular bisector of $\overline{AX}$.

        b $\triangle MAX$ is isosceles.

20

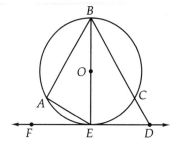

Given: Diameter $\overline{BE}$ of circle O, $\overleftrightarrow{FE}$ tangent to O at E, chords $\overline{AB}$, $\overline{AE}$, and $\overline{BC}$, with $\overline{BC}$ extended to meet $\overleftrightarrow{FE}$ at point D. $\overarc{AE} \cong \overarc{CE}$.

Prove: $\dfrac{BD}{BE} = \dfrac{BE}{BA}$

Geometry Regents Examinations

Reference Sheet

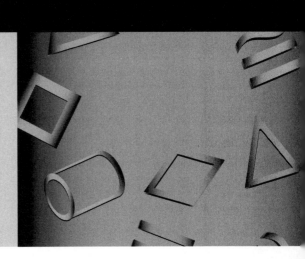

Volume	Cylinder	$V = Bh$ where B is the area of the base
	Pyramid	$V = \frac{1}{3} Bh$ where B is the area of the base
	Right Circular Cone	$V = \frac{1}{3} Bh$ where B is the area of the base
	Sphere	$V = \frac{4}{3} \pi r^3$

Lateral Area (L)	Right Circular Cylinder	$L = 2\pi rh$
	Right Circular Cone	$L = \pi rl$ where l is the slant height

Surface Area	Sphere	$SA = 4\pi r^2$

Part I

Answer all 28 questions in this part. Each correct answer will receive 2 credits. No partial credit will be allowed. For each question, write on the separate answer sheet the numeral preceeding the word or expression that best completes the statement or answers the question. [56]

1. In the diagram below of trapezoid $RSUT$, $\overline{RS} \parallel \overline{TU}$, X is the midpoint of $\overline{RT}$, and V is the midpoint of $\overline{SU}$.

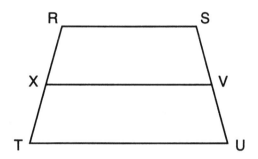

   If $RS = 30$ and $XV = 44$, what is the length of $\overline{TU}$?
   (1) 37   (2) 58   (3) 74   (4) 118

2. In $\triangle ABC$, $m\angle A = x$, $m\angle B = 2x + 2$, and $m\angle C = 3x + 4$. What is the value of x?
   (1) 29   (2) 31   (3) 59   (4) 61

3. Which expression best describes the transformation shown in the diagram below?

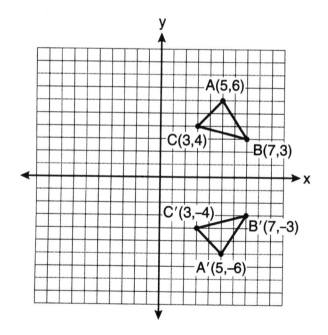

   (1) same orientation; reflection
   (2) opposite orientation; reflection
   (3) same orientation; translation
   (4) opposite orientation; translation

4. Based on the construction below, which statement must be true?

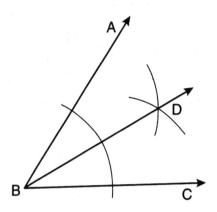

(1) $m\angle ABD = \frac{1}{2}m\angle CBD$ (3) $m\angle ABD = m\angle ABC$

(2) $m\angle ABD = m\angle CBD$ (4) $m\angle CBD = \frac{1}{2}m\angle ABD$

5. In the diagram below, $\angle ABC$ is inscribed in circle P. The distances from the center of circle P to each side of the triangle are shown.

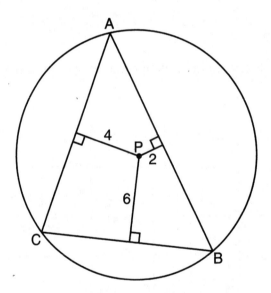

Which statement about the sides of the triangle is true?

(1) $AB > AC > BC$ (3) $AC > AB > BC$

(2) $AB < AC$ and $AC > BC$ (4) $AC = AB$ and $AB > BC$

6. Which transformation is *not* always an isometry?

(1) rotation   (2) dilation   (3) reflection   (4) translation

7. In $\triangle ABC$, $\overline{AB} \cong \overline{BC}$. An altitude is drawn from B to $\overline{AC}$ and intersects $\overline{AC}$ at D. Which statement is *not* always true?

(1) $\angle ABD \cong \angle CBD$ (3) $\overline{AD} \cong \overline{BD}$

(2) $\angle BDA \cong \angle BDC$ (4) $\overline{AD} \cong \overline{DC}$

8. In the diagram below, tangent $\overline{PA}$ and secant $\overline{PBC}$ are drawn to circle O from external point P.

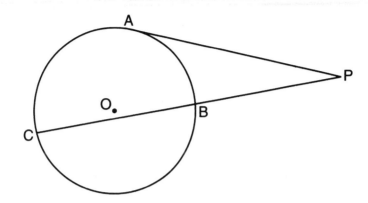

If $PB = 4$ and $BC = 5$, what is the length of $\overline{PA}$?
(1) 20   (2) 9   (3) 8   (4) 6

9. Which geometric principle is used to justify the construction below?

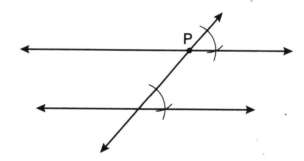

(1) A line perpendicular to one of two parallel lines is perpendicular to the other.
(2) Two lines are perpendicular if they intersect to form congruent adjacent angles.
(3) When two lines are intersected by a transversal and alternate interior angles are congruent, the lines are parallel.
(4) When two lines are intersected by a transversal and the corresponding angles are congruent, the lines are parallel.

10. Which equation represents the circle whose center is $(-2, 3)$ and whose radius is 5?
(1) $(x - 2)^2 + (y + 3)^2 = 5$ (3) $(x + 2)^2 + (y - 3)^2 = 25$
(2) $(x + 2)^2 + (y - 3)^2 = 5$ (4) $(x - 2)^2 + (y + 3)^2 = 25$

11. Towns A and B are 16 miles apart. How many points are 10 miles from town A and 12 miles from town B?
(1) 1   (2) 2   (3) 3   (4) 0

12. Lines j and k intersect at point P. Line m is drawn so that it is perpendicular to lines j and k at point P. Which statement is correct?
(1) Lines j and k are in perpendicular planes.
(2) Line m is in the same plane as lines j and k.
(3) Line m is parallel to the plane containing lines j and k.
(4) Line m is perpendicular to the plane containing lines j and k.

13. In the diagram below of parallelogram $STUV$, $SV = x + 3$, $VU = 2x - 1$, and $TU = 4x - 3$.

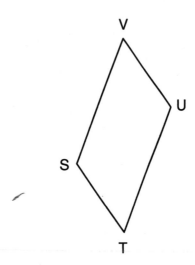

What is the length of $\overline{SV}$?
(1) 5   (2) 2   (3) 7   (4) 4

14. Which equation represents a line parallel to the line whose equation is $2y - 5x = 10$?
(1) $5y - 2x = 25$ (2) $5y + 2x = 10$ (3) $4y - 10x = 12$ (4) $2y + 10x = 8$

15. In the diagram below of circle O, chords $\overline{AD}$ and $\overline{BC}$ intersect at E, $m\widehat{AC} = 87$, and $m\widehat{BD} = 35$.

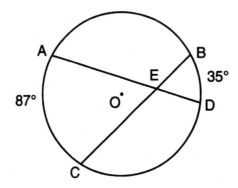

What is the degree measure of $\angle CEA$?
(1) 87   (2) 61   (3) 43.5   (4) 26

16. In the diagram at the right of $\triangle ADB$, $m\angle BDA = 90$, $AD = 5\sqrt{2}$, $AB = 2\sqrt{15}$.

What is the length of $\overline{BD}$?
(1) $\sqrt{10}$ (2) $\sqrt{20}$ (3) $\sqrt{50}$ (4) $\sqrt{110}$

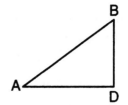

17. What is the distance between the points (−3, 2) and (1, 0)?
    (1) $2\sqrt{2}$ (2) $2\sqrt{3}$ (3) $5\sqrt{2}$ (4) $2\sqrt{5}$

18. What is an equation of the line that contains the point (3, −1) and is perpendicular to the line whose equation is $y = -3x + 2$?

    (1) $y = -3x + 8$ (2) $y = -3x$ (3) $y = \frac{1}{3}x$ (4) $y = \frac{1}{3}x - 2$

19. In the diagram below, $\overline{SQ}$ and $\overline{PR}$ intersect at T, $\overline{PQ}$ is drawn, and $\overline{PS} \parallel \overline{QR}$.

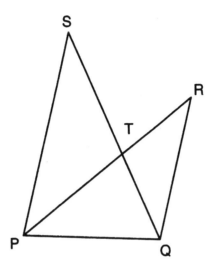

    Which technique can be used to prove $\triangle PST \sim \triangle RQT$?
    (1) SAS   (2) SSS   (3) ASA   (4) AA

20. The equation of a circle is $(x - 2)^2 + (y + 4)^2 = 4$. Which diagram is the graph of the circle?

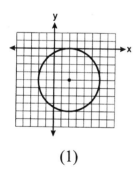
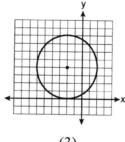
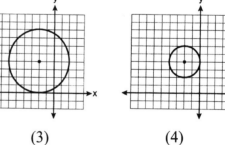

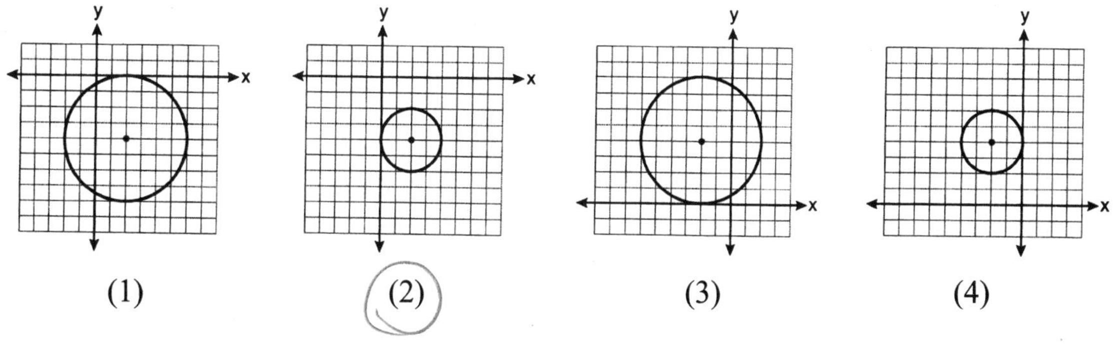

(1)   (2)   (3)   (4)

21. In the diagram below, $\triangle ABC$ is shown with $\overline{AC}$ extended through point D.

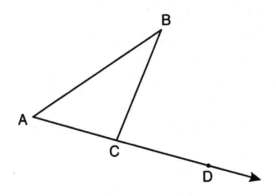

If m$\angle BCD = 6x + 2$, m$\angle BAC = 3x + 15$, and m$\angle ABC = 2x - 1$, what is the value of x?

(1) 12   (2) $14\frac{10}{11}$ (3) 16   (4) $18\frac{1}{9}$

22. Given $\triangle ABC \sim \triangle DEF$ such that $\frac{AB}{DE} = \frac{3}{2}$. Which statement is *not* true?

(1) $\dfrac{BC}{EF} = \dfrac{3}{2}$ (3) $\dfrac{\text{area of } \triangle ABC}{\text{area of } \triangle DEF} = \dfrac{9}{4}$

(2) $\dfrac{m\angle A}{m\angle D} = \dfrac{3}{2}$ (4) $\dfrac{\text{perimeter of } \triangle ABC}{\text{perimeter of } \triangle DEF} = \dfrac{3}{2}$

23. The pentagon in the diagram below is formed by five rays.

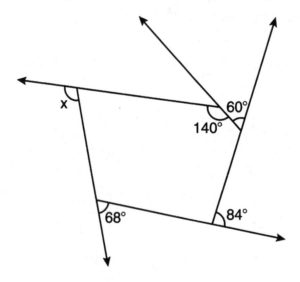

What is the degree measure of angle x?
(1) 72   (2) 96   (3) 108   (4) 112

24. Through a given point, P, on a plane, how many lines can be drawn that are perpendicular to that plane?
    (1) 1   (2) 2   (3) more than 2   (4) none

25. What is the slope of a line that is perpendicular to the line whose equation is $3x + 4y = 12$?
    (1) $\frac{3}{4}$ (2) $-\frac{3}{4}$ (3) $\frac{4}{3}$ (4) $-\frac{4}{3}$

26. What is the image of point $A(4, 2)$ after the composition of transformations defined by $R_{90°} \circ r_{y=x}$?
    (1) $(-4, 2)$ (2) $(4, -2)$ (3) $(-4, -2)$ (4) $(2, -4)$

27. Which expression represents the volume, in cubic centimeters, of the cylinder represented in the diagram below?

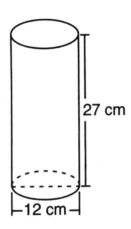

27 cm

12 cm

    (1) 162π (2) 324π (3) 972π (4) $3,888\pi$

28. What is the inverse of the statement "If two triangles are not similar, their corresponding angles are not congruent"?
    (1) If two triangles are similar, their corresponding angles are not congruent.
    (2) If corresponding angles of two triangles are not congruent, the triangles are not similar.
    (3) If two triangles are similar, their corresponding angles are congruent.
    (4) If corresponding angles of two triangles are congruent, the triangles are similar.

Part II

Answer all 6 questions in this part. Each correct answer will receive 2 credits. Clearly indicate the necessary steps, including appropriate formula substitutions, diagrams, graphs, charts, etc. For all questions in this part, a correct numerical answer with no work shown will receive only 1 credit. All answers should be written in pen, except for graphs and drawings, which should be done in pencil. [12]

29. In $\triangle RST$, m$\angle RST = 46$ and $\overline{RS} \cong \overline{ST}$. Find m$\angle STR$.

30. Tim has a rectangular prism with a length of 10 centimeters, a width of 2 centimeters, and an unknown height. He needs to build another rectangular prism with a length of 5 centimeters and the same height as the original prism. The volume of the two prisms will be the same. Find the width, in centimeters, of the new prism.

31. In the diagram below of circle C, $\overline{QR}$ is a diameter, and $Q(1, 8)$ and $C(3.5, 2)$ are points on a coordinate plane.

    Find and state the coordinates of point R.

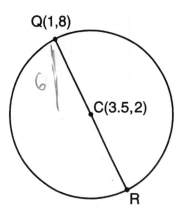

32. Using a compass and straightedge, and $\overline{AB}$ below, construct an equilateral triangle with all sides congruent to $\overline{AB}$. [Leave all construction marks.]

33. In the diagram below of $\triangle ACD$, E is a point on $\overline{AD}$ and B is a point on $\overline{AC}$, such that $\overline{EB} \parallel \overline{DC}$. If $AE = 3$, $ED = 6$, and $DC = 15$, find the length of $\overline{EB}$.

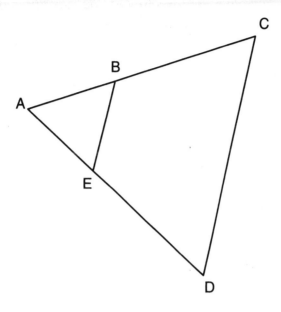

34. In the diagram below of $\triangle TEM$, medians $\overline{TB}$, $\overline{EC}$, and $\overline{MA}$ intersect at D, and $TB = 9$. Find the length of $\overline{TD}$.

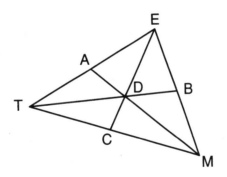

Part III

Answer all 3 questions in this part. Each correct answer will receive 4 credits. Clearly indicate the necessary steps, including appropriate formula substitutions, diagrams, graphs, charts, etc. For all questions in this part, a correct numerical answer with no work shown will receive only 1 credit. All answers should be written in pen, except for graphs and drawings, which should be done in pencil. [12]

35. In $\triangle KLM$, $m\angle K = 36$ and $KM = 5$. The transformation D_2 is performed on $\triangle KLM$ to form $\triangle K'L'M'$.

    Find $m\angle K'$. Justify your answer.

    Find the length of $\overline{K'M'}$. Justify your answer.

36. Given: *JKLM* is a parallelogram.

    $\overline{JM} \cong \overline{LN}$

    $\angle LMN \cong \angle LNM$

    Prove: *JKLM* is a rhombus.

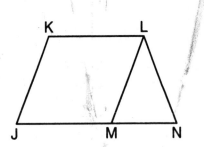

are equidistant from both the x and y axes and
n. Label with an **X** all points that satisfy both

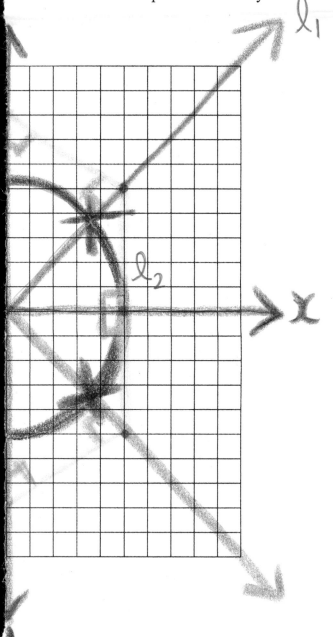

Part

Answer the question in this part. A correct an
necessary steps, including appropriate formul
A correct numerical answer with no work show
be written in pen. [6]

38. On the set of axes below, solve the foll
   values of x and y.

Axis of Symmetry $= \dfrac{-b}{2a} = \dfrac{4}{2} = 2$

$y = (x -$

$4x + 2$

$-4x$

$y = -2x + 7$ ← y

x	y
-1	13
0	8
1	5
2	4
3	5
4	8
5	13

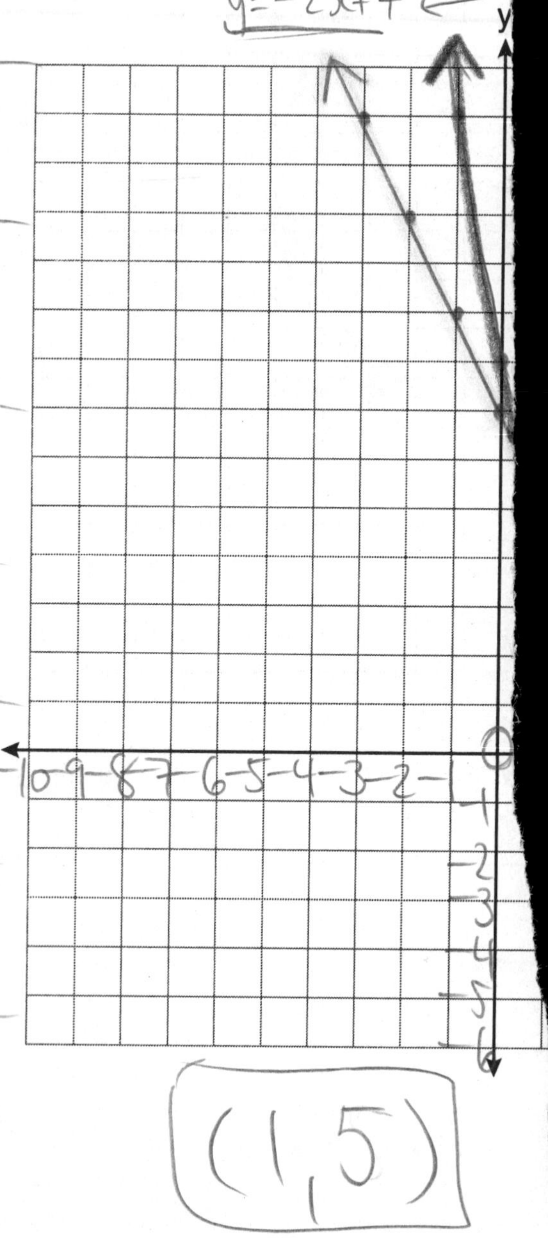

$(1, 5)$

37. On the grid below, graph the points that
the points that are 5 units from the origi
conditions.

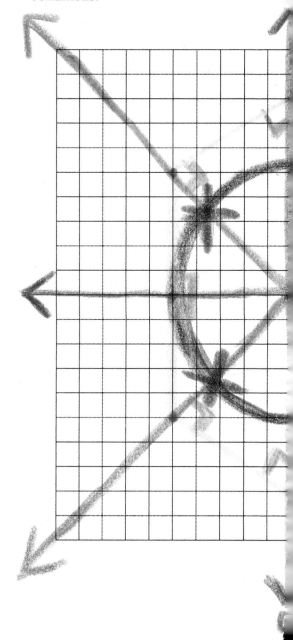

IV

swer will receive 6 credits. Clearly indicate the
a substitutions, diagrams, graphs, charts, etc.
n will receive only 1 credit. The answer should

wing system of equations graphically for all

$2)^2 + 4$ = $y = (x-2)(x-2)+4$
$v = 14$ $y = x^2 - 4x + 4 + 4$
$-4x$ $y = x^2 - 4x + 8$
$2y = -4x + 14$
$\quad 2$

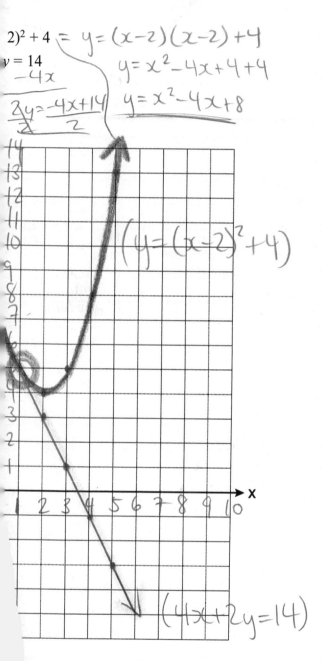

$(y = (x-2)^2 + 4)$

$(4x + 2y = 14)$

Part I

Answer all 28 questions in this part. Each correct answer will receive 2 credits. No partial credit will be allowed. For each question, write on the separate answer sheet the numeral preceeding the word or expression that best completes the statement or answers the question. [56]

1. In the diagram to the right of circle O, chord $\overline{AB} \parallel$ chord $\overline{CD}$, and chord $\overline{CD} \parallel$ chord $\overline{EF}$.

   Which statement must be true?

   (1) $\overset{\frown}{CE} \cong \overset{\frown}{DF}$ (3) $\overset{\frown}{AC} \cong \overset{\frown}{CD}$

   (2) $\overset{\frown}{AC} \cong \overset{\frown}{DF}$ (4) $\overset{\frown}{EF} \cong \overset{\frown}{CD}$

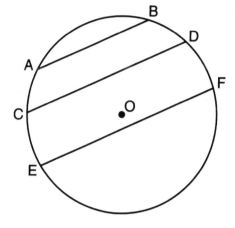

2. What is the negation of the statement "I am not going to eat ice cream"?
   (1) I like ice cream.
   (2) I am going to eat ice cream.
   (3) If I eat ice cream, then I like ice cream.
   (4) If I don't like ice cream, then I don't eat ice cream.

3. The diagram below shows a right pentagonal prism.

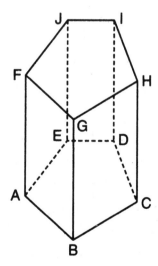

   Which statement is always true?

   (1) $\overline{BC} \parallel \overline{ED}$ (3) $\overline{FJ} \parallel \overline{IH}$

   (2) $\overline{FG} \parallel \overline{CD}$ (4) $\overline{GB} \parallel \overline{HC}$

4. In isosceles triangle ABC, $AB = BC$. Which statement will always be true?
   (1) $m\angle B = m\angle A$ (3) $m\angle A = m\angle C$
   (2) $m\angle A > m\angle B$ (4) $m\angle C < m\angle B$

5. The rectangle $ABCD$ shown in the diagram below will be reflected across the x-axis.

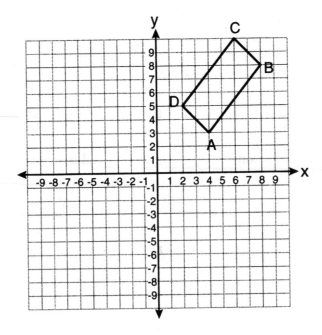

   What will *not* be preserved?
   (1) slope of $\overline{AB}$ (3) Length of $\overline{AB}$
   (2) parallelism of $\overline{AB}$ and $\overline{CD}$ (4) measure of $\angle A$

6. A right circular cylinder has an altitude of 11 feet and a radius of 5 feet. What is the lateral area, in square feet, of the cylinder, to the *nearest tenth*?
   (1) 172.7   (2) 172.8   (3) 345.4   (4) 345.6

7. A traversal intersects two lines. Which condition would always make the two lines parallel?
   (1) Vertical angles are congruent.
   (2) Alternate interior angles are congruent.
   (3) Corresponding angles are supplementary.
   (4) Same-side interior angles are complementary.

8. If the diagonals of a quadrilateral do *not* bisect each other, then the quadrilateral could be a
   (1) rectangle   (2) rhombus   (3) square   (4) trapezoid

9. What is the converse of the statement "If Bob does his homework, then George gets candy"?
   (1) If George gets candy, then Bob does his homework.
   (2) Bob does his homework if and only if George gets candy.
   (3) If George does not get candy, then Bob does not do his homework.
   (4) If Bob does not do his homework, then George does not get candy.

10. If $\triangle PQR$, $PQ = 8$, $QR = 12$, and $RP = 13$. Which statement about the angles of $\triangle PQR$ must be true?
    (1) $m\angle Q > m\angle P > m\angle R$ (3) $m\angle R > m\angle P > m\angle Q$
    (2) $m\angle Q > m\angle R > m\angle P$ (4) $m\angle P > m\angle R > m\angle Q$

11. Given:

$$y = \frac{1}{4}x - 3$$

$$y = x^2 + 8x + 12$$

In which quadrant will the graphs of the given equations intersect?
(1) I   (2) II   (3) III   (4) IV

12. Which diagram shows the construction of an equilateral triangle?

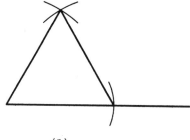

(1)

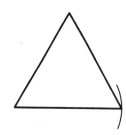

(3)

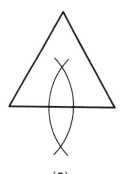

(2)

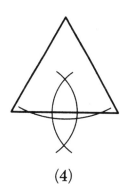

(4)

13. Line segment AB is tangent to circle O at A. Which type of triangle is always formed when points A, B, and O are connected?
    (1) right   (3) scalene
    (2) obtuse   (4) isosceles

14. What is an equation for the circle shown in the graph below?

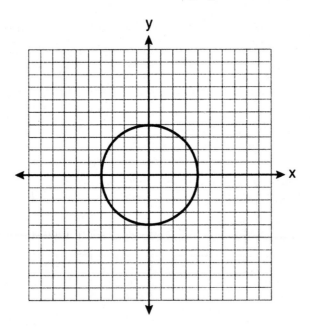

   (1) $x^2 + y^2 = 2$ (2) $x^2 + y^2 = 4$ (3) $x^2 + y^2 = 8$ (4) $x^2 + y^2 = 16$

15. Which transformation can map the letter **S** onto itself?
   (1) glide reflection   (3) line reflection
   (2) translation   (4) rotation

16. In isosceles trapezoid $ABCD$, $\overline{AB} \cong \overline{CD}$. If $BC = 20$, $AD = 36$, and $AB = 17$, what is the length of the altitude of the trapezoid?
   (1) 10   (2) 12   (3) 15   (4) 16

17. In plane P, lines m and n intersect at point A. If line k is perpendicular to line m and line n at point A, then line k is
   (1) contained in plane P (3) perpendicular to plane P
   (2) parallel to plane P (4) skew to plane P

18. The diagram below shows $\overline{AB}$ and $\overline{DE}$.

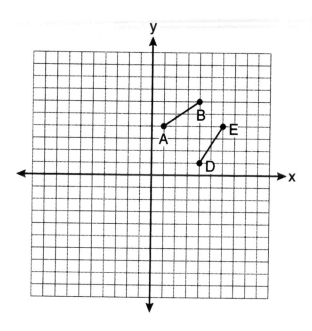

Which transformation will move $\overline{AB}$ onto $\overline{DE}$ such that point D is the image of point A and point E is the image of point B?

(1) $T_{3,-3}$ (2) $D_{\frac{1}{2}}$ (3) $R_{90°}$ (4) $r_{y=x}$

19. In the diagram below of circle O, chords $\overline{AE}$ and $\overline{DC}$ intersect at point B, such that $m\widehat{AC} = 36$ and $m\widehat{DE} = 20$.

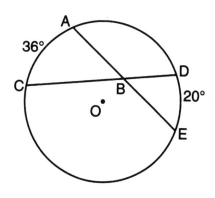

What is $m\angle ABC$?
(1) 56   (2) 36   (3) 28   (4) 8

20. The diagram below shows the construction of a line through point *P* perpendicular to line *m*.

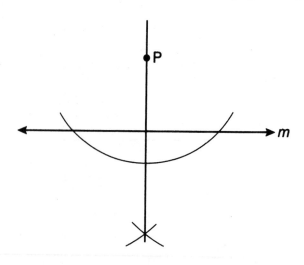

Which statement is demonstrated by this construction?
(1) If a line is parallel to a line that is perpendicular to a third line, then the line is also perpendicular to the third line.
(2) The set of points equidistant from the endpoints of a line segment is the perpendicular bisector of the segment.
(3) Two lines are perpendicular if they are equidistant from a given point.
(4) Two lines are perpendicular if they intersect to form a vertical line.

21. What is the length, to the *nearest tenth*, of the line segment joining the points (−4, 2) and (146, 52)?
(1) 141.4   (2) 150.5   (3) 151.9   (4) 158.1

22. What is the slope of a line perpendicular to the line whose equation is $y = 3x + 4$?

(1) $\dfrac{1}{3}$ (2) $-\dfrac{1}{3}$ (3) 3   (4) −3

23. In the diagram below of circle O, secant $\overline{AB}$ intersects circle O at D, secant $\overline{AOC}$ intersects circle O at E, $AE = 4$, $AB = 12$, and $DB = 6$.

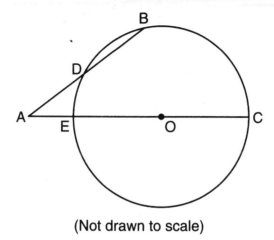

(Not drawn to scale)

What is the length of $\overline{OC}$?
(1) 4.5   (2) 7   (3) 9   (4) 14

24. The diagram below shows a pennant in the shape of an isosceles triangle. The equal sides each measure 13, the altitude is $x + 7$, and the base is $2x$.

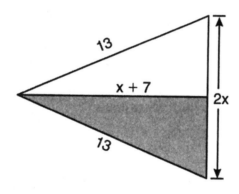

What is the length of the base?
(1) 5   (2) 10   (3) 12   (4) 24

25. In the diagram below of △*ABC*, $\overline{CD}$ is the bisector of ∠*BCA*, $\overline{AE}$ is the bisector of ∠*CAB*, and $\overline{BG}$ is drawn.

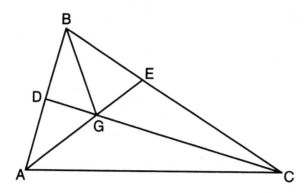

Which statement must be true?
(1) *DG* = *EG*   (2) *AG* = *BG*   (3) ∠*AEB* ≅ ∠*AEC*   (4) ∠*DBG* ≅ ∠*EBG*

26. In the diagram below of circle *O*, chords $\overline{AD}$ and $\overline{BC}$ intersect at *E*.

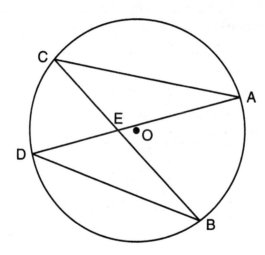

Which relationship must be true?
(1) △*CAE* ≅ △*DBE*   (2) △*AEC* ~ △*BED*   (3) ∠*ACB* ≅ ∠*CBD*   (4) $\overset{\frown}{CA}$ ≅ $\overset{\frown}{DB}$

27. Two lines are represented by the equations $-\frac{1}{2}y = 6x + 10$ and $y = mx$. For which value of *m* will the lines be parallel?
(1) −12   (2) −3   (3) 3   (4) 12

28. The coordinates of the vertices of parallelogram *ABCD* are *A*(−3, 2), *B*(−2, −1), *C*(4, 1), and *D*(3, 4). The slopes of which line segments could be calculated to show that *ABCD* is a rectangle?
(1) $\overline{AB}$ and $\overline{DC}$ (2) $\overline{AB}$ and $\overline{BC}$ (3) $\overline{AD}$ and $\overline{BC}$ (4) $\overline{AC}$ and $\overline{BD}$

Part II

Answer all 6 questions in this part. Each correct answer will receive 2 credits. Clearly indicate the necessary steps, including appropriate formula substitutions, diagrams, graphs, charts, etc. For all questions in this part, a correct numerical answer with no work shown will receive only 1 credit. All answers should be written in pen, except for graphs and drawings, which should be done in pencil. [12]

29. Tim is going to paint a wooden sphere that has a diameter of 12 inches. Find the surface area of the sphere, to the *nearest square inch*.

30. In the diagram below of $\triangle ABC$, $\overline{DE}$ is a midsegment of $\triangle ABC$, $DE = 7$, $AB = 10$, and $BC = 13$. Find the perimeter of $\triangle ABC$.

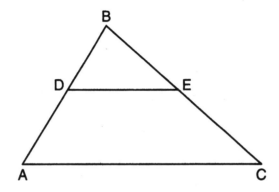

31. In right $\triangle DEF$, m$\angle D = 90$ and m$\angle F$ is 12 degrees less than twice m$\angle E$. Find m$\angle E$.

32. Triangle *XYZ*, shown in the diagram below, is reflected over the line $x = 2$. State the coordinates of $\triangle X'Y'Z'$, the image of $\triangle XYZ$.

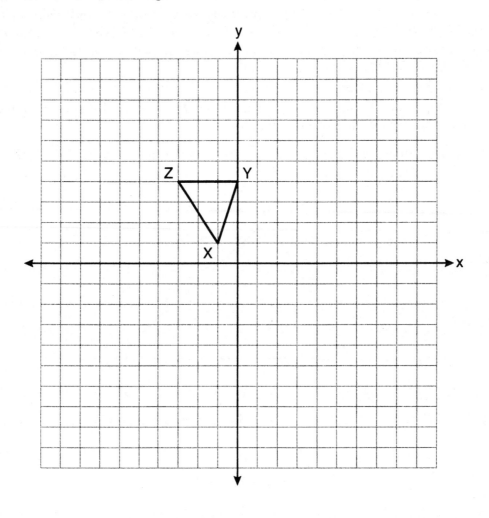

33. Two lines, $\overleftrightarrow{AB}$ and $\overleftrightarrow{CRD}$, are parallel and 10 inches apart. Sketch the locus of all points that are equidistant from $\overleftrightarrow{AB}$ and $\overleftrightarrow{CRD}$ and 7 inches from point *R*. Label with an **X** each point that satisfies both conditions.

34. The base of a pyramid is a rectangle with a width of 6 cm and a length of 8 cm. Find, in centimeters, the height of the pyramid if the volume is 288 cm³.

Part III

Answer all 3 questions in this part. Each correct answer will receive 4 credits. Clearly indicate the necessary steps, including appropriate formula substitutions, diagrams, graphs, charts, etc. For all questions in this part, a correct numerical answer with no work shown will receive only 1 credit. All answers should be written in pen, except for graphs and drawings, which should be done in pencil. [12]

35. Given: Quadrilateral $ABCD$ with $\overline{AB} \cong \overline{CD}$, $\overline{AD} \cong \overline{BC}$, and diagonal $\overline{BD}$ is drawn

    Prove: $\angle BDC \cong \angle ABD$

36. Find an equation of the line passing through the point (6, 5) and perpendicular to the line whose equation is $2y + 3x = 6$.

37. Write an equation of the circle whose diameter $\overline{AB}$ has endpoints $A(-4, 2)$ and $B(4, -4)$. [The use of the grid below is optional.]

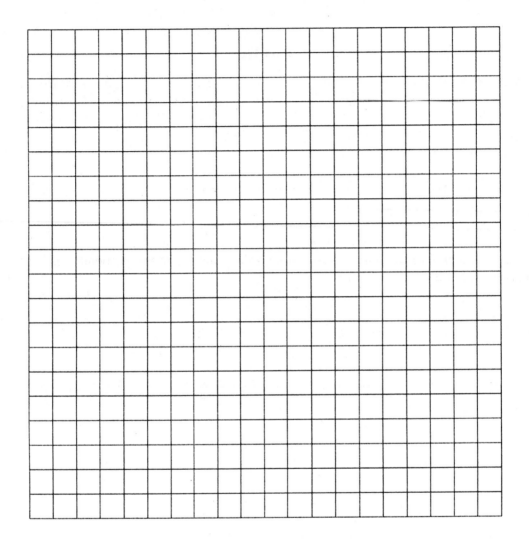

Part IV

Answer the question in this part. A correct answer will receive 6 credits. Clearly indicate the necessary steps, including appropriate formula substitutions, diagrams, graphs, charts, etc. A correct numerical answer with no work shown will receive only 1 credit. The answer should be written in pen. [6]

38. In the diagram below, quadrilateral *STAR* is a rhombus with diagonals $\overline{SA}$ and $\overline{TR}$ intersecting at *E*. $ST = 3x + 30$, $SR = 8x - 5$, $SE = 3z$, $TE = 5z + 5$, $AE = 4z - 8$, m∠*RTA* = $5y - 2$, and m∠*TAS* = $9y + 8$. Find *SR*, *RT*, and m∠*TAS*.

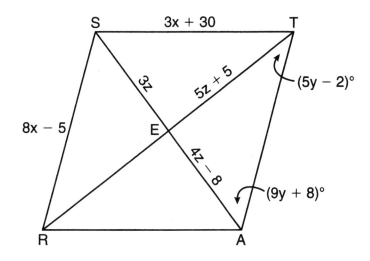

Part I

Answer all 28 questions in this part. Each correct answer will receive 2 credits. No partial credit will be allowed. For each question, write on the separate answer sheet the numeral preceeding the word or expression that best completes the statement or answers the question. [56]

1. In the diagram below, $\triangle ABC \cong \triangle XYZ$.

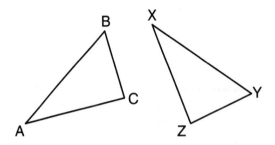

Which two statements identify corresponding congruent parts for these triangles?

(1) $\overline{AB} \cong \overline{XY}$ and $\angle C \cong \angle Y$ (3) $\overline{BC} \cong \overline{XY}$ and $\angle A \cong \angle Y$

(2) $\overline{AB} \cong \overline{YZ}$ and $\angle C \cong \angle X$ (4) $\overline{BC} \cong \overline{YZ}$ and $\angle A \cong \angle X$

2. A support beam between the floor and ceiling of a house forms a 90° angle with the floor. The builder wants to make sure that the floor and ceiling are parallel. Which angle should the support beam form with the ceiling?
   (1) 45°   (2) 60°   (3) 90°   (4) 180°

3. In the diagram below, the vertices of $\triangle DEF$ are midpoints of the sides of equilateral triangle ABC, and the perimeter of $\triangle ABC$ is 36 cm.

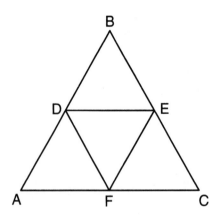

What is the length, in centimeters, of $\overline{EF}$?
(1) 6   (2) 12   (3) 18   (4) 4

4. What is the solution of the following system of equations?

$$y - (x + 3)^2 = 4$$
$$y = 2x + 5$$

(1) (0, −4)   (2) (−4, 0)   (3) (−4, −3) and (0, 5)   (4) (−3, −4) and (5, 0)

5. One step in a construction uses the endpoints of $\overline{AB}$ to create arcs with the same radii. The arcs intersect above and below the segment. What is the relationship of $\overline{AB}$ and the line connecting the points of intersection of these arcs?
(1) collinear   (2) congruent   (3) parallel   (4) perpendicular

6. If $\triangle ABC \sim \triangle ZXY$, $m\angle A = 50$, and $m\angle C = 30$, what is $m\angle X$?
(1) 30   (2) 50   (3) 80   (4) 100

7. In the diagram below of $\triangle AGE$ and $\triangle OLD$, $\angle GAE \cong \angle LOD$, and $\overline{AE} \cong \overline{OD}$.

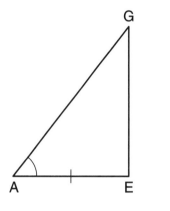 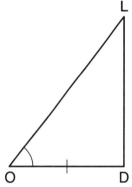

To prove that $\triangle AGE$ and $\triangle OLD$ are congruent by SAS, what other information is needed?
(1) $\overline{GE} \cong \overline{LD}$ (3) $\angle AGE \cong \angle OLD$
(2) $\overline{AG} \cong \overline{OL}$ (4) $\angle AEG \cong \angle ODL$

8. Point A is not contained in plane β. How many lines can be drawn through point A that will be perpendicular to plane β?
(1) one   (2) two   (3) zero   (4) infinite

9. The equation of a circle is $x^2 + (y - 7)^2 = 16$. What are the center and radius of the circle?
(1) center = (0, 7); radius = 4   (3) center = (0, −7); radius = 4
(2) center = (0, 7); radius = 16   (4) center = (0, −7); radius = 16

10. What is an equation of the line that passes through the point (7, 3) and is parallel to the line $4x + 2y = 10$?

(1) $y = \dfrac{1}{2}x - \dfrac{1}{2}$ (3) $y = 2x - 11$

(2) $y = -\dfrac{1}{2}x + \dfrac{13}{2}$ (4) $y = -2x + 17$

11. In $\triangle ABC$, $AB = 7$, $BC = 8$, and $AC = 9$. Which list has the angles of $\triangle ABC$ in order from smallest to largest?
(1) $\angle A$, $\angle B$, $\angle C$ (3) $\angle C$, $\angle B$, $\angle A$
(2) $\angle B$, $\angle A$, $\angle C$ (4) $\angle C$, $\angle A$, $\angle B$

12. Tangents $\overline{PA}$ and $\overline{PB}$ are drawn to circle O from an external point, P, and radii OA and OB are drawn. If m$\angle APB = 40$, what is the measure of $\angle AOB$?
(1) 140°   (2) 100°   (3) 70°   (4) 50°

13. What is the length of the line segment with endpoints $A(-6, 4)$ and $B(2, -5)$?
(1) $\sqrt{13}$ (2) $\sqrt{17}$ (3) $\sqrt{72}$ (4) $\sqrt{145}$

14. The lines represented by the equations $y + \frac{1}{2}x = 4$ and $3x + 6y = 12$ are

(1) the same line   (3) perpendicular
(2) parallel   (4) neither parallel nor perpendicular

15. A transformation of a polygon that always preserves both length and orientation is
(1) dilation   (2) translation   (3) line reflection   (4) glide reflection

16. In which polygon does the sum of the measures of the interior angles equal the sum of the measures of the exterior angles?
(1) triangle   (2) hexagon   (3) octagon   (4) quadrilateral

17. In the diagram below of circle O, chords $\overline{AB}$ and $\overline{CD}$ intersect at E.

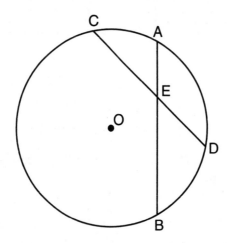

If $CE = 10$, $ED = 6$, and $AE = 4$, what is the length of $\overline{EB}$?
(1) 15   (2) 12   (3) 6.7   (4) 2.4

18. In the diagram below of $\triangle ABC$, medians $\overline{AD}$, $\overline{BE}$, and $\overline{CF}$ intersect at G.

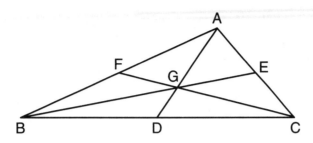

    If $CF = 24$, what is the length of $\overline{FG}$?
    (1) 8   (2) 10   (3) 12   (4) 16

19. If a line segment has endpoints $A(3x + 5, 3y)$ and $B(x - 1, -y)$, what are the coordinates of the midpoint of $\overline{AB}$?
    (1) $(x + 3, 2y)$ (3) $(2x + 3, y)$
    (2) $(2x + 2, y)$ (4) $(4x + 4, 2y)$

20. If the surface area of a sphere is represented by 144π, what is the volume in terms of π?
    (1) 36π (2) 48π (3) 216π (4) 288π

21. Which transformation of the line $x = 3$ results in an image that is perpendicular to the given line?
    (1) $r_{x\text{-axis}}$ (2) $r_{y\text{-axis}}$ (3) $r_{y = x}$ (4) $r_{x = 1}$

22. In the diagram below of regular pentagon $ABCDE$, $\overline{EB}$ is drawn.

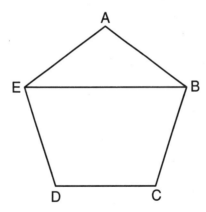

    What is the measure of $\angle AEB$?
    (1) 36°   (2) 54°   (3) 72°   (4) 108°

23. $\triangle ABC$ is similar to $\triangle EDF$. The ratio of the length of $\overline{AB}$ to the length of $\overline{DE}$ is 3:1. Which ratio is also equal to 3:1?
    (1) $\dfrac{m\angle A}{m\angle D}$ (3) $\dfrac{\text{area of } \triangle ABC}{\text{area of } \triangle DEF}$

    (2) $\dfrac{m\angle B}{m\angle F}$ (4) $\dfrac{\text{perimeter of } \triangle ABC}{\text{perimeter of } \triangle DEF}$

24. What is the slope of a line perpendicular to the line whose equation is $2y = -6x + 8$?

    (1) −3   (2) $\frac{1}{6}$ (3) $\frac{1}{3}$ (4) −6

25. In the diagram below of circle C, $m\overset{\frown}{QT} = 140$ and $m\angle P = 40$.

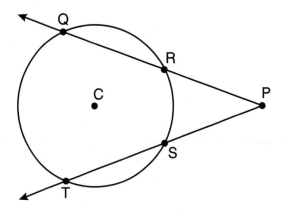

    What is $m\overset{\frown}{RS}$?
    (1) 50   (2) 60   (3) 90   (4) 100

26. Which statement is logically equivalent to "If it is warm, then I go swimming"?
    (1) If I go swimming, then it is warm.
    (2) If it is warm, then I do not go swimming.
    (3) If I do not go swimming, then it is not warm.
    (4) If it is not warm, then I do not go swimming.

27. In the diagram below of $\triangle ACT$, $\overleftrightarrow{BE} \parallel \overline{AT}$.

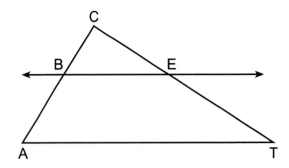

    If $CB = 3$, $CA = 10$, and $CE = 6$, what is the length of $\overline{ET}$?
    (1) 5   (3) 20
    (2) 14   (4) 26

28. Which geometric principle is used in the construction shown below?

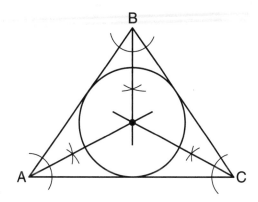

(1) The intersection of the angle bisectors of a triangle is the center of the inscribed circle.
(2) The intersection of the angle bisectors of a triangle is the center of the circumscribed circle.
(3) The intersection of the perpendicular bisectors of the sides of a triangle is the center of the inscribed circle.
(4) The intersection of the perpendicular bisectors of the sides of a triangle is the center of the circumscribed circle.

Part II

Answer all 6 questions in this part. Each correct answer will receive 2 credits. Clearly indicate the necessary steps, including appropriate formula substitutions, diagrams, graphs, charts, etc. For all questions in this part, a correct numerical answer with no work shown will receive only 1 credit. All answers should be written in pen, except for graphs and drawings, which should be done in pencil.   [12]

29. The diagram below shows isosceles trapezoid $ABCD$ with $\overline{AB} \| \overline{DC}$ and $\overline{AD} \cong \overline{BC}$. If $m\angle BAD = 2x$ and $m\angle BCD = 3x + 5$, find $m\angle BAD$.

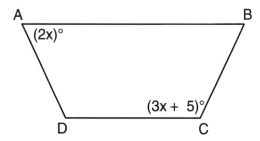

30. A right circular cone has a base with a radius of 15 cm, a vertical height of 20 cm, and a slant height of 25 cm. Find, in terms of π, the number of square centimeters in the lateral area of the cone.

31. In the diagram below of $\triangle HQP$, side $\overline{HP}$ is extended through P to T, $m\angle QPT = 6x + 20$, $m\angle HQP = x + 40$, and $m\angle PHQ = 4x - 5$. Find $m\angle QPT$.

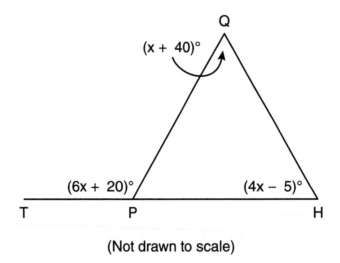

(Not drawn to scale)

32. On the line segment below, use a compass and straightedge to construct equilateral triangle ABC. [Leave all construction marks.]

A   B

33. In the diagram below, car A is parked 7 miles from car B. Sketch the points that are 4 miles from car A and sketch the points that are 4 miles from car B. Label with an **X** all points that satisfy both conditions.

Car A
•

Car B
•

34. Write an equation for circle O shown on the graph below.

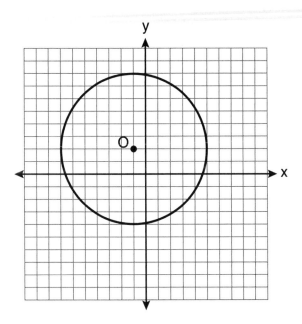

Part III

Answer all 3 questions in this part. Each correct answer will receive 4 credits. Clearly indicate the necessary steps, including appropriate formula substitutions, diagrams, graphs, charts, etc. For all questions in this part, a correct numerical answer with no work shown will receive only 1 credit. All answers should be written in pen, except for graphs and drawings, which should be done in pencil. [12]

35. In the diagram below of quadrilateral $ABCD$ with diagonal $\overline{BD}$, $m\angle A = 93$, $m\angle ADB = 43$, $m\angle C = 3x + 5$, $m\angle BDC = x + 19$, and $m\angle DBC = 2x + 6$. Determine if $\overline{AB}$ is parallel to $\overline{DC}$. Explain your reasoning.

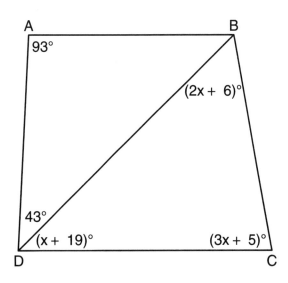

36. The coordinates of the vertices of △ABC are A(1, 3), B(−2, 2), and C(0, −2). On the grid below, graph and label △A″B″C″, the result of the composite transformation $D_2 \circ T_{3,\,-2}$. State the coordinates of A″, B″, and C″.

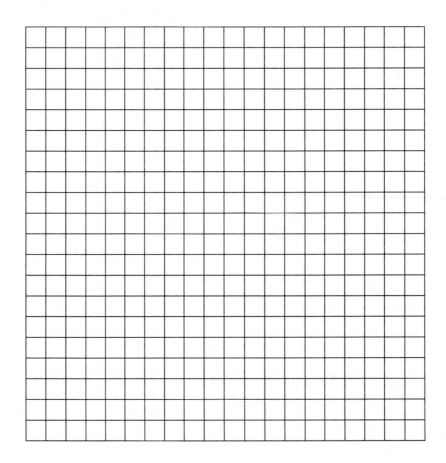

37. In the diagram below, △RST is a 3-4-5 right triangle. The altitude, h, to the hypotenuse has been drawn. Determine the length of h.

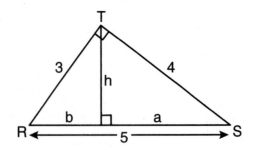

Part IV

Answer the question in this part. A correct answer will receive 6 credits. Clearly indicate the necessary steps, including appropriate formula substitutions, diagrams, graphs, charts, etc. A correct numerical answer with no work shown will receive only 1 credit. The answer should be written in pen. [6]

38. Given: Quadrilateral *ABCD* has vertices *A*(−5, 6), *B*(6, 6), *C*(8, −3), and *D*(−3, −3).

    Prove: Quadrilateral *ABCD* is a parallelogram but is neither a rhombus nor a rectangle.

    [The use of the grid below is optional.]

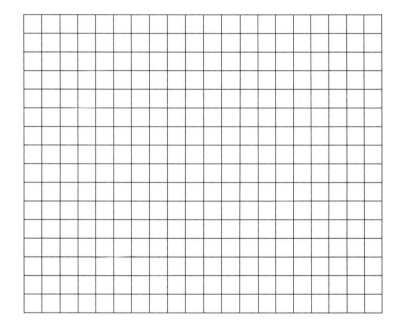

Index

Index